MALE NUDITY IN THE GREEK IRON AGE

Why did the male nude come to occupy such an important place in ancient Greek culture? Despite extended debate, the answer to this question remains obscure. In this book, Sarah C. Murray demonstrates that evidence from the Early Iron Age Aegean has much to add to the discussion. Her research shows that aesthetics and practices involving male nudity in the Aegean had a complicated origin in prehistory. Murray offers a close analysis of the earliest male nudes from the Late Bronze and Early Iron Ages, which mostly take the form of small bronze votive figurines deposited in rural sanctuaries. Datable to the late second and early first millennia BCE, these figurines, she argues, enlighten the ritual and material contexts in which nude athletics originated, complicating the rationalizing accounts present in the earliest textual evidence for such practices. Murray's book breaks new ground by reconstructing a scenario for the ritual and ideological origins of nudity in Greek art and culture.

Sarah C. Murray is Assistant Professor of Classics at the University of Toronto. An archaeologist of the Aegean Late Bronze and Early Iron Ages, she is the author of *The Collapse of the Mycenaean Economy*.

MALE NUDITY IN THE GREEK IRON AGE

REPRESENTATION AND RITUAL CONTEXT IN AEGEAN SOCIETIES

SARAH C. MURRAY

University of Toronto

CAMBRIDGE
UNIVERSITY PRESS

CAMBRIDGE
UNIVERSITY PRESS

University Printing House, Cambridge CB2 8BS, United Kingdom

One Liberty Plaza, 20th Floor, New York, NY 10006, USA

477 Williamstown Road, Port Melbourne, VIC 3207, Australia

314–321, 3rd Floor, Plot 3, Splendor Forum, Jasola District Centre, New Delhi – 110025, India

103 Penang Road, #05-06/07, Visioncrest Commercial, Singapore 238467

Cambridge University Press is part of the University of Cambridge.

It furthers the University's mission by disseminating knowledge in the pursuit of
education, learning, and research at the highest international levels of excellence.

www.cambridge.org
Information on this title: www.cambridge.org/9781316510933
DOI: 10.1017/9781009039079

First published 2022

Printed in the United Kingdom by TJ Books Ltd, Padstow Cornwall

A catalogue record for this publication is available from the British Library.

ISBN 978-1-316-51093-3 Hardback

Cambridge University Press has no responsibility for the persistence or accuracy
of URLs for external or third-party internet websites referred to in this publication
and does not guarantee that any content on such websites is, or will remain,
accurate or appropriate.

Publication of this book has been aided by a grant from the von Bothmer Publication Fund of
the Archaeological Institute of America.

This book is dedicated, with immense gratitude, to Paul Christesen

CONTENTS

PLATES

FIGURES

TABLES

PREFACE

WHY AND WHEN DID THE MALE NUDE COME TO OCCUPY SUCH AN IMPORTANT place in ancient Greek culture? Despite extended debate, the answer to this question remains obscure. In this book, I show that the evidence from the Early Iron Age (EIA, *ca.* 1100–700 BCE) has much to add to the discussion, although it has not received a complete treatment to date.

I suspect that many readers will wonder, based on my publication record and previous research, why and how I came to write a book focused on EIA figurines and ritual. I therefore thought it might be helpful to include a preface to this book to ground the current project in my intellectual history as a researcher and to contextualize how I came to embark on this vector of investigation into nudity in early Greece.

The first reason that I came to be interested in writing a new book on EIA figurines, and that I continued to pursue the project despite many dead ends, is a simple matter of curiosity. The bronze figurines at the center of the study here have always struck me as extremely interesting, even mysterious. I wanted to do a research project on these figurines because I wanted to understand them better. However, it turned out that the project also had useful and thoroughgoing methodological intersections with some of my previous research, even though it was very different in its subject matter, and here I try to explain how these intersections are manifest.

My first professional research project, a dissertation-turned-monograph, covered changes in the intensity and nature of trade and institutions across the Bronze to Iron Age transition in the Aegean. I sought to understand how we might best use material evidence to assess dynamism in economic systems, especially institutions and mechanisms for long-distance exchange in commodities and finished value-added goods.[1] In the course of this work, I continually found that the story of the topic was almost completely dominated by thinking drawn from earlier and later textual evidence. For example, based on textual evidence from the eastern Mediterranean, such as the Amarna letters, the nature of trade in the palatial/Mycenaean Late Bronze Age has

---

[1] Murray 2017.

usually been reconstructed as kingly exchange occurring mainly among palatial agents and aimed at providing rulers with extraordinary objects that could be used for elite self-fashioning. Despite the fact that these texts and the economic and political systems that produced them were clearly no longer extant in the twelfth century, material from this period was often being interpreted the way that palatial – era texts would suggest it should be – as related to elite exchange and self-fashioning.

However, if one removed the assumptions based on these texts while thinking about postpalatial material, it seemed to me that the nature and contexts of the material suggested that exchanged objects were doing something else entirely. For example, at the site of Perati in east Attica, I argued that imported *exotica* were personally or ritually meaningful objects that had little or nothing to do with self-aggrandizement or elites, based on some of their archaeological characteristics: they are highly worn and visually unimpressive, seemed related to non-local mortuary ritual, and were not located in particularly wealthy tombs.[2]

When it comes to the EIA, the Homeric texts still dominate many discussions of trade. For example, because Homer talks about gift exchange, when we find imported objects from sites like Lefkandi, they are usually interpreted as evidence for Homeric-style gift exchange. But in the case of the EIA, reasoning according to a paradigm drawn from texts is not optimal, because it does not take into account the fact that the relevant objects are dated to the tenth or ninth centuries, a considerable remove from whatever society Homer is talking about. If we take away assumptions that the EIA world resembles the world Homer presents, the archaeological record does not independently lead to the conclusion that exchanged objects must relate to Homeric *xenia*.[3]

Questions concerning the relationship between text and archaeology have been at the center of much excellent scholarship, and this book builds on that body of work. In general, untangling inferences drawn from texts from reconstructions of society based on archaeological evidence is a central concern of my research. Ultimately, I am trying to identify places where the material record seems to be at odds with interpretations that have been imposed from texts. I then seek, as best as possible, to resuscitate the material record, and to build new interpretations that are built up primarily from archaeological evidence, often informed by analogical reasoning drawn from parallel contexts in the ethnographic or anthropological literature.

That general aim is consistent with the work I am doing in this book, on the emergence of cultural institutions revolving around male nudity in the Aegean. My interest in nudity in ancient Greece began when I was an

---

[2] Murray 2018.   [3] Arrington 2016.

undergraduate research assistant for Paul Christesen, a prominent scholar of ancient athletics and athletic nudity, and grew during my career as I taught courses and published a few pieces on topics related to ancient sport and spectacle.[4] Engaging in this work led me to two conclusions that ultimately resulted in my embarking on this research project. First, it convinced me that the history of practical and visual cultures of nudity in ancient Greece was an interesting and important topic worthy of study. Extant scholarship on the Archaic and Classical emergence of regular practices of male nudity in the context of athletics, ritual, and civic activities is of extremely high quality and does an excellent job of demonstrating how functionally important the culture of male nudity was within ancient Greek history overall. It also makes clear that the Greek obsession with male nudity in art and in life was apparently unique in the ancient Mediterranean; even the Romans thought the Greek penchant for nude practice was off-kilter. This stimulating body of research inspires curiosity about the origins and impetus behind such unusual developments.

The second thing I saw in the scholarship was that the origins and impetus behind a culture in which male nudity played a prominent role were poorly understood. This lack of understanding seemed connected to their origin in the EIA, and the concomitant lack of interest within extant EIA scholarship on the question of nudity and nude athletics. While historians of the Archaic and Classical periods working on these questions occasionally brushed up against the EIA evidence, it was not the focus of their analysis, and so they had not pursued a complete treatment of it. Moreover, because the EIA evidence is not enlightened by texts, but exists in the form of material culture alone, scholars trained as historians were not in an ideal position to deal with it thoroughly. As a scholar trained as an EIA archaeologist who has also acquired some expertise in the topic of ancient athletics, it seemed to me that I was in good position to make this contribution. I set out to do so through a detailed study of the earliest evidence for a visual and practical culture of nudity in the EIA.

Academic projects tend to evolve as they move forward and this one has not been an exception. As I researched and wrote about naked males in the EIA, I was increasingly convinced that this material demonstrated a number of patterns and details that might both complement and complicate current views on the history of a Greek culture of nudity. However, I also began to see that the EIA evidence for nudity had been treated in a way that was elegantly expressive of two enduring issues of method that confront researchers dealing with EIA material culture in the Aegean. The first is the issue of Homer's influence on interpretations of EIA Aegean society. The second is the way the

---

[4] Murray 2013, 2015, 2021.

transitional status of the EIA within the master narratives of Aegean prehistory and Greek archaeology imposes unhelpful interpretative frameworks that hinder our ability to reconstruct EIA society independent from expectations that we bring to it from better-documented earlier and later contexts.

For the first several years that I was working on the project, I did not get very far in terms of new interpretations or new insights because I was working within the intellectual corridors where existing disciplinary frameworks tend to lead. I was thinking about naked EIA males in terms of origins (of Greek athletic nudity) and evolutions (whether there was continuity or discontinuity in nude practice and imagery between the collapse of Mycenaean states and the Archaic period), and I was bothered by the fact that Homer did not seem to be interested in nudity at all. However, while I was inspecting the bronze figurines at the center of the study to understand some technical details about methods of manufacture, I reached a point of clarity with the material which led me to believe that it had been fundamentally misunderstood specifically because of a lot of the baggage that the structure of the field has imposed onto it. In the case of depictions of unclothed males from the EIA, interpretations influenced by Homer and history have impeded a contextual understanding of the material that is relevant to the specific social and cultural world of the EIA, rather than to earlier and later periods.

While the content of the book remains centered on naked males in the EIA Aegean, I think that much of its value resides in its contribution as a case study that illustrates some persistent issues in the way that EIA material is usually framed. The research demonstrates how treating EIA material as transitional or subordinating it to inferences drawn from Homer hinders the accurate recon-struction of social and political realities of the EIA itself. Treating the EIA archaeological evidence in its context, without letting either Homer or the ideological frame of a "transition" lead interpretation, enables the reconstruc-tion of a complex social history of ritual practice, metal working, and initiatory nudity that bears little resemblance to extant narratives about social, political, economic and religious developments in the EIA. A study of early male nudity therefore provides an ideal nexus for exploring important issues of method and approach, while also constituting a full treatment of evidence that has not been forthcoming to date.

I did not expect for the research project to end in this way. Instead, when I began writing the book, I intended for the main conclusion to be an extension of the history of nude athletics in Greece into the EIA, and a revision of the view that this cultural institution could not be identified with any confidence prior to the sixth century. In that sense, I started out expecting to find something in the EIA that was familiar from historical Greece and thus to bridge the divide between prehistory and history as the current disciplinary paradigm would suggest is desirable. Although I ended up finding something different, the intellectual design of the project remains embedded in the master narratives of the field, and it seems likely that the main reason that people will be interested in the book is because it relates to the origins of male nudity, which is a topic of general interest among many historians and art historians. However, I now think of this framing as a hook rather than as the project's substance. I hope that focusing on an issue that is of broad general interest might open up the readership of the book to scholarly communities unlikely to otherwise take a great interest in the EIA, who may then be surprised by the complexity of what the EIA evidence can reveal. In a way, then, I am trying to make a kind of advertisement for the importance of the EIA by starting with a topic many people are already interested in, but then demonstrating how rich the EIA is as grounds for new and unexpected insights in the cultural history of the Aegean.

Along these lines the book contains three often interlocking but ultimately separate vectors. One seeks to correct the distortions introduced into the interpretation of the EIA because of periodization and framing. As a corrective to the distortions that have been introduced into our interpretations of the EIA by the structure of the field, I produce a reconstruction of EIA ritual and visual culture independent from the idea of this era as a transitional period primarily important for developments that led from the Bronze Age to the historical Greek era. Instead, I recast the EIA as a self-contained phase with a structure and logic that does not relate very closely to the institutions that we know about from the preceding Late Bronze Age or the subsequent historical period. In the case of the earliest depictions of naked males from the Aegean, I show that interpreting these figures within their EIA context, rather than seeing them primarily as primitive forbears of something (heroic, athletic, or civic nudity) that comes later allows us to reconstruct a dense web of meaning around them in ways that have not emerged from analysis that positions them within an evolutionary narrative.

A second vector in the book aims to engage with the idea that ancient Greco-Roman textual sources provide useful evidence for interpreting archaeological material from the EIA. Although Homeric epic continues to pervade many archaeological works that deal with the EIA, viewing EIA material through a Homeric lens usually does more interpretative harm than good. In the case of EIA nudity, the Homeric evidence has led scholarship astray in important ways. On the other hand, reconstructing the apparent ideological and material histories of nudity based on material evidence alone helps to explain a number of aspects of the textual record that had previously seemed perplexing. The study thus demonstrates how the usual model in Classics – where we use texts to enlighten material evidence – can actually be reversed, so that material evidence provides a logic to explain the content of some Greco-Roman texts.

These two methodological points are pursued by means of the third substantive vector: the presentation of a thorough treatment of a category of EIA
material evidence that has been mostly considered meaningless within extant
scholarly discourse on nudity in early Greece, and the demonstration of how
much these objects can contribute to a reconstruction of complex social and
ritual worlds in the prehistoric Aegean.

ACKNOWLEDGMENTS

It is always strange to arrive at the end of a research and writing project, look back at the origins of the ideas it contains, and realize how many years have passed since the project began. I have been thinking about the origins of some kind of meaningful practice or iconography involving nudity in the ancient Greek world for almost exactly half my life. In 2002, Paul Christesen hired me as an undergraduate research assistant at Dartmouth College. He was finishing a long article on nude athletics in Archaic and Classical Greece, and one of my jobs was to read and check the manuscript. At the time, of course, I hardly knew anything about Greek social history, but – typical of Christesen's work – the writing and argumentation of the paper were extremely lucid, so that even a novice reading it could immediately grasp how unusual athletic nudity was as a form of politically meaningful civic practice embedded in Greek social life. In the early years of my PhD program at Stanford I started to tinker with some ideas about the strange obsession with the male nude in Greek art and culture – I wrote a short paper on nudity in Homer during my first-year Ancient Greek survey course, and then a longer paper on theories of embodiment and Greek athletic nudity for my archaeological theory seminar. But eventually I settled on a different research area for my dissertation (Late Bronze and EIA trade and exchange) and set my vague ideas about the naked Greeks aside.

Between 2010 and 2016 I wrote a couple of short papers on topics related to ancient athletics, and taught about sport and nudity in undergraduate courses several times, but I was too busy working up various dissertation-related projects for publication to start any kind of fresh research. With all that finally winding down during the winter of 2016, I was ready to have an intellectual break from thinking about prehistoric trade and exchange, and that is when I began working on EIA figurines in earnest. After a hectic semester of teaching, I had an uninterrupted stretch of time (three weeks or so) during the winter holiday break, which I spent at my favorite 'battle stations' in the American School of Classical Studies at Athens' Blegen library, the perfect place to start scaffolding up a big new research project. My original plan was to write a long article arguing against the idea that evidence from Homer serves as a suitable *terminus post quem* for the beginning of nude athletics, and then providing a new analysis of naked figurines from the EIA to show what they might reveal about such beginnings. But the first draft of that 'article' weighed in around 50,000 words and was still far from doing justice to the topic. I tried to think of ways to break the piece down into two or more articles, but, in the end, I felt that the material should be treated all together, so it seemed like the best route forward was to reorganize and expand the text of the article draft into the beginnings of a book.

That draft was written a long time ago. While at first it seemed like the text and argument of the book might come together relatively rapidly – I'd already put a lot of thought into the article draft – in reality the process of writing this book has not been straightforward at all. The structure and argument have gone through so many major evolutions that it is hard even for me to keep track of or reconstruct the pieces at this point. I initially came to the material with a lot of ideas rooted in my previous work on EIA archaeology and engagement with extant research on ancient athletics and festivals, but eventually I found that a lot of those ideas were at odds with the details that I was seeing in the material evidence. Attending to those details yielded a major reinvigoration and transformation of the whole trajectory of the research project, so that this book is completely different in approach and argument to the article draft I started with nearly five years ago. I do not wish to insult the glory of the natural world by directly comparing the process to a caterpillar's transformation into a butterfly, and I am aware that this book is far less spectacular and perfect than any specimen of that insect, but it is not an exaggeration to say that the first article draft bears about the same resemblance to the final manuscript as those two entities do to one another.

While it was often frustrating to continuously restructure and revise the text, it was rewarding to find that a long period of iterative and open-minded research eventually yielded results, insofar as a set of material evidence that first seemed extremely perplexing eventually began to make more sense to me. The EIA nude figurines at the center of this book are a difficult nut to crack. I read and wrote about them for several years before I had an opportunity to handle and study them, in the summer of 2019, which encounter completely changed my view of their function and meaning. That is when things got fun. I am sure that most other academics know the feeling of finally having a sense of what your project is about and what you must do to bring it to a conclusion after many years of fruitless, aimless toil. It is the best and most exciting moment of the research process, usually (at least for me) followed by an obsessive phase of manic writing. This tends to be a nearly out-of-body experience, where the neuroses associated with being a human in the world fade away, and you are totally consumed by the task of working out new ideas through the text. To me those are fleeting and special moments, similar to the weird euphoria a person experiences after running very fast for several hours and beginning to feel that there is no other reasonable state of being, so that one could keep running fast for an infinite amount of time. Maybe the greatest scholars and intellectuals feel like that all the time, because they are constantly having great ideas and getting excited about writing them down, which sounds exhausting. But for the more average among us, it is nice to get that exhilarating experience once in a while, and I have had a really amazing time writing up this project over the last year, once I figured out what I had to say that was actually original and maybe convincing (but that last part is up to the reader to decide).

Like anyone coming to the end of a project that has undergone such a long period of gestation, I've incurred many debts to colleagues and friends who have brought their intelligence, ideas, or advice to bear on the material in one way or another. The book is dedicated to Paul Christesen for many reasons. I would never have thought of working on the topic of athletic nudity without his influence, but much more is owed than that. I was not a confident undergraduate student, and Paul was the first person who told me that my ideas were good and that I might have something important and interesting to contribute if I put some effort into it. He has supported my intellectual development as a scholar and my professional advancement in many ways since then: advising my (voluminous and tedious!) undergraduate thesis, hiring me as a teaching assistant for two Dartmouth Foreign Study Programs in Greece, and bringing me on as a collaborator or coauthor in a number of enriching research and writing projects. It is not an exaggeration to say that this book, my career, and my reasonably high-functioning adult life in the world would almost certainly not exist without his help and influence.

There are others to thank, although to some degree this has been something of a secret project, and I never really circulated drafts to my Bronze and Iron Age archaeology colleagues, for fear that the text would bore them or that they might think I was too crazy for writing a book on a topic that is superficially unrelated to my dissertation research. As I mentioned above, some seeds of the project were sown in papers that I wrote in graduate school at Stanford University (way back in 2007 and 2008). I am thankful to Richard P. Martin and Ian Hodder for feedback on those papers and for running excellent and thought-provoking graduate seminars on early Greek literature and archaeological theory, respectively. I presented some aspects of the research at the 2018 meeting of the Society for Classical Studies in Boston and the 2018 International Scholars' Symposium at the International Olympic Academy in Olympia, and in the context of invited lectures at Princeton University, Simon Fraser University, and Dalhousie University in 2019 and 2020. I received important and valuable feedback from the audiences and panel members at all of these events, and especially would like to thank Princeton University faculty members Dan-el Padilla Peralta, Marco Gygax, and Michael Flower for very thought-provoking comments on the way that Homeric poetry has been used in the context of historical treatments of nude athletics. Additional conversations with Philip Sapirstein, Carl Knappett, Sylvian Fachard, Maeve McHugh, Charles Stocking, Dimitri Nakassis, and Catherine Pratt have been challenging and valuable.

More generally, my interest in the transition between the Bronze and Iron Ages emerged from many years of productive mentorship from Jeremy Rutter and Ian Morris. My experience at Stanford also brought me into contact with anthropological and theoretical archaeology, especially in the context of courses taught by Lynn Meskell and Ian Hodder. The perceptive and creative scholarship of other EIA archaeologists, especially Anthony Snodgrass, John Papadopoulos, Sarah Morris, Susan Langdon, Angeliki Lebessi, Anna Lucia D'Agata, Antonis Kotsonas, and Mieke Prent, has influenced my views about and interpretations of the period and/or proven very useful to me as I've written this book in particular. I've generally benefited from the recent explosion in sophisticated work on the social archaeology of the Aegean EIA; it is an exciting time to work on this period, and it is encouraging to meet so many other junior scholars who are constantly invigorating many areas of research within the field.

Throughout my career, I have also benefited from generous interlocution with many, many other colleagues. In roughly chronological order of how long I have known them, this list would include Roger Ulrich, Jared Benton, Bartek Lis, Thanos Webb, Matthew Loar, Mary Dabney, Jim Wright, Sabrina Higgins, Robert Stephan, John Sutherland, Lela Urquhart, Darian Totten, Melissa Bailey, Tom Tartaron, Daniel Pullen, Miriam Clinton, Amy Dill, Adam Stack, Hüseyin Özturk, Elissa Faro, Alex Clapp, Eph Lytle, Lindsay Montgomery, Hans Weitzke, Tom Strasser, Louis Ruprecht, Alex Knodell, John Cherry, Sue Alcock, Chris Cloke, Effie Athanassopoulos, Sarah Craft, Fotini Kondyli, and Catie Steidl. I'm constantly inspired by the enthusiasm of students both in and out of the classroom and field, and I want to thank my graduate students – Katerina Apokatanidis, Elliott Fuller, and Taylor – and other graduate students with whom I have worked – Grace Erny, Joey Frankl, Melanie Godsey, Matthias Kalisch, and Aikaterini Psoma – for keeping me excited about the future of the field. Thanks are also due to Megan (Leah) Stephens who assisted me with collecting images as a Research Assistant in the winter of 2019. I'd also like to thank my Toronto Ancient History colleagues Eph Lytle, Seth Bernard, Katherine Blouin, Ben Akrigg, Carrie Atkins, Boris Chrubasik, and Kevin Wilkinson for constant good cheer and enriching interlocution my Toronto archaeology colleagues Carl Knappett, Ed Swenson, Michael Chazan, Tim Harrison, and Ted Banning, who have cultivated an active and stimulating community at the Toronto Archaeology Centre, my departmental mentor Alison Keith for excellent guidance through the early phases of my career in a large, complex institution, and the three chairs that I worked with during the production of this book, Christer Bruun, Jonathan Burgess, and Victoria Wohl, for facilitating institutional support for my research.

Funding for travel to study objects in Greek museums during the summer of 2019 was provided by the University of Toronto Classics department's Norwood Travel Grant. Additional resources for travel to the American School of Classical Studies at Athens and work in the Blegen Library were made available through a start-up grant provided by the University of Toronto's faculty of Arts & Sciences. Additional thanks are due to Ioanna Damanaki, Administrative Assistant to the Director and Archaeological Heritage Director at the American School of Classical Studies at Athens, who facilitated applications for and management of a series of permits to study materials in the Olympia, Delphi, and Heraklion Archaeological Museums, as well as the National Archaeological and Acropolis Museums in Athens. I would also like to thank the French and German schools who gave permission for me to study objects from their excavations, and the museum staff who facilitated these visits for their patience and collegiality: Panagiotis Kalpakos and Kostas Antonopoulos at the Olympia Archaeological Museum, Maria Karimi of the Heraklion Archaeological Museum, Nikolaos Petrocheilos at the Delphi Museum, and Mrs. Hatzipanagiotou, Mrs. Avronidaki, and Giorgos Kavvadias at the National and Acropolis Museums in Athens. I always do my best writing in the Blegen Library of the American School of Classical Studies at Athens, and, indeed, essentially the entirety of the research, writing, and revision for this book took place there. I would like to thank all of the library staff and administrators of the school for maintaining such a magnificent space for archaeological research. The final revisions were undertaken in the spring and summer of 2020, and thanks are also due to the University of Toronto and its library staff for facilitating access to a large amount of HathiTrust resources that made at least a little research possible during the sweeping library closures induced by the global pandemic. A generous grant from the Archaeological Institute of America made possible the inclusion of color plates, and the book is much improved by their inclusion. I would like to thank Beatrice Rehl for editorial her very patient guidance through the extensive duration of the project, three anonymous reviewers who provided helpful feedback and suggestions during the review process, and the staff at Cambridge University Press for their assistance during the production process.

Writing this book has taken a long time, but it has been a very fulfilling process. I am mostly thankful to all of my friends in the field of Aegean archaeology for constituting such a wonderful community within which to work, and for forgiving all of the shortcomings and blunders that probably still exist in this book. I hope that some of the ideas in it prove useful or interesting to others, despite its flaws.

CHAPTER ONE

INTRODUCTION

To be really medieval one should have no body, to be really modern one should have no soul, to be really Greek one should have no clothes. –

Oscar Wilde[1]

Greeks and nudity are closely linked in the popular imagination, a result of the fact that a great deal of Archaic (700–480) and Classical (480–323) Greek art prominently features depictions of naked men. In part, the prominence of the naked male relates to the popularity of athletes as subject matter and the fact that ancient Greek athletes really did train and compete while naked. However, not all images of naked men in Greek art are imitative of real conditions, the actual practice of going about in the world without any clothes on, and it is clear that nudity represented a complex 'costume' and a cultural ideal, suitable for heroes, warriors, and gods as well as athletes. While we have become used to this feature of Greek art, it was unusual in its original ancient Mediterranean context, as was the social practice of nude athletics that developed into an important part of civic life in Greece by the Archaic period.[2] Why and how did the Greeks develop these highly unusual practical and aesthetic relationships with the naked male body?

[1] Wilde in Foreman, ed., 1966, 1203. All dates given in this book are BCE unless otherwise indicated.

[2] See also Bonfante 1993, 7 (quoting Broneer): "We always take the Greeks as our model, forgetting that they did everything differently from everyone else."

Insightful scholarly treatments of the role of male nudity in Greek art and history have improved our understanding of its role as the standard outfit for athletic activity in ritual and civic contexts, as a 'costume' prevalent in iconography, and as an element of the heroic ideal in the Greek Archaic and Classical periods.[3] However, many questions about male nudity in ancient Greece remain unanswered. Greek attitudes toward nudity were already considered an aberration in antiquity,[4] and existing texts do not help very much in clarifying just what ancient Greeks thought about the meaning of nudity in society or art, especially during the apparently formative Archaic period.[5] Though considerable progress has been made in situating nudity in Greek history and culture, the processes through which nudity became a feature of Greek art and daily practice are not well understood.[6] In particular, the origins of both the practice of regular male nudity in the context of Greek athletic contests and the development of a visual system in which nudity was a normal costume for males remain a matter of some obscurity.

This book aims to mitigate some of that obscurity via a detailed treatment of images of naked males from the Early Iron Age (EIA, *ca.* 1100–700). Depictions of naked males exist from many EIA contexts in the Aegean. However, extant scholarship seeking to explain historical Greek nudity has largely turned to literary and iconographical sources from the Archaic and Classical periods, when nudity was *already* a prominent aspect of Greek culture, to the almost

---

[3] Bonfante 1989; Osborne 1997; Hurwit 2007; Lee 2015, 172–197.

[4] For example, Lucian *Anacharsis* 1–5. See discussion in Boardman 2004, 49.

[5] In Greek literature, the word *gymnos* was often used to describe light-armed troops or shamefully exposed women rather than indicating nudity, but there is no evidence in Greek textual evidence for an ideal of nudity comparable to that found in Classical Greek art. Some Archaic examples of the word's usage include Hipponax: Iamb. Frag. 62.1 (*Et. Gen.* (p. 46 Calame)): ἐν ταμείωι τε καὶ χαμευνίωι γυμνόν, "you and a bed naked"; Iamb. Frag. 84.13–14 (P. Oxy 2174 fr. 16 col. ii + addit.): μὴ ἥμεας λάβ [. . .] γυμνοὺς ἔρυ, "lest we be caught naked"; Epode fr. 115 (P. Argent. 3 fr. 1.16, ed. Reitzenstein; disputed authorship, possibly Archilochus): κύμ[ατι] πλα[ζόμ]ενος κἀν Σαλμυδ[ησσ]ῷι γυμνὸν εὐφρονέσ[τατα θρήϊκες ἀκρό [κ]ομοι λάβοιεν, ". . .drifting about on the wave. And at Salmydessus may the top-knotted Thracians give him naked a most kindly reception."; Pindar: Nemean 1.52: γυμνὸν. . . <φάσγανον>, "an unsheathed sword"; Isthmian 1.22–24: λάμπει δὲ σαφὴς ἀρετά ἔν τε γυμνοῖσι σταδίοις σφίσιν ἔν τ᾽ ἀσπιδοδούποισιν ὁπλίταις δρόμοις, ". . .and their excellence shines clearly in the naked foot races and in the races of armor with clanging shields. . ."; Olympian 3.23–24: τούτων ἔδοξεν γυμνὸς αὐτῷ κᾶπος ὀξείαις ὑπακουέμεν αὐγαῖς ἀελίου, "without [trees] the enclosure seemed naked to him and subject to the piercing rays of the sun."; Pythian 11.48–51: ἔσχον θοὰν ἀκτῖνα σὺν ἵπποις, Πυθοῖ τε γυμνὸν ἐπὶ στάδιον καταβάντες ἤλεγξαν Ἑλλανίδα στρατιὰν ὠκύτατι, ". . .captured swift brilliance with their horses, but also when they entered the naked foot race at Pytho they put to shame the Hellenic host with their speed." In Herodotus, being seen naked (ὀφθῆναι γυμνόν) is a barbarian taboo (1.10.3); on dress and undress in Herodotus, see Soares 2014.

[6] Scholarship on the origins of nudity in Geometric art includes Müller 1906, 85–87; Heilmeyer 1972, 61; Bonfante 1989, 549; Stewart 1990, 106; 1997, 34–42; Osborne 1997, 507–510; Hurwit 2007, 46, n. 52; Langdon 2008, 245–246; Stansbury-O'Donnell 2015, 88. On the origins of athletic nudity, see also Arieti 1975; McDonnell 1991; Christesen 2012b, 2013.

total exclusion of the visual evidence from *before* the period when nudity was firmly established throughout Aegean culture, especially the evidence from the EIA. A detailed treatment of naked males in iconography from the EIA thus promises to contribute original information to the discussion among scholars seeking to understand the cultural history of an interesting phenomenon in ancient Aegean culture: the establishment of ideals and cultural practices entailing the nude male.

The earliest consistent artistic tradition featuring male nudity in the Aegean comes in the form of small-scale bronze votive figurines. Because of their primacy as a coherent body of depictions of naked males in the material culture of a region in which naked males would become a dominant iconographic motif, these figurines are at the core of the analysis in this book. Although EIA bronze figurines comprise crucial early evidence for the development of visual and practical cultures of male nudity, they have generally been dismissed as a source of insight into these topics for reasons discussed below. The primary substantive contribution of this book is therefore to bring a critical and thorough discussion of this group of objects to bear on questions related to male nudity in Aegean culture, in dialogue with an increasingly sophisticated body of scholarly work on the social archaeology of the EIA Aegean. In doing so, the book advances scholarship on several axes: the history and geography of evidence for nudity in Aegean ritual contexts (especially those featuring physical contests), the regional diversity of ritual practice in the EIA Aegean in general, and the role of metallurgists and metallurgy in EIA ritual and society. Moreover, the book demonstrates how detailed analysis of archaeological evidence from the EIA can provide insight into and explanation of some aspects of later textual evidence, a departure from the more traditional model used in Classical archaeology, where texts are used to explain or enlighten material evidence.

THE HISTORY AND DEVELOPMENT OF SOCIETY AND FIGURAL ART FROM THE LATE BRONZE TO THE EARLY IRON AGE IN THE AEGEAN

This section provides an abbreviated introduction to the chronological and historical background of the Late Bronze Age (LBA) and EIA in the Aegean, the context in which the material presented in this book belongs. It is intended to be helpful for readers not familiar with the regional and chronological context. Details about the history and archaeology of the period continue to emerge from ongoing fieldwork and new syntheses frequently offer revisions to the big picture, so a universally satisfying, yet brief, account is impossible to produce. What follows represents an attempt to fairly encapsulate the current consensus.

Discussion of the Bronze Age in the Aegean typically divides the area into three regions.[7] On the mainland, the three phases of the Bronze Age (*ca.* 3000–1100) are known as Early, Middle, and Late Helladic, with the Late Helladic (LH) period (*ca.* 1600–1100) often referred to as Mycenaean, a designation derived from the type site of Mycenae and descriptive of the political development of somewhat complex states described below.[8] The phases of the Bronze Age on the Cycladic islands are labeled Early, Middle, and Late Cycladic. Finally, the island of Crete follows a sequence labeled Minoan after the legendary king Minos, accordingly Early, Middle, and Late Minoan.[9] However, Cretan archaeologists also refer to periods on the island according to terms derived from architectural developments: Protopalatial, Neopalatial, Final Palatial, and Postpalatial.

This terminology reflects one of the defining characteristics of the Middle and Late Bronze Ages in the Aegean, the appearance of large structures, termed palaces in the literature, that are probably related to the sociopolitical rise of complex, somewhat hierarchical states. On Crete, these states emerge in the Middle Bronze Age (*ca.* 2000–1600), alongside the appearance of large court-centered structures (palaces), communal sanctuaries, and signs of increasing sociopolitical complexity.[10] Among these are the appearance of a writing system, called Linear A, which remains undeciphered, and flourishing craft production industries with an extraordinary iconographic tradition that demonstrates a keen interest in the natural environment.

Influence from Neopalatial society on Crete probably played some role in the appearance of complex states on the mainland.[11] Few and far between during the Middle Bronze Age, signs of social and political complexity become more pronounced in the LH period, when large architectural complexes, also known as palaces and probably occupied by socially and politically powerful groups, also appear on the mainland. Late Bronze Age states on Crete and the mainland made use of a modified form of the preceding Linear A script called Linear B (mostly) in order to record economic transactions. Thanks to the

---

[7] Tartaron 2008, 83–84.

[8] The dates given are approximate; debate is ongoing regarding nearly all aspects of prehistoric Aegean chronology. LBA chronology has been recently discussed in Knapp and Manning 2016. For a brief summary of the current state of the field regarding LB III and EIA chronology, Dickinson 2020, 46–50.

[9] According to Thucydides and other historical Greek sources, Minos was a king of Crete who established the first known thalassocracy in the Aegean (Thuc. 1.3–8). The fact that the Cretan Bronze Age bears this name is a legacy of the early history of Aegean archaeology, during which it was normal disciplinary practice to associate mythical Greek and Homeric characters with Bronze Age remains (the Treasury of Atreus, the Mask of Agamemnon, etc.).

[10] Manning 2008.

[11] On Mycenaean state formation see, for example, Wright 2008; Maran and Wright 2020, 102–112.

decipherment of Linear B in the middle of the twentieth century, scholars are able to read these texts, which record an early form of the Greek language. As a result, we possess a reasonably granular understanding of the activities in which the palatial states took an economic interest and the various roles of individuals within the political structures at Pylos and Knossos, the two sites where the majority of the texts have been excavated.[12]

As was the case with the Linear B script, the architecture and material culture of mainland LBA states were influenced by and demonstrably similar to predecessors on Crete, although they were distinct in important ways.[13] Most notably, Cretan art is characterized by a wider range of media and greater technical virtuosity than imitative arts that appear on the mainland, and it is generally recognized that artists from Crete had a hand in crafting some of the finest material objects found in mainland palatial deposits.[14] However, Mycenaean pottery on the mainland developed a distinct and recognizably widespread, if regionally complex, figural style characterized by decoration that often included images of humans as well as stylized representations of natural phenomena or animals, like octopi.[15] Although artistic and political developments on Crete anticipated those on the mainland, it seems clear that the mainland states either conquered or became influential over Cretan society during the fourteenth century, after which the spatial organization and seeming hierarchy of Cretan sites is reconfigured somewhat.[16]

Eastern Mediterranean palatial states, including Aegean ones, confronted a series of crises around the turn of the twelfth century, the nature and exact outcomes of which continue to evade certain reconstruction.[17] What is not disputed is that the palatial states cease to exist in any meaningful operational terms by the early stages of the twelfth century. The palatial structures are mostly destroyed, information is no longer written down in Linear B or any other script, and ceramic styles and shapes change noticeably.[18] There is little doubt that whatever supra-regional political power palatial states and their leaders had accrued during the Bronze Age dissolved, and political structures were probably limited to local and regional influence during the following several centuries. There are good reasons to believe that the population of the

---

[12] Galaty and Parkinson 2007; Shelmerdine 2008; Shelmerdine and Bennet 2008.

[13] Often cited are the seemingly Hittite-influenced architectural characteristics of mainland palaces (e.g., Maner 2012; Blackwell 2014), burial customs, and an interest in large-scale engineering projects (e.g., the draining of the Kopaic basin; Knauss, Heinrich, and Kalcyk 1984).

[14] Crowley 2008, 261.   [15] Mountjoy 1999; Mommsen, Beier, and Hein 2002.

[16] The degree to which this influence was the result of cultural appropriation and borrowing or military conquest has been debated. Relevant discussions include Palaima 1987, 254–265, 2003; Olivier 1997; Nafplioti 2008; Alberti 2014.

[17] Cline 2014; Knapp and Manning 2016; papers in Middleton 2020.

[18] Dickinson 2020, 46.

mainland decreased substantially in some regions, although a stable population on Crete and some mainland regions, like Thessaly, is suggested by relatively stable numbers of sites throughout the twelfth and eleventh centuries.[19] It seems almost certain that some of the human attrition evident in the material record was the result of movements of people, especially emigration to other parts of the Mediterranean.[20] There is especially good evidence for a strong Aegean element in material culture on Cyprus during the twelfth century.[21] Although there is significant debate about the exact ramifications that these developments had for society, it is likely that some degree of insecurity and instability may have characterized life in some regions, as existing institutions were broken apart and reconstituted in somewhat different configurations.[22]

The series of events that precipitated apparent institutional change, known as the LBA collapse, ushered in the period that is known as the "Early Iron Age" because iron began to replace bronze as a material used to make some weapons and tools around this time.[23] Although manufactured iron artifacts appear in the Aegean starting around 1200, the final phase of the LBA (LB IIIC) in the twelfth century is considered part of the Bronze Age, because much of the material culture produced during this period continues to be recognizably similar to earlier Bronze Age types, before a significant change in style occurs during the eleventh century, the formal beginning of the Iron Age. In terms of material culture, many traditions of art in media large and small were no longer part of the repertoire of craftspeople working in the Aegean by the eleventh century. These included large-scale wall painting, most work in precious metals and materials like ivory and gold (which are rarely found in the postpalatial archaeological record), glassmaking, and glyptic. On the mainland, the relatively standardized designs of Mycenaean ceramic decoration develop into simple, usually geometric, schemes such as bands, triangles, and abstract patterns.[24] Most ceramicists recognize the existence of a phase characterized by transitional styles – called Subminoan and Submycenaean on Crete and the mainland, respectively – at least in some regions.[25] Figural decoration on ceramics becomes

---

[19] See evidence presented in Murray 2017, 210–246; 2018, 34, fig. 2.

[20] Yasur-Landau 2010.   [21] Iacovou 2012.

[22] For regional developments see, for example, Adrimi-Sismani 2006; Eder 2006a; Deger-Jalkotzy 2008; papers in Lemos and Kotsonas 2020, volume 2. On institutional change, Murray 2017, 254–249; Maran and Wright 2020, 117–120.

[23] On the reasons for and mechanisms of the introduction of iron production in the Aegean, see Waldbaum 1978; Snodgrass 1989; Sherratt 1994; Maddin 2011, 204–207.

[24] Dickinson 2006, 124.

[25] Some contend that Submycenaean should not be considered a distinct chronological division, but rather a particular subtype of LH IIIC pottery that was used exclusively in burials within particular regions (Papadopoulos, Damiata, and Marston 2011; but see Deger-Jalkotzy 2014). The Subminoan sequence is better defined and its existence as a separate chronological phase not as aggressively questioned.

increasingly rare during the course of the twelfth century, and by the eleventh century most of the remaining forms of material culture being produced are fully aniconic, which is to say that the human figure is not a prominent feature of the few crafts that continue to appear in the archaeological record – ceramics and bronze and iron objects – although anthropomorphic and zoomorphic figurines continue to be produced.[26] The existence of figural art in organic media that do not often survive archaeologically in Greece, like textiles, has been frequently posited but is yet to be definitively proven.[27]

The EIA is usually broken down into sub-phases according to ceramic chronology, since ceramics are prominent among the archaeological remains that have come down to us from the period. The main phases are the Protogeometric (PG; *ca.* 1050–900) and Geometric (900–700), both divided into Early, Middle, and Late; both use Attic ceramic development as a baseline.[28] However, regionalism is a prominent characteristic of both styles, and each area of the Aegean followed its own trajectory to some extent.[29] In some regions, such as Euboea and Crete, alternative phasing systems have been developed to describe sequences of EIA ceramics that are sufficiently distinct from the core Attic-derived chronology to merit such treatment.[30] In general, the PG style is decorated almost exclusively with geometric shapes, usually employing dark rectilinear shapes like zigzags, triangles, checkerboard patterns, and groups of bars or bands organized in horizontal registers on a buff surface. A concentric semicircle motif is also popular in some regional workshops.[31] During the ninth century, the PG style developed into the Geometric style. Geometric decoration is mostly rectilinear, and covers most of the surface of the pot, as opposed to PG decoration which was usually more limited in coverage.[32] Figural decoration in the form of birds and animals is evident from the beginning of the sequence of Geometric pottery. By the Late Geometric

---

[26] See discussion in Chapter 2.

[27] An EIA tradition of making figural scenes in basket-weaving or textiles seems like one of the only ways to explain the extraordinarily close resemblance between some examples of LBA and EIA iconography, for example, the *prothesis* scene on an LH IIIC krater from Aghia Triada in Elis and later Greek *prothesis* scenes (see Schoinas 1999, 258, fig. 1), or the line dance scene from an LH IIIC hydria from Kamini on Naxos (Mastrapas 1996, 798, figs. 1–2) and the line dancers in Peloponnesian art from the Geometric period. See also discussion on continuity in the iconography of mourning after the LBA in Papadopoulos 1993, 2014; Vikatou 2001, Kramer-Hajos 2015).

[28] Coldstream 2008. These dates are conventional; PG probably ought to end a bit earlier, while Geometric styles probably persisted after 700 in Athens, as elsewhere, for example, Crete and Euboea (Papadopoulos 2003, 146; Coulié 2013, 111, 198).

[29] Dickinson 2020, 46–47.   [30] Gauß and Ruppenstein 2020, 449–457.

[31] Lemos 2002, 3–26; on concentric circles, see Eiteljorg 1980; Papadopoulos, Vedder, and Schreiber 1998.

[32] See Coulié 2013, 36–37, fig. 2, which shows clearly the main features of the transition from the Submycenaean to Late Geometric styles.

period (the eighth century), human beings are regularly depicted on pottery in the region of Attica and occasionally but less regularly elsewhere. The human beings that decorate Geometric ceramics are represented as schematic silhouettes that follow the overall logic of the decorative schemes. Conventions for the depiction of the human figure are probably imitative of decoration on elaborate textiles, which mostly do not survive in the archaeological record but were likely to have been among the most prestigious craft goods during the period.[33]

The organization of society and political structure in the EIA are difficult to reconstruct with certainty, but it seems likely that the low levels of population on the mainland were accompanied by a situation in which most communities were small in scale and relatively simple in hierarchical organization. Cemeteries outnumber settlements in the archaeological record for the earlier part of the EIA. Burial offerings are mostly modest, limited to pottery or a few bronze and iron pins or weapons in most cases, although a few rich cemeteries at sites like Lefkandi in Euboea and Knossos on Crete contain a much wider variety of offerings. These exceptional sites show that at least some Aegean communities had ample contacts with the wider Mediterranean, especially Cyprus and Phoenicia, and access to sources of precious materials like ivory and gold through the eleventh and tenth centuries.[34] Excavated PG settlements on the mainland, like Nichoria in Messenia, Mitrou in East Lokris, and Asine in the Argolid, seem best described as villages, with simple architecture and few distinct differences in scale or elaboration from one structure to the next, although preliminary reports from recent excavations at Lefkandi demonstrate that this site was exceptional in its architecture as well as its burials.[35] However, there is little evidence for second-order institutions, like states, on the EIA mainland, and most scholars reconstruct simple political structures, perhaps centered around one important household, for this period.[36] A few rural sanctuaries (the most important being Olympia) were in use from at least the eleventh or tenth centuries, and at some (like Kalapodi) there is extant, if vestigial, evidence for continuity of cult from the Late Mycenaean period through to the EIA.[37]

---

[33] On the possibility that the designs imitate textiles, Benson 1982, 542; Barber 1991, 365–72; Murray, Chorghay, and MacPherson 2020. On the discovery of some textiles from seemingly elite burials during the EIA, see Popham, Touloupa, and Sackett 1982, 173; Spantidaki and Moulhérat 2011; Kolonas et al. 2017.

[34] See review of evidence for burial offerings in PG tombs on the mainland in Lemos 2002, 151–190. On the Knossos cemeteries see, for example, Antoniadis 2017.

[35] Nichoria (MacDonald et al. 1983); Asine (Wells 1983); Mitrou (Rückl 2008); Lefkandi (Lemos 2010, 2011–2012).

[36] Whitley 1991b; Mazarakis Ainian 1997; Thomas and Conant 1999; Whitley 2020.

[37] On both sanctuaries see discussion in Chapter 2. For ritual developments on the mainland in general, see Morgan 1990.

Crete follows a considerably different trajectory after the twelfth century. As noted above, population levels look to have been more stable on Crete, but there are still signs that not all was well. The Late Minoan (LM) IIIC and Subminoan periods are characterized by the establishment of new sites in dramatic defensible locations in the mountains.[38] These were largely abandoned for more convenient locations in the Cretan PG.[39] There is demonstrable continuity in the use of a number of sanctuaries, especially the cave sanctuaries of Mts. Ida and Dikte where large quantities of local and imported luxury goods were deposited throughout the EIA, and the site of Syme Viannou, a rural sanctuary located on the southern shoulders of the Lasithi massif in central-eastern Crete.[40]

The eighth century is usually considered a major watershed in the history of Greece, with developments therein constituting something of a 'renaissance' when cultural and social complexity reemerged after a long period of stagnation in the earlier EIA. Archaeological evidence dated to the turn of the eighth century and later is certainly more abundant, as the number of documented settlements increases, urban organization at most sites appears to become more complex, and indications of greater material prosperity among artifactual assemblages from tombs and settlements become apparent. Sanctuaries sites like Olympia and Delphi that appear to have been of regional importance in the eleventh to ninth centuries begin to accrue large quantities of votive offerings that suggest an increase in visitors from across the Aegean. According to much later chronicles, the first Olympic games were held in the eighth century, although this dating is far from secure, and debate continues about the exact nature of ritual and social interaction that occurred during the early phases of activity at interregional sanctuaries.[41] An important eighth-century development is the adaptation of the Phoenician alphabet and the advent of writing in alphabetic Greek script, although this has recently been pushed back into at least the ninth century by new finds at the site of Methone in coastal northern Greece.[42] Figural art becomes more abundant during the eighth century, both in decorated vase-painting and other media, such as metalwork and three-dimensional sculpture in bronze and terracotta. Some but not all of this change in the material record is related in complex ways to an increase in population, but scholars are not in agreement about how exactly to logically connect demography to social and political developments. Much discussion about the eighth century has centered on the way that the

---

[38] Nowicki 2000.   [39] Wallace 2010, 233–262.

[40] On the cave sanctuaries, see Rutkowski and Nowicki 1996; Coldstream 2006a; Sakellarakis 2013. On Syme Viannou see discussion in Chapter 4.

[41] On offerings, Morgan 1990, 1997, 2003; Crielaard 2015. On monumental structures, Verdan 2013, 2015; Petropoulos 2002; Kolia 2011. On the earliest Olympics, see Christesen 2007.

[42] Bessios, Tzifopoulos, and Kotsonas 2012.

changes in the archaeological record at the end of the EIA relate to "rise of the *polis*", the quintessential Archaic and Classical Greek city-state.

Trajectories established in the eighth century continue and accelerate in the succeeding Archaic period (*ca.* 700–480), which is where most scholars would place widespread establishment of city-states and related institutions for organizing and arbitrating political and military disputes among citizens. In addition to the presence of urban structures that were probably erected by collectives rather than individuals, archaeological evidence from the Archaic period demonstrates increasing, probably at least also partly collective, investment in monumental art and architecture, including the construction of the first monumental stone temples and gigantic stone sculptures of standing nude males and clothed females, known as *kouroi* and *korai*. By the seventh century, sanctuaries like Delphi and Olympia were holding regularly scheduled 'Panhellenic' (all Greek) festivals, where people from all around the Greek-speaking Mediterranean would gather to celebrate and participate in rituals like animal sacrifice and sporting contests. Elaborate metalwork, often influenced by designs known from the eastern Mediterranean, is increasingly associated with votive activity at interregional sanctuaries, and the Geometric style of the preceding period is largely abandoned, to be replaced with an elaborate figural style that likewise takes many cues from artistic traditions outside of the Aegean.[43] In general, the quantity and quality of material evidence surviving from the Archaic period indicates that this was a period of increasing prosperity and extensive connectivity for communities living in the Aegean. The Archaic is considered the first 'historical' period in Greek antiquity, due to the survival of substantial literary and epigraphic evidence datable to the seventh and sixth centuries and the fact that the first Greek historian, Herodotus, although writing in the fifth century, has much to say about events that notionally took place during the sixth century.

THE HISTORY AND ICONOGRAPHY OF THE NAKED MALE IN THE AEGEAN

Within this general narrative of Greek history and archaeology, male nudity has been examined along two axes. The first deals with practical nudity: when and why did people begin conducting activities, such as athletic contests, while unclothed? The second considers the history and development of a visual ideal of nudity: when and why did an identifiable and consistent iconography of nudity appear in material culture? Although scholarship is not so neatly divided

---

[43] Some relatively recent discussions on pertinent aspects of Archaic Greek history and archaeology are available in the following volumes: Raaflaub and van Wees 2009; Charalambidou and Morgan 2017; Duplouy and Brock 2018.

along such lines, these are two largely separate issues that should be dealt with separately in introducing the state of scholarship on the topic dealt with in the chapters that follow. In this section, I therefore review existing scholarship on the origins of both practical and visual cultures of nudity in ancient Greece.

Part of the purpose of this section is to introduce the reader to current understanding on these issues, but it is also intended to explain why the earliest images of naked males from the ancient Aegean – the EIA figurines that I deal with in this book – have never been the central analytical target of scholarship, even though the earliest images of naked males in the regional tradition would seem like the most obvious place to start in trying to answer the questions stated above. The critique presented here establishes the need for a project along the lines of this book, which is novel in pressing the search for answers to questions about the origin of Aegean developments regarding the relationship between practical and aesthetic nudity back into the late second millennium.

Nudity in Ancient Greek History and Society

From the point of view of the ancient historian, a compelling question concerns the history of social practice involving regular nudity in ancient Greece: its chronology, behavioral context, and sociopolitical circumstances. Ancient Greece was not a nudist culture – the prominence of nudity in Greek art does not represent reality, in the sense that most Greeks did not engage in activities like warfare and work while entirely naked.[44] The practice of male nudity in ancient Greece was instead limited to particular events and special locations. Historians generally accept that there was male initiatory nudity present in Greece prior to the Archaic period.[45] However, since evidence for these initiatory nude events is separated considerably in time and space from most of the evidence for historically documented practices of nudity,[46] existing studies largely concern the historically most prominent forms of practical male nudity: athletic nudity and civic nudity.

---

[44] Osborne 1997, 506; David 2010, 152; Lee 2015, 179.

[45] For example, Bonfante 1989, 547–548, 553; McDonnell 1991, 193; Leitao 1995; Stewart 1997, 28–29, 240; Christesen 2013, 227.

[46] Christesen (2002, 19–20, n. 20) and Scanlon (2002, 360–361, n. 48) both lay out the extant evidence in a long footnote before concluding that this evidence is likely not relevant to historical Greece. Although familiar with Koehl's thesis (Koehl 1986, 2016) that Aegean athletic contests in ritual contexts originated on Crete, Scanlon rejects it, asserting that "no archaeological or other evidence from Crete indicates a continuity of athletic contests attached to these rituals" and that "the Dorian occupation and the devastation of the Dark Age make the continuity less likely." David (2010, 138) suggests but then dismisses a prehistoric origin for nude athletics. See also Thommen 1996.

These two forms of nudity were first defined by Larissa Bonfante.[47] Athletic nudity is the practice of performing physical exercise or competition while in a state of complete undress. There is good reason to believe that the majority of athletic contests in Archaic and Classical Greek society involved a state of total undress on the part of the participants.[48] Civic nudity is a more complex phenomenon involving the more-or-less compulsory practice of collective nude exercise in a gymnasium that served to symbolically circumscribe a group of enfranchised citizens and to create some kind of unity among them.[49] The latter institution was clearly and certainly a development of the late Archaic and Classical periods. More controversial are the origins of athletic nudity.

The History of Nude Athletic Competition in the Aegean

When did Greeks begin exercising and competing in athletics while naked? There is some textual evidence for the history of regular male nudity in the context of athletic training and competition. Late traditions connecting the inception of athletic nudity with early Olympic victors would place the beginnings of athletic nudity in the eighth or seventh centuries, but these traditions are internally inconsistent and have therefore been viewed skeptically by historians.[50] Passages from the fifth- and fourth-century authors Thucydides and Plato provide accounts of the beginnings of athletic nudity that have been afforded greater credibility in scholarly discourse. Thucydides states that athletic nudity was invented at Sparta in the Peloponnese and

---

[47] Bonfante 1989.

[48] Bonfante 1989, 556–557; Christesen 2007, 353–359; Christesen 2013, 227.

[49] On civic nudity, see Bonfante 1989, 557–558; Christesen 2002; Hurwit 2007, 57; Lee 2015, 179–181.

[50] These traditions attribute the innovation of athletic nudity to individual athletes. Three different individuals are credited with inventing nude sport in the sources: Orsippos of Megara or Sparta, Akanthos of Sparta, and an anonymous Athenian athlete. See McDonnell 1991, 183, n. 2 for a summary of the relevant sources (they include Dionysios of Halikarnassos *Rom. Arch.* 7.72.2–3; Pausanias 1.44.1; Isidorus of Seville *Etymologiae* 18.7.2). These texts date the onset of athletic nudity to the fourteenth (724), fifteenth (720), or thirty-second (652) Olympiads. Moretti (1957) has rejected the latter date as an outright mistake. The earliest source is purported to be an epigram composed by Simonides, but this text is transmitted quite late, via a Hadrianic or fifth century CE inscription from Megara (*CIG* I 1050 = *IG* 7.52 = Kaibel, *Epig. Gr.* 843). A whole separate discussion would be required to review historians' explanations for why Greek society began to integrate nude exercise as a regular form of behavior in everyday life. Most of the explanations fall into one of three categories: practical, erotic, and sociopolitical. For practical explanations (and related discussions) see Erbse 1969; Sweet 1985; Hannah 1998; David 2010, 139; Christesen 2013, 227. For erotic explanations see Arieti 1975, 436; Ludwig 2002, 263, 318. For sociopolitical explanations, see Crowther 1982; Christesen 2012a, 2012b, 2013; Ducat 2006. I return to this issue briefly in Chapter 6.

suggests that the practice did not begin long before his own time (Thuc. 1.6.5):[51]

> ἐγυμνώθησάν τε πρῶτοι καὶ ἐς τὸ φανερὸν ἀποδύντες λίπα μετὰ τοῦ γυμνάζεσθαι ἠλείψαντο τὸ δὲ πάλαι καὶ ἐν τῷ Ὀλυμπικῷ ἀγῶνι διαζώματα ἔχοντες περὶ τὰ αἰδοῖα οἱ ἀθληταὶ ἠγωνίζοντο καὶ οὐ πολλὰ ἔτη ἐπειδὴ πέπαυται.

> [The Lakedaemonians] were the first to bare their bodies and, after stripping openly, to anoint themselves with oil when they engaged in athletic exercise; for in early times, even in the Olympic games, the athletes wore girdles about their loins in the contests, and it is not many years since the practice has ceased. (trans. Smith)

Likewise, Plato (*Republic* V 452c) states that the Greeks had not been accustomed to nudity for very long. In contrast to Thucydides, he assigns the geographical origin of the practice of regular nudity to Crete, which is where he believes the Spartans learned it.[52]

> ...οὐ πολὺς χρόνος ἐξ οὗ τοῖς Ἕλλησιν ἐδόκει αἰσχρὰ εἶναι καὶ γελοῖα ἅπερ νῦν τοῖς πολλοῖς τῶν βαρβάρων, γυμνοὺς ἄνδρας ὁρᾶσθαι, καὶ ὅτε ἤρχοντο τῶν γυμναίων πρῶτοι μὲν Κρῆτες. ἔπειτα Λακεδαιμόνιοι, ἐξῆν τοῖς τότε ἀστείοις πάντα ταῦτα κωμῳδεῖν.

> ...it is not so long since the Greeks thought it shameful and ridiculous, as the majority of foreigners do now, to see men naked, and when the Cretans first began to exercise naked, followed by the Spartans, the wits of the day made fun of all this. (trans. Emlyn-Jones and Preddy)

Considerable scholarly debate concerns the degree of skepticism with which we should view these statements.[53] Read at face value, Thucydides' and Plato's assertions would indicate that athletic nudity was introduced in the fifth century, or at the earliest in the late sixth century. Thucydides' account is, however, made in the context of a rationalizing argument about the trajectory

---

[51] On the meaning of the adjective *gymnos*, the linguistic history of its denominative, and the likelihood that 'nude' rather than 'lightly clad' is meant in this context, see Sturtevant 1912, 324–329; Mann 1947; Christesen 2002.

[52] Other accounts linking Cretan and Spartan institutions include Hdt. 1.65.4–5; Aristotle *Pol.* 1271b 20, 1272a 1f; Strabo 10.4.17–19.

[53] For scholars generally convinced by the Thucydidean and Platonic dating, see Gomme 1945–1951, 106; Sansone 1988, 109; Harris 1964, 64; Arieti 1975, 431–432. Both Boekh (*CIG* I 1050, 555) and Howland (1983, *OCD*², 142) sought to make sense of the evidence by limiting early nude athletics to one sort of contest or another (e.g., boxing or running). McDonnell (1991, 184) is more skeptical of Thucydides and places more weight on the evidence from visual culture for an early date: "...scholars who simply reject the early 'Orsippos-Akanthos' tradition in favor of the later date of Thucydides and Plato ignore a considerable amount of evidence which indicates both an early innovation and the prevalence of athletic nudity in Athens, from, at the latest, 550." On the history of combat sports in Greece, see Poliakoff 1987.

of Greek civilization, and this might give us pause in assigning it verisimilitude to actual historical events.[54] The context of the statement, part of a general commentary on the way in which Greeks have lately distinguished themselves from non-Greeks, underlines the rhetorical purpose of the passage. In turn, Plato is probably drawing upon Thucydides' account or a common source in his statements in the *Republic*.[55] He also seeks to position the practice of athletic nudity as a civilized act special to the Greeks which others do not understand.

While some have taken the statements by Thucydides and Plato at face value, concluding that athletic nudity could not have been introduced before the fifth century, it is not clear that either Thucydides or Plato had good evidence for the earliest history of nude athletics.[56] Both were Athenians, and as such they likely had limited access to information about the genesis of institutions and norms that most likely arose in regions such as the western Peloponnese or Crete where record keeping may have been limited.[57] In general, it is probably safest to proceed on the assumption that Thucydides and Plato are not reliable guides to the timing of the advent of athletic nudity in early Greece.

There is, moreover, compelling evidence in the archaeological and art historical record to suggest that athletic nudity arose prior to the fifth century.[58] It has generally been accepted that the presence of nudity in Archaic Greek art dated to the seventh and sixth centuries proves that athletic nudity was practiced prior to the fifth century,[59] provided we can accept that art gives

[54] On the context of Thucydides' account in regard to athletics, see McDonnell 1991, 189–193.

[55] McDonnell 1991, 190–193.

[56] Schröder 1927, 22–23; Gardiner 1930, 191; Mouratidis 1985, 213–214; Beck 1988, 421; Sansone 1988, 108.

[57] Müller (1906, 91–95) suggested that Thucydides had poor or little information regarding the origins of athletic nudity, making his account of little use. Crowther (1982) argued that Thucydides was describing a recent development separate from the original innovation of regular athletic nudity. In this argument, the more recent (likely sixth century) advent of nudity is positioned as especially designed to increase contrasts between Greeks and barbarians after the Persian wars. See also Christesen 2013, 228.

[58] Until the early 1990s, a group of vases that Myles McDonnell called the *perizomata* vases was thought to provide a *terminus post quem* for the widespread adoption of athletic nudity (McDonnell 1991, 186–189). The *perizomata* vases depict athletes competing while wearing loincloths and date to the end of the sixth century. In combination with Thucydides' assertion that athletic nudity was a fifth-century innovation, this iconography supported the idea that athletic nudity may not have been widely adopted in a durable tradition as a cultural practice until the fifth century. However, McDonnell argued that the *perizomata* vases were probably produced for consumers in Magna Graecia who did not exercise while naked, and thus should not be taken as evidence for the history of athletic nudity in the Aegean.

[59] See McDonnell 1991, 184, nn. 7, 9–11, for a review of the evidence. Especially revealing is the evidence collected in Legakis 1977, which comprises over 800 representations of naked athletes in art of the sixth century.

us a faithful and accurate window into developments in real life.[60] Based on this evidence, most scholars posit a date for the introduction of athletic nudity sometime prior to the fifth century.

While the evidence from Plato and Thucydides provides a *terminus ante quem* for the origins of the practice, and the artistic evidence suggests that it must have begun significantly prior to the fifth century, the lack of nude athletics in LBA art in combination with evidence from the *Homeric Iliad and Odyssey*, usually dated to the eighth or seventh centuries BCE, has been taken to provide a reliable *terminus post quem* for the beginnings of athletic nudity. Total nudity is not generally apparent in LBA depictions of physical contests that might be called athletics.[61] In addition, the Homeric poems do not seem to include nude athletics.[62] The wrestlers in Patroklos' funeral games, for example, put on a loincloth before competing.[63]

Based on this combination of artistic and literary evidence, historians are generally in agreement that nudity was not a feature of athletic competitions prior to the sixth century.[64] According to the consensus, the origin of nude athletics is placed in the later Archaic period because the absence of nudity in the Homeric poems obviates the possibility that this practice had its origins prior to the eighth century, because Thucydides and Plato prove that it must have been common by the fifth century, and because a critical mass of visual evidence of nude athletes appears only in the sixth century.[65]

---

[60] One exception is Thuillier (1988) who argued that artists' decision to depict young naked males led to imitative practices whereby young men began stripping down before exercising and competing. Most historians have not been convinced by Thuillier's model, and instead follow the more orthodox logic whereby the appearance of nude males in art provides convincing evidence for a practice of athletic nudity.

[61] Bonfante 1989, 548; McDonnell 1991, 182, n. 1; Christesen 2013, 227. Most scholars do not think that athletics played an important part in the societies of the Aegean Bronze Age. However, LBA experts are not entirely in agreement, see, for example, Younger 1976; Rystedt 1986, 1988; Demakopoulou 1989; Younger 1995; Rehak 1996; Militello 2003; Lebessi, Muhly, and Papasavvas 2004, 11–21; Rutter 2006.

[62] For example, Bonfante 1989, 543–570, esp. 547–548; McDonnell 1991, 182, n. 1; Christesen 2013, 227; Lear 2013, 253.

[63] Examples can be found at *Il.* 23.685; *Il.* 23.710; *Od.* 18.66–69; 18.76. See Karouzou 1960, 60–71; Gordon 1950–1951; McDonnell 1991, 182, n. 1. See also Dionysios of Halikarnassos (7.72.3) for an ancient argument that these passages prove that ancient Greek athletes did not compete while naked.

[64] An exception to this rule is Mouratidis 1985. There is a very cursory treatment in Müller 1906, 72–74.

[65] McDonnell 1991, 182: "…fairly certain that athletic nudity was not practiced before the late eighth century"; Percy 1996, 114: "Everyone agrees that nudity in gymnastics, even when performed before the public, began among the literate rather than the preliterate Greeks."; Christesen 2002, 17: "…the custom of performing athletics in the nude was not common in Greece until the sixth century."; Christesen 2013, 227; Christesen 2018, 547: "Before the sixth century, Greek athletes typically wore a loincloth."

Homer and Nudity

The Homeric evidence has thus proven crucial in reconstructing the history of nudity in Greek culture. Historians have interpreted Homer's treatment of nudity as a convenient *terminus post quem* allowing them to to bracket a limited period within the Archaic period when nude athletics was introduced. They have then proceeded to rationally situate the origins of this peculiar phenomenon within a particular Archaic sociopolitical and cultural context that may be reconstructed with some granularity.

In this section, I review the Homeric evidence in some detail, so that the reader may assess the basis of historians' conclusions, which are important here because they have implications for the interpretation of the EIA evidence I present in the rest of the book. If historians seem correct in stating that the Homeric poems provide convincing proof of an Archaic origin for most meaningful nude activity in the EIA, there is no use examining EIA evidence for insights into the cultural history of naked males in Aegean life and art. However, if the Homeric evidence seems unsatisfying from this perspective, then it eliminates any *terminus post quem* for the date at which naked activities began to constitute an element of Aegean cultural practice and sets the stage for a reevaluation of EIA evidence along these lines.

There is little to suggest the presence of a positive or idealistic connotation for nudity in the Homeric poems.[66] The adjective *gymnos* (γυμνός, naked/lightly clad) occurs eight times in the *Iliad*, once in the *Odyssey*, and three times (in one passage) in Hesiod's corpus.[67] Perhaps because of the rarity of its appearance in early Greek poetry, nudity in Homer has not drawn a great deal of comment from scholars of the Homeric poems.[68] In the few existing discussions of Homeric *gymnos* in scholarship, the most frequent interpretation is that nudity represents "shame, vulnerability, death, and dishonor."[69] *Gymnos* can also simply indicate a state of being "lightly clad/armed" (it was used throughout antiquity to denote both).[70] In the most detailed existing

---

[66] Percy 1996, 114.

[67] The adjective can also be used to describe an arrow or bow that has been removed from its quiver or case (*Od.* 11.607; *Od.* 21.417).

[68] Himmelmann 1985; 1990; Bonfante 1989; 1990; Stewart 1997, 24–42; Ferrari 2002, 114–15; Hurwit 2007.

[69] MacCary 1982, 153–154; Bonfante 1989, 547; Yamagata 2005; Hurwit 2007, 55; Thommen 2007, 17–22.

[70] Himmelmann 1985; 1990; Osborne 1997, 504–528; Stewart 1997, 25; Christesen 2002, 23–24. Chantraine (1968) gives the definition as "nu, sans vêtement, sans arme" in its Homeric sense, and the denominative γυμνόομαι (*gymnoomai*) as "se mettre nu, se denuder, être sans defense, être nue, en parlant d'une épée" (also see this entry for the inexplicable development of the initial γ from a presumptive dental initial sound; cf. Sturtevant 1912; Knobloch 1993). Likewise, Frisk (1960) gives a definition of "nackt, unbedeckt, unbewaffnet" for the Homeric use. Already by the Archaic period (Tyrtaean and Herodotean use) the derivative γυμνής, -ῆτος (*gymnes, etos*) for "leichtbewaffneter Krieger" appears.

treatment of *gymnos* in Homer, MacCary argued that the Homeric *gymnos* indicates a man who has been stripped of his armor and is therefore incapable of actually fulfilling his function as a man.[71] In MacCary's view, being *gymnos* implies having been "symbolically castrated" (153) because (154) "the man who has no armor cannot fight, the man who cannot fight is not a man." Being *gymnos* is equivalent to being like a woman, as suggested by Hektor's statement about being *gymnos* in book 22, when he worries that if he goes as a suppliant to Achilleus in that state "like a woman," it would be shameful and worse than dying while fighting like a man. MacCary was primarily interested in a Freudian analysis of the nudity of heroes. To him, armor is part of the "phallic" manhood that distinguishes Homeric heroes, without which they are no longer either men or heroes.[72]

For the reader interested in the basis for these arguments, I present a discussion of the relevant passages in Appendix A. In the current context, it is efficient to accept the general conclusion that nudity in the Homeric poems is usually associated with vulnerability and shame, or it is a characteristic of a corpse.[73] Being unclothed in public and being unarmored in battle are indications of an undesirable state of weakness. The masculinity of Homeric characters is defined by external accessories rather than by heroic nudity.[74] The notions of recognition, deception, and identity in Homer have been treated extensively in existing scholarship, and this work has established a clear relationship between clothing, armor, and persona/identity in the worlds of early epic.[75]

Moreover, there is no explicit association between nudity and athletic activity in Homeric poetry and, according to scholarly orthodoxy, Homeric athletes always wore loincloths.[76]

Despite the confidence with which most historians state this latter point, there is room for considerable skepticism about the notion that Homeric characters were always clothed when participating in athletic contests, because it does not necessarily follow explicitly from the relevant passages in the poems. Athletic activities are encountered in several scenes of the *Iliad* and *Odyssey*. While Homer often describes the clothing, accessories, or accoutrements of his characters in some detail, athletic attire is afforded little attention.[77] Brief descriptions

---

[71] MacCary 1982, 152–154.   [72] MacCary 1982, 160–161.

[73] See also Osborne 1997, 507.   [74] Yamagata 2005; van Wees 2010.

[75] Beidelmann 1989, 235; Yamagata 2005; van Wees 2010. Block (1985) stresses that the importance of clothing as a maker of the man can be seen at many moments in the action and dialogue of the poem, for example, *Od.* 14.503–506.

[76] See sources in n. 65.

[77] On clothing in Homer, see, for example, Block 1985; van Wees 1995. As opposed to that of athletes, the clothing of dancers is specified in detail, for example, *Od.* 17.166–169; for the clothing of festival dancers, *Il.* 18.593–6: "There, youths and marriageable girls/were

of informal athletic activity can be found at *Iliad* 2.773–775, where Achilleus' army practices discus and javelin throws on the beach, and *Odyssey* 17.166–169, where the suitors in Ithaka do the same to work up an appetite for dinner.

Il. 2.773–775:
λαοὶ δὲ παρὰ ῥηγμῖνι θαλάσσης
δίσκοισιν τέρποντο καὶ αἰγανέῃσιν ἱέντες
τόξοισίν θ᾽;

And his men along the shore of the sea
amused themselves in casting the discus and the javelin
and with archery.[78]

Od. 17.167–169
μνηστῆρες δὲ πάροιθεν Ὀδυσσῆος μεγάροιο
δίσκοισιν τέρποντο καὶ αἰγανέῃσιν ἱέντες,
ἐν τυκτῷ δαπέδῳ, ὅθι περ πάρος, ὕβριν ἔχοντες.

And the suitors meanwhile in front of the palace of Odysseus
were making merry, throwing the discus and the javelin
as their custom was in insolence of heart.

Neither passage provides information about attire. More expansive descriptions of Homeric sport are found in two places: the long section of *Iliad* 23 detailing the funeral games for Patroklos and the description of athletic contests in the context of a festival at Phaiakia in *Odyssey* 8. The funeral games for Patroklos involve chariot racing, boxing, wrestling, running, armed combat, a sort of discus throw using a mass of iron, archery, and the javelin throw. In general, the attire of the participants is not discussed. However, passages regarding boxing and wrestling events mention that combatants gird themselves with a *zoma* prior to competing.[79] According to *Iliad* 23.683–687 and *Iliad* 23.710, the contestants in the boxing prepare for the contest by casting belts around their waists, and the shade of Agamemnon remembers this feature of such contests after his death:

Iliad 23.683–687
ζῶμα δέ οἱ πρῶτον παρακάββαλεν, αὐτὰρ ἔπειτα
δῶκεν ἱμάντας ἐϋτμήτους βοὸς ἀγραύλοιο.
τὼ δὲ ζωσαμένω βήτην ἐς μέσσον ἀγῶνα,
ἄντα δ᾽ ἀνασχομένω χερσὶ στιβαρῇσιν ἅμ᾽ ἄμφω
σύν ῥ᾽ ἔπεσον, σὺν δέ σφι βαρεῖαι χεῖρες ἔμιχθεν.

---

dancing, with their hands on each other's wrists/the girls wore fine linen dresses, the youths' tunics/well-woven, faintly gleaming with oil."

[78] All translations of Homer in the text are based on A. T. Murray's translation in the Loeb Classical Library editions (LCL Nos. 104–105, 170–171).

[79] On belts in early Greece and Homer see Bennett 1997, 103–115. Bennett connects the limited use of belting in combat sports to a general association of belts with warriors in the contemporary eastern Mediterranean context (105–110, esp. n. 29).

A belt he first cast about him and then
gave him well-cut thongs of the hide of an ox of the field.
So, the two, girded, stepped into the center of the assembly,
and lifting their mighty hands on high one against the other
fell on one another and their hands clashed together in heavy blows.

Iliad 23.710
ζωσαμένω δ' ἄρα τώ γε βάτην ἐς μέσσον ἀγῶνα

Girded, they stepped into the center of the assembly

Odyssey 24.87–89
ἤδη μὲν πολέων τάφῳ ἀνδρῶν ἀντεβόλησας
ἡρώων, ὅτε κέν ποτ' ἀποφθιμένου βασιλῆος
ζώννυνταί τε νέοι καὶ ἐπεντύνονται ἄεθλα.

Before now you have been present at the funeral games of many men,
heroes, when at the death of a king
the young men gird themselves and prepare to win prizes.

An important issue is the precise meaning of the term *zoma* and related verbal constructions in these contexts. Although it is often translated as loincloth, there is no reason to assume that the *zoma* functioned in the way that the English word would suggest, that is, to cover the loins.[80] Instead, parallels from the broader Mediterranean in a comparable chronological timeframe suggest that the Homeric *zoma* was probably a garment worn around the waist that did not cover the loins.[81] Comparative evidence indicates that the EIA and Archaic meaning of *zoma* in the Mediterranean was a leather or cloth belt specifically worn in combat sports and associated with heroic acts and warriors.[82] Parallels from EIA art support the fact that this may be a preferable definition of the *zoma*: there are many belts on EIA figurines, but they do not cover the groin.[83]

Turning to the *Odyssey's* Phaiakian festival games, the events included a running race, a wrestling contest, a long jump, a discus throw, and a boxing match. There is no mention of attire, except for the description of Odysseus "leaping up with his cloak about him as it was" in a fit of anger to compete

---

[80] For translation/reception as loincloth, for example, Leaf 1900–1902, 579–81; Lorimer 1950, 250; Scanlon 2002, 297; Christesen 2013, 227. A frequent point made in favor of the fact that the *zoma* must mean a loincloth is that Dionysios of Halikarnassos uses the term to support his argument that there were no nude athletics in early Greece. Dionysios was writing in the first century (7.72.3), so his testimony has limited value for reconstructing EIA practice. As Bennett (1997, 109; following Bonfante 1989, 548, n. 26) points out, his comments "need only indicate that in his day *zoma* meant an article of clothing that covered the genitals."

[81] Gordon 1950–1951, 131–136. Gordon provides Near Eastern and Egyptian parallels in which wrestlers wear belts around their waists for competition but are otherwise entirely naked. For example, wrestlers painted in the eleventh dynasty Egyptian tomb of Baqti III at Beni Hasan wear belts that only cover the waist (Decker 1978, 73–78).

[82] Bennett 1997, 111. [83] Naumann 1969; Byrne 1991, 113–116.

when he is accused of being incapable of athletic excellence (*Od.* 8.186–188). Given the extenuating circumstances, Homer might have mentioned the cloak precisely because throwing a discus with a cloak on is exceptional, not because clothed athletics was the norm:

ἦ ῥα καὶ αὐτῷ φάρει ἀναΐξας λάβε δίσκον
μείζονα καὶ πάχετον, στιβαρώτερον οὐκ ὀλίγον περ
ἢ οἵῳ Φαίηκες ἐδίσκεον ἀλλήλοισι.

He spoke, and leaping up with his cloak about him as it was
seized a discus larger than the rest, and thick, heavier by no slight amount
than those with which the Phaeacians were accustomed to contend with one
    another.

In sum, although it has become scholarly orthodoxy to assert that these passages prove Homer's athletes do not compete while nude, on closer inspection it seems apparent that they could just as easily be interpreted to mean that the athletes were naked for most events, but put on belts for boxing and wrestling.[84] The evidence may indicate that removing unnecesary clothing and donning special equipment normally took place directly prior to the start of competition, and that precise attire depended on the event scheduled to take place next (*Il.* 23.739). When Ajax, Odysseus, and Antilochus prepare for the running race, no mention is made of their attire – they do not gird themselves before competing, unlike the boxers and wrestlers – so a logical conclusion could be that, having stripped off their tunics and not put on a belt, they ran unclothed. The lack of information given about girding prior to events other than wrestling might, in general, just as well indicate that most athletes competed in most events naked, but put a belt on for the heavy events of wrestling and boxing.

Overall, it seems concerning that the evidentiary basis for assigning the advent of nude athletics to a post-seventh century date is limited to a few lines in Homeric epic, even though it is not clear from these lines that Homeric athletes always compete while wearing a loincloth. Although there seem to be some fragments of an ideology connecting nudity with vulnerability or weakness in a military context in the *Iliad* and *Odyssey*, there is no convincing reason to deny the possibility that Homeric athletes may have been unclothed. In sum, the Homeric evidence upon which a *terminus post quem* for nude competitions in Greek history has been erected should be considered shaky, even if one accepts a straightforward connection between Homeric poetry and historical institutions.

---

[84] Likewise, the athletes must put on armor in order to participate in the clash of arms at *Il.* 23.802–805. For accounts of warriors putting on a *zoma* covered in bronze in preparation for battle, see Bennett 1997, 67–102.

Homer, History, and the Archaeological Record

However, it should be stated at this point that most EIA archaeologists do not currently think that it is possible to generalize about EIA practices or ideas based on the practices and ideologies present in the Homeric poems. Much of the history of debate on this topic is well known to scholars of early Greece, but I review it very briefly here.[85] After a long period in the nineteenth century during which scholars dismissed Homer's stories of the Trojan War as mere myth and fantasy, Heinrich Schliemann confounded the world when he excavated a major Bronze Age citadel at the site of Hissarlik in the Troad, which he proclaimed to be the site of Troy.[86] Schliemann believed that the remains he discovered proved the historical accuracy of the poems, which he read as an eyewitness account of a war that happened during Homer's lifetime.[87] This hypothesis ran into serious problems when it became clear that Homer's texts could not have been written down until the invention of the Greek alphabet, at least half a millennium after the date of the final walled phase of the citadel at Troy.[88] In the 1950s, Moses Finley argued, *contra* Schliemann, that the society described in Homer's poetry was not a guide to the Bronze Age, but provided a reasonably accurate depiction of life during the period between the collapse of the Mycenaean palaces and the birth of the *polis*, of which he saw few signs in Homer's world.[89]

While Finley's view proved influential and led to a great deal of work describing the EIA as a fundamentally Homeric world, it was largely vitiated in the 1980s by scholarship demolishing the idea that oral poetry should be used as a reliable historical document for any period.[90] Instead, oral poetry constitutes a highly versatile narrative genre whose content changes rapidly in the hands of its practitioners in order to suit contemporary audiences and their view of how society ought to work.[91] It is therefore clear that, even if we wish to place the composition of the versions of the *Iliad* and the *Odyssey* that have come down to us in the eighth century, we cannot 'read' eighth century Greek society (let alone tenth or ninth century society) from these texts.

Developments in Homeric studies since the 1980s have produced updated views on the relationship between Homer and history. One such view grows from an increasingly widespread recognition that the original manuscript

---

[85] See Crielaard 1995, 201–207; Latacz 2004; Grethlein 2009.
[86] Grote 1846–1856, vol. 1, 321; Schliemann 1880, 336–345.
[87] Schliemann's argument gained acceptance in the scholarly community by the early twentieth century. See Allen 1921; Page 1959; papers in Wace and Stubbings 1962; Mylonas 1966; Luce 1975.
[88] Morris 2000, 87–88.
[89] Finley 1954; 1981, 199–212, 232. See also Andrewes 1961; Dickinson 1986.
[90] Morris 1986; cf. van Wees 1992; 1994, comments and discussion in Crielaard 1995; Bakker 2018; Segal 2018, 113–141; Dickinson 2020, 38.
[91] For example, Cook 2004, 49.

tradition of the Homeric poems should not be dated to the eighth century, but rather well into the Archaic period.[92] If this dating for the fixing of the manuscripts is correct, and if we accept that the society described in the poems would have constantly evolved to remain relevant to its audience, there is little secure grounds on which to argue that the *Iliad* and the *Odyssey* provide good evidence from which to reconstruct society or institutions between the thirteenth and eighth centuries, whether or not the poems contain some memories of that period.[93]

Even those favoring an optimistic reading of the relationship between Homer and history must admit that there are likely to be many social practices and historical realities that epic poetry is not likely to enlighten at all.[94] As over a century of scholarship on early hexameter poetry has demonstrated, almost every aspect the Homeric poems is complicated and difficult to understand and interpret.[95] Homeric poetry probably served a particular purpose in the imaginative and mythical cognitive landscapes of the societies in which it circulated.[96] It is likely that there were regionally specific variations on the stories in the poems, and that distinct traditions developed and evolved through time.[97] Literary scholars with whom I have discussed the outsized influence Homeric poetry has had on interpretations of EIA archaeology express inverse annoyance with the idea anyone should ever expect a literary text to reveal underlying social realities with fidelity.

In general, then, the current scholarly consensus on the EIA in the Aegean is that it represents a long period for which no extant textual evidence is clearly relevant.[98] While it may once have been acceptable to attribute the existence

---

[92] Nagy 2003; West 2011, 185–186; Bendall and West 2020, 58. However there is not universal agreement on a later dating of the poems, see, for example, Rutherford 2019, 34, n. 80.

[93] Sherratt 1990; Bennet 2014; West 2014.

[94] Although it is not impossible to imagine that select elements within the epic do tell us something about the EIA, see, for example, Korfmann 1995; Bennet 1997; Gottschall 2008; Monroe 2009, 227–230; Olsen 2014, 95–100.

[95] The volume and sophistication of literary work on Homer is a truly awesome testament to this complexity. Debate continues on even basic aspects of the identity or identities of the author/s of the poems (see, e.g., Rutherford 2013, 1–29) or their likely audiences (e.g., Dalby 1995). Issues of orality and textuality, including not only the date when the poems were originally written down but also the extent and timing of later editing and interference, likewise continue to divide scholars (see discussion in, e.g., Currie 2016, 55–72; Ready 2019).

[96] For a range of cosmological readings of just a single object in the poem, the shield of Achilleus, see, for example, Buffière 1956, 155–172; Taplin 1980; Hardie 1985.

[97] Hall 2002, 56–89; Sherratt 1990; Rutherford 2019, 38.

[98] A resurgent link between Homer and historical events has been advocated by Latacz, and followed by some other scholars (Niemeier 1999; Latacz 2004, 2005; Schrott 2008. For a critical review, see Ulf 2003). According to Latacz, the resemblance between the archaeological remains of Troy VIIa and the city and environment described in the *Iliad* provides a compelling case for the facticity of a Trojan War along the lines of what Homer describes. But even Latacz's position, currently among the staunchest still advocating a link between real historical events and Homer's stories, admits that the texts have only the kernel

or absence of cultural institutions from the EIA based on a reading of a few lines of Homer, this is no longer true. Put simply, Homeric poetry is not describing how nudity worked in the EIA in any general or specific sense. The conclusion that Homer gives us a *terminus post quem* for the introduction of regular nude athletics in early Greece should therefore be set aside.

Summary

Because there is no explicit heroic or athletic nudity present in Homeric epic, and because of a few comments by Athenian authors placing the development of nude athletics recently before their lifetimes in the Classical period, historians have agreed that meaningful practices and aesthetics associated with male nudity did not develop until the later Archaic period. However, it is not consistent with best practices in current archaeological or literary analysis to contend that Homer can serve as a general proxy for cultural practices or beliefs in any historical period, let alone the EIA, which is probably considerably removed chronologically from the composition of the versions of Homer's poems that have come down to us. In general, placing too much credence on the textual tradition when it comes to interpreting the EIA will almost certainly distort our impression of the dynamics inherent to the period, especially causing us to underestimate the importance of regional developments outside of Attica, since most Classical authors are from Athens and thus probably had little information about EIA developments elsewhere.[99]

Removing Homeric evidence from the equation prompts an important modification to our understanding of the history of nude practices in the EIA. The first phase of the history of nude practice in the Aegean is almost universally located in ritual contexts, in particular in liminal or initiatory rites that took place in sanctuaries. The earliest evidence for these kinds of rites comes from LBA and EIA sites or regions that are marginal from the point of view of the historical geography of Greek *poleis*. It is especially abundant in Cretan material culture.

---

of the war at Troy as the truth at their center, while the rest of the material would have developed and changed over the hundreds of years of its performance history. Grethlein (2009, 124–126) provides a helpful review of the new German orthodoxy of an historical Trojan War. See also Bachvarova 2016 on the presence of older Anatolian elements embedded in the Homeric poems due to their long and geographically rangy performance history. Some idiosyncratic outliers continue to insist that Homer has unambiguous relevance for reconstructing EIA society. For example, as recently as 2008, Gottschall presented an interpretation of Homeric poetry contending that the obsession with feuds over women in the poems resulted from a shortage of women in the EIA, in his words that "the Homeric poems reflect life in the last moments of the Greek Dark Ages" (Gottschall 2008, 22).

[99] See recent discussion about the relevance of the Greek tradition for the EIA in Dickinson 2020.

With a Homeric *terminus post quem* for the onset of meaningful activities associated with nudity in place, there was compelling reason to believe that this earlier evidence for initiatory nudity was either unrelated or only loosely related to developments located in the Archaic period, including the regular practice of nude athletics. However, recognizing that the Homeric evidence is not an adequate basis upon which to reconstruct a totalizing historical trajectory of any aspect of Aegean society in the EIA eliminates the logical basis for placing a *terminus post quem* for the adoption of such practices after the eighth century. In the absence of such a *terminus post quem,* unless we are prepared to believe that Thucydides and Plato had any idea about what was going on several hundred years before they were born, we should accept that we do not know anything about the timing or advent of something like nude athletics in ancient Greece. Accepting this makes imperative a careful consideration of the EIA evidence and its relevance as a source for interesting information about the beginning of meaningful ritual practice involving nudity, including ritual athletic contests, prior to the Archaic period.

Nudity in Early Iron Age Art

Indeed, naked males begin to appear in Aegean art almost immediately after the demise of LBA palatial societies, around the twelfth century, and they are quite well represented amongst depictions of the human figure throughout the PG and Geometric periods.[100] This is a novel feature of Aegean iconography that first appears in the period between the end of the LBA and the EIA. In most LBA Aegean art, neither women nor men are regularly depicted unclothed. Minoan women frequently bare their breasts, but males and females are distinguished from one other mainly on the basis of clothing and skin color.[101] Clothing is present on performers and participants in physical contests

---

[100] Production of bronze figurines persisted without interruption between the Bronze and Iron Ages on Crete (as noted in Müller 1906, 76–91; see extensive discussion in Chapter 2). On nudity in Geometric human figures, Langdon 2008, 245:

> from the outset the human figure is depicted nude... of the 226 ninth- and eighth-century independent and tripod handle figurines of known provenance, 210 or 93% are identifiable by gender. Of figures with sufficiently preserved anatomical detail, 81% have clear sexual attributes, with a male emphasis: 87% of males and 75% of females are gendered by anatomy rather than or in addition to attributes.

[101] However, in some cases the idea that gender corresponds to skin color in Minoan Art (generally speaking white was used for the skin of females and red for males, a convention borrowed from Egyptian painting) is clearly problematic. See Immerwahr 1990, 90–92; Damiani-Indelicato 1988; Marinatos 1993, 219–220; Morgan 2000, 939–940; Rehak 1996, 41; Hitchcock 2000; Alberti 2002, 109. A possible nude female is known from the Late

in Minoan art.[102] Males are athletically muscled and are frequently lightly clad, but the genitalia are almost always concealed by a codpiece or loincloth.[103] The exceptions to this rule are children and adolescents, who sometimes appear naked.[104] Late Bronze Age Aegean traditions in this respect are significantly distinct from the norms of later Greek art, in which adult males are depicted nude in a variety of circumstances, but represent something closer to the norm than the exception for Mediterranean societies as a whole.

The basic facts of chronological development– consistently naked males first appear in the final phases of the LBA and the beginning phases of the EIA in a break with LBA tradition – suggest that the transition from the Bronze to the Iron age would be an obvious place to seek the origins of this tradition in iconographical practice. Moreover, it is conventional to see the seeds of Greek art as a set of technical and aesthetic achievements that began in the EIA, so a move along these lines would be consistent with general ideas about how Aegean art developed in the first millennium.[105] Nonetheless, scholars have generally not accepted the idea that the earliest naked figures in EIA art should be treated as evidence for a meaningful culture or ideology of nudity beginning in the twelfth century.[106]

EIA Male Nudes in Art Historical Perspective

Instead, the two extant arguments positing an explanation of the function of naked figures in EIA art both conjecture that nudity in EIA art was little more than an artistic convention that provides minimal insight into the reality of

---

Minoan IB site of Makrigialos on Crete (Mantzourani 2012) and two are among finds from the Cretan peak sanctuary of Petsofas (Rutkowski 1991, pl. 43.1–4).

[102] For example, the combatants on the boxer rhyton from Aghia Triada wear loincloths (McDonnell 1991, 182, n. 1). See also Rethemiotakis (2001, 126–128) on figurines representing athletic worshippers from peak sanctuaries.

[103] Mouratidis 1985, 217 ("athletic nudity was unknown in Minoan Crete"); Hitchcock 2000, 69–70; Rethemiotakis 2001, 68; Morris 2017, 667; Vetters and Weilhartner 2017, 34. For possibly nude male figurines from Vrysinas, see Tzachili 2012 (but paint seems to indicate a codpiece, 237).

[104] Chapin 2007a; see also Chapin 2007b; 2009; 2012; 2014, 22–24. There are naked figures in golden plaques of eastern origin from the shaft graves at Mycenae, but these were not manufactured as part of an Aegean tradition, so their relevance to local conceptions of nudity is difficult to assess (Karo 1930, pl. 25, nos. 27–28).

[105] Schefold 1966, 15, 22–23; Snodgrass 1971, 416–436; Robertson 1975, 14–33; Hägg 1983; Murray 1993, 8.

[106] Beginning with Furtwängler (1890, 43). Kunze made the first attempt to write a cultural history of EIA figurines (in a series of publications; 1930; 1944; 1961; 1967) but did not bother to treat most of the earliest figurines on account of their lack of aesthetic sophistication (1930, 141, 153). The importance of this early material is likewise underappreciated in Scott's (2010) more recent monograph about Olympia and Delphi, which does not really discuss material dated prior to the mid-seventh century.

social or cultural practices. The first and more elaborate argument is that genitals and breasts appear in EIA art because artists working within a rudimentary and primitive figural style were not capable of naturalistically rendering the human form, making the depiction of breasts and genitals necessary to differentiate males from females.[107] A related idea concerns the reconstruction of an ideology, reflected in early art, that males were normal and natural and hence required no clothing, while females were incomplete and inadequate and therefore often needed to be clothed.

The most thorough treatment along these lines has been presented by Stewart.[108] Stewart defines two phases in early Greek nudity. In the first, both males and females are depicted nude. In the second, nudity is restricted to males only.[109] Stewart considers these phases as sequential in the progression of Greek artists' rediscovery of the human form, and then their discovery of misogyny.[110] In the first phase, the body "*constitutes* the person" while clothing is only a supplement. The penis is a marker of man, while woman is defined by the lack of penis.[111] By the second phase, in the eighth century, only men are "real" and "act freely in the world" and so women must always be shrouded in garments while men may continue to be naked.[112] In sum, we should conclude that while many of the earliest images of humans from the EIA represent nudity, the depiction of males in a state of total undress does not reflect any actual practice of nudity, but instead adheres to a conventional visual logic

---

[107] Hurwit 1985, 98–99; Bonfante 1989, 549; Osborne 1997, 507–508; Stähli 2006, Langdon 2008, 245–246:

> From the outset the human figure is depicted nude, a convention introduced to facilitate unambiguous identification of sex . . . in the second half of the eighth century, social constructions augment nudity in both sculpture and painting . . . although male figures remain nude and "normal", female figures are dressed . . . the nude male body is complete even in and of itself, the essence of humanity.

It has been generally accepted that this distinction became increasingly important as circumscribed social roles for males and females "emerged" along with the *polis* in the eighth century. Heilmeyer's interpretation of the nudity of the early terracotta figurines from Olympia follows a similar tack (Heilmeyer 1972, 60). Heilmeyer's objection to the association of the nudity of early figurines with the nudity of early Olympic athletes rests on ascribing the origin of the Olympic games to *ca.* 720 (Heilmeyer 1972, 60, n. 132). Cf. Hurwit 1985, 98–99; Bol 2004, 283: "Die menschliche Figur kann nicht angemessen durch die sie umgebende Kleidung repräsentiert werden."

[108] Stewart 1997, 34–42.   [109] Bonfante 1989, 549; Stewart 1997, 39–42.

[110] Stewart 1997, 39–42.   [111] Stewart 1997, 40.

[112] Benson 1970, 106; Stewart 1997, 40; Bol 2004, 286; Lee 2015, 173: ". . .positive associations of nudity are generally ascribed to male figures, while the negative connotations of nakedness are frequently associated with female figures."; Müller (1906, 87) calls nudity a "naïve artifice"; these arguments are also summarized in Osborne 1997, 512; Christesen 2002, 18–19, n. 17.

rooted in a semiotic understanding in which males are marked by having a penis while females are unmarked.

The other extant argument for the logic of the appearance of nude males in EIA art is that early nudes mostly represent the divine, ithyphallic potency of a god (usually Zeus or Apollo).[113] The prominent male genitalia of early Greek figurines thus relate to superstitious fears surrounding taboo, magical, or divine nudity.[114]

Although apparently naked individuals appear with some regularity in EIA art, then, it is not agreed that indicate any kind of cultural practice or aesthetic associated with nudity that was operational during the EIA.[115] Several aspects of the evidence for EIA nudity should cause us to question these explanations. To take the latter explanation, that nudity in the EIA most often represents the ithyphallic potency of a god, this seems to be contradicted by the fact that, although there are a few isolated cases of ithyphallism among EIA figurines, most naked males from the EIA are not ithyphallic. Moreover, while a few early nude figurines are characterized by gestures that are attributed to divinities throughout the prehistoric Mediterranean,[116] most figurines are characterized by gestures that are typical of worshippers.[117] Other nude figures seem to be participating in physical activities, like boxing, playing music, or dancing together or individually, that are not usually associated with divine iconography.[118] Figures of all kinds, from horse-leaders to worshippers, musicians to warriors, appear naked in the corpus of EIA art.[119] This information all seems to undermine the idea that most naked figures in the EIA were intended to represent powerful deities or the taboo of ithyphallism.[120]

The argument from semiotics has proven more popular than the appeal to ithyphallic potency as an explanation for the appearance of nudity in EIA art.[121] However, there are some logical issues with this interpretation. The

---

[113] Schweitzer 1969, 127–129; Böhm 1990; see also Kunze 1944, pls. 38–39; 42–46; 1946, figs. 1–13; 1961.

[114] For nudity interpreted as an indication of divinity, see Heilmeyer 1972, 61. For the explanation of nudity as divine or ritual rather than ideal, Müller 1906, 90–91: "Aber noch erschien uns die Nacktheit nicht als ideale ästhetische Forderung. Sie tritt, wie wir glaubten, der Wirklichkeit gemäß, wie bei den Frauen im Kultus der Toten und Götter auf."

[115] McDonnell 1991, 183–184.

[116] Some examples are the early Olympia and Delphi figurines with arms extended directly to the side; see Byrne 1991, 120–121.

[117] References to examples from Crete, the Near East, and Cyprus are cited in Byrne 1991, 127, n. 91.

[118] Some early examples include a figurine from Patso Cave (Lebessi 2002, fig. 26); a figurine from the Idaean cave (Lebessi 2002, fig. 44); and a figurine from Syme Viannou (Lebessi 2002, pl. 11. No. 13;, pl. 15, no. 15).

[119] Müller 1906, 91.

[120] Knapp 1986, 8: "until proven divine, these figures must be regarded as human"; cf. Moorey and Fleming 1984, 79.

[121] Accepted in, for example, McDonnell 1991, 183–184; Christesen 2002, 18, n. 17.

argument contains two separate but related ideas which are unsatisfactory on separate grounds.

The first idea is that EIA artists working in a schematic style could not distinguish gender without the addition of primary sex characteristics. If it were true that the gender of primitive silhouette figures like the ones that often occur in EIA art could not be distinguished without the inclusion of primary sexual characteristics, we should expect most or all schematic depictions of males and females in similar artistic traditions to be thus differentiated. But this is not the case. There are many extant traditions of schematic or abstract silhouette art in which nudity need not be, and is indeed rarely, a factor.[122] Modern examples include the standard bathroom signs which render abstractions of man and woman. Nudity is not implied.

The second idea is that Greek artists (and society) eventually determined that men and women were distinct, and used the depiction of male genitalia and the consistent covering up of the female body to strongly differentiate males and females within an iconographic system. As this semiotic argument suggests, male genitalia are depicted with greater frequency than female genitalia in EIA art. However, while naked men are proportionally more common in EIA art, naked women do appear with some regularity and men and women both appear clothed in many cases. Thus, nudity as a semiotic device is not universally or systematically employed. As demonstrated already by Haug,[123] there is regional and intraregional variation in the treatment and demeanor of individuals who are nude and clothed, and dramatic changes through time that belie a churning world of real communities and individuals reckoning with social and political changes through ideology and imagery. If the lack of a penis rendered a man not a man, then what are we to make of the fact that many depictions of men in EIA art do not include this feature? While EIA artists may have been interested in creating a distinction between males and females in some cases, and while EIA society may have conceived of the genders as distinct in regard to the appropriateness of nudity, the complex demeanor of nudity in EIA art is not adequately explained by the semiotic argument. There is surely much to gain by examining the diverse choices made in the depiction of the human figure in EIA art rather than masking this complexity with a universalizing appeal to semiotics.

Beyond Art History: A Contextual and Process-Oriented Approach to EIA Naked Figurines

Overall, the current scholarly consensus posits that, although there is a lot of nudity present in EIA art, it relates primarily to artistic convention concerning

---

[122] Boardman 2004, 49.   [123] Haug 2012.

the differentation of males and females, and is therefore of limited utility for scholars interested in actual practices associated with nudity or in the ideological role of nudity in society overall. Haug's thorough study of the images of men in eighth and seventh century Attic art is an exception to this rule in identifying meaningful and complex patterns of nudity in Geometric art.[124] She points out that there is meaningful nudity present in the vase-painting tradition from Athens and distinguishes it from contemporary trends in three-dimensional art, for example noting that three-dimensional wagon drivers in Athenian art are naked, as opposed to those in ceramic depictions.[125] She identifies nascent concepts of military and athletic *arete* in some images of nude males in Geometric vase painting.[126] Another exception to the general trend is Lebessi, who has asserted that the naked arms-bearing figurines from the transition between the Late Bronze and Early Iron Ages represent "the beginnings of the idealized nudity of the Archaic period."[127] Despite the strength of Lebessi's argument regarding EIA figurines (discussed at greater length in Chapter 3), which is rooted in a thorough treatment of the material, it has not been widely accepted or dealt with in the scholarship. The work of both scholars demonstrates that there is much more interpretative ground to be gained in the study of these bodies of evidence, despite the current consensus.

If there is so much interesting evidence for EIA nudity, why should it have been treated so cursorily to date? It might be related to the position of EIA art within the overarching narrative of Greek art history and archaeology.[128] EIA art has usually been approached from a relational and evolutionary point of

[124] Haug 2012.
[125] The latter, she thinks, are "vom einem athletischen, aber gänzlich unkriegerischen Wagenlenker-Rollenbild vor." On athletics, see Haug 2012, 373. On the chariot drivers, Haug 2012, 215, 233–234.
[126] Haug 2012, 284: "Im plastichen Medium werden, wie sicht zeigt, Details ausformuliert, die den zweidimensionalen Bildern implizit eingeschrieben sind – Athletik und Nacktheit. Der Krieferkörper wird hier als gestählter, trainierter Körper konzipiert, er ist Produkt einer kulturellen Praxis."
[127] Lebessi 2002, 214.
[128] The tendency to treat EIA art as primitive predates even the discovery of most EIA art, for example, Müller 1852, 19:

> Of all the branches of the Indo-Germanic race, the Greeks were that in which sensible and spiritual, internal and external life were found in the finest equipoise; hence they have been from the first most peculiarly fitted for the independent cultivation of artistic forms, although it required a long process of development and many favourable circumstances before this feeling for art, which showed its activity so early in poetry and mythology, could be also transferred to external matters and ripen into sculpture.

> 58 "the forms passed over from their original poverty and rudeness in characterizing into an exuberance of expression, directed on the one hand to the exhibition of strength, energy, and activity, and on the other to the display of elegance which at this period had to supply the want of grace."

view. Protogeometric and Geometric art has often been discussed in terms of stagnation and then renaissance. According to such discussion, after a period of slumber in the mainly aniconic PG and Early Geometric periods, Late Geometric artists engaged in a period of awkward but innovative experimentation, the primitive ideas from which slowly coagulated into the sophisticated cultural matrix of the Archaic and Classical periods.[129]

Due to the important role that the ideal of naturalism has played in the study of Greek art, much art from the tenth to the fifth centuries is valued in relation to the achievement of this ideal.[130] Perhaps for this reason, schematic images in PG and Geometric art have often been described with openly disdainful language.[131] It is generally suggested that Geometric artists were grasping at something resembling Classical naturalism, but were incapable of achieving it.[132] Regionally distinct Geometric and Archaic styles and techniques are described as being engaged in a race, the goal of which is achieving the naturalistic depiction of the human form, which eventually emerges from the struggle of the preceding several centuries.[133] There is a decline in the art after the Classical period associated with a notional descent into decadence and/or mass production.[134]

Thinking about EIA material culture according to this narrative of rise and fall undermines our ability to understand EIA objects as contextual to society at the time of their creation and use, or to reconstruct the purposes that they

[129] For example, Müller 1906, 90–91; Schefold 1966, 15; Schweitzer 1969, 26–27; Hurwit 1985, 36–37, 70; Osborne 1998, 30; Langdon 2007.

[130] The effects of Winckelmann's evolutionary scheme of rise and fall (Winckelmann 1763, 4–5) in the conception of Classical art have been discussed at length (e.g., Harloe 2013). Boardman compared the Geometric period to childhood, a time during which Greek artists gained discipline before their wayward adolescence led them to the naturalism of the mature Classical (Boardman 1967, 73); De la Croix and Tansey 1986, 128–130; Hartt 1989, 139; Janson and Janson 1991, 153; Cook 1997, 2; Hurwit 1985, 37; Snodgrass 2008, 25.

[131] Nicholls 1970, 1: "This study is devoted to one of the humblest of all periods of Greek art, not from any convictions as to its aesthetic merits, which are scant enough in all honesty...."; Cook 1997, 1, 21. The idea that there was a quintessential ideal embedded in Classical art that was the result of a special genius is inherent in many early philosophical treatments on aesthetics dating back to the Renaissance (e.g., Herder in Moore ed. 2006, 84); according to Hegel, one of the main purposes of life was to proceed to the naturalistic human form as the one and only sensuous appearance appropriate to the Spirit within (Podro 1982, 20). A good example is Gombrich's theory of the Greek revolution in art, requiring artists to break away from symmetry and schemata in order to arrive at the pinnacle of naturalistic narrative art (Gombrich 1960, 29).

[132] Austin 1937, 20–21; Benson 1970, 9; Carter 1972, 35, 39.

[133] Schweitzer 1967, 26; Hurwit 1985, 70; Cook 1997, 3. For the great leap forward of the human figure, see Austin 1937, 18; Desborough 1952, 298; Schweitzer 1969, 12; Carter 1972, 27, 29, 37; Benson 1982, 539–40, 542; Bohen 1991, 59–61. The most hyperbolic statements along these lines are those of Nottbohm (1943).

[134] For example, Cook 1997, 3: "Hellenistic vase-painters, if they can be called that, mostly made do with a few tatty ornaments from the conventional stock."

served for the contemporary humans that made and consumed them.[135] Such an evolutionary paradigm for the understanding of EIA art introduces two separate but related issues for the way that we approach art as value laden. The first is the assumption that naturalism is the ultimate goal of artistic production. Looking at art from the EIA makes it seem clear that EIA artists may not have been interested in generating naturalistic images; nor were they aware of what Classical art would look like, so it is hardly reasonable to assess the images they produced using a standard drawn from several hundred years after they were working.[136] The fact that the images EIA people made are not naturalistic does not mean that the details, like primary sexual characteristics, that people added to figurines and figures in vase painting were not meant to communicate important information.[137]

The second issue that this discussion brings to the fore is the disciplinary tendency to evaluate artifacts through the lens of consumption, as finished objects valued for their material, visual, and aesthetic performance. This focus on objects aligns with a general archaeological emphasis, since the publication of Appadurai's influential volume in the 1980s, on things and materiality.[138] Enlightening as related approaches have been, they are problematic in assuming that the ways archaeologists interact with and value artifacts overlap significantly with those of past peoples.

In particular, our aesthetically and materially attuned encounters with ancient artifacts focus our attention on finished products, often eliding consideration of the social value of the processes embedded in their creation.[139] Although the *chaîne opératoire* concept has been well received in ancient technical studies, in practice, archaeologists have been concerned primarily with the behavioral sequences connected to particular categories of artifact, and rather less with their roles in the reflection and shaping of ideology. The view of technological systems as a form of ritual, whereby transformative

---

[135] Criticism of the notion that art should be judged by a universal standard or ideal dates back to the beginnings of art history. In the late eighteenth century, the German critic and intellectual Johann Gottfried Herder was challenging the notion that the aesthetics of Egyptian art should be evaluated according to standards of visual culture in Greece. Instead, he suggested, the Egyptians produced their art according to the ideas and expectations of their own society. According to Herder, "it would be manifestly stupid to consider yourself to be quintessence of all things and all peoples." See Herder 1877, vol. 8, 476; Bernard 1969; summary in Podro 1982, 1–4.

[136] Hurwit 1985, 54; Garrison 2010, 9. For the notion that Geometric art is primitive, see, for example, Austin 1937, 18; Herrmann 1964, 17; Carter 1972, 37; Bouzek 1983, 73; Bohen 1997, 53.

[137] Joyce 1993, 256.

[138] Appadurai 1986; the influence can be seen, for example, in scholarship published in *The Journal of Material Culture*.

[139] Pálsson 1994; Gosselain 1998; Dobres 2010; Lemonnier 2012; Ingold 2013.

power is expressed through valorized acts, has rich but still underexploited potential.[140] The approach in this book is especially influenced by Lemonnier's anthropological work on technology and production which emphasizes the performativity embedded in the making of objects – even those that are not visually impressive – and recommends muddying the distinction between the communicative functions of things and the ritualized acts that bring them into the world.[141] Lemmonier reminds us that "[p]eople do not merely look at...objects. They produce them, manipulate them, and perform material actions with them" and that "the ability of diversified material practices to convey non-verbal shared references to the past and to gather people together is by no means limited to exotic ritual objects."[142]

One example, among many, that demonstrates how objects do not always accrue value because of their visual appearance is the phenomenon of the *tupilaq*, used among traditional peoples in Greenland.[143] Made by a shaman out of concrete objects like stone, bone, wood, antlers, or whale tooth, the *tupilaq* is classifiable as an object from a certain point of view. However, within the cosmology of the Inuit religion of Greenland, the *tupilaq* was not an object but a living thing, an avenging monster, that could swim through the water to destroy the enemy whom it is bidden to find.[144] The *tupilaq* was made by a shaman in secret, at night, and its effectiveness depended on its use, which involved its being immediately cast into the sea and thus deployed to its mission, remaining completely secret and invisible.[145] Its characteristic as an object for visual consumption, then, was essentially nonexistent: there was no intention for the object to be seen by anyone, let alone valued for its aesthetic performance – quite the opposite, in fact. The reason that these objects were made was not to appear before the eye as an object for visible consumption, but to participate in society in an entirely different fashion. Due to the demand of the modern tourist industry in Greenland, approximations of *tupilaq* are now made for the consumption of curious visitors.[146] But if we did see a real *tupilaq*, perhaps having encountered one in the archaeological record, conceiving it as an object for aesthetic consumption would entail a fundamental misunderstanding of its role within the social, ritual, and spiritual context of its original production and use. It would therefore be pointless, except from an antiquarian point of view, to describe it or try to situate it historically as a source of information about aesthetic capabilities of artists working in ancient Greenland. Such examples encourage us to account for not only the productive outputs of past artisans, but also the experiences and participation of ancient

---

[140] Gell 1998; Lemonnier 2012; Swenson 2015.
[141] For example, Lemonnier 1992; 2012, 77, 134–136.   [142] Lemonnier 2012, 98.
[143] Romalis 1983.   [144] Rink 1885, 53; Rasmussen 1938, 159.   [145] Rasmussen 1938, 168.
[146] Romalis 1983, 154–155.

communities with the making of objects, in interpreting the role that these objects played in societies.[147] Indeed, much evidence suggests that experiences associated with acts of creation often overshadow their material outcomes as the locus of critical value within social and political systems.[148]

Following on these observations, one of the main innovations of this book is to take the earliest images of naked males from the Aegean and move beyond a consideration of their performance as art objects designed to be viewed and evaluated aesthetically. I seek to reconstruct a more complex material history of bronze figurines in full archaeological perspective: as artifacts that pertain in material ways to their own EIA social and ritual context. Rather than evaluating them as visual art or as failed attempts to produce the kinds of naturalistic images of the human body that would become popular hundreds of years later, I attend primarily to the symbolic and performative context of their production and use.

Summary

The EIA figurines that constitute the beginning of a long tradition of nude males in Aegean material culture have usually been interrogated as art objects and placed in a developmental narrative of Greek art in which they represent a primitive beginning. The fact that these naked figurines are schematic, small, and unprepossessing has been taken as evidence for the rudimentary character of EIA art, a lack of skill among EIA craftsmen, and a general absence of much meaning behind iconographic choices made in the production of the figurines. All of this discussion is couched within art historical narratives that attend to the figurines' visual rather than material attributes, taking as a given that their main function would have been as objects for aesthetic consumption.

Bringing these assumptions to bear on the material has limited the utility of EIA figurines as a source of meaningful insight into the development of EIA society in general, and the history of nude practices and aesthetics in an EIA context in particular. I therefore make two revisions to existing approaches in the argument that follows. First, I do not presume that the goal of the people that made these objects was to generate beautiful or naturalistic images of humans. Second, I prioritize consideration of the material characteristics of the objects, and the processes required for making them, instead of only focusing on the appearance of the final products. As I hope to show in this book, reinterpreting the figurines squarely in the context of their production and use in EIA sanctuaries, and taking an approach informed by anthropological rather than art historical reasoning, prompts a reevaluation of the role of bronze figurines in EIA society and ritual, as well as new insights into the history of nudity in the Aegean.

---

[147] Dobres 2010, 109–110. [148] Swenson and Warner 2012.

PRELIMINARY MATTERS: CATEGORIES, DEFINITIONS, AND CHRONOLOGY

I divide the discussion of archaeological evidence in the book into categories, and it is necessary to address the logic behind this categorization (and some generally relevant issues with categorization that will come into play throughout the argument) before I proceed. This section also sets out the working definitions that I use here in my discussion of issues related to the complicated social and material concepts of ritual, nudity, and technology.

Categories

Categorization, the sorting or division of objects, people, or any other entity based on shared characteristics, is at the core of archaeological practice. Categorizing ceramic sherds according to their evolving styles and shapes allows us to construct relative chronologies that let us date deposits. Logistically, dividing classes of material culture by material, size, or type reduces the quantity of material that needs to be assigned to specialists, who can then focus their efforts on making clear trends or divergences among and across sites. Heuristically, breaking down archaeological evidence into categories is helpful when it comes to analysis because it limits the material we are seeking to make sense of into manageable chunks; our limited human intellects simply cannot make sense of all of the evidence at once. Archaeologists need categories in order to help limit bodies of material for analysis and to structure available information, but they can be problematic.

Archaeological categories are ultimately an imposition on the material record, and it is important to think about how and why this implicates archaeologists' efforts to put together a realistic story about ancient experiences of the material world. The categories that archaeologists use are often fixed: an artifact is a potsherd, or a spindle whorl, or a lithic; a space is a house or a temple or a palace, etc. However, as humans we realize that many of the categories that we use as we go about the world are rather ad hoc categories. For example, we might think about *things I need to take with me on a work trip* or *things I need in order to bake a cake*, categorical groupings that do not correspond to any fixed, externally observable logic. These kinds of ad hoc categories tend to be governed by goal orientation – these are the things I will need in order to accomplish some goal.[149] The way that we put together these categories or think of grouping these things together varies according to our cognitive and social environments.

---

[149] Barsalou 1983; 1985.

Research on the degree to which there are fixed categories experienced in a common way across human cognition suggests that there is a 'basic' level at which people categorize certain things often encountered in the world, like shapes and colors. However, even at a basic level "categorization is not independent of who is doing the categorization."[150] For example, when an adult and a child are both shown a leopard, the adult may categorize the animal as a leopard while the child categorizes it as a cat, because the child does not know about as many categories as the adult. Shown a bank shaped like a pig, one person may categorize it as a bank, attending to the characteristics of the object pertaining to storing money, while another categorizes it as a pig, attending to the characteristic of the object as pig-shaped. Which category is chosen will be determined by the salience of the different attributes to the person doing the categorizing. This example serves to demonstrate that categories are not inherent in objects or independent of people, but are instead interactional, having to do with the way that humans perceive, think about, behave toward, and interact with objects and the world around them.[151]

Appreciating this aspect of categorization reveals the obstacles archaeologists erect toward understanding by means of our conventional approaches to categorizing objects. I thought about this issue quite a lot while writing about imports, a common category of analysis within the study of the archaeology of the Mediterranean.[152] It makes sense for archaeologists to categorize things as imports because we are interested in trade patterns, and in the absence of robust textual documentation of exchange or an abundant corpus of shipwrecked trading vessels, the deposition of artifacts in regions far from their location of production is the best guide we have to reconstructing this aspect of the ancient economy.[153] However, there are many reasons to believe that grouping imports together as a unit of meaningful analysis is not likely to yield coherent results. Again, thinking about this from my own perspective, among the imports that I own are an expensive Japanese camera purchased through my professional research fund, a fuzzy hat made of sheepskin that was a gift from a herder in the Caucasus region of Georgia, and a bag of extremely chunky sea salt from a street market in Athens, Greece. While all three are imported, they function very differently in my life and I obtained and value them for very different reasons and through a diverse range of mechanisms. It is very difficult to intellectually make them cohere as a category outside of the ultimately (to me) unimportant fact that they were made somewhere far away

---

[150] Mervis and Rosch 1981; Mervis 1986.   [151] Lakoff 1987, 51.

[152] Murray 2017; Murray 2018, 35.

[153] However, for some recent work that complicates the definition and evaluation of imports in the context of the LBA and EIA Aegean see, for example, Cohen, Maran, and Vetters 2010; Heymans and van Wijngaarden 2011, 125; Vetters 2011; Brysbaert and Vetters 2013; Arrington 2016.

from where I live. Thus, while the logic of the archaeological category of imports pertains to the way that archaeologists interact with these objects, it is likely that the way that people in the prehistoric past interacted with imports was different in ways that perhaps render our archaeological category of limited heuristic value for understanding the role of imports in ancient society. This is not to say that we should eliminate or entirely revise this categorization, but that we need to be aware of its ad hoc, interactional nature when we approach material for interpretation. Processing the massive quantities of information that we have from the ancient world obviously requires categorization, but it must be the case that the intellectual effects of this reality sometimes cause us to wander down the wrong imaginative and interpretative corridors when it comes to reconstructing ancient societies.

In the context of this book, there are a number of issues with categorization that emerge, spanning the treatment of material objects, their depositional contexts, and the social roles of people that interacted with them. In reconstructions of the EIA, analysis tends to conceptually link particular sorts of social actors with certain kinds of motives and activities that seem often to be fixed. Thus, elites are political actors who pursue political gain, while craftspeople are economic actors who pursue material gain. I believe that the tendency to maintain a barrier between and strictly divide these kinds of social roles is a mistake, because there is no evidence that such discreet roles existed in the EIA. I discuss the impact that this tendency to fix social roles within rigid categories has had on interpretations of EIA ritual and society toward the end of the book, especially in Chapter 5.

A related issue that I want to foreground is the fact that archaeologists tend to divide finds from excavations up by material. The staff on archaeological field projects is composed of specialists with expertise broken down by a somewhat idiosyncratic set of categories that are usually based on function or material: pottery, terracotta roof tiles, weaving implements, chipped stone, ground stone, architectural stone, bronzes, jewelry, etc.[154] These categories obviously relate to the way that archaeologists interact with objects. It is not necessarily always true that they relate clearly to the way that ancient people did, although synthetic studies often also break down along lines that suggest we often confuse the two sets of cognitive logic. For example, treating all

---

[154] The tendency for analysis to break down along these lines is most visible in the structure of publications that result from a typical excavation, in which different volumes are dedicated to different types of material (e.g., Furtwängler 1890; Heilmeyer 1969, 1972; Jarosch 1994; Lebessi 2002; Felsch 2007), but has reverberations in the nature and conception of synthetic studies that break along the same lines (to somewhat randomly cite a sample of works I have used in writing this book, e.g., de Ridder 1896; Demargne 1929; Higgins 1967; Coldstream 1968; Badre 1980; Margreiter 1988; Bianchi 1990; Guggisberg 1996; Mattusch 1988; Babbi 2007).

bronze votive objects as a single category might be problematic, because it seems unlikely that a large bronze tripod cauldron had the same social value or meaning as a tiny metal figurine the size of a paperclip.[155]

Thinking about this encourages us to take care in the design of synthetic, interpretative research projects focusing on one category of prehistoric artifact if that category resides in our thinking as such only because of archaeological convention. The categories we use to organize archaeological information are ultimately arbitrary and need not be faithful to ancient categorization. When it comes to the EIA, we certainly have difficulty reconstructing any kind of internally coherent cognitive landscape that would help us understand how people thought of and grouped artifacts. This means I need to defend the logic according to which I am centering the synthetic treatment in this book on nude male anthropomorphic bronze figurines, which strikes one immediately as a category of interaction not self-evidently pertinent to EIA people. Obvious components of this categorization that are open to criticism are the separation of bronze figurines from terracotta or ivory ones, the separation of anthropomorphic figurines from zoomorphic figurines, and the distinction of nude and clothed, male and female. That is to say, there are grounds for criticizing every aspect of this categorization.

It is obvious that part of the reason I constructed this category as I did relates to issues that may be external to their original EIA social context. Because Greek historians have been interested in the prominence of nude males in Archaic and Classical Greek art, the first male nudes from the EIA are interesting and of course the investigation of an origin for this phenomenon underpins the research project presented here. And certainly, there is a sort of freestanding logic that supports the separation of EIA naked males as a nexus of inquiry, in the sense that the naked male did have a distinct trajectory of development from other iconographical topics. But it should be made clear that part of the point of honing in on the naked male is to draw readers who would normally ignore the period into a study on the EIA, rather than a necessarily ironclad case that the naked male was *particularly* meaningful in an EIA context. I would expect that many of the conclusions drawn here might be applicable to other forms of small votive object in the EIA, too.

In terms of the material distinction (bronze vs. terracotta or ivory), treating bronzes separately is defensible from the point of view of ancient interactional categories. As I elucidate in Chapters 4 and 5, the experiential aspects of the production of bronze figurines, as well as the material characteristics of the finished products, were very dramatic, and dramatically different than those associated with the production of clay and ivory figurines. I also argue that the

---

[155] cf. Osborne 2004, 3.

way people interacted with bronze votive figurines was distinct, and that the history and depositional context of bronze figurines shows that they were an interactively different sort of object than figurines made of other materials. In this sense, if categories should be human sized and interactive, I think that EIA bronze figurines logically fit into a distinct cognitive basket.

However, aside from a potentially defensible material distinction between bronze (or at least metal) and non-metal figurines, the focus on the unholy category of EIA bronze nude males is mainly driven by the rhetorical aims of the argument rather than the internal logic of the archaeological record. I accept that this is problematic, and I can see many reasons that this analysis might be expanded and nuanced if the categories were reorganized. Ultimately, however, I believe the methodological points I want to make are better served by keeping the category of the nude human male at the center.

Terms and Working Definitions: Ritual, Nude/Naked, Technology

When archaeologists talk about ancient societies we often appeal to certain abstract concepts that can be difficult to define in ways that are universally satisfactory. For the sake of discussion, the important thing is to set out what these terms will be used to indicate in the current context from the start. In this book, I use three such concepts – ritual, nude/naked, and technology – so I will explain what I take them to mean before moving on with the argument.

Ritual

A common criticism, or joke, leveled at archaeologists that we tend to interpret any aspect of the archaeological record that is strange, seemingly non-functional, or hard to explain by appeal to ritual.[156] That said, it is probably not controversial to state that the material that I am dealing with in this book is ritual in nature; I am not aware of any scholars that have produced an alternative interpretation of the EIA bronze votives that I will be discussing, or any work contesting that the EIA sites of Syme Viannou, Olympia, and Delphi were locations where ritual took place.[157] It is nevertheless useful to restate some views on the way that archaeologists think about ritual in ancient society in order to clarify what I mean when I discuss it in the pages that follow.

---

[156] Hodder 1982c, 164; Renfrew 1994. For some recent reviews of ritual in archaeological perspective see Fogelin 2007; Howey and O'Shea 2009; Insoll 2011.

[157] The sites satisfy most of the archaeological characteristics of ritual places set out by Renfrew, including the presence of sacrificed plants or animals, a location in a special geographical locale, and distinct material cultural elements (Renfrew 1985, 19).

It has often been observed that archaeologists might be best served by thinking of ritual as action or practice.[158] Thinking about ritual as practice is convenient because ritual practice usually has a material component that is repetitive and patterned, so that it leaves recognizable traces in the archaeological record.[159] Along these lines, ritual practice can be defined as a set of behaviors that are conventional, externalized material correlates of a participant's internal experience of belief that serve to express these inner states to some other entity, either other participants in the behaviors or those intended to accept or receive them, human or supernatural.[160] As Lemonnier has shown, this definition of ritual allows us to expand the use of related contexts beyond the normal 'religious' or 'sacred' realms.[161] Ritual objects, then, are the physical objects that are coopted into these behaviors and that aid in the communication of internal states to external audiences. While ritual objects need not be extraordinary, they often tend to be, perhaps because the extraordinary nature of a material or a type can help to add emphasis to the messages and meanings meant to be transmitted through extraordinary actions, processes, and events.[162] The use of extraordinary objects made of expensive materials in ritual also often occurs because ritual is used in the service of regulating or delineating power.[163] If communication with the supernatural requires special objects, and only certain individuals may access those objects, it becomes possible for those controlling the materials or means of producing ritual objects to make a special claim to social or political authority.[164]

The conspicuous signaling of ritual practice also tends to communicate something about sets of shared ideologies or identities, so that groups of people that hold similar rituals materially express a sense of shared sacred beliefs by doing so. These shared beliefs are part of the religion rather than the ritual. While identifying ritual action in the material record is often not problematic, when it comes to understanding ancient religion we are on shakier ground. Geertz recommended breaking the study of religion down into two stages, first identifying the systems of meaning that underlay the symbols embedded in religious practice, and then working to define the relationships between systems of meaning and the structures of society and psychology.[165]

When we are dealing with the EIA we can look at the symbols associated with ritual practice, but we struggle with all of the other parts of this analytical process because the evidence presents substantial obstacles to understanding

---

[158] Walker 1998, 296; cf. discussion in the Aegean context in Wright 1995.
[159] Howey and O'Shea 2009, 194.
[160] Jordan 2003. On a behavioral approach to ritual, see, for example, Hill 2003; Osborne 2004; Bradley 2005.
[161] Lemonnier 2012, 140–145.   [162] Bell 2009 [1992], 1997; Humphrey and Laidlaw 1994.
[163] Fogelin 2007, 65.   [164] Yoffee 1985, 43.
[165] Geertz 1973, 125; discussion in Fogelin 2007, 57.

meaning and social structure, let alone the psychologies of people's ritual experiences.[166] Since it is essentially impossible to access these beliefs in any systematic way for the EIA and because the range of different sets of evidence across its complicated ritual landscape seems to militate against the reconstruction of any 'Greek' religion during this period, I restrict my discussion to ritual as practice.

Naked and Nude Males

The lack of clothing on human bodies, usually called naked or nude in such a state, provides the logic circumscribing the main group of objects that I am subjecting to analysis, so it is important to discuss these terms before setting out on the argument. What does the term nudity entail? Most art historians distinguish between nudity and nakedness. In 1960, Clark articulated a distinction between nakedness, which reflects a material reality (the natural state of the unclothed body), and nudity, a transcendent state of cultural disguise.[167] Berger, along the same lines, argued that nakedness is the state of revealing oneself, whereas nudity must be seen, must be placed on display.[168] More recently, the naked/nude duality has been criticized as an immaterial artifact of western civilization, philosophical artifice, and the patriarchy.[169] Nonetheless, a persistent distinction between nudity as an idealizing or artistic state of undress and nakedness as a state of natural, shameful, and/or sexual undress seems to persist in literature on undressed human bodies in art.[170] In the context of the EIA, little progress has been made in sorting out various categories of undress. The nature of the evidence makes it difficult to establish a meaningful distinction between nude and naked in this period. In the interest of avoiding any overinterpretation of the images in question during the descriptive portions of what follows, I mostly use the term naked to describe figurines in a state of undress, since nudity is the more loaded term. However, in relating information about the scholarly discourse on nudity, I retain this term.

This book concerns the emergence of a set of developments concerning the ideological, visual, and practical culture of naked men.[171] It has therefore been necessary to assign male and female identifications to depictions of the human figure. The existence of such terms, and their meanings, has been controversial.[172] Although archeologists have often used the terms sex and gender

---

[166] Hayes 1993; Fogelin 2007, 56.   [167] Clark 1960, 1–7.   [168] Berger 1972, 54.
[169] Neal 1992, 12–22; see also Asher-Greve and Sweeney 2006, 130.
[170] Relevant discussions in König 1990, 27–59 (arguing that nakedness should be opposed not to nudeness, but to the clothed body, which often constitutes the norm in society); Duerr 1988–1999; Jullien 2000.
[171] The development of the nude female in Greek art is a distinct phenomenon.
[172] On the variety in assumed meanings for these terms, Moore 1994, 6. For continuing debate on the identification of gender in figurines, Bailey 2013, 246–249; Morris 2017, 661–662.

interchangeably, the two should be distinguished according to the usual practice followed by sociologists and historians of gender.[173] The distinction of male and female gender and sex was once thought to be relatively straightforward, with gender representing little more than the cultural elaboration of the two biological sexes.[174] Recent work on the history of gender and sexuality has nuanced this view, demonstrating that (like the nude/naked dichotomy) the binary distinction between male and female should not be taken as given, but represents a cultural construction that has governed many but not all historical societies.[175] Not all historians of art and society have accepted the fact that binary sex systems are imposed by culture, and the question of whether a binary system of clearly defined sexes is a natural or fundamental aspect of human society remains the subject of debate. Fausto-Sterling sought to demonstrate that at least five sexes could be biologically proven, and her data showed that nearly 2% of live births represent intersex individuals having both male and female sex characteristics.[176] Saxe later restated the evidence for various configurations of sex characteristics, but contested the high rate of occurrence as unsubstantiated.[177] In any case, it is obvious that even when it comes to a straightforward identification of genetic sex, dependent on chromosomes and physically apparent sexual attributes, things are not always as simple as has been historically assumed. The question of gender in society is a far more problematic issue that must be dealt with from the point of view of cultural history, since gender has been shown to be conceived and performed differently in particular historical contexts.[178]

In the specific context of the Aegean, textual evidence does not leave any doubt that, by the Archaic and Classical periods, Greeks had a binary system of sex and gender in which male and female were clearly distinguished from one another. While it is not entirely possible to extend surety about the state of gender definition into the LBA and EIA, it seems likely from the preponderance of the evidence that there were strong conceptions of gender difference throughout Aegean prehistory.[179] In this book, I accept the general idea that

[173] Hamilton 2000, 22; discussion in Knapp and Meskell 1997, 186–187.

[174] Riggsby 1992, 23, 26 (gender represents how "biological differences are interpreted and translated into social expectations of everyday life."); Yates (1993) demonstrates that in Swedish rock art, men acquire accoutrements of gender over time as the figural tradition develops. Also relevant are Butler 1993; Brod and Kaufman 1994; Cornwall and Lindisfarne 1994; Connell 1995; Grosz 1995; Moore 1994; Knapp 1997; Knapp 1998.

[175] See discussion in Knapp and Meskell 1997, 185–186; Halpern (2000, 30–31) argues that sex and gender are not easily separable terms; other overviews of perceptions of sex and gender include Beal 1994; Mealey 2000; Helgeson 2002.

[176] Fausto-Sterling 1993, 20.   [177] Saxe 2002, 174–178.   [178] Hamilton 2000.

[179] Reasons for believing that there were probably clear divisions between men and women in EIA society include the distinct way in which the sexes are depicted in EIA art (Waldstein 1905, 3–10; Langdon 1984; Lebessi 2002) and relatively clearly demarcated sets of grave goods for men and women, at least where this is apparent (Dickinson 2006, 185;

male and female were distinct genders in the EIA, and that these genders should be identifiable by primary sex characteristics. In some cases, subsidiary features probably related to gender like beards or mustaches and physique for males, and visible pregnancy or the holding of infants for females, can also be used to distinguish the gender of a figurine. When relevant, I also consider elements such as clothing and jewelry in identifying the gender of individual figures in early Greek art.[180]

Technology

In the later sections of the book I use the term technology quite a bit. Since this term carries some modern baggage, it should be briefly unpacked in order to avoid confusion. In the study of prehistoric metalworking it is common to employ terms like technology, industry, and metallurgy that strongly connote an assumption that metalworkers in the prehistoric past were essentially rational practitioners that had more in common with scientists than other artisanal producers like basket makers or potters.[181] This assumption is problematic because it imposes a certain social role on the persona of the metalworker (as a rational and perhaps innovation-driven visionary with a fundamental understanding of the material science behind metal production) that encourages a certain assumptions about the intentions and motivations of individuals inherent to an industrial rather than a pre-industrial context. Indeed, one of the arguments I make toward the end of the book is that these preconceptions have caused us to fundamentally misunderstand the role of the smith in EIA society. However, for the sake of convenience and because it is conventional in discussions of ancient metalworking, I use the term technology when I am referring to the processes used to cast early votive figurines from EIA sanctuaries. When I do so I am using the term only as a useful shorthand for the sum of procedures used in the production of the figurines rather than a more formal description of a branch of knowledge that deals with the application of scientific knowledge for practical purposes.

Chronology

A few caveats about the way that I deal with chronology in this book should be mentioned at this juncture. Although the EIA is usually broken down

---

Papadopoulos and Smithson 2017, 660–667. See also Morris 1999). However, on difficulties in assigning gender to buried individuals based on finds like weapons in EIA burials, see Whitley 2002.

[180] A reasonably logical method is laid out in Christou 2012, 9.

[181] Budd and Taylor 1995, 134.

internally into a number of sub-phases, I often use the term EIA to discuss all of the bronze figurines on which the study focuses. The reason for this is that the archaeological contexts from which most of these figurines issued are mixed, so that they are mostly dated by style rather than stratigraphy.[182] Their precise dating is controversial and the schemes according to which period designations have been assigned are not secure. Moreover, many of my general points apply to the entire range of the material rather than to chronologically specific subsets of it, so it is convenient to call it EIA rather than to use a more specific term. As I have argued elsewhere, although the end of the LBA is usually placed around 1100, many of the most important changes in the archaeological record that mark likely systemic change are already apparent in thoroughgoing ways from around 1200.[183] For functional purposes then, when I use the term EIA in the book, I am using this term as a shorthand to encompass the entire period between the demise of palatial Bronze Age states and roughly 700, the traditional start of the Archaic period. This date is an appropriate end point for the study in ways that do not relate to traditional periodization, but to major changes that occur in the material culture of the specific sites and assemblages that I focus on in particular, as I discuss in Chapter 6.

PLAN AND STRUCTURE OF THE BOOK

This introduction has argued that there is much more analytical ground to be gained for scholars seeking to clarify the origins of various institutions surrounding nudity through study of the EIA figurines that are among the earliest relevant imagery in the Aegean. That is not to say that existing scholarship which runs up against the material is of poor quality, just that it is not really engaged in doing interesting things around EIA archaeological evidence. This book aims to develop a more interesting set of ideas about how these EIA nude males function in the social archaeology of their particular chronological and social context through a focus that is squarely on the figurines, rather than what precedes or follows them.

Chapter 2 presents a review and discussion of the main body of evidence under analysis here, EIA figurines representing apparently naked males. I discuss the chronology, iconographic characteristics, and likely ritual context of deposition of these objects. I show that the earliest tradition of naked male figurines begins in the final phases of the LBA, and continues in the twelfth

---

[182] The figurines that are at the center of the research project are mostly from mixed sanctuary fill deposits that postdate the LBA and predate the seventh century, but for which more detailed chronology is difficult to determine, as discussed in Chapter 2.

[183] Murray 2017, 280–281.

through eighth centuries on Crete, which has a continuous tradition of solid-cast small-scale bronze nude male votive statues throughout this period. Similar figurines are among the earliest votive objects deposited at the newly established sanctuaries at Olympia and Delphi on the mainland in the late tenth and early ninth centuries. With some exceptions, most of the figurines seem to represent worshippers, that is, the people who visited the sanctuary to participate in rituals, rather than gods, both on Crete and on the mainland.

Chapter 3 begins by considering the iconographic and regional patterns in the appearance of the earliest naked bronze figurines in EIA sanctuaries. The types of naked male figurines that appear in the EIA include a few popular types, especially warriors and charioteers. However, the variation in types and stylistic approaches to the human figure challenges any attempt at thorough categorization. Naked figurines on the mainland are concentrated at two sites: Olympia and Delphi. The geography of the other sites where scattered examples of naked bronze figurines have been found suggests that their production and deposition on the mainland was largely, not to say exclusively, a western Greek phenomenon. This might suggest that any attitudes or practices about male nudity that they evince were also regionally circumscribed. I check these conclusions against the appearance and demeanor of naked males in vase painting. In the eighth century, representations of naked males appear in Geometric figured vase painting produced in several regions, but the way that nudity works in iconography varies according to region. In Argive and Lakonian pottery, nudity usually appears in scenes showing people engaged in dances or competing in some kind of physical challenge. On the other hand, in Attic and Cycladic pottery, nudity is a characteristic of the dead or the endangered. I argue that this evidence, taken together with the patterns in the deposition of naked male figurines, provides a good basis on which to reconstruct the existence of multiple ideologies surrounding nudity in the EIA: a generally Cretan and western ideology identifying nudity mainly with ritual activity and an eastern ideology identifying nudity with weakness and death.

Having established the likely existence of these two ideologies, I turn to the question of the origin and meaning of the figurines. The precedence of the Cretan tradition of cast bronze figurines, along with the strong formal and iconographic relationship between EIA Cretan figurines and the earliest figurines from the mainland sanctuaries of Olympia and Delphi, creates a logical basis on which to infer that the mainland figurines were influenced by a Cretan tradition. I argue that any such influence is unlikely to have occurred as a purely material phenomenon (i.e., to have entailed only the transfer of a formal and iconographic type) but probably involved developments in ritual practice as well. I come to two conclusions. First, the iconography of western Greek nudes, most of which seem to be involved in ritual action, dancing, or competing in some kind of physical challenge, suggests that these images represent actual practices in which males participated while unclothed. Second, I argue that it is most likely that the naked EIA figurines were deposited in the context of liminal initiatory rites that, like the tradition of cast bronze figurines, originated on Crete.

Taken together, all of this suggests a model along the following lines. The appearance of naked male figurines on the mainland in the late tenth and early ninth centuries probably occurred in tandem with the inception of novel ritual practice associated with initiatory rites at rural, open air sanctuaries. By the time that figural vase painting became popular in the eighth century, male nudity was especially associated with dancing and physical contests in the context of liminal festivals, but this association is evident mostly outside of an Attic or eastern Aegean regional context. Overall, the geographical and temporal patterns which emerge from the archaeological evidence converge to support the conclusion that there were at least two different ideologies of nudity in the EIA Aegean: a western and Cretan ideology in which nudity served an important role in socializing ritual practice among or within communities, and an eastern ideology in which nudity represented shame, weakness, and death. Thus, the analysis of the EIA material points to a previously unappreciated aspect of EIA culture: the existence of a set of conflicting, regionally distinct ideologies about the meaning of nudity. This conclusion also helps make sense of the disconnect between the Homeric evidence and the visual evidence for nudity – they do not relate to one another because they come from two separate parts of the Aegean at a time that this world was not operating as an ideologically unified culture. It provides convincing reason to believe that early ritual at Olympia and Delphi did not emerge entirely based on internal sociopolitical developments on the mainland, but entailed a decisive catalyst from Crete, although we will surely always struggle to reconstruct what the mechanism for this might have been. An important point to make based on the conclusions in this chapter is that the discussion should not be taken to constitute general points about the EIA Aegean as a whole but a limited set of conclusions about ritual practice that relates to the specific sanctuaries in which naked bronze figurines were deposited.

In Chapter 4 I turn from the formal and iconographical characteristics of EIA figurines to consider how we might interpret them as the products of a particular set of technological processes. I do this partly in order to confirm the connection between Cretan and mainland figurines suggested by formal and iconographic analyses. However, I contend that thinking about the production of the figurines provides an analytical key that opens up a better understanding of both the idiosyncrasies of their appearance and the role that they played in ritual worship at the rural sanctuaries where they were deposited. I present a technical discussion of the lost wax casting process and its limitations and then show that the craftsmen of both the Cretan and mainland figurines approached this process in the same way, seemingly confirming a Cretan influence on the artifacts from the mainland. I also show how the generally unprepossessing and often imperfect qualities of the figurines can be best appreciated in light of their production through direct lost-wax casting, a process during which such imperfections can be introduced by even minor mistakes at virtually every stage. However, I argue that the imperfections of the figurines are so thoroughgoing that we should probably assume that they were not valued for their performance as aesthetic objects, which is why the people making them did not take special care about their final appearance. Usually, the fact that these figurines are schematic, small, and unprepossessing has been taken as evidence for the primitive character of EIA art and the lack of skill among EIA craftsmen. Instead, I suggest a more elegant explanation for the consistently rough and careless appearance of the figurines: that their performative value resided in the transformational and dramatically elemental process of metallurgical work inherent in their production, not in their final appearance.

In Chapter 5 I develop the implications of this conclusion, the result of which is a new reconstruction of the nature of EIA ritual at rural sanctuaries and the role of the smith therein. I argue that metalwork was probably not an incidental economic activity that took place alongside ritual activity in sanctuaries, but that the smith and his work were central and inherent to the ritual itself. The earliest naked figurines from these sanctuaries should be considered as the material outcomes of ritual practices that were more closely related to the method of their production rather than their final appearance. The nudity of the figurines probably reflects a belief among individual worshippers, who I argue were involved in the production of votives, that nudity was an important aspect of the transformational rituals that they underwent at sites where the figurines appear. Chapter 6 outlines the way in which the story that I have been able to tell about these figurines (and the fact that they are naked) is distinct from existing reconstructions of EIA nudity, ritual, and society overall. I also point out a few questions that Archaic historians might find it interesting to consider in light of this revised interpretation of EIA ritual, nudity, and society.

A brief final chapter steps back and places the arguments made in the book in the context of larger issues of method and approach that continue to hamper progress in research on the Aegean EIA. The material in this book may interest those who want to know more about EIA institutions and ideologies surrounding nudity and ritual practices. However, perhaps equally important are the methodological implications pertaining to the reconstruction of a robust and materially grounded cultural history of the EIA Aegean. First, even though interpretational certainty can be elusive in this context, EIA archaeological evidence can be mustered to provide quite compelling insights about regional and historical trajectories of cultural history that are distinct from those we might arrive at if we viewed the EIA in exclusively relational terms based on the better-documented periods that came before and after. Second, starting from the texts will lead us astray more often than not when we are dealing with the EIA Aegean. Third, prehistorians may benefit from thinking more carefully about processes of production rather than assessing ancient objects primarily based on their aesthetic performance.

Setting aside the Homeric evidence that has long served as a *terminus post quem* for the introduction of meaningful practices and iconography associated with nudity among males in the ancient Aegean opens up analytical possibilities for EIA material that has often been ignored. Moreover, analysis of this material produces new insights and avenues of interpretation into the details of the beginnings of nude iconography and naked activities in the Aegean. It also demonstrates that the EIA in the Aegean need not only interest us because it bridged an imaginary gap between two ages, which are an entirely modern invention, or because it was an incubation chamber for the later Greek achievements, which we value for reasons that are ultimately more about modern than about ancient societies. It constituted a rich, lively social, political, economic, and ritual environment with immense regional diversity in culture that can sustain much interest in its own right.

CHAPTER TWO

NAKED MALE FIGURINES
IN THE EIA AEGEAN

The material record datable to the early phases of the Aegean EIA is relatively short on figural art. According to the usual diachronic narrative, the turn of the first millennium involves a relatively long-lasting period during which images of humans and animals are mostly absent from visual culture – as Benson originally called it, a "long pictureless hiatus."[1] In place of figural decoration, geometric designs are most characteristic of Aegean iconography during the EIA. According to some art historical accounts, this period of aniconic art represents a reset, during which the traditions of LBA iconography were mostly wiped away. The figural art of the Geometric period is then usually presented as the start of a new tradition.[2]

This narrative is not entirely accurate.[3] While the human figure is not especially common in material culture from the eleventh to ninth centuries,

---

[1] Benson 1970, 10; Coldstream 2006b; cf. Rystedt 1999.

[2] For example, Buschor 1951, 35: "Aus dieser spröden, körperlosen, phantastischen Figurenwelt erheben sich–wie wir annehmen: um die Jahrhundertwende–neue Gestalten, die geometrische Grundform mit quellendem Leben durchdringen." The choice of the Geometric period as a starting point for Greek art history is driven in part by the traditional subdisciplinary divide between prehistoric and historic archaeology. The largely artificial nature of this break is increasingly being recognized, criticized, and dismantled by archaeologists working across the LBA/EIA divide (see, e.g., Papadopoulos 2019; Lemos and Kotsonas 2020, xiii).

[3] One could also object that it does not accurately reflect the complexity of what is going on with Greek material culture following the collapse of the Mycenaean palatial system. As has

anthropomorphic figurines continued to be produced and deposited in sanctuaries on Crete throughout the transition from the LBA to the EIA. Many of these earliest EIA figurines represent nude males. Likewise, nude male figurines appear among the earliest extant ritual deposits at several mainland sanctuary sites and precede the thoroughgoing reappearance of humans on figure-decorated pottery in the EIA by at least a century. Thus, nude figurines constitute an important set of evidence when considering the social archaeology of the EIA Aegean. As some of the only images of humans from the period, they provide a limited but important resource from which to reconstruct some EIA ideas about people and, perhaps, ritual practice.

In this chapter I lay out the basic evidence for the appearance and archaeological context of these figurines. First, I briefly discuss the history of naked males and naked male figurines in Aegean art in order to demonstrate that the bronze male figurines of the EIA are not unrelated to LBA iconography, but depart from LBA traditions in significant ways. While male nudity is not entirely absent from LBA Aegean art, the examples of naked male figurines that do exist from the Bronze Age are materially and thematically quite distinct from EIA examples. These distinctions suggest that the nude bronze figurines under study here represent a type new to the Aegean that appears at roughly the same time as the demise of palatial LBA states. This type is likely to have been inspired or influenced by eastern Mediterranean traditions, but tracing these with any kind of certainty or granularity is probably impossible given the current state of the evidence. Turning to the development of the EIA type of the cast bronze naked male, I describe the current state of the evidence.[4] I discuss the chronology of the development of the EIA figurines while also laying out matters concerning the iconography and depositional context of the figurines. While my main focus in this book is on bronze figurines, some of the discussion in this chapter covers the related phenomenon of votive terracotta figurines. I introduce this discussion primarily to establish that the depositional practices associated with the bronze figurines seem substantially distinct from

---

been noted elsewhere, the collapse of the palaces and their institutions is likely to have impacted different regions in dramatically different ways (e.g., Salavoura 2015 on Arkadia; Kramer-Hajos 2016; Knodell 2021 on central Greece). While some regions with a particularly prominent palatial presence – for example Messenia, the Argolid, and Boeotia – may have experienced considerable social and political change after 1200, and while apparent migrations and movements of peoples (and perhaps a change in climate) apparently impacted each region in ways that are difficult to reconstruct, the notion that a clean breaking off of artistic traditions went along with a high level political collapse is difficult to sustain based on available evidence (see, e.g., Papadopoulos 1994 on potters' marks). Many areas of the mainland do not preserve much in the way of figural art from the duration of the EIA, but it is plausible that artists continued to illustrate scenes with human figures in organic media like wood, basketry, and textiles that do not survive in the archaeological record. See sources cited in Chapter 1, n. 27.

[4] A catalog of the EIA figurines dealt with in this book is presented in Appendix B.

those associated with terracotta ones, which indicates that these two bodies of evidence probably require independent analysis as ritual phenomena.

It is important to set out this evidence in some detail because it serves as the foundation for the argument that will follow in the rest of the book. Some aspects of the basic evidence that are useful to keep in mind include: (a) that total undress seems to be an important, but not universal, characteristic of bronze votive figurines from the very beginning of the EIA, (b) that the contexts from which any significant corpus of naked bronze figurines have been recovered are quite limited in number but cohere typologically as rural sanctuaries, and (c) that the demeanor of EIA naked figurines is highly variable in terms of both style and iconography. Once I have reviewed the basic evidence for the development of nude male figurines in this chapter, I consider what these figurines might indicate about nudity, cultural history, and ritual in the chapters that follow.

NAKED MALE FIGURINES IN THE AEGEAN LATE BRONZE AGE

Figurines representing the human form are present in Mediterranean material culture beginning in the Neolithic period and persist as a feature of the archaeological record more or less consistently after that.[5] The comprehensive history and scholarly consensus on the meaning and function of figurines in Mediterranean prehistory is a large topic beyond the scope of the current project.[6] Here I provide only a brief introduction to the history of figurines representing apparently unclothed males in Late Bronze and EIA Aegean contexts.

Naked Males in LBA Art

Representational art is a prominent feature of material culture dated to the Middle and Late Bronze Ages in the Aegean, but nudity does not figure

---

[5] See research on a range of topics in Insoll 2017. On figurines and their functions generally, Lesure 2001; Bailey 2005.

[6] During the best-documented periods, the majority of figurines seem to have a ritual function as votives, although small-scale figures in the round can also serve other purposes – for example as playthings (dolls) for children (Bailey 2005, 66–87; Langdon 2008, 134, fig. 3.2; Lee 2015, 185). Sometimes male and female figurines appear in distinct proportions, with one gender dominating (as females do in the Neolithic and LBA Aegean; or as males do in second millennium Byblos), while males and females appear together in relatively equal quantities among other assemblages. Seeden has suggested that females tend to dominate votive figurine assemblages when agricultural is of greatest concern to a society, while males appear in greater number when hunting or warfare predominate in the concerns of a community (Seeden 1980, 152).

prominently in iconography during these periods.[7] In general, females dominate extant assemblages of Mycenaean and Minoan figurines, although males occasionally appear as horse-riders.[8] Freestanding male figurines are present on Crete beginning in the Early Bronze Age (*ca.* 3000–2100), and appear in votive assemblages at sanctuaries from the Middle Bronze (*ca.* 2100–1500) period onward (appearing with special frequency at peak sanctuaries, e.g. Petsofas).[9] Male figurines from this period are usually interpreted as worshippers and typically appear in a distinctive pose with one hand raised to the forehead.[10] Figurines representing the human body are naturalistically modeled throughout the Minoan period, with exaggerations of musculature and stylization of certain features.[11] Breasts were regularly exposed in depictions of females; men could be nearly naked but almost always wore a codpiece.[12] These iconographic rules seem to indicate a general taboo against showing the groin, which extended from the palatial elite to members of society who appear to be lower down the political hierarchy. The exceptions to the rule were the very young; on occasion, children, including young boys, appear naked in Minoan and Mycenaean art.[13] However, toward the end of the Bronze Age, this rule appears to have changed or lapsed. Aside from an unpainted male figurine that may have had its genitalia broken off from an LM IIIA2/IIIB Early (*ca.* fourteenth–thirteenth centuries) deposit at the harbor site of Poros-Katsambas near Knossos on Crete,[14] the earliest appearance of something approximating a tradition of adult naked males in Aegean iconography dates to the very end of the thirteenth century.

In the West Shrine at the site of Phylakopi on Melos a group of terracotta male figurines was excavated in a deposit dated to the end of the thirteenth century or early twelfth century (LH IIIB or LH IIIC periods).[15] Such male figurines were not found elsewhere on the site, but were exclusive to the West Shrine.[16] One figurine appears to represent a

---

[7] Vetters and Weilhartner 2017, 35.

[8] For overviews of Mycenaean figurines, see French 1971, 1981; Morris 2017, 672–676; on male riders see Hood 1953.

[9] Myres 1903, pl. X.

[10] Biesantz 1954, 169. An example of this genre is known from Kea (from an LB I context; Caskey 1964, pl. 56a).

[11] Rethemiotakis 2001, 23.

[12] A hunter on a Mycenaean krater in the British Museum (London British Museum Inv. No. C342 (Karageorghis 1958, 385, figs. 5–6)) is an exception. For nudity in Late Bronze Age Crete and Greece see, Müller 1906, 90–91; French 1985; Stewart 1997, 31–35; Hitchcock 2000, 69–70; Morris 2017, 667; Vetters and Weilhartner 2017, 34–37.

[13] Davis 1986; Koehl 1986; Chapin 2009.

[14] Rethemiotakis 1998, 163, pl. 84; 2001, 68, 143.

[15] The finds are discussed in French 1985, 223–230.

[16] French 1985, 223. One fragment (Object No. SF 817, French 1985, fig. 6.11) from the East Shrine might represent a male, but the evidence does not allow for a confident attribution of the gender. The Phylakopi excavation find numbers for the figures are (from Assemblage A) SF 1550, SF 1553, SF 2340; from Assemblage G (SF 1544, SF 1520).

warrior.[17] He wears a conical helmet and probably carries a sword in his baldric. On his back, long wavy lines suggest a flowing mane of hair. Another figurine from the deposit is decorated with long vertical lines on both front and back.[18] These may represent clothing, but the modeling of the figure suggests nudity.[19] A third handmade nude figurine is decorated with hatched lines on the chest and back, and wavy lines on the arms and legs.[20] The break where the figure's buttocks should be suggests that the figurine may have been a centaur.[21] Two additional male figurines were found in a separate deposit.[22] The first is naked and wears a conical cap.[23] His torso and arms are decorated by criss-crossing painted lines. The second is in a poor state of repair that presents obstacles for precise reconstruction of its appearance—the bottom half of the figurine is missing, and it may or may not have been naked.[24] As is apparent from the name of the context in which the deposit was found, the excavators of the site interpreted the figurines as ritual in nature, an identification supported by the architecture of the building and the associated finds, which included a considerable quantity of large, wheel-made bovine figurines.[25] Renfrew argued that the West Shrine at Phylakopi should be interpreted as evidence for an inflection point in Aegean cult history. While both cows and male figurines are rare at Mycenaean and Minoan cult sites dated prior to LH IIIB, they appear in relative abundance at Phylakopi beginning in the final stage of LH IIIB (ca. late thirteenth/early twelfth century), and would thereafter become common material correlates of Aegean ritual practice.[26]

[17] French 1985, 226, fig. 6.12 (Phylakopi Object No. SF 2340).
[18] French 1985, 229, fig. 6.14 (Phylakopi Object No. SF 1550).
[19] Vetters and Weilhartner 2017, 36.
[20] French 1985, 226, fig. 6.12 (Phylakopi Object No. SF 1553).
[21] Langdon (2007, 178) suggests that this figurine is a piece from a centaur and formed a group with the nude warrior (no. 2340) in anticipation of later groups of warriors paired with centaurs from the EIA. However, French (1985, 223, 226, fig. 6.12) reconstructs the figurine as a standing male originally supported by a prop that did not survive, but allows that it could have been a centaur based on comparison with the PG centaur from Lefkandi (for which see Desborough, Nicholls, and Popham 1970). See also discussion in Lebessi 1996, 148–149. There is a good comparandum for such a centaur from Cyprus (Tatton-Brown 1979, no. 290).
[22] French 1985, 225, 228, fig. 6.13.
[23] French 1985, 228, fig. 6.13 (Phylakopi Object No. SF 1544).
[24] French 1985, 228, fig. 6.13 (Phylakopi Object No. SF 1520).
[25] French 1985, 236–253. Wheelmade bull figurines do not appear in significant quantities in the Aegean until the LB IIIB period. The majority of such figurines date to the LB IIIC period (Guggisberg 1996; Zeimbekis 1998, 172–173). The only assemblage similar in size and preservation to the Phylakopi group comes from the Amyklaion near Sparta (Demakopoulou 1982).
[26] Renfrew 1985, 420:

> The five male terracotta figures from Phylakopi constitute a remarkable document for the Aegean religions of the late bronze age. They are almost without parallel among Mycenaean finds . . . for the contrast between Greek religion as reflected in Homer and Hesiod and in the art of the Geometric period, on the one hand, with

Aegean Bronze Age comparanda for the Phylakopi figurines are not numerous. A fragmentary naked male figure from Tiryns, originally cited as a parallel for the Phylakopi finds by French, has recently been reanalyzed by Vetters and Weilhartner.[27] The fragments of the figure constitute (1) an 11 cm hollow wheel-made phallus with three fingers grasping its base and (2) two fragments of hollow wheel-made arms that do not join the phallus but appear to come from the same figure.[28] The figure's right hand is grasping the phallus, while the other arm is reconstructed as reaching forward from the body, presumably to indicate a ritual gesture.[29] The fully constituted figure must have been quite formidable. Voigtländer estimated that it would originally have stood at least 40 cm tall.[30] The three fragments were found in the Epichosis deposit, a dump of material from outside of the citadel's fortification wall, southwest of the palace.[31] Given this depositional context, the fragments' original use context cannot be determined with precision, but the material from the Epichosis is thought to have come from somewhere in the Upper Citadel. Vetters and Weilhartner argue that the figure would have served as a libation vessel in a ritual context. This conclusion is partly based on the associated ceramic and other artifact types in the Epichosis deposit, and partly based on the formal characteristics of the object.[32] In their words, "this three-dimensional model of a masturbating anthropomorph male literally spouts forth semen and in a context of religious libations actually enacts a fertility rite."[33]

Ceramics and terracotta figurines date the majority of the deposit to the late or final phase of LH IIIB, corresponding to the end of the thirteenth century. Voigtländer dated the figurine to the LH IIIC period based on stylistic analysis.[34] Vetters and Weilhartner reject this dating, and prefer to place the

its strong emphasis on male deities, and the late bronze age, on the other, has always been a striking one . . .;

on the bovine figures from Phylakopi, Renfrew 1985, 425–427.

[27] French 1985, pl. 37, e–h; Vetters and Weilhartner 2017, 41–49. Catalog numbers and excavation contexts for the fragments can be found in Vetters 2009 (DB-nos. 2679–2681); see also Voigtländer 2003, 130, taf. 41; 229, pl. 94.

[28] The attribution of the fragments to a single figure is based on the "clay fabric, manufacturing techniques, and strong similarities in surface finish and coloring" (Vetters and Weilhartner 2017, 44).

[29] Vetters and Weilhartner 2017, 42–43, fig. 5.   [30] Voigtländer 2003, 229.

[31] The lengthy bibliography on the Epichosis deposit includes: Verdelis 1959; Ålin 1962, 26–28; Schachermeyr 1962, 222, 251; Verdelis, French, and French 1965; Voigtländer 1973, 245–255; 2003; Vetters 2009, 249–281. It is alternatively known as the West Wall Deposit.

[32] Other unusual finds from the Epichosis indicating that a special, perhaps Levantine-inspired libation ritual may have taken place here include two fish rhyta and a conical rhyton decorated with painted figures (Vetters and Weilhartner 2017, 52–53).

[33] Vetters and Weilhartner 2017, 56.

[34] He dated the stratum within the Epichosis deposit to which the figure fragments belong in general to the twelfth century (Voigtländer 2003, 130).

figure in the palatial period.[35] Given its lack of parallels in the Mycenaean world, the resemblance of some of the object's features to Hittite coroplastic technology, and stylistic similarities to Cypriot and Western Anatolian ceramics, the possibility has been raised that the object itself was an import, but the fabric appears to be local.[36] In addition to this large-scale figure, a few hand-made-burnished-ware figurines of nude males come from LH IIIC levels at the site, seemingly from habitation contexts including hearths and doorways.[37]

Several naked male figurines, including one apparently playing a flute and one with outstretched arms, were discovered in fill deposits from wells associated with an industrial installation at the site of Kontopigado near Athens.[38] The figurines have been dated to the LH IIIB/LH IIIC transition. Although they cannot be associated with a primary depositional context, the fact that they were found together with a number of bovine figurines has suggested to the excavators that they may have come from a shrine or ritual context.[39] Kardamaki points out that the figurine with the outstretched arms bears a close resemblance to the Phylakopi statuette with outstretched arms, which has been interpreted as a cult statue.[40]

On Crete, naked male figurines from the end of the Bronze Age were excavated in the Piazzale dei Sacelli at Aghia Triada in the Mesara. The history of ritual activity at Aghia Triada is not understood precisely because the site was excavated in the nineteenth century CE, when record keeping was not particularly thorough.[41] However, current thinking holds that the Piazzale dei Sacelli was a shrine to the Minoan Goddess with Upraised Arms prior to the LM IIIC period. At the start of the LM IIIC period, this older shrine was abandoned, and subsequent deposits are characterized by new kinds of votives.[42] The LM IIIC and later deposits produced an unusual quantity of male figurines, including nudes, in association with animal figurines, such as bulls.[43] Unlike the Phylakopi, Tiryns, and Kontopigado examples, which were exclusively made of clay, the LM IIIC and later Aghia Triada figurines are made of both bronze and clay. Rethemiotakis identified these figurines as worshippers rather than as deities, partly due to their small size (especially compared with the older Goddess with

---

[35] Vetters and Weilhartner 2017, 48–49.   [36] Vetters and Weilhartner 2017, 47.

[37] Vetters 2020, 550. A similar example is known from LH IIIC Middle levels at Lefkandi (French 2006, 259, 262).

[38] Kardamaki 2015, 49, 62–66. A similar male figurine head comes from the south slope of the Athenian Acropolis (Casson 1921, 345; French 1971, 148). Since the deposit was unstratified, the figurine's date cannot be determined with certainty although it has generally been assigned to the Late Mycenaean period (Demakopoulou 1970, 174–183, pl. 58).

[39] Kardamaki 2015, 80. Bulls were also associated with the find of the male head on the south slope of the Acropolis. See also Pilafidis-Williams, who suggested that the bovine figurines from the LBA in general were associated with the worship of male deities (Pilafidis-Williams 1998).

[40] Kardamaki 2015, 65–66.   [41] Paribeni 1903.

[42] Banti 1943, 52; Alexiou 1958, 217; D'Agata 1999, 213–249.

[43] Banti 1943; Renfrew 1985, 423 D'Agata 1999.

Upraised Arms figures) and lack of particular details that would serve as notional attributes of a deity.[44] A clearly distinguished cult figure was not found, nor was any sign of architectural elaboration, leading the excavators to conclude that the sanctuary was the site of open air worship.

Naked LBA Males in Their Mediterranean Context

It is interesting that the finds from Phylakopi, Tiryns, Kontopigado, and Aghia Triada all seem to suggest a new association of naked male figurines with cult activity at approximately the same date, around the end of the thirteenth century. As Renfrew noted, "the finding of these figures highlights the astonishing dearth of male cult images from the Aegean bronze age."[45] The relatively sudden appearance of naked male figurines in apparently ritual contexts, often associated with bovine figurines, in an Aegean cultural environment where they were not part of a visible preexisting tradition demands historical explanation. One possibility that seems compelling is that the impetus for the introduction of such figurines to Aegean cult assemblages came from beyond the Aegean.[46] Bronze and terracotta naked male votive figurines had a long history of use in several regions of the eastern Mediterranean during the Bronze Age. Assemblages characterized by the presence of an armed naked male figure and bull figurines can be observed in the archaeological record from the Syro-Palestinian coast, especially the area around Byblos, dating back to the second millennium and extending into the early first millennium.[47] The function of the figurines, both bulls and humans, as votive deposits at ritual sites is parallel to the apparent use context of the few examples of naked male figurines identified at late thirteenth and twelfth century Aegean sites. Identical gestures on the part of some female and many male figurines from the Aegean, Cyprus, and Byblos suggest that they may be part of the same iconographic, if not ritual, tradition.[48] Renfrew made this

[44] Rethemiotakis 2001, 143. At Aghia Triada nude female figurines are also apparent in the repository, probably dated to the Subminoan period (Rethemiotakis 2001, 144). The bronze figurines are discussed in several publications (Borda 1946; Zervos 1956; Naumann 1976). The definitive study is provided in D'Agata 1999.

[45] Renfrew 1985, 438.

[46] As argued in Negbi 1988 (but see Gilmour 1993). For the notion that nude figures in the EIA represent the reemergence of a tradition that was common prior to the LBA, see Waldstein 1905, 16.

[47] Catalog and analysis in Seeden 1980. On the contrast between the situation in the Near East and that in the Aegean, see Kardamaki 2015, 63, 65; Vetters and Weilhartner 2017, 51–52.

[48] Compare, for example, the Tell el-Judeidah female figurines with arms clasped around their breasts (Seeden 1980, pl. 1, nos. 1a; 2a), Bronze Age Cypriot female figurines with the same gesture (Karageorghis 1993, pls. 9–10), and fragments of a votive plaque from Aegina (Sinn 1988, 153, abb. 4). The armed male smiting gods from the Levant, Crete, and the mainland are formally compared in Byrne 1991 (especially 109–157, 181–195).

comparison in his discussion of the Phylakopi figurines, drawing attention to the resemblance between armed bronze figurines of Negbi's 'Anatolian' type from the Levant (especially those from the site of el-Judeidah) and the Phylakopi figurines.[49] The resemblances are not limited to gesture (with the hands held forward around shoulder height) but also include attire, for example, the dagger in the belt and the conical helmet.[50]

Vetters and Weilhartner argue that two objects from the site of Tell Kazel on the coast near the modern border between Syria and Lebanon are closely related to the naked male figure from Tiryns.[51] Tell Kazel is identified with the ancient site of Amurru, a major LBA trade center mentioned in the Amarna letters.[52] The site yielded a large quantity of imported LBA pottery from Cyprus and the Mycenaean world, with local imitations of postpalatial Mycenaean wares indicating the possible presence of immigrant Mycenaeans starting in the twelfth century.[53] The parallels cited for the Tiryns figure are a wheelmade jug with an ithyphallic spout and a fragmentary vessel with a face and an ithyphallic spout being grasped by the figure's two hands.[54] Like the Tiryns figure, the Tell Kazel objects have no known local parallels. They were found in a ritual context associated with LH IIIA2 Mycenaean[55] and Cypriot[56] ceramics. Some or perhaps all of the Cypriot vessels may have served as containers for naked figurines made of sheet bronze.[57] The latter object type is known from a number of sites in the Syro-Palestinian region, including Hazor, Gezer, Megiddo, Tell el Ajjul, and Kamid el Loz (in the LBA temple).[58]

The association of the naked bronze figurines with Cypriot pottery is interesting in light of the presence of naked male figurines sharing many formal characteristics with the Phylakopi figurines in the relevant coroplastic assemblages from the LC II (1400–1250) period on Cyprus. The ithyphallic figurine from Grave 44 at Kourion, for example, seems quite similar in form

---

[49] Renfrew 1985, 422–423.   [50] Negbi 1976, 8, 11, fig. 13.

[51] Vetters and Weilhartner 2017, 51.

[52] Badre et al. 1994, 354; Badre and Gubel 1999/2000, 198.

[53] Badre 2006, 65–66; Badre 2011; Badre, Boileau, and Jung 2005; Jung 2007; Badre and Capet 2014.

[54] Badre and Gubel 1999/2000, 148–149, figs. 18a–b.

[55] See Badre and Gubel 1999/2000, 148; comparanda for the Mycenaean piriform amphoriskos come from Nafplio (Mountjoy 1986, 70, fig. 81.1) and Ugarit (Hirschfeld 2000, 80, no. 23).

[56] Badre and Gubel 1999/2000, 149. The Cypriot pottery mostly comprises White Shaved juglets with pointed bases.

[57] Badre and Gubel 1999/2000, 148–149.

[58] Negbi 1976, 97; Hachmann 1980, pls. 15–16. The excavators are unsure of the origin of the bronze sheet figurines; based on their association with Cypriot ceramics, they might be of Cypriot origin. The other possibility is that the figurines are local imitations of a Cypriot type (Badre 2006, 77).

and idea to the naked male figure from Tiryns.[59] In later periods, Cypriot figurines representing naked males carrying offerings are common.[60] In general, this period saw the simultaneous increase in hypaethral sanctuaries, votive offerings including naked males, and the deposition of bull figurines in Cyprus.[61] French argued that some of the idiosyncrasies in the terracotta assemblage at Phylakopi might also be related to Cypriot imports at the site.[62]

The evidence therefore seems to suggest that the earliest adult naked males to appear in the iconographic repertoire of the Aegean Bronze Age appeared under Cypriot or Syro-Levantine influence, influence that was either purely iconographic or both iconographic and ritual. This conclusion is made more persuasive by the spatial distribution of early naked figurines in the LBA Aegean, because the earliest sites where these appear are, or are near, harbor sites where long-distance exchange might have facilitated particularly close connections across sociocultural boundaries. Excavations at Poros–Katsambas have yielded bronze ingots and evidence for metalworking; it is likely that the site was an important harbor for northern central Crete during the

[59] Karageorghis 1993, 3–5, for naked females; 15 for the naked male (D4: LC II/III "a standing male figure with solid cylindrical body, right arm raised to touch the mouth, left arm curved obliquely across the body to touch the genital part. Short legs, no feet shown. Height 8.2 cm. From Kourion, T.44, British Museum Inv. No. 96/2-1/19"; comments at p. 23:

> D4 is very unusual. The fabric is the same as that of the figurines described above, including the use of paint, but the rendering of the facial characteristics differs. The long body, the short legs and the accentuated genitals recall a group of male figurines from Phylakopi. The attitude of the arms, especially the raised right arm, the short legs and the accentuated mouth may recall some Cretan adorants dating to the LM III period but the left hand touching or holding the genitals is not known in Cretan iconography.)

[60] For later Cypriot votive males, see Myres 1897.
[61] Karageorghis 1993, 1:

> "ca. 1200 . . . votive figurines are now produced not only to be offered as gifts to the dead but also to be placed as votive offerings to a divinity in a sacred place. Such figurines occur not only in clay, but also in other materials, particularly bronze. Furthermore, apart from the female figurines we now have the introduction of male figurines, obviously as the emergence of the male god as a partner of the Great Goddess in the Cypriote pantheon . . . the bull, a symbol of virile fertility, takes a predominant place in coroplastic iconography, either by itself or as an affix to other objects such as wall brackets."

Whether there is a uni-, bi-, or multi-directional connection between early Cretan, mainland, and Cypriot Greek nudity and cult worship, similarities among the iconographical systems are evident. For example, man-leading-bull compositions from twelfth century Cyprus are nearly identical to ones from EIA Crete and the mainland: compare Karageorghis 1993, pl. 14 (from Kazafani; Cyprus Museum no. CS 1829/136 [date, LC IIC, twelfth century]) with Lebessi 2002, pl. 32 (Syme Viannou, no. 36) and Rolley 1969, no. 42 (Delphi Archaeological Museum Inv. No. 6571).

[62] French 1985, 277.

LBA.[63] Phylakopi on Melos was a natural stopping point for people seeking to exploit Melian obsidian throughout prehistory; imported finds (e.g., a scarab and two bronze Reshef figurines of Syrian type) testify to the site's cosmopolitan nature in the LBA.[64] Kontopigado, an LH IIIB/LH IIIC settlement near the natural harbor of Palaio Faliro, was a site of industrial activity, perhaps related to commercial activities at the harbor.[65] Aghia Triada is located just inland from the harbor site of Kommos, where an extraordinary amount of ceramic evidence for long distance trade and craftwork in metal and jewelry attests to the presence of a busy port town.[66] Finally, excavations at Tiryns, which is thought to have been a port for LBA settlements in the Argolid, have uncovered installations for faience and metal production from the final periods of the LBA; the site probably served as the home to resident craftsmen practicing nonlocal ritual traditions.[67] Taken together, geographical patterns and iconographical particularities in the corpus of LBA Aegean naked males suggest that the adoption of this type was likely to have been influenced by an eastern Mediterranean tradition of ritual practice which involved the votive deposition of naked male figurines.[68]

[63] Reports about the Poros-Katsambas excavations are given in Dimopoulou 1997; 2004; 2012.

[64] Renfrew and Cherry 1985, 300–301, 303–310; Renfrew 1985, 424–425.

[65] Kardamaki 2015.

[66] Publications concerning ceramic imports from the site include Watrous 1985; 1992, 149–183; Knapp and Cherry 1994, 138–141; Rutter 1999; 2006; Tomlinson, Rutter, and Hoffmann 2010. On the relationship between Kommos and Aghia Triada, see Shaw 2006, 866–871. It is likely but not certain that Kommos was the main port for goods entering Crete through a polity centered at Aghia Triada and/or Phaistos from LM IA until at least the end of LM IB. That port continued in use through the end of LM IIIB, but the political configuration of the region after the LM IB period is not entirely clear.

[67] The evidence is reviewed with bibliography in Vetters and Weilhartner 2017. Connections between Tiryns and Tell Kazel may also be indicated by the presence at the latter site of several Syro-Palestinian armor plates (Badre and Gubel 1999/2000, 185–186, pl. 39lm). An example of this artifact type was also apparently deposited in a ritual/industrial context at Tiryns (Maran 2004, 21, fig. 14). It is interesting that such plates are also known from Kamid el Loz, where naked male bronze figurines have also been documented (Miron 1990, figs. 12–14). On armor scales in the eastern Mediterranean in general, see Karageorghis and Masson 1975.

[68] For the same conclusion, Byrne 1991, 198–200; Kardamaki 2015, 66, 80; Vetters and Weilhartner 2017, 51–52; on early bronze figurines, see Alexiou 1958; Negbi 1976; Sapouna-Sakellarakis 1995, 140–142. See also Rethemiotakis 2001, 31, for the suggestion that anthropomorphic head vases were likewise imitations of a Cypriot and Syro-Palestinian type during the LM IIIB/C periods:

> . . . in addition to the Moires rhyton a series of plastic anthropomorphic vases bears witness to the continuity of the type from LM IIIC into the early Greek period. Anthropomorphic vases of different type are the head-vases (examples from Phaistos and Gortyn) that date from the LM IIIB and probably imitate head-vases from Cyprus and the Syro-Palestinian littoral, which are dated in the fourteenth and thirteenth centuries BC.

Naked Males and Ritual Developments at the End of the LBA

While it is likely that the form itself was probably adopted at least in part due to influence from the eastern Mediterranean, the question of why this influence occurred when it did remains difficult to answer with precision.[69] It would notionally be possible to explain the transfer of the idea of nude male divine imagery from the eastern Mediterranean to the Aegean along two axes of discourse prominent in our understanding of the final stages of the Mycenaean period – the movement of peoples and an increase in violent coercion as a structuring force of society. On the former point, it is generally understood that Aegean LBA states probably employed immigrant labor in workshops under palatial control. This is indicated by the extraordinary evidence from Tiryns mentioned above, but also by some of the textual evidence in the Linear B tablets mentioning foreign names and groups of possibly nonlocal women receiving allocations or work orders.[70] Furthermore, Aegean LBA states were clearly engaged with the wider eastern Mediterranean world in the thirteenth century.[71] Along these lines, we might imagine that fourteenth and thirteenth century port towns hosted cosmopolitan communities among which various ritual practices and supernatural views coexisted. It is not implausible that ideas about and artifacts associated with ritual may have been among the things exchanged in the context of these port and harbor environments in the LBA Aegean.

It is also interesting to consider the potential relationship between the appearance of naked male figurines in the Aegean and changes in the role of violent or coercive force in society. Naked male figurines begin to appear around the transition between the LB IIIB and LB IIIC periods at a small number of sites. This period is contemporary with the demise of the Mycenaean palatial states. Although this coincidence need not indicate a causal relationship, it is plausible that one existed. It seems worth considering whether there may have been some connection between the physical appearance of armed male figures in ritual contexts and the social, political, and military environment in which this new iconographical tradition was adopted in the Aegean.[72] Seeden has suggested that the appearance of male gods in any given repertoire of figurines could be interpreted as an indication of underlying

---

[69] See Renfrew's discussion on the social and political underpinnings of cultic change across the LBA collapse (Renfrew 1981, 29–31).

[70] Chadwick 1988a, 83, 91–93; Hiller 1988; Palaima 1991, 279–80; Olsen 2014.

[71] See review of evidence in Sherratt 2020, 191–196.

[72] Renfrew 1985, 438–439. Although he suggests a relationship between the transformations of the cult at Phylakopi and the collapse of Mycenaean states, he does not make a clear connection between the nature of these transformations and the sudden turn to male cult statues in particular.

social values that emphasize hunting or warfare.[73] Periods in which a formerly strong state authority gives way to anarchy and entropy are often characterized by the rise of strong men and an increase in violence.[74] We could therefore reconstruct a scenario in which increased sociopolitical turmoil, and the increasing salience of coercive violence as a force structuring society, during the late LB IIIB and LB IIIC periods created a shift in cultural values that resulted in the appearance of a new type in material culture – a virile, masculine war god. This line of thinking would link the appearance of nude armed male figurines to the onset of an era of social uncertainty during which preexisting structures of power and authority were called into question or openly rejected through violent resistance. A warrior god might take on a new importance in a period of Hobbesian conflict where might made right.[75] In sum, it seems reasonable to explain the appearance of nude males in the Aegean at the end of the LBA by appeal to eastern Mediterranean influence, probably related to the movement of people, especially traders or craft specialists, and perhaps aligned with changing sociopolitical circumstances in which violence became a more important force in structuring relationships within and among communities.

NAKED MALE FIGURINES IN THE AEGEAN EARLY IRON AGE

Naked Male Figurines after the Bronze Age on Crete

Although the human figure is not frequently encountered in mainland material culture for a period of about a century after *ca.* 1200,[76] a tradition of

---

[73] Seeden 1980, 152.

[74] On the interaction between violence and order in society in general, see North, Wallis, and Weingast 2009. On the connection between strong states and the suppression of internal violence, see Tilly's classic study (1990) and Morris's extension of the thesis (2014). In a Mycenaean context, Kramer-Hajos (2016, 100–104) discusses the way in which the Mycenaean state sought to domesticate the warrior through a redirection of ideology from violence as a path to authority to a more institutional basis of state control. The period after the Mycenaean collapse saw the reemergence of a warrior class (Kramer-Hajos 2016, 149–166).

[75] One could instead possibly speculate that the association of Near Eastern gods resembling the Aegean Zeus/Apollo with rain, sun, thunder, and/or disease might have something to do with special attention afforded to such phenomena in a period of apparent climate change (at least in some regions: see Kaniewski et al. 2010; Finne et al. 2017).

[76] Coldstream 2006b. Two archers on a hydria from Lefkandi, dated to *ca.* 1000, are an interesting exception (Popham, Sackett, and Themelis 1980, pls. 254b, 270d, e). Representations of centaurs, at least part-human, are present at a few sites. A wheelmade terracotta figurine of a centaur standing 36-cm tall was found broken and divided between Tombs 1 and 3 of the Toumba cemetery at Lefkandi (Desborough, Nicholls, and Popham 1970, 24–25). On the basis of the finds from the associated burials, the excavators date the centaur to the final decades of the tenth century (Desborough, Nicholls, and Popham 1970, 23–24). Earlier centaur models date to the twelfth and eleventh centuries and come from Cypriot and Cretan sanctuaries (Desborough, Nicholls, and Popham 1970, 27, with

three-dimensional depictions of humans, especially in the form of bronze and terracotta figurines, continued throughout the LBA to EIA transition on Crete.[77]

The history of human figurines on Crete differs from the tradition on the mainland in a variety of ways. Virtually all figurines manufactured throughout the Bronze Age on the mainland and in the Cycladic islands were made of clay or stone. A couple of exceptions from the Early Bronze Age – one lead figurine from Antiparos[78] and one bronze figurine from Pavlopetri – demonstrate the near universality of this rule.[79] While Crete also preserves a continuous sequence of clay figurines (both anthropomorphic and zoomorphic), figurines cast in bronze appear alongside clay figurines starting in the Middle Minoan III period (approximately the seventeenth century) on the island. From this date onward, there was a continuous Cretan tradition of cast bronze figurine production.[80]

Figurines (both clay and bronze) from prehistoric Crete most often appear in ritual contexts. Clay figurines have been documented in all kinds of sanctuaries (cave, peak, extra-urban, and urban),[81] while bronze figurines do not appear in the archaeological record of peak sanctuaries or urban sanctuaries,[82]

references; see also discussion in Karageorghis 1966). Another possible centaur figurine was recovered from excavations in the Lefkandi settlement in 2004 (Lemos 2006; Thurston 2015, 198). It seems almost certain that the Lefkandi centaur/s was/were either imported from Cyprus or Crete or made under strong Cypro-Cretan influence (Lebessi 1996). The original excavators of the Toumba centaur raise the possibility that it was a nonlocal product, but ultimately argued that a local craftsperson was primarily responsible for its manufacture (Desborough, Nicholls, and Popham 1970, 30: "... it is to be seen as the product of an essentially Greek development."). A couple of wheelmade figurines, including centaurs, were discovered in tenth and ninth century deposits at the sanctuary at Ayia Irini on Kea (Gjerstad et al., 1935, 671, 675, 785, 817, pls. 227–228). In general, the dedication of wheelmade animal figurines in the Aegean final LBA and EIA can be traced in more or less continuous sequences at Athens (Nicholls 1970; Higgins 1967, 20–22) and at the Amyklaion (Buschor and von Marrow 1927).

[77] This point was originally emphasized by Müller 1906, 76. See also Lebessi 2002, 7.
[78] Sapouna-Sakellarakis 1995, no. 149.   [79] Sapouna-Sakellarakis 1995, no. 73.
[80] Biesantz 1954; Sapouna-Sakellarakis 1995, 6–7. See studies and discussion in Verlinden 1984; Sapouna-Sakellarakis 1995; Lebessi 2002. There remains no consensus about whether the appearance of bronze votive figurines on Crete was an instance of cultural diffusion, the result of imports and their influence on local craftsmen, or some other sort of outside impetus. See Müller 1929, 51; Alexiou 1958; Negbi 1976; Sapouna-Sakellarakis 1995, 140–142. In addition to the bronze figurines from Crete, two bronze figurines, one male and one female, come from a tholos tomb dated to LM/LH III at Kampos in Lakonia (Sapouna-Sakellarakis 1995, 83, nos. 144–145; Bossert 1923, fig. 250). The male is shown standing upright with open legs and is characterized anatomically by strong musculature. The inner surfaces of his hands point down. He is not naked, but wears a conical cap and a "schaumtasche" to cover the genitalia (Sapouna-Sakellarakis 1995, taf. 33, no. 144).
[81] See summary of clay figurines from peak sanctuaries in Faro 2008, 140–143 and data on figurines from extra-urban sanctuaries in Faro 2008, 229, table 6.1.
[82] Faro 2008, 145. For scholarship on the range of types and gestures present in these assemblages, see Rizza 1974; Rutkowski 1989; 1991; Morris 1993; 2001; 2009; Rethemiotakis 1997; Morris and Peatfield 2002.

but are preferentially found in cave sanctuaries[83] and other extra-urban sanctuaries.[84]

Male figurines in clay and bronze are clothed at least minimally (with a loincloth or 'codpiece') during most of the LBA, but begin to appear naked during the Subminoan period. This is also the "Blütezeit" for male figurines in bronze on Crete, when they overtake female figurines in variety and quantity within the corpus.[85] Bronze figurines from Crete that postdate the Minoan period have been collected by Naumann (1976) and reviewed in Byrne (1991) and Lebessi (2002). Significant assemblages come from Cretan cult places, including Aghia Triada (as discussed above), and the Psychro, Phaneromeni, and Idaean caves; the figurines are especially numerous at the sanctuary of Syme Viannou.[86] Isolated or small groups of naked male figurines are also known from the Subminoan and PG sanctuaries at Patsos,[87] Amnisos,[88] and Lato.[89]

Most of the figurines appear to represent worshippers or devotees.[90] Their poses, including the most frequently encountered gesture of one arm raised to the head and one at the side, are consistent with those of Minoan figurines usually identified as worshippers, but the Minoan gestures gradually become less marked over time, and largely disappear as the EIA progresses.[91] Terracotta figurines of a variety of types also continue to be produced throughout the Subminoan and Cretan PG periods, although such figurines from the EIA are relatively rare.[92] The types that occur are comparable to the bronze figurines, including males in a variety of poses and attitudes. Nude male terracottas from some Cretan sites are comparable in style and gesture to the Phylakopi terracottas.[93]

---

[83] Renfrew 1985, 423; Faro 2008, 79, table 3.3.

[84] These patterns are emphatic, but it is worth noting that the lack of bronze figurines at peak sanctuaries might be an accident of preservation, since metal is likely to be preserved better in cave deposits than exposed areas on mountaintops. An important early example of a bronze male figurine is a votary from the shrine of the double axes (LM IIIB) at Knossos (Evans 1928, 340, fig. 192). He is clothed, as is a contemporary warrior figurine from the villa at Kannia (Mitropolis) near Gortyn (Levi 1959, fig. 6.6).

[85] Naumann 1976, 11.

[86] For the Aghia Triada finds, D'Agata 1999; On the finds from Dikte, see Boardman 1961, 7. On the Idaean cave, Sakellarakis 2013. Syme Viannou is discussed in detail below.

[87] Naumann 1976, 94, no. P1, pl. 19; 96, nos. P23, P26, pls. 28, 31; 220, no. 228, fig. 89; Kourou and Karetsou 1994, 118, 145, nos. 83–84, figs. 95–96; 119, no. 89; 145, no. 85, fig. 97; Lebessi 2002, 59, fig. 26; 70–71, fig. 39; 80–81, fig. 49; 82, fig. 51.

[88] Stürmer 1992, 248, D1. b1; Lebessi 2002, 71–72, fig. 38.

[89] Demargne 1929, 383–384 (Heraklion Archaeological Museum Inv. No. 1483).

[90] Prent 2005, 391.   [91] Langdon 1991.

[92] Gesell 1985, 50. A group of bearded males from Aghia Triada has been interpreted as votive in nature, but is exceptional (see Halbherr 1903, 73–74).

[93] The naked male warriors from Vrokastro (Hayden 1991, 133–142, nos. 34, 35) and dated to the PG and Geometric period "resemble the body type of the Phylakopi males" (137). One holds his arms forward, perhaps to hold a weapon. Another naked terracotta figurine, with crossed straps that resemble those on the body of the Phylakopi warriors, is known from the Unexplored Mansion at Knossos (Higgins 1984, pl. 193.6).

Since most Cretan bronze figurines do not come from well-stratified deposits, they have usually been dated on stylistic grounds.[94] It has been assumed that the pieces wearing the traditional Minoan codpiece and saluting in a recognizably Minoan manner should be dated earlier in the sequence, to the Subminoan period, while those without clothing or a salute should belong to the PG period.[95] These kinds of formal characteristics are not ideal criteria for dating, and it may be that both types coexisted for a time around the end of the Bronze Age. The schema of typology and dating developed by Naumann in the 1970s, prior to the discovery of LBA nude males at Phylakopi, rested in part on the notion that nudity categorically did not belong in Late Bronze Age contexts. This conviction had a strong impact on the determination of dates for early naked figurines from Crete because it established a default *terminus post quem* for nudity, but this assumption can now be called into question given the information summarized in the first part of this chapter.[96] The fact that there are strong stylistic resemblances between the earliest nude Cretan bronze and terracotta figurines and the figurines from Phylakopi suggests, as Renfrew points out, that, through the matrix of Cretan figurines, "[t]here may be a thread of continuity linking these first LBA nude plastic representations of the male figure with those of Geometric Greece."[97]

EIA Naked Males at Syme Viannou

A strong local tradition of naked figurines is especially apparent in the finds from the sanctuary of Syme Viannou in south central Crete, where this tradition persists through the end of the LBA and into the Geometric and Archaic periods. Since the site is one of the few shrines that remained in use as a site of ritual activity throughout the EIA, and since an unusually large number of naked figurines has been recovered from EIA deposits at Syme Viannou, it is worth reviewing the evidence from the site in some detail.[98]

The sanctuary of Syme Viannou is located in a mountainous environment, nestled at the base of a cliff on the southern shoulders of the Lasithi massif at an elevation of 1,200 masl. The site occupies a spectacular natural setting, a verdant woodland surrounded by dramatic topography that is well-watered even in the high summer months. The first signs of human use and occupation date to the Protopalatial period, and although there is architecture associated

---

[94] Boardman 1961, 7; Naumann 1976, 51; Other figurines with arms extended to hold a weapon or offering are known from Kannia near Gortyn, the palace at Knossos, and Kommos. See Gesell 1985, 50; Hayden 1991, 138, n. 103.

[95] Boardman 1961, 7; Sapouna-Sakellarakis 1995; cf. Renfrew 1985, 423.

[96] Hayden 1991, 137.

[97] Renfrew 1985, 424: "The stance, the near nudity (at least in the modelling) and the style of many of these is anticipated at Phylakopi."

[98] Lebessi 1996; 2002; Faro 2008, 219–222.

with each phase, it seems likely that open-air ritual practice was characteristic of activity at the site throughout its history of use.[99] The phasing of the site's architecture is complex and reflects some changes in the organization of cult activity over the thousand-year life of the sanctuary. During the Neopalatial period, cult architecture consisted of a large rectangular built structure, accessed via a paved road, inside of which a thick black stratum was excavated. The black stratum contained a large quantity of animal remains along with pottery and other apparently votive offerings.[100] Among the votive offerings were bronze figurines, weapons, libation tables, and ceramic and stone ritual vessels.[101]

Activity at the site continued through the end of the Bronze Age and into the EIA, with substantial changes appearing in votive assemblages beginning in the LM IIIC/SM period, including the introduction of wheelmade bovine figurines that are common to many Cretan votive assemblages during this period.[102] The quantity of votive dedications increased during the EIA phases, with most coming from a substantial black layer that was spread across the central area of the site. The black layer is probably best interpreted as the remains of animal sacrifices that would have constituted an element of ritual activity. The main altar has two EIA phases, one dated to the PG and another to Late Geometric (LG), and the presence of at least some relatively flimsy architectural foundations dated to the PG period suggest that additional structures were present here throughout the period of the sanctuary's use.[103] However, there is a noticeable increase in building at the site around 700, including the construction of a new stone altar and substantial terracing.[104]

Among the votive offerings recovered from the EIA black layer were forty-one bronze anthropomorphic figurines, many of which represent naked males, datable from the LM IIIC to LG/Orientalizing periods. As an assemblage of nude male figurines, the material from Syme Viannou is unique in its size, iconographical variety, and chronological span which ranges across the Bronze to Iron Age transition.[105]

Although the ashy layer in which the early votives were deposited was mixed, making it necessary to date the bronzes based mainly on style, Lebessi has constructed a plausible chronological sequence.[106] The earliest (LM IIIB)

---

[99] Prent 2005, 170.

[100] For review of the site and its phasing, see Lebessi and Muhly 1990, 320–323; Prent 2005, 170–174.

[101] It is the only Minoan sanctuary where chalices have been found (Lebessi and Muhly 1987, 110).

[102] Continuous use throughout the LBA to EIA transition is a common characteristic of sanctuary sites on Crete (e.g., the Idaean, Psychro, Patsos, and Tsoutsouros sanctuaries, for which see Boardman 1961; Alexiou 1963a; Sakellarakis 1983; 1988; 1992; Kanta 1991; Rutkowski and Nowicki 1996, 1–45; Watrous 1996, 101–111; Erickson 2002). For a brief review of the LM IIIC/SM phases see Prent 2005, 172–173.

[103] See the phase plan published in Lebessi and Muhly 1976, 3; Lebessi and Muhly 1990, 318, abb. 3.

[104] For a thorough review of the architecture of the site, see Zarifis 2007.

[105] The bronzes are described in Lebessi 2002, 13–27.   [106] Lebessi 2002, 27–32.

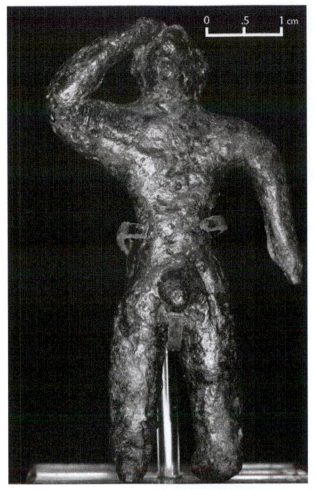

2.1. An LM IIIC transitional bronze figurine of a naked male from the sanctuary of Syme Viannou on Crete (Syme Viannou Excavation Inv. No. 5055, photo by author; with permission of the Heraklion Archaeological Museum; © Hellenic Ministry of Culture and Sports – Hellenic Organization of Cultural Resources Development)

figurines from the assemblage are equipped with the usual Minoan costume – the men are muscular and mostly unclothed but wear a small skirt or codpiece. They also make traditional Minoan gestures, including the pose of the worshipper holding one hand to the head and the other straight down the side.[107] However, already in some of these early examples the absence of the loincloth is suggested.[108] A transitional figurine, dated by Lebessi to LM IIIB/C, has the same pose as earlier Minoan worshipper figurines, but is entirely naked, without a loincloth (Figure 2.1).[109] A naked warrior figurine is also dated to the LM IIIC

---

[107] Lebessi 2002, 32–49, pls. 1–7.
[108] See, for example, Lebessi 2002, 35–39, pl. 2, nos. 2–3 (Syme Viannou Excavation Inv. Nos. MH4304, MH 4305).
[109] Lebessi 2002, 50–54, pl. 8 (Syme Viannou Excavation Inv. No. MH 5055).

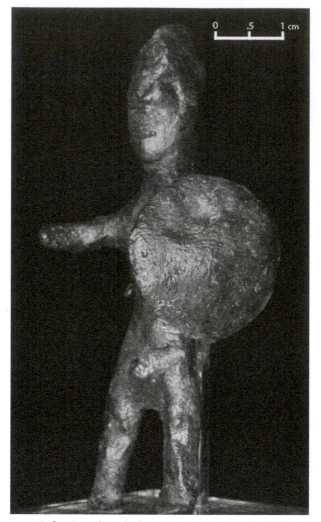

2.2. A figurine of a naked warrior dated to the LM IIIC period from the sanctuary of Syme Viannou on Crete (Syme Viannou Excavation Inv. No. MH 4959, photo by author; with permission of the Heraklion Archaeological Museum; © Hellenic Ministry of Culture and Sports – Hellenic Organization of Cultural Resources Development)

phase. He wears a conical hat and holds a spear in his right hand, a shield in his left.[110] A second figurine is very similar in style, although the weapon probably held in this statuette's right hand may have been cast separately and is no longer attached to the object (Figure 2.2).[111] Figurines from the site dated to the PG period include not only freestanding figures but elements of larger compositions,

[110] Lebessi 2002, 54–56, pl. 8 (Syme Viannou Excavation Inv. No. MH 3700).
[111] Lebessi 2002, 50–54, pl. 8 (Syme Viannou Excavation Inv. No. MH 4959).

for example, a naked bronze male playing a flute that was probably part of a group that originally decorated a Cypriot-style rod tripod along with other naked males.[112] Animal figurines also figure prominently in the corpus of EIA votives from Syme Viannou; their deposition begins in the eleventh century and the corpus mainly comprises bovines.[113]

The quantity of Geometric period votives deposited at Syme Viannou is greater than those dated to the PG period. The Geometric figurines from Syme Viannou are also more varied and complex in iconography than earlier material.[114] To the local Early Geometric period (850–790) are dated a figure interpreted as a flagellant (Figure 2.3), a group composed of two naked helmeted figures holding hands, and a naked cup-bearer.[115] Early to mid-eighth century figurines include a young naked boy with his hands at his sides and a pair of naked dancers.[116] To the end of the eighth century dates another standing naked male with his arms out in a pose usually interpreted as that of a warrior, based on the assumption that weapons would have been attached to the arms in the original design.[117] These figurines all come from the open-air phase of the EIA sanctuary; as noted above, an explosion of building starting around 700 and represented a turn in the nature of ritual worship at the site.[118]

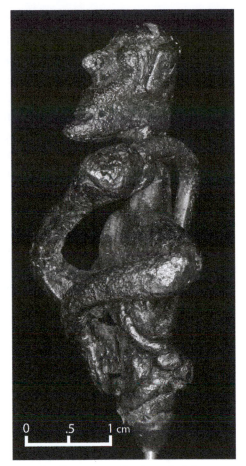

2.3. A fragmentary figurine depicting a flagellant from the sanctuary of Syme Viannou on Crete (Syme Viannou Excavation Inv. No. MH 4301, photo by author; with permission of the Heraklion Archaeological Museum; © Hellenic Ministry of Culture and Sports – Hellenic Organization of Cultural Resources Development)

[112] Syme Viannou Excavation Inv. No. MH 3147. For the rod tripod fragments, see Lebessi 2002, 71–74. On the rod tripods and their manufacture, distribution, and sociopolitical implications, see Papasavvas 2001, 2014.

[113] Schürmann 1996; Muhly 2008.   [114] Lebessi 2002, 74–97, pls. 14–20.

[115] Lebessi 2002, 74–85, pls. 14–16 (Syme Viannou Excavation Inv. Nos. MH 4301, MH 3137 (see **Plate 2 D**), MH 4357).

[116] Lebessi 2002, 86–92, pls. 17–19 (Syme Viannou Excavation Inv. Nos. MH 4360, MH 4358, MH 4359).

[117] Lebessi 2002, 92–97, pl. 20 (Syme Viannou Excavation Inv. No. MH 3699).

[118] Lebessi 1975; Kanta 1991, 325.

Naked Male Figurines at Other Cretan Sites

While the assemblage of naked bronze male votive figurines from the site of Syme Viannou is exceptional, scattered finds from other sanctuaries across Crete and dated to the same period attest to the fact that it was not the only site where such votives were being used and deposited during the EIA.[119] The evidence is thoroughly reviewed in Lebessi's publication of the Syme Viannou figurines; a few examples will suffice to provide a good impression of the material in in the current context.[120] From the Subminoan period, a pair of bronze figurines from Psychro Cave echo the transition, seen in Figure 2.1, from the Minoan to Postminoan style, with the traditional Minoan worshipper pose in a figure that is apparently lacking a loin-cloth.[121] The same attributes belong to a pair of figurines from the Phaneromeni Cave and likewise dated to the Subminoan period.[122] Outside of Syme Viannou, naked bronze figurines from the PG period are known from Patsos, the Idaean Cave, the Psychro Cave, Aghia Triada, Amnisos, and Kalamafka.[123]

Notwithstanding the long tradition of ritual practice involving the deposition of bronze votive figurines on Crete, the consistent appearance of naked males among Cretan votive figurines in the twelfth century is a novel phenomenon.[124] The proximate source of influence on Cretan naked votives might be Phylakopi, as Renfrew argued.[125] The early date of the naked male figures at Phylakopi relative to the earliest identified naked males on Crete may indicate that Cretan ritual iconography was influenced by new developments in the Aegean at the end of the LBA.[126] Alternatively, there may instead be cause to rethink the absolute dating of some of the naked figurines from Crete, since their sequencing has partly been

---

[119] Lebessi 2002, 50–74.

[120] Lebessi (2002) provides images and comparanda for all of the Syme Viannou figurines. Her publication constitutes a complete treatment of the genre for the Cretan LBA/EIA transition.

[121] Lebessi 2002, 50–51, figs. 16–17. See also examples from Archanes (Heraklion Archaeological Museum Inv. No. 4351; Lebessi 2002, 50, fig. 15); Crete Unspecified (Athens National Archaeological Museum Inv. No. 8914; Lebessi 2002, 52, fig.18); and Crete Unspecified (Heraklion Giamalaki Collection Inv. No. 527; Lebessi 2002, 53, fig. 19).

[122] Lebessi 2002, 54, figs. 20–21; see also **Plate 2 A**.

[123] From Patsos, Heraklion Archaeological Museum Inv. No. 207 (see **Plate 6 C**) and Oxford Ashmolean Museum Inv. No. G 392; Psychro Cave, Heraklion Archaeological Museum Inv. No. 431; Aghia Triada, Heraklion Archaeological Museum Inv. No. 746; Amnisos, Heraklion Archaeological Museum Inv. No 2316 (see **Plate 3 C**); and Kalamafka, London British Museum Inv. No. 1930.6-17.1. On the Idaean Cave, Lagogianni-Georgakarakos 2000 (there is an interesting concentration of naked female figurines here, but at least one naked male is also present).

[124] The dating of most votives from early Cretan religious sites depends on style, since votive deposits are not generally *in situ* or stratified and contain finds that appear to be attributable to a range of different dates.

[125] Renfrew 1985, 424.

[126] The sanctuary at Phylakopi remained in use after 1200; the same is true of the Cycladic town sanctuary at Ayia Irini, which was used in the LBA as well as during the PG (Renfrew 1985, 361–363; Mazarakis Ainian 1997, 170–171).

based on presumptions about whether naked human figures should be expected to occur in deposits from certain periods.[127]

Naked EIA Figurines on the Mainland: Olympia and Delphi

On the mainland, EIA bronze figurines represent a new feature of the archaeological record that is not preceded by an equivalent LBA tradition.[128] Votive figurines (often zoomorphic but occasionally anthropomorphic), usually interpreted as dedications to a deity,[129] have been recovered from largely mixed but probably early deposits at some sanctuary sites. The figurines are generally dated to the end of the tenth century or the ninth century.[130] Many of the figurines are associated with "black layers", deposits rich in ash and animal bones, at sites where the earliest ritual activity is usually identified as comprising some combination of open-air sacrifices and feasts.[131] The anthropomorphic bronze figures among the votives include both males and females, but males outnumber females by a considerable margin.[132] The naked males and females both include a variety of iconographic types.[133]

The site of Olympia has produced the largest and earliest assemblage of bronze and terracotta naked votive figurines on the mainland.[134] The earliest figurines from Olympia probably date to the tenth century, and the sequence of bronze male figurines from the site extends through the end of the eighth century.[135] The majority of the early bronze and terracotta anthropomorphic figurines from Olympia come from a black, ashy layer excavated across the

---

[127] The amount of clothing on the figurines has served as the criterion for dating each individual piece to the Subminoan or PG period, respectively, based on the assumption that nudity does not occur prior to the EIA (e.g., Boardman 1961, 7; Naumann 1976; cf. Renfrew 1985, 424: "It seems likely that had [the Phylakopi figurines] been available when the Cretan bronzes were being studied, an earlier date might have been found acceptable for some of the latter.").

[128] Herrmann 1964, 17–18; Higgins 1967, 17; Schweitzer 1967, 133–135; Langdon 1984, 27–28, 272.

[129] This assumption is justified mainly by appeal to evidence pertaining to later votive practice, for example, the inscription on the Mantiklos Apollo (Thebes, ca. 700–675): "Mantiklos dedicated me as an offering to the far-shooter, and you Phoibos give me something pleasing in return." See also Boardman 1978, fig. 10; Van Straten 1981, 73; Grottanelli 1989–1990, 52; Bremer 1998, 130–131; Parker 1998, 110–111.

[130] Langdon 1984, 2–3. One bronze figurine of a horse is known from a Geometric settlement deposit at Vitsa Zagoriou in Epirus (Vokotopoulou 1968, 291). A few figurines are known from Geometric burial contexts, but these are all animal figurines, not anthropomorphic ones (the sites including such burials are Chamilovrisi near Thebes (Spyropoulos 1971, 215–216), Tiryns (Müller and Oelmann 1912, 132, fig. 6); Kalamata (Themelis 1965, 207); Amfikleia (Courbin 1954, 132); Halikyrna (Dekoulakou 1972, 438–439); Kainourgion (Liagkouras 1963, 144); Anavra (Theocharis 1964a, 242)). Langdon suggests the bronze figurines in these burials may represent secondary deposition of objects originally made for votive use in sanctuaries (Langdon 1984, 45–46).

[131] Bergquist 1988, 25; Simon 1997, 125–126.   [132] Langdon 2008, 245–246.

[133] Langdon 1984, 171–201.

[134] In total, 2,221 EIA terracotta figurines are reported (Heilmeyer 1972, 6–8).

[135] Heilmeyer 1972; Rolley 1977, 133.

center of the site that lay stratigraphically between the structural remains of the Middle Helladic 'Pelopeion' and the foundations of the early sixth century Hera temple.[136] The black layer probably represents the remains of a large ash altar accumulating detritus from many years of sacrificial activity that was demolished, and its contents then distributed horizontally across the site, during the early seventh century, when the sanctuary seems to have been significantly reorganized.[137] Fragments of early figurines have turned up from other deposits at Olympia. For example, several were excavated from within the foundation trenches of the sixth-century Heraion.[138] Heilmeyer is probably correct in stating that although many figurines (both bronze and terracotta) have been recovered from the site, they likely represent only a fraction of the original quantity deposited.[139]

The bronze figurines from Olympia were originally published in 1880 and 1890 by Adolf Furtwängler. He organized the material in a sequence according to what he perceived to be developmental stages, partly based on technique and partly based on style. Furtwängler's chronology has been mostly accepted but somewhat refined in subsequent studies by Kunze, Herrmann, and Heilmeyer.[140] According to the scheme developed by the iterative work of these scholars, the earliest bronze representations of naked males from Olympia date to the late tenth century, although this could now plausibly be pushed back to the eleventh century, given recent redating of the earliest cult activity at the site.[141] The majority of the figurines are dated to the ninth and eighth centuries.[142]

The black layer from which most of the figurines were excavated contained a mixture of animal bones, ash, and votive offerings that was probably laid down gradually over a long period of time, but whose original stratigraphy was not preserved. Efforts to understand the development of these figurines over time have therefore by necessity relied on evolutionary models and notions of

---

[136] On the excavation of the black layer, see Furtwängler 1890–1897, 43; Dörpfeld 1935, 9–28; Mallwitz 1966. An excellent color photograph showing the black layer sandwiched between the prehistoric architecture and the Pelopion *temenos* wall can be found in Kyrieleis 2002, 217, abb. 3. Although there is increasing evidence for use of the sanctuary in the eleventh century (Eder 2001a; 2001b; Kyrieleis 2006), it has thus far not been possible to demonstrate cult continuity from the Bronze Age (Kyrieleis 2002, 217; review of evidence in Papakonstantinou 1992).

[137] Kyrieleis 2002.   [138] Heilmeyer 1972, 4–5; Langdon 1984, 234.

[139] Heilmeyer 1972, 5.

[140] Furtwängler 1880; 1890. Further discussion in Willemsen 1954–1955; Himmelmann-Wildschutz 1974; Hiller 1977. See also Heilmeyer 1979, Langdon 1984, 14–25 for a survey of the history of the research on Geometric figurines at Olympia.

[141] Eder 2001, 206.

[142] Although some have attempted to date the earliest terracotta figurines to the LBA based on stylistic similarities to Mycenaean terracottas (Furtwängler 1890–1897, 44; Herrmann 1964, 59), Heilmeyer (1972, 42) dates the earliest terracottas to the PG period. The earliest bronze figurines are likewise dated to the PG period (see discussion in Müller 1929, 71; Herrmann 1964, 59, 272; Kunze 1967, 214–215).

stylistic development rather than stratigraphic sequencing.[143] According to Kunze, the crudest figurines are dated to the earliest phases, while the finer and more naturalistic figurines belong later in the sequence. However, one could just as easily assume that figurines of various styles and qualities were dedicated at random, because the style of each figurine is largely independent of any other, so we need not necessarily accept the established dating on logical grounds.[144] That said, given the archaeological context, it is certainly impossible to improve upon the existing, stylistic seriation of the figurines, which was produced through exemplary and careful work on the part of the excavators and subsequent analysts affiliated with the Olympia excavations. Nonetheless, I suggest that classing all of the finds as generally EIA without accepting an internal sequencing is most prudent, given the near-total lack of certainty regarding the relative date of the bronze figurines.

The chronological relationship between the terracotta and bronze figurines from Olympia also remains ambiguous because of their mixed depositional context. It has been suggested that the terracotta figurines were deposited prior to the bronze ones, because most of the terracotta figurines come from the lower sections of the black layer. However, these deposits also contained bronze finds, so the stratigraphic relationship between the two cannot be determined with certainty.[145] The earliest examples of naked male figures, both bronze and terracotta, have consistently both been dated to the late tenth century.[146] Some the terracotta anthropomorphic figurines which Heilmeyer dated to the PG

---

[143] Herrmann (1964) produced the seminal article on this front, distinguishing a number of workshops or schools of production. Although he relied on style for the most part, he also derived some of his groupings from his detailed knowledge of the find spots of the figurines. His system remains in place today, with some modifications (e.g., Rolley 1969, 73–76; Heilmeyer 1979, 12–13). See discussion in Kyrieleis 2006, 91–95. Lebessi (1996, 146, 152, n. 23) has suggested that the chronology of the mainland figurines be reconsidered because the dating in part relied on the notion that better-crafted bronzes could not have been made during the 'primitive' phase of PG art.

[144] Kunze 1967, 220–223.

[145] The terracottas almost all come from the older of two strata of black soil located between the Heraion and the Pelopion that were separated by sand (Kunze 1944, 139; Willemsen 1957, 166). However, bronzes including tripods and figurines were found together with terracottas in this layer, making the sequence of the two media of figurines difficult to parse with certainty. For arguments that the terracottas are earlier, see Heilmeyer 1972; Rolley 1977, 133. The hypothesis that bronze figurines instead inspired imitations in clay (suggested by Hayden [1991, 137] for Cretan terracotta figurines) is also not implausible, since the former could notionally have been more valuable than the latter. For additional discussion of the dating of the figurines, see Cook 1975; Nicholls 1975, 289; Cooper 1977, 345.

[146] For the early terracotta males, Heilmeyer 1972, 60–78. Some female terracotta and bronze figurines appear to be unclothed (Heilmeyer 1972, 56–61; Byrne 1991, 23–25, 229–230). Eder's restudy of the EIA ceramics from Olympia shows a continuous sequence into the eleventh century. This raises the possibility that some of the figurines could likewise be dated prior to the tenth century (Eder 2001a, 2001b).

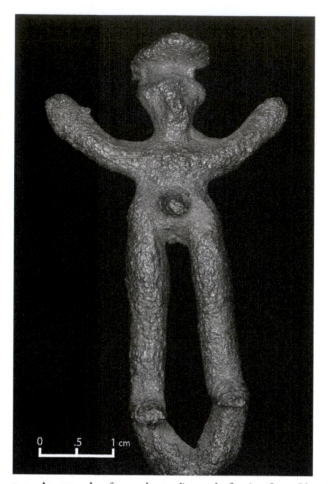

2.4. An example of an early standing male figurine from Olympia (Olympia Archaeological Museum Inv. No. B 4245, photo by author, published with permission of the Archaeological Ephorate of Elis; © Hellenic Ministry of Culture and Sports – Hellenic Organization of Cultural Resources Development)

and EG I period are clearly male and naked.[147] Within the sample of 242 figurines published by Heilmeyer,[148] 27 are naked males with weapons and 21 are standing naked males (Figure 2.4).[149] All but six of these are dated to the very end of the EIA, the LG period. The other significant class of terracotta votives from Olympia

[147] Furtwängler 1890, pl. 17, nos. 279–296. The figurine no. 288 bears a strong resemblance to the Phylakopi figurines in posture and attire. On the lack of good parallels elsewhere, see Heilmeyer 1979, 19–26; Langdon 1984, 66–67.

[148] Heilmeyer found few parallels elsewhere on the mainland from the same period to assist with dating, so his chronology for the figurines is based on comparing their style to images in early vase painting (Heilmeyer 1972).

[149] See also a more recently excavated naked male bronze figurine from Olympia illustrated in Kyrieleis 2006, taf. 49, 6–8 (Kat. 132).

are the charioteers and wagoneers, which are far more numerous (nearly 100) than the bronze ones (15) from the site. According to Heilmeyer, the chariots in both terracotta and bronze seem to have been dedicated at the same time, between MG and LG I.[150] Most of the terracotta charioteers are naked; two wear a hat, the flat broad type usually called a *petasos*.[151]

Other terracotta figurines from Olympia often wear a small conical cap, perhaps some kind of helmet, and have their arms outstretched. On the basis of the belts and hats, Heilmeyer suggested that the figures were probably originally armed, with weapons attached as separate pieces.[152] While Heilmeyer, Kunze, Byrne, and others have interpreted the male figurines as representations of a deity (presumably Zeus), there is no reason to assume this must be true.[153] The argument is based on the fact that early depictions may have been armed and striding in the fashion of later depictions of Zeus, and that they bear some distant resemblance to cult images from the Bronze Age. However, as Himmelmann has pointed out, it is just as plausible that the votives represent worshippers.[154]

Of the sixty EIA bronze figurines from Olympia that can be assigned a gender with confidence, thiry-seven are naked males.[155] Within this group, a wide range of types is represented. A group of twenty-three naked bronze figures represent frontally facing males standing with their legs apart and arms outstretched. While this group coheres in terms of general posture, the figurines within it do not have a great deal in common with one another otherwise.[156] According to Kunze, the earliest of all the bronze figurines are the standing males with legs apart, arms extended to the sides and either a flat hat, along the lines of a *petasos*, or no apparent headgear (see Figure 2.4).[157]

---

[150] On the phasing of the terracotta charioteers, see Heilmeyer 1972, 41–55. Heilmeyer (1972, nos. 148–149) suggested that the chariot drivers represented wealthy aristocrats who visited the sanctuary in order to make a dedication.

[151] Heilmeyer 1972, nos. 148–149. [152] Heilmeyer 1972, 62.

[153] Heilmeyer 1972, 64–65; see also Weege 1911; Kunze 1946; Riemann 1946/1947; Kunze 1948, 9; Mallwitz 1966, 325; Kunze 1967; Byrne 1991, 27–30. The argument is based on the notion that the figures must represent early stages in the development of cult statues, and on the view that nudity should signal the supernatural in the EIA.

[154] The position that all early figurines at the sanctuary were images of Zeus was viewed critically by Himmelmann (2002, 96). Although he identifies a few statues of the seventh century as potentially Zeus-like, he rejects the idea that the earliest EIA figurines represent Zeus (99–102). He appeals to the fact that the Subminoan comparanda cited by those identifying the figures as Zeus are likely to be worshippers rather than deities. For the idea that the EIA figurines inspired or influenced later artists creating images of the striding Zeus, see Smith 1962; Burkert 1992, 19. On the interesting phenomenon of a longstanding German interest in identifying the earliest images of gods, see Bruer 2010.

[155] Langdon (1984, 301–310) catalogued 81 figurines, but many could not be identified as either male or female due to their state of preservation.

[156] Langdon 1984, 88–94.

[157] For example, Furtwängler 1890, pl. 15, no. 238; pl. 16, no. 237.

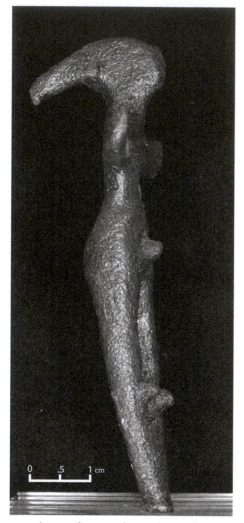

2.5. A standing nude male with arms outstretched and a peculiar pointed hat from Olympia (Olympia Archaeological Museum Inv. No. B 1698, photo by author, published with permission of the Archaeological Ephorate of Elis; © Hellenic Ministry of Culture and Sports – Hellenic Organization of Cultural Resources Development)

Kunze reconstructed the development of a subsequent class of figurine that seems to be specific to Olympia – the standing naked male with arms raised upward, wearing a special crested hat that arcs backward like an *agrimi* horn (Figure 2.5).[158] These examples are indeed unusual. They have been interpreted as epiphanies of the deity on analogy with the old Mycenaean/Minoan image of the deity with upraised arms, but their hats also bear a close resemblance to those worn by some Minoan figurines (Figure 2.6).

These unusual figurines are not representative of the pose and demeanor of the group overall. Other classes of figurines include individuals portrayed with arms that seem designed to bear weaponry and shields, horse riders, and chariot drivers.[159] The armed figurines usually wear some kind of headgear, a simple conical cap or sometimes a more elaborate crested helmet (e.g., Figure 2.7).[160] The riders and charioteers are also usually naked except for a belt and/or a hat, sometimes the *petasos* or a conical cap.[161] Formal outliers include a figurine holding both hands over his abdomen,[162] a young boy who appears to be riding a bull or ram,[163] and a seated figure who appears to be whistling or playing an instrument.[164]

A second significant mainland assemblage of EIA bronze figurines comes from Delphi. According to Rolley's dating, bronze figurines begin to appear at Delphi in the Middle Geometric II period, considerably later than the appearance of the first such objects at

---

[158] For example, Furtwängler 1890, pl. 16, nos. 240–241.
[159] Some of the EIA figurines that have been described as arms bearers do not seem well-designed to receive attachments. Instead, they bear close resemblance to the Minoan pose of the worshipper, with one hand to the head (compare, e.g., Lebessi 2002, figs. 13, 20 (LM IIIA–C figurines from Knossos and the Phaneromeni cave) and Kunze 1944, taf. 16 (from Olympia)).
[160] For example, Furtwängler 1890, pl. 15, no. 247, pl. 16, nos. 242–246.
[161] Furtwängler 1890, pl. 15, nos. 249–251, 256, pl. 16, nos. 251, 258.
[162] Furtwängler 1890, pl. 16, no. 239.   [163] Furtwängler 1890, pl. 16, no. 255.
[164] Langdon 1984, 137. There are also two centaurs (Furtwängler 1890, pl. 13, no. 215). The centaurs may be compared with a celebrated group now in the Metropolitan Museum and said to come from Olympia, showing a naked male locked in some fashion of embrace or combat with a centaur (Metropolitan Museum 17.190.2072; see images and bibliography in Padgett, Childs, and Tsiafakis 2003, 133–136).

2.6. A Minoan figurine of a worshipper on display in the Heraklion Museum (photo by author; with permission of the Heraklion Archaeological Museum; © Hellenic Ministry of Culture and Sports – Hellenic Organization of Cultural Resources Development)

Olympia.[165] However, it should be noted that most of the earliest bronze dedications from the site come from dumps of earlier material buried within the sixth century leveling fills of the sanctuary, so there are issues with dating the material according to any criterion other than style.[166] The formal similarity in style and execution between the bronze figurines from Olympia and those from Delphi suggests that there may have been a close relationship between early rituals or the earliest craftspeople who made figurines at the two sanctuaries. For example, the so-called 'clothes-peg' figures from the sites, two from Olympia and one from Delphi, are virtually identical (Figure 2.8). Each is composed of a flat-hammered rod split at the legs, with a head, eyes, and mouth rendered, and what may be a hat indicated in excess metal material

[165] For an account of the early history of cult practice at the site, see Rolley 1977, 134–138.
[166] Scott 2010, 48.

2.7. A figurine of an armed male from Olympia (Athens, National Archaeological Museum Inv. No. 6096; Olympia Excavation No. Br 9788, published with permission of the National Archaeological Museum, Athens, © Hellenic Ministry of Culture and Sports/Archaeological Receipts Fund)

on top of the head.[167] A group of five striding armed males likewise bears strong resemblance to comparable material from Olympia. It has previously been suggested that these objects were made in the same workshop.[168] Another small figurine holding a conical round shield in its left hand looks very similar to comparably designed figurines from Olympia and Crete (compare Figures 2.2, 2.7, 2.9).[169] It is thought that the figurine once had additional attachments, including a helmet crest and a spear.[170]

A total of ten naked warrior figurines belong to the assemblage from Delphi.[171] Three other standing naked males are unlikely to be warriors because their hands hang at their sides.[172] One figurine represents an

---

[167] Langdon 1984, 203, nos. C74 and C123.
[168] Herrmann 1964, 47–49; Rolley 1969, 25–26.
[169] However, see also Müller 1929, 168, 188; Rolley 1969, 40; Byrne 1991, 51. All comment on the object's Near Eastern affinities.
[170] Langdon 1984, 103.   [171] They are described at Langdon 1984, 102–104.
[172] Langdon 1984, 148–149.

archer in the act of stringing a bow, and another might represent a boxer (see Plate I C).[173]

Mainland EIA Figurines of Naked Males from Other Sites

Some naked male bronzes have been discovered at other sanctuary sites on the mainland, including sites in the Peloponnese (Sparta, Tegea, Mavriki), Thessaly (Pherai, Philia), and Aetolia (Thermon). The largest known assemblage of mainland naked male bronze figurines outside of Olympia and Delphi comes from the site of Philia (later the sanctuary of Athena Itonia)[174] in Thessaly, near modern Karditsa. The site was excavated by Theocharis beginning in the 1960s after residents of the area notified the archaeological service of looting.[175] The excavators uncovered a burnt layer containing artifacts dated to the Geometric and Archaic periods, sealed by what were apparently fluvial deposits. The majority of the Geometric bronze finds comprised fibulae, jewelry, weapons, and ivory plaques. Seven naked male figurines from the deposit date to the Geometric period.[176] Three of the figurines are of the typical Delphic/Olympic type of the naked male standing with arms raised in a posture that suggests they were designed to hold a weapon in one hand and a shield in the other.[177] Another with an unusually attenuated neck stands with its legs apart and arms curving forward (see Figure 3.2). The figure may be pouring or offering a libation.[178] Two figurines definitely represent naked dedicants offering or pouring libations; while one holds both hands out

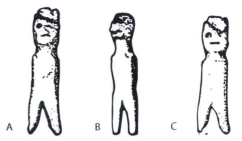

2.8. Three "clothes-peg" figurines, two (A, B) from Olympia and one (C) from Delphi (Redrawn from Langdon 1984, 203, her catalogue nos. C74 [Olympia Excavation Inv. No. Br 7378], C75 [Olympia Excavation Inv. No. Br 11831], and C123 [Delphi Archaeological Museum Inv. No. 10102])

---

[173] Rolley 1969, nos. 10 and 26, pl. 10. Casting issues with the hands of figures are common in EIA figurines, as discussed below in Chapter 4; the lumps of metal at the end of the notional 'boxer' figure's right hand could therefore have been the result of flaws in the mold or the metal pour, rather than a design feature intended to make the figure look like a boxer. However, the figure is belted, as other EIA images of boxers and wrestlers are, so an identification of the figurine as representing a participant in combat sports is plausible.

[174] According to Theocharis 1963, who was drawing from Strabo's account (9.5.17).

[175] Theocharis 1963, 135.

[176] Objects and votives from the site are currently split between the Ny Carlsberg Glyptothek (Inv. Nos. 3309, 3310, 3311, 3359, 3360, 3607; see Johansen 1982; Christiansen 1992, 13, 50–51, 54–56, 58–59) and the Volos and Karditsa Archaeological Museums (Theocharis 1964b, 247, pl. 291a, b). See Kilian-Dirlmeier 2002 for thorough publication of the small finds from the site, including three additional figurines, datable only roughly to the period from 750–575 BCE (Kilian-Dirlmeier 2002, 207–211). These three figures are standing naked males, two with one hand raised. One wears a belt.

[177] Theocharis 1964b, pl. 291; Langdon 1984, nos. C91–93.

[178] Johansen 1982, 73, fig. 1; Christiansen 1992, 59, no. 23.

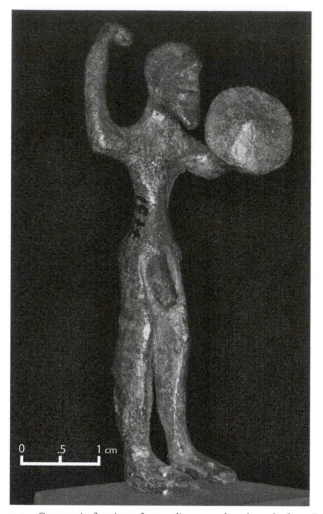

2.9. Geometric figurine of a standing armed nude male from Delphi (Delphi Archaeological Museum Inv. No. 7731, photo by author; with permission of the Delphi Archaeological Museum; © Hellenic Ministry of Culture and Sports – Hellenic Organization of Cultural Resources Development)

away from his body,[179] the second holds his erect penis with one hand while pouring a libation with the other.[180] One of the Philia figurines is a remarkable nude rider/warrior with an elaborately crested helmet.[181] A seated naked male, apparently a smith, is a unique find (Figure 2.10).[182]

[179] Johansen 1982, 74, fig. 2; Christiansen 1992, 58, no. 58.
[180] Johansen 1982, 74, fig. 3; Christiansen 1992, 56, no. 20. A connection might be drawn between this figure and an anthropomorphic vase from a seventh century deposit at the Heraion on Samos that holds its erect penis in one hand (Buschor 1951). The figurine also recalls the pose of the Tiryns figurine discussed above (Vetters and Weilhartner 2017).
[181] Johansen 1982, 75, fig. 4; Christiansen 1992, 50–51, no. 17.
[182] Johansen 1982, 76, fig. 5; Christiansen 1992, 54–55, no. 19.

2.10. Late Geometric figurine of a smith working at an anvil from the sanctuary of Philia in Thessaly (Ny Carlsberg Glyptotek Inv. No. 3360, Photo by Anders Sune Berg, courtesy Ny Carlsberg Glyptotek, Copenhagen)

One other Geometric anthropomorphic figurine is known from Thessaly. It was found at the site of Pherai, which would later become an important regional sanctuary. The sanctuary has yielded a massive quantity of bronze dedications rivaling the scale of the assemblages from Olympia and Delphi, including dedications of fibulae that number in the thousands.[183] While a number of animal figurines were apparently dedicated at the site, thus far only two bronze anthropomorphic figurines have been published. One is too badly preserved to be identifiable,[184] while the other is a standing naked male.[185]

The sanctuary of Athena Alea at Tegea in the central Peloponnese began as an open-air sanctuary in the LG period. Many votive offerings from a black layer filled with charred organic remains, probably to be associated with an early altar, date to this early phase. The three naked male figurines that came from this deposit include one seated and one standing figure, the latter with a conical hat,[186] and a group showing a naked man seeming to save a goat from an attacking canine.[187] At the nearby sanctuary of Mavriki (Artemis Knakeatis) a naked seated male was among the early dedications, dated to around 700.[188] Excavations at the Spartan sanctuary of Athena Chalkioikos have turned up

[183] On the fibulae, see Kilian 1975; Kilian-Dirlmeier 1985. On EIA finds from the sanctuary, see Georganas 2008, 278–279.
[184] Kilian 1975, 185, pl. 88.4.   [185] Biesantz 1965, no. L63.
[186] Dugas 1921, 355–356, nos. 53–54, fig. 19; Kilian 1980, fig. 5.1
[187] Dugas 1921, 354, no. 51, fig. 17; Rolley 1967, no. 9.   [188] Romaiou 1952, 26, pl. 20d.

deposits rich in Geometric dedications, including a figurine of a naked male with outstretched arms.[189] From the sanctuary of Artemis Orthia near Sparta, a seated naked male who appears to be playing a musical instrument dates to the LG period.[190] A Geometric bronze group of male dancers with zoomorphic heads from near the temple at Petrovouni in the Mani may represent a dance or fight of naked boys wearing masks.[191]

Outside the Peloponnese, Delphi, and Philia,[192] the only site on the mainland from which multiple naked male figurines are known is the sanctuary of Thermon in Aetolia. Several figurines were excavated from a black layer in the uppermost floor levels of Megaron B, including a bronze helmeted figure with arms extended to the side and a naked figure wearing a belt.[193] Isolated examples have appeared at sites elsewhere in the Aegean. The provenance of two bronze figurines from Zakynthos is not well known: they were originally part of a group of five, but the others are now lost.[194] A naked standing male with arms akimbo in the manner of some examples from Olympia was among the offerings at the sanctuary of Aetos on Ithaka,[195] where ceramics suggest that cult activity began as early as the ninth century.[196] Geometric finds from the sanctuary on Delos largely comprise Cycladic ceramics, but also include offerings of tripod fragments, four bronze animal figurines, and two male figurines, one of which is a standing nude male with arms held out at his sides.[197] A handful of bronze figurines have been found in other sanctuary deposits in central and eastern mainland, but they are not representations of naked males.[198] A handful of bronze figurines have been

---

[189] Woodward, Droop, and Lamb 1926–1927, 82, pl. 8.

[190] Woodward, Droop, and Lamb 1926–1927, 99, pl. 11; Rolley 1967, no. 26.

[191] Letterman and Hiller von Gaertringen 1911, 252. For the idea that the boys are not dancing in a circle but rather engaging as two sets of pairs, perhaps in order to wrestle, while wearing monstrous masks, see Langdon 2008, 115. There are nine figurine groups representing ring dancers from Geometric Olympia. Most represent groups of females (see discussion in Tölle 1964; Langdon 1984, 187–191). On terracotta ring dancing groups dated to the eleventh and early tenth centuries from Cyprus, see Mikrakis 2016, 60–61. The Olympia groups may represent Cypriot influence. However, circular dance groups are also known from Minoan Crete (e.g., the LM IIIA group from Palaikastro [Heraklion Museum no. 3903]; Rethemiotakis 1998, 19, 64, 109, 118, 147, no. 1, figs. 20–23, 99)

[192] On apparent cultural connections between Delphi and Thessaly from an early date, see Lerat 1961, 352–357; Morgan 1990, 108.

[193] Romaiou 1915, 273–274, figs. 40–41. Langdon (1984, 239) suggests that the statuette is supposed to represent "the polemic aspect of Apollo."

[194] Benton 1932, 216.   [195] Benton 1935.   [196] Benton 1953, 259.

[197] Déonna 1938, 223–224, fig. 1; Rolley 1973, no. 19.

[198] One Geometric male bronze figurine was found at Kalapodi (Felsch 1983, 126–127, fig. 12; on Kalapodi, offerings in the sanctuary, and evidence for religious continuity, Felsch 1996; 2001; 2007). The figurine was broken at the waist. Two Geometric bronze figurines are known from the Athenian Acropolis (from which also come a few figures of naked males that would have been attached to tripod cauldron handles from the end of the eighth or early seventh century, for which see Papaspyridi-Karouzou 1952, 137–149). One of the

found in sanctuary deposits in central and eastern mainland, but they are not representations of naked males.

In the eastern Aegean, very few sites have produced bronze figurines of naked males.[199] There is a sizable collection of bronze votive figurines among the remarkable and rich early ritual deposits at the Samian Heraion. The depositional contexts of the figurines are mixed, so the chronology is not entirely secure.[200] Many of the bronze figurines from the site are imports from the eastern Mediterranean that are completely different in type from the bronze anthropomorphic figurines known from sites like Olympia and Delphi. These imports include some figurines of naked females, but no imported Samian bronzes represent naked men.[201] Out of three non-imported bronze figurines from Samos dated to the Geometric period, only one shows a naked male.[202] This figure is part of a remarkable group in which a man and his hunting dogs are engaged in a battle with a lion.[203] The scene is probably related to a type encountered in Geometric vase painting and metalwork, depicting a (sometimes naked) man involved in an altercation with a lion or two lions.[204]

A thorough understanding of the geographical and chronological distribution of the bronze figurines from EIA sanctuaries is hindered by the fact that a sizable fraction of the corpus lacks any kind of provenience data – many of the highest quality EIA naked male bronze figurines currently reside in North American and British museum collections but cannot be assigned to a particular region or date.[205] Even if this body of evidence could be linked to

freestanding figurines from the Acropolis is naked (de Ridder 1896, no. 771; Boardman 1961, p. 9, pl. 6; Herrmann 1964, 49, figs. 36–38). A seated male bronze figurine, probably a musician, from Eretria may be naked, but this is not made explicit through the modeling of primary sexual characteristics (Aupert 1976, 701, fig. 277).

[199] A group of bronze figurines from Kameiros on Rhodes might represent naked males. Unfortunately, they are extremely corroded and their anatomical characteristics are therefore not discernable (Jacopi 1932–33, 344–345, fig. 80.5–9). Of the two EIA bronze figurines from Lindos, one represents a standing naked female, and the other is a small male with outstretched arms, but he seems not to be naked (Blinkenberg 1931, 399, nos. 1575–1576).

[200] Gehrig 1964, 3–6, 12–17.

[201] They are presented in Jantzen 1972. The history of ritual activity at the site is reviewed in Walter 2019.

[202] The other two are females, a standing nude (Gehrig 1964, no. 2) and a woman carrying a vessel on her head (Gehrig 1964, no. 1). They seem to be influenced by eastern Mediterranean types.

[203] Samos Museum Inv. B190 (Kunze 1930, 146–147).

[204] For parallels and discussion, see Ahlberg-Cornell 1987, 56; Snodgrass 1998, 14, for example, fig. 1; Langdon 2008, 46–47; they are briefly discussed here in Chapter 3). The earliest example of this type of scene in the Aegean may be the one on a krater from a Cretan tomb dated to the late ninth century (Kunze 1931, 205, fig. 30, Beil. 1; Sackett 1976, 117–119).

[205] Of the 202 figurines Langdon (1984) catalogued, over thirty lack any secure provenance information.

individual sites, it is unlikely that the assignments would change the general patterns, especially the remarkable concentration of EIA bronze figurines at two mainland sanctuary sites: Delphi and Olympia.

Terracotta Anthropomorphic Figurines

Terracotta figurines are not present in large numbers in EIA deposits at most sanctuaries.[206] Where they are present (with some exceptions), they do not coincide with the contexts where naked bronze figurines have been found.[207] Naked males are also not prominent among EIA terracotta figurines. I review the evidence here briefly to justify my choice to set aside the analysis of terracotta figurines for the remainder of the book. As is the case with naked female figurines, terracotta figurines and their distribution are eminently worthy of careful study, but patterns in their manufacture and use seem to require separate analysis.[208]

Male terracotta figurines are not common during the LH IIIC period (see the section "Naked Males in LBA Art") . EIA terracotta figurines from ritual deposits have a circumscribed geographic distribution, mainly occurring in sanctuaries on Crete, in the Peloponnese, and in the eastern Aegean. While handmade terracotta figurines of both anthropomorphic and zoomorphic types are common on Crete throughout the Bronze and Iron Ages, terracotta male figurines remain relatively rare – female figurines are much more common at Cretan sites throughout the earlier part of the EIA.[209] A smattering of male terracotta figurines on Crete comes from transitional Bronze Age/Iron Age contexts, including the Unexplored Mansion at Knossos and the sanctuary at Vrokastro, but few are known from the later phases of the EIA.[210] The site of Aghia Triada, discussed above with regard to its final Bronze Age finds, is exceptional in preserving a corpus of clay anthropomorphic male figurines that appear alongside terracotta zoomorphic figurines and bronze anthropomorphic

---

[206] Langdon 1984, 233.

[207] See Pilz 2011 for groups of dedicatory terracotta plaques from LG and Archaic Cretan sanctuaries.

[208] See discussion of categorization in Chapter 1. Thurston (2015) produced an excellent study of the terracotta figurines from the period covered here in her doctoral thesis.

[209] Hayden 1991, 138; Vetters 2020, 555. However, it should be acknowledged that detailed study of these figurines remains lacking (Prent 2005, 418). A better-studied type is the large wheelmade figure (e.g., at particular sites, Forster 1901–1902, 278–279; Demargne 1931, 391; Rizza 1967–1968, 214; in general, Kourou 2002a). I do not discuss them here because the scale of these objects and their likely use as cult statues rather than votives sets them apart from the topic of current study. They also never represent naked males. There is a period at most sanctuaries between the final phases of the Bronze Age and the Geometric period during which wheelmade figurines are not represented (Kourou 2002a, 21).

[210] On Vrokastro, Hayden 1991.

figurines throughout the EIA sequence.[211] Many of the males are naked, and they bear a close stylistic resemblance to early terracotta figurines from Olympia.

The situation at Syme Viannou cannot be dealt with in much detail for this book, because the terracotta anthropomorphic figurines from the sanctuary are currently still under study by Lebessi in preparation for publication. However, in existing publications, Lebessi has mentioned that "there are 157 preserved and identifiable clay anthropomorphic votives of various categories from Syme that range in date from the early PG period down to the fourth century."[212] While she specifies that 46 of these 157 represent females, it is not clear how many of the remainder date to the EIA and represent naked males. With these two exceptions, it seems that on Crete most sites where bronze figurines were dedicated in any quantity, especially cave sanctuaries, are notable for the absence of terracotta anthropomorphic figurines.[213]

Few sites on the mainland have produced sizeable assemblages of anthropomorphic terracotta EIA figurines, and those that have preserve few representations of naked males. One broken figurine from an eighth century level at Eretria probably represented a naked male.[214] Terracotta male figurines have not been found in EIA sanctuary deposits in Attica.[215] There are apparently no terracotta figurines from Geometric deposits at Delphi, although a cache of Mycenaean figurines may have been deposited in eighth century levels.[216] Anthropomorphic clay male figurines dated to the EIA have not been recorded at Kalapodi.[217] Terracotta figurines in Boeotia are found exclusively in mortuary deposits, and do not represent naked males.[218] At the Argive Heraion, thousands of clay figurines were excavated in the early twentieth century from the black ashy layer below the foundations of the second temple, but it appears that most of these date to the seventh century and later.[219]

---

[211] D'Agata 1999, 127–145.

[212] Lebessi 2009, 524. Muhly 2008 presents the EIA zoomorphic clay figurines from the site.

[213] For Patsos, see Kourou and Karetsou 1994. The site produced a group of eleven bronze human figurines and a large assemblage of bovine figurines, but there were no clay anthropomorphic figures. There are more EIA sites on Crete with sizable assemblages of zoomorphic clay figurines than there are sites with many anthropomorphic ones. A good example is Kommos, which has produced no clay anthropomorphic figures but ample zoomorphic ones; Shaw and Shaw 2000, 136–142).

[214] Huber 2003, 48, no. 14.

[215] Mazarakis Ainian 1997, 314–318. The possible exceptions are four handmade figurines that could date to the LG. However due to the absence of information about their context, it is not possible to date these with any certainty or to assign them to a ritual context (Averett 2007, 36, n. 30).

[216] Rolley 1969, 1977; Morgan 1990, 137–147.

[217] For Kalapodi, Felsch 1980; 1983; 1987; 1996.   [218] Averett 2007, 9, 35, n. 23.

[219] Waldstein 1905, 3–10. The excavators originally dated the majority of the figurines to the pre-Mycenaean period, but this dating is not based on stratigraphic evidence and should not be considered reliable. Some of the figurines from the Heraion bear a close formal resemblance to those found in early layers at Olympia, suggesting that they could notionally

I have discussed the clay figurines from Olympia (see the section "Naked EIA Figurines on the Mainland: Olympia and Delphi"); terracotta figurines of both humans and animals appear at other sanctuaries in the Peloponnese. Near to Olympia in Elis, at the site of Kombothekra, eleven naked male terracotta figurines were found in fill deposits that were disturbed by looters. These appear to be very close in style to early figurines from Olympia, and were probably also made in the EIA.[220] The sanctuary of Poseidon at Isthmia received clay figurine dedications, but they are almost exclusively zoo-morphic.[221] At the Lakonian site of Amyklai, mixed ashy deposits, probably from an early open-air shrine with possible roots in the Bronze Age, produced two anthropomorphic figurine heads, one of which is probably a warrior. However, since the accompanying bodies were never recovered, it is impos-sible to know whether the figurines were naked; their size also makes it plausible that they were intended to serve as representations of deities rather than votives.[222] Also in Lakonia, terracotta anthropomorphic figurines have been recovered from votive deposits at the sanctuary of Artemis Orthia, but such figurines are extremely rare in deposits dated prior to the seventh century.[223] A similar situation is encountered at Tegea, where large quantities of terracotta figurines dated to the sixth and fifth centuries were recovered, compared with only about ten from earlier periods. None of the early examples represent males.[224] A similar pattern holds at other Arkadian sanctu-aries including Mavriki, Lousoi, and Gortsouli.[225] In general, outside of Olympia, anthropomorphic terracotta figurines of naked males are present but very rare, echoing the distribution of the bronze figurines.

In the eastern Aegean, terracotta votive figurines are more common than they are on the mainland during the EIA, with figurines occurring in a wide variety of sanctuaries. However, in contrast with the situation in the central and western Aegean, female figurines tend to dominate these assemblages. The Samian Heraion has produced an immense quantity of votive material dated to the earliest phases of the EIA.[226] Clay votive male figurines are, however, "rare and late."[227] The number of female clay figurines from EIA deposits at Samos is far greater than the number of males. Four male figurines might be

be redated to the EIA, for example, Waldstein 1905, 17, no. 16 (fig. 10). However, absent further excavations to establish a stratigraphic sequence, the dating of this corpus remains problematic.

[220] Sinn 1981.

[221] Morgan 1999, 167–175. For the single EIA anthropomorphic figurine head from the site, Morgan 1999, 168, F8.

[222] Langdon 1998, 253–254.   [223] Higgins 1967, 24.

[224] Voyatzis 1990, 252; 1995, 273–275.   [225] Voyatzis 1990, 239.   [226] Jarosch 1994.

[227] Averett 2007, 65.

naked.[228] These figurines bear some resemblance to examples from Olympia. Based on the minimal stylistic variation in the group, Jarosch suggests that they all probably date to a period circumscribed within approximately twenty years at the end of the eighth century.[229] Four male figurines are recorded from Emporio on Chios, all dated to the mid to late seventh century. The earlier clay figurines from both the acropolis and the harbor sanctuaries depict only females and animals.[230] A similar scenario applies to the Geometric figurines from the site of Lindos on Rhodes; anthropomorphic figurines are present, but with the exception of a male musician that is part of a group of female ring dancers and a group of clothed male figurines imported from Cyprus, they mainly represent females.[231] At the Hephaesteion on Lemnos three female figurines were found in LG levels and figurines of cows have been recovered from the sanctuary of Iria on Naxos and the sanctuary of Apollo on Kalymnos.[232]

Generally, then, there are regional patterns in the evidence for practices associated with the deposition of votive figurines in the EIA Aegean. Sizable assemblages of terracotta figurines occur in eastern Aegean sanctuaries, but in general female figurines are more common than male figurines.[233] Assemblages of terracotta figurines on the mainland are rare outside of Olympia; in the few sanctuaries where there are considerable numbers of EIA figurines, they are most often zoomorphic. On Crete, naked male clay figurines do not occur with much frequency, and the general distribution of clay anthropomorphic figurines does not align well with the distribution of bronze ones, except at Aghia Triada and (maybe) Syme Viannou. Olympia and Aghia Triada therefore stand out as exceptional sites where bronze and clay anthropomorphic figurines of nude males are dedicated in seemingly significant quantities in the

---

[228] Jarosch 1994, 147–157 (catalogue of female figurines); 157–158 for male figurines. In addition to the freestanding male figurines, there is a LG figurine of a naked horse rider (Jarosch 1994, 129, no. 469).

[229] Although it is dated to the early seventh century, an anthropomorphic vessel with a phallus from the southwestern deposits of the sanctuary near the Imbratos river bears mentioning here (Buschor 1951). When he originally published it, Buschor dated the vessel to the third quarter of the seventh century (Buschor 1943, 10), but after further research he argued that it must belong earlier, either to the late eighth or early seventh century (Buschor 1951, 34). The dating is almost entirely based on stylistic comparisons. For instance, it is placed prior to the Hera figurines because it is too crude to have been made at the same time as those, and after the eighth century because "die über die spröde Strenge der geometrischen Form hinausführt und etwa als subgeometrisch bezeichnet werden darf." A similar object is known from Rhodes (London British Museum Inv. No. 94.7–18.3; see Buschor 1943, 10–11).

[230] Boardman 1967, 191. Present in the assemblage was also a ceramic phallus (Boardman 1967, no. 75, pl. 77), which could have belonged to an anthropomorphic vessel, but it was not pierced in order to serve as a spout as was the phallus associated with the Tiryns figure.

[231] Blinkenberg 1931.   [232] Lambrounidakis 1992, 215; Kourou 2002a, 27.

[233] See quantified material presented in the graph at Averett 2007, 298.

same sanctuary during the EIA. These regional patterns in figurine deposition suggest that there were probably regionally distinct forms of ritual practice, and perhaps belief, both in different parts of the Aegean and within individual regions, and that an interest in small-scale three-dimensional images of naked males was limited to a few ritual contexts in mainland Greece and Crete for most of the EIA.

CONCLUSIONS

An examination of the history of archaeological deposition of naked male figurines prior to and during the EIA Aegean demonstrates that this category of artifact begins to appear in increasing numbers at the very end of the LBA, but only develops into a relatively coherent iconographic and material type during the EIA. The adoption of the type may have been influenced by Syro-Palestinian or Cypriot models, as suggested by the appearance of a few depictions of naked males from the final phases of the LBA at Tiryns and Phylakopi, but these terracotta figurines do not appear to have had an immediate impact on material culture in their proximate regional contexts. While there is no subsequent tradition of naked male figurines in most of the Aegean area between the LBA and the EIA, naked male figurines persist as part of the archaeological record at some ritual sites (especially Syme Viannou) on Crete during this entire period, most often taking the shape of solid cast bronzes. The appearance of similar naked male figurines at open air mainland sanctuaries begins in the late tenth or early ninth century. While naked male bronze figurines appear at a number of mainland sites after this, the largest assemblages come from Olympia and Delphi. Terracotta votive figurines are present in EIA contexts on both Crete and elsewhere, but to date it appears that the majority of extant, published naked male figurines from the EIA are made of bronze.

Taken together, the figurines reviewed in this chapter represent the earliest evidence for an aesthetic tradition of the depiction of naked males in ritual contexts in the Aegean. In Chapter 3, I will describe the iconographic and regional patterns of these objects, and consider how those patterns might relate to corresponding ideas or ideologies surrounding nudity in the EIA Aegean.

CHAPTER THREE

ICONOGRAPHIC AND REGIONAL PATTERNS IN EIA NAKED MALE FIGURINES AND THE HISTORY OF RITUAL ACTION

The purpose of this chapter is to add iconographic and spatial analyses to the diachronic presentation of the history of nude figurines in Chapter 2, and to consider whether the iconographic patterns and spatial distribution of naked figurines might indicate the existence of different attitudes and practices related to naked males in EIA Greece. Iconographic patterns are somewhat difficult to pin down, although a few identifiable types, like warriors and worshippers, bind together disparate regional traditions. The spatial patterns in the figurine data show that the practice of depositing bronze anthropomorphic figurines, including nude figurines, was likely quite circumscribed during the EIA. The distribution shows a mainly Cretan and western pattern. In order to test whether this geography of EIA nude male figurines should be taken only to indicate the spatial limits of ritual practices associated with dedicating bronze figurines or whether it might indicate the presence of distinct regional iconographies and practices associated with nudity, I check these patterns against patterns in the depiction of nudity in Geometric vase painting. Although this evidence is considerably later than many of the naked figurines discussed in the previous chapter, it suggests that, at least during the eighth century, people in different regions of the Aegean probably had distinct ideas about nudity. I argue that it is not unreasonable to reconstruct, based on the combined spatial patterns in EIA figurines and EIA vase painting, that these distinct ideas can be extrapolated back into the earlier phases of the EIA. I therefore posit a Cretan and western EIA ideology in which nudity was often associated with ritual practice, and an eastern EIA ideology in which nudity was most often associated with death and vulnerability.

ICONOGRAPHIC THEMES AND PATTERNS IN EIA FIGURINES

Characterizing general themes or patterns of EIA bronze figurines is challenging, because the assemblage is distinguished most of all by its internal heterogeneity, an observation emphasized also by Langdon in her pioneering study of EIA bronze figurines.[1] The figurines of naked males frequently represent individuals in generic poses, often bearing arms, but there are also clear representations of individuals participating in a variety of ritual acts including dancing, leading bulls, playing music, fighting, shooting arrows, boxing, riding horses, driving chariots, holding offering cups, and self-flagellating. Although there are strong iconographic similarities among some small groups of figurines – such as pairs of figurines that share a generally comparable pose – each figurine can legitimately be called unique. The extreme heterogeneity of the figurines under study makes a review of iconographic themes more of an exercise in list-making than analytical generalization. The distribution of naked male figurines under study here that can be assigned a general type are broken down by site in Table 3.1. Not all figurines are represented in the table, since some are too fragmentary to be assigned to an iconographic category, and others that are complete do not fit into an identifiable type. Within the general fog of unique representations and intra-site variation, some identifiable patterns, and distinct characteristics of the assemblages from each site or region, may be observed.

Figures probably identifiable as worshippers, based on comparison with poses known from earlier Minoan iconography, are prominent among Cretan figurines. Cretan figurines dated to the earliest phases of the Iron Age bear a close resemblance to Bronze Age figurines representing worshippers shown with one hand raised to the forehead, and some figurines from cave sanctuaries remain somewhat conservative in retaining an identifiable Minoan style. Overall, the Cretan material retains elements recognizable from the Minoan tradition through the twelfth and eleventh centuries. However, the poses and demeanor of figurines from Cretan sites are more varied than those of mainland figurines. PG and Geometric figurines from Syme Viannou are especially diverse in subject matter, including dancers, musicians, and warriors. Some of these figurines, including the dancers and several warriors, wear belts.

Among Cretan figurines, the treatment and pose of the human figure varies widely from figurine to figurine. Close attention to details like facial and

[1] Langdon 1984.

TABLE 3.1. *Distribution of iconographic types represented among assemblages of ELA naked figurines from different sites*

Site	Worshipper	Outstretched arms	Warrior/armed	Rider/charioteer	Hunter	Musician	Flagellant	Dancer or athlete
Crete								
Syme Viannou	4	1	2			3	1	3
Archanes	1							
Psychro Cave	3							
Phaneromeni	2	1						
Kommos		1						
Patsos	4							
Aghia Triada	1	2	1					
Amnisos								1
Kalamafka							1	
Mainland								
Olympia	3	23	2	7		1		1
Delphi	1	2	10	1				2
Philia	4	1		1				
Tegea		2			1			
Sparta		1						
Mavriki	3	1						
Thermon	1	1						
Pherai	1							
Argive Heraion	1			1				
Athens	1							
Ionian Islands								
Aetos		1						
Zakynthos		2						
Cyclades/East Aegean								
Samos					1			
Delos	1							

89

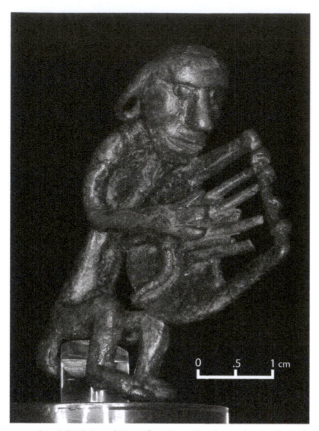

3.1. An LG/Orientalizing figurine of a lyre player from Syme Viannou (Syme Viannou Excavation Inv. No. MH 2064, photo by author; published with permission of the Heraklion Archaeological Museum; © Hellenic Ministry of Culture and Sports – Hellenic Organization of Cultural Resources Development)

anatomical details, such as eyes, noses, mouths, nipples, and musculature, is especially apparent in Cretan figurines dated to the PG and LG periods. For example, a seated musician singing at the lyre (dated to the LG-Orientalizing period) includes substantial anatomical detail, despite a lack of convincing naturalism (Figure 3.1).

The standing male with outstretched arms is the most common iconographical type among EIA figurines from Olympia. However, there is quite a lot of formal variation even within this group. Some figurines clearly have both arms extended upward, others have arms that stretch out laterally, and still others hold one arm up and the other directly out or sometimes down. Many of the figurines wear hats, and their hats can take a number of different shapes or forms. Variations include the flat *petasos* type discussed in Chapter 2, a pointed *pilos* cap, and a long, curving, fin-shaped helmet. It is likely that some figurines were designed to hold weapons or shields that would have been added separately, so some individuals classed as generic standing males might rather have been designed to be warriors.

Naked male charioteers are also present among the charioteer figurines at Olympia and Delphi (charioteers are not present in the Cretan material). While the standing males that do not wear armor are never belted, clearly identifiable charioteers, warriors, and riders often are depicted with a belt.

In terms of additional detail, the majority of the Olympia figurines do not demonstrate any interest in anatomical detail, with minimal to nonexistent attention paid to modeling realistic facial features or any body parts aside from the basic shape of the human body, headgear, and genitalia. Scattered finds around the western Aegean, such as those from Zakynthos and Thermon, are closely related to the Olympia model of the standing naked male with outstretched arms, and often bearing the same distinctive fin-shaped headgear.

At Delphi, there is a notable preponderance of warrior figurines. The group of striding warriors from Delphi are all belted, as are many other of the other figurines from Delphi, including a group of standing males with both hands raised in the air, which might represent warriors, worshippers, or athletes engaged in a combat sport, such as boxing or wrestling. Two of the figurines from Delphi seem to represent worshippers carrying or leading an animal, in one case clearly a bovine. An archer figurine from Delphi is unique.

The group of figurines from Philia is thematically consistent with the general types encountered elsewhere – worshippers and warriors – with the exception of the seated smith, although the sorts of close stylistic similarities observable between the assemblages of figurines from Olympia and Delphi are not apparent between the Philia figurines and those from any other site. These figurines have a distinctive style of slightly attenuated but generally carefully modeled human anatomy, although some features, like the 'Frankenstein' bolts emerging from the neck of one worshipper figurine, lend them something of an otherworldly appearance (Figure 3.2).

Perhaps the only overarching generalization that may be made about this corpus of material is that it largely defies iconographic generalization, in that heterogeneity in form and iconography is the norm. At the same time, a few general remarks about the iconography of the figurines hold true. First, while the specific pose and design is usually distinctive to the individual figurine, there are some clearly identifiable types: standing unarmed figures gesturing with their arms, standing armed figures, riders, and charioteers. Second, notwithstanding the existence of such types, each site's assemblage has distinctive characteristics, such as the preference for warriors at Delphi and charioteers at Olympia. Finally, although EIA figurines have often been called ithyphallic, a review of the evidence shows that the majority of early nude males in the iconographic record are definitely naked, but not usually ithyphallic. Although it cannot be denied that the artists often made special effort to distinguish the nudity of even the most roughly modeled figurines, the few actually ithyphallic males in the material presented above are the exception rather than the rule.

3.2. An LG bronze votive figurine depicting a standing naked male, probably a worshipper, from Philia (Ny Carlsberg Glyptotek Inv. No. 3310, Photo by Anders Sune Berg, courtesy Ny Carlsberg Glyptotek, Copenhagen)

THE SPATIAL DISTRIBUTION OF EIA BRONZE FIGURINES

Table 3.2 and Figure 3.3A lay out the regional distribution of naked male EIA bronze figurines from mainland sanctuaries, and Figure 3.3B shows the distribution of such figurines at sites on Crete. Several clear trends are apparent in this distribution. First, the assemblages from the sites of Olympia and Delphi are extraordinary and have produced the bulk of the evidence for the deposition of naked male bronze figurines from the EIA mainland. The distribution of the rest of the figurines demonstrates another feature of the known corpus of Geometric bronzes – they are generally a western and central Greek phenomenon. Only two nude male figurines from the EIA come from sites in Attica or the east Aegean. Although some of these sites have turned up modest numbers of bronze figurines, they are most often either female or not clearly naked. Given the quantity of material that has been excavated and published from eastern Aegean

TABLE 3.2. *Regional distribution of Aegean EIA bronze figurines outside of Crete (ca. 1000–700)*

Site	Region	Bronze Figurines	Naked Males
Olympia	Peloponnese	59	36
Delphi	Phokis	34	20
Philia	Thessaly	7	7
Tegea	Peloponnese	5	4
Kameiros	Dodecanese	5	? (corroded)
Samos	East Aegean	3	1
Delos	Cyclades	2	1
Sparta	Peloponnese	2	2
Mavriki	Peloponnese	2	1
Lousoi	Peloponnese	2	0
Athens	Central Greece	2	1
Zakynthos	West Greece	2	2
Thermon	West Greece	3	2
Pherai	Thessaly	2	1
Lindos	East Aegean	2	0
Argive Heraion	Peloponnese	2	2
Aetos	West Greece	1	1
Petrovouni	Peloponnese	1	1
Eretria	Central Greece	1	0
Kalapodi	Central Greece	1	0

sanctuaries like Delos, Kalapodi, Eretria, Emporio, and the Samian Heraion, the extreme rarity of naked figurines from these sites seems likely to be a real phenomenon rather than an artifact of differential excavation history or preservation. It is likewise notable that one of the only bronze naked male figurines from the east Aegean, a bronze group from Samos, shows a naked male being attacked by a lion, a very different kind of scene than those present in the assemblages of naked bronze males from Olympia and Delphi.

The observation that most naked male bronze figurines in the non-Cretan Aegean come from ritual contexts at a limited number of sanctuaries could be interpreted in a number of different ways, each with different implications for an attempt to understand the history of attitudes and ideologies associated with naked ritual practice and the iconography of nudity in the EIA Aegean. One way to interpret the relatively limited distribution of naked male figurines would be to suggest that any attitudes or practices about male nakedness that they might evince were regionally circumscribed. However, it is important to distinguish between the presence of naked figurines in the archaeological record and the presence of a certain set of ideas in society. For example, an alternative interpretation of the limited distribution of bronze figurines would be that the practice of depositing bronze anthropomorphic figurines in sanctuary sites was regionally circumscribed or limited to a select group of

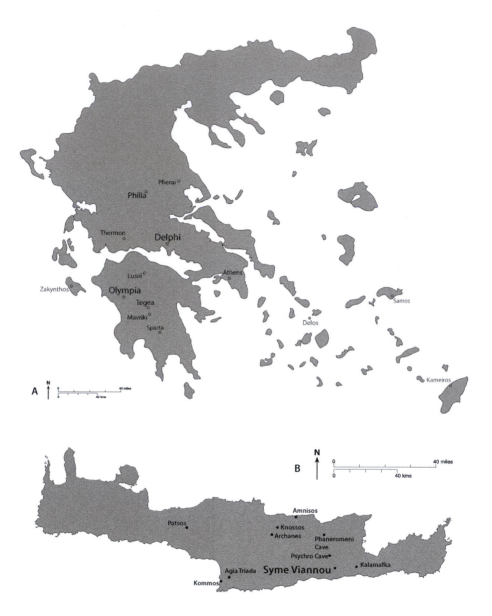

3.3. (A) Regional distribution of bronze naked male figurines from sites on the mainland and in the islands. The labels of sites are scaled roughly according to the number of nude bronze figurines known from each site where at least one is present. (B) Map of Cretan sites that have produced naked bronze figurines datable to the LM IIIC–Geometric periods.

sanctuaries. Or, since access to bronze in the EIA may have been at least somewhat limited or restricted, it might be the case that bronze figurines were only deposited in some areas because only some groups had access to metal resources. In either scenario, we would only have material evidence of what-ever ideas bronze figurines represent from sanctuaries where their deposition inhered in ritual practice or was made available through preferential access to bronze, even if such ideas were prevalent elsewhere. Without an alternative means of assessing these possibilities, it is hazardous to extend an argument about the regional distribution of figurines to include any statement about the regional nature of ideological systems in the EIA.

The possibility that the distribution of naked bronze figurines aligns more closely with availability or a particular set of ritual practices involving bronze figurines rather than with a specific set of ideas about the human body is made somewhat less likely by the distribution of terracotta figurines, discussed in Chapter 2. While terracotta figurines of males and females are present at sanctuaries around the Aegean, including sites in the East Aegean, naked male terracotta figurines map reasonably well onto the regional distribution of bronze ones. This suggests that there might be a set of ritual practices or ideologies associated with the regions or sanctuaries where such figurines were deposited, and that we might be able to reconstruct regionally distinct ideas about naked males in the EIA from patterns in the appearance of naked male figurines. However, the relatively small number of figurines available from which to draw this conclusion is a weak analytical rung upon which to hang such a conclusion, and does not elide the possibility that regional patterns concerning the deposition of votive figurines in general, rather than of bronze figurines in particular, lay behind the distributon of male nude iconography in the EIA. Thus, adding another layer of evidence to test the potential relationship between regional distributions of male naked figurines and societal attitudes toward nudity seems necessary. The only other roughly contemporary and sizable corpus of imagery against which one could check the data from the EIA bronze and terracotta figurines is the figural repertoire of LG vase painting. In the following section that corpus is examined in order to assess the likelihood that attitudes and ideas about nudity were regionally diverse in the EIA Aegean.

NAKED MALES IN GEOMETRIC POTTERY

Figure-decorated ceramics are found in Geometric deposits beginning in the late ninth and eighth centuries. After many decades during which patterns and shapes, as well as an attractive black gloss, predominated in ceramic decoration, animals are the first figures to reappear as iconographic motifs on Geometric pottery. By the second half of the eighth century, the human form begins to be depicted with regularity in figural scenes on Geometric vessels.[2] Study of Attic

---

[2] Cook 1997, 1; Stewart 1997, 16; Snodgrass 1998, 12–15; Stansbury-O'Donnell 2015, 76–77.

pottery has dominated scholarship on the history of Geometric art, but other craft traditions of Argive, Corinthian, Lakonian, and Boeotian pottery did develop figural traditions toward the end of the EIA as well.

There are a number of ways in which EIA vase-painting iconography is not an ideal body of evidence to serve as an iconographic comparandum for EIA figurines. While the evidence for figurines spans the EIA, anthropomorphic imagery in ceramic iconography is mainly limited to the very end of the EIA, especially the second half of the eighth century. Even then, a robust tradition of human figural representation is basically limited to Attica, with much smaller bodies of evidence available from other regional ceramic decorative traditions. Moreover, the schematic nature of the silhouette technique used to depict humans in Geometric vase painting presents challenges for distinguishing an artist's intent to indicate nakedness. These issues all create interpretative complications for any attempt to interrogate ideas about naked males from EIA ceramic iconography, and undermine the certainty with which patterns apparent in the images on Geometric pottery can be read as evidence for ideas or practices related to nudity in the Aegean. They also call into question the degree to which evidence from ceramic iconography can be combined with analysis of bronze figurines, since the chronological and spatial attributes of these two bodies of evidence do not overlap neatly.

Despite these difficulties, it remains worth making some effort to think about the evidence for naked imagery in art across the two genres. The first reason such effort may be justified is that EIA anthropomorphic iconography is sufficiently sparse that it makes sense to investigate the possibilities of deriving analytical value from all available evidence, however problematic. The second reason that such effort seems worthwhile is that there are interesting points of intersection between the two bodies of evidence that suggest intriguing conclusions about regional distinctions in ideas about nudity that may well pertain only to the later part of the EIA, but could also represent the legacy of prior traditions. A third reason to interrogate iconography in extant EIA ceramic figural repertoires is that the regional distinctions evident in the nature of material cultural assemblages highlight a disunity in the way that material production and visual culture were constituted across the Aegean in the EIA. Recognizing this disunity helps underline the value of taking into account the likelihood that there was a concomitant disunity in the way that both objects and nakedness functioned within different communities.

With these considerations in mind, I review the treatment of the human body across several regional styles of Geometric ceramic decoration in what follows. Rather than attempting to be exhaustive, the purpose of the treatment here is to produce a general review of the contexts in which nudity seems to appear in the painted decoration added to EIA pottery, and to get a sense of the differences in the demeanor of naked individuals across different regions and genres of vase painting.[3] To summarize the main conclusions, the naked human body appears in a variety of circumstances in EIA pottery, but the most common context for clearly naked males is ritual. There is also proportionally less interest in depictions of naked males engaged in ritual within Attic and Cycladic iconography than there is in iconography from Lakonia and the Argolid. While there are a number of ways that we could interpret these patterns, I argue that they are probably meaningfully related to both the patterns observable in the figurine data and some practices and ideas associated with naked males in EIA life and art.

Attica

The human figure is rendered in schematic and roughly geometrical forms in painted decoration on Attic Geometric pottery.[4] Among the first figured vases from the Attic Geometric tradition are monumental kraters and amphorae that were intended to mark graves. Because of the monumental scale and elaborate decoration of the vessels, they have usually been interpreted as markers of conspicuous consumption, an expression of material well-being through signaling within performative funerary contexts.[5] Figural scenes populate a wider range of Attic ceramics dated to the later eighth century, especially vessels designed for the symposium, such as cups and pouring vessels.[6]

Because my intent here is merely to develop a general sense of how the human body is treated in Attic Geometric ceramic decoration, I analyzed a sample of 200 individual iconographical contexts within the overall corpus of Attic iconography, rather than pursuing a complete treatment of the material, especially because Haug has treated this evidence exhaustively and recently.[7] The notion of sampling is widespread in archaeological research, and holds that

---

[3] A list of the museum inventory numbers of and references for objects analysed in this chapter is available in Appendix C.

[4] The schematic and abstract appearance of most human and animal figures in EIA art has been interpreted in a variety of ways. One interpretation is that the dominance of geometric forms arises from an overridingly geometric logic inherent to the decorative style, for example, Schefold 1966, 17; Himmelmann 1990, 31–32: "...the reproduction of man does not proceed from the observed reality, but develops the figures of characterizing features ... these features not only refer to physical functions, but also constitute an ethical statement."; Ahlberg-Cornell 1992, 18–19; Snodgrass 1998, 16: "what has clearly happened is that the artists, wishing to incorporate representational scenes as well as abstract ones, have made their figures observe 'geometric' principles similar to those of the rest of their repertoire." For the idea that the figures represent a generic social type, Langdon 2008, 82. See also the recent treatment by Haug (2012) which is very thorough. She describes the development of the human body and all of its parts, including noses, ears, mouths, and hair, during the eighth and seventh centuries. Haug's observations on the topic of nudity are discussed above in Chapter 1 (see also Osborne 2014).

[5] Ahlberg 1971b; Whitley 1991a, 181–183; Stansbury-O'Donnell 2015, 77.

[6] Neer 2012, 79.   [7] Haug 2012; Coulié 2013.

generalizations drawn from a random sample of units selected out of a population can be extrapolated as representative of the trends in a larger population if there is no reason to suspect that the sample units are skewed in ways that would make the sample unrepresentative. The sample is essentially random, and was compiled mainly by systematically going through collections of figured Geometric pottery from museum collections published in *Corpus Vasorum Antiquorum* (*CVA*) volumes. Haug's exhaustive study presents just over 400 iconographical scenes, and a 50% sample is generally far more than is necessary to produce a representative result for any given dataset.[8] Thus, the patterns evident in the sample should provide a reasonable sense of the general approach to depicting nakedness among Attic Geometric painters.

Within the sample of 200 figured Attic Geometric vessels and vessel fragments, 64 of the 148 pieces that could be attributed to a vessel type were amphorae, and 23 were kraters. A group of twenty-two oinochoai date to the LG II period (late eighth century), as do nineteen drinking vessels (including cups, chalices, tankards, and kantharoi). Other shapes represented include hydriae (7), pyxides (3), a louterion (1), a lebes (1), a cauldron (1), a psychter (1), and a tripod stand (1). The range of shapes with human-figural decoration is therefore largely limited to kraters, amphorae, drinking vessels, and oinochoai. The scenes painted on the monumental vessels from the earlier phases of this sequence most often relate to funerals, especially the *prothesis* and *ekphora* which are inherent to the treatment and commemoration of the dead, and scenes of warriors either marching to battle, where presumably they frequently met their death, or participating in a funerary procession.[9] Overall, images of chariots or warriors in groups, often interpreted to indicate departure for war, or images of combat at land or sea constitute the primary decorative scene on 92 of the sample of 200 Geometric Attic figure-decorated vessels or fragments collected for analysis here. Scenes involving dancing (35 examples) and those related to funerals – the *prothesis, ekphora,* and mourning – make up the next largest iconographical groups in the sample, with 32 examples. Thus, the majority (78%) of the images relate to dancing, war, or death. Two-thirds of the corpus deals with the latter subjects. The two themes of war and death could certainly have been closely linked in the eighth century, since the first often leads to the second.[10] The remaining third of the depictions contains an idiosyncratic mix of iconographic motifs.

---

[8] See lists provided in Haug 2012, 669–716.

[9] The iconography and subject matter of Geometric vase-painting has been the subject of much discussion. See, for example, Webster 1955; Schefold 1966; Schweitzer 1967; Ahlberg 1971a; 1971b; Rombos 1988; Ahlberg-Cornell 1992; S. Morris 1997; Snodgrass 1998; Langdon 2008; Morgan 2010; Haug 2015; Stansbury-O'Donnell 2015, 77–79.

[10] Several other vessels, for instance the LG oinochoe from Munich depicting a shipwreck (Munich AM Inv. No. 8696; Coulié 2013, 93, fig. 68), a kantharos dated to 730 in

Dancers often appear on shapes other than amphorae and kraters, especially cups and oinochoai. The range of shapes associated with images of dance in Geometric Attic vases may suggest that such images were considered appropriate in different social contexts than representations of mourning, which usually appears on amphorae or kraters. There are also sixteen master-of-animals scenes, in which a man holds one or two animals, most often horses. However, there is also one example of a man with griffons and one with a centaur.[11] Otherwise, two depictions of what seems to be a festival,[12] two scenes of a hunt,[13] two scenes of music-playing,[14] one scene of sitting with a bird,[15] one scene of wrestling,[16] one scene of sailing,[17] and one scene of boxing[18] are present. The sample of human figures studied here is therefore quite diverse in terms of both the types of vessels upon which they appear and the types of scenes depicted, although there are some popular vessels and themes that stand out. Shapes associated with wine consumption are decorated with human figures more often than other shapes, and scenes associated with war and funerals are generally the most popular.

Before discussing the presence or absence of naked individuals in Attic Geometric vase painting, it is necessary to confront the question of whether all of the humans in Attic Geometric vase painting are intended to be naked. The answer to this question is not settled. Most human figures in Geometric ceramic iconography are painted as silhouettes without much added detail to indicate clothing.[19] However, women are often clearly clothed below the waist; instead of legs their lower halves consist of painted panels which surely represent skirts. In some cases, feminine gender is indicated by breasts, which may or may not indicate nudity (breasts are usually apparent underneath clothing).[20] Some have argued that the schematic nature of the figural style

Copenhagen depicting monsters eating a man (Copenhagen Museum Inv. No. 727), and a louterion in the British Museum depicting an abduction on one side and a row of chariots on the other (London British Museum Inv. No. 1899; Coulié 2013, 89, fig. 60; Langdon 2008, 20–21, figs. 1.1–1.3) show images with thematically related violent or mortal content.

[11] The horse-leader scene is more common in Argive Geometric iconography (Langdon 1989). For the man with griffons, see Louvre Inv. No. CA 1780 (Louvre *CVA* no. 16, pl. 39). The man with a centaur is rendered on Copenhagen Inv. No. 7029 (*CVA* no. 3, pl. 73).

[12] See Coulié 2013, 92–93, figs. 65–66 (Copenhagen Inv. No. 7029, Copenhagen *CVA* no. 3, pl. 73); Prague Museum Inv. No. 6016 (Prague *CVA* no. 1, pl. 11).

[13] Boston Museum of Fine Arts Inv. No. 25.42 (Haug 2015, 105, abb. 42); Kerameikos Museum Inv. No. 407 (Rombos 1988, pl. 37b).

[14] Athens National Archaeological Museum Inv. No. 17497 (Athens *CVA* 3, pl. 12; Coulié 2013, 93, fig. 67) and Paris Louvre Inv. No. CA 1940 (France *CVA* 17, pl. 25).

[15] Brussels Museum Inv. No. A 1941 (Brussels *CVA* 3, pl. 1).

[16] Athens, Piraeus museum no number (see Haug 2012, 369, abb. 302).

[17] Coulié 2013, 76, fig. 46.   [18] Kerameikos Museum Inv. No. 812 (Rombos 1988, pl. 74a).

[19] Osborne 1997, 507; Bol 2004, 282: "Die geometrische Normalfigur ist nackt."

[20] There are numerous Mediterranean parallels for women baring their breasts as part of mourning rituals but not going entirely unclothed otherwise. See Werbrouck 1938; De Garis

required apparent nudity as a convention meant to aid viewers in determining whether a figure was male or female, while others suggest that all figures were indeed meant to be interpreted as unclothed.[21]

In general, I do not accept that all figures in Attic Geometric vase painting were intended to be seen as entirely naked. While males appear to be lightly clad and women's breasts are sometimes indicated, individuals are generally not rendered as explicitly naked in most figured scenes.[22] In scenes of arming and departing for war, male gender is typically indicated by the presence of weapons and/or a shield which completely obscures the body.[23] Although it is impossible to determine exactly whether Attic Geometric vase painters intended to indicate that people were naked or not, it is very rare for total nakedness to be explicitly emphasized in Attic Geometric scenes.

It seems to me most likely that the majority of figures in EIA vase painting were not intended to be conceived of as naked, for two main reasons. The first reason is that the decision to explicitly indicate exposed genitalia was unusual, the exception rather than the norm. In the 200 depictions of Attic Geometric vase painting that I analysed in this project, only 16 scenes (8%) include clear indications of primary sexual characteristics aside from breasts, by far a minority in the corpus overall.[24]

Second, the indication of total nudity appears to have been reserved for a relatively limited range of vessel types and iconographic contexts, suggesting that nudity itself was probably seen as acceptable or informative in some rather than all such contexts. Figure 3.4 illustrates some examples of Attic Geometric painting where nudity is clearly indicated. Six of the naked figures in Attic vase-painting appear on sherds that preclude a determination of vessel shape,

---

Davies 1925, pl. xxi; Asher-Greve and Sweeney 2006, 138. Women are likewise depicted with bare breasts but not otherwise unclothed in Bronze Age art from Crete.

[21] Müller 1906, 86–87; Himmelmann 1990, 32–33:

> In geometrical narrative, there is no room for covering clothing, which is why the figures often give the impression of nudity. This impression is, however, misleading, because, of course, no naked participants are conceivable in the case of the *prothesis* and the *ekphora*. In addition, there are often references to clothing or armor...As a rule, geometrical figures are not conceived as naked but clothed, as conformed to the Homeric custom.

Himmelmann (1990, 34) goes on to argue that the Geometric ideal of the male body with broad triangular shoulders corresponded to an ideal applied to gods in literature of the time, appealing to the case of Apollo who is described in the *Hymn to Pythian Apollo* as (450–451): "bearing the form of a man, brisk and sturdy, in the prime of his youth, while his broad shoulders were covered with his hair."

[22] Langdon 2008, 246; Haug 2012, 215.

[23] Osborne 1997, 507: "Maleness is positively indicated not by clothing but by arms and armor and by such occupations as driving a chariot."

[24] For a scene that may show a naked female mourner, see New York Metropolitan Museum Inv. No. 14.130.15 (Coulié 2013, 87, fig. 58).

3.4. Naked males in Attic LG iconography: (A) hunting scene (Kerameikos Museum Inv. No. 407, redrawn from a photograph); (B) hunting scene (Boston Museum of Fine Arts Inv. No. 25.42, after Haug 2015, 105, Abb. 42); (C) corpse in ekphora scene (Thorikos Inv. No. T C 65.666, after Rombos 1988, pl. 11a); (D) battle scene (Paris Louvre Inv. No. A 560, after Louvre CVA v. 3, pl. 8); (E), shipwreck (Munich Staatliche Antikensammlungen, Inv. No. 8696, after Coulié 2013, 93, fig. 68); (F, H, and I) three panels from a festival or wedding scene (Copenhagen Mus. Inv. No. 727, after Copenhagen CVA v. 3, pl. 73); (G) dancing in a line (Tübingen Museum Inv. No. 2657, after Tübingen CVA v. 2, pls. 14–15).

but the general collection of shapes is idiosyncratic. Only one scene is painted on an amphora and none decorate kraters. Otherwise, the images appear on oinochoai (3), kantharoi (3), a cup, a pyxis, and a tripod stand. The vases illustrated in Figure 3.4 provide a good sense of the range of iconographic contexts in which nudity seems to be indicated clearly. On the leg of a tripod stand from the Kerameikos, an armed, naked man is engaged in a fight with a large boar whose ferocity is expressed by his rampant pose and toothy, gnashing maw (Figure 3.4A). The belly of an oinochoe currently in Boston shows naked men holding objects that look like whips amidst an unruly group of dogs and foxes, probably best interpreted as a scene of a hunt in the countryside (Figure 3.4B). On a sherd from Thorikos, a naked dead man lies on the funeral bier, while mourners above are not obviously naked (Figure 3.4C). Another sherd currently in the Louvre shows two warriors (Figure 3.4D). The one to the left with an arrow through his torso and another through his head while the one to the right carries a sword sheathed in a baldric and has his hands raised. The figure to the left appears to be naked, while the figure to the right does not. Finally, an oinochoe currently in Munich shows a shipwreck scene on its neck

3.5. Depiction of an apparently naked hunter from an Attic pyxis in the National Museum in Athens. (Athens National Archaeological Museum Inv. No. 14960, photo by author, published with permission of the National Archaeological Museum, © Hellenic Ministry of Culture and Sports – Hellenic Organization of Cultural Resources Development)

(Figure 3.4E).[25] There is a beaked ship, probably a *pentekonter*, upside down in the center of the scene. One man sits astride upturned keel of the ship, waving one hand in the air. Around him, the scene is filled with ten naked men, surrounded by fish – these probably represent men drowning in the sea as a result of the wreck. The scenes on a kantharos in Copenhagen have been interpreted as depicting a wedding or festival of some kind; they include images of naked men fighting and dancing (Figure 3.4F, H, and I).[26] Finally, the belly of an oinochoe in the Tübingen museum shows a line of naked men and women dancing and holding garlands (Figure 3.4G).

The contexts in which apparently naked figures are included repay close attention. One circumstance in which nakedness seems to be explicitly indicated is the context of the hunt, as illustrated in Figure 3.4A,B and Figure 3.5.[27] Several of the scenes show individuals who are dead or probably

[25] On which see Schefold 1964, 25, pl. 8; Fittschen 1969, 49–51, sch. B I, fig. 13; Ahlberg-Cornell 1992, 27–28; fig. 31; Schefold 1993, 155–156, fig. 160; Snodgrass 1998, 35–36, fig. 14; Langdon 2008, 120–121, fig. 2.28; Hurwit 2011; Coulié 2013, 93, fig. 68.

[26] The vase is currently in the Copenhagen National Museum (Inv. No. 727). Due to its complex iconography, the piece has attracted considerable commentary: some of the extant bibliography includes Ahlberg-Cornell 1987; Langdon 2008, 197–200 (she argues that it shows a scene of abduction); Haug 2012, 139, 365–367, with references.

[27] Boston Museum of Fine Arts Inv. No. 25.42 (Haug 2015, 105, abb. 42); Athens National Archaeological Museum 14960 (Haug 2012, 369, abb. 302).

in danger of dying. In the Munich oinochoe shipwreck, the man sitting on the vessel's upturned hull is not obviously naked, while those in the sea seem to be – a contrast that likely emphasizes the fact that one is alive and the rest are literally dead in the water (Figure 3.4E).[28] An association with nudity and death might also be suggested by the fact that the naked male individual on the Louvre sherd is shot through with an arrow (Figure 3.4D). Likewise, although most of the figures depicted on a sherd from Thorikos (Figure 3.4C) are not explicitly naked, the corpse being mourned apparently is.

Other scenes that indicate nudity may depict festivals, or at least occasions that involve dancing and music. The elaborate program of scenes on the kantharos from Copenhagen, dated to around 730, provides an unusually vivid glimpse into what these occasions might have entailed (Figure 3.4F, H, I). On one side of the vessel, a central scene shows a headless body being gored by two wild animals.[29] Surrounding this vignette are several other scenes: two pairs of youths engaged in what might be mock battles,[30] another pair that appear to be boxing, two pairs of youths carrying tree branches, two lyre-players, and three youths dancing to the music. The most common interpretation of this scene is that it depicts a festival.[31]

The corpus of Attic Geometric vases showing apparent nudity also includes three master of horses scenes, four scenes of dancing,[32] one image that appears to show a footrace, and one image of a warrior whose context is difficult to determine due to the fragmentary nature of the piece in question.[33] The horse

---

[28] Munich Staatliche Antikensammlungen Inv. No. 8696 (Coulié 2013, 93, fig. 68); cf. discussion in Snodgrass 1998, 35–36.

[29] This is a version of a repeated type scene that first seems to appear on Crete in the EIA (on a krater now in the Heraklion museum, see Sackett 1976, 117–129; Snodgrass 1998, 14, fig. 1). It also occurs on metalwork (Kunze 1931, 205, fig. 30, Beil 1; Coldstream 2003 [1977], 179, fig. 64 (Vienna AM Inv. No. 124, from Eretria, dated to 725)). See also Coldstream's discussion (2003 [1977], 102) of the lion hunt motif. The scene is probably influenced by eastern motifs, as are a number of type scenes in Attic vase-painting, for example, the 'rattler' scenes, as argued by Ahlberg (1967).

[30] Ahlberg-Cornell 1987, 75: "a mock combat rather than a real one."

[31] Rombos 1988, 314–315; Markoe 1989, 113; Ahlberg-Cornell 1987; Langdon 2008, 197–200 (Langdon suggests that the scene might depict a wedding festival).

[32] For discussion of the dancers on the Tübingen vessel, see Snodgrass 1998, 65. He interprets them as youths and girls on analogy with Homer's description of a dance in the shield of Achilleus. In the Bochum piece, it appears that the musician at the lyre is naked while the female dancers are not.

[33] Objects with horse leader scenes are Laon Museum Inv. No. 37769 (Haug 2012, 340–341, abb. 283b), Kerameikos Museum Inv. No. 268 (Haug 2012, 326, Abb. 270), and Oxford Ashmolean Museum Inv. No. 1929.24 (Haug 2012, 340, Abb. 284). The four scenes of dancing are represented on Amsterdam Allard Pierson Museum Inv. No. APM 3491 (Haug 2012, 157, abb. 126a), Bochum Museum Inv. No. 1066 (Haug 2012, 162, abb. 130a), Brauron Museum Inv. No. 315 (Rombos 1988, pl. 66a), and Tübingen Museum Inv. No. 2657 (Rombos 1988, pl. 71a; Haug 2012, 136, abb. 98). The footrace is on two joining sherds, Athens GM Inv. Nos. 136–137 (Haug 2012, 368, abb. 301). The warrior is Paris Louvre Inv. No. CA 4615 (Louvre CVA 18, pl. 18).

leader scenes probably demonstrate Argive influence, while the dancing and race scenes could also belong to festival contexts.

The iconographic characteristics of explicitly naked males in Attic vase painting is, therefore, varied and complex, resisting simple characterization. Still, some general observations can be made about the way in which naked individuals are depicted in this group of vases. They do not appear to belong to a single workshop or a unified stylistic group in any other regard. Although a couple of the vases that seem to show nudity belong to the Burly workshop, the assemblage in general is not stylistically uniform.[34] For example, the two possibly naked lyre players on the vases from Bochum and Copenhagen are rendered with distinct conventions.[35] The musician on the Copenhagen vase has a reserved eye, a mouth jauntily open in song, clearly defined calf muscles, and a stout chest, while his counterpart on the Bochum vase has a straight, narrow stick-like torso, no reserved eye, and calves and lower legs of a uniform thickness from the knees downward. The rendering of the two lyres is not comparable. The naked dancers on an oenochoe from Tübingen and the amphora from Amsterdam likewise do not appear to belong to the same workshop or hand.[36] The men on the latter vessel are stoutly rendered with their hands joined to their arms by zig-zagging, sharp elbows, and they have several individually delineated fingers. Each figure is separated from its neighbors by additional zigzags. On the Tübingen vase male and female dancers join their hands in a variety of poses, including curvilinear ones. Space in between the figures is filled with branches held by the dancers or by circular patterns of dots. The hunter on the Kerameikos tripod stand seems to wear a belt and baldric, left in reserve, and he is given a crest, perhaps indicating a helmet, to complete the impression of an armed hunter.[37] Based on figural style, then, there is no reason to connect the painterly convention of rendering explicit nakedness to a particular Attic Geometric artist or workshop.

Argolid

A significant corpus of figured Geometric vase painting has been recovered from archaeological excavations of graves and sanctuaries in the Argolid.[38] The chronological sequence for Argive Geometric pottery is relatively

---

[34] On the Burly workshop, which may have produced both Copenhagen National Museum Inv. No. 727 and Tübingen Inv. No. 2657, see Davison 1961, 83–86.

[35] Bochum Museum Inv. No. S 1066 (Haug 2012, 162, abb. 130a) and Copenhagen National Museum Inv. No. 727 (Haug 2012, 162, abb. 130c).

[36] Tübingen Museum Inv. No. 2657 (Rombos 1988, pl. 71a; Haug 2012, 136, abb. 98) and Amsterdam Allard Pierson Museum Inv. No. APM 3491 (Haug 2012, 157, abb. 126a).

[37] Kerameikos Museum Inv. No. 407 (Rombos 1988, pl. 37b; Haug 2012, 209, abb. 170).

[38] See treatment of Argive Geometric painting in Courbin 1966. A considerable proportion of the known corpus of Argive figural iconography comes from artifacts excavated at the Argive Heraion in the early twentieth century (Waldstein 1905).

well-understood because of many decades of careful work by French and Greek archaeologists.[39] Figural decoration first appears in the local LG, starting around 750. Dance and male figures leading horses are the most common motifs in Argive pottery.[40] For the purpose of this study, I looked at forty examples of LG Argive pottery decorated with human figures; in this case, the sample essentially comprises all examples of eighth century Argive figured scenes published in Courbin's study from 1966 and more recent works by Zimmermann, Courbin, and Croissant.[41] In general, the frequency of anthropomorphic iconography is less in Argive Geometric than in Attic Geometric.

The characteristics of the overall assemblage of Argive pottery showing figural scenes differ considerably from those of the Attic material.[42] While many of the Argive pieces are fragmentary (16), the shapes of the ceramic vessels featuring painted decoration are relatively evenly distributed between kraters (12) and drinking vessels (7). Amphorae (3) are not as frequently decorated with human figures as they are in Attica. There are also three figure-decorated pyxides. The iconographical range of the Argive artists is mainly limited to two types of scenes: dances (14) and the master of horses (22), which together compose 88% of the human-figured scenes in the sample (see Figure 3.6B, C, D, F, G).[43] In extant scenes of dancing in Argive Geometric pottery, nine depictions show females dancing, and the other five show males dancing. Argives scene that focus on males dancing almost always indicate nudity.[44] In the horse-leader scenes that are most characteristic of Argive Geometric iconography, the majority (13 of 22) show men who appear to be naked.

Other scenes with naked males include one scene of battle, one scene of a chariot departure, one horse rider, one fight over a tripod, a flagellant

[39] See review and references in Papadimitriou 2006.   [40] Langdon 2008, 160–164.

[41] Courbin 1966; 1992; Zimmermann 1989.

[42] For some areas of contrast between Argive and Attic Geometric vase painting not related to the rendering of the human figure, see Coldstream 2003 [1977], 120–121. Differences include treatments of the meander and variation in bird forms. Coldstream attributes the latter to the possibility that "the marshlands between Argos and the sea allowed the painters more scope of firsthand observation."

[43] Coldstream 2003 [1977], 121: "The Argives and Lakonians showed a preference for the row of dancers, who always join hands and usually carry branches ... in the Argolid ... the subject was especially popular near the end of Geometric. But the favorite Argive theme is the horse-tamer, who persists throughout LG, controlling either one or two horses." One fragment, from the Argive Heraion (Waldstein 1905, pl. 57, no. 6), appears to show a flagellant, calling to mind the bronze flagellant from Syme Viannou shown in Figure 2.3.

[44] All these sherds are from the Argive Heraion: two are illustrated in Courbin 1966, pl. 147, and the others are published in Waldstein 1905, pl. 57, nos. 6, 7, 19. One exception is a vase (Argos Archaeological Museum Inv. No. C 240; Courbin 1966, 40) that shows a horse-tamer in the foreground and a line of dancers in the background. Coldstream (2003 [1977], 121) suggests that "perhaps these activities formed part of a local festival by the sea." See also discussion in Langdon 1989; 2008, 165–166.

3.6. Naked males in Argive LG iconography: (A) possible flagellant, sherd from the Argive Heraion (after Waldstein 1905, pl. 57, no. 7); (B) individual at a festival, sherd from the Argive Heraion, (after Waldstein 1905, pl. 57, no. 19); (C) horse leader, sherd from the Argive Heraion (after Waldstein 1905, pl. 57, no. 4); (D) horse leader (Argos Archaeological Museum Inv. No. C 1263, after Courbin 1966, pl. 141); (E) combatants under handle (Argos Archaeological Museum Inv. No. C 209, after Courbin 1966, pl. 102); (F) dancing, probably at a festival, sherd from the Argive Heraion (after Waldstein 1905, pl. 57, no. 17); (G) horse leaders (Argos Archaeological Museum Inv. No. C 201, after Courbin 1966, pl. 43).

(Figure 3.6A), and one amphora, dated *ca.* 735–725, that shows two pairs of wrestlers, one under each handle (Figure 3.6E).[45] The scene of wrestling is a remarkable and unusual depiction. The two combatants are highly attenuated in form, perhaps recalling the characteristics of some Geometric bronzes from Olympia and Delphi.[46] The scene of the chariot departure also includes apparently naked males.[47]

The Cyclades

The Cycladic Geometric tradition of painted pottery has produced few scenes showing the human figure. Extant Parian material appears to draw heavily from Attic Geometric in the earlier phases of the EIA before diverging into a

---

[45] Courbin 1966, pl. 102; discussion in Coldstream 2003 [1977], 120.

[46] Argos Archaeological Museum Inv. No. C 209. It certainly does not seem out of the question that this scene depicts an early form of naked athletics. McDonnell (1991, 183–184) is, however, skeptical. For Geometric boxers and wrestlers, see Laurent 1901, 150, fig. 3; Waldstein 1905, 113, no. 11; Ahlberg-Cornell 1987, 55–86, esp. 62–63.

[47] It appears on a sherd from the Argive Heraion (Waldstein 1905, pl. 57, no. 12).

3.7. Painting on an LG amphora from Paros showing a battle, ca. 750 (Paros Archaeological Museum Inv. No. 3524, photo by author; © Hellenic Ministry of Culture and Sports – Hellenic Organization of Cultural Resources Development)

recognizable figural tradition in the late eighth century (*ca.* 730).[48] There are also painted Geometric vessels from the island of Delos, although only one, a depiction of females dancing on a vessel probably made in Naxos, shows human figures.[49] On the Parian vessels, figural scenes show battle or warriors (3) and a prothesis (1). Nakedness is only indicated in figures on one vessel, and it is reserved for individuals who appear to be on the losing end of a missile barrage (Figure 3.7).[50]

The other corpus of Cycladic material involving the depiction of human figures takes the form of relief-decorated pottery.[51] The distinctive product of Tenian workshops were large coarse pithoi with figured friezes added in relief to the surface of ceramic vessels.[52] This relief-decorated ceramic tradition flourished primarily in the final stages of the Geometric period (the late eighth century) and the Archaic period, but relief-decorated Cycladic vessels

---

[48] Coldstream 2003 [1977], 195–196; on the relationship between Parian battle scenes and Attic vase painting, see Croissant 2008.

[49] Mykonos Archaeological Museum Inv. No. B.4.208 (Coulié 2013, 98, fig. 73).

[50] Paros Archaeological Museum Inv. No. 3524; for discussion of the Paros vase see, for example, Coldstream 2003 [1977], 195; Zafeiropoulou 2000; Zafeiropoulou and Agelarakis 2005; Zafeiropoulou 2006; Croissant 2008. For discussion of Cycladic vase-painting in the Geometric period, Coulié 2013, 97–104.

[51] Simantoni-Bournia 2004, 64; Kourou 2008.

[52] Coldstream 2003 [1977], 193: "The figures were made separately, freely modeled and pressed on to the wall of the vase when it was still leather-hard."

continued to be produced through the sixth century.[53] On Tenos, the vessels were almost all recovered from the island's primary sanctuary at Xobourgo.[54] At Xobourgo, the pithoi were kept in the cella of the temple, suggesting that they had a close connection to ritual.[55] A number of pithoi of the same type have been found at other sites in the Aegean, including at Thebes in Boeotia (the workshop that produced the Xobourgo pithoi was originally thought to be Boeotian)[56], at Zagora on Andros, at Eretria on Euboea, and elsewhere in the Cyclades.[57] Most Cycladic relief pithoi with elaborate human-figural decoration postdate the Geometric period; prior to this, Cycladic relief vessels were decorated with geometric designs that relate stylistically to designs on painted Attic and Euboean ceramics.[58] The iconography of seventh century Cycladic relief pithoi includes an extraordinary number of scenes that contain identifiable treatments of stories known from myth and literature, including episodes from the Trojan War.[59] A notable example is the monumental pithos from Mykonos with, among other scenes from the Trojan cycle, what seems to be a depiction of the Trojan Horse.[60]

While the most famous examples of the style were produced in the Early Archaic period, the relief pithoi from the LG (750–700) period present an interesting treatment of nudity. In the LG period, Cycladic relief vessel decoration favors the depiction of animals (horses, centaurs, and goats) rather than humans. When human figures appear, they are usually either warriors or dancers, neither of which are generally depicted naked.[61] Instead, they are usually clothed in elaborate textiles or bearing ample armor. On the other hand, naked figures from the repertoire include a depiction of an apparently naked dead man that is being attacked by a bird (Figure 3.8)[62] and an image of a man leading a goat.[63] The iconographic tradition of relief pithoi in the Archaic period seems to echo the trend identified in Attic painted pottery, in which warriors and women are associated with armor and elaborate textiles,

[53] Caskey 1976, 20.
[54] On excavations at Xobourgo see Kontoleon 1950; 1952; 1953; 1955; 1958; Kourou 1996.
[55] Kontoleon 1953, 259; Kourou 1996, 262–266, pl. 67b; Kourou 2008, 78–82.
[56] See De Ridder 1898. On the Tenian material, Graindor 1905, 286–291; Courby 1922, 81–82; Kontoleon 1961; Ervin 1963.
[57] On the distribution of these vessels see Caskey 1976, 20–22; see also Cambitoglou 1971, figs. 31–32; Ervin 1963 on Mykonos.
[58] Coldstream 2003 [1977], 193; on affinities with Attica, see Kourou 2008, 86.
[59] Anderson 1975, 3; Kourou 2008, 82–85; Simantoni-Bournia 2017, 36.
[60] For the initial publication, see Ervin 1963. Other explicit depictions of episodes from the Trojan War include the "Death of Priam" pithos (see Caskey 1976, 34–36).
[61] Anderson 1975, 18–19.
[62] Athens National Archaeological Museum Inv. No. 2495 (Courby 1922, 81, fig. 17; Caskey 1976, pl. 2, fig. 10).
[63] Munich Antikensammlung Inv. No. 7697 (Caskey 1976, pl. 4 fig. 5).

3.8. Sherd of a Cycladic relief vase showing a naked, probably dead man being attacked by a bird (Athens National Archaeological Museum Inv. No. 2495, photo by author, published with permission from the National Archaeological Museum, Athens, © Hellenic Ministry of Culture and Sports – Hellenic Organization of Cultural Resources Development)

while death and interactions with wild animals may serve as appropriate occasions for the depiction of the unclothed body.[64]

Lakonia

Lakonian Geometric pottery does not feature a large number of human-figure-decorated scenes. However, a figured style developed in Lakonia during the second half of the eighth century, usually appearing on drinking vessels such as skyphoi and kraters.[65] Geometric pottery with figured decoration has been excavated at the sanctuaries of the Amyklaion and Artemis Orthia and a few sherds come from the Spartan Acropolis.[66] This corpus of material shows some affinities with Argive Geometric in terms of the normal context for its

---

[64] For example, *ArchEph* 1969, pl. 46; Schäfer 1957, pl. X, no. 2.   [65] Vlachou 2012, 119.

[66] Margreiter 1988 remains the best source for this material. The Lakonian vessels in question are the pyxis Athens National Archaeological Museum Inv. No. 234 (Coldstream 1968, pl. 46n), a pyxis and a krater from Sparta that are not numbered but are illustrated in Coldstream 1968 (pl. 46j, p), and the fragments from Sparta (the Amyklaion, Artemis Orthia sanctuary, and acropolis) illustrated at Margreiter 1988, taf. 25, nos. 290, 294 and abb. 12–47; taf. 26, no. 304; taf. 40, no. 472; and taf. 41, no. 481. Two additional figured scenes have come from recent excavations at the Amyklaion (see Vlachou 2012, 120, fig. 5 and Vlachou 2018, 112, fig. 4.10).

3.9. Lakonian Geometric pyxis showing nude dancers (Athens National Archaeological Museum Inv. No. 234, photo by author, published with permission from the National Archaeological Museum, Athens, © Hellenic Ministry of Culture and Sports – Hellenic Organization of Cultural Resources Development)

deposition (sanctuaries) and the typical iconography of human figural scenes (dancing scenes and horses are popular).[67] A large pyxis fragment, for example, shows a group of naked males holding hands in a line; the presence of a lyre between two of them and a garland in the hands of two others suggest that this is a scene of a dance (Figure 3.9).[68] Nude dancers are also probably depicted on six other fragments from Lakonian sanctuaries. One sherd from an unknown location in Sparta shows a naked man next to three horses, a scene potentially influenced by Argive horse-leader scenes.[69] A ritual scene may be indicated on a sherd from the Amyklaion recently published by Vlachou, in which a man, not obviously naked, holds a switch or whip aimed at something in front of him.[70] Proportional to the number of figured scenes, which is admittedly small, apparently naked males figure relatively prominently in Geometric Lakonian vase painting. Dancing scenes showing men are most popular.[71]

[67] Vlachou 2012, 119.

[68] Athens National Archaeological Museum Inv. No. 234 (Coldstream 1968, pl. 46n; Margreiter 1988, abb. 12, no. 46).

[69] Coldstream 1968, pl. 46j.   [70] Vlachou 2018, 112, fig. 4.10.   [71] Vlachou 2012, 120.

In all except one of the scenes showing males dancing, genitalia are rendered, suggesting that the figures are explicitly supposed to be seen as naked.[72]

Boeotia

The tradition of figure-decorated Geometric pottery in Boeotia begins around 740, with strong external influences. Designs seem influenced by Attic, Corinthian, and Euboean material, although the iconography also overlaps with that observed on southern Peloponnesian pottery.[73] The most characteristic Boeotian shapes are the pyxis, kantharos, and krater.[74] Boeotian Geometric pottery decorated with human figures does not represent a large corpus of material, but the iconographic repertoire is varied.[75] Scenes pictured in Boeotian LG pottery include hand-to-hand combat (3), lion fights (3), dancing (2), a mistress of animals (1), the *prothesis* (1), warriors (1), an abduction (1), and warriors departing on a ship (1). This variety has been interpreted as the result of a late-developing repertoire that was influenced by outside traditions.[76]

Of the thirteen examples of human-figured scenes sampled here, eight show males. Five of these eight scenes include apparent nudity. The most remarkable among them is probably a scene on one side of a complete LG pedestalled krater. In the center of the scene, two male figures, each with one hand wrapped in a glove and one hand extended with five fingers to the front, might be interpreted as engaged in a fight, perhaps a boxing match.[77] Behind them, smaller male figures, their size perhaps indicating youth, carry swords in baldrics and hold the reins of horses that flank the central scene. All four of the figures are naked. An even smaller figure depicted underneath the horse to the left does not appear to be naked. Another scene of males in combat appears on a sherd in Sarajevo, where two naked men appear to be engaging in fisticuffs, this time over a tripod.[78] A fragmentary kantharos in the Röhss museum

---

[72] An exception is a sherd showing two dancing or running males from recent excavations at the Amyklaion (Vlachou 2012, 120, fig. 5).

[73] On stylistic influences, see Coldstream 2003 [1977], 210–211.

[74] Coldstream 2003 [1977], 210.

[75] Nine vessels with depictions of males: Athens National Archaeological Museum Inv. No. 12896 (Coldstream 1968, pl. 44j), Paris Louvre Museum Inv. No. A 568 (Coulié 2013, 103, fig. 80), Hamburg Museum Inv. No. 1936.2 (Hamburg *CVA* No. 1, pl. 1), Göteborg Museum Inv. No. GA 1641 (Göteborg *CVA* No. 1, pl. 18), Sarajevo Museum Inv. No. 36 (Rombos 1988, pl. 57b; Yugoslavia *CVA*, pl. 11, no. 36), Athens National Archaeological Museum Inv. No. 5893 (Coldstream 1968, pl. 45d), Paris Louvre Museum Inv. No. A 575 (Coulié 2013, 102, fig. 79), Heidelberg Museum Inv. No. G 60 (Heidelberg *CVA* No. 3, pl. 119), London British Museum Inv. No. 1910.10-13.1 (Coldstream 1968, pl. 44b).

[76] Coldstream 2003 [1977], 182.

[77] Athens National Archaeological Museum Inv. No. 12896 (Coldstream 2003 [1977], pl. 44j).

[78] Sarajevo Museum Inv. No. 36 (Rombos 1988, pl. 57b; Yugoslavia *CVA*, pl. 11, no. 36).

showing either a race or a dance also includes naked men.[79] Men being attacked by lions on two vessels currently in the Louvre are apparently naked.[80] Two recently discovered sherds of dinoi from the sanctuary of Herakles in Thebes and dated to the turn of the eighth or early seventh centuries show a centaur abducting a woman and a fight between a man and a lion, neither of which indicate nudity.[81] Likewise, the remaining figural scenes in Boeotian material surveyed for this study, including those showing boxers, a charioteer, and warriors do not explicitly indicate nudity.[82]

Crete

On Crete, the human figure appears occasionally on decorated pottery.[83] Anthropomorphic figural decoration is, however, limited to the local Cretan PGB (*ca.* 840–810) and LG (*ca.* 750–700) periods.[84] An early PG krater from a settlement context at Thronos Kefala (ancient Syvrita) and dated to the tenth century is an exception.[85] The krater shows armed warriors on the bands of decoration on both sides, probably engaged in a kind of ritual dance.[86] The figures carry round shields that obscure their bodies, and given their isolated appearance in the early PG, they could be interpreted in connection with earlier images of warriors on LH IIIC kraters, although the iconography of the Thronos Kefala krater is distinct from depictions of LH IIIC warriors in its emphasis on a ritual dance.[87] Nonetheless, it might be connected to the ideology of a dominant warrior elite or a liminal rite, something like the Pyrrhic dance attested in much later historical sources.[88]

In terms of spatial distribution, human figures on pottery occur at only a few sites on Crete, with a heavy concentration at Knossos, and the normal context for complex figured scenes is mortuary.[89] Most of the tombs in which figured vessels have been found are wealthy, suggesting to some that the purpose of the elaborate decoration was to underscore the elite status of the dead.[90] A couple of vessels dated to the middle PG and late PG from the site show males that appear to be hunting, although one is clearly related to a type scene that involves a male being eaten by a pair of facing lions or monsters.[91] In the local PGB period, decoration featuring the human figure is usually limited to a

---

[79] Röhss Museum Inv. No. 55.59 (Göteborg *CVA* 1, pl. 17–18).

[80] Paris Louvre Museum Inv. No. A 575 and Paris Louvre Museum Inv. No. CA 284 (Coulié 2013, 102, fig. 79).

[81] Aravantinos 2014, 202; 2015, 103; 2017, 227.

[82] For example, Paris Louvre Museum Inv. No. A 568 (Coulié 2013, 103, fig. 80).

[83] For early Cretan figured pottery, see Levi 1945; Blome 1982; D'Agata 2012; Kaiser 2013; D'Agata 2014.

[84] Kaiser 2013, 142.   [85] For its archaeological context, D'Agata 2012, 213–219.

[86] D'Agata 2012, 219–229.   [87] D'Agata 2012, 231.   [88] D'Agata 2012, 232–236.

[89] Pilz 2014, 246.   [90] D'Agata 2012, 211.   [91] Coldstream, Eiring, and Foster 2001, 50.

particular shape, the straight-sided pithos, which was also introduced in the PGB period, although a couple of figured scenes appear on kraters and amphoras. The ninth century figured repertoire of Knossian pottery contains themes that are common in the east, especially on metalwork, as well as some that probably relate to earlier Minoan iconography, like women in long robes.[92] In the eighth century, the figures on Cretan pottery mostly appear in Central Crete, are strongly influenced by Attic style, and usually come from funerary contexts.[93]

Women are depicted more frequently than men on both PGB and LG pottery from Crete.[94] In PGB and LG pottery males are usually depicted wearing clothing, most often a short skirt probably derived in its design from the longer skirts that adorn females. Examples include the male figure under a fragmentary handle from Siderospilia/Prinias in central Crete and the hunter on a krater from Knossos Tekke Tomb F.[95] When female figures appear in figured PGB Cretan pottery they are often interpreted as depictions of deities, and this interpretation has generally been extended to the male figures.[96] For example, the man approaching a tripod holding a bird depicted on a lid from an LG tomb at Knossos has been interpreted as a depiction of Zeus.[97] However, one scene on an amphora from Andromyloi, in the mountains of southeastern Crete, depicts what appears to be a ring dance including both males and females.[98] None of these depictions indicate that any figures, male or female, are naked.

[92] D'Agata 2012, 211; Pilz 2014, 246. On the influence of eastern Mediterranean metalwork on Cretan EIA imagery, see Matthaus 2005.

[93] Coldstream 1981, 183; Pilz 2014, 246. An LG/Early Orientalizing pyxis from a funerary context at Itanos in east Crete is on display in the Sitia museum and shows three males fighting. It is not easy to discern whether they are naked or clothed.

[94] From the PGB, Knossos North Necropolis vessels MF 107.114 (two robed females) and 107.214 (two robed females) show humans. From the Knossos Fortetsa Necropolis Inv. Nos. F 339 (two males and six females) and 1440 (a female figure) show humans. See Kaiser 2013, 142–148. From the LG period humans appear on Knossos Fortetsa Tomb F 1414 (one male), Knossos G 19 (one female), Praisos AN 1600 (one female, perhaps giving birth), and Andromyloi H3205 (eight females and three males).

[95] Tomb F 1414 (Coldstream and Catling 1996, 8, no. 1; fig. 59, pl. 48); Praisos Inv. No. G 122 (Rizza 1974; 1978, 136, abb. 56; Kaiser 2013, 151). On the male figures on painted pottery from Prinias see, for example, Pautasso 2018, 2019.

[96] Kaiser 2013, 148. Benson (1970, 68) initially interpreted the male figure on the Siderospilia sherd as a worshipper, while Coldstream (1981, 70) suggested that it could represent a painter's attempt to depict a cult statue. Kaiser (2013, 151–152) rejects both positions and advocates leaving open the possibility that the figure represents someone engaged in a ritual activity.

[97] Coldstream 1981, 153.

[98] Coldstream 1981, 155; Tsipopoulou 2005, 208, abb. 319, taf. 23, 501.

TABLE 3.3. *Distribution of painted scenes in Geometric pottery showing naked males organized by region and indicating themes and contexts present in the scenes from each region*

Ware	Total	Naked males	Scenes with nudity
Attic	200	16	Dance (4), hunt (3), master of horses (3), corpse (3), festival (1), warrior (1), race (1)
Argive	41	18	Master of horses (11), dance (5), wrestling (1), chariot (1)
Cycladic	26	3	Dead or dying men (2),[a] goat-leader (1)
Boeotian	9	5	Hunt (2), dance (1), boxing (1), contest (1)
Lakonian	9	8	Dance (5), master of horses (1), undetermined (2)
Cretan	10	0	N/A (perhaps 1 from Itanos showing a battle)

[a] The data for Cycladic relief pottery dated to the eighth century was assembled from Anderson 1975.

Summary and Discussion[99]

To conclude the review of evidence, I summarize the trends apparent in the depiction of nudity in vase painting in Table 3.3. This table shows the regional distribution of (a) human-figured scenes analyzed in the current study, (b) the number of naked males present in these figured scenes, and (c) the activities or scene types in which the naked individuals are engaged.

Apparently naked males in Geometric vase painting are engaged in a variety of activities, including those we could categorize as ritual (dancers and participants in festivals), vulnerable (death), and athletic, or at least competitive in some sense (wrestling, boxing, running). Analysing the scenes showing naked male figures according to regional workshops demonstrates some potentially interesting patterns. In the few extant examples of painted Geometric pottery showing human figures from the Cyclades (e.g., the amphora from Paros) naked individuals appear to be coterminous with individuals who are dead or about to die. A connection between nudity and death can be traced more generally in the relief-decorated pottery from the Cyclades, dated to the very end of the Geometric and the Early Archaic period. In this tradition, elaborate robes and armor, rather than nudity, are the rule for heroic males.[100]

[99] Other regional traditions of painted Geometric pottery do not often feature the human figure, so I do not discuss them in detail here. Three sherds of an oinochoe from Nikoleika in Achaia show clothed figures in a ring dance (Gadolou 2017, 282, 290, fig. 4) and a roof model from the same sanctuary shows a pair of seated men with a tripod, an abduction, and chariot drivers (Gadolou 2017, 291, fig. 6). An early PG krater from Euboea shows two archers, but Euboean Geometric pottery does not feature many depictions of human figures (an amphora showing chariot racing from Eretria is dated to the seventh century [Coulié 2013, 96, fig. 71]). Only a few human figure-decorated sherds have been found at Delphi (e.g., Laistner 1912/1913, 67).

[100] For example, Simantoni-Bournia 2004, pl. 36, a relief-decorated amphora from Tinos.

When nudity occurs it is most often associated with the weak and the dying.[101]

On the other hand, in Lakonian and Argive Geometric scenes, naked males often appear in contexts that do not imply vulnerability or death. Individuals leading horses in Argive ceramic iconography, usually identified as participants in some sort of ritual, are commonly depicted naked.[102] In Lakonian Geometric, the most common context for all human figures is a ritual dance, and most of the males that are painted on pottery made in the region appear to be clearly naked. Male figures are not commonly found on EIA pottery from Crete. Most of the few anthropomorphic figures on painted EIA Cretan pottery come from funerary contexts at Knossos and females are more commonly depicted than males. The males that do occur in EIA Cretan ceramic decoration are always clothed. They are often interpreted as images of deities.

The iconography of naked men in the Attic and Boeotian Geometric traditions are more complex. In Attic vase-painting, nudity occurs in a relatively wide variety of contexts: scenes of violence and death including warfare and hunting. In such violent scenes, the guise of nudity might be meant to indicate the fact that death is imminent or has already occurred. However, in the hunting scenes it might just as easily be meant to indicate the hunter's immersion in a wild natural environment or to emphasize the virility of such a daring man who can confront and kill a wild beast. Naked figures are sometimes present in scenes that show ritual activity, especially on oinochoai from the end of the eighth century. Figures engaged in funerals or arming for war, on the other hand, may be lightly clad but are essentially never marked out as explicitly naked.

Boeotian Geometric scenes likewise run the gamut, from nude hunters and boxers to participants in festivals and dancers. One possible explanation for the diversity of scenes including explicitly naked figures in Boeotian and Attic vase painting might be that painters in these traditions were influenced by both Peloponnesian and eastern iconographic traditions, each of which had its own conventions regarding the appropriate context for naked figures.

Another explanation for this discrepancy might be the depositional context of the finds and the likely social function that we might assign to ceramics based on different such contexts. There is significant variation in the contexts where figure-decorated pottery occurs in material culture across the regions surveyed. In Attica, figure-decorated pottery was usually deposited in mortuary contexts and seems often to have been designed for such use. Its

---

[101] See Haug 2012, 241–246; Simantoni-Bournia (2017) suggested that the scenes from Cycladic relief pithoi should be read as "visual translations of Homeric verses." She discusses scenes involving corpses being eaten by birds specifically (2017, 36).

[102] Courbin 1966, GR 2c C.201/B, pls. 43–45; Courbin 1966, GR 2c C. 890 pl. 64.

iconography is therefore unsurprisingly concerned with funerals, and with the kinds of scenes that might have preceded or been associated with death, such as departing for or engaging in armed combat. On the other hand, many of the figure-decorated ceramics from Lakonia and from the Argolid come from ritual rather than mortuary contexts. It therefore might be logical to conclude that the images painted on the pottery reflect the sorts of activities, especially group dance and perhaps ritual competitions, that are likely to have taken place in such contexts.[103] That is to say, the figural repertoires and their thematic differences might, to some degree, relate to the intended function and audience of the objects.

The intended meaning of the iconography present in Geometric vase painting has been the topic of much discussion. Several scholars have connected this iconography and scale of Attic Geometric figured vases with the development of status warfare associated with the negotiation of relationships among elites and between elites and the community.[104] It may be true that the scenes of elaborate funerals and chariot-riding in Attic Geometric pottery were painted on mortuary vessels because they were activities with which elites hoped to link their identities (and the identity of their families). On the other hand, iconography designed to be seen in the context of communal rituals at sanctuaries was presumably intended to be relevant in the context of those rituals. If we accept that different figural traditions diverge in their iconographic repertoires because they were designed for different audiences engaging in different sorts of activities in different performative contexts, this could help explain the patterns apparent in nudity. It may have been true that elaborate funerals among the elite and those departing for war were not contexts in which nudity was considered to be appropriate, while dancing at a festival was such an occasion.

In other words, if art can be taken to imitate life and nudity was restricted to certain contexts, the divergent patterns of nudity in, for example, Attic and Lakonian vase-painting may reflect not a geographical difference in approaches to nudity, but local choices about what kinds of activities and what sorts of occasions merit investment in special craft objects, like figure-decorated pottery. Although scenes showing nonmortuary ritual activity are not frequently

---

[103] Geometric pottery decorated with images of naked male figures engaging in activities such as boxing and dancing is concentrated in Lakonia, the Argolid, and, to a limited extent, in Boeotia (boxers: Courbin 1966, GR 1 C. 209 details, pl. 102; dancers: Courbin 1966, GR 2b Fr. de l'Heraion; Waldstein 1905, pl. 57, no. 17, pl. 147; Argive Heraeum pl. LVII, nos. 6, 7). The possibility that early contests and dances may have involved actual nudity is usually dismissed because dancers at festivals and athletic competitors are clothed in the Homeric poems. For the clothing of athletes in Homer, see discussion in Chapter 1 and Appendix A; for the clothing of festival dancers in Homer, *Il.* 593–596.

[104] For example, Morris 1996; 2000, 157; Stewart 1997, 16; Snodgrass 2008.

depicted in Attic LG pottery, this may indicate that such activity occurred with some regularity in Attica, but were not depicted in figure-decorated pottery. We cannot, therefore, conclude that the absence of many figural scenes showing ritual occasions when some kind of naked activity occurred necessarily indicates that such occasions were not a part of life in EIA Attica.

However, there are problems with explaining regional distinctions in the use of nudity in Geometric vase painting as a product of the depositional context. Some of the Attic vessels featuring naked males, including some engaged in a ritual activity, come from mortuary contexts. Cretan figure-decorated pottery does not show funerals, even though it comes mainly from mortuary contexts. In the Cyclades, scenes that seem to draw from myth and legend, rather than images that show ritual activities, are popular on vessels from the sanctuary of Xobourgo. Argive human-figure decorated pottery has been excavated from both mortuary contexts and from the sanctuary of the Argive Heraion, but neither assemblage features imagery of funerals.[105] We could perhaps reconstruct a scenario in which distinctions between iconography in pottery from mortuary and ritual contexts across these regions could be explained by regional variation in mortuary and ritual *activities* (e.g., that Attic funerals involved the *prothesis* while Argive ones entailed horse-taming rituals). However, this conclusion is made unsatisfying by the fact that horse-taming scenes also appear on pottery from the Argive Heraion and sometimes from Attic mortuary contexts.[106]

A better explanation for the complexities inherent in the evidence is that each region had a distinct tradition of both cultural practices and ceramic decoration, such that iconographic choices were impacted by complex local legacies and ideas, while occasionally reflecting outside influence. Rather than rendering the evidence useless in dealing with questions of naked behavior in EIA Greece, this explanation encourages an appreciation of how much there is to gain by recognizing that disunity and regional distinction must be central to our interpretations. Material culture is not only shaped by, but has a function in shaping ideologies, social relations, and behavioral modalities. The artists and patrons of eighth century Athens, Argos, and Sparta made conscious choices about what kinds of scenes should be commemorated in the medium of painted pottery, and these choices mattered. Thus, the fact that the most impressive Attic Geometric art glorifies funerals constitutes not just a happenstance of the material record, but a manifestation of choices made by people

---

[105] The monumental kraters that marked the tombs of prominent Argive elites do not show scenes that are explicitly funerary in nature. Instead, the most common motif on these funerary markers is the scene of a man or youth leading horses.

[106] Argive horse-master scenes may provide evidence for some sort of ritual involving the taming of stallions, possibly in the context of a festival. See Langdon 1989 for review of scholarship on this topic.

and communities. By the same token, the different choices made by Argive and Spartan patrons and artists are likely to represent meaningful differences in the ideas and ideals that they hoped to reproduce by creating permanent images of individuals and communities. We should take these differences as laden with meaning, as indications of where communities and individuals saw, or hoped to generate, value in material culture. This suggests that we should take distinctions in the representation of nudity among these different ceramic traditions as indications that different EIA communities may have had different ideas about nudity and its role in society during the LG period.

It also encourages us to consider the tensions that may have been present *within* communities during the EIA. Multiple ideas about where and when figures ought to be represented naked are evident in Attic and Boeotian figured scenes, suggesting that multiple ideas about the meaning and valence of naked-ness could have been present within one region at the same time. In this context, it is worth considering the fact that the archaeological contexts of figural scenes in ceramics do not align well with archaeological contexts of naked male figurines: the only sites that have produced both naked male figurines and figural scenes on pottery from the EIA are Knossos, Sparta, and Athens. Even at these sites, only one or two naked figurines are present. The sites from which the most bronze figurines have been recovered (cave sanctuaries on Crete, Syme Viannou, Olympia, Delphi) do not seem to have been the site of production or consumption of EIA figure-decorated ceramics. Indeed, the extreme variance in the kinds of material culture that are abundant at different sites from the EIA is a potent reminder of how different cultural practices associated with material culture across sites and regions must have been during this period.

The comportment of the Cretan evidence is elegantly expressive of the complexity of the situation. While naked males are relatively widespread and occur very early in particular archaeological contexts on Crete, ceramic icon-ography from EIA Crete includes no naked males whatsoever. Whether or not the lack of alignment across these genres can be explained by the influence of Attic pottery on Cretan LG style or the mortuary rather than ritual depos-itional context of most Cretan figure-decorated pottery, recognizing the variance in treatments of the body across material categories complicates an attempt to draw conclusions about what people thought and how people behaved around concepts of naked men based on a synthetic approach. It seems likely, then, that even within regions, different craft communities (i.e., potters vs. metallurgists) were not necessarily operating within the same traditions or serving the same communities, so material from each site should be carefully considered as meaningful within a quite limited social context.

It is thus best to draw a relatively limited conclusion from the way that naked males are depicted in Geometric pottery rather than to reconstruct a granular or thoroughgoing set of ideas about nudity from the combination of ceramic evidence and the evidence of the figurines. While the evidence is quite complex and resists simplification, it seems to me that three statements about it can be made with relative confidence. First, while Attic and Cycladic iconography demonstrates that nakedness and death were connected in some contexts in these regions, there is no connection between nakedness and death or weakness evident in the images on pottery from Cretan, Lakonian, and Argive sites. Second, it is generally evident that naked males most often appear in ritual contexts across all regional traditions. Third, as a proportion of the overall evidence, both bronze and ceramic, the most evidence for an iconographic interest in ritual nakedness comes from Crete and the southwestern and central mainland. While it is impossible to be sure whether these material patterns relate in straightforward ways to social practices or ideas about nudity, they do suggest that naked ritual practice may have been more important in the regions or communities where it appears most prominently in art..

FORMAL AND ICONOGRAPHIC ARGUMENTS FOR CRETAN INFLUENCE ON MAINLAND BRONZES

Taken together, the evidence indicates that there may have been some special connection between ritual behaviors involving nudity on Crete and in central and western mainland Greece prior to and during the EIA. Such a connection is supported by the patterns in bronze figurine deposition discussed in Chapter 2. Scholars working on mainland EIA material culture have usually associated the appearance of bronze naked male figurines at Olympia and Delphi with local sociopolitical and economic developments related to state formation or community coherence in early Greece.[107] Art historical studies have often asserted that EIA figurines provided the impetus for the onset of a new tradition of figural art in mainland material culture.[108] But, given the long history of depositing bronze figurines in ritual contexts on Crete prior to the EIA, it is plausible that these figurines primarily represent the result of Cretan influence on mainland ritual practice, rather than the manifestation of endogenous developments.[109]

---

[107] For a local invention, Rolley 1977, 106–113; Langdon 1984, 98–99; Morgan 1990, 61–89. For the idea of influence from the nebulous east, which sometimes arises in the context of the discussion of the origins of the figurines, see Müller 1929, 167–176; Langdon 1984, 272–276; Fuchs and Floren 1987, 29–31.

[108] For EIA figurines as a "wholly native" phenomenon: Nicholls 1970, 20; Lamb 1929, 36–52; Schweitzer 1967, 133–173; 1969, 127; "The balkanization of the new Greek world and its return to a primitive condition broke the connections between Asia and Europe for a long time. Greece, finally reunited after upheaval and fierce wars, faced, as far as small-scale sculpture in bronze and terracotta was concerned, a completely new problem."; Langdon 1984, 3, 32, 98; Haug 2012, 3–4: "Die neue, verdichtete Form der Gemeinschaftlichkeit bildet den Rahmen füre die Genese einer Bild- und Schriftkultur."

[109] Naumann 1976, 85–86; Byrne 1991; Lebessi 1996; 2002; *contra* Nicholls 1970, 19.

Although understanding the mechanisms for such a technological and ritual transfer remains challenging, the case for Cretan influence on the tradition of depositing nude figurines in mainland votive contexts based on formal and iconographic elements is relatively strong. I state that case in what follows. I then consider the ritual context of the production and deposition of these votives on Crete, and assess the likelihood that a transfer of the material type of the naked male bronze figurine occurred in tandem with the transfer of a set of ritual practices. The preponderance of the evidence from both Crete and the mainland suggests that the appearance of EIA naked bronze figurines was connected to initiatory rituals that were probably meant to usher young people into a new life phase at remote rural sanctuaries.

On the mainland, there is no extant tradition of cast bronze sculpture in the round prior to the appearance of figurines in EIA sanctuaries.[110] Thus, the bronze figurines dedicated at Olympia and Delphi in the EIA represent an entirely new development for the region. On the other hand, EIA Cretan figurines were deposited within the context of a long tradition, dating back to the Middle Minoan period, of dedicating small cast bronze statuettes in ritual contexts, which continued through the eleventh and tenth centuries.[111] These figurines thus represent a direct development following the Minoan, and post-Minoan sequences on the island.

Is there a clear connection between this tradition and the cast bronze figurines that appear at Olympia and Delphi? The case that early bronze figurines from Olympia and Delphi were made under some sort of influence from Cretan examples was first made by Burkert in 1975. According to Burkert, EIA bronze figurines from mainland sites were the end result of a chain of transmission of ideas from the east via Cyprus, then Crete, then the Peloponnese, but his case was made primarily on the basis of a logical hypothesis rather than systematic examination of the evidence.[112] His argument did draw somewhat from archaeological study of bronzes at Delphi, many of which are considered to be Cretan imports.[113] The origin of mainland figurines was also addressed by de Santerre, who thought that artists on the mainland were using imported Reshef figurines from the Bronze Age as models, but the long chronological remove between those imported figurines and the appearance of bronze figurines at Olympia and Delphi undermines the

---

[110] Hood 1978, 112–14; Mattusch 1988, 31; Sapouna-Sakellarakis 1995, 99; Lebessi 2002, 354. There is some vestigial evidence for the production of cast bronze rod tripods that seem to represent a Cypriot tradition at Akovitika and Lefkandi (Zimmer 1990, 20–21) through the EIA, but these tripods probably represent a different set of ideas and cultural practices than do small-scale sculptures of human figures dedicated at sanctuaries (see also discussion of evidence for their production in Chapter 5).

[111] Bol 1985, 21.   [112] Burkert 1975, 52, 62–74.

[113] See discussion and sources cited in Kotsonas 2009, 1053–1054.

plausibility of this conclusion.[114] Both Byrne and Lebessi have subsequently conducted thorough research on the relevant artifacts. Both conclude that the aesthetic characteristics of the earliest figurines at Olympia and Delphi demonstrate extremely close connections between the bronze figurines from Crete in the Postminoan and PG period, and argue that the Cretan examples did in fact provide the basis or inspiration for production of bronze figurines in ritual contexts at mainland sites.[115]

In a monograph based on his doctoral thesis and published in 1991, Michael Byrne attempted to trace the historical development of earliest bronze warrior figurines that appear at mainland sanctuaries in the Geometric period in their Mediterranean context using an essentially iconological method.[116] Starting from the hypotheses of Burkert and de Santerre, Byrne's study compares and contrasts the standard motif of the bronze warrior figurines from the LBA and EIA in the Levant, Cyprus, Crete, and the mainland. By compiling a database of characteristics including the postures and gestures of the figurines, he generated a quantitative metric for comparing these several bodies of evidence.[117] According to this metric, the material from the EIA mainland shares the most features with Cretan figurines, including the manner of modeling facial features and attenuation in the neck and the limbs.[118] Particular mainland motifs that can be directly traced from early Cretan figurines include postures with the arms extended horizontally sideways from the body, with the arms extended directly forward from the body, with one or both arms held over the stomach, with one arm held to the head and the other at the side, the motif of the nude figure wearing only a belt, and standing with bent knees.[119]

Lebessi's study of the important assemblage of bronze figurines from Syme Viannou includes a lengthy treatment of the historical development of such votive figurines in the context of the history of three-dimensional bronze sculpture in the Aegean, part of her effort to place the Syme Viannou figurines in a chronological sequence.[120] This treatment traces possible predecessors and

---

[114] Gallet de Santerre 1987.
[115] Byrne 1991, 109–157; Lebessi 1996, 146; 2002, 353–357; See also Hogarth 1899–1900, 107; Demargne 1947, 356; Kunze 1967, 216–222; Heilmeyer 1972, 10. Other aspects of the ritual archaeological record in Crete during the EIA, such as the concentration of imported objects in ritual deposits, likewise prefigure developments on the Greek mainland of the eighth century. See also Boardman 1961, 1, 118; Renfrew and Cherry 1985, 308: "The . . . finds from Delphi are not readily distinguished from those of Aghia Triada or the Dictaean Cave in Crete . . . some elements in the modeling of the nude male figures can in consequence now be traced back to Crete." Kotsonas (2009, 1053–1058) also identifies the strong Cretan influence on EIA central Greek metalwork and reviews a number of theories about the agency behind this influence. See also Borrell and Rittig 1998, 154–161 for an argument that a group of early bronze reliefs from Olympia were made by Cretan smiths.
[116] Byrne 1991.   [117] Byrne 1991, 222–224.
[118] Byrne 1991, 17, 132–135, 147–151. See also discussion in Prent 2005, 390.
[119] Byrne 1991, 113–129, 138–139.   [120] Lebessi 2002, 29–157.

successors for each of the figurines excavated from the sanctuary. In addition to standing alone as the most authoritative extant aesthetic analysis of EIA bronze figurines on Crete, Lebessi's discussion concurs with Byrne's in asserting a strong stylistic influence from Crete on early figurines from Olympia and Delphi.[121] Rather than relying on quantitative metrics to reach this conclusion as Byrne did, Lebessi focuses on individual figurines from the mainland that appear to draw directly on particular Cretan models for their inspiration in terms of modeling and design. She concludes her study with a strong statement to the effect that the bronze figurines from mainland Greece were made by artists who must have learned the technique from Cretan artists, or who may have been Cretan artists themselves.[122]

The arguments made by Byrne and Lebessi are sufficiently thorough to demonstrate the point, and sufficiently complex to obviate their complete rehearsal here. A few examples serve to demonstrate the strength of their aesthetic case for a Cretan influence on EIA bronze figurines from the mainland. There is a strong visual resemblance between some classes of figurine from Olympia and Crete, like the so-called clothespin figurines discussed by Langdon (see Figure 2.8) and several other poses (Figure 3.10). Likewise, warrior figurines from Delphi and Syme Viannou are quite close in style and conception. Connections between Olympia and Delphi, on the one hand, and Crete, on the other, are also supported by the large number of other Cretan or Cretan-influenced dedications in early deposits at Delphi,[123] and the Cretan influence apparent in the earliest bronze objects, not including figurines, from Olympia.[124] Deposits at Syme Viannou dating to the tenth century contained dedications of bronze bovine figurines, another type that was popular as a dedication at mainland sanctuaries.[125] From a formal and archaeological point of view, then, early Cretan influence on the practice of depositing metal figurines looks very likely because of stylistic similarities between the earliest such figurines discovered on the mainland, and other circumstantial evidence linking EIA Crete and mainland sanctuaries established in the late tenth and ninth centuries.[126]

---

[121] Lebessi 2002, 297–311.   [122] Lebessi 2002, 311–313; 353–357.

[123] Rolley 1977, 146; Langdon 1984, 243.

[124] For these, see Morgan 1990, 142–146; 1999, 379–381; Lebessi 2002, 299–304; Himmelmann 2002, 95–102.

[125] Schürmann 1996, 215. Twenty-three cattle figurines date to the last quarter of the tenth century, while another forty-nine are dated to the ninth century. Cattle and rams are the earliest types of animal figurine attested in the sanctuary. Horses are largely absent from the assemblage. Like naked male figurines, bovine figurines are attested from the LH IIIB and IIIC phases at Phylakopi (Renfrew 1985, 425–427), among the assemblage of figurines at Kontopigado (Kardamaki 2015, 80), at the sanctuary of Aphaia on Aegina (Pilafidis-Williams 1998), and at Tell Kazel (Badre and Gubel 1999–2000).

[126] Renfrew and Cherry (1985, 307–308) raised this possibility. The argument is supported by the presence on Crete of the "intermediate" or Subminoan figurines published in Naumann 1976; cf. discussion and conclusions in Lebessi 2002.

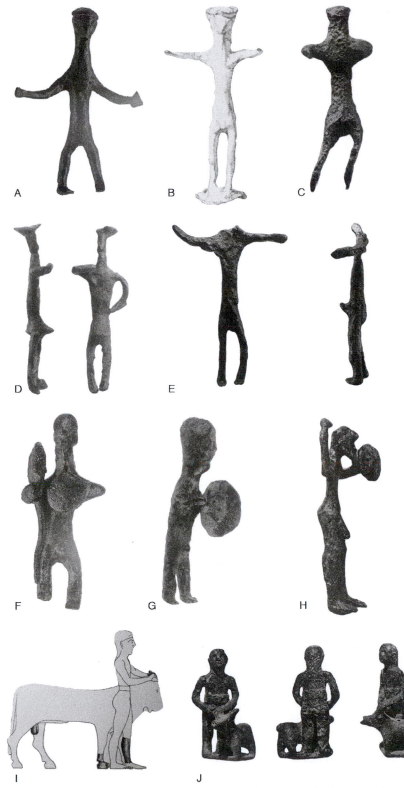

3.10. Select LM III C–Geometric figurines from Crete (left) and Olympia and Delphi (right) that demonstrate the existence of similar iconographic types present in votive sanctuary deposits:

A CRETAN INFLUENCE ON EIA MAINLAND RITUAL: RURAL SITES AND INITIATORY RITES

It is thus relatively convincingly established that the material and aesthetic type of the naked bronze Aegean figurine originated in Cretan workshops during the final phase of the LBA and that the earliest such figurines on the EIA mainland were made under direct influence from Crete. There is some evidence to suggest that the formal influence of Cretan figurines and other votives on the earliest votives dedicated at EIA sanctuaries was the result of a substantive influence of Cretan ritual practice on developments in mainland ritual during the EIA.[127]

In this section I argue that the adoption of a practice of depositing bronze votives that included naked anthropomorphic figurines probably occurred alongside the adoption of a particular kind of ritual practice, rather than constituting a merely superficial or technological development. There is some compelling, albeit circumstantial, evidence to suggest that an important aspect of this development involved initiatory rituals that originated on Crete and were integrated into ritual practice on the mainland during the EIA.

One of the enduring questions regarding the new establishment of cult locations at Olympia and Delphi in the early first millennium has revolved around the question of siting – why did sites in marginal locations that do not seem to have been used for ritual practice in the LBA suddenly accrue ritual importance in the EIA?[128] There does not appear to have been a strong tradition of worship at open air sites or in caves during the LBA on the mainland.[129] With the exception of mortuary rituals, evidence for extensive

---

3.10. (*cont.*) (A) Syme Viannou Excavation Inv. No. MH 4300 (after Lebessi 2002, pl. 11); (B) Olympia Archaeological Museum Inv. No. Br 11194 (after Furtwängler 1890, pl. 16, n. 237); (C) Oxford Ashmolean Museum Inv. No. 1946.113 (after Lebessi 2002, 63, fig. 30); (D) Olympia Archaeological Museum Inv. No. B 6269 (photo by author); (E), Syme Viannou Excavation Inv. No. MH 3700 (after Lebessi 2002, pl. 9); (F) Syme Viannou Excavation Inv. No. MH 4959 (after Lebessi 2002, pl. 10); (G) Delphi Archaeological Museum Inv. No. 7731 (after Lebessi 2002, 310, fig. 184); (H) Syme Viannou Excavation Inv. Nos. MH 4631, 3701, 3803, 3620 (after Lebessi 2002, pl. 32); (I) Delphi Archaeological Museum Inv. No. 6571 (after Rolley 1969, pl. 12, n. 42).

---

[127] Lebessi and Muhly 2003; D'Agata 2006; Haysom 2011, 100–103.

[128] Desborough 1952, 199–200; McDonald and Rapp 1972, 317; Demakopoulou 1982; Morgan 1990, 1, 20–25; Østby et al. 1994; de Polignac 1995; Morgan 1996, 53–54; 1999, 379–384; Østby 1997; Eder 2001a; Eder 2001b; 2006b; Kyrieleis 2002, 627–628;. The majority of sanctuaries in EIA Greece first preserve unambiguous evidence of ritual use beginning in the ninth and eighth centuries, although many may have been used for domestic purposes in the Bronze Age (Lemos 2002, 146).

[129] Renfrew 1985, 398. It is plausible that this situation is an artifact of the history of archaeological research in the landscapes of Crete and the mainland, respectively, since Cretan wild places and mountaintops have been explored more thoroughly than mainland ones. Minoan archaeologists have aggressively scoured the Cretan landscape for rural sites

ritual practice outside of the confines of LBA palatial settlements or their immediate surroundings on the mainland is rare.[130] The newly established cults in the Iron Age were likely distinctive from LBA predecessors, constituting open air sanctuaries usually located outside of urban centers in remote places of natural beauty.[131]

On Crete, such rural communal sanctuaries receiving votive deposits of animal and human figurines were part of the ritual landscape during the Bronze Age. The best-known types of rural Minoan sanctuaries on Crete are peak sanctuaries and sacred caves. However, Minoan Crete was also characterized by extra-urban ritual spaces situated elsewhere in the landscape.[132] Ritual activities at these sanctuaries were "focused on aspects of nature, located in rural settings, and produced material culture that links them closely with rituals performed at sanctuaries and sacred caves."[133] The best known and most thoroughly published such rural open-air sanctuary is Syme Viannou, but other sites of a similar nature exist in the Cretan archaeological record. In his treatment of the subject, Rutkowski identified fourteen open-air rural sanctuaries in Minoan Crete.[134] Ritual practice at these sites was centered on a built

(Rutkowski 1988, 23; Faro 2008, 195). Paul Faure, who was interested in Cretan sacred caves, seemingly explored every cave on Crete between 1956 and 1978, publishing his results in a series of ten articles over that period (for example, Faure 1967; 1969; 1972). Since then, archaeologists like Bogdan Rutkowski and Krzysztof Nowicki have taken up the torch of tireless explorers of the Cretan landscape, visiting nearly every mountaintop and cliff on the island in the second half of the twentieth century (Rutkowski 1988; Nowicki 2000). For the mainland, the Linear B evidence has been influential, so the idea that the religious sector was 'controlled' by the palace may have led to the limitation of identified religious spaces to areas that could nominally be controlled by the palatial authorities – that is, areas within or near settlements, especially palaces (Hiller 1981, 95). In some cases, it seems very likely that ritual centers were in fact located inside of palaces, for example, at Mycenae (French 1981b) but this does not obviate the possibility that extrapalatial sanctuaries also existed.

[130] van Leuven 1978; Chadwick 1988b; Aravantinos 1989–1990; Albers 1994; Bendall 2007; Lupack 2010. There are exceptions. Rural sites such as Mount Lykaion (Romano 2005; 2013, 187–188; Romano and Voyatzis 2010) and Kalapodi may have been used for ritual purposes throughout the LBA/EIA transition (Felsch 1996; 2007). Increasing investigation of mainland hinterlands is generating "growing evidence for Mycenaean sanctuaries...located in the countryside beyond the palace" (Eder 2016, 178). Eder has produced a list of twelve sites that are likely to have represented extra-urban sanctuaries on the Mycenaean mainland, which include locations on mountains, peaks, and passes (Eder 2016, 178–182).

[131] Renfrew 1985, 398.

[132] Rutkowski 1988, 23. The term "open-air shrine" was first used by Dessenne (1949); see also Faure 1967; 1969; 1972.

[133] Faro 2008, 195.

[134] The sites identified by Rutkowski (1988) are Stous Anthropolithous, Gazi, Syme Viannou, Katsamba, Kamilari Tymbakiou Pyrgotissis, Kavousi Pachlitsani Agriada and Kavousi Plai tou Kastrou, Keramoutsi Kavrochoriou, Kemasma, Pankalochori, Piskokephalo, Poros, Rousses, Sachtouria, and Vaveloi.

stone or ash altar.[135] The worship of sacred trees may also have taken place.[136] Such extra-urban open air sanctuaries in Minoan Crete served as locations for ritual action in a natural setting distinct from the surroundings of everyday life.[137] In many cases, the absence of any ritual architecture may suggest that it was the dramatic topography and natural situation of the sanctuaries themselves that invested the space with ritual importance. The material record indicates that ritual practice at such sites involved the deposition of animal and human figurines in bronze or clay, weapons, and jewelry as votives.[138] Bronze figurines are most commonly associated with deposition in caves,[139] and male bronze figurines outnumber female ones.[140]

Rural and cave sanctuaries were a regular feature of ritual topography in the Cretan Bronze Age, and some remained in use during the EIA.[141] In addition, some new extra-urban ritual sites (including caves or rock shelters (Patsos, Phaneromeni) and open air or altar-centered sanctuaries (Aghia Triada)) appear on Crete in the twelfth century, indicating that communal, rural worship gained in popularity following the end of the LBA on the

---

[135] On the architectural remains at Kavousi, Alexiou 1956; at Gazi, Gesell 1972. On the finds from these sites see Dessenne 1949; Platon 1951; Gesell 1976; Brown and Peatfield 1987. Ash altars are evident in the archaeological record and dated to the earliest phases of the Iron Age at Syme Viannou, Amnisos, Kommos, and Aghia Triada (see summary in Wallace 2010, 137). On ash altars, in general, Wallace 2010, 137; at Kavousi, Alexiou 1956; at Gazi, Gesell 1972; on animal figures, Nicholls 1970; Renfrew 1985, 439–440; Zeimbekis 1998; on bulls at Phaistos, see Maraghiannis n.d. pl. XV, nos. 3, 5; at Aghia Triada, Banti 1943, fig. 37.

[136] Rutkowski (1986, 1989) reached this conclusion after detailed study of such sites; see also updated information in Faro 2008.

[137] Faro 2008, 204.

[138] Hogarth 1903; Boardman 1961; Rutkowski 1986, 47–73; Prent 2005, 174–182; Morris 2017, 664. Morris notes that the majority of all figurines documented from Minoan Crete come from peak sanctuaries.

[139] Morris 2017, 670. Morris suggests that the limited distribution of bronze figurines may be related to the greater availability or wider distribution of clay as compared to bronze, and to the exclusivity of rites taking place in caves, which could have only been accessible to elites. Alternatively, it might be the case that the use of different materials seemed appropriate due to the different nature of rituals being performed at each site. An interesting observation from the ethnographic record is that caves and underground places are often associated with forges and smithies. It also seems important to take postdepositional factors into consideration when evaluating the importance of this trend, since bronzes at open air sites might have been more easily corroded and destroyed or discovered and removed by later visitors than those at sites hidden deep in caves.

[140] Hitchcock 1997.

[141] See overview of Cretan sanctuaries in Sporn 2002; Wallace 2010, 136–139. For discussion of the extraordinary, early, and widespread investment by Cretans in sanctuaries on borders and in nature, and of the function and meaning of the associated cults, see Chaniotis 2006. For caves, see Alexiou 1963; Rutkowski 1986, 47–99; Rutkowski and Nowicki 1986; Watrous 1996, 47–98. For Syme Viannou see Lebessi 1975, 1985; Kanta 1991. For Amnisos see Marinatos 1929; 1996; Schäfer 1991; 1992, 182–3; Watrous 1996, 100–102. Ritual activities at the Amnisos cave may, at some point in the EIA, have been transferred to an open-air sanctuary nearby on the coast, although the relationship between the two sites is not certain.

island.[142] Continuing in the Bronze Age tradition, almost all bronze anthropomorphic figurines from EIA Cretan sanctuaries come from rural sanctuaries, often but not always the same cave sanctuaries that received such dedications in the Bronze Age.[143]

The position of rural sanctuaries like the Idaean cave and Syme Viannou within the Cretan landscape bears some resemblance to the siting of rural sanctuaries that appear on the mainland during the EIA, which seem to be preferentially established in areas of limited habitation with distinctive topography or natural environs.[144] It does not seem entirely implausible, then, to reconstruct a situation in which the bronze figurines deposited at Delphi and Olympia in the EIA may represent the adoption of a set of ritual practices closely related to preexisting such practices characteristic of Cretan ritual at rural sites in extraordinary natural environments.

Supporting evidence for a connection between Cretan ritual practice and mainland developments during the EIA is available in the form of patterns in the deposition of bull figurines. Beginning in the LH IIIB period, wheelmade bull figurines appear in possible cult contexts at Phylakopi, Tiryns, the Argive Heraion, Apollo Maleatas at Epidauros, Agios Konstantinos on Methana, the Menelaion, Amyklaion, and Delphi.[145] In the LM IIIC period, Cretan cult assemblages likewise contain a large quantity of animal figures, especially bulls; these bulls appear at the same sites that preserve early examples of male nudes, like Aghia Triada, Syme Viannou, and Phaistos, but also at other long-established extra-urban sites of worship, like Mount Joutkas, where over a hundred LM IIIC bull figurines were recovered.[146] They continue to appear at these sites on Crete throughout the PG period, although they cease to appear at shrines in the twelfth century on the mainland and in the Cyclades. On Crete, the bovine figurines are always distinct in geographical location and ritual context from the old Cretan Goddess with the Upraised Arms.[147] Another new feature of the Cretan cult landscape in the EIA is the dedication

[142] For Patsos and Phaneromeni cave, see Kourou and Karetsou 1994; Rutkowski and Nowicki 1996, 34–6, 42–45; on Aghia Triada, D'Agata 1997; 1998; 1999. On Kommos, which was established in the later tenth century, see Shaw and Shaw 2000, 8–14.

[143] Prent 2005, 390. Prent suggests a distance–value function to this distribution: "there may have been a tendency to dedicate more expensive or more lasting votives in cult places farther away from one's home, indicating the special character of the occasion."

[144] Prent 2005, 565.

[145] Nicholls 1970; Renfrew 1985, 439–440; Zeimbekis 1998, 186, 223. See also the data compiled by Guggisberg and reproduced in Zeimbekis 1998, 223, table 9. The number of bovine figurines per period is as follows: LH II–IIIA, 4; LH IIIA-B, 3; LH IIIB, 26; LH IIIB-C, 39; LH IIIC, 64. On Agios Konstantinos, see Konsolaki-Yannopoulou 2004.

[146] Zeimbekis 1998, 182. For the idea that the appearance of ritual bulls related to social change accompanying the collapse of the palaces, see Renfrew 1985, 439–440. On bulls at Phaistos, see Maraghiannis n.d. pl. XV, nos. 3, 5; at Aghia Triada, Banti 1943, fig. 37.

[147] Zeimbekis 1998, 227.

of bronze zoomorphic figurines alongside clay ones. The distribution of these bronze animal figurines fits well with the distribution of bronze anthropomorphic figures, with 535 coming from Syme Viannou, and the majority of the remainder from the Idaean and Psychro caves.[148] The chronological and regional and distribution of the bovine figures may suggest that they are related to the production or deposition of naked male figurines, insofar as their material manifestations seem to follow a generally similar trajectory – from several mainland sites in the LH IIIC period, to Crete over the EIA transition, and eventually to Olympia and Delphi during the tenth and ninth centuries.[149]

What ritual activities might have called for the deposition of these kinds of objects? Evidence for cult practice on Crete allows the plausible reconstruction of a long history of ritual activity focused around ceremonies of initiation for young men of military age.[150] According to anthropologists of ritual, initiation involves "a body of rites and oral teachings whose purpose is to produce a decisive alteration in the religious and social status of the person to be initiated."[151] Such rites and teachings generate a ritual environment in which liminal rites are understood to be fundamentally transformative, so that the pre-initiate emerges from the ritual ceremony as an ontologically distinct being. Initiatory rituals often play a part in ushering individuals through the transition from childhood to adulthood. Such *rites de passage* are widely documented in human. They tend to involve three stages: removal from normal society, a period of isolation (which often takes place in a natural setting), and subsequent reintegration into society as the new, transformed individual. The person undergoing a period of isolation in such rites is often made to partake in exceptional behavior (such as the completion of a physical challenge or contest), engage in compulsory sexual activity, wear an unusual costume, or consume a restricted diet. The endurance of the ordeal serves simultaneously to introduce an adolescent to institutional norms or rituals of society and assess the likelihood that he or she will succeed as a functioning adult in that society. Rites of passage tend to be most prevalent in societies that are not governed by strong, small elite class, because these societies are

[148] Prent 2005, 393.

[149] Guggisberg 1996, 375. Guggisberg notes that such bovine figurines are rare at EIA sanctuaries in the Cyclades, at Athens, and at Lefkandi on Euboea. A different pattern is evident in the appearance of bird-shaped vessels, which disappear from most of the Aegean after the twelfth century, but continue to occur at Athens and Lefkandi. Thus, there are multiple strands of evidence that suggest separate regional developments in ritual iconography in the EIA Aegean, with naked males and bovines in Crete, the Peloponnese, and parts of Central Greece, and naked females and avian imagery in Attica, Euboea, the Cyclades, and the East Aegean.

[150] Lebessi 1985; Koehl 1986; Watrous 1995, 399; Koehl 2016.   [151] Eliade 1958, 7.

dependent on the direct participation and thus buy-in from a large proportion of their members.[152]

There is iconographical evidence for reconstructing such initiatory rites on Crete during the LBA. Scholars of Minoan art, especially Koehl, have identified iconographical indications that individuals in Minoan Cretan society were ushered through the stages of childhood, youth, and adulthood via rites of passage.[153] The relevant evidence includes a gold signet ring of Minoan manufacture from a tholos tomb at Pylos, which seems to show two males of different ages engaged in a rite of passage taking place in a mountainous setting and involving sexual activity accompanied by a caprid,[154] and a group of three sealings from the palace of Kato Zakro. Like the ring, the sealings appear to depict males of different ages engaged in ritual activities that include sexual acts and dances.[155] Additional evidence for the early appearance of rites of passages in ritual settings in Minoan Crete is provided by a gold signet ring showing a runner in action from Syme Viannou. The iconography of the ring suggests that foot races could have been among the contests involved in such rituals already in the Bronze Age, at least on Crete.[156] According to Koehl, these images can plausibly be connected not only to rites of passage, but to rites of passage specifically involving young males engaging in transformative physical contests, in rural locations, and in the company of older males.[157]

Koehl connects these images to elements in the historical and literary record to support the notion that initiatory rituals involving nudity were present in late second and early first millennium Crete. He draws special attention to Ephoros' account, quoted in Strabo, of a Cretan rite of passage involving younger and older males. This account explicitly links eroticism, pederasty, and coming of age rituals in a Cretan context. The degree to which it can be relied upon as a guide to Bronze Age practice is, of course, questionable. However, taken together, the iconographical resemblances between the images highlighted in Koehl's work and the material aspects of the rite that Strabo describes provide compelling evidence that something like this may have been taking place on Crete during the Bronze Age.[158]

---

[152] For example, such rites of passage have been observed among the Marind-Anim people in Papua New Guinea, who utilized a system of age-classes involving homosexual relationships with interesting structural similarities to those that may have characterized the Spartan *agoge* (van Baal 1966, 669–672; 817–818; 950).

[153] Koehl 2000, 135–137. On the identification of age grades by hairstyle in Minoan art, Davis 1986; Koehl 1986; Chapin 2007a; 2009.

[154] Blegen et al. 1973, 113, fig. 192.9a–b.   [155] Koehl 2016, 118–128.

[156] Lebessi, Muhly, and Papasavvas 2004; Koehl 2016, 117–118. The figures are not obviously naked on either the runner's ring or the Sybrita krater.

[157] Koehl 2016.   [158] See also Stewart 1997, 140; Scanlon 2002, 75–76.

Beyond the detailed description provided by Ephoros, additional literary evidence for such initiatory rites include sets of antonyms present in the Archaic-period Gortyn Law code and other Cretan texts: *apagelos* ("preherder") and *agelaos* ("herd member"); *apodromos* ("pre-racer") and *dromeus* ("runner"); *skotios* ("obscure") and *kleinos* ("renowned").[159] These terms document the existence of a series of stages in childhood separated by liminal activities within Cretan culture at least as early as the Archaic period.[160] Additional, albeit later, epigraphic evidence for similar institutions comes from a late-third century inscription from Dreros that describes youths leaving the ritual of the *agela* as ἀγελάοι πανάζωστοι (*agelaoi panazostoi*, A 1.10), "members of an *agela*, completely naked." Additional historical evidence documents a ritual at Phaistos called the *apellai* or *ekdysia* that was probably related to initiation.[161]

An old Cretan tradition of initiation involving young men and nudity has also been connected to certain peculiarities of the historically documented Cretan Zeus cult. Classical Cretan Zeus was associated with the creation of social order, a central concern of initiatory ceremonies designed to induct notionally 'wild/untamed' children into the life of the community as mature adults.[162] The Cretan Zeus *Hetaireios* in particular was closely associated with the notion that boys grew into manhood in the wilderness under the watchful stewardship of the god.[163] In historical Crete, the initiation of young men occurred when they reached military age and involved casting off the clothing of their youth and putting on the accoutrements of the warrior, as well as an extended period of camping in the mountains and hunting. It may be that these texts represent enduring cultural memories of an early version of Cretan initiation ceremonies that involved nudity, exclusion from the community, physical contests, and the dedication of votive objects.

Some aspects of male votive figurines dedicated at sanctuaries on Crete during the transition from the LBA to the EIA support the idea that they were offered in the context of initiation rites for young male community members.[164] The earliest naked male votive figurines from Syme Viannou

---

[159] Percy 1996, 61. See also the evidence discussed in Koehl 2016.

[160] According to Cole, initiation rites in Ionia seem to have been distinct from Cretan ones, involving the offering of a lock of the boy's hair and service as an *ephebe* rather than remote isolation, hunting, and the exchange of one costume for another (Cole 1984, 233–244).

[161] Ducat 2006, 188; on the *apellai* or *ekdysia* see discussion in Willetts 1955, 120–123; Watrous 1995, 401. Koehl has connected the *agela* of Dreros to possible Minoan prototypes associated with youths attached to palatial elites, who might be depicted on LBA artifacts like the Chieftain Cup and the camp stool fresco (Koehl 2016, 108).

[162] Willetts 1962, 231–251; Verbruggen 1981, n. 45; Watrous 1995, 400.

[163] Watrous 1995, 400.

[164] For example, Watrous 1995, 400–401; it is generally agreed that most or all represent worshippers instead of deities (Byrne 1991; Prent 2005, 391).

and cave sanctuaries in the EIA often represent young naked men carrying weapons.[165] While these figurines are difficult to interpret, they are thematically and geographically connected to later material that is more forthcoming about its likely communicative meaning, for example, a series of bronze plaques that date to the seventh century and show scenes that are clearly related to youthful initiations.[166] The mountainous setting of Syme Viannou would have provided a suitable location for the kinds of ritual activities described in later texts, including hunting, seclusion, and feasting.[167] Outside of Syme Viannou, a krater from ancient Syvrita on Crete dated to the tenth century depicting several armed men dancing to the music of a lyre has been connected to preparatory ritual performances designed to ensure male readiness for warfare.[168] D'Agata has suggested that this krater is evidence for the early onset of initiation rituals for young warriors involving group dance.[169]

Although the iconographical and textual evidence for early mainland ritual initiatory practices is less robust, it does not require a great conceptual stretch to reconstruct a situation in which initiatory rites for young males were important elements of ritual practice on the mainland as well.[170] Among the earliest theorists of the early development of Greek religion, van Gennep, Jeanmaire, and Brelich all posited that primitive initiatory events formed the earliest basis for Olympic athletic contests.[171] In *Homo Necans,* Burkert reiterated the conclusions of his predecessors, asserting again that the basis for the development of athletic contests at Greek sanctuaries lay in rituals of initiation into adulthood, which were formative elements of cult at sites like Olympia and Delphi. Nagy later elaborated on Burkert's view, demonstrating the way

---

[165] Lebessi 2002, 269–282; D'Agata 2006, 405.   [166] See discussion in Prent 2005, 574–590.

[167] As noted by Koehl 2016, 108.

[168] D'Agata 2012; 2014, 77–78, fig. 3; Mikrakis 2015, 283. Training in dance and warfare likewise went hand in hand in Archaic Cyprus (Mikrakis 2017, 63):

> The intermingling of music and dance within the sphere of warfare appears to have served as a distinctive feature of social identities during the formative period of the Archaic city-kingdoms of Cyprus. The eagerness to demonstrate performing skills from the Late Cypriot IIIB onward, as manifested in a sharp increase in the production of musical scenes and the incorporation of this theme into the coroplastic repertoires, partly draws on the local tradition of music making by the ruling elite rather than by specialized performers of lower social rank.

[169] D'Agata 2014. For initiation rituals on EIA Crete and Crete in general see also Willetts 1955, 15–17, 120–123; 1962, 46–53; 1965, 112–118; Brelich 1969, 196–207; Lebessi 1991b, 103–113; Chaniotis 1996, 21, n. 83.

[170] On the importance of initiation rites at sanctuaries for the integration of social groups in the community, see de Polignac 1984, 15–92; on the long history of initiation rites in the LBA and EIA Aegean, Langdon 2007, 191.

[171] Van Gennep 1909; Jeanmaire 1939; Brelich 1962, 1969.

that the ordeal of the athlete at the festival mirrored the original experience of the initiates.[172]

Scanlon opposed this view, asserting that ancient athletic competitions and initiatory rites arose only in the Archaic period, independent of any EIA institutions, due to sociopolitical developments emerging at that time. However, his opposition to the argument that EIA initiatory rituals formed the basis of later athletic contests at rural sanctuaries was in large part grounded on the absence of such rituals in the Homeric poems. According to this argument, the absence of a prestigious footrace, age categories, and recurring festivals in Homeric poetry should be interpreted as convincing evidence for the absence of such institutions in the EIA overall and the lack of connection between initiation and contests at Panhellenic festivals.[173] However, such objections are no longer tenable in light of more recent developments in scholarly understanding of the relationship between Homer, history, and archaeology, discussed in Chapter 1. To briefly restate the central issue, the idea that Homeric texts can serve as a reliable shorthand for all EIA Aegean ritual institutions is not concordant with current understanding of the relationship between EIA society and the Homeric texts.

Aside from Scanlon's objections, historians of Greek religion are generally in agreement that the earliest activities at rural sanctuaries like Olympia and Delphi involved contests, probably running races, that were related to initiatory or liminal ritual, and that these contests represent the foundational core of the athletic contests that would later form an important part of standard Greek festival practice at sanctuaries.[174] The importance of initiatory rites involving physical contests is supported not only by back-projecting source material and institutions from later periods, but also by the apparently early presence of a racetrack at Olympia prior to the construction of permanent or monumental architecture, which has been suggested based on the spatial arrangement of the earliest wells at the site (Figure 3.11).[175]

The likelihood that liminal initiatory rituals for young people were prominent activities taking place at rural sanctuaries in the EIA mainland is also supported by the thoroughgoing presence of imagery related to coming of age rituals in EIA art, which has been treated at length by Langdon.[176] Langdon has shown that the art and visual culture of the Geometric mainland seems to be

---

[172] Burkert 1983, 84–103; Nagy 1986, 73, 77.   [173] Scanlon 2002, 69.

[174] Scanlon 2002, 64–198 reviews the evidence for and scholarship on the relationship between the foundation of early sanctuaries and initiation ceremonies for young men and women. For the probably important role of initiatory rites in Sparta from an early date, see Ducat 2006, 179–222.

[175] Mallwitz 1999, Beil. 11; cf. comments in Gauer's review (2003, 245). Earlier Mallwitz (1988, 79–109) argued against an early racecourse.

[176] Langdon 2008.

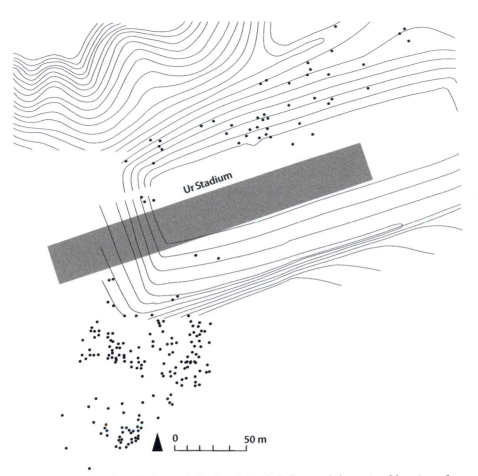

3.11. Layout of early wells (ca. 700), indicated by black dots, and the notional location of an early running track in the sanctuary at Olympia (modified from Mallwitz 1999, Beilage 11).

centered on children and adolescents. This focus extends from imagery depicting young initiates to the production of toy horses and dolls, the considerable investment in children's graves,[177] and the production of elaborate material culture designed to commemorate children's experience of the world, especially as they moved through youth's stages. Her account of the central role of liminal rites in structuring community relations and social roles is convincing and richly supported by the archaeological and iconographical evidence. There is indeed a surprising quantity of material evidence related to the rites of passages associated with children coming of age in EIA Greece.[178] Among the vestiges of such rituals in the archaeological record related to the maturation of young men are, in addition to the figurines under study here, a series of masks from Tiryns and Mycenae. While the function of

[177] Houby-Nielsen 2000.   [178] Langdon 2007, 174–191.

these masks cannot be determined with certainty, Jameson suggested they were involved in a coming of age ritual in which masked boys fought with a sickle.[179] Similar masks from the sanctuary of Artemis Orthia at Sparta and dated to approximately 650 may have been used for a similar ritual.[180]

Another EIA motif that may pertain to the initiation of young men in the wilderness are centaurs. Two LG bronze tripod handle groups from Olympia depict men and centaurs,[181] bronze centaur figurines have been recovered from votive deposits at Olympia[182] and Phigaleia,[183] a large centaur figurine was found in two pieces from two separate tombs at Lefkandi,[184] and centaurs often appear in Geometric vase-paintings.[185] Langdon's interpretation of the meaning of the centaurs in EIA art and material culture draws on the mythologically attested role of the centaur as a trainer of young heroes, which role made the centaur a suitable iconographic correlate for ritual contexts in which the rearing and development of young men played a central role.

In general, Langdon argued that the social institutions we can observe in the material record of mainland Greece in the EIA are often connected to "ritual occasions, in which a community reaffirms its roles and values, offer critical opportunities for introducing systemic change by building hierarchies of class, age, and gender."[186] While patterns in the evidence suggests a new focus on such institutions on the mainland in the EIA, such institutions are likely to have existed already in the later phases of the LBA on Crete, as discussed above.

CONCLUSIONS

Taken together, then, a preponderance of evidence suggests two conclusions about the chronological and regional development of ideas and practices involving ritual, perhaps athletic, nudity in EIA Greece. First, regional patterns in both figurine deposition and iconography indicate that such ideas and practices were primarily present on Crete and in a few mainland sanctuaries

---

[179] Jameson 1990; Langdon 2007, 175.

[180] It is interesting to note that, much like the evidence for early initiatory nudity, these masks seem to be a mainly Peloponnesian phenomenon. In this light, the presence of a small clay figurine of a naked boy with a mask over his face in the earliest layers of the sanctuary of Zeus at Nemea is of interest, though it seems to date to the sixth century (Miller 2002, 242, fig. 4).

[181] Athens National Archaeological Museum Inv. No. 6179 and Paris Louvre Museum Inv. No. C 7286 (Langdon 2007, 181–182).

[182] Langdon 1984, 202, no. C73.   [183] Langdon 1984, 202–203, no. C152.

[184] For a bronze votive centaur from Syme Viannou, see Lebessi 1996, pl. 53c. Centaurs also appear in the archaeological record at Nemea and Athens, although they postdate the EIA (Miller 2002, 244, figs. 16, 18).

[185] Langdon 2008, 95–109.   [186] Langdon 2007, 173.

during the EIA. Second, there is a strong case to be made that the establishment of rural festivals centered on initiation rites and animal sacrifice at Olympia and Delphi, and perhaps other Peloponnesian sanctuaries, was somehow connected to Cretan influence.

An interesting methodological point raised by these conclusions is the potential for even the relatively scarce and gappy archaeological evidence available for the EIA to clarify aspects of the historical record that have proven perplexing to scholars dealing primarily with textual sources. Many ancient textual sources generally point to an early, possibly even Bronze Age, Cretan influence on both ritual and athletic festivals at Olympia and Delphi and the origins of nude initiatory rituals with some homoerotic component.[187]

I have already mentioned Plato's comments to the effect that the Cretans were the first to practice athletic nudity in Chapter 1. Other literary sources from the Classical period onward tie the history of both Olympia and Delphi to Crete. According to one version of the story of the origin of the Olympic games, Herakles, the oldest of the Daktyls from Cretan Ida, came to Olympia and set up a race for his brothers, the prize for which was an olive crown.[188] The presence of an altar supposedly set up by the Cretan Clymenus to Idaean Herakles and the Kouretes and the shrines of Eileithyia and Sosipolis attest to the enduring presence of Cretan connections at the sanctuary.[189] Finally, there was reportedly an Idaean Cave at Olympia where Cretan rituals took place in the Classical period.[190] Regarding Delphi, the Homeric Hymn to Apollo recounts a story in which the god waylays a boat full of Cretans and coopts them into forming the original priesthood of his sanctuary at Delphi.[191] According to the story, Apollo travels a great distant around the Aegean searching for a place to found his new sanctuary, and eventually is advised to choose the mountainous dell near Chryse (partly because chariots will not

---

[187] The evidence was originally reviewed by Bethe 1907, 441, 444; followed by Percy 1996. Sixth-century inscriptions from Thera relating Apollo Delphinios, cults of initiation, and intimate relationships, may be relevant in this context as well (Bethe 1907, 449–453; Jeanmaire 1939, 456–460; Bremmer 1980, 283).

[188] Paus. 5.7.4.   [189] Paus. 5.8.1; 6.20.3.

[190] Pindar *Ol.* 5.20. There is considerable evidence to suggest that the manifestation of Zeus worshipped on Classical Crete was associated with older cults related to mountaintops and peak sanctuaries (Cook 1925, 117–186; Verbruggen 1981).

[191] *Hymn. Hom. Ap.* 388–544:

> Then Phoebus Apollo pondered in his heart what men he should bring in to be his minsters in sacrifice and to serve him in rocky Pytho. And while he considered this, he became aware of a swift ship upon the wine-like sea in which were many man and goodly, Cretans from Knossos, the city of Minos, they who do sacrifice to the prince and announce his decrees, whatsoever Phoebus Apollo, bearer of the golden blade, speaks in answer from his laurel tree below the dells of Parnassus. These men were sailing in their ship for traffic and for profit to sandy Pylos... (trans. Evelyn-White).

come there to annoy him and steal his spotlight with their loud noises and magnificent displays).[192] He then happens upon a boat of Cretan sailors heading to Pylos to do business, and, flopping onto the deck in the guise of a dolphin, redirects the ship to the harbor below the sanctuary, joins the sailors in a feast, and breaks the news to them that they will never return home, but must stay and attend to the sacred rites at the Delphinion. Later, when Apollo slays Python, he must go to Crete to purify himself.[193]

Several myths also attribute the origin of organized pederasty, which may have been related to the initiation rites associated with early physical contests, to behavior inspired by the acts of male divinities who abduct or take young lovers; most of these relationships are either consummated on Crete or involve Cretans.[194] According to Aristotle (*Pol.* 1272a), the Dorians in Crete institutionalized pederasty as a means of population control.[195] Other writers who link institutional pederasty with the Cretans include Timaeus of Taormina, writing around 300, who states that "The practice...came into Greece from the Cretans first."[196]

Despite these several textual sources gesturing toward Crete as an important point of origin for the development of institutions surrounding nude athletics, ancient historians writing on the history of the complex nexus between education, initiation, pederasty, and nudity in the Archaic Greek world have been skeptical of the connection between early Cretan society and early mainland ritual and community institutions for various reasons.[197] However, the analysis presented here suggests that these textual attestations actually represent quite accurately the direction of influence that is evident in the material record.

Thus, by first setting aside prior assumptions based on some texts (Thucydides, Homer), and focusing solely on the archaeological record, we may reach a point of clarity that turns our attention to and provides support for the potential veracity of a separate, less canonical set of textual sources (Ephoros, Homeric Hymns, Timaeus). This reverses the usual model of classical archaeology, in which texts are used to prove or disprove material

---

[192] On chariots and Apollo's sanctuary, see *Hymn. Hom. Ap.* 229–240:

> And further still you went, O far-shooting Apollo, and came to Onchestus, Poseidon's bright grove: there the new-broken colt distressed with drawing the trim chariot gets spirit again, and the skilled driver springs from his car and goes on his way. Then the horses for a while rattle the empty car, being rid of guidance; and if they break the chariot in the woody grove, men look after the horses, but tilt the chariot and leave it there; for this was the rite from the very first. And the drivers pray to the lord of the shrine; but the chariot falls to the lot of the god. (trans. Evelyn-White).

[193] Paus. 3.7.7.   [194] Percy 1996, 61.   [195] Sallares 1991, 169–171.   [196] Ath. 13.602.
[197] For example, Scanlon 2002, 74, 96, 360–361, n. 48; Lear 2013, 253.

from the archaeological record, to flesh out vestigial evidence, or to provide a narrative structure in which to frame material evidence.

In general, there is an irony at play in the EIA archaeology of Greece that the material presented in this chapter highlights. On the one hand, the period is often viewed as a time of stagnation and poverty which society muddled through between peaks of innovation and prosperity in the Late Bronze and Archaic periods. On the other hand, the archaeological record from the EIA demonstrates that all sorts of entirely new solutions to social problems were being developed in this period. From the adoption and development of ironworking technology to the elaboration of many new kinds of funerary ritual, to the development of a remarkably distinctive ceramic style, novel forms of material and social practice are commonplace in this period. On the mainland, one of these novelties was the establishment of rural sanctuaries where ritual practice was conducted in remote, extra-urban locations with little evidence of prior Bronze Age ritual. The new rituals centered on two primary activities – animal sacrifice and the deposition of votive objects, including bronze figurines – in open air sanctuaries.

It is generally agreed that this set of new material realities must align with the adoption of a new form of social practice revolving around liminal initiatory rites. Here, I suggest that such rites on the mainland were begun under some kind of Cretan influence. The evidence for this includes formal and iconographic similarities between the material correlates of worship at rural sanctuaries on the mainland and on Crete, especially the shared presence of ash layers, solid cast bronze naked male figurines, and animal figurines, especially bulls. The likely prominence of initiatory rituals at Cretan and select early ritual sites on the EIA mainland, further supports a situation in which there may have been a strong connection between the early establishment of ritual space at a few mainland sanctuaries and previous traditions on Crete. Such traditions are quite limited in their distribution, and cannot be said to represent any kind of unified 'Greek' approach to ritual practice in the EIA, but seem to have been characteristic of particular places, especially Olympia and Delphi.[198]

---

[198] On the likelihood that regional variation and rapid change through time was characteristic of ritual practice in the LBA as well, see discussion in Renfrew 1981.

CHAPTER FOUR

THE LOST WAX METHOD OF PRODUCTION OF EIA BRONZE FIGURINES

The votive deposition of naked bronze male figurines and the adoption of actual naked activities in ritual contexts probably cohere as elements of a set of social and ritual practices that were novel in the Aegean during the EIA. In this chapter, I make a case that this ritual system cannot be understood in the absence of an extended consideration of its material underpinnings, specifically the material realities entailed in the production of bronze votives, with a focus on the figurines with which I am concerned in this book.

As I discussed in Chapter 3, the case for a Cretan influence on the production of bronze votive figurines at mainland sites in the EIA has been made based on the aesthetic and formal characteristics of the figurines, that is, from an art historical perspective. A Cretan influence is also suggested by circumstantial evidence surrounding the appearance of the type in the context of initiatory rituals at extra-urban sanctuaries embedded in striking natural landscapes. The case for a Cretan influence based on these formal and circumstantial factors alone is relatively compelling. In this chapter, I argue that such a case can be bolstered by a consideration of the craft processes used to make bronze figurines. This perspective is also beneficial because it brings into focus some important factors underlying the physical particularities of the figurines.

The contribution of this chapter is therefore to layer a consideration of the methods and techniques of manufacturing bronze figurines over a discussion of material that has mainly been evaluated on formal and aesthetic grounds.[1] This discussion is valuable for three reasons. First, detailed evidence for production processes, including the kinds of manufacturing flaws and mistakes that are commonly evident in EIA votive figurines, lends additional support to the case for a connection between Cretan and mainland bronze figurines. The implication is that the appearance of bronze figurines on the mainland does not only represent the transfer of an iconographical and artefactual type, but also of technological knowledge. Taken together with the iconographical and formal arguments already advanced by other scholars, this evidence presents a very strong case for the fact that the idea of dedicating small cast bronze votives at EIA sanctuaries on the mainland was both preceded and decisively influenced by Cretan ritual practice.

Second, understanding the nature of the production process contributes to an enhanced understanding of the idiosyncratic characteristics of the figurines. Many of these characteristics, including miniature scale and maximal individual variation, flow naturally from the limitations of the direct method of lost-wax casting by which they were produced. For example, solid bronze figurines generally cannot be produced at large scales, which explains why the figurines are often so tiny, and the roughness of the surfaces and incompleteness of some casts can be attributed to challenges encountered while pouring molten metal.

Third, looking at the assemblage, with the process of bronze casting in mind, encourages an original conclusion about bronze figurines' meaning and value in the context of EIA sanctuaries. The manufactory characteristics of the figurines indicate that the people who made them were almost certainly not trying to make naturalistic or aesthetically pleasing finished objects for visual consumption. Based on this observation, I suggest that the likely value of the figurines in the context of ritual practice did not reside in their physical appearance, but in the transformative power of the pyrotechnological process of metal casting which brought them into existence. This conclusion should lead us to reinterpret the purpose and meaning behind the earliest figurines from EIA sanctuaries in ways that are unrelated to normal narratives of Greek history and art history.

---

[1] Byrne (1991) argues that Cretan figurines had a decisive influence on mainland ones, but does not discuss the technology of bronze production. Lebessi (2002) makes a strong case for Cretan influence and also discusses technical characteristics, but she does not bring the two lines of argument together to link the evidence of the production process to her case for a decisive Cretan influence on mainland figurines. Heilmeyer discusses the technologies required for manufacture of the Olympia figurines but does not address the Cretan evidence, instead suggesting that the inspiration to make cast bronze figurines came from a regional tradition of sculpture in wood and ivory that he speculates may have been common in the EIA (Heilmeyer 1969, 29).

Consideration of the social and technological processes of production is therefore triply useful. It takes us from the study of objects themselves to an appreciation of the capabilities and technical knowledge of the people that made them. It also opens up novel intellectual space in which to reconsider the sociopolitical structures that may have been related to metallurgical production and the ritual deposition of votives. This consideration provides an intellectual bridge between the observation that a Cretan form of material and visual culture seems to have been adopted at mainland sanctuaries and a new reconstruction of social and technological reality that might cause us to think differently about the nature of ritual and the function of naked figurines the EIA Aegean.

Part of my goal in this book is to show how setting aside preconceptions about EIA archaeology and society, and thinking through archaeological contexts without reference to earlier or later periods for which evidence is perhaps more abundant, can open up complicated and rich new landscapes of interpretation. Putting this exercise in reframing to work in this chapter, I offer an extended consideration of the material realities that must have attended the inclusion of bronze votive figurines in EIA ritual at rural sanctuaries. I first review the likely processes involved in making bronze figurines and, in dialogue with the physical details of EIA figurines, connect their features with the technicalities of production. I show that the art historical case for Cretan influence on the development of a mainland tradition of figurine production is strengthened by a consideration of the processes required for the production of cast bronze objects. Finally, I reinterpret the meaning, appearance, and social value of the figurines with the technology of their production in mind. Following this, in Chapter 5, I put the ritual implications of the process of making figurines into a Mediterranean and broader human context, then proceed to reinterpret the value and meaning of bronze working and naked bronze figurines in EIA sanctuaries.

MAKING BRONZE FIGURINES

It is necessary to preface inspection of EIA figurines with a description of the technology and expertise that would have been required to produce them, because it is impossible to appreciate the objects and their makers in the absence of at least some knowledge about the casting process. EIA bronze figurines were made by the direct method of lost-wax or investment casting, a technique that allows the creation of a precise replica of a wax object through metal casting.[2] In this process, a figure is formed out of wax, appended to

---

[2] Lapatin 2014, 225. For discussions of the lost-wax casting method in the ancient
Mediterranean and Aegean, see Lucas and Harris 1962, 211–217; Mattusch 1975; Gehrig 1979,

which are pouring channels and a funnel (known as gate and door systems). The wax model is coated in a refractory matrix (the investment) that is resistant to very high temperatures and can reproduce all of the elements present in the model, then heated in a furnace so that the wax melts out of the form, leaving a negative impression of the wax figure. Molten metal is subsequently poured into this mold and allowed to cool, after which the mold is broken to release the casting and the metal cleaned and finished.

Among the benefits of this method of casting is that it allows a wide range of designs to be implemented, including shapes with dramatic undercuts and complex curves that would be very difficult to render in metal using other techniques.[3] Unlike clay, wax does not need to be worked while wet, so that the artist need not worry about the material drying out and cracking during the modeling process.[4] Wax requires very little special equipment to work, and working with it creates less of a mess than working with clay. Moreover, the use of hard wax as a modelling material ensures that details can be sharply rendered and extremely thin sections created without sacrificing strength.[5] Bronze's material characteristics make it sensitive to detail, so that bronzes that are cast properly will accurately mimic every nuance of the wax mold.[6] Metalworkers in the LG and Archaic periods also made larger bronze artworks out of hammered sheet bronze instead of casts; they would eventually develop more elaborate and very sophisticated methods for lost wax casting, including indirect casting and large-scale casting from models with a hollow core, but the bronze figurines dealt with in this book were made by the simplest version of lost wax casting, which produces a solid metal object.[7]

547–550; Seeden 1980, 34–39; Moorey and Fleming 1984, 81–82; Bol 1985, 18–29; Verlinden 1986, 41–52; Haynes 1992, 24–56; Thomas 1992, 14–20.

[3] Smith 1981, 134.   [4] Thomas 1995, 33.

[5] Beeley and Smart 1995, 16. It is also possible to create casts that replicate models made from other sorts of organic or easily combustible materials like light wood, fabric, or flowers, which will incinerate under similar conditions as those used to melt the wax out of the mold. There are some examples of ancient Greek bronzes that were probably made using this method, for example the bronze bay leaves dedicated at the Archaic temple of Apollo in Kerkyra (Kalligas 1968: 309–13; 1969: 54–55).

[6] Feinberg 1983, 9; Thomas 1995, 7.

[7] For the most part, bronze figurines that date prior to the seventh century are cast solidly, with very few, seemingly experimental exceptions from the Minoan Bronze Age, on which see Lebessi 2002, 159–160. One figurine from Syme Viannou was also cast in two pieces and joined together with tenons, but this is an exception among EIA bronze figurines (Lebessi 2002, 122–125). There are many advantages to working with a hollow mold rather than a solid one, among the foremost of which is that it requires much less metal per unit area; it also allows for the creation of much larger casts. The body of scholarship on the development of technology for indirect lost-wax casting over a hollow core to produce large-scale sculpture in bronze in Greece is voluminous; some includes Mattusch 1988; Haynes 1992; Hemingway 2000.

The lost-wax process of casting figurines was known among ancient Mesopotamian craftspeople by the early stages of the second millennium.[8] The discovery that molten metal would easily adopt the characteristics of any surface against which it solidified probably must have followed relatively rapidly after bronze metallurgy began, and it is not difficult to imagine that casting bronze objects in molds was adopted as a matter of craft practice in such circumstances.[9]

The earliest and simplest molds for metals were stone or clay open and bivalve molds, which were often used to make weapons in prehistory.[10] Eventually, however, collaborations between ceramicists (with their sophisticated knowledge of refractory materials) and metallurgists produced the more elaborate technique of lost wax, which eliminated the mold joints that resulted from older methods.[11] Examples of cast bronze figurines from the Middle Bronze Age are known from a number of sites in the Levant and Cyprus, including Byblos, Nahariya, and Tell el-Hayyat.[12] By the fourteenth century, the technique was commonly used to produce human figures in Egypt and throughout the Levant. Late Bronze Age casting practices are especially illuminated by finds from sites like Akko, Tell Nami, and Timna.[13] Above all, Cyprus has produced a great deal of evidence for bronze casting technologies, including the production of ritual figurines. In an Aegean context, lost wax casting is first practiced on Crete in the Middle Bronze Age[14] and on the mainland starting in the tenth century, although the historical Greek textual tradition argues that bronze casting in the Aegean was invented by Samians in the seventh century.[15]

[8] Smith 1981, 134; Bianchi 1990, 61; Beeley and Smart 1995, 14–18; Ali Khan, Sheikh, and Al-Shaer 2017, 2.

[9] Smith 1981, 127.

[10] Smith 1981, 128; Ali Khan, Sheikh, and Al-Shaer 2017, 2. Most evidence for Bronze Age metal production in the Aegean suggests that this was the main technology used for casts with the exception of Minoan ritual figurines that must have been made using the lost-wax method. For example, at the LBA site of Poros-Katsambas numerous bivalve molds were found, to the exclusion of investments for or detritus (e.g., discarded gate systems, miscast objects) from lost-wax casting (Dimopoulou 2012, 136–137). On evidence for metal production in the form of specialized tools, molds, and other materials from the LBA, see Blackwell 2018, 528; 2020. The manufacturing technique for various Bronze Age tool types is discussed in Evely 1993.

[11] Smith 1981, 134.

[12] Dothan 1956, 21–22; Dunand 1958, 651, 805, 846–847; Homès Fredericq, and Hennessey 1989, 257–259.

[13] Beeley and Smart 1995, 18; Dardaillon 2012, 175.   [14] Bol 1985, 19; Thomas 1992, 39–49.

[15] Pausanias (8.14.5–8) comments on the invention of bronze sculpture in Greece; see discussion in Kyrieleis 1990, 15.

THE PROCESS OF LOST WAX CASTING: PROCEDURES AND POTENTIAL PROBLEMS

While the process of direct lost wax casting was therefore not a novel technology at the time it was used to make EIA bronze figurines, and while it is elegantly simple in principal, it was new to the Greek mainland in the EIA. In order to understand some of the flaws apparent in the EIA figurines under study here, it is important to emphasize the variety of skills and technologies that would have gone into making them. The need for skill and expertise is made most evident by a relatively thorough consideration of the stages of the production of a lost-wax cast and the many potential pitfalls therein. A great deal of labor is involved in casting, and considerable expertise in the control of thermodynamics is needed to produce a successful outcome.

The Wax Model

The first and often decisive step for any craft process is identifying and selecting the correct raw materials. In the case of bronze casting, the main materials required would have been (a) wax, (b) clay and dung for building the investiture, (c) wood or charcoal for firing, and (d) metal, either in the form of ores to be smelted into bronze or pre-prepared metal in the form of scrap or ingots to be melted down in a furnace.

Selecting an appropriate material in which to model figurines would have required the artisan to have a sense of the material desiderata that would result in an optimal outcome of the modeling. An optimal modeling wax should be firm enough to hold its shape but pliable enough so that it may be worked with hands or simple tools, and it should melt at about the same temperature at which water boils. It should have a relatively poor memory, so that when modeled a certain way it will not seek to return to its former position, and should not expand more than 8–10% in volume when heated. Most importantly, the artist must be sure to use a wax that will melt out of the mold completely, leaving no traces behind; if there is wax left over in the mold after the burn-out the resulting casting will be porous and incomplete because of gases produced by the interaction of the wax and the molten metal.[16]

It is logical to presume that the wax used in ancient bronze production was beeswax, although modern casters tend to supplement such wax with additives like paraffin and petroleum to optimize its properties for casting.[17] In an

---

[16] Feinberg 1983, 13.
[17] See Noble's brief note reporting on his serendipitous discovery of two Egyptian wax models dated to about 600 in "a box of oddments in a dealer's shop" (Noble 1975). The models were made of pure beeswax containing only 1% of other substances (Noble 1975, 369).

ancient context, it is plausible that artisans may have modified beeswax with locally available materials like tree resins or tallow rendered from animal fat along similar lines.[18] However, even when the founder uses pure beeswax, a considerable amount of processing is required to bring this material to a state of suitability for modeling. Beeswax in its natural state will contain all kinds of solid matter, including but not limited to dead bees and dirt. This material needs to be removed or filtered.[19] Moreover, when beeswax is melted down it tends to be transparent, which is not optimal for the artist wishing to see the model clearly during the production process.[20] In modern workshops the wax is melted with warm water and kneaded, which results in a wax matrix that is essentially opaque and thus easier to work with.[21]

Once the wax is prepared, there are multiple approaches available to the artist creating the model. One approach is to carve a model out of a solid block of wax, using a process and tools strongly analogous to those expedient for carving a block of wood, a purely subtractive rather than additive process.[22] Alternatively, the sculptor can construct the model by cutting wax into pieces, rolling or bending these into shape, and then heating the wax to join the separate parts into one model.[23]

Additional details can likewise be elaborated using either an additive (joining units of wax to the model usually by slightly heating them first) or subtractive (incising or applying a mold) process.[24] If the model is to be solid cast, as in the case of the EIA figurines, an important consideration is that no section of the model should be greater than 2.5 cm in diameter. Attempts to cast solid bronzes that are greater than this thickness will result in a great deal of porosity in the surface of the final object because of the way in which thick bronze cools down.[25] Moreover, solid-cast bronzes are extremely heavy, so casting a large statue from solid bronze would impose serious constraints on the possibilities available to the designer.

After the model is completed, further waxwork is required in the form of the so-called running-up process, in which a system of wax rods that will allow

The Athena Promachos building accounts may include a mention of wax, but the word can only be restored in the text once, and then uncertainly (Dinsmoor 1921).

[18] Cavanagh 1990, 148. Lebessi (2002, 165–166) attributes change in the style of figurines after the end of the Minoan period to a change in the medium of modeling from soft to hard wax, suggesting that ancient wax preparations could have differed from period to period.

[19] Noble suspects that the wax of his Egyptian models was likewise warmed, strained, and kneaded, because it was "very fine-grained and highly birefringent." (Noble 1975, 369).

[20] Haynes 1992, 31, n. 2.

[21] Feinberg 2010, 12. This is the process used in the experiment described in Willer 2007.

[22] Thomas 1995, 37. Raven-Hart (1958) argued that this was the primary technique used by EIA artists, but it is not necessary to be prescriptive, as the figures in question are highly diverse.

[23] Thomas 1995, 39.   [24] Sapouna-Sakellarakis 1995, 100; Thomas 1995, 37–41, 85–91.

[25] Haynes 1992, 24–25, 31, n. 4; Thomas 1995, 7, 37.

the molten metal to flow into the mold is appended to one or more smooth surfaces (i.e., surfaces without detail) of the model. Thicker rods, called runners or jets, provide the channels through which to introduce molten metal, while thinner rods, risers or vents, allow gas and air to escape the mold during the metal pouring process.[26] A filling cup (sprue cup) to allow the molten metal to enter the system is appended. While one point of influx is typically sufficient for simple models, additional wax runners might need to be formed in order to ensure that the metal flows smoothly and completely to areas of the casting that have restricted access to its main body or other tricky areas to which the metal might not naturally flow due to gravity.[27] An important consideration is the need to minimize turbulence in the molten metal, which can happen if it is forced to change direction rapidly during the pour; a turbulent flow will introduce bubbles and thus porosity in the resulting solid bronze. If sufficient risers are not introduced in the model, gases will not be able to escape the mold and will either expand explosively, blowing the entire thing to pieces, or introduce turbulence to the bronze, which will, again, compromise the surface quality of the final product.[28] In modern foundries, a unique running-up system is designed for each sculpture to be cast, and the design process requires a certain amount of ingenuity, experience, and expertise with the casting process.[29]

The Investment Mold and Burnout

Of equal importance is the selection and mixing of the material used to form the investment, the material packed around the wax model that will be baked into a mold. As stated above, the key characteristics of the investment are that it can withstand high temperatures (specifically temperatures greater than 1000°C) and undergo extremes of heating and cooling without cracking or breaking, at the same time reproducing a smooth surface that retains all of the features of the wax model.[30] It is almost certain that the investment in an ancient Greek context would have been composed of clay mixed with some other materials, but pure clay is unlikely to have been suitably sturdy to withstand the shock of encounters with molten metal or knocking about during the casting process.[31] In modern nonindustrial workshops dung, ash, and charcoal are the most common additives to clay investment coatings, and these common materials would likewise have been available to ancient metalworkers experimenting with different recipes for investment material.[32] Modern foundries often use sand as a matrix for lost-wax molds, but the sands

[26] Mattusch 1975, 3; Haynes 1992, 26; Thomas 1995, 97. [27] Feinberg 2010, 21.
[28] Willer 2007, 50. [29] Thomas 1995, 97. [30] Thomas 1995, 98.
[31] Cavanagh 1990, 151. [32] Feinberg 1983, 23–24.

in Greece, which are mostly made of limestone particles rather than silicate ones, are not thermally stable enough to accommodate molten metal.[33]

In order to ensure a smooth surface on the finished metal cast while also generating a mold that is sturdy, the investment should have multiple layers or components. The first layer, added directly to the wax model, should be composed of fine rather than coarse clay, ideally mixed with dung, and carefully applied so that it hews precisely to the details in the wax.[34] Any pockets of air or cracks in the investment material will be opened up during firing and reproduced in the bronze, resulting in imperfections known as 'potatoes' (lumps) and 'feathers' (flashing marks).[35] Once the initial coat has dried, coarser and thus stronger layers of investment could be added to the model to complete the mold.[36]

After the investment has been added, the mold needs to be dried out thoroughly and slowly, to prevent cracks due to uneven shrinkage of its inner and outer parts.[37] The part of the investment material covering the wax funnel that will become the point of egress for melted wax and ingress of molten metal must be scraped off. The next step is to heat the investment containing the wax model to both melt out the wax and harden the mold in preparation for the introduction of molten metal. This process does not need to take place in a special facility: the fire can be lit in a simple pit, with the fire made over or around the mold.[38] Nonetheless, the burnout stage requires delicate mastery of pyrotechnics in order to produce the correct heating environment, since cracks in the shell can result from exposure to improper conditions during the dewaxing process.[39] The optimal firing of the mold probably varied quite a bit according to the precise characteristics of the clay being used. According to modern burnout manuals, the process should ideally take place in three stages. First, the mold is heated to approximately 400°C, a temperature that is maintained for approximately eighteen hours. A second stage of firing, designed to eliminate volatility in the clay investment and thus produce a suitably inert mold for casting, requires higher temperatures, about 650°C, which must be maintained for approximately six hours. Finally, the temperature is reduced again to 450°C and maintained for another twelve hours or so.[40] While the wax will melt out of the mold in a matter of hours, at least a day of firing would probably have been required to remove all of the carbon

---

[33] Rostocker and Gebhard 1980, 353.
[34] Mattusch 1975, 5; Feinberg 1983, 9; Haynes 1992, 26.   [35] Thomas 1995, 98.
[36] Haynes 1992, 27.   [37] Feinberg 1983, 9; Willer 2007, 50.
[38] Feinberg 1983, 7. The use of an oven for the burnout does not affect the final product, but will increase the speed and efficiency of production.
[39] Beeley and Smart 1995, 15.   [40] Thomas 1995, 99.

deposits and all water vapor in the mold.[41] If carbon deposits or moisture are left in the mold, this will react with the molten metal when it is poured causing spitting, volatility, and porosity in the final product; in the worst case, catastrophic scenario, the entire mold can explode due to the reaction between the carbon and the metal.[42] The mold should be allowed to cool very slowly once the oven is turned off, in order to prevent cracking that results from too rapid a change in temperature. Any cracks in the mold will be reproduced in the bronze figures when they are cast, again causing characteristic surface 'feathers'.

The process of burnout would have taken a long time and required a great deal of fuel to complete. Gathering or procuring sufficient organic fuel for the duration of the firing process and competence in controlling the temperature of the fire are two aspects of lost-wax casting that are not readily apparent or discussed at length in the extant literature on these production processes, but that certainly would have impacted the artisans at work on production in nontrivial ways. One important consideration that any bronze working crew would have needed to take into account was the availability of fuel.[43] Whether incidentally or by design, the rural and often mountainous nature of early sanctuary sites would have facilitated the easy availability of organic material for the furnace. Olympia, for example, would have provided an excellent environment for metalworking from the point of view of fuel, since it is surrounded by ample forests and significant lignite deposits, which could have also been added to the furnaces.[44]

Casting and Finishing

All of the considerations discussed above precede what must have been the most technically challenging aspect of making cast bronzes – the metallurgical aspect. Bronze metallurgy entailed a number of different stages, beginning with the smelting of the raw copper ores and the production of an alloy by the addition of tin, arsenic, or other elements to pure molten copper.[45] While

[41] Cavanagh 1990, 152; Thomas 1995, 7. There is a great deal of variation in published prescriptions for the firing of the mold at the burnout stage. According to Feinberg (1983, 10), good results could be achieved with 800°C temperatures applied for only 4–6 hours.

[42] Mattusch 1975, 6; Cavanagh 1990, 151.

[43] Wertime 1983, 447. An inscription from the Classical period detailing the production of the bronze statue of Athena Promachos on the acropolis mentions the need for coal and firewood repeatedly (Dinsmoor 1921).

[44] Bol 1985, 23. Other natural resources especially available at Olympia might have been wax, since beekeeping was more common in rural areas, and the clayey loam of the Olympia valley system, which would have been optimal for mixing a suitable investment jacket for casting.

[45] For a review of the material processes required for smelting and alloying copper see Rehder 2000, 113–121.

there is considerable evidence that bronze figurines were *cast* at many early Greek sanctuaries (see Chapter 5), the evidence that the copper and alloys that composed them were actually smelted from the raw ores and alloyed in these contexts during the EIA is ambiguous. The presence of slags that suggest smelting has been documented at some sites, but at others the only evidence of bronze casting comes in the indirect form of miscast bronzes or discarded elements of the running up system, so that it is possible to reconstruct a situation in which bronzes may have been cast, but metals not prepared from scratch on site. It seems plausible that such waste products were present in but not retained or documented from deposits excavated prior to the middle of the twentieth century, although other equipment, like crucibles and tuyéres, likely would have been.[46] Given the relatively patchy and lacunose nature of all finds related to metalworking installations at EIA sites, it is not out of the question that the entire process of metallurgical production, from smelting raw ores to casting final products, could have taken place at such sites in ways that are no longer evident in the archaeological record. However, on current evidence it is not possible to reach a certain conclusion on this question.

If ore were being smelted from scratch at EIA sanctuaries, the most likely method used would have been what is known as the carbothermic smelting process, in which ore is pulverized and mixed with a flux (usually a silicate, which bonds with impurities in the ore to produce slag) and charcoal, then heated to $1100-1400°C$. Because of the addition of the flux, this mixture can be smelted in a biomass-fueled open-draft environment (ore without such a mixture cannot be smelted in this kind of oxidizing atmosphere).[47] However, such a process requires that ore be heated in a crucible, because it will result in the production of molten copper under a layer of molten slag, which needs to be sloughed off before the copper can be used. The fact that very few crucibles clearly datable to the EIA have been discovered at sanctuary sites suggests that smelting probably did not occur locally.[48] Moreover, the highly variable range

---

[46] Mattusch (1975, 185) notes "bronze left over from crucibles of various sizes, with some flat-bottomed pieces and some hemispherical pieces" in the storerooms of Olympia, but given that most of the evidence for bronze production at the site postdates the Geometric period, it seems most likely that this material does, too.

[47] Rehder 2000, 104.

[48] On the process of smelting copper and alloying it with tin, Mattusch 1975, 60; Rehder 2000, 107–108. Querns found at EIA sites with other evidence of metalworking might indicate people were processing ores locally. See Rehder's comments (2000, 108):

> For copper, this could have been either in several crucibles on the hearth of a kiln or in a vertical biomass fueled natural draft furnace holding a single crucible. This could explain two seemingly unrelated archaeological puzzles. One is the many cases – worldwide but particularly documented in the eastern Mediterranean and Near East – where there are fields of slag of considerable amount, a notable example being Cyprus, but only minor evidence of furnaces or tuyéres. This could be understandable if pottery kilns or similar structures

of alloys present in the bronzes from the sanctuaries suggests that the molten metal being cast may have been a mixture of various lots of scrap metal.[49] Thus, what we are dealing with in early Greek sanctuaries are probably best termed foundries, a specific term used for places where objects are cast from molten metal, rather than generalized smithies.

Whether metallurgists were smelting, alloying, and casting or merely casting bronze at early Greek sites, a sophisticated understanding of pyrotechnics and knowledge about controlling and manipulating high temperatures would have been necessary to produce and deploy molten metal for the casts. There is ample evidence that, from the Neolithic period onward, one of the most important technological advances made by humans was in the area of pyrotechnological competence. Ceramic kilns capable of developing temperatures in the neighborhood of 1200°C, a temperature sufficient for either smelting copper ore or remelting and alloying copper and bronze, are present in the archaeological record already in the Neolithic period.[50] By the EIA founders would have had no problem producing the heat necessary to bring copper or bronze ingots and scrap to a molten state. When bronze is being melted with fire, as it surely was in antiquity, it is important that the flame be adjusted so that it is as neutral as possible, since both reducing and oxidizing flames introduce contaminants that can alter the metal. It is especially important that the bronze remain free of hydrogen.

The founder will usually weigh the total amount of bronze to be melted in order to ensure that sufficient quantities of molten metal would result to fill the investment molds.[51] A normal rule of thumb is that ten times as much weight of metal is needed to cast as the weight of wax used in the models.[52] If a considerable quantity of metal were needed at once, for example if a number of figurines were being cast all together, it would have been expedient to heat several crucibles of metal on the flat hearth of the kiln; however, if these were heated and then removed in sequence, the temperature loss during the removal process may have resulted in variable temperatures among the batches when poured, thus producing a molten metal agglomerate of varied viscosity that would not pour into casts correctly. If metal were heated in a single mass, on the other hand, it would have been more ungainly to pour but would be more likely to produce a solid metal of uniform composition.[53] One possibility is to heat solid masses of metal in a furnace from which gravity takes molten metal through channels cut into the earth directly to molds set into sand at a

---

had been used as smelting furnaces. The other puzzle that would be elucidated is the ubiquity of querns and similar grinding stones that seem to be far in excess of need for flour milling.

[49] Heilmeyer 1979, 45. [50] Rehder 2000, 42. [51] Cavanagh 1990, 147.
[52] Mattusch 1975, 4. [53] Rehder 2000, 52–53.

lower elevation. Even in the best cases, dealing with molten metal would always and still does entail something of a risky guessing game, as there is no sure way to tell whether molten bronze has reached the optimal temperature to fill a mold correctly.[54]

Once the mold and the molten metal have been prepared, the mold is packed in a bed of sand, which helps to support the mold when the metallostatic pressure of the pour is introduced.[55] The pouring should take place while the mold is still hot (*ca.* 600°C) from the burnout process, but not directly after, when the temperature of the mold would be sufficiently hot (*ca.* 800°C) to cause the molten metal to boil.[56] Even if the mold has been made correctly, problems with the cast can be introduced during the casting phase, as the introduction of molten metal produces immense amounts of pressure on the mold. This pressure will often result in swelling in the mold and will also ensure that any defects or cracks in the interior surface of the mold will be reproduced in the surface of the hardened bronze.[57] The pour should be steady, because any kind of turbulence in the metal will (as already discussed) negatively affect the surface quality of the resulting bronze.[58] If the molten metal is not heated to the correct temperature, if the molten metal is introduced to a mold that has been allowed to cool too much after the burnout stage, or if the pouring channels, runners, and risers have been designed improperly, the molten metal may fail to flow into the entirety of the mold, resulting in hollows in the cast.[59] If any water is present in the crucible or the mold an explosion or the introduction of gaseous porosity in the metal could occur.[60]

Once the molten metal appears glowing at the top of the filling cup(s) or riser holes, the pour is complete. After about forty-five minutes, the bronze should be cool and the molds removed from their sand bed.[61] When the cooling is complete, the outer part of the investment is carefully hammered or otherwise broken off of the bronze. Generally, the softer inner layer of investment would be gently scraped or brushed off in order to prevent any damage to the surface of the sculpture.[62]

Considerable work remains to be done upon the completion of the casting. The running-up system is usually removed with a file or chisel. However, in some examples of early Greek figurines, the pouring funnel was designed so that it could also serve as the base of the figurine, and sometimes casting channels are left as flanges that could be used to insert the figurines into (presumably wooden or other perishable) bases. In such cases, the funnel would not need to be removed and discarded, reducing the amount of scrap

---

[54] Cavanagh 1990, 147.   [55] Thomas 1995, 7.   [56] Feinberg 1983, 10.
[57] Beeley and Smart 1995, 3.   [58] Thomas 1995, 99–100.   [59] Beeley and Smart 1995, 3.
[60] Feinberg 1983, 62.   [61] Thomas 1995, 100.   [62] Feinberg 1983, 8; Lapatin 2014, 226.

metal generated by each cast.[63] Usually there are casting defects that need to be repaired, for example by patching with additional molten metal or with mechanical cleaning, again with a file or a chisel (although post-casting surface treatment is not always apparent on EIA bronze figurines; see section below on "Finishing").[64] Cold-working to add details is also possible at this point.

Summary

The production of solid sculpture in bronze using the lost-wax casting method was a complex, multistep process that required considerable expertise as well as major inputs of time and energy. While the procedure sounds quite simple and elegant when described in its essence, success or failure in a casting came down to the skill of the founder.[65] The cast could be ruined or compromised at any stage, from the selection of the raw materials, to the application of pyrotechnic heat, to the final pouring of the molten metal.[66] It is also apparent that the founder responsible for producing bronze sculpture needed a wide variety of craft skills, not only those of the founder but many associated with ceramic production, because the founder needed to fashion models in a plastic art homologous to that of the coroplast and to fire molds using technical knowledge similar to that required for firing pottery. This speaks not only to the likelihood of cross-craft interaction in the EIA Aegean, but also to the unusual and impressive range of abilities that the individuals responsible for producing EIA figurines must have possessed.[67]

THE TESTIMONY OF THE FIGURINES

It is instructive to bring this granular outline of the procedures involved in lost wax casting to bear on a close inspection of the figurines from Olympia, Delphi, and Crete. An examination of the details of these artifacts demonstrates that the people who created the three sets of material probably brought similar approaches to bear on molding and casting.[68] A range of similarities amongst the figurines suggests the compelling possibility that the craftspeople involved in manufacturing all of these artifacts had a close relationship. Moreover, considering the figurines with the lost-wax casting process in mind helps us to comprehend many of their characteristics that seem highly irregular, unusual, or inexplicable upon first inspection.

---

[63] Lebessi 2002, 169.
[64] Willer 2007, 49, notes the same absence of evidence for repairs in a smiting god figurine in the Bonn museum.
[65] Papasavvas 2003, 28.   [66] Feinberg 1983, 9.   [67] Lapatin 2014, 229.
[68] See comments by Lebessi 2002, 159.

All LBA and EIA bronze figurines from Crete were made using the lost-wax casting method, and all bear material markers of the production technique that went into their manufacture. Many of the same material markers are evident in the earliest figurines from the Greek mainland. Of course, there are certain limitations to what can be achieved with the raw materials – wax, clay, metal – and the lost-wax technique, so it is not entirely necessary that the similarities I note in what follows prove direct technological influence of one community of craftspeople on the other. However, given the similarities of production evident in the treatment of the figurines, the similarities in their use context (votive deposition in extra-urban sanctuaries) and their aesthetic similarities (described in Chapter 3) it seems logical to reconstruct a situation in which the mainland bronzes resulted from at least some degree of influence from Cretan practice. I discuss similarities in the formal characteristics of the figurines according to the stages involved in lost wax casting.

The Wax Model

Bronze figurines made using the lost-wax process will most often retain the soft appearance of wax in ways that demonstrate the method by which the artist worked the original wax model.[69] Wrinkles where limbs and bodies bend reflect the characteristic response of the wax to contortion, rather than a feature inherent to metalwork.[70] A figurine may clearly have been built up and then elaborated through an additive process, where the main segments are formed by rolling wax between the fingers, while additional pieces, such as small spheres for the eyes, are appended to the main body of the figurine. This method of production is totally alien to any kind of process inherent to direct work in metal, and it is often possible to observe points at which the pressure applied to the wax during this process of construction resulted in characteristic withdrawals and contortions of material that must relate to the features of work in wax. Alternatively, the wax may be carved away in order to make features, so that details like the eyes are hollow. Forms like arms and torsos can likewise be made by carving a figure away from a larger block or chunk of wax. Features like notches suggesting facial features or the manes of horses would likewise have been cut into the wax model. Both additive and subtractive techniques are commonly used, and both are apparent in the physical characteristics of EIA figurines. (Plate 1). It appears that a flat scraping tool was often used to remove and shape wax on the torsos and arms of both Cretan and mainland figurines (Plate 2). In Minoan cast figurines, long tendrils of hair would have been produced by rolling thin strips of wax between the fingers, and then applying

---

[69] Bol 1985, 20.   [70] Papasavvas 2003, 29.

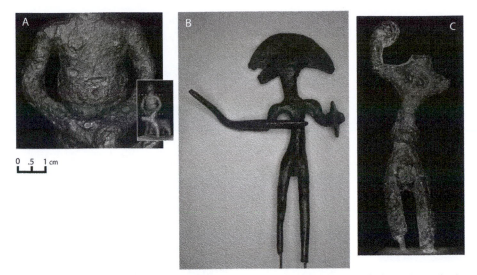

0 .5 1 cm

PLATE 1. Figurines demonstrating a range of wax modeling techniques (all photos by author): (A) Torso of a Geometric figurine of a young naked male leading a small cow from Delphi with details like belt and nipples probably built using additive technique (Delphi Archaeological Museum Inv. No. 6571; published with permission of the Delphi Archaeological Museum; © Hellenic Ministry of Culture and Sports – Hellenic Organization of Cultural Resources Development); (B) PG figurine of a warrior from Olympia built up using additive technique (Olympia Excavation Inv. No. Br 9788, Athens National Archaeological Museum Inv. No. 6096, published with permission from the National Archaeological Museum, Athens, © Hellenic Ministry of Culture and Sports/Archaeological Receipts Fund); (C) Geometric figurine, perhaps of a belted boxer, from Delphi with added details (Delphi Archaeological Museum Inv. No. 2978; published with permission of the Delphi Archaeological Museum; © Hellenic Ministry of Culture and Sports – Hellenic Organization of Cultural Resources Development) [A black and white version of this figure will appear in some formats. For the color version, please refer to the plate section.]

them to the main body of the figure.[71] A similar technique is apparent in the treatment of the lyre player from Syme Viannou, whose instrument is likewise built up out of a series of individual strands of wax (see Figure 3.1). Most early zoomorphic figurines appear to have been created in a like manner, from a series of rolled pieces of wax, and the same is probably true of the legs, arms, and other appendages of most of the early figurines from the mainland.

Investment and Burnout

EIA cast makers adopted a variety of different approaches to building the investment jackets for their casts. While the smooth surfaces of some figurines, especially Minoan (early) and Geometric (late) ones, indicate that the creators took care to assure the fineness of adherence of the investment's inner surface to the surface of the wax, the graininess of other figurines indicates that

[71] Bol 1985, 20.

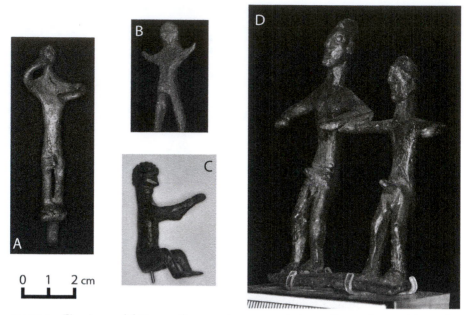

PLATE 2. Figurines exhibiting surface scraping as a technique of manufacture (photos by author): (A) Subminoan figurine of a naked male with a plank-like appearance probably resulting from a subtractive modeling technique (Heraklion Archaeological Museum Inv. No. 2960; published with permission of the Heraklion Archaeological Museum; © Hellenic Ministry of Culture and Sports – Hellenic Organization of Cultural Resources Development); (B) PG figurine modeled by scraping (Olympia Archaeological Museum Inv. No. B. 1754, permission of the Archaeological Ephorate of Elis, © Hellenic Ministry of Culture and Sports – Hellenic Organization of Cultural Resources Development); (C) Geometric figurine of a rider worked using both additive and subtractive techniques (Olympia Excavation Inv. No. Br 8131, Athens National Archaeological Museum Inv. No. 6150; published with permission from the National Archaeological Museum, Athens, © Hellenic Ministry of Culture and Sports – Hellenic Organization of Cultural Resources Development); (D) PG figurine of two naked males holding hands, with flat surfaces indicating modeling by a subtractive, scraping technique (Syme Viannou Excavation Inv. No. MH 3137; published with permission of the Heraklion Archaeological Museum; © Hellenic Ministry of Culture and Sports – Hellenic Organization of Cultural Resources Development) [A black and white version of this figure will appear in some formats. For the color version, please refer to the plate section.]

some founders applied a single, rough coat of clay for the investment (see, e.g., Plate 2A).[72] As discussed above, the firing of the investment requires careful control of pyrotechnological conditions, the poor management of which will result in lumps and cracks in the investment that will fill with bronze, yielding imperfections known as potatoes and feathers. These sorts of imperfections are common on the surfaces of both Cretan and mainland EIA bronze figurines (Plate 3).[73]

---

[72] cf. Heilmeyer 1979, 41–42.

[73] Heilmeyer 1979, 42; Bol 1985, 26. See also Willer 2007, 49, for similar issues in the surface of a statuette of a smiting god from Bonn.

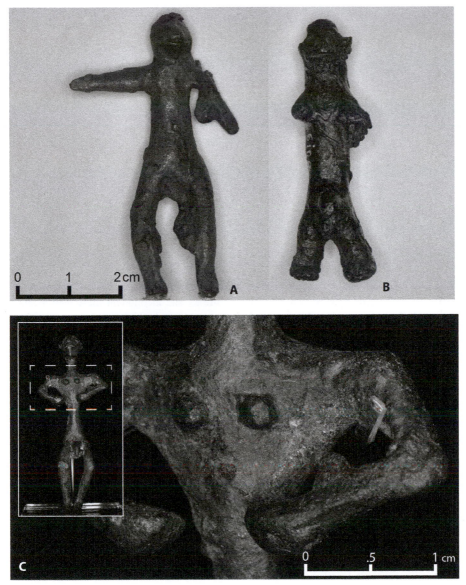

PLATE 3. Figurines with extensive flashing and/or 'potatoes' (photos by author): (A) PG humanoid figurine from Olympia showing major problems with flashing and a few potatoes (Athens National Archaeological Museum Inv. No. 6105, published with permission from the National Archaeological Museum, Athens, © Hellenic Ministry of Culture and Sports/ Archaeological Receipts Fund); (B) PG humanoid figurine from Olympia showing evidence of multiple casting issues, including flashing (Olympia Excavation Inv. No. Br 6364, Athens National Archaeological Museum Inv. No. 6100; published with permission of the National Archaeological Museum, © Hellenic Ministry of Culture and Sports – Hellenic Organization of Cultural Resources Development); (C) Detail of PG figurine from Amnisos with flashing on interior surface of akimbo arms (Heraklion Archaeological Museum Inv. No. 2316; published with permission of the Heraklion Archaeological Museum; © Hellenic Ministry of Culture and Sports – Hellenic Organization of Cultural Resources Development) [A black and white version of this figure will appear in some formats. For the color version, please refer to the plate section.]

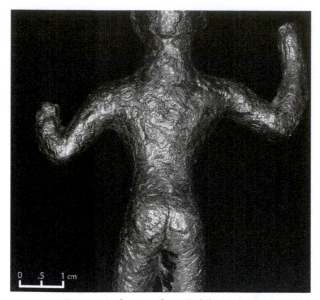

PLATE 4. Geometric figurine from Delphi with streaky and inconsistent metal alloy (Delphi Archaeological Museum Inv. No. 3649, photo by author; published with permission of the Heraklion Archaeological Museum; © Hellenic Ministry of Culture and Sports – Hellenic Organization of Cultural Resources Development) [A black and white version of this figure will appear in some formats. For the color version, please refer to the plate section.]

Casting

One striking feature of the corpus of EIA figurines on both Crete and the mainland is the wide range of colors and qualities of bronze from which they are cast. Even accounting for differences in surface treatment and modern curatorial cleaning to remove patinas, the colors of EIA bronze figurines range widely from the bright, shiny copper of a new penny to a dull greyish brown. Some figurines are not even consistent in color across their entire surface, presenting a streaky effect (Plate 4).[74] This variation in color is most likely the result of the employment of inconsistent alloys in the casting of the EIA figurines, perhaps related to the use of mixed scrap metal. Such a conclusion is supported by the results of Heilmeyer's chemical analyses, which showed that the metallographic characteristics of EIA bronze figurines were not only inconsistent from one figurine to another, but also inconsistent within individual casts (so that tests applied to different parts of the figurines yielded different results).[75] In her analytical work on Minoan bronze figurines,

---

[74] cf. Heilmeyer 1979, 45. Streakiness will result when scrap metals with different alloys are being melted together, if the metal is not heated up to a sufficient temperature to properly integrate the mixture.

[75] Heilmeyer 1979, 276–277. The tin content in the five bronzes analyzed by Heilmeyer was 4, 4, 8, 0, and 0 percent. The amount of lead in the alloy also ranged from essentially zero to nearly 1 percent.

Sapouna-Sakellarakis likewise noted this feature in Bronze Age figurines from Crete. She interpreted the data as evidence that varying mixtures of elements were employed in figurine manufacture at the behest of individual founders with greater or lesser knowledge of the casting process.[76] For example, some, but not all, of the Minoan figurines contain lead, which helps to guarantee a good casting because it increases plasticity and lubricity of the metal.[77] An interesting observation by Sapouna-Sakellarakis is that apparent skill in the preparation of the metal for casting often did not match the skillfulness of the figurine's formal execution. This phenomenon can be observed in EIA figurines generally – figurines that seem to have been cast with technical acumen do not necessarily correspond to the most aesthetically elaborate or expertly molded figurines.

This mismatch between the quality of the metalwork and the formal execution of the figure could be interpreted in a variety of ways. Sapouna-Sakellarakis suggests that the presence of well-executed figurines in poor casting alloys should attest to the skill of the metallurgists, who could create a satisfactory final product even when their access to alloying elements was suboptimal.[78] It may also be worth considering that foundries in the EIA functioned along the same lines as modern foundries do; for the most part, the sculptors who create wax models to be invested, molded, and cast in contemporary foundries are separate agents from the founders themselves. The bronze workers are paid a fee in order to produce bronze end products from wax models provided by the artists. Along the same lines, it may be that multiple individuals were involved in the production of EIA bronze figurines – the metallurgist who was responsible for casting the figure and some other individual who provided the wax model to be cast. This separation of steps along the *chaîne opératoire* might explain the disconnect between the metallurgical and formal quality of many EIA figurines, since a model made by a clumsy hand could have been turned over to an expert founder for casting, or vice versa.

The bronze surfaces of most EIA figurines contain flaws and blemishes, perhaps a testament to the many challenges that a founder would have encountered in a relatively simple and unpredictable casting environment. The metal is often full of air bubbles and blisters that could have resulted from an overly volatile pour, a poorly designed running up system, or an inadequate treatment of the investment jacket leading to gaseous reactions with carbon or moisture left in its matrix (Plate 5).[79] Sunken depressions in the bronze are also

---

[76] Sapouna-Sakellarakis 1995, 98–99.   [77] Haynes 1992, 83.

[78] Sapouna-Sakellarakis 1995, 99.

[79] Heilmeyer 1979, 46; Bol 1985, 20, 24; Sapouna-Sakellarakis 1995, 101; Lebessi 2002, 173. On Minoan figurines, Morris 2017, 670 (she attributes the flaws to low levels of tin in the alloy, but this is not compatible with Sapouna-Sakellarakis' results from metallographic analysis). Unfortunately, without the discovery of a foundry context that can be associated with these early figurines, it is impossible to say for certain how the pour would have been executed, whether from a crucible or direct from a furnace through cut earthen channels. Bol (1985, 26)

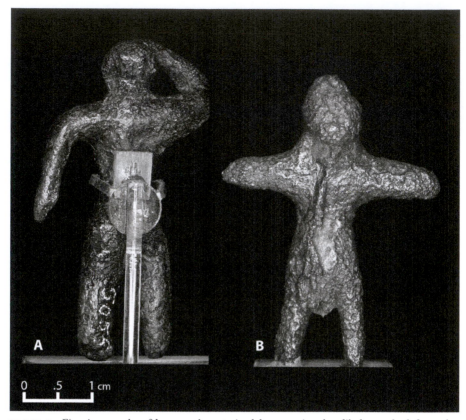

PLATE 5. Figurines made of bronze characterized by porosity that likely resulted from the presence of excessive gas in the casting environment (photos by author): (A) Rear view of an LM IIIC figurine of a saluting naked male with porosity from gaseous casting (Syme Viannou Excavation Inv. No. MH 5055; published with permission of the Heraklion Archaeological Museum; © Hellenic Ministry of Culture and Sports – Hellenic Organization of Cultural Resources Development): (B) PG anthropoid figurine from Olympia with multiple issues in the cast, including flashing and porous metal (Olympia Archaeological Museum Inv. No. B 5994, permission of the Archaeological Ephorate of Elis; © Hellenic Ministry of Culture and Sports – Hellenic Organization of Cultural Resources Development) [A black and white version of this figure will appear in some formats. For the color version, please refer to the plate section.]

common; these probably resulted from the uneven cooling and shrinkage of the bronze after the molten metal was poured. Moreover, it often seems to be the case that the pour did not reach all of the parts of the mold, so that many figurines have incomplete or missing appendages (Plate 6). Such outcomes probably resulted from either a poorly designed mold/running up system or from pouring metal that was not at the correct temperature, and therefore cooled and hardened before it could reach all of the extremities of the mold. In at least one figurine from Olympia, it is obvious that the metal cooled and

observed that there is no indication in the remaining pouring funnels on extant figurines to suggest that a channel of bronze flowed directly into them, making the use of crucibles more likely.

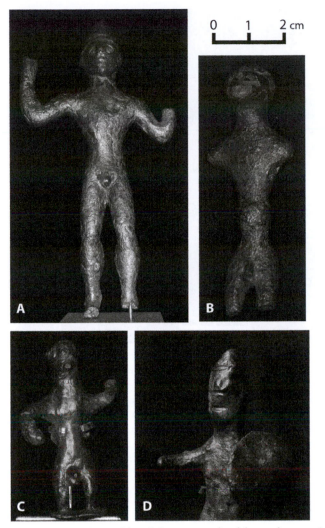

PLATE 6. Figurines with missing or poorly elaborated extremities (photos by author): (A) Geometric figurine of a standing naked male from Delphi with missing hands and feet (Delphi Archaeological Museum Inv. No. 3649; published with permission of the Delphi Archaeological Museum, © Hellenic Ministry of Culture and Sports – Hellenic Organization of Cultural Resources Development); (B) Geometric figurine of a naked, belted male missing all extremities from Delphi (Delphi Archaeological Museum Inv. No. 3240; published with permission of the Delphi Archaeological Museum, © Hellenic Ministry of Culture and Sports – Hellenic Organization of Cultural Resources Development); (C) PG figurine of a naked male with casting problems around the hands from Patso Cave (Heraklion Archaeological Museum Inv. No. 207; published with permission of the Heraklion Archaeological Museum; © Hellenic Ministry of Culture and Sports – Hellenic Organization of Cultural Resources Development); (D) PG figurine of a naked armed male from Syme Viannou with a poorly articulated right hand (Syme Viannou Excavation Inv. No. MH 4959; published with permission of the Heraklion Archaeological Museum; © Hellenic Ministry of Culture and Sports – Hellenic Organization of Cultural Resources Development) [A black and white version of this figure will appear in some formats. For the color version, please refer to the plate section.]

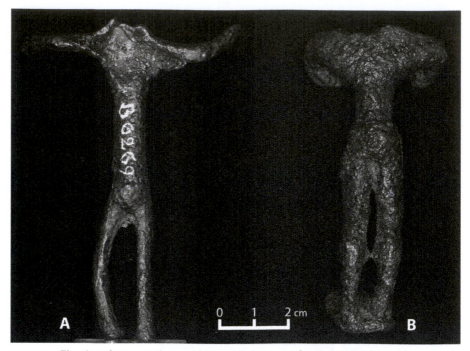

PLATE 7. Figurines demonstrating problems with the pour of molten metal (photos by author):
(A) Rear view of a PG figurine from Olympia showing problems with the casting pour
(Olympia Archaeological Museum Inv. No. B 6269, © Hellenic Ministry of Culture and
Sports – Hellenic Organization of Cultural Resources Development); (B) Rear view of a
headless Geometric figurine from Delphi, showing that the molten metal never reached the
head (Delphi Archaeological Museum Inv. No. 3976, published with permission of the Delphi
Archaeological Museum; © Hellenic Ministry of Culture and Sports – Hellenic Organization of
Cultural Resources Development) [A black and white version of this figure will appear in some
formats. For the color version, please refer to the plate section.]

became extremely brittle before the casting process was complete, resulting in
a deformed and cracked figurine missing its entire head, a problem also
encountered in the cast of a Geometric figurine from Delphi (Plate 7).

These examples notwithstanding, the most frequent structural problems with
the figurines are encountered around the hands and feet. Although at first glance it
appears that these could have been broken off after their dedication and deposition, a close inspection of the figurines suggests that, more often than not, the
extremities were absent from the cast due to problems with the manufacturing
process. The reason for this is likely that these extremities, already shaped like
runners, were often used as part of the channeling system through which the
molten bronze was introduced to the mold. If a foundry worker underestimated
the quantity of metal needed for the pour, these extremities would be the last to
fill up with molten metal, resulting in figurines that are missing their hands and
feet. In addition, carelessness in removing the pouring funnel attached to the hands
or feet might also have resulted in frequent damage to them.

An extraordinary and unique find from Olympia, probably dated to the
eighth century, demonstrates that the use of the extremities as elements of the

running up system provides a plausible explanation for persistent issues with these parts of the figurines. The find is a bronze statuette, probably intended to be a ring-handle-holder for a tripod, found still encased in its original invest-ment coating in the northern wall of the stadium in 1960.[80] The statuette was originally assumed to be made of highly corroded iron, but subsequent study in the late 1970s revealed that the gnarly exterior surface of the artifact was not iron but a fired jacket of clay, inside of which the bronze figurine was still almost fully encased.[81] An X-ray analysis of the artifact demonstrated that the investment comprised two layers of clay, a fine inner coat and a rough outer coat.[82] The reason that the figurine was never freed from its casting jacket may be that the cast went amiss at its hands, which either never poured correctly or were broken off with the pouring funnel during some kind of accident late in the casting process.[83] It is not clear why the investment was not broken off and the metal re-melted and reused. Similar accidents probably resulted in the many deformed or missing hands and feet among the corpus of EIA figurines, and a nearly identical accident probably explains the state of a figurine from Kommos, dated to the tenth/ninth century (Plate 8).[84] The fact that molten metal was sometimes introduced through the feet instead of the hands is shown by the remnant of sprues below the feet of a number of figurines, including those among the earliest from Olympia and older Minoan examples (Plate 9).

Finishing

Both Cretan and mainland figurines display a wide variety of finishing tech-niques. In some cases, it is clear that the sprues and funnels from the pour system have been filed or chiseled off, but both Cretan and mainland artists often designed the wax models so that the pouring funnel or parts of the running up system would remain to serve as part of the finished product.[85] In the case of some Minoan female figurines, the bronze was probably poured through the skirt,[86] but more often (and especially for male figures, i.e., figures without a skirt) the feet and legs served as the main point of egress for wax and ingress for molten bronze.[87] Here, the sprues from the pour were often left wholly or partly intact, perhaps in order to facilitate the insertion of the figures

---

[80] Born and Moustaka 1982; Zimmer 1990, 21–24.   [81] Born and Moustaka 1982, 17.
[82] Born and Moustaka 1982, 18; Zimmer 1990, 22.   [83] Zimmer 1990, 22.
[84] Koutroumbaki-Shaw 1987, 371–382.   [85] Sapouna-Sakellarakis 1995, 100.
[86] Sapouna-Sakellarakis 1995, 100.
[87] Sapouna-Sakellarakis 1995, 100. For figurines representing quadrupeds, the thickest parts of the animals, like the body and the nose, were used for the attachment of wax channels (Bol 1985, 25).

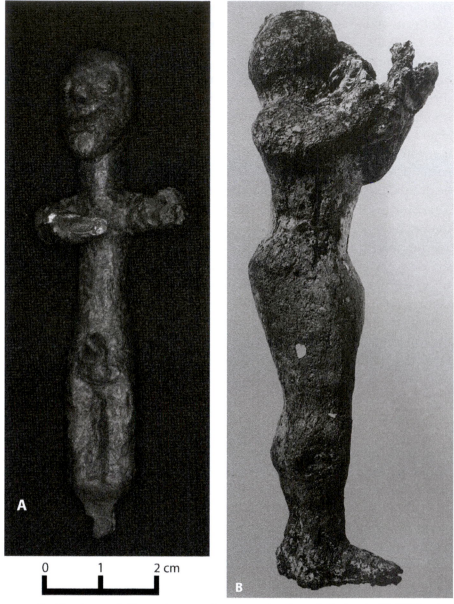

0   1   2 cm

PLATE 8. Figurines probably cast by a metal pour entering through the hands: (A) PG figurine of a naked male with damaged hands from Kommos that was originally designed to be installed in a stone plinth with a bull figurine (Heraklion Archaeological Museum Inv. No. 5416, photo by author; published with permission of the Heraklion Archaeological Museum; © Hellenic Ministry of Culture and Sports – Hellenic Organization of Cultural Resources Development); (B) Geometric figure of a flute player from Olympia still encased in the casting investment (photo courtesy of the German Archaeological Institute, D-DAI-ATH-Olympia 4877, photographer Eva-Marie Czakó) [A black and white version of this figure will appear in some formats. For the color version, please refer to the plate section.]

PLATE 9. LBA and EIA figurines with sprues attached at the feet (photos by author): (A) Minoan figurine of a worshipper on display in the Heraklion Museum; (B) PG figurine of a naked male from Olympia (Olympia Excavations Inv. No. Br 8900, Athens National Archaeological Museum Inv. No. 6249, published with permission from the National Archaeological Museum, Athens, © Hellenic Ministry of Culture and Sports/Archaeological Receipts Fund); (C) PG figurine of a naked male from Olympia (Olympia Archaeological Museum Inv. No. B 4245, permission of the Archaeological Ephorate of Elis; © Hellenic Ministry of Culture and Sports – Hellenic Organization of Cultural Resources Development) [A black and white version of this figure will appear in some formats. For the color version, please refer to the plate section.]

into wooden or stone bases, without which it is impossible for most of them to stand upright.[88]

In some cases (usually relatively late, i.e., LG) figurines, the metal has been worked or smoothed with a hammer in order to create a regular final surface finish.[89] Details, especially belts around human waists or stamps and zigzags on animal figurines, are sometimes added by cold chasing after the figurine was

---

[88] While we know that the figurines were intended to serve as votives, and later dedicatory inscriptions suggest they were personal dedications, it is difficult to reconstruct the actions involved in the dedication process, or to be certain about the way that the votives would have been displayed. Some of the lower extremities of later figurines were encased in lead, perhaps so that they could be easily installed in a wood or stone base. A small-scale figurine from Kalapodi dated to the Archaic period (see discussion in Rolley 1986, 32) and at least one EIA figurine, from Kommos, were definitely displayed in this fashion (Koutroumbaki-Shaw 1987). This might indicate that the tiny statuettes could have been on display in the sanctuary for some time after their production, although the relevance of the Kalapodi and Kommos examples for the material at Olympia and Delphi is not certain, given the very distinct find contexts. On stands attached to Minoan figurines see Morris 2017, 667.

[89] Sapouna-Sakellarakis 1995, 100.

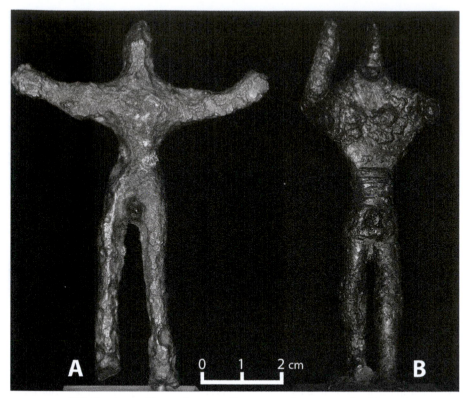

PLATE 10. EIA figurines with rough cast surfaces, suggesting an unrefined inner investment layer and lack of cold working after casting (photos by author): (A) PG figurine of a standing naked male from Olympia with a rough and unfinished surface (Olympia Archaeological Museum Inv. No. B 5377, Olympia museum, permission of the Archaeological Ephorate of Elis; © Hellenic Ministry of Culture and Sports – Hellenic Organization of Cultural Resources Development); (B) Geometric figurine of a standing belted male from Delphi with a rough surface (Delphi Archaeological Museum Inv. No. 2903; published with permission of the Delphi Archaeological Museum; © Hellenic Ministry of Culture and Sports – Hellenic Organization of Cultural Resources Development) [A black and white version of this figure will appear in some formats. For the color version, please refer to the plate section.]

finished.[90] But aside from the minimum step of removing the casting apparatus, most figurines are apparently left in a very raw state, with little or no attempt to machine, polish to smoothness, or otherwise work the surface after casting (Plate 10).[91] Overall, the finishing of the figurines does not seem to have been a major concern.[92]

EVALUATING EIA FIGURINES IN LIGHT OF THE PROCESS OF PRODUCTION

EIA bronze figurines are usually positioned fairly low in the hierarchy of aesthetic masterpieces of Greek art. Taken individually and as a collective,

[90] Bol 1985, 29.   [91] Bol 1985, 29; Lebessi 2002, 170–171.
[92] Bol 1985, 20; Lebessi 2002, 171.

they are a rough and unprepossessing set of objects that are not really a wonder to behold. Their lack of aesthetic virtuosity does not, however, take away from the many details that they can reveal about EIA ritual, especially if we appreciate the figurines' formal qualities within the context of their production and use. In this vein, it worth highlighting some aspects of the figurines that make the most sense when they are considered in the context of the casting process.

One of the most beguiling characteristics of EIA bronze figurines is their tiny size. It is difficult to appreciate the miniature scale of these figurines without encountering them in person. The smallest figurines in the corpus of EIA material from Olympia, for example, are of the order of 3.5–5 cm tall, or slightly greater than the long dimension of a standard paperclip (Plate 11). The maximum size of any of these cast bronzes down to the end of the Geometric period is 47 cm, but the majority are considerably smaller than that, usually between 5 and 8 cm.[93] When the figurines begin to get taller, they become extremely attenuated and appear strangely stretched out, like a character from a cartoon show (Plate 12). These characteristics make a great deal of sense when considered in the context of the limitations of casting in solid bronze.[94]

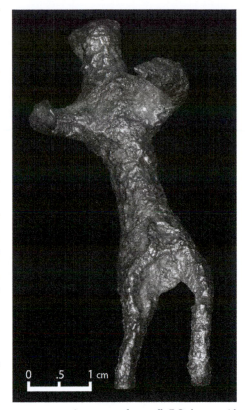

PLATE 11. An extremely small PG humanoid figurine from Olympia (Olympia Archaeological Museum Inv. No. B 5378, photo by author, published with permission of the Archaeological Ephorate of Elis; © Hellenic Ministry of Culture and Sports – Hellenic Organization of Cultural Resources Development) [A black and white version of this figure will appear in some formats. For the color version, please refer to the plate section.]

First, because the objects are solid casts, even small ones would have required a considerable amount of metal to create; the solidity of the bronze would also create a major scaling factor in terms of bronze required for the cast that would need to be taken into consideration by the designer. Along with the relative dearness of metal resources for alloying in the EIA, these factors probably

[93] Maximum figure according to Bol 1985, 28; see also Haynes 1992, 31, n. 4, where the two largest are a horse from Olympia (45.5 cm; Heilmeyer 1979, 262, no. 823) and a flute-player from Samos (42 cm; Buschor 1934, 61, figs. 146–149). The average height of the figurines in Langdon's study (1984) is 7.2 cm and the median is 6.7 cm.

[94] For a theoretical discussion of the potential meanings of miniaturization in clay figurines, see Bailey 2005, 29–44. For the bronze figurines, I prefer a more pragmatic interpretation that emphasizes the realities of production and the identities of the producers, as laid out in this section.

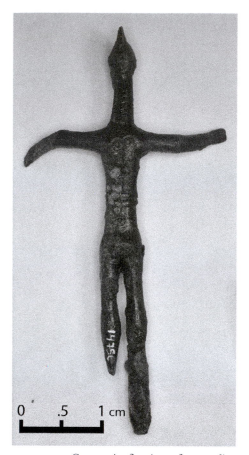

PLATE 12. Geometric figurine of a standing naked male from Thermon with highly attenuated proportions (Athens National Archaeological Museum Inv. No. 14756, photo by author, published with permission from the National Archaeological Museum, Athens, © Hellenic Ministry of Culture and Sports – Hellenic Organization of Cultural Resources Development) [A black and white version of this figure will appear in some formats. For the color version, please refer to the plate section.]

contributed to a tendency toward miniaturization. Second, the cooling properties of the bronze needed to be taken into consideration – once the thickness of the cast exceeded about 2.5 cm there would have been major risk of cracking and sunken areas because of the differential rates at which bronze through the section of the cast would have cooled. This aspect of the casting technology helps make sense of both the small scale of most early bronze figurines and the tendency toward attenuation apparent in figures that aspire to greater heights in the Geometric period.

In addition to being small, EIA bronze figurines represent an extraordinarily idiosyncratic group of objects, so much so that they effectively defy any thoroughgoing categorization or typology.[95] This has often been interpreted in light of the perceived adolescence or immaturity of EIA art, in which the figures represent an experimental phase prior to the establishment of an iconographic canon.[96] However, understanding the manufacturing processes brings us from speculation about the state of mind of EIA artists to the material realities of direct lost-wax casting. Since the only mold created during the direct lost-wax casting process (the investment) was destroyed at the conclusion of the cast, it would have been difficult or impossible to replicate a figurine exactly. Even in the few cases of figurines from the EIA that seem to have been made from a shared template

[95] Langdon's treatment of the body of evidence as a coherent group in her dissertation (1984) is characteristically full of insight. Even given Langdon's analytical prowess, the best criterion available for making a categorization was body position (sitting, standing, etc.) within which categorization there is great variation for each individual (Langdon 1984, 8–12, 84–231). Lebessi (2002) eschews any attempt at categorization, proceeding to analyze each individual figurine on its own. See also the various styles introduced by Müller 1929. For an attempt to identify workshops for the figurines, Kunze 1967. For general comments on the stylistic variation in the bronzes, Thomas 1992, 49–57.
[96] E.g., Furtwängler 1890, 43; Kunze 1930; Matz 1950; Langdon 1984, 2–3.

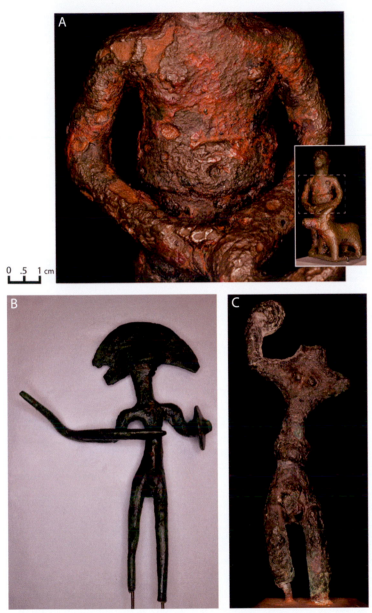

PLATE 1. Figurines demonstrating a range of wax modeling techniques (all photos by author): (A) Torso of a Geometric figurine of a young naked male leading a small cow from Delphi with details like belt and nipples probably built using additive technique (Delphi Archaeological Museum Inv. No. 6571; published with permission of the Delphi Archaeological Museum; © Hellenic Ministry of Culture and Sports – Hellenic Organization of Cultural Resources Development); (B) PG figurine of a warrior from Olympia built up using additive technique (Olympia Excavation Inv. No. Br 9788, Athens National Archaeological Museum Inv. No. 6096, published with permission from the National Archaeological Museum, Athens, © Hellenic Ministry of Culture and Sports/Archaeological Receipts Fund); (C) Geometric figurine, perhaps of a belted boxer, from Delphi with added details (Delphi Archaeological Museum Inv. No. 2978; published with permission of the Delphi Archaeological Museum; © Hellenic Ministry of Culture and Sports – Hellenic Organization of Cultural Resources Development).

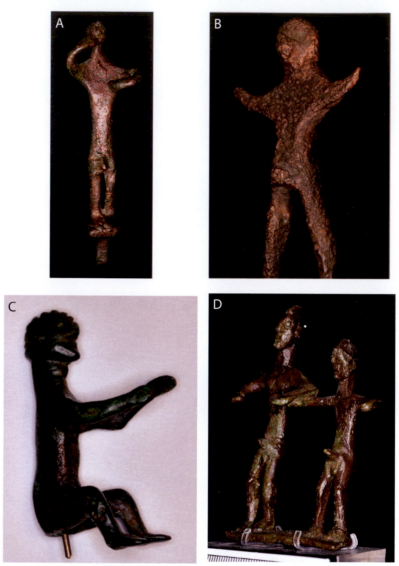

0   1   2 cm

PLATE 2. Figurines exhibiting surface scraping as a technique of manufacture (photos by author): (A) Subminoan figurine of a naked male with a plank-like appearance probably resulting from a subtractive modeling technique (Heraklion Archaeological Museum Inv. No. 2960; published with permission of the Heraklion Archaeological Museum; © Hellenic Ministry of Culture and Sports – Hellenic Organization of Cultural Resources Development); (B) PG figurine modeled by scraping (Olympia Archaeological Museum Inv. No. B. 1754, permission of the Archaeological Ephorate of Elis, © Hellenic Ministry of Culture and Sports – Hellenic Organization of Cultural Resources Development); (C) Geometric figurine of a rider worked using both additive and subtractive techniques (Olympia Excavation Inv. No. Br 8131, Athens National Archaeological Museum Inv. No. 6150; published with permission from the National Archaeological Museum, Athens, © Hellenic Ministry of Culture and Sports – Hellenic Organization of Cultural Resources Development); (D) PG figurine of two naked males holding hands, with flat surfaces indicating modeling by a subtractive, scraping technique (Syme Viannou Excavation Inv. No. MH 3137; published with permission of the Heraklion Archaeological Museum; © Hellenic Ministry of Culture and Sports – Hellenic Organization of Cultural Resources Development).

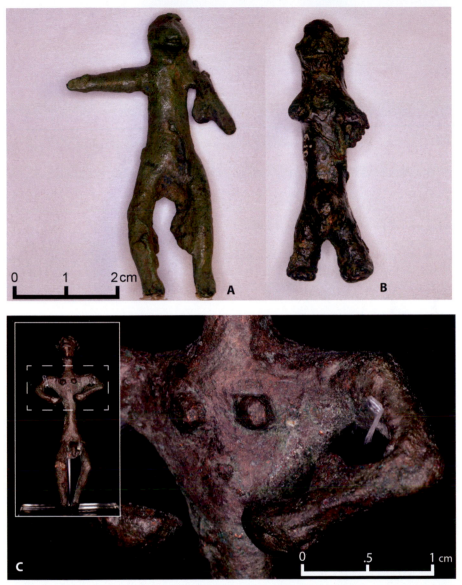

PLATE 3. Figurines with extensive flashing and/or "potatoes" (photos by author): (A) PG humanoid figurine from Olympia showing major problems with flashing and a few potatoes (Athens National Archaeological Museum Inv. No. 6105, published with permission from the National Archaeological Museum, Athens, © Hellenic Ministry of Culture and Sports/ Archaeological Receipts Fund); (B) PG humanoid figurine from Olympia showing evidence of multiple casting issues, including flashing (Olympia Excavation Inv. No. Br 6364, Athens National Archaeological Museum Inv. No. 6100; published with permission of the National Archaeological Museum, © Hellenic Ministry of Culture and Sports – Hellenic Organization of Cultural Resources Development); (C) Detail of PG figurine from Amnisos with flashing on interior surface of akimbo arms (Heraklion Archaeological Museum Inv. No. 2316; published with permission of the Heraklion Archaeological Museum; © Hellenic Ministry of Culture and Sports – Hellenic Organization of Cultural Resources Development).

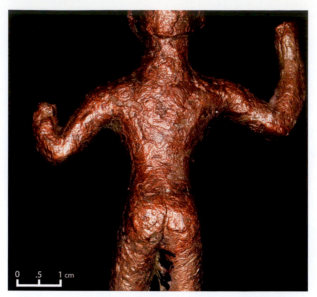

PLATE 4. Geometric figurine from Delphi with streaky and inconsistent metal alloy (Delphi Archaeological Museum Inv. No. 3649, photo by author; published with permission of the Heraklion Archaeological Museum; © Hellenic Ministry of Culture and Sports – Hellenic Organization of Cultural Resources Development).

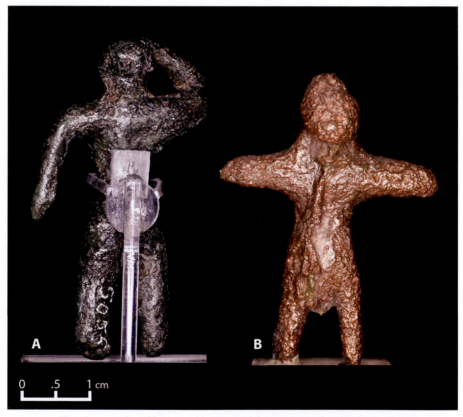

PLATE 5. Figurines made of bronze characterized by porosity that likely resulted from the presence of excessive gas in the casting environment (photos by author): (A) Rear view of an LM IIIC figurine of a saluting naked male with porosity from gaseous casting (Syme Viannou Excavation Inv. No. MH 5055; published with permission of the Heraklion Archaeological Museum; © Hellenic Ministry of Culture and Sports – Hellenic Organization of Cultural Resources Development): (B) PG anthropoid figurine from Olympia with multiple issues in the cast, including flashing and porous metal (Olympia Archaeological Museum Inv. No. B 5994, permission of the Archaeological Ephorate of Elis; © Hellenic Ministry of Culture and Sports – Hellenic Organization of Cultural Resources Development).

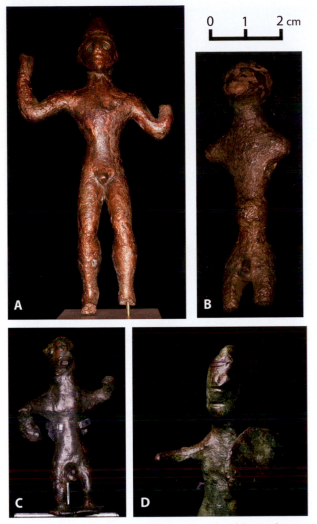

PLATE 6. Figurines with missing or poorly elaborated extremities (photos by author): (A) Geometric figurine of a standing naked male from Delphi with missing hands and feet (Delphi Archaeological Museum Inv. No. 3649; published with permission of the Delphi Archaeological Museum, © Hellenic Ministry of Culture and Sports – Hellenic Organization of Cultural Resources Development); (B) Geometric figurine of a naked, belted male missing all extremities from Delphi (Delphi Archaeological Museum Inv. No. 3240; published with permission of the Delphi Archaeological Museum, © Hellenic Ministry of Culture and Sports – Hellenic Organization of Cultural Resources Development); (C) PG figurine of a naked male with casting problems around the hands from Patsos (Heraklion Archaeological Museum Inv. No. 207; published with permission of the Heraklion Archaeological Museum; © Hellenic Ministry of Culture and Sports – Hellenic Organization of Cultural Resources Development); (D) PG figurine of a naked armed male from Syme Viannou with a poorly articulated right hand (Syme Viannou Excavation Inv. No. MH 4959; published with permission of the Heraklion Archaeological Museum; © Hellenic Ministry of Culture and Sports – Hellenic Organization of Cultural Resources Development).

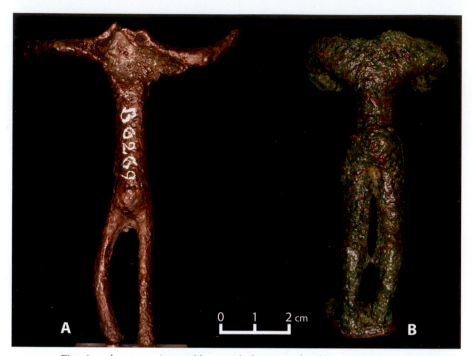

PLATE 7. Figurines demonstrating problems with the pour of molten metal (photos by author): (A) Rear view of a PG figurine from Olympia showing problems with the casting pour (Olympia Archaeological Museum Inv. No. B 6269, © Hellenic Ministry of Culture and Sports – Hellenic Organization of Cultural Resources Development); (B) Rear view of a headless Geometric figurine from Delphi in which the molten metal never reached the head (Delphi Archaeological Museum Inv. No. 3976, published with permission of the Delphi Archaeological Museum; © Hellenic Ministry of Culture and Sports – Hellenic Organization of Cultural Resources Development).

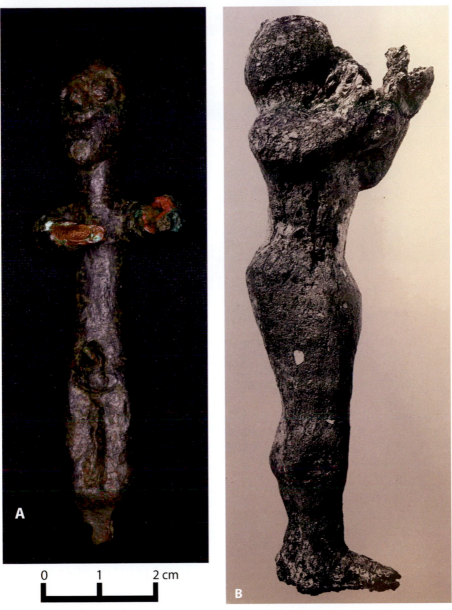

0   1   2 cm

PLATE 8. Figurines probably cast by a metal pour entering through the hands: (A) PG figurine of a naked male with damaged hands from Kommos that was originally designed to be installed in a stone plinth with a bull figurine (Heraklion Archaeological Museum Inv. No. 5416, photo by author; published with permission of the Heraklion Archaeological Museum; © Hellenic Ministry of Culture and Sports – Hellenic Organization of Cultural Resources Development); (B) Geometric figure of a flute player from Olympia still encased in the casting investment (photo courtesy of the German Archaeological Institute, D-DAI-ATH-Olympia 4877, photographer Eva–Marie Czakó).

PLATE 9. LBA and EIA figurines with sprues attached at the feet (photos by author): (A) Minoan figurine of a worshipper on display in the Heraklion Museum; (B) PG figurine of a naked male from Olympia (Olympia Excavations Inv. No. Br 8900, Athens National Archaeological Museum Inv. No. 6249, published with permission from the National Archaeological Museum, Athens, © Hellenic Ministry of Culture and Sports/Archaeological Receipts Fund); (C) PG figurine of a naked male from Olympia (Olympia Archaeological Museum Inv. No. B 4245, permission of the Archaeological Ephorate of Elis; © Hellenic Ministry of Culture and Sports – Hellenic Organization of Cultural Resources Development).

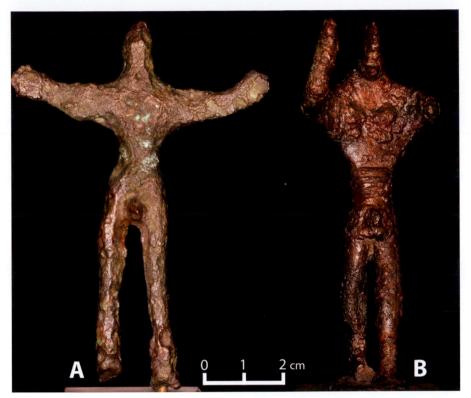

PLATE 10. EIA figurines with rough cast surfaces, suggesting an unrefined inner investment layer and lack of cold working after casting (photos by author): (A) PG figurine of a standing naked male from Olympia with a rough and unfinished surface (Olympia Archaeological Museum Inv. No. B 5377, Olympia museum, permission of the Archaeological Ephorate of Elis; © Hellenic Ministry of Culture and Sports – Hellenic Organization of Cultural Resources Development); (B) Geometric figurine of a standing belted male from Delphi with a rough surface (Delphi Archaeological Museum Inv. No. 2903; published with permission of the Delphi Archaeological Museum; © Hellenic Ministry of Culture and Sports – Hellenic Organization of Cultural Resources Development).

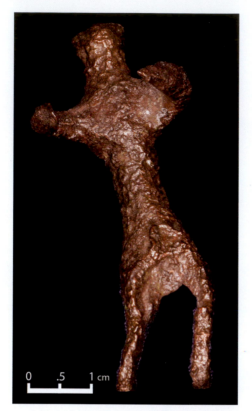

PLATE 11. An extremely small PG humanoid figurine from Olympia (Olympia Archaeological Museum Inv. No. B 5378, photo by author, published with permission of the Archaeological Ephorate of Elis; © Hellenic Ministry of Culture and Sports – Hellenic Organization of Cultural Resources Development).

PLATE 12. Geometric figurine of a standing naked male from Thermon with highly attenuated proportions (Athens National Archaeological Museum Inv. No. 14756, photo by author, published with permission from the National Archaeological Museum, Athens, © Hellenic Ministry of Culture and Sports – Hellenic Organization of Cultural Resources Development).

PLATE 13. Two similar, but not quite identical, PG naked standing male figurines from Olympia. Left: Olympia Archaeological Museum Inv. No. B 1391, Right: Olympia Archaeological Museum Inv. No. B 4245. (Photo by author, published with permission of the Archaeological Ephorate of Elis; © Hellenic Ministry of Culture and Sports – Hellenic Organization of Cultural Resources Development).

PLATE 14. Students pouring molten metal in an art studio class at the University of Nebraska (photo courtesy Philip Sapirstein).

PLATE 15. Detail of a Geometric standing nude figurine from Delphi (Delphi Archaeological Museum Inv. No. 2910, photo by author; published with permission of the Delphi Archaeological Museum; © Hellenic Ministry of Culture and Sports – Hellenic Organization of Cultural Resources Development).

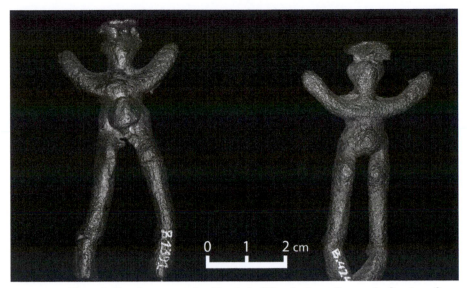

PLATE 13. Two similar, but not quite identical, PG naked standing male figurines from Olympia. Left: Olympia Archaeological Museum Inv. No. B 1391, Right: Olympia Archaeological Museum Inv. No. B 4245. (Photo by author, published with permission of the Archaeological Ephorate of Elis; © Hellenic Ministry of Culture and Sports – Hellenic Organization of Cultural Resources Development). [A black and white version of this figure will appear in some formats. For the color version, please refer to the plate section.]

(perhaps a model made of clay or some other material), slight differences attest to the fact that each figurine had to be originally modeled separately in wax (Plate 13). Indeed, each solid-cast figurine must have begun life as a *sui generis* creation built up or carved out from wax by hand before being committed to a permanent form in metal.[97]

Moving from this insight, it is possible to rethink the implications of the immense variety of forms and iconographical choices apparent among the human figurines from the EIA. If each figurine was made by hand from wax, perhaps with the design and production distributed among multiple individuals (e.g., a designer/modeler and a founder), it may be that the range of aesthetic and formal characteristics of the figurines reflects a variety of individual ideas about what the important characteristics of a human representation related to ritual worship were.

Returning to the topic of the naked male as an iconographic choice, it is relevant to raise the point of the frequency (but not uniformity) with which genitalia are modeled and added to the simple figures, which does not seem likely to have been an incidental or accidental generic default meant to distinguish male from female, as some have argued. The decision to create extra wax elements and to append them to the basic armature of the figure was

---

[97] On variation and repetition in early Greek bronzes, see Mattusch 1990, 128; 2008, 422.

intentional and must indicate that the makers of the wax models considered the unclothed state of the individual to be an important feature to make permanent through the casting process.

However, the fact that these elements were not always appended, and that the parts of the human anatomy and accoutrements afforded to the figurines is generally highly variable, suggests that each visitor to the sanctuary was able to design a vision of a human or animal in wax that aligned with their own ideas about what a votive object ought to look like, and what it ought to convey. Appreciating this aspect of the EIA figurines positions the corpus as a remarkable source of insight into individual action and intentionality from a period for which such insights are rare. In the case of these bronze figurines, it is necessarily true that the creator of the wax model needed to make decisions about what features to add and what to leave out. The wide range of decisions that were made about modeling EIA figurines in this regard may give us a sense of a range of expressions and actions of otherwise highly elusive EIA individuals.

In considering the choices made by individual modelers, compelling insights are available from engagement with existing theoretical scholarship that deals with the meaning and iconography of prehistoric figurines. Rosemary Joyce's discussion of Honduran figurines is particularly productive in that it assists us in coming to terms with the significance of representational choices made during figurine production. Joyce reminds us that representational choices that establish resemblance to 'nature' are not symbolically or ideologically meaningless, but are made in order to reinforce "stereotypes of natural or essential human behavior."[98] Each figurine, then, provides a sort of narrative of choice, wherein makers can produce and promulgate important aspects of their social identities through representation.[99]

In general, extant work on prehistoric figurines makes it seem likely that ephemeral votive offerings are likely to reflect both personal values and the social systems within which those values operated.[100] The choices made in the production of figurines were either deliberate or based on ideas that were so deeply ingrained in the maker's mind that no choice need be made. In either case, the ideas and symbols communicated by figurine modeling ought to reveal either individual or collective values and social systems.[101]

While the relatively schematic style of EIA figurines makes it difficult to read particularly "pregnant moments" of narrative from their iconography, the makers of the figurines seem often to have decided that it was important to indicate that the humans they represent were not clothed.[102] The frequent

---

[98] Joyce 1993, 256.   [99] Joyce 1993, 257.
[100] On the capability of figurines to offer intimate glimpses into the minds of ancient people, see, e.g., Ucko 1962; 1968; Talalay 1987; 1993; Bolger 1996.
[101] Joyce 1993; Lesure 2001, 51–52; Bailey 2005, 66–87, esp. 82–83.   [102] Barthes 1977, 73.

occurrence of nudity in EIA figurines from ritual contexts therefore suggests that the fact of going without clothes in the particular context of ritual often (though not always) was conceived as significant within the system of symbols associated with participation in rural ritual practice.

Aside from their small size and idiosyncratic modeling, another perplexing aspect of EIA bronze figurines is that flawed and broken figurines, and even detritus from casting, were all dedicated alongside more refined and complete ones in votive deposits at Syme Viannou, Olympia, and Delphi. Considering the process of lost wax casting sheds light on the possible reasons behind the seemingly illogical practice of dedicating flawed objects and production waste alongside rather more refined pieces. The labor and care that went into the design, modeling, and investment of any given figurine would have been significant, even before the addition of the molten bronze to the mold. Since so much time and energy had already been sunk into the object through the modeling, investment, and burnout process, and since it was very difficult and time-consuming to start over, the choice to dedicate an imperfect object may often have seemed more appealing than melting down the metal into scrap and beginning the process from scratch. We may even imagine that the process of designing the figurine, and engaging with a symbolic system of images and ideology through that process, was more important to the dedica-tor than the appearance or quality of the final cast, so that broken votives had the same personal value as complete ones.

Thinking along these lines brings us to a relatively radical interpretation that emerges naturally from the observation that imperfect votives were dedicated in sanctuaries, and that almost all of these objects are flawed and largely unrefined by surface treatment. This observation implicates the way that we tend to understand and reconstruct the value of objects in the archaeological record. Because EIA bronze figurines are not very aesthetically pleasing or formally sophisticated, they have often been treated cursorily in an art histor-ical perspective wherein value accrues to objects primarily based on their performance as objects for visual consumption.[103] Along these lines, the normal interpretation of the rough appearance of early bronze figurines is that they were made by inexperienced craftsmen who were incapable of producing better art. The figurines were the result of a primitive stage of technological and artistic development, when artisans learning how to cast bronze for the first time struggled to master the pyrotechnic and metallurgical techniques needed to generate fine products. It is certainly logical to come to this

---

[103] However, see Langdon's work (e.g., 1984; 2007; 2008) which has consistently sought to place the figurines into a cultural historical context regardless of their aesthetic characteristics, following valuable efforts by Kunze (1930; 1944; 1948; 1961; 1967) and Rolley (e.g., 1984; 1993; 1998) along these lines.

conclusion if we reconstruct a scenario in which the aim of the craftsperson was to create objects of aesthetic beauty and naturalism.[104]

On the other hand, looking carefully at EIA bronze figurines as an assemblage provides a strong basis upon which to question the plausibility of an interpretation that the figurines are flawed because the artists who made them lacked skill. The figurines are indeed consistently flawed. From an art historical perspective, perhaps the most obvious explanation for these flaws in execution is the failure of the artist to achieve a desired intent, where the desired intent is a beautiful and naturalistic figurine. However, the thoroughgoing lack of care evident in the production of the figurines undermines this conclusion. Errors and manufacturing flaws are so strongly characteristic of EIA bronze figurines that it is more economical to suggest that the people who made the figurines did not care a great deal about effecting a polished and refined final appearance. We should conclude, in other words, not that the people who made these figurines were unskilled craftspeople who could not do better work, but that they did not really care about making a visually refined final product.[105]

Why would anyone make a work of art if they did not actually care what the end product looked like? This would be the case if the aesthetic quality of the output of the production process was not where the value in an object's production resided. In other words, it may be the case that we have been interpreting these figurines incorrectly because the original social and ritual value or function of these figurines does not align with the criteria of value according to which we appraise them.

As discussed in Chapter 1, archaeologists tend to approach ancient artifacts as objects whose purpose was to perform as an object for consumption. However, we need not take as a given that all ancient technological practice aimed at the production of beautiful or useful artifacts.[106] Instead, the

---

[104] It seems to be true that 'later' figurines are in general more technically accomplished than 'earlier' ones which could support the notion that the production of a refined outcome was always the goal of EIA bronze casting. However, perhaps the conventional chronology of the figurines – which is based on the idea that the least refined figurines should be placed earlier in the sequence and the more ambitious ones later – rather than on stratified context – is simply playing tricks on us.

[105] Kiderlen suggests that the earliest bronze tripod cauldrons from EIA sanctuaries might date to a period roughly contemporary with the earliest bronze figurines (Kiderlen 2010). If he is correct, this would constitute another grounds on which to question a theory positing that EIA bronze workers were unskilled, since tripods were very complicated to manufacture. However, the earlier date for the tripods cannot be determined stratigraphically. Kiderlen's argument relies on the logic that, since molds for tripods from Lefkandi date to earlier in the EIA, the examples from sanctuaries of the same type should also date to the eleventh and tenth centuries. This revises the later dating suggested in Willemsen 1957 and the chronology later discussed by Maass 1978. See Papasavvas 2003 for discussion of the skill required to successfully cast a rod tripod in a single piece; multi-part tripods might have taken less skill to cast.

[106] Dobres 2010, 109–110.

performance of technology required for craft production may have contained as much or more social meaning than the outcomes of that performance. In this sense, dedicatory assemblages including both indifferent, imperfect, and broken castings and more refined and carefully modeled ones in EIA sanctuaries may point toward a situation in which the performance of technological knowledge inherent in the production of EIA bronze figurines was more important than the final product.[107] This is also suggested by the minimal attention paid to the aesthetic appearance most EIA figurines through the entire *chaîne opératoire*. Rather than attributing this to incompetence or inexperience on the part of the artists and founders, it is possible that these attributes reflect a general indifference to the appearance of the final cast bronzes. In Chapter 5, I will argue that the physical characteristics of the figurines make the most sense if we appreciate that it was not really the product of bronze casting but rather the process of the casting that had value in the context of ritual practice at EIA sanctuaries.

CONCLUSIONS

In this chapter, I have argued that reconstructing the casting process involved in the production of EIA bronze votive figurines opens up new avenues of insight into the meaning and history of these artifacts. First, although lost-wax casting seems elegant and simple in theory, in practice the successful casting of bronze figurines required significant pyrotechnical and material knowledge, and there were many opportunities for things to go wrong during the procedure, with significant implications for the quality of the final products. Second, the technical details of the earliest figurines from the Greek mainland and earlier examples from Crete strongly support the case for a strong influence of the manufacture of the latter on the former, a case that has already been made based on formal characteristics and other circumstantial evidence elsewhere. Third, understanding the technological processes required for manufacturing solid bronze votives sheds significant light on many of their unusual features and flaws, including the fact that each is totally *sui generis* and that they are uniformly small in stature. Finally, a close examination of the figurines with metal casting processes in mind suggests that one of the reasons these objects are not very visually impressive is because the people who made them did not care what they looked like. In Chapter 5, I build on this conclusion, arguing that metalworking and metalworkers played central roles in the rituals that took place at some rural EIA sanctuaries, and that it was the transformational aspect of the bronze casting process itself, not the appearance of the final product, that invested EIA cast bronzes with their ritual value.

[107] Heilmeyer 1979, 35.

CHAPTER FIVE

BRONZE FIGURINES, TRANSFORMATIVE PROCESSES, AND RITUAL POWER

In the last chapter I suggested that the most likely explanation for the appearance of a new kind of votive dedication at EIA mainland sanctuaries sites was a process of both technological and ritual transfer from Crete, and that the metal casting processes that went into votive production explain many peculiar characteristics of EIA bronze figurines, including their small size, stylistic variety, and many flaws and defects. I closed this discussion by suggesting that the craft processes involved in making the figurines were more fundamental to their meaning in the context of ritual practice than the aesthetic outcome of those processes.

In this chapter, I turn from the figurines themselves to the ritual context of their production in order to make the case that casting bronzes was a central rather than ancillary activity at some EIA rural sanctuaries. I first establish that metalworking did take place in many of these sanctuaries, reviewing the relevant archaeological evidence. Usually this phenomenon has been interpreted as essentially economic in nature, the outcome of a demand for votives generated by a culture of competitive elite display in ritual contexts. Instead, on the basis of comparative evidence from the Bronze and Iron Age Eastern Mediterranean and from the ethnoarchaeological record, I argue that metal production in ritual spaces at some EIA sanctuaries was not an incidental means to an end (the need for votives) but a fundamental aspect of ritual practice itself. This conclusion suggests some revisions to the way that we reconstruct a number of aspects of early first millennium Aegean society: relationships between Bronze and Iron Age society and culture, the history of connections between the Aegean and the Eastern Mediterranean, and the social location of ritual power. Within this modified broader perspective, it is possible to put forward a new interpretation of the earliest bronze figurines under study here.

EVIDENCE FOR BRONZE CASTING IN EARLY GREEK SANCTUARIES

To make the case that production processes were embedded within and contributed significantly to dynamics of ritual, power, and votive deposition in some EIA sanctuaries, it is necessary to demonstrate that votive production in addition to votive deposition took place at these sanctuaries. Most scholarship on the archaeology of EIA sanctuaries has emphasized ritual activities that are familiar features of later Greek ritual practice, especially the deposition of votives and animal sacrifices and feasts, because they are easily recognizable from a perspective informed by Archaic and Classical sources.[1] Less attention has been paid to the productive craft activity that is evident, if in fragmentary and small quantities, in the archaeological record of these sanctuaries.[2] This evidence indicates that bronze votives were not only dedicated at EIA sanctuaries but were also being created on site. In this section, I review the nature of this evidence.

The location of artistic production in the EIA is often difficult to discern due to the general scarcity of archaeological evidence for workshops from EIA sites. Although it is certain that fine pottery and metal objects were being produced during this period, durable industrial installations are scarce in the archaeological record.[3] This scarcity is probably related to the likely small scale and temporary nature of many production facilities in the context of the relatively simple EIA economy, but has also probably also been impacted by intensive later occupation and intervention at most sites, like Athens, Argos, Sparta, Olympia, and Delphi, where we might expect EIA production centers

---

[1] For example, Bergquist 1988; Morgan 1996, 46–55; Niemeier 2016; Lupack 2020.

[2] But see treatments by Morgan 1990, 85–86; Risberg 1992; 1998.

[3] On the scarcity of evidence for well-preserved remains of ceramic workshops in the EIA, see Papadopoulos 1989, appendix 1; Hasaki 2002, 220–225. The limited evidence for metal production is presented below. Mattusch has published a few metallurgical workshop contexts from the Agora (1975) and Corinth (1991) which have produced impressive quantities of foundry debris including crucibles and pieces of investment molds, but these date considerably later than the EIA. From Corinth, the Penteskouphia plaques show pictures of kilns dated to the Archaic period, but so far there is no archaeological correlate of these for the EIA (Raubitschek 1988: 119–20. On the Penteskouphia plaques see Greiveldinger 2003; Palmieri 2009; D'Agostino et al. 2017). Earlier metalworking tools and contexts from the Bronze Age have been documented more commonly as well (e.g., Dimopoulou 1997; 2004; 2012; Blackwell 2020), especially from Crete and Cyprus (e.g., Evely 1993; Kassianidou 2012, 97), but in situ facilities for metalworking in the archaeological record of the Aegean are rare (Mattusch 2008, 418).

to have been located. The situation in Athens is a good example of this impact – while Papadopoulos has documented quite a lot of waste in wells of the Agora that must have been associated with an EIA ceramic production center, *in situ* installations for craft production, like kilns, have apparently not survived millennia of later activity on the site.[4]

Notwithstanding these difficulties with the evidence, it is possible to say without too much doubt that metalworking took place at a number of EIA sanctuaries. In the absence of the remains of an actual foundry, lacking at all EIA sanctuaries with the possible exception of Eretria, there are other archaeological indicators that metal production was taking place. These include quantities of bronze scrap broken into pieces that could fit inside a crucible; vessels used to melt or pour molten metal, usually crucibles; evidence of mold systems, including pieces of broken molds or the leftover bronze gates, runners, and risers that facilitated the filling and venting of molds; failed or defective bronze casts; and pieces of bronze spills or drips that are unlikely to have been removed from the location of bronze production due to their small size.[5]

Many such indicators of metal production have been recovered from EIA sanctuaries.[6] At Olympia, the existence of on-site bronze foundries is documented as early as the ninth century.[7] The EIA evidence for metalworking is effectively circumstantial but still convincing, and includes the presence of mold fragments, miscast figurines that have not had their riser and runner systems or pouring funnels removed, and a figurine found still encased in its original investment cast (discussed in Chapter 4).[8] An interesting depositional characteristic of the unsuccessful castings is that they come from the same contexts as finished figurines, suggesting that a failed cast need not obviate the possibility of offering the votive object to the god.[9]

---

[4] Papadopoulos 2003.   [5] Rostocker and Gebhard 1980, 350.

[6] Delphi is an exception (Mattusch 2008, 431).

[7] Furtwängler 1890, 29, 37; Hampe and Jantzen 1937, 28–41; Herrmann 1964; Heilmeyer 1969, 1–28; Heilmeyer 1979, 35; Bol 1985, 22; Risberg 1992, 32; Orfanou 2020, 56–57.

[8] As Mattusch (1975, 184) has noted, the small, miscast pieces from Olympia mostly date to the Geometric period, with few dating to later periods. Presumably this could be the result of the fact that the founders became technically more competent over time, resulting in fewer later pieces that were obviously miscast. Alternatively, this may represent a change in the way that the figurines were valued and an evolution in the role of metalworkers in ritual contexts.

[9] Heilmeyer 1969, 1; 1979, 35, 52–3; cf. Born and Moustaka 1982. Heilmeyer argued that the sacred nature of the votives prevented them from being melted down and reused even in the case of a failed casting (the argument is echoed by Bocher (2006–2007) in her discussion of votive bronze sheet objects). Neugebauer (1931) argued that the different qualities/finishes of dedicated figurines indicated a difference in class or economic means, but this would be difficult to substantiate (See discussion in Kyrieleis 2006, 95–102). Another possibility is that it was the process of productive transformation and surrender to the deity more than the quality of the finished object itself that formed the fundamental core of the ritual process. On the importance of the process of ritual action as a behavioral rather than a product-oriented

In addition to circumstantial evidence for local bronze casting, Olympia has produced several original production contexts that may have been in use during the Geometric period. Based on the distribution of scraps and crucible fragments, Heilmeyer has argued that EIA bronze manufacturing at the site would have taken place on the later treasury terrace or just below it, within the core of the sacred *altis* and directly adjacent to the site of the earliest sacrificial activity.[10] In this area, just to the northwest of the stadium, the remarkable remains of a metallurgical workshop were discovered in an old streambed during German campaigns of the 1930s (Figure 5.1).[11] Among the finds were ten simple open-air furnaces made of stone. The furnaces were deliberately built adjacent to naturally occurring beds of fireproof sand in the streambed, which served as packing for the investment casting molds. Clay-lined canals led from the bases of the ovens to the casting pits, so that the molten bronze could flow directly from the furnace to the casting pit. A great deal of detritus, including charcoal, crucibles, vitrified bricks, bronze scrap, mold fragments, and nozzles of bellows, alongside pieces of failed bronze castings, funnels, and gate systems, was found tossed about the industrial area.[12] Although the extant remains of these establishments seem to belong to the seventh to fifth centuries, the presence of the still-invested flute player figurine in the same area suggests that manufacturing may have taken place in similar installations of an earlier date that were destroyed by the reuse of the site in subsequent periods.[13] A considerable amount of metallurgical detritus was also found in the area of the Phidias workshop, and although there are some early objects among the remains indicating that it could have begun its use in the eighth century, it is not clear that any foundry activity here predated the Classical period.[14]

A building excavated just to the east of the temple of Apollo Daphnephoros at Eretria and dated to the Geometric period (eighth century) provides perhaps the only well-preserved context of a bronze smith's workshop with a secure EIA date, and makes it certain that the presence of a metalworker was a fixture

experience, see, e.g., Bradley 2000; Fogelin 2003; 2004; 2006; Inomata 2006; Inomata and Coben 2006.

[10] Heilmeyer 1969, 6–14, 21; Heilmeyer, Zimmer, and Schneider 1987; Heilmeyer suggested (1979, 35) that the debris from the early workshops was used as part of the black layer when this was distributed across the *altis* in the early seventh century. Kyrieleis (2006, 95–102) argued that there was no bronze production occurring at Olympia in the earliest periods, but this argument is now perhaps contradicted by analytical work (Kiderlen 2010; Kiderlen, et al. 2017).

[11] Hampe and Jantzen 1937, 34–35.   [12] Mattusch 2008, 432.

[13] Born and Moustaka 1982.

[14] Mallwitz and Schiering 1964, 43–45, 158; Maass 1978, 26, pl. 27; Maass 1981; Schneider and Zimmer 1984; Heilmeyer, Zimmer, and Schneider 1987, 266–268.

5.1. Reconstruction of the bronze foundry excavated at Olympia (Heilmeyer 1969, Abb. 35, drawing used with permission of the artist, Gerhard Zimmer)

of the ritual landscape within the *temenos* of the sanctuary.[15] The building was made of mud-brick set on a stone foundation and contained a casting pit, interpreted as such because it contained large quantities of ash, burnt pieces of clay, abundant slag, and unformed pieces of bronze. The building also contained a number of benches that could have served as the location for other stages of the smithing process, that is, work benches. The finds from the building also include tuyéres and crucibles which could have been used for melting or smelting metal, including bronze, although the evidence indicates that a range of metals work worked here, including not only bronze but also gold and iron. Additional scatters of metal waste have been recovered in more recent excavations in the same area.[16] While the presence of large amounts of slag at the site demonstrates that ore processing may have occurred here, a smelting furnace has not yet been found *in situ* and the excavators suggest that the foundry would have acquired its metals in finished form.[17] It is interesting to note that, while there is an unusual abundance of evidence for metalworking on the site, there is little reason to believe that the deposition of votive figurines formed an important part of the rituals carried out in the sanctuary.

[15] Preliminary report in Krause 1981, 70–87; cf. Huber 1991; 1997; see now the authoritative publication by Verdan 2013.

[16] Verdan 2013, 145–151.

[17] Verdan 2013, 148. Slag can also be produced during the melting and alloying process.

Only one locally made bronze figurine is among the finds, a major contrast to the situation at sites like Olympia and Delphi.[18]

Other sanctuaries with convincing evidence for some metal production in the EIA include the Heraion on Samos, the sanctuary of Athenia Itonia at Philia in Thessaly, and the sanctuary of Aphrodite on Aegina. On Samos, a number of leftover bronze pieces from gate systems and filling funnels, along with the presence of some copper ingots, indicate that casting and perhaps even alloying took place in the early sanctuary.[19] The remains at Philia demonstrate that metal production was taking place, although there is more convincing evidence for ironworking than bronze working. Nonetheless, the remains of misshapen bronze castings, debris, and raw materials show that both metals were probably produced at the site.[20] On Aegina, early seventh century bronze production is evident at the sanctuary of Aphrodite in the form of a pit full of slag and a mold for a metal vessel.[21] Bronze working debris and miscast objects suggesting that production was taking place locally have been excavated at other sanctuaries, including Isthmia,[22] Delphi,[23] Delos,[24] Bassae,[25] Aetos on Ithaka,[26] and Kalapodi,[27] although in some cases this material seems unlikely to predate the Archaic period.

A few scraps of evidence for bronze working have been identified in excavated EIA settlements, although the most artistically productive locales

[18] Verdan 2013, 23, nos. 394. Also of interest is the near-total absence of molds or casting investments from the context, despite its excellent state of preservation (only two very fragmentary pieces survive). Verdan suggests it may be that the casting process at Eretria involved bivalve molds rather than lost-wax casting for the most part (2013, 147).

[19] Jantzen 1955, 57–60; Kopcke 1968, 250–314; Gehrig 1979, 547–558; Bol 1985, 23; Kyrieleis 1990, 23.

[20] Kilian 1983, 131–146.   [21] Wolters 1925, 8.

[22] Rostocker and Gebhard 1980, 350–351.

[23] Perdrizet 1908, 97, fig. 339; Rolley 1977, 82–83, 86. The miscast pieces include part of a tripod cauldron that clearly came from a mold that did not fill properly with metal, as well as several pieces that are full of large holes or bubbles probably caused by air or gas in the mold.

[24] Deonna 1938, 209–235; Rolley 1973, 491–524; Langdon 1984, 318, no. 153.

[25] Yalouris 1959, 155–159; 1978, 91–94. While the majority of the finds from the site are dated to the Archaic and Classical periods, Yalouris notes (1978, 91) at least three LG bronze figurines as well as abundant slag from the northwest sector of the sanctuary.

[26] Benton 1953, 343, 352. The evidence for a forge is limited to the excavation of a single iron hammer, a few pieces of slag, and a mold.

[27] Felsch 1983, 123 (the only evidence cited here is one poorly cast male figurine); preliminary reports with brief discussion of other evidence for metalworking include Catling 1980–81, 24 (of the late eighth century temple, "[s]everal small contemporary buildings of which traces have been found outside the *temenos* may have been workshops"); Touchais 1980, 625:

> Quant à l'existence d'ateliers de bronziers à cet endroit dès le VIIIe siècle av. J.-C., elle est confirmée par les nombreux déchets de fonte et par la présence d'un kouros géométrique tardif jeté dans une couche à peine plus récente. On a d'ailleurs detrouvé dans le sanctuaire lui-même une dizaine de trépieds géométriques en bronze et un masse d'objets votifs en métal (plus de 1,600 en bronze et plus de 1,200 en fer) qui témoignent d'une grande activité métallurgique locale.

of the period, including Argos, Sparta, Corinth, and Athens, have not yielded any such evidence that clearly dates to the EIA.[28] The presence of hearths and furnaces along with pieces of slag and ingots makes clear that bronze and iron smelting and casting took place at Oropos in northeastern Attica toward the end of the LG period.[29] Roughly 350 molds from a Geometric pit at Lefkandi and 30 from a pit of rubble at Akovitika, testify that at least one kind of bronze object, the rod tripod, may have been occasionally manufactured in EIA settlements.[30] So far, however, there is no evidence that figurines were produced in settlements.[31] In general, the majority of evidence for bronze production on the mainland in the EIA published to date comes from sanctuary sites.

The evidence from Crete supports a similar picture. Of the many sanctuaries that have been investigated across the island, several have produced compelling, if ambiguous, evidence for metalworking. At the sanctuary of Diktaean Zeus at Palaikastro, the presence of bits of metal bars and pieces of rough castings suggested to the excavator that bronze-working was occurring in the sacred areas of the site.[32] Evidence for ironworking has been documented in cult contexts at Vrokastro and Kommos.[33] Industrial activities are attested to the west of the sanctuary at Prinias Patela, though the remains are not clearly metallurgical installations.[34] By far the most abundant and convincing evidence for bronze working in a sanctuary context on Crete comes from Syme Viannou. The evidence is difficult to date with certainty, but occurs in deposits containing material dating as early as the eleventh century. It is similar in nature to the early evidence for bronze working from sites on the mainland, especially Olympia. While *in situ* industrial installations have not been found, ample quantities of bronze waste, a piece of a clay crucible, and many miscast figurines and leftover pieces of running up systems likely point to the fact that bronze figurines were being cast in the sanctuary as well as deposited there.[35]

Overall, then the evidence that metallurgy was taking place in the context of ritual practice at some early Greek sanctuaries is lacunose, as is often the case with archaeological evidence for craft production from the EIA. However, it

[28] Mattusch 2008, 432–433. See also Courbin 1957, 677, 680, fig. 31; Daux 1959, 768 for a possible EPG ore-smelting furnace from Argos, and Verdelis 1963, 61–62 for the importance of metalworking in EIA Argos.

[29] Doonan and Mazarakis Ainian 2007, 364–365.

[30] Zimmer 1990, 20–21. The two assemblages of molds demonstrate a relatively sophisticated grasp of what was necessary to produce a proper cast from wax, comprising – in both cases – a two-layer investment shell with an inner, fine clay and a rougher outer clay.

[31] Relevant here is Langdon's observation (1984, 282): "...the bronze objects produced only for cult must have been largely manufactured within the *temenoi*."

[32] Dawkins, Hawes, and Bosanquet 1904–5, 307; MacVeigh Thorne, and Prent 2000.

[33] Hall 1914, 110–111; Shaw 2000, 28–30; Birringer 2015.   [34] Rizza 1991, 334–335, 344–346.

[35] Lebessi 1991a, 313, pl. 201e; Schürmann 1996, 189–193; Lebessi 2002, 187.

seems hard to dispute the fact that many EIA bronze votive objects deposited in EIA sanctuaries, including the figurines that are the main topic of this book, were being cast in or near the *temenoi* of those same sanctuaries.[36]

INTERPRETING THE FUNCTION OF BRONZE CASTING IN EARLY GREEK SANCTUARIES

Previous discussions taking note of this evidence have focused exclusively on economic aspects of metal votive production in sanctuary contexts.[37] In this section, I consider whether it is reasonable instead to view the production of bronze votives as a ritual component of the events that took place at some EIA sanctuaries. I argue that metalworking in early Greek sanctuaries was probably a fundamental and significant part of ritual practice, rather than an ancillary or economic activity that was a means to an end (the production of votives).

Previous Discussions of Metallurgy in Sanctuaries: A Focus on the Economy and Markets

Existing scholarship treating the question of metallurgical workshops in early sanctuaries is situated within a broader set of ideas about the emergence of these sanctuaries in the context of early Greek state formation and religious institutions. Influential work by Snodgrass that was elaborated upon and expanded by Morgan's authoritative contributions has connected the presence of large quantities of bronze dedications at regional and interregional sanctuaries to a number of developments, especially those related to state formation.[38] From the point of view of the political economy, it is thought that major interregional sanctuaries like Olympia and Delphi were important because they served as neutral sites where elites from nascent *poleis* could exchange information and engage in agonistic practices of votive dedication.[39] Both of these activities are thought to have contributed to the formation of a recognizably Greek identity and the mediation of intra and inter-community

---

[36] Lebessi 2002, 187; Prent 2005, 344.

[37] Heilmeyer 1969, 2, 21; 1979, 35, 52; Risberg 1992, 39–40; Schürmann 1996; Kilian-Dirlmeier 2002, 207–211; Lebessi 2002, 185–192.

[38] Snodgrass 1980, 52–54; Starr 1986, 40–41; Morgan 1990; 1993, 19; 1994; 1996, 47–48; Treister 1996, 20; Blakely 1999, 88; Auffarth 2006; Linke 2006, 107–111; Scott 2014, 53–55.

[39] Murray 1980, 65; 1991, 26; Snodgrass 1980, 27–28, 58, 60–61, 85–86; de Polignac 1984; 1994, 11–12; Morgan 1990, 3–4; Morris 1997, 30; Risberg 1998, 674; Coldstream 2003 [1977], 321–322; Kiderlen 2010; Hall 2013, 301–305; Lyttkens 2013, 31; Eder and Lemos 2020, 148–149; Vetters 2020, 549.

tensions among growing populations.[40] In this context, the dedication of bronze votives functioned within a system of ritualized elite competition, with the votives themselves serving as important visual correlates of wealth and status.[41] The dedication of bronze votives has likewise been interpreted as a visually conspicuous way for elite members of society to demonstrate a connection to and hence the favor of supernatural powers.[42]

If we think about early bronze votives within this model, it makes sense to reconstruct a role for the metallurgist within the sanctuary as an economic opportunist. Indeed, the predominant explanation for the presence of metallurgists at early sanctuaries is related to the idea of the market, with craftsmen working at sanctuaries to cast and sell votives for purchase.[43] Elites traveled to and gathered within interregional sanctuaries, and artisans (often described as itinerant craftsmen) followed in order to benefit from the temporarily hot market for votives these gatherings precipitated.[44] The logic is straightforwardly drawn from a system of market economics – temporary demand is generated by the traveling elites and the artisans respond by producing the supply of votives in due course.[45] In his study of the figurines from Olympia, for example, Heilmeyer argued that the bronze votives produced and dedicated in the EIA were made by itinerant craftsmen who came to the sanctuary for major festivals and then returned home afterwards.[46] Schürmann and

[40] Snodgrass 1977, 15, 34; Coldstream 1984, 10; Morris 1991, 41–42; Snodgrass 1993, 39; Osborne 2009 [1996], 60; Eder 2019. On Hellenization and identity formation, for example, Sourvinou-Inwood 1988, 259, 267; 1990, 300–301; Eder and Lemos 2020, 142. The notion that shared religious practices bind Greeks together in a community is stated by Herodotus in the fifth century (8.144.2).

[41] For example, Langdon 1987, 113; Morgan 1990, 86–88; Hall 2013, 303.

[42] Kurke 1999, 151; Rivière 2016; 2018.

[43] Brock 1957, 218; Kardara 1968, 222–227; Coldstream 1977, 100; Rolley 1977, 144; Boardman 1980, 56–58; Morgan 1990, 35–39, 89–90 (from which the quote); Burkert 1992, 9–11; Risberg 1992, 38; 1998, 674–675; Morgan 1993, 23; Treister 1996, 77, 122–123; Blakely 1999, 88; Spivey 2004, 233; Osborne 2009 [1996], 57. Starr (1986, 40), drawing on Snodgrass, frames this quite explicitly: "before true cities appeared, other types of artisans found their markets in the gatherings at sanctuaries whereas Mycenaean smiths and artists worked for the lords of the palaces."

[44] The phenomenon of the itinerant craftsmen has been discussed a great deal in scholarship on early Greece. For itinerant metalworkers in the LBA and EIA, Bass 1967, 163; Zaccagnini 1983; Rolley 1986, 68; Morris 1992a, 103–105; Blakely 2006, 205–206; Dickinson 2006, 34, 118–120, 145–146; Wallace 2010, 216; On itinerant craftspeople in general, for example, Burkert 1992, 9–40; Stampolidis 1992; Bloedow 1997; Donlan 1997; Ulf 2009, 93; Blackwell 2014. On itinerant potters in the LBA and EIA, Morgan and Whitelaw 1991, 91–92; Papadopoulos 1997; Crielaard 1999, 55; 2011, 97; Morris 2007, 233–234; Langdon 2008, 23–24; Papadopoulos and Smithson 2017, 893.

[45] For example, Morgan 1990, 92: "Since neither the quantity of figurines nor our knowledge of prevailing social values would support the idea that travelling craftsmen were employed at Olympia on a long-term basis, it seems likely that . . . their visits were confined to a short period in the year."

[46] Heilmeyer 1979, 52–53; Zimmermann 1989; Prent 2005, 573. On the question of identifiable workshops for the production of tripods, Willemsen 1957, 174–180; Maass 1977.

Lebessi reached the same conclusion in their respective studies of animal and human bronze figurines from Syme Viannou, which they argue constitute the collective output of traveling artisans who visited the sanctuary from different parts of the island in order to serve the votive needs of worshippers.[47] Morgan's influential work on EIA evidence from Olympia and Delphi has been instrumental in cementing a model placing the production of votive figurines in the hands of EIA travelling craftsman.[48] Such interpretations have been supported at least in part by the taxonomization of votive figurines. Analysts charged with categorizing and publishing massive corpora of votive figurines have tended to observe the lack of internal stylistic unity in groups of votives and to respond by assigning them to regional schools that can be connected to the hypothetical traveling artisans.[49]

Although it remains the most popular explanation for the production of bronze figurines in EIA sanctuaries, there are several problematic points of this interpretation that deserve discussion: the assumption that EIA figurines relate to elite status competition, the strict social roles assigned to people within the logic of the model, and its incompatibility with our understanding of the realities of economic and social structures in the EIA, as well as recent metallographic evidence from the bronze votive objects themselves.

One aspect of the current interpretation that is open to critique is the notion that the earliest votive dedications should be connected to elite status competition and self-aggrandizing behavior. Along these lines, it is generally accepted that EIA bronze dedications "should . . . be seen in a dynamic social framework of 'cumulative emulation' or 'ritualized competition' between aristocratic members of society . . . the dedication of prestigious offering made visible and perpetuated a donor's claim to special relations with higher powers, similarly enhancing his position in society."[50] This interpretation is not unreasonable for some kinds of artifacts dedicated in sanctuaries – such as large tripod cauldrons that might have remained on display in *temenoi* or temples for years (Figure 5.2).[51] However, the figurines I am analyzing in this book are hardly suitable for demonstrating extraordinary wealth and the favor of the god. As I discussed in Chapter 4, these early votive figurines are quite small and not made particularly carefully. It is necessary to consider these objects and the power they might have as agents in elite status competition based on their own

[47] Schürmann 1996; Lebessi 2002, 185–192.

[48] For Morgan's reconstruction of the economics of the sanctuary and votive production see especially Morgan 1990, 35–47.

[49] See extensive discussions in Gehrig 1964; Herrmann 1964; Heilmeyer 1969; 1979, 73–179; Schmaltz 1980; Croissant 1992. Much work has focused on breaking down the votives into schools, for example, Argive, Lakonian, Olympian. For general discussion of regional schools of bronze production in the LG period, Rolley 1986, 66–72; 1994, 144.

[50] Prent 2005, 356.

[51] Aurigny 2019 provides an up-to-date and well-illustrated catalog of tripod cauldrons from late eighth and seventh century dates at Delphi.

5.2. Bronze tripod from Olympia, ca. 900 (photo courtesy of the German Archaeological Institute, D-DAI-ATH-1974/1108, photographer Gösta Hellner)

characteristics, rather than simply classing them together with more impressive votive dedications that we interpret in that light, just because they are both made of bronze. This brings us back to some questions of categorization that were discussed in the introduction.

When we attend to the particular characteristics of EIA figurines instead of to their basic material category (votive bronzes), it becomes rather implausible to reconstruct a scenario in which these objects were functional adjuncts to a process of self-aggrandizing elite status competition.[52] Besides their diminutive stature and unfinished appearance, the figurines probably would not have been on display for an extended of time, but appear instead to have been cast more or less directly into the waste from the animal sacrifices that accompanied the

[52] For an elaborate formulation postulating a strong role for very tiny bronze figurines in socio-political competition see, for example, Prost 2018, 156, where a group of diminutive bronze horses are created by Lakonian craftsmen "through a desire to distinguish themselves . . . from their powerful Peloponnesian neighbor [Argos] . . . at the very moment when the city of Sparta, no doubt, is being formed, the Olympic connections established, and a veiled rivalry with Corinth setting in."

rituals for which they were produced.[53] This does not mean that a model whereby some kind of elite display was happening at Olympia is totally incorrect, and certainly this model goes some way in explaining some of the evidence from the site (e.g., the dedication of large and impressive bronze cauldrons). However, accepting that one set of material objects can be interpreted in one way does not necessitate interpreting adjacent material objects in that same way, especially if doing so presses against the limits of interpretative plausibility.[54] In my view, it does not seem like elite self-aggrandizement or status competition provides a compelling explanation of the social function of the earliest bronze figurines dedicated at EIA sanctuaries.

A second issue with the standing interpretation of the production of these votives likewise pertains the issue of categorization, but relates to the categories that we impose on people rather than objects. The existing model assumes the existence of a number of distinct social roles: the political elites of the nascent *poleis* who visit the interregional sanctuaries, the craftspeople that travel to meet elite demand for votives, and (presumably) the religious personnel that mediate ritual practice on behalf of the divine authority.[55] These actors, moreover, belong to distinct spheres of behavior to which categorically different motivations attend. The elites visit the sanctuary to enhance their political standing relative to other elites. The craftsmen ply their trade at the sanctuary in order to augment their economic well-being within a market peopled by itinerant experts in craft production. The religious personnel, often assumed rather than named, presumably benefit as intermediaries, facilitating the ritual procedures in order to produce social standing within the wider community through the cultivation of a certain ideology that values their intermediation between elites and supernatural powers.

---

[53] It is difficult to reconstruct the exact series of events that might have transpired around the production and dedication of the votives, because the black layers in which the majority of the figurines were excavated are probably not in primary deposition. However, the fact that the votives are mostly mixed in with the remains of the ash and bones from animal sacrifice suggests that they may have been set up or thrown into the ashes directly after or during the cooking of the animal. See discussion of the archaeological contexts of the figurines in Chapter 2.

[54] It is interesting to note that the distribution of bronze anthropomorphic figurines on Crete does not overlap with the dedication of large and impressive metal votives, for the most part (Prent 2005, 390).

[55] The idea of a 'priestly class' has not played much of a role in discussions of EIA religion and society, for reasons that remain unclear. However, see Murray 1980, 66: "Professional priests existed at certain shrines, but they stood outside the normal organization of society; it is a characteristic of early Greece that the nobility performed most civic religious rituals by virtue of themselves holding priesthoods."; also relevant is Murray 1991, 26, where the idea that there was effectively no such group mediating between elites and the supernatural in early Greece is presented.

From a modern, or even an Archaic and Classical perspective, it might make sense to think about craftspeople as largely or even exclusively economic actors, and thus to cordon off productive activity from political or ritual behavior. That line of thinking also makes sense within the context of extant models for understanding the development of worship in rural sanctuaries and the importance of the activities that took place within them.[56] However, I do not think that kind of categorization is helpful when it comes to understanding the evidence for bronze production from EIA sanctuaries.[57] Rather, there are many reasons to break this distinction down and to reconfigure an understanding of EIA ritual and metallurgical production in which the two were closely intertwined and perhaps even inseparable.

In keeping with the methodological goals of this project, it is worth pausing briefly to note the way in which this point illustrates the issues with the master narratives that drive much of our reconstruction of EIA society. The model of elite competition and identity formation at EIA sanctuaries is straightforwardly derived from the way that these sanctuaries functioned in the Archaic period.[58] But nothing about these models necessarily belongs in or fits well with the evidence from the EIA itself. We are dealing with a period that is at a significant chronological remove from the Archaic period, during which all kinds of structural, demographic, cultural, and institutional aspects of life in Greece were likely to have been totally different than they were in the seventh century. While it is difficult to reconstruct the exact nature of these differences, thinking through the models proposed for the production of the earliest Greek figurines, even in an abstract way, presents some sense of how they might not easily transfer back to an EIA context.

For example, the current model for reconstructing the logistics of bronze votive manufacture at sanctuary sites is difficult to square with some widely accepted aspects of the material conditions in which people probably lived during the tenth and ninth centuries. A model attributing the production of bronze votives at sanctuaries to itinerant or wandering tinkers who opportunistically set up shop at rural sanctuaries during festivals implicitly assumes that a number of conditions obtained. The first would be that the pilgrims traveling

---

[56] On the economic importance of sanctuaries see, for example, Snodgrass 1980, 49–58; sources cited in discussion above.

[57] It generally seems problematic to work with models of society in which individuals are conceptualized as having a fixed and single social role in society, as we can easily understand when we think about our own lives and the many social roles that we play, even on a daily basis (within families, jobs, friendship groups, socioeconomic encounters, political lives, etc.). On discussion of such complexities of social status in Archaic Greece, with a review of some relevant sociological literature, see Davies 2017.

[58] For Blok (2014), participation in cults constituted the core claim to citizenship among male members of *polis* communities. For Archaic agonistic competition in sanctuaries see, for example, Hodkinson 1999; Hall 2013, 142, 303–305.

to the sanctuary had access to scrap or ingot bronze, since the model posits that the pilgrims supplied the bronze to the tinkers upon arrival at the sanctuary.[59] The large number of bronze votives dedicated would then require us to reconstruct a situation in which many members of different communities had access to metal resources, which is not really supported by the archaeological distribution of bronze. Some small items made of bronze appear in mortuary contexts in EIA Greece, but the quantities are very limited. The only sizable deposits of bronze from the ninth and eighth centuries come from the very sanctuaries where these votives are dedicated.[60] This could be attributable to distortions in the archaeological record introduced by depositional habits, but there is also room to speculate that the majority of bronzes exist in sanctuary contexts because the majority of the bronze resources in circulation in the EIA regularly resided in sanctuary contexts, rather than that such resources were widely distributed and brought to sanctuaries by worshippers.

Another issue with a model positioning metalworkers as itinerant economic actors is the evidence for the origin of the copper used to make EIA votives. In a distributed model where each worshipper brought bronze for votives to the sanctuary or each tinker traveled around gathering bronze to make votives, we would expect that such metal resources would be highly variable as to their origin, since it is logical that people from different regions might be acquiring bronze scrap from a variety of different sources. However, all of the copper used to produce metal objects from Olympia and Delphi that have been analyzed by Kiderlen and colleagues seems to come from the exact same metal source (the Faynan mines in Israel's Negev desert).[61] Additional work by Kiderlen indicates not only that most EIA bronze tripods excavated at Olympia were made at Olympia but that tripods dedicated at Kalapodi were also manufactured at Olympia.[62] We must therefore try to square a model where metal access was widespread and probably heterogeneous with metallographic and Neutron Activation Analysis evidence that suggests a metal source and location of bronze manufacturing that was limited and homogenous.

---

[59] This is a system that is widely known from well-documented cultural contexts, as discussed in Rowlands 1971, 210–224; Risberg 1992, 39–40; 1998, 675. On the possibility that the *ta-ra-si-ja* system in the LBA Pylian state involved a regular distribution of metal to smiths for special purposes along something like these lines, see Hiller 1972, 51–72; 1979; Leukart 1979; Gillis 1997, 509–511; Del Freo 2005; discussion in Blackwell 2018. On the role of the smith in Mycenaean society, see Gillis 1997, who believes they were wholly independent workers who were powerful within their own villages and in their capacity as suppliers to the palace. Also relevant are comments by Nakassis (2013, 170).

[60] Morgan 1993, 46; Murray 2017, 271.   [61] Kiderlen et al. 2016.

[62] Kiderlen et al. 2017, 339: "... a large percentage of the tripods dedicated at Kalapodi were made at Olympia."

If bronze workers were going to the trouble of traveling to sanctuaries, setting up workshops and making votives for customers, we must also consider what sort of profit they accrued for these efforts. In the context of a simple, probably household-centered, certainly pre-monetary EIA economy, it is difficult to reconstruct a coherent system whereby itinerant smiths would have been compensated for their labor in a way that was logistically convenient.[63] While there has been extensive scholarly discussion about the evolution of Mediterranean trade and exchange systems in the EIA, less thinking has gone into sorting out how local and small-scale exchanges would have taken place, such as how an itinerant smith might have been paid.[64] Since currency was nonexistent and precious materials relatively scarce in the EIA, the option that makes the most sense would be exchange in kind.[65] We might conjecture that the smith would have demanded something durable in exchange for votive production, since the sanctuary calendar probably resulted in an uneven 'boom and bust' cycle, so that the smith had huge amounts of gains in concentrated moments and less robust opportunities for income other times of year. This makes it unlikely that the staple goods available to most households would have constituted an ideal form of payment. Herd animals or perhaps a share of the feast at the sanctuary are easier to imagine as plausible forms of compensation. Overall, many of the logical underpinnings of the system of the itinerant tinker and votive maker sit somewhat awkwardly with current understandings of the EIA economy (though it makes sense from an Archaic and Classical point of view).

An Alternative Model: Metalworking as Central to Ritual Action

A more elegant model might situate possession, production, and distribution of bronze as a closed system that was at the core of ritual action at some sanctuaries. In other words, I propose reconfiguring the role of the smith in ritual practice at some EIA sanctuaries. Instead of seeing the smith as an

---

[63] For recent reviews of evidence for the nature of production and exchange in the EIA economy, see Murray 2020, 202–203; Nakassis 2020, 280–281.

[64] Rations for smiths are not attested in the Pylos texts (Gillis 1997, 513). In the EIA we do not have good evidence from which to reconstruct mechanisms of exchange, but most speculation involves household-based economies in which specialization was unusual and luxury goods scarce (Zurbach 2016) and in which most identifiable exchange involved ceramics (and hence perhaps surplus agricultural goods; for example, Lemos 2002, 212–217; Gimatzidis 2010, 258–269; Kotsonas 2012b, 155–162; Lemos 2012; Pratt 2015).

[65] Kroll (2008) suggests that silver might have been used for transactions in early Greece. Some readings of Homer push the idea that gold was used for transactions in the EIA (Zurbach 2016, 366), but the very small amounts of gold evident in the archaeological record give reason for skepticism about whether this could have been generally true for the vast majority of exchanges taking place, especially prior to the late eighth century.

economic actor, metallurgical workers may have been priestly figures with jurisdiction over ritual actions which included the production of metal artifacts. One reason to prefer this model is that the metallographic evidence makes more sense if we place the ritual personnel of the sanctuary and the physical location of the sanctuary at the center of the both the production of votives and the management of the resources for production. A model along these lines also eliminates many of the problems associated with solving the archaeological record against the notional career of the economically motivated itinerant bronze worker: bronze from the period is concentrated at sanctuaries because sanctuary personnel managed bronze acquisition and deposition, and votives were produced as part of ritual spectacle itself, accruing social and political capital, rather than economic gain, to the persona of the smith, whose presence and productive practice were both essential to the sanctity of the space.

In considering the merits of this model, it is worth revisiting the way our contemporary categorizations of social roles can undermine our ability to think creatively about past social systems. In the context of Aegean archaeology, it has been normal to categorize metalworking and metalworkers as economic actions and actors. It is also usually assumed that these actors must or probably should be specialists in metalworking, to the exclusion of other kinds of expertise. These views derive their logic from the way that we construct technologists as somewhat scientific and ultimately economically driven individuals, but it is easy to break apart these assumptions.

Named smiths in the Pylian Linear B tablets were not specialists, but also did other things, appearing in some texts as smiths but in others as herders.[66] Since systems of production in the EIA are usually considered to have featured *less* craft specialization than Mycenaean ones, this evidence provides *ipso facto* grounds for suspecting that EIA smiths were very unlikely to have been specialists, but instead may have done all sorts of different things to make a living. Recognizing this goes some way toward relieving us from the need to reconstruct the traveling bronze smith, because the main grounds for doing so is that these economic actors would have had nothing to do at sanctuaries during the times that festivals and rituals were not taking place, *ergo* they must have been itinerant.

If smiths occupied many different, sometimes overlapping, but seasonally distinct roles in society, we need not imagine that their lives entailed an endless tour of road tripping for festival gigs. Instead, the smiths may have varied their pursuits throughout the year. During festivals, these could have included producing bronze votives, but during non-festival periods smiths could have

---

[66] Gillis 1997, 512, n. 41; Nakassis 2013, 73–116.

attended to the care and provision of herd animals in the remote areas around sanctuaries (maybe even those that would be sacrificed for ritual feasts during festivals) or to the acquisition of metal resources through trade or travel.[67] Alternatively, we might retain the view of smiths as itinerant, but posit that they traveled in their capacity as ritual authorities rather than economic actors, so that it was their very presence at EIA sanctuaries that precipitated the enactment of a festival.[68] This model could account for the remarkable alignment of the early ritual assemblages from the spatially dispersed sites of Syme Viannou, Olympia, and Delphi, which all include black layers full of similar kinds of votives that share many formal characteristics, evidence for metalworking, and probably some kind of initiatory or liminal rites.[69] The mechanism for the correspondence among the assemblages would then be the shared identity of the officials that presided over rites at all of these sites, that is, a traveling group of priest-smiths. Rather than profiting materially from their work in sanctuaries *sensu* the market, we would conclude that metalworkers were producing votives at sanctuaries as part of a linked suite of activities that they conducted in order to acquire and maintain ideological and social capital – or even political power.

One of the many reasons to prefer a model that ties metalworkers and metalworking to ritual rather than economic aspects of early sanctuaries is the state of the archaeological record at the sanctuaries themselves. At Olympia, the evidence suggests that smithing took place just to the north of the old ash altar. At Syme Viannou, where bronze working evidence dates from the early first millennium, this evidence also comes from the center of the ritual space of the sanctuary. The close spatial association between the ritual heart of early sanctuaries and metalworking spaces provides some vestigial but compelling reason to believe that there may have been a close connection between the ritual activities and metal production.

The possibility of such a connection seems even more compelling if we take into account the sensory implications of a close spatial relationship between

---

[67] Burkert (1996, 29, n. 45) notes that the etymology of the word *altis*, the name for the area of the sacred grove at Olympia, plausibly refers to its use as an open area where livestock were fed.

[68] It is interesting to note that the population of metallurgical workers buried in the vicinity of the Wadi Faynan metallurgical work sites is thought to have been nomadic (perhaps connected with the Shasu nomads mentioned in contemporary Egyptian texts), representing groups that came together and engaged in smelting periodically but did not otherwise constitute a permanent community (Levy, Adams, and Muniz 2004; Levy et al. 2004; Levy 2009). Likewise, the dispersed networks of LBA and EIA metallurgical production recently investigated in the south Caucasus region are not accompanied by buildings or habitations, suggesting that the community that used them may have been nomadic or semi-nomadic (Erb-Satullo, Gilmour, and Khakhutaishvili 2014).

[69] For example, the earliest bronze votive tripods from Cretan sanctuaries "sind kaum zu unterscheiden" (can hardly be distinguished) from one another (Maass 1979, 50).

metalworking and the heart of EIA sanctuaries. If metalwork was taking place within close range of ritual space, it would not have been inconspicuous, like a souvenir shop at the entrance to an archaeological site. Bronze casting is elemental, producing heat, noise, smoke and steam, not to mention unsavory smells and the persistent risk of explosions and dangerous accidents. If metallurgy were happening in or near the ritual space of an EIA sanctuary, everyone present would have noticed. The disruptive sensory qualities of metal production (not to mention the need for large amounts of charcoal and wood for the furnaces, which would have been abundant in these areas) may even go some way toward explaining the logic underlying sanctuaries' rural locations, in environments far from residential communities that could be disturbed or frightened by this pyrotechnological activity.[70]

Like burnt animal sacrifice, metalworking was apparently taking place at rural sanctuaries from very early in their history of use as ritual gathering spaces.[71] However, the possible ritual connotations of this apparently foundational tandem of metalwork and rural worship have not been fully explored, probably because of the persistent tendency to see craftwork as functioning economically rather than ritually within society. In what follows I demonstrate how our interpretation of EIA figurine production transforms if we situate it as embedded in the ritual anthropology of metalwork and metalworkers, rather than placing it within a model of state formation and elite political competition. Situating metalworking within ritual practice is logical because it is suggested in a straightforward way by the archaeological evidence, which shows a close spatial correlation between evidence for metalworking and other ritual activities. It is also made plausible by a broader assessment of ritual and metal work in eastern Mediterranean and general human contexts.

Comparative Evidence: Metallurgy and Ritual Authority in the Eastern Mediterranean

Greek archaeologists tend to place metallurgy, with other craft activities, in the domain of economic activity. Likewise, the metallurgist is seen as an economic, rather than a ritual or political actor, in the context of early Greece. However, in other eastern Mediterranean societies bronze working and

---

[70] On the usual location of smithies near wooded areas and areas where people did not live, see Forbes 1964, 69; Childs and Killick 1993, 325; Treister 1996, 79.

[71] Unlike the scanty literature on metalworking in sanctuaries, discussions of the sacrifice and commensality through feasting as important elements of cult activity in Greece from the Mycenaean to the Archaic period are abundant. Some of many discussions include Schmitt-Pantel 1990; Wright 1994; Morgan 1996; Palaima 2004; Sherratt 2004; van den Eijnde 2010; Niemeier 2016; Eder and Lemos 2020, 142; Lupack 2020, 161–163.

bronze workers are known to have inhabited important political and religious roles, rather than just economic ones, during the LBA and EIA.

The most thorough case for the embeddedness of metallurgy within a system of ritual and political authority has been made for Bronze Age Cyprus.[72] At Cypriot sites such as Enkomi, Athienou, Kalopsidha, and Kition-Kathari, the presence of metallurgical workshops, as well as the votive deposition of scrap metal and metallurgical waste in temple contexts provides the archaeological basis for reconstructing a connection between bronze workers and ritual practice in the Bronze Age.[73] For example, at Kition a building complex with clear evidence for copper production was excavated directly adjacent to a temple and a sacred *temenos* and dated to the thirteenth century.[74] The appearance of the so-called ingot god who is depicted standing on an ingot and to whom miniature ingots were dedicated as votives likewise supports the connection between metallurgy and ritual power in Cyprus; the cast bronze figurines representing this god, have been extensively discussed by scholars of the Cypriot Bronze Age, most of whom agree that the only reasonable interpretation of the type is some kind of religious worship centered on the production of copper and bronze.[75] Knapp has argued convincingly that the ritual authority connected with metal production also implicated systems of political authority, and that skill in and control over copper production was not simply a matter of craft or economic ability, but a nexus for the negotiation and reification of religious and state power as well.

Evidence for other kinds of connections between religious institutions, divine or political authority, and metal production is relatively widespread in the EIA eastern Mediterranean. Inscriptions on two eighth century Phoenician bowls dedicated at Limassol in Cyprus indicate that the first fruits of copper production were dedicated to Baal of Lebanon, presumably because the god had some kind of claim to the products of Cypriot mines.[76] One possible interpretation of these bowls is that temples "played a role in the sourcing and trade of bronze."[77] Biblical texts describe a king of Tyre named Hiram, who not only had political authority but was also a smith connected with the production and trade of bronze.[78] According to the relevant accounts,

---

[72] Knapp 1986.

[73] Dietrich 1983, 89; Webb 1999, 237; Dardaillon 2012, 175. On Kition see Karageorghis 1976; 1985. On Enkomi and Athienou see Knapp 1986 with exhaustive previous bibliography. On Kalopsidha, Åstrom 1987, 177–179.

[74] Karageorghis 1976, fig. 11.

[75] Catling 1969, 86; 1971, 29–30; Karageorghis 1973, 108–9; Knapp 1986, 10.

[76] Grottanelli 1988, 244–246; Zamora Lopez 2015, 31. The inscriptions are very similar, each reading something along the lines of "PN, governer of Qartihadast, servant of Hiram, king of the Sidonians, gave this to Baal of Lebanon, his lord, as the first fruits of copper from H..."

[77] Zamora Lopez 2015, 21.   [78] 2 Sam. 5:11; Kings 5:1–11; 10:11; 1 Kings 7:13–51.

Hiram was summoned by Solomon to create bronze objects with which to elaborate his temple. The details demonstrate that the author had substantial understanding of and interest in the manufacturing process, including the use of clay molds by Hiram.[79] The book of Exodus describes another powerful bronze worker, Bezalel, the god-given artistic merits he possessed, and his divine mandate to craft wonderful objects for the glorification of the cult place:

> Then the Lord said to Moses, "See, I have chosen Bezalel son of Uri, the son of Hur, of the tribe of Judah, and I have filled him with the Spirit of God, with wisdom, with understanding, with knowledge and with all kinds of skills – to make artistic designs for work in gold, silver and bronze, to cut and set stones, to work in wood, and to engage in all kinds of crafts. Moreover, I have appointed Oholiab son of Ahisamak, of the tribe of Dan, to help him. Also, I have given ability to all the skilled workers to make everything I have commanded you."[80]

The close association of acumen in metal crafts and divine or political authority is also apparent in EIA Assyrian texts, especially the annals that describe the careers of Sargon II and his son Sennacherib, who ruled in the eighth and seventh centuries. Sennacherib's accounts of his improvements of the palace at Nineveh (the "palace without a rival") are remarkable in promulgating a direct and extensively elaborated connection between the king's metallurgical skills, his authority as the ruler of the kingdom, and the divine agency behind the skills the king needed to achieve impressive results. The annals include a number of boasts about massive bronze smithing projects including the casting of huge herds of bronze lions "constructed out of 11,400 talents" of metal by "the workmanship of the god Nin-a-gal" and adorning architectural elements with bronze at similar expense.[81] In several inscriptions, Sennacherib describes the way that his metallurgical skills exceed those of his predecessors and the god-given cunning that he requires to manage his accomplishments as a craftsman:

> In times past, when the kings, my fathers, fashioned a bronze image in the likeness of their members, to set up in their temples, the labor on them exhausted every workman; in their ignorance and their lack of knowledge, 'they drank oil and wore sheepskins to carry on the work they wished to do in the midst of their mountains'. But I, Sennacherib, first among all princes, wise in all craftsmanship, great pillars of bronze, colossal lions, open at the knees, which no king before my time had fashioned, through the clever understanding which the noble

---

[79] 1 Kings 7.
[80] Exodus 31.1–6. See also Exodus 36–39 for a long appreciation of the artisans making wonders for the tabernacle and the association of their work with the glory of god.
[81] Excerpts from text of "The Palace without a Rival" translated by Luckenbill (1924, vol. I) I.83–84.

Nin–igi–Kug had given me, and in my own wisdom, I pondered deeply the matter of carrying out that task, following the advice of my head (will) and the prompting of my heart, I fashioned a work of bronze and cunningly wrought it...I built a form of clay and poured bronze into it, as in making half-shekel pieces, and finished their construction.[82]

The annals of Sennacherib demonstrate both a remarkable understanding of the technological acumen required for the achievement of impressive results in bronze casting and an unambiguous ideology connecting the divine authority over distribution of this acumen, the divine sanction of the political authority, and the degree to which skilled craftsmanship was connected to the cult of the ruler in eighth-century Assyria. As Thomason comments, "the ultimate message is that the object arrived in its finished form via the capable and powerful hands of king Sennacherib."[83] While Sennacherib emphasized his role as a craftsperson and artist more than most Mesopotamian kings, similar albeit less extensive claims were made by his father Sargon II and by kings of Sumer in the preceding periods.[84]

As opposed to the situation in Bronze Age Cyprus and the EIA in the Eastern Mediterranean more generally, evidence of a connection between bronze working and ritual is sparse for the LBA in the Aegean. On Crete, Poros-Katsambas was obviously the site of a major metallurgical operation until the twelfth century but does not seem to have had any ritual importance.[85] Workshops at Kato Zakro and Malia have been interpreted as adjuncts to ritual institutions, although based on quite tenuous circumstantial evidence.[86] Votive assemblages from the transition between the Middle Minoan and LM I periods at the peak sanctuary of Kophinas yielded a considerable

---

[82] Luckenbill 1924, vol. II, 108–109. For a nearly identical inscription see also Luckenbill 1924, vol. II, 122–123 ('undated bull inscription'). Similar boasts are made in a description of the building of the armory (133: "With the keen understanding which Ea, lord of wisdom gave me, I made clay molds for all the copper work needed (desired) for my palace which I built at Nineveh, according to the command of the god, and poured bronze therein. The work of my hands was successful and these female protecting deities of shining bronze I flanked (lit. caused to bear) with slabs of ashnan-stone . . .") and the temple of the new year (139–142: "Sennacherib, king of Assyria, maker of the images of Assur and the great gods"; "A gate of burnished copper, with all kinds of ___, in the workmanship of the smith-god, by my own artistic ability, I made, and the image of Assur, who is advancing to battle into the midst of Tiamat, as he raises his bow, riding in a chariot, bringing on the storm...and the image of Amurru, who rides with him as charioteer, these I engraved upon that gate, at the command of Shamash and Adad as they gave it through the oracle.)"

[83] Thomason 2004, 156.   [84] See Winter 2003 on the Sumerian kings.

[85] Dimopoulou 1997; 2004; 2012.

[86] At Malia, the presence of ritual objects that appear to have fallen from above the workshops of Quartier Mu led the excavators to speculate that they might have been situated underneath a shrine (Poursat 1983). At Zakro the west wing, which has been interpreted as having a sacred function, contained considerable evidence for craft activity, but not for metalworking in particular (Chrysoulaki and Platon 1987, 81).

amount of bronze waste and several fragments of bronze talents along with two bronze anthropomorphic figurines.[87] Marinatos suggested that the massive metal hoard at Arkalochori might indicate the presence of a smith or foundry at the sacred cave, since the hoard contained unfinished items alongside ingots.[88] A votive deposit from the Neopalatial period at the recently excavated Anetaki plot at Knossos might suggest that rituals involving metalworkers comprised a part of the politico-religious system in Bronze Age Crete. The deposit in question was placed inside of a rock-cut pit and sealed with a round plaque made of stone. Most of the votives consisted of pieces of raw materials rather than finished objects – pieces of gold, silver, and copper bars, a copper bun ingot, and raw chunks of rock crystal, amethyst, sardonyx, and a bluish-white stone – and could thus plausibly have been deposited by a craft worker who used these raw materials.[89]

For the Mycenaean mainland, some connection between divine institutions and metal production may lie behind the formulation *ka-ko na-wi-jo* in a Linear B text PY Jn 829 from Pylos, which could construe something along the lines of 'temple bronze'.[90] However, scholars are not in agreement about the interpretation of this text, and the majority seem not to favor an interpretation that connects the bronze (*ka-ko*) in question to any kind of temple.[91] The cult center at Mycenae may have been affiliated with artisans who made votive objects from exotic materials stored in the complex, but other than this, there is scant archaeological evidence to substantiate a link between sacred and productive spaces from the Mycenaean world.[92] Suffice it to say that a link between craftspeople and cult practice in the LBA Aegean is tenuous at best on current evidence. If ritual craft production of some kind did exist in this context, it does not seem to have constituted a dominant sector of the LBA economy.[93]

In sum, a connection between metallurgical production, metalworkers, and ritual authority was not an unusual feature in societies of the late second and early first millennium in the eastern Mediterranean. Such connections are, on the other hand, not unambiguously apparent in the Aegean prior to the EIA.

---

[87] Platon and Davaras 1961–1962, 287–288; Alexiou 1963b, 384; Karetsou and Rethemiotakis 1990, 429.
[88] Marinatos 1962, 87–94.   [89] Stampolidis et al. 2019, 253.
[90] Discussion in Hiller 1979, 190. Borgna (1995, 19–21, 40–43) has connected hoards of bronze metals with a ritual, competitive, elite practice designed to conspicuously remove metals from circulation, but even if this argument is to be accepted, it is not clearly related to the production of bronzes. See also comments by Blackwell (2018, 527).
[91] Michailidou 2001; Del Freo 2005; Palaima 2015; Blackwell 2018, 528.
[92] French 1981b, 45.   [93] Hägg 1992, 32.

*Comparative Evidence: Metallurgy and Ritual in Historical
and Ethnographic Perspective*

The situation in the eastern Mediterranean around the turn of the first
millennium can be helpfully informed by evidence for connections between
metallurgical practice and ritual power in human history more generally. This
association was quite common in ancient and modern society up until the
Industrial Revolution introduced a rift between science and religion.[94]
Prehistorians have largely followed Childe in retaining a distinction between
the industrial and technological knowledge and economic role of smiths and
the ritual and religious realm in human prehistory.[95] Aegeanists have in turn
also followed Childe's distinction both because of Childe's immense influence
and because a distinction between craft and industrial production and ritual
power and practice is discernible in the texts produced by the literate proto-
urban and urban societies of Greece and Rome.

However, there is reason to believe that this separation was not typical in
premodern societies, especially those with limited literacy and minimal urban-
ization.[96] In the ancient Andes, mining and metallurgical processes were highly
mystical: mines were sacred places that were worshipped and given offerings.[97]
In his interpretation of the blending of ritual and metalworking structures in
the earthen enclosure at Mšecké Zehrovice in Bohemia, Bradley argued for
the interpretation of the site as a sacred location where the transformational
practice of metalworking produced its magical and sacred character as well as
utilitarian artifacts, rejecting as fundamentally flawed the distinction archaeologists normally maintain between sacred and functional activities.[98] There is
widespread evidence that iron production and politico-ritual power were
intimately connected historically in Sub-Saharan Africa.[99] In general, historical
traditions preserve a number of narrative tropes whereby metalworkers
acquired political power in tandem with the ritual power invested in their
mastery over fire, perhaps in part because warriors relied upon them to create
weapons.[100] Traditions involving smiths that came to political power include
an account according to which Genghis Khan began his life as one, and an
Iranian myth according to which the founder of the Kayva dynasty was a smith
who one day "fixed his leather apron to a spear head thus raising the standard
of revolt against the dragon king."[101]

---

[94] Budd and Taylor 1995, 133.   [95] Budd and Taylor 1995, 135–138.
[96] Helms 1993; 2006, 452.   [97] Petersen 2010, xix.
[98] Bradley 2005, 21–23; for the site itself, Venclová 1998.
[99] As summarized and brought into engagement with Greco-Roman literature in Blakely
2006, 166–179. For some of the original ethnographic accounts and work by Africanists see,
for example, Barnes and Ben-Amos 1983; Bernus 1983; Schmidt and Mapunda 1997;
Barndon 1999.
[100] On the smith and the warrior see Eliade 1955, 208.   [101] Altheim 1952, 33, 126.

Folk customs from late antique and early modern European history likewise bind together magic/ritual and metal production with regularity. In certain western European traditions dating to the early Middle Ages, Jesus' father Joseph was a smith and thus imbued with supernatural powers appropriate to the rearing of the son of the Judeo-Christian god.[102] The same association between smiths and supernatural power is apparent in the lore of many traditional societies that have been studied by anthropologists and ethnographers. For example, according to a proverb from the tradition of the Sakha, a traditional herding people in the central Asian steppe, "smiths and shamans come from the same nest." The smith was, however, considered to be far more powerful than and senior to the shaman and was involved in the initiation of new shamans, a process that was viewed as akin to the tempering of iron.[103] Siberian people in general see the role of the smith in society as a spiritual rather than a commercial one, and in their societies the smithy is used as a place of worship in lieu of discrete buildings (i.e., churches or temples) specifically set aside for ritual.[104] Traditional Indonesian society imagined a strong connection between the metallurgist and control over human fate that imbued metalworkers with important religious and magical powers.[105] Moreover, the locations of metalworking themselves were collocational with shrines, a characteristic that is not limited to the Indonesian context, for example, the same situation existed in the Iron Age culture of the Irish midlands.[106]

In sum, cross-cultural examinations of preindustrial societies often attest to a widespread belief that artisans in general and smiths in particular were privy to wonderful secrets and magical knowledge that allowed them to effect fundamental transformations of base materials into fine things through mastery of fire. These beliefs often extend ritual control over transformative rites or life events such as initiations and death to smiths, and imbue the locations where metalworking took place with ritual significance.[107]

Although common, ritual veneration for smiths is not a universal feature of premodern societies. An obvious counterexample is the familiar Greek textual evidence attesting to the fact that smiths and other craftsmen were base and

---

[102] Budd and Taylor 1995, 133. These folktales often equate the smith with the darker aspects of magic, and smiths are often seen in such stories making ill-advised deals with the devil (see, e.g., Eliade 1955, 207; Graça da Silva and Tehrani 2016). On Joseph the Smith, see Le Goff 1988, 207; Helms 2006.

[103] Eliade 1955, 206–208.   [104] Jochelson 1931, 172.

[105] Baumann 1950, 89; Evans 1953, 15–17; O'Connor 1975; 1985.

[106] Zerner 1981, 95. On smithies as sacred spaces see Robins 1953, 26; Eliade 1962, 79–86, 107; Forbes 1964, 75.

[107] Edsman 1949, 96–98, 166–171; Eco 2004, 102–103; Helms 2006, 460. For hilltop spectacles of metallurgical production, see Dolan 2016.

often despised members of society from the Archaic period onward.[108] It is important to emphasize one generalization about the societies in which reverence for smiths is apparent, which is that they tend to be preliterate societies or societies in which literacy is quite limited. The reason for the alignment between low levels of literacy and associating technology with magic probably has to do with the way in which procedures that needed to be followed with some precision were embedded in memory where they could not be transmitted by text.[109] Most often, when magical metalwork has been documented, its complex procedures are remembered through ritualization by way of something like a spell.[110] Access to this ritualized knowledge is often kept secret, so that metalworkers with access to it form closed and mysterious groups that pass on information through apprenticeships.[111] The perception of metalworkers as secretive was reinforced by the fact that the location of metallurgical work sites was often remote.[112]

It is possible to summarize the situation as follows. There is much comparative evidence for the commonplace investment of ritual and social power in the persona of the smith from a wide variety of human societies in which literacy was either nonexistent or highly limited. It is therefore not necessary or natural to bring the assumption that smiths, social and political elites, and ritual personnel occupied distinct social roles in the EIA, which was by all accounts a period of limited literacy during which metalworking and ritual spaces are often closely associated in the archaeological record.

EIA Ritual Practice: The Role of Bronze Production

In the context of the Aegean, the close and consistent spatial association between early sanctuaries and metallurgy is a novel feature of the EIA

---

[108] Herodotus (2.167.2) indicates that craftspeople were despised in most Greek cities in his time. Examples of Classical authors expressing distaste for or making fun of craftspeople include but are not limited to Xen. *Oec.* 4.2–3; Xen. *Mem.* 3.7.5–6; Ar. *Eq.* 733–740; Ar. *Plut.* 507–526; Lucian, *Somn.* 22; Andoc. 1.146; Dem. 25.38; Dem. 57.30–36. See also Ober 1989, 274–277, 310–311. For the low status of artisans under the democracy see de Ste. Croix 1981, 274–275; Vickers and Gill 1994, 93–96. However, Feyel (2006) argues a sensible point that artisans were always a mixed group in terms of background and socioeconomic status. It is also important to distinguish between regular craftspeople who were serial producers of ordinary, low-cost goods, and people in charge of making bespoke commissions for the rich or the state (including such famous craftsmen as Phidias, Praxiteles, etc.) and professional architects, who held generally higher social esteem (Sapirstein 2018, 101).

[109] Schmidt and Mapunda 1997; Dobres 2000.

[110] Budd and Taylor 1995, 139. According to ancient Indonesian myth, for example, smiths rely upon *mantras* (sacred formulas) that are used for forging and for the ritual of the dead (Goris 1960).

[111] Tylecote 1976, 1–36; Harper 1987, 652.

[112] Forbes 1964, 69; Childs and Killick 1993, 325, 327; Treister 1996, 79.

archaeological record. It also coincides, in part, with another development in the archaeological record, whereby bronze artifacts that had previously been associated primarily with political centers or elaborate burials begin to be redirected into sanctuary deposits. These new features of the archaeological record, which surely align with new social and ritual realities, could have arisen due to purely internal factors, constituting new religious institutions designed to serve as venues for elite competition and the response of craftsmen to those new markets. However, this interpretation is problematic because it projects features of Archaic and Classical Greece, such as the stark separation of social roles for craftspeople (economic), elites (socio-political), and ritual personnel (religious), and an economic model positing markets with supply and demand, into a period for which we have no evidence for such a breakdown of social roles and for which the reconstruction of a developed market economy seems unnecessary and perhaps inappropriate.

An alternative interpretation is that the association between metallurgy and ritual arose in part because of connections between the Aegean and the eastern Mediterranean and a concomitant realignment of the role of metallurgy in society in the EIA Aegean.[113] Archaeological evidence demonstrates that connections sufficient to facilitate this kind of realignment are likely to have existed in the EIA.[114] Connections between Cypriots, Phoenicians, and Crete in the areas of craft production are suggested by some EIA archaeological evidence.[115] Cretan ceramicists appear to have manufactured containers for oil that closely imitated Cypriot containers, and the ceramic evidence in general supports relatively close connections between the two islands during the tenth to seventh centuries.[116] The presence of non-local craftsmen on Crete during the EIA has been posited for a variety of reasons, especially the appearance of metal artifacts produced using techniques that seem new to the island.[117]

Later mythological sources suggest that Cypriot and Phoenician connections and influences might have extended from the realm of craftwork to the area of ritual in EIA Crete.[118] In her thorough treatment of this subject, Sarah Morris stated that "the tradition of *demioergoi*, who practiced religious as well as artistic specialties, seems closely linked on Crete, such that these innovations may have

---

[113] Blakely (1999) raises this possibility, but then rejects it based in part on the lack of evidence for such evidence for ritual metallurgists in Greek textual sources. I suggest instead that textual evidence from the Archaic and Classical periods mostly pertain to those periods, and are not very helpful when it comes to reconstructing ritual systems of the EIA.

[114] Burkert 1992; Hoffman 1997.

[115] Sakellarakis 1992; Hoffman 1997; papers in Karageorghis and Stampolidis 1998; Matthäus 2000; Stampolidis and Kotsonas 2006; Karageorghis et al. 2014.

[116] Kotsonas 2012b.

[117] Hoffman 1997; Coldstream 2000; Matthäus 2000, 270; Papasavvas 2001; 2014; Stampolidis and Kotsonas 2006; Hatzaki and Kotsonas 2020, 1044–45.

[118] Burkert 1992, 19–25.

migrated, together, from the Orient."[119] A figurine from Syme Viannou that closely resembles the Cypriot Bronze Age ingot god provides material evidence that some form of ritual belief and practice linking metal production and divine power may have become part of a Cretan tradition through Cypriot influence during the transition from the Bronze to the Iron Age.[120] The presence of an ivory throne in the Idaean cave and faience statuettes of non-Aegean deities have, in turn, been taken as evidence for Near Eastern influence on Cretan EIA ritual practice.[121] In addition, Temple B at the site of Kommos has been interpreted as a Phoenician-type shrine that must have involved non-Cretan agency of some variety.[122] Since the connection between metallurgy and ritual is not evident in the Aegean prior to the end of the Bronze Age, but is quite common among Cypriot and Phoenician communities with whom Cretans apparently had close contacts in the EIA, it might be reasonable to guess that a new spatial association of metalworking and sanctuaries in the EIA was connected to new ritual systems that were somehow connected to influential contact between Aegean communities and other groups.

To summarize the previous discussion, an association of metalwork and ritual authority is not uncommon in eastern Mediterranean societies of the LBA and EIA. There is considerable evidence for cultural and ritual influence flowing from elsewhere in the Mediterranean into the Aegean, especially via Crete, during the transition between the Bronze and Iron Ages. This is the same period when a close association between metalwork and sanctuary sites first becomes apparent in the material record in the Aegean. If there was a connection between metal production and ritual practice in the EIA Aegean, that would not be particularly surprising from the broader point of view, because such a relationship is well-documented in many human societies, especially ones in which knowledge about technical procedures cannot be recorded in texts and is held or controlled by a limited group of people.

If we accept that metallurgical production was not incidental but central to ritual practice at sites like Syme Viannou, Olympia, and Delphi, it is necessary to rethink the way in which ritual at these sanctuaries worked. In other words, if we place metallurgy into the mix of early Greek ritual practice, and consider it as a ritual rather than economic element of the activities that took place in these sanctuaries, it is necessary to consider how metallurgical production might have functioned within a sacred space as an experiential and material aspect of ritual.

It seems generally agreed that the ritual activities taking place at early Greek sanctuaries like Olympia and Syme Viannou often involved initiation rites for

---

[119] Morris 1992a, 164.   [120] Dietrich 1983, 89.
[121] Stampolidis and Kotsonas 2006, 343–346.
[122] For the shrine, Shaw 1989; 2000, 711–713; Pappalardo 2002.

young members of the community. These rites often required the completion of physical challenges or competitions of some sort. Another activity that is clearly documented to have taken place at early sanctuaries was burnt animal sacrifice. Finally, as discussed above, bronze working occurred alongside these initiatory rituals and animal sacrifices.[123]

One feature that these three activities share in common is transformation: young boys or girls into men and women, living animals into smoke and meat, and wax models into solid bronzes. Initiatory rituals involve something "equivalent to an ontological mutation of the existential condition," so that the initiate in fact emerges from the ritual as a different sort of being than the one that entered into the ritual.[124] In *Homo Necans*, Burkert specifically emphasized the close relationship between an initiatory footrace for participants in ritual at early Olympia and the purifying fire of the ritual sacrifice on an ash altar: "The end of the race, its goal, is the top of the ancient heap of ash, the place where fire must blaze and burn up the thigh bones. The race marks the transition from blood to purifying fire, from encountering death to the joyful satisfaction of surviving as manifested in the strength of the victor."[125] Many aspects of myths related to early Olympia also speak to the recognition that a fiery transformation of youths constituted an important nexus of discourse around the foundation of athletic festivals. The eponymous founder of the Lykaia festival in Arkadia was supposedly killed by his father, cooked in a cauldron by the gods, and then brought back to life through divine intervention. A similar story exists about Pelops, sometimes credited as the founder of the Olympic festival: he was supposedly cooked in a tripod cauldron, eaten by the gods, and then reconstituted in the same cauldron through divine agency. According to another story, Poseidon fell in love with the young Pelops after he was taken out of a purifying fire by Fate.[126]

The transformative quality of bronze casting, set alongside these parallel fiery transformations of initiation and burnt sacrifice, may therefore have been an important reason that it was valued in these ritual contexts. For anyone who has not spent time around molten metal in the foundry, it is worth emphasizing the remarkable visual and material characteristics of this substance and the wonder that must have attended the process of turning a wax model into a metal one (Plate 14). Anyone observing the smithing and casting process would have witnessed something extremely impressive, and this was probably

[123] On the role of initiation ceremonies at these sanctuaries see discussion in Chapter 3. It is worth noting as an aside that animal sacrifice and metallurgy might have been complementary activities, as Knapp has noted, since bone ash is an optimal fluxing agent (Knapp 1986, 43).

[124] Eliade 1958, 7.   [125] Burkert 1983, 98.   [126] Nagy 1986, 79–80, 86.

PLATE 14. Students pouring molten metal in an art studio class at the University of Nebraska (photo courtesy Philip Sapirstein). [A black and white version of this figure will appear in some formats. For the color version, please refer to the plate section.]

especially so in the context of a preindustrial world in which the transformation of materials, glowing lights, and shining objects were not regularly encountered.[127] The craftsman, manipulating a charcoal fire with bellows to a particular temperature, was transforming lumps of heavy, brown material into glowing, molten, liquid fire, which he then used to further transform a dull, soft, waxen figure into a shining, solid, gold-colored object, creating something entirely new and extraordinary from ordinary objects found in nature.

Surely this process of transformation – brown lumps destroyed and reborn in a polished red gold; a wax figure reborn as a solid, heavy, shining metal figure – and the expertise wielded to effect it was an impressive spectacle to behold.[128] The magic of metalworking in the prehistoric past is somewhat difficult to grasp for us because of the thoroughness with which such processes have been embedded in the context of industrial economic production in the modern world. However, only a little bit of imagination is required to begin to come to terms with the amazing visual impression that the EIA foundry probably would have made, and the wonder that would have been expressed toward those who had mastered its management. Indeed, ancient sources consistently attest to the wonder inspired by transformative technological processes in the

[127] Bol 1985, 22.   [128] Wertime 1983, 447; Cavanagh 1990, 145–146.

Greco-Roman world generally.[129] It is not difficult to reconstruct a scenario in which such a spectacle could have been meaningfully and seamlessly integrated into rituals involving the transformation of youths into adults and the transformation of livestock into meat for a ritual feast.

It is, moreover, not difficult to move from an appreciation of the dramatic transformational process of bronze casting to a relocation of the persona of the metallurgist from economic opportunist to a figure who was more integral to ritual institutions and claims to divine authority. In other words, if ritual authority and metallurgical practice were linked, it is likely to also be the case that the metallurgists themselves were ritual authorities rather than economic actors who frequented sanctuaries to profit from extraordinary markets.[130] The role of metallurgists as ritual figures, masters of a universally feared element, and arbiters of divine power in the EIA may be preserved in a number of myths about powerful divine metallurgists, many of which are associated with Cretan religion.[131] Magical Cretan smiths from ancient Greek traditions include the Telchines, the Kouretes, the Korybantes, and the Dactyles, not to mention Daidalos, while others like the Sintians and the Kabeiroi hail from elsewhere.[132] Their powers accrue to the transformative abilities they possess on account of their knowledge of the manipulation of materials, but extend beyond skills explicitly related to metallurgy to incantatory powers,[133] shamanistic abilities, and influence over fertility.[134] Their ability to create one substance from another is often equated to the divine power of human procreation, and their creative process thereby often likened to the mechanisms and means of sexual reproduction.[135] While these strands of Greek myth have been elucidated by previous scholarly work, the ritual role of the metallurgist has not been integrated into the reconstruction of ritual practice and its material cultural correlates in the archaeological record of the EIA because evidence for later Greek religion does not suggest an important ritual role for the metallurgist during historical periods.[136]

It is interesting, nonetheless, to set aside the preconceptions that we have based on our knowledge of later evidence and to think about how we might reconstruct the social position of the metallurgist in an EIA context. In many

---

[129] For example, Hdt. 1.68.1; Pliny *Nat. Hist.* 36.10.159–160.

[130] It is interesting in this respect to note that two of the only extant images of metallurgists in the round from early Greece were probably bronze votives cast in sanctuaries (Figure 2.10, from Philia, and a figurine now New York Metropolitan Museum Inv. No. 42.11.42; Richter 1944, 1–5).

[131] Morris (1992a) provides a wide-ranging and erudite discussion of magical artisans in the Greek tradition. Blakely (2006) also presents evidence for and discussion of metallurgists in Greco-Roman literature. On the Sintians, see Hom. *Od.* 8.294.

[132] Dietrich 1983, 89; Morris 1992a, 87.   [133] Diodorus 5.64.

[134] Delcourt 1957; Blakely 2006, 80–81.   [135] Blakely 2006, 99.

[136] For example, Blakely 1999, 2006.

myths from the ancient Mediterranean, and in many historically documented cultural constructs of the shamanistic or magical metallurgist, these characters are often marked by some kind of physical deformity or disability.[137] There are many ideas about why this might be so. Working with arsenic (as the earliest bronze smiths, who used it as an alloy instead of tin, did) can cause physical problems, so the lame craftsmen might represent a garbled memory of the health problems encountered among smiths working with arsenic.[138] Aristotle attributed the unseemly appearance and unhealthy bodies of smiths and other artisans to the fact that they spent too much time near the heat of the fire.[139] Both of these suggestions reconstruct a causal chain – that working metal *induces* disability – but Blakely has suggested an inverse model, that entering craftsmanship like metallurgical work was a strategy for those born with physical impairments.[140] In the context of the EIA, when every member of a household was probably expected to contribute to agricultural work and in which power was probably arbitrated by physical or martial prowess, it seems unlikely that the world would have been kind to those with limited physical capabilities. An appealing possibility to consider is that such individuals could, by virtue of wit and skill with materials rather than brawn and good looks, carve out a path to sociopolitical power and influence through the practice of craft work. Thus, the appearance of a socially powerful but physically compromised magical metalworker may be reconstructed as pertinent to a certain kind of economic opportunism, just not quite in the way that the model of the itinerant tinker reconstructs it.

VALUING EIA FIGURINES FROM PROCESSES RATHER THAN PRODUCTS

With the potentially ritual persona of the EIA bronze worker in mind, it is opportune to turn back to the topic with which I began this book – EIA bronze figurines from sanctuaries – and begin to reconstruct a robust set of explanations for the idiosyncratic nature of their characteristics as an assemblage. I argue that the most important aspect of the EIA bronze votive figurines at sites like Syme Viannou, Olympia, and Delphi was the production process of bronze casting, rather than the final aesthetic appearance or visual power of the finished products.

A first point in support of this interpretation relates to the existence and distribution of these figurines. As discussed in Chapter 4, anthropomorphic and zoomorphic bronze figurines have a very particular distribution in the

---

[137] Rosner 1955.

[138] Harper 1987, 654–656. One of the long-term effects of chronic exposure to arsenic is "the development of a peripheral neuritis which may lead to weakness in the legs and feet." See also Nriagu 1983, 316–317, 365–373.

[139] Ar. *Pol.* 8 1337b.   [140] Blakely 2006, 32.

archaeological record in the EIA: they are almost all dedicated as votives at sanctuaries, but they appear mainly at a limited number of sanctuaries – the majority of the early figurines come from (a) Syme Viannou and a few cave sanctuaries on Crete, (b) Delphi, and (c) Olympia. Moreover, these figurines appear during a time when figural art does not seem to be a major concern of society. In other art forms, such as vase-painting, the human figure is rare until well into the eighth century, when the figurines had been in production for several hundred years. The limited distribution of these figurines, along with their diminutive size and rough finishing begs the question of what the figurines were doing within society. In other words, why do these objects exist at all? Although the obvious and easy answer might be that the objects were made in order to be dedicated as votive objects, this is only a proximate answer. Why go to the trouble of making these figurines of bronze? What could these diminutive and barely human-looking votive objects have meant to someone participating in a ritual (Plate 15)? What value might a bronze representation of a human (or an animal) have had to the dedicant or the community?

A potential answer is available if we take into account the transformative and magical qualities of the production of the figurine. The figurine is of value because it is the material manifestation of the initiatory rite that the human participant in the ritual has undergone. In other words, if there was a parallel between the transformation of the wax figure to the bronze figure and the transformation of the initiate from youth to adult and between the transformative power of the divine ritual and the transformative power of the metallurgist's skills, then it would be sensible to reconstruct a value invested in the figurine that flowed from the transformation that the object had undergone, the casting process itself, rather than from its formal performance characteristics.[141] In this light, it would not be surprising to find that miscast objects and waste from the metallurgical process were often dedicated alongside finished figurines, or to find that little attention was paid to the polishing or finishing of the objects.[142] In short, the best explanation for the unprepossessing

---

[141] Legends of magical smiths often describe the processes by which they acquire their powers, which require an initiation (Delcourt 1957). The initiatory rites for shamans among Siberian people are often described in terms of the process of being forged in metal, for example, the autobiographical description of an Avam-Savoyed Shaman who saw himself enter into a smithy inside a mountain, where the smith cut off his head and broke up his body into pieces, then remade him from a simmered mixture of all the parts together (Eliade 1955, 207). In some societies, smiths are not only important in political and religious life but specifically preside over initiation rites within the community (Eliade 1955, 211–215).

[142] On the dedication of waste from bronze casting alongside bronzes, see discussion above in this chapter. The explanation usually provided for the dedication of waste products alongside finished ones is that the bronze itself is considered to belong to the god and so could not be discarded elsewhere or reused for profane purposes (Kyrieleis 1990, 23; Risberg 1992, 34; cf. Webb 1999, 237). Bol (1985, 26) suggests that the figurine from Olympia found

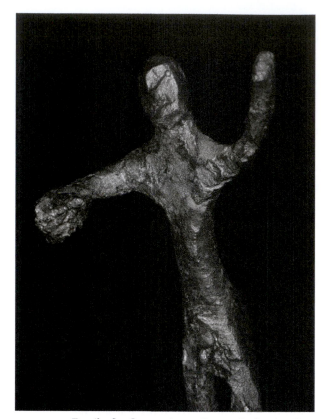

PLATE 15. Detail of a Geometric standing nude figurine from Delphi (Delphi Archaeological Museum Inv. No. 2910, photo by author; published with permission of the Delphi Archaeological Museum; © Hellenic Ministry of Culture and Sports – Hellenic Organization of Cultural Resources Development). [A black and white version of this figure will appear in some formats. For the colour version, please refer to the plate section.]

appearance of EIA figurines could be that it was not the product but the process that imbued these figurines with their value.

Instances in which it is clear that the importance of production processes as spectacles superseded the value of the products in which they resulted are commonplace in prehistoric societies. In a preindustrial context, major construction works or exceptional displays of technical knowledge could have been valued for the spectacular and extraordinary, probably often collective, sensory experience that they provided, which surely provoked both wonder at the power demonstrated and reverence for the special individuals that could muster these performances. That the impression of watching something amazing being made or done in social environments was valued as much as the outcome of the processes is suggested by the fact that the products of many amazing feats of building and lifting would have been hidden from view most of the time. Looking to the prehistoric Aegean, an example is available in the form of the massive stones used in the construction of some Mycenaean tholos tombs, which would have spent most of their existence buried under many tons of dirt.[143] Another testament to the importance of processes as spectacle are the depictions of hauling and building contained within the iconographic program

still in its cast jacket may have been a dedication by the craftsman in recognition of the risks involved in bronze casting.

[143] According to Cavanagh and Mee's energetics analysis of the Treasury of Atreus, the construction would have required over 20,000 person-days of work (Cavanagh and Mee 1999). While most studies of energetics embed these sorts of numbers in an economic analysis, it is worth keeping in mind how visible this construction process would have been over what was likely a longer period of time than the actual funeral, so that the elite display

of reliefs decorating Sennacherib's throne room at the palace in Nineveh. Several of the reliefs show the process of dragging colossal *lamassu* statues from the mountains and bringing them over difficult terrain to their final place of display.[144] Sapirstein presents an argument along these lines in connection with the erection of monumental stone objects like monolithic columns and super-sized *kouroi* in the Archaic period, reconstructing their value as actors within a collective spectacle of visually exciting engineering feats.[145]

The general point to press is that although we tend to value and express wonder at the products of technological processes, there is a case to be made that ancient people and communities might often have valued the spectacle of watching extraordinary mastery over nature being achieved instead.[146] This would be especially true if the best opportunity for the maker or patron to show off their mastery of production was the moment or process of production itself. If people were likely to gather at a festival to watch a monolithic column being raised, to see molten metal being poured, or to view huge stones being dragged through the countryside for a special construction for the king, they may have been much less likely to frequently see or gaze rapturously on the final products, as we are used to doing in the contexts of museums, sites, and art galleries.

VARIATION IN EIA FIGURINE STYLE AND THE RITUAL MEANING OF METAL MAKING

Reconstructing a metalworking presence that was essential rather than ancillary to ritual at sanctuaries solves some problems but introduces another: the problem of explaining the high rate of variation in styles among votives, even those from a single period at a single sanctuary. As discussed above, this

---

would have inhered just as much in the process of making the tomb as in the product of the tomb, which would have been underground most of the time.

[144] A series of reliefs showing the process of quarrying and transportation of *lamassu* adorned two walls of the inner court of Sennacherib's palace (Barnett, Bleibtreu, and Turner 1998, 64–70, nos. 135–183, pls. 98–125). The choice to include this event (or series of events) in the palatial iconography is a likely testament to the importance that the spectacle of acquiring the colossal statues had for Sennacherib's presentation of himself as an immensely powerful political leader (Russell 1987). The images, moreover, remind us that these sorts of objects, regularly consumed by modern viewers as finished works of monumental art, would likely have been experienced by most of Sennacherib's subjects (who did not regularly visit the palace) as spectacular interventions into and throughout the territory by the strong arm of the state.

[145] Sapirstein 2021, 459: "Though the huge size of the building elements at Syracuse would have been difficult to discern after the completion of the project, their manipulation would have made for a spectacle when construction was underway. The lifting of gigantic blocks would have advertised to outsiders the power of the patrons, while occupying the workers with challenging construction problems."

[146] Dobres 2010, 109–110.

variation has often been explained by appeal to the agency of itinerant craftsmen who opportunistically traveled to sanctuaries from regional centers to make votives. If the manufacture of the votives was undertaken by ritual actors associated with the sanctuary, we might expect their style to be more consistent. Thus, if the latter model is correct, a new explanation for the high level of variation in the style of EIA votives is needed.

Such an explanation is supported by the specificities of the production process associated with lost-wax casting and by the formal characteristics of the figurines themselves. One of the interesting aspects of lost-wax casting as it is usually carried out among modern artists is the collaborative nature of the work. The purpose of most modern foundries is not to produce bronze sculptures from the design phase to the finishing phase, but to cast models brought to the foundry by sculptors who prepare models or molds in wax ahead of time in their studios. The production process is therefore divided into two clear phases – the conception and execution of the model, on the one hand, and the technical processes that transform the model into bronze: investment, burnout, casting, and finishing. These phases generally reside with two separate agents: the sculptor/artist and the founder/metalworker.

It is interesting to consider that EIA votive figurines might have been created according to a similar division of labor, so that when we look at these figurines we are not looking at the product of a craftsman or a bronze worker but at the result of a collaboration among multiple individuals, each of whom contributed to one stage of the production process. An idea worth considering is that some of the agents involved in the process of production were the devotees themselves, specifically the youthful initiates taking part in ritual acts of liminal transition. While many craft activities require considerable technical expertise, making a simple animal or human figure out of a soft, malleable material is something that anyone can do, including children.[147] Perhaps initiates or other worshippers at early sanctuaries were responsible for creating their own votives in wax, then turned them over to smiths associated with the sanctuary for casting. The childlike, inexpert treatment and immense formal variation among the figurines might then be explained by the fact that it was indeed young and inexpert hands that made them, rather than by the fact that the figurines appear at an early and so-called primitive/developmental stage of Greek art.[148]

This explanation is especially appealing because it allows us to move beyond an interpretation of the aesthetic characteristics of EIA figurines that grows from our own formal valuations of artistic periods or cultures (such as primitive

---

[147] Murphy 2020.
[148] The regional schools and styles identified for EIA bronze figurines generally only pertain to relatively advanced groups from the later eighth century, while the earliest figurines consistently defy classification.

5.3. A group of PG zoomorphic figurines from the black layer at Olympia (Furtwängler 1890, pl. 10)

arts vs. developed arts) to one that attributes the characteristics of the figurines to the life stage of the people that made them (immature/young humans vs. experienced/older humans).[149] Looking again at the EIA figurines in this light, it is easy to see in them the kinds of art that most children produce – representations of living beings tend to be reduced to their simplest and most basic forms (body, arms, legs, head, tail), although idiosyncratic choices and wildly distorted proportions are common (Figure 5.3). It also helps to make sense of the fact that specialists have struggled to assign many of the figurines from Olympia to a recognizable regional school, even within the homogenous content of the bronze animal figurines, 99% of which represent horses, oxen, or deer.[150]

[149] See Langdon 2015 on methods for identifying childlike artwork and on the likelihood that some children were involved in the production of Geometric art.
[150] Heilmeyer 1979, 195–196.

Within his sample, Heilmeyer sought to distinguish regional schools, but assigned fully two thirds of the sample to a 'local' category that did not correspond to any identifiable regional style.[151] Overall, the highly idiosyncratic and inexpert treatment of human and animal forms apparent in the EIA figurines might be best explained if we reconstruct the identities of their designers and modelers and their dedicators as one and the same: young initiates engaging in transformative ritual processes.

NAKED FIGURINES, INITIATES, AND RITUAL PRACTICE

A scenario in which the dedicants visiting the sanctuary were involved in designing and executing the models from which early figurines were cast returns us to the question of nudity. To understand the importance of the frequently and explicitly naked depiction of the humans represented in the corpus of EIA figurines it is first necessary to address the question of who these figures represent. Most scholars have identified many early Greek figurines, and especially those that are clearly naked, as images of a god.[152] With some exceptions, however, it seems likely that the majority of naked males depicted in the EIA are intended to represent the youthful initiates who participated in liminal rites at the sanctuaries where they were dedicated. This conclusion follows partly from the limited depositional contexts – the figurines come almost exclusively from rural sanctuaries associated with initiatory rites, and it is not obvious why these particular sanctuaries would exclusively seem like an appropriate context for dedicating images of deities.

More decisively, several characteristics of the figurines themselves make it likely that they are meant to represent initiates or worshippers instead of deities. Ithyphallism is sometimes associated with epiphanies of the god but the majority of EIA naked male figurines are not ithyphallic. Moreover, it is probably not coincidental that most of EIA naked figurines are engaged in the sorts of activities that could be connected with male initiatory rites – wearing armor, dancing, taming horses, hunting, driving chariots, making offerings, and occasionally participating in physical challenges. Indeed, scholars like Byrne and Lebessi who have spent the most time studying the formal characteristics of the figurines believe that the vast majority are designed to represent the people who came to the sanctuary to worship, and this seems like the correct solution.[153]

Overall, I consider it most likely that many EIA naked male figurines are meant to represent worshippers at sanctuaries Less likely, but certainly possible, is that these worshippers also designed the figurines in wax before turning

---

[151] Heilmeyer 1979, 139–179. According to Rolley (Rolley 1986, 68), "the principles of classification on which [regional] attributions are based are very insecure," suggesting that they may not really represent a robustly coherent taxonomy. See also Lebessi 2009, 533 on the variety of styles among votives at Syme Viannou.

[152] See review of scholarship in Chapter 1.   [153] See discussion in Chapter 3.

them over to sanctuary personnel for casting. Someone sitting down to make a model out of a plastic material is always faced with a new design problem – each figurine must be made from scratch. The wide variety of approaches to the modeling of the figurines makes it look like they were not usually made with reference to any kind of template. Thus, any features that were added to the model would have taken a certain amount of effort and imagination to append.[154] We should assume that the common occurrence of nudity among the individual specimens of this artifact class represents a choice that was made because it was thought to be meaningful and important in the context of the production of the votive, at least in many cases.

The fact that nudity is not always explicitly indicated, on the other hand, suggests that some individuals did not imagine that nudity formed a central part of their own experience of ritual and votive activity. A natural conclusion to reach, then, would be that nudity was not represented because it was a primitive default or because it was necessary to distinguish men from women. Instead, nudity was variably represented because the variety of people taking part in the production of the figurines had diverse ideas regarding what was important about their ritual experience. More often than not, however, it does seem that individuals made a deliberate choice to model and append genitalia to the figurines. The fact that nudity is often explicitly indicated on these figurines mostly likely attests to the fact that nudity was an important aspect of the rituals that took place where they were deposited.

This assertion should not be particularly surprising, because nudity is generally common in the kinds of initiatory rituals that were probably among the activities that took place in EIA sanctuaries. While it is not entirely intuitive to associate coming-of-age rituals involving physical challenges like hunting and wielding sharp objects with total nudity, such ordeals often do involve the ritual costume of nudity, as is attested in anthropological and ethnographic parallels.[155]

---

[154] Joyce 1993, 256.

[155] Ducat 2006, 187–189. Dover (1992, 120–122) reviews liminal rites involving both nudity and sex. Given the close connection between initiatory rituals and bovine imagery at sites such as Syme Viannou, Olympia, and Delphi, a potentially interesting parallel is the tradition of initiatory cow jumping among the Hamar tribes in eastern Africa. The economic basis of the Hamar, a small group of approximately 42,000 members, remains largely tied to agropastoralism, and cows are an important basis for subsistence and social status. Young men are required to complete the cow-jumping ceremony before they are allowed to marry. The cow-jumping ceremony is a community affair, in which the whole village participates. The festivities last all day and involve dancing and drinking coffee and sorghum beer. The culmination of the event is the cow-jumping ritual. The ceremony is overseen by older boys (Maza), who wear special jewelry and carry thin branches to be used as whips to get and keep the cows in place. The initiates, called Ukuli, must mount the back of a line of castrated male cows and traverse the backs of the cows four times, back and forth, without falling off. They are completely naked during the process, which is accompanied by the rhythmical jangling of jewelry created by the dancing of the crowd of tribesmen who are present to watch the spectacle. If the Ukuli completes the task without falling, he then becomes a

Such rituals are also attested to have occurred in the historical Aegean.[156] Moreover, nudity would ultimately become the normal costume for participants in ritual activities at the same sites where the majority of EIA figurines appear. The logic of extending these rites back into the EIA is the kind of Occam's Razor argument that seems too obvious to need explicit construction, but which is necessary in the context of a scholarly tradition that has continually rejected EIA figurines as evidence for the early onset of meaningful social and visual practices associated with athletic nudity in the Aegean. Taking the process of production into account goes some way toward generating robust logical grounds for treating these early depictions of nudity as evidence for a meaningful cultural and ritual position for nudity in the EIA, because it demonstrates that the depiction of nudity was probably a deliberate choice taken by the designers of figurines seeking to express the meaningful aspects of their own participation in EIA ritual practices.

CONCLUSIONS

This chapter has presented the argument that EIA bronze figurines, considered as the material outcome of a complex technological process, allow us to reconstruct some interesting aspects of EIA ritual belief and practice. The production of figurines and other bronzes in the EIA took place in several rural sanctuaries. I have argued that the role of metalworking in these sanctuaries was not an economic one, but had mainly ritual importance. Moreover, I suggest that the metalworkers in charge of bronze production at sanctuaries were not one-dimensional economic actors. Instead, they were probably invested with ritual power by virtue of their control over a dangerous element and their ability to transform one element into another. A scenario in which the transformative technology of metallurgy held an important role in ritual practice fits nicely with the generally transformative nature of other events that took place at EIA sanctuaries – the transformation of animals into meat through burnt sacrifice and the transformation of initiates through liminal rites. The naked males that appear among the figurines produced by the foundries at these sanctuaries are not naked because artists relied on nudity to distinguish between men and women. Rather, the depiction of naked bodies represents an active design choice related to the context of production, embedded in a complex and visually remarkable transformative metallurgical procedure that, I suggest, was itself an important constituent of EIA ritual in some rural sanctuaries.

Maza, and spends the immediate future traveling around to other villages in the area to assist in the supervision of initiation ceremonies for other Ukuli.

[156] Jeanmaire 1939, 442, 518; Brelich 1969, 31, 72, 158, 200, 452; Vidal-Naquet 1986, 106–128; Scanlon 2002, 64–174.

CHAPTER SIX

EIA NUDITY AND RITUAL IN HISTORICAL PERSPECTIVE

The purpose of this last substantive chapter of the book is twofold. First, I reiterate a number of differences between the interpretation of the naked EIA males that I have presented here and views about them that arose from previous interpretations of the same material. Second, I articulate a number of new questions that may be posed of cultural and ritual history based on these interpretations, questions that might not have occurred to historians to ask based on previous reconstructions of the evidence. The goal of this chapter is therefore to highlight how the results of this study may move understanding of EIA nudity forward, while the concluding chapter that follows will comment on the value of the study from the point of view of methodological challenges involved in understanding EIA society.

REVISIONS TO THE HISTORY OF EARLY GREEK NUDITY AND RITUAL PRACTICE

My reconstruction of the cultural history of images of naked males and their role in EIA society and ritual differs in substantial ways from previous interpretations. The main revisions include (a) an appreciation of regional dynamics shaping the manifestation of naked males in material culture and an assertion of the decisive influence of Crete in shaping early practices involving naked males at mainland sanctuaries, (b) a rebuttal of the widespread view that EIA figurines do not inform us about nude ritual practice but merely constitute an artistic convention, (c) a clearer appreciation of the many reasons why texts postdating the EIA, including Homer, should not determine our reconstructions of the history of practices involving nudity in the Aegean, and (d) a new evaluation of the material characteristics of EIA bronze figurines that takes the process of their production into account.

A Cretan Origin for Naked Figurines and Initiation Rites

I begin with some basic empirical patterns in the evidence that emerge from systematic study of EIA naked figurines. Most of the earliest depictions of naked males in Aegean material culture date to the Late/Final Mycenaean period (*ca.* 1300–1100), and are likely to have been created in the context of cultural interaction with and probably under the influence of prior traditions of male nudity in the Levant, where standing, armed, nude, male figurines were common throughout the second millennium. However, the tradition of making cast, three-dimensional bronze votive figurines in the Aegean origin-ated on Crete during the LBA, and this is also where the earliest naked male bronze figurines occur in the EIA, appearing exclusively in the context of votive deposits from sanctuaries in caves and other extra-urban locations. The earliest male nudes on the mainland likewise comprise a corpus of closely related cast bronze figurines dedicated as votives at the rural sanctuary sites of Olympia and Delphi starting in the late tenth and early ninth centuries. It is likely that the appearance of these votives was related to Cretan influence. The conclusion that the production of the earliest bronze figurines at mainland EIA sanctuaries was directly related to preexisting craft practices on Crete is sup-ported by circumstantial, formal, iconographical, and technical lines of evi-dence. Re-asserting the decisive role of Cretan influence represents a departure from older views according to which EIA figurines represent a novel form of cultural expression developed on the mainland and representing the fresh start of a new iconographic tradition distinct from that which characterized LBA art.

The geographical distribution of EIA naked bronze figurines is mostly limited to a few sanctuaries in the Aegean. Most such sanctuaries are located on Crete or in the Peloponnese, with the exception of Delphi and a couple of sites in Thessaly. The fact that naked iconography within ritual contexts in the EIA was a primarily western, central, and Cretan phenomenon in the EIA is supported by patterns in LG ceramic iconography. Nudity with probably ritual connotations appears in Argive and Lakonian vase-painting with some regu-larity, but is rare within the large corpus of Attic and Cycladic Geometric figured scenes. When nudity appears in the iconography of Attic and Cycladic wares, it often seems meant to indicate vulnerability, a wild environment, or death. The spatial and chronological distributions within the early archaeological evidence for naked males thus support a reconstruction of a range of regionally distinct practices associated with both the ideology of nudity and the deposition of anthropomorphic naked bronze votives. This conclusion, which posits at least two, probably partly overlapping, sets of ideas about the appropriate role and meaning of nudity within society, represents a modification of previous scholarship which assumed that we could probably imagine EIA attitudes toward nudity and its iconography as a single indivisible whole. One important implication is that we must keep in mind the limited conclusions that may be drawn based on EIA bronze figurines: these votives do not tell us about EIA ritual or beliefs about nudity in a totalizing or general way, but can only shed light on a specific set of rituals and ideas that were relevant in certain regional contexts.

While some previous approaches to the EIA figurines have considered them important primarily as evidence of new aesthetic or artistic trends, I focus instead on the ritual practices that may have resulted in their appearance at EIA sanctuaries and the likely material activities that would have accompanied their production and deposition. It seems most likely that the earliest naked bronze anthropomorphic figurines on the EIA mainland began to be produced in Olympia and Delphi during the later PG or early Geometric period in the context of new cultural institutions involving religious worship in open-air rural sanctuaries, burnt animal sacrifice, and nude initiatory rituals, probably with strong influence from Crete. There is good reason to believe that artistic depictions of naked males and the ritual practice of male nudity, occasionally encompassing athletic competitions, arose on mainland Greece simultaneously with these new institutions. While many treatments of the EIA naked figurines have contested the notion that we may infer the enactment of nude activities at sanctuaries based on their deposition (that is, that art imitated life in this context) there are both empirical and logical grounds upon which to base the opposite position, that the presence of naked figurines does in fact indicate that naked physical activities probably took place at EIA sanctuaries.

The first is the circumscribed distribution of early naked figurines and the information that we can reconstruct about what occurred in the context of their deposition. Most EIA naked figurines come from ritual deposits at EIA sanctuaries, especially Syme Viannou, Olympia, and Delphi. They probably represent worshippers/votaries that attended rites at the sanctuaries. The ritual context of their votive deposition probably involved initiatory or liminal rites that were designed to usher young members of the community into a new life phase. Such liminal rites frequently entail the requirement that the initiate undergo some kind of physical ordeal or contest while 'clothed' in the special costume of total nudity, which visually signals the extraordinary nature of the transitional state and the rebirth constituted by the completion of the rites involved.

The same pattern is true in the case of nudity in Greek painted pottery – the majority of apparently naked males in this iconographic tradition represent individuals participating in activities, such as dancing and physical contests, conducted in ritual contexts or festivals.[1] The consistency across genres for the context of naked figures suggests that the images showing nudity in LG vase painting are probably representing events where people were actually naked, and that the inclusion of primary sexual characteristics was not just an iconographical mechanism for signaling gender. While others have argued that the decision to depict an individual as unambiguously naked or undeterminedly silhouetted may have been taken at random by individual vase-painters or workshops, I do not think this conclusion can be sustained in light of the different conventions for depicting the human body that prevail depending on the genre of the scene under scrutiny. If EIA artists only depicted humans naked in order to indicate gender, we would expect a much more random distribution of depictions of explicitly naked humans, since this would be a general problem encountered by artists working in a schematic iconographic tradition. However, this is not what the patterns in the evidence show. There is a consistent association of naked individuals with certain iconographic scenes, especially dances, festivals, hunts, and contests, while nakedness is rarely indicated in images of funerals or battles. I suggest that the geographical distribution and particular contexts of naked figures in both small sculpture and painting on pottery, taken together, provide plausible logical grounds on which to posit that naked figures in EIA art are really imitating life.

The likelihood that naked figures from the EIA probably represent something meaningful, such as actual practices that were undertaken in a state of undress, rather than something conventional, like a default means of indicating gender, is also supported by a consideration of the process of producing bronze

---

[1] This point could be extended to apply to extant depictions of naked males from the LBA. The youths in the fish-holding fresco in room 5 of the west house at Akrotiri were originally interpreted as "fishermen," but in light of their physique ("broadening shoulders, swelling arms and leg muscles, trim waists, and developing genitalia") and hair styles have been reinterpreted as youths in mid-puberty engaged in some kind of ritual involving the offering of fish to the deity being worshipped in the shrine (Chapin 2014, 22; cf. Chapin 2007a; 2007b; 2009). Likewise, the boxing boys from Santorini are nude except for a belt and one glove, and are clearly represented as relatively pudgy youths (Rehak 1999b). As Chapin notes, the fact that they are engaged in a boxing contest "confirms the importance of athletic training in prehistoric Aegean culture." (Chapin 2014, 24). Underscoring the possible presence of initiatory athletic training in early Greece is the evidence for bull-jumping and boxing elsewhere in the Minoan iconographic record. While the bull-jumpers in late Mycenaean iconography always wear a codpiece, it has been suggested that they are adolescents at various stages of some kind of initiation, which would explain their powerful yet youthful physiques and the variation in skin color that some have observed (Chapin 2014, 13). Finally, the boxer rhyton has been reconstructed as a representation of an extra-urban initiatory ritual for young men by Koehl (1986). For discussion of imagery possibly related to an initiation rite on a larnax from Tanagra, see Benzi 1999.

figurines. Each figurine had to be individually modeled in wax, meaning that the design and execution of each figurine represented a unique creative process that allows us at least some insight into the thought-processes of EIA individuals. In most cases, the artist would have needed to take special steps to ensure that the viewer knew that the figure being depicted was meant to be naked. For example, primary sexual characteristics sometimes had to be modeled independent of the main figure in separate pieces of wax, then affixed to the figure by heating the two surfaces and bonding them together. This process required a conscious set of decisions and the expenditure of additional effort, time, and care. We should probably assume that the frequency with which this effort was expended relates to the fact that nakedness was an important visual marker of some sort of meaning in the context of the making and dedication of the figurines.

Based on the evidence presented in Chapters 4 and 5, I reconstruct a situation where the figurines represent participants in liminal rites at sanctuaries. I also suggest that these participants may also have had a hand in designing and modeling the wax figures that were later remade into cast bronze. If this is correct, it might also go some way toward explaining why there is such a great variety of design choices evident in the ultimate formal appearance of figurines, since we might imagine that each initiate would prioritize different physical features or elements of a costume (such as belts or hats) based on their own experience as an initiate or their own ideas about what was important to include in the medium of the figurine.

Finally, there is a simple logical case for positing that naked practices explain the nudity apparent in EIA visual evidence. The majority of the EIA naked figurines represent individuals that are often engaged in some kind of physical contest and come from sanctuaries like Syme Viannou, Olympia, and Delphi where we know that nude physical contests were a part of ritual activities starting in the Archaic period. It therefore requires far more argumentative contortionism and contrarianism to argue that these naked figurines do not represent something along these same lines rather than to accept that they do.

Homer, EIA Nudity, and Nude Athletics

If this case seems so logical, why has it been so consistently resisted by historians and art historians? I believe the main reason for the hesitancy to believe that naked contests were a central part of EIA ritual has been the influence of Homer. If naked contests were taking place in the EIA, then why does Homer not mention this? Instead, nudity in Homeric poetry is typically a negative attribute especially associated with the bodies of unarmed warriors who are dead or about to be killed, or with a shameful state of undress in unusual circumstances. Moreover, Homer's heroes are not explicitly said to be naked when they participate in the funeral games of Patroklos or semi-formal athletics in other contexts.

The demeanor of Homeric nudity has long served as a backstop for histories of nudity in Greek culture. The fact that EIA objects are interpreted with Homer in mind is predicated on the assumption that there was a relatively close and special relationship between the Homeric epic, EIA art, and a generally shared Greek culture in the EIA.[2] The manifestation of this notional shared culture has often been termed 'cultural poetics' by scholars reconstructing a relatively unified cultural landscape of the early Greek world.[3] Against this view, an important observation to register is the regionally distinct nature of the iconographic evidence. The way that Homer presents nudity – as a characteristic of those who are vulnerable, about to die, or already dead – is consistent with the iconographic appearance of nudity in EIA Attica and the east Aegean in general.[4] However, the earliest evidence for ritual and athletic nudity from the EIA comes from Crete and from a few scattered rural sanctuaries, mostly in the Peloponnese. It seems worth considering that Homer does not enlighten the earliest EIA nudes because Homeric poetry reflects a set of ideas that were not only chronologically but also regionally distinct from the one within and for which EIA naked figurines were produced.[5]

One aim of this study is to challenge the existing view that the nature of nudity in the Homeric poems provides a *terminus post quem* for the introduction of meaningful forms of male undress in both practice and imagery in the Aegean. While it is true that Homer's wrestlers put on belts, there is no reason to extend this evidence as a convincing proof of a late, post-eighth century onset for the practice of nude athletics. Homer's testimony about nudity may reflect a particular, and perhaps old, eastern/Ionian set of ideas about practices and ideologies associated with nudity, but this is not necessarily a guide to the complicated history of nudity in the EIA Aegean.[6] This is especially apparent if we do not consider EIA culture as a unified whole, but as a world of many different ideologies, traditions, and social systems. The ideologies of nudity apparent in the evidence seem roughly in alignment with the geography of

---

[2] For example, Himmelmann 1990, 32; Snodgrass 1998; 2008, 24: "I see the Geometric vase paintings as the visual counterpart to the literary message that others have read into the Homeric epics."; Haug 2012, 3: "Die neue, verdichtete Form der Gemeinschaftlichkeit bildet den Rahmen füre die Genese einer Bild- und Schriftkultur."; see also Morris 1986, 127–129.

[3] For example, Dougherty and Kurke 1993; Kurke 1999.

[4] On the eastern/Ionian dialect in which the Homeric poems were composed, see Ruijgh 1995, 13–17.

[5] For the view that Homeric epic is antagonistic to Cretan ideologies in general, see Sherratt 1996.

[6] For the idea that Homeric poetry expresses an 'Anatolianizing' view of nudity, see Mouratidis 1985, 217.

notionally Dorian and Ionian tribal divisions as described by later Greek authors, but we need not imagine that these two traditions were the dominant or only sets of ideas circulating in the EIA or that there were internally coherent communities that identified as such in the early first millennium.[7]

The evidence from Crete and from a few mainland sanctuaries shows that naked initiatory rites were probably being conducted as part of ritual practice in at least some parts of the Aegean around the turn of the first millennium. Stating this is not necessarily equivalent to a straightforward extension of the history of nude athletics into the EIA, because most historians have drawn a distinction between ritual/liminal nudity, limited to special occasions, and profane/normative athletic nudity, which was part of everyday life. This distinction seems natural from a modern perspective and is useful in some ways, especially in helping to distinguish between different, well-documented ideas about nude physical exercise that arose in the Classical and Hellenistic periods. On the other hand, a distinction between ritual and profane sport is hard to sustain from the point of view of anthropological theory, which maintains that realms of sacred and profane were probably not categories relevant to most premodern societies.[8] Stylized activities like sport and theater essentially share all of the formal characteristics of what we usually identify as rituals, so that – in the absence of some insight into the way people thought in the EIA – it is very difficult to define something like athletics in opposition to what we might identify as ritual activity. It seems more reasonable to conclude that there were in fact nude physical contests taking place at EIA sanctuaries, and that, by most definitions, these were essentially equivalent in all formal senses to what we now call athletic contests. Accepting this does not amount to saying that nude athletics was common throughout the Aegean in the EIA, but that some such activities did in fact occur in some places prior to the sixth century.

Early Figurines and their Makers at Syme Viannou, Olympia, and Delphi

An understanding of the likely regional fragmentation of EIA ideologies and ritual systems cautions against extending any simple or totalizing interpretations of society based on EIA naked bronze figurines. The limited distribution of the EIA naked male bronzes requires that the conclusions we draw from them be limited in relevance to the regional contexts from which they have

---

[7] This reconstruction effectively hearkens back to arguments made by Müller (1906) in the early twentieth century. Although Müller's arguments were not properly substantiated when he put them forward in the beginning of the twentieth century, and as a result have been mainly dismissed by scholars, in retrospect they appear quite prescient. For explicit criticism of Müller's reconstruction, see, for example, McDonnell 1991, 185.

[8] Insoll 2004, 22; Fogelin 2007, 58, 60.

been recovered. Within these contexts, some aspects of the figurines reveal a few new insights into ritual practice and systems of ritual authority.

The first aspect is the aesthetic quality of the figurines. Existing scholarship is nearly unanimous in attributing the unprepossessing, often clumsy visual appearance of EIA figurines to the unskilled or primitive nature of the art of the EIA. These interpretations and evaluations are effectively relational, anticipating what we know about later developments in the technical and aesthetic quality of art, including bronze statuary, that appears in later periods, and appreciating the contrast to the aesthetic outcomes of three-dimensional statuary made on Crete in the Bronze Age.[9] In this book, I have done my best to set aside this relational evaluation of the aesthetics of the EIA figurines in order to try to understand them contextually as a product of a certain set of craft and ritual practices.

The lost-wax casting procedure used to make the figurines required the mastery of a number of stages in the *chaîne opératoire*. Each of these stages provided many opportunities to make mistakes that would introduce flaws in the products of the casting, and the material outcomes of many such mistakes are identifiable in the figurines. However, the thoroughgoing presence of such mistakes – and the generally raw and unfinished nature of bronze cast figurines deposited in the sanctuaries overall – suggests that technical incompetence is probably not the best explanation for the lack of aesthetic virtuosity in the earliest EIA figurines. Technical incompetence among bronze workers at EIA sanctuaries is also made difficult to sustain by the presence of complex tripod cauldrons dedicated alongside bronze figurines in the same deposits, because it is likely that the same metalworkers cast both kinds of objects. The fact that the figurines are tiny, unrefined, poorly crafted, and often broken probably suggests that their appearance was not important to the people who made them rather than that the people who made them were not capable of making nicer figurines. I have argued that the important part of the production of the figurines was the process of transformation through fire inherent in the casting process rather than the final aesthetic qualities of the product of the cast. It may also be the case that the immense variation in style and modeling approach, and the inexpert execution of the style of the figurines, relates to a collective process of production, with ritual initiates themselves modeling wax figures that were then cast by smiths, in the same way that modern founders cast artwork made by unattached sculptors.[10]

Placing the production of the figurines rather than their final appearance at the center of interpretation encourages a reevaluation of the role of bronze working and bronze workers in EIA ritual practice at rural sanctuaries. This

---

[9] For example, Sapouna-Sakellarakis 1995, 99.   [10] See, for example, Thomas 1995, 93.

represents the second aspect of our understanding of EIA ritual that should be revised in light of the argument presented in this book. The most common interpretation of the presence of evidence for metalworking within early Greek sanctuaries has rested on the assumption that the social role of the bronze worker was mainly an economic one. Along these lines, most scholars reconstruct a situation in which roving smiths attended sanctuaries on a temporary basis in order to take advantage of the unusual market produced by the desire of worshippers to dedicate votives.

However, the evidence I presented in Chapter 5 might encourage a reevaluation of this reconstruction. I propose that metalwork and metalworkers were not ancillary economic entities that parasitically leveraged ritual events to their material benefit, but were central to the ritual itself. I reconstruct a central role of smiths in EIA religion as magical, shamanesque figures invested with power to oversee a variety of transformational rites, including the initiation of young community members, the casting of wax into solid bronze, and the fiery sacrifice of valuable livestock for the ritual feast. Seen in this context, we may rethink old interpretations that see the figurines as the product of some sort of EIA *zeitgeist*, which determined a particular schematic style, the clumsy artistic product of artists who did not know what they were doing, or a primitive effort within a chain of iconographical developments leading to a naturalistic ideal. These views impose the aspect of images that we value (aesthetic quality and technical mastery) onto images that may instead have been produced for the sake of the visual spectacle of transformation entailed in the process of their production. I propose instead that the earliest EIA bronze figurines should be understood as embedded in a ritual system where value was placed on transformative processes, especially processes involving transformation of bodies from one state to another.

Summary

Taken together, the value of these three revisions to the story of the EIA naked figurines serve to complicate and undermine the linear, unified logic of the narrative in which they have usually been nested from the points of view of the history of nude practice, art, and ritual ideology. The revisions make evident that the situation regarding practices and ideas about nudity in the EIA is probably much more complicated than the Homeric texts let on. Nothing in this interpretation seems to tell us about the ambitions or achievements of great art in the Classical tradition. It is not clear at all that the system of ritual practice I reconstruct has anything to do with state formation or the nascent agonism of elites and aristocrats from early Greek *poleis*. A Classical tradition casting aspersions on any kind of work that required artisanal labor is not evident in the model I reconstruct, in which metalworkers were revered as holders of secret knowledge with access to supernatural powers. In many ways, the world that I have described, uninterested in art for art's sake and populated with magical smith shamans conducting mysterious ceremonies in woods and mountains, seems at odds with the world that we think we know about from the Bronze Age or the Classical period. While this may seem disturbing from some perspectives seeking to find a unity and coherence to the grand narrative of Classical antiquity, I believe this is really where the value of the study lies, in showing that EIA society is about more than the birth of Archaic and Classical institutions or a set of structures and communities to be compared and contrasted with Minoan and Mycenaean ones. The evidence from the EIA can stand on its own as a basis for rich reconstructions of cultural and social institutions that need not be part of an evolutionary trajectory.

SOME NEW QUESTIONS FOR HISTORIANS

That said, I hope that Archaic historians will also find this evidence useful as a basis for formulating future research questions about Aegean ritual and cultural institutions. Here I present some of the questions that have occurred to me during the process of writing this book. I am not a historian of Archaic Greece, so I am not qualified to answer any of these questions myself. Moreover, the purpose of this book was not to answer questions about Archaic Greece, but to deal with the EIA as a period of interest on its own merits. For these reasons, I will not treat any of the questions I raise here in any detail, or attempt to produce anything approximating convincing or thoroughly argued solutions for them. Instead, the purpose of this section is to suggest some strands of future research that the evidence and argument I have made in this book make me eager to see addressed, and that Archaic historians would be better suited to answer.

The History and Function of Nude Liminal Rites in Archaic Greece

Ritual practices and the contexts in which they took place underwent meaningful transformations in the Aegean during the early first millennium. I have suggested that the proximate source of these transformations should be sought on Crete. While EIA scholars, especially Sarah Morris, have argued for such a ritual influence on mainland developments,[11] Archaic historians have more

---

[11] For the reconstruction of ritual influence from Crete on mainland religion, see Morris 1992a, 164:

> The Greeks themselves remembered Crete for its contributions to religion, claiming that its natives invented [honors and sacrifices and other things about initiations] (Diodorus 5.77), all of which appear first in the Levant. In legend, the Telchines

often attributed the florescence of worship at sites like Olympia to processes related to state formation or population growth and related social needs within and between communities. In light of the evidence presented here, perhaps historians should reconsider the importance of Cretan influence when modeling the early trajectory of Greek religion.

Nonetheless, it would be reductive to assert that the adoption of these novel cultural practices was a simple process of diffusion that occurred in a vacuum of the sorts of social and political developments that historians usually discuss when situating developments in EIA and Archaic ritual practice. Cretan ritual traditions probably would not have been taken up by communities on the mainland if they did not have some perceived utility within these communities. The material indicators of ritual change in the EIA probably constitute evidence for an active series of choices taken to solve problems or address thoroughgoing issues confronting mainland communities in the late tenth and ninth centuries. This is especially true given the particularities of the way that ritual usually functions in human society. In general, ritual and religion are usually among the most conservative aspects of societies, and will usually resist change over time more than other kinds of social institutions.[12] However, while ritual can sometimes form an inherently stable core for social institutions, the fact that it plays such an important role in structuring identities and societies makes it a potentially powerful tool for transformation, for producing social change through manipulation of traditional elements.[13] Thus, modeling or reconstructing the agents and dynamics that surrounded the adoption of new ritual practices in the mainland during the EIA represents a probably interesting potential vector for analysis.

This underlines a point made by Langdon and discussed in Chapter 3 – that rites of passage and the movement of youths through the stages of life form a social institution of fundamental importance to understanding the EIA. Why did these rites of passage become so important in the EIA? In order to address this question, it is necessary to consider some of the extensive anthropological literature on the function of ritual in society. This literature emphasizes that ritual is work, not simply an idealized or symbolic rite. A substantial amount of labor, time, and effort would have been necessary to enact initiatory rituals,

of Crete were renowned not only for their art but for their invention of divine images (Diodorus 5.55.2) and were thought to practice [initiations and mysteries] (5.64). The island was the birthplace of Zeus, home to priests for Delphi and of Cretans like Epimenides who purify Athens.

[12] Buikstra and Douglas 1999; Van Dyke 2004; Fogelin 2007, 58.
[13] Aldenderfer 1993; Howey and O'Shea 2009, 195.

and the community as a whole would have to be complicit in removing youths of a certain age from the group, subjecting them to various ordeals, and then reabsorbing them into the normal life of the village or state. Anyone who has endured any kind of initiation ceremony, be it a baptism, a fraternity induction, or a graduation, will know that these events are often highly unpleasant and traumatic to the participants. Why do such rituals exist; why do families allow their children to be removed from the household and subjected to the ritual demands of outside institutions? We should be skeptical of the notion that these kinds of rites would have been adopted or developed in the absence of some kind of pressing need for the kinds of social or political goods that rituals provide.[14]

Could the need for a new form of ritual practicein the EIA mainland have been related to population growth or state formation? One thing that is apparent about the period subsequent to the dissolution of the Mycenaean states of the LBA is that it probably entailed significant population contraction, especially in the Peloponnese. Although the exact cadence and degree of population growth in the EIA has been debated, it is clear that, probably beginning in the tenth and ninth centuries, the population began to grow from the low levels sustained through the twelfth and eleventh centuries.[15] Given the timing of the appearance of evidence for rural initiatory rites at Olympia and Delphi, among other sites on the mainland, it is not implausible to connect demography to an increased interest in framing young peoples' progress to adulthood. Increasing social pressures might have characterized a period during which small communities were gradually becoming larger. Within communities, increasing population might have generated conflicts between families and clans, and these conflicts could have partly been solved by the introduction of ritual practices that encouraged the development of clearly defined social roles, hierarchies, and solidarities on a suprahousehold level. An increase in population could have also resulted in greater tensions between communities, as resources such as land and quarry become dearer. It is not difficult to imagine that these tensions drove the need to create a structured way of training and educating children about their place in the community and the skills that would be needed to serve that community in the form of military service. Thus, perhaps there were some social goods that were fulfilled in part by the introduction of a bundle of ritual practices designed to structure and order individual roles in the community while simultaneously encouraging a sense of community loyalty and coherence.[16]

[14] Smith 1987, 198.

[15] For population fluctuations and their likely cadence see Morris 2007, 216–217; Murray 2017, 210–246; review of evidence in Nakassis 2020, 277.

[16] See, for example, Whitley 2020, 177: "Cult and commensality then seem to be the forms of social and ritual glue that kept the political communities of AR Greece functioning … citizen states were therefore equally communities of cult held together by participation in major feasts and festivals to the gods."

Indeed, ritual has an active role in shaping human communities, especially regarding the conditioning of behavior and the structuring of individual roles related to the community. Rituals in general and rites of passage in particular are thought to provide a number of sociopolitical goods important for the proper functioning of communities, most obviously in their function as a tool for social control. The nature of social control "wielded by ritual" is not uniform, and has not been theorized along a single axis. In some ways theories about ritual − which can either abet reactionary conservatism or aid in transformative revolution − can seem inherently contradictory.[17] Durkheim constructed a model of ritual that situated the social control it attends along four lines: social solidarity, channeling conflict, repressing natural instincts, and defining reality.[18] According to Durkheim, ritual "dramatizes collective representations and endows them with a mystical ethos that in the course of the communal experience did not merely promote acceptance of those representations but inculcated deep-seated affective responses to them."[19] Edelman, alternatively, described ritual action as a mechanism for maintaining the social fabric during times of strain and fragmentation by providing an artificial context for conflict in which the conflict must and can be resolved.[20] According to Turner, ritual involves a dialectic between structure and anti-structure. In this regard, it serves to imbue functionally useful norms and values with positive emotions, therefore transforming "the irksomeness of moral constraint" to an unquestioning enthusiasm for pursuing socially desirable norms and values which take on the guise of virtue.[21]

The intellectual landscapes in which liminal ritual has been enmeshed are therefore complex, but taken together can help situate change in the importance of certain rituals to certain communities over time within a sociopolitical context. Initiation rituals are thought to function most strongly as a ritual mechanism for the definition of reality. This function of ritual prioritizes the modeling of relations and the structuring of values.[22] In other words, rituals that serve to define reality provide participants with a model of social order, a central institution that (a) communicates culture, (b) internalizes values, and (c) inculcates participants with a perception of the universe that suits these values.[23] Initiation rituals furthermore assist youths in progressing past "the universal infantile experience of helpless dependency" to a state of adulthood

---

[17] Kertzer 1988; Bell 2009 [1992], 169. It may not be coincidental that sport is likewise considered to be contradictory in these terms − it encourages cohesion and a sense of solidarity while also serving as a venue for fierce competition.

[18] Durkheim 1965 [1915].   [19] Bell 2009 [1992], 171.   [20] Edelman 1971.

[21] Turner 1967; Bell 2009 [1992], 172.

[22] This approach has been put forward by several anthropologists, including Douglas (1966, 1970) and Geertz (1980).

[23] Bell 2009 [1992], 176.

in which personal responsibility for defensive violence and independence are plausible and indeed imperative.[24] In the context of ancient Greece, Burkert's *Homo Necans* and subsequent studies discuss how all of these functions pertain to initiation rituals in ancient Greece. In particular, rites for young men emphasized the clear delineation of masculine expectations, the removal of the boy from the realm of the household, the articulation of his new role as a citizen and soldier poised to take on roles related to the community and not to the clan, and the preparation of the boy in terms of military fitness. Athletic contests were naturally suited to the latter objective; the ancient literary sources on athletic training also specifically assign it a primary role in preparing a formidable military.[25] Ancient cultures likewise connected training in group dance with the expression of masculinity and with military training.[26]

If the anthropological and philological study of ritual overall and initiatory ritual has given us sophisticated intellectual tools for understanding, at any given time, how ritual functions in society, it does not necessarily spell out how rituals come into being, adapt to changing social needs, or lapse over time. Such an inquiry must fall to the historian. From this point of view, Mary Douglas' work in *Purity and Danger* and *Natural Symbols* provides an historical lever for envisioning when and where rituals might be most important in the historical trajectories of communities. In Douglas's view, initiation rituals function like a form of speech, which transmits culture and social relations in clear and emphatic ways to the participants in ritual.[27] The effectiveness of the ritual arises from the physical communication of these cultures and relations through embodied experience and projection through images of the symbolic and structural schemes to which the initiate is being introduced.[28] Douglas observes that this kind of transmission and its use as a form of social control is fundamental only in certain types of societies. She goes on to ask a historical question: in what sorts of societies will these rituals tend to be most fundamentally important? According to Douglas, the answer is: "(1) closed social groups with (2) restricted codes of linguistic and symbolic communication in

---

[24] Bell 2009 [1992], 175, commenting on Burkert 1983, 27.
[25] For example, Solon *Anacharsis* 25.
[26] For a modern Cretan parallel, Herzfeld 1985, 67: "... the agile men dancing with implications of aggressive masculinity, and, by extension, of the skills of the good raider."
[27] Bell 2009 [1992], 178.
[28] Bell 2009 [1992], 180. Also relevant in this line of thinking is Goffman's (1956, 10) notion of "Belief in the Part One Is Playing":

> when an individual plays a part he implicitly requests his observers to take seriously the impression that is fostered before them. They are asked to believe that the character they see actually possesses the attributes he appears to possess, that the task he performs will have the consequences that are implicitly claimed for it, and that, in general, matters are what they appear to be.

Both the performer and audience are taken in by the act.

which (3) there is a great emphasis on hierarchical position as opposed to personal identity and (4) yet a general consensus still upholds the system." In other words, rituals might come into being when communities need to cement strong hierarchies, in which individuals and their relations are subordinated to ordered roles and positions. The ritual is aimed at fostering a collective that "is simultaneously both highly differentiated and exalted as a corporate unity above the interests of the self."[29]

According to Douglas, initiatory rituals would come to the fore during periods that also involve a progression from a relatively simple and non-hierarchical community structure to one in which the functioning and success of a community increasingly depended on a complex set of hierarchies that govern decision making, distribution of authority, and the organization of social relations as well as the reorientation of individual loyalties away from the household and toward the community overall. This set of ideas may give us a useful heuristic for historically situating the importance of initiatory rituals in the EIA, at least insofar as they appear to lay behind a significant quantity of the images and objects that constitute EIA ritual material culture. The production of material cultural associated with liminal rites might have been related to the kinds of meaningful signaling desirable in the context of such rituals.[30]

While some historians have argued that Archaic Greek athletic nudity and rites of passage should be considered as distinct from the primitive initiations of prehistoric peoples, material culture from the EIA strongly suggests that nude physical contests in the Archaic world were directly connected to earlier developments, especially the initiatory rites present in EIA ritual.[31] It seems unlikely to be coincidental that a majority of EIA naked figurines are engaged in exactly the sorts of activities that are we would associate with male initiatory rites related to the acquisition of the status of manhood in early Greece – wearing armor, dancing, taming horses, hunting, driving chariots, making offerings, and occasionally participating in physical challenges that look like early iterations of Greek sport. A live question would seem to concern the particular social logic behind the adoption of such rituals in particular places and times between the EIA and the Archaic period.

Later Developments in the Greek Nude Male: Why Did the Phallus Reign?

The evidence from early Greek material culture therefore suggests that physical contests were associated with male nudity and coming of age from the very beginnings of both of these forms of cultural practice. If it is reasonable to ascribe the origins of male undress in Greek society to initiatory and liminal

---

[29] Bell 2009 [1992], 178–179.   [30] Faro 2008, 138–139.
[31] See also Thuillier 1988; McDonnell 1991, 182–193; Shapiro 2000, 313–337.

rites, this explanation does not help us to address later developments in the iconography and practice of male nudity. There are many societies in which initiatory nudity exists, so we need not necessarily seek special explanations for reconstructing initiatory rituals that involved nudity in early Greece. However, the degree to which the presence of this form of social practice eventually impacted Greek life and art is not ordinary. The question of how and why the nude Greek male become such a dominant force in Greek art remains vexed.

It may be that positing an explicit connection between EIA nudity and Cretan institutions could provide some grounds for making sense of the later Greek obsession with male nudes. It seems relatively clear that the initiation rituals for young males in Crete had erotic and homosexual overtones from the beginning of their existence, and that these rites can be related in straightforward ways to institutional pederasty on the part of the Cretans.[32] Strabo's account of ancient Cretan initiatory rituals links eroticism, pederasty, and coming of age rituals in very explicit terms.[33] The degree to which it can be relied upon as a guide to EIA practice is, of course, questionable. The iconographical resemblance between the finds at Syme Viannou and the material aspects of the rite that Strabo describes nonetheless might suggest that something like the homosocial bonding activities described by Strabo could have been taking place on Crete in the EIA.[34] The gifts provided to the initiate in Strabo's account include a set of arms, an ox, and a wine cup, three objects that seem designed to loudly declare the initiate's arrival into the world of men, since men fight in battles, rear and sacrifice cattle, and drink wine.[35] The finds from Syme Viannou include dedications of figurines that include both cows and nude males bearing arms and wine cups, and leading cows, as well as images that suggest a connection between all of these objects, the rites at the sanctuary, and homoerotic relationships. As discussed in Chapter 3, many references from ancient literature assert that Greek pederastic institutions should be traced on the mainland to Sparta, but that ultimately the Spartans acquired this institution from Crete.[36] Ancient historians writing on the history of the complex nexus between education, initiation, pederasty, and nudity have been skeptical of the connection between early Cretan society and mainland city-states,[37] but it seems that the archaeological evidence may support a Cretan origin for initiatory rituals and festivals related to homoerotic pederasty.[38]

[32] Koehl 2016.   [33] Strabo 10.4.21. The original source is probably Ephoros.
[34] See also Stewart 1997, 140; Scanlon 2002, 75–76.
[35] Bremmer argues that none of these signifiers would have been relevant to young boys, who probably served as wine-attendants because they were not allowed to consume the alcohol (Bremmer 1980, 286).
[36] See, for example, Bethe 1907, 441, 444; followed by Percy 1996.
[37] Scanlon 2002, 360–361, n. 48; Lear 2013, 253.   [38] Nagy 1986, 83–86.

Aside from the fraught question of its origins, there is a general consensus that institutional pederasty played an important part in the upbringing and cultural conditioning of young men, especially elite young men.[39] The educational benefits of a system of institutionalized pederasty were considered to be of fundamental importance to developing soldiers for a strong military – indeed the entire educational system at Sparta was designed to fulfill military objectives.[40] The enforced public nudity and general bodily control that the state-sponsored *agôgê* entailed may have been designed to create cohesion and an incentive for physical well-being among Spartiate males, but as Christesen has argued, it also had the end result of creating a powerful psychological effect of subordination among the male members of Spartan society.[41] From a young age, the Spartiate citizenry as a whole was, through required and long-term participation in public nude training and homoerotic partnerships, submitted to the penetrating surveillance of the centralized state.[42] This surveillance led to the sorts of "docile bodies" that Foucault discusses, whose ideal nature was dictated and enforced by the means and norms established by the surveyor.[43] There is evidence that this surveillance formed a very important aspect of the Spartan state from an early date. As Powell states, "the assumption that sexual intercourse in public was a feature of pre-Lycurgan festivals would also supply a possible origin for the (by general Greek standards) extraordinary uses of public nudity at Sparta for purposes of the Lycurgan state."[44] Ultimately some permutation of this system became characteristic of education in most places.[45] Education involving initiatory rites, athletic contests, and homoerotic characteristics was, in the Classical world, "virtually omnipresent."[46]

---

[39] See also discussion in Cartledge 1981; Winkler 1990; Spivey 2004, 44–53; Scanlon 2005; David 2010.

[40] Cartledge 1981, 26.   [41] Christesen 2012b.

[42] Aelian (*Historical Miscellany* 14.7) mentions a Spartan law pertaining to the surveillance of bodies:

> The law contains the following provisions. No one from among the Lakedaemonians is to appear effeminate or to have a body bulkier than that produced by exercise. For it seemed to them that the latter corresponded to idleness, while the former was not suitable for a man. It was also written in the law that every ten days the ephebes should stand nude in public, before the ephors. And if they were strong and healthy and had been sculpted and carved by exercise, they were lavishly praised. But if there was any flabbiness or softness in their limbs, any swelling or growing fat on account of laziness, they were beaten and punished there and then.

[43] Foucault 1985, 69–70.   [44] Powell 1998, 131–135.

[45] Scanlon 2002, 66–72; Ducat 2006, 196–201; David 2010, 144–146; for a summary and bibliography of work on the relationship between pederasty and Greek sport, see Lear 2013, 253–255.

[46] Scanlon 2002, 70.

Connecting the origins of athletic/initiatory nudity with homoeroticism in the form of institutional pederasty provides some traction for understanding the prominent position and nature of male nudity in Greek art. The ideal of the male nude involves men of a specific age – young men on the cusp of adulthood. If the upbringing of young men in Greek culture were at least in part underpinned by institutions involving liminal rites that bonded younger and older males to one another through homoerotic relationships, the saturation of visual culture with social cues related to the attractiveness and appeal of young boys on the cusp of adulthood, but ready to engage in the cultural hallmarks of manhood, makes sense. And if such an important institution as the education of the male citizen body revolved around a world of initiatory rites encouraging male homosexual bonding, material culture could have played a role in reifying the appeal of young males. These complex ritual, cultural, erotic, and social institutions may have precipitated a situation in which attractive young males participating in activities that pertained to bonding rites became pervasive in visual culture.

Seventh Century Imagery, Smiths, and Elites in Greek Sanctuaries

An interesting aspect of the material evidence, however, is that the tradition of the naked male in Archaic Greek art did not follow directly on from the material from the EIA that I have dealt with in this book. Scholars seeking to elucidate the historical development of images and practices associated with nude males in Archaic Greece have noted that nudity is not a prominent feature of imagery from the seventh century. Images of nude males begin to appear once again in the sixth century, but only in certain regions. I suggest these uneven patterns in nude iconography may relate to the presence of competing ideologies concerning the appropriate role of nudity in society that were contested over time and regionally distinctive.

Archaeologists have identified many signs of such competing ideologies in the material record of the EIA. While wealthy tombs dominate the archaeological record during the early part of the Geometric period, large communal temples and the mass dedication of small objects in sanctuaries became widespread phenomena during the second half of the eighth century.[47] At the same time, *prothesis* and *ekphora* scenes and monumental kraters designed to commemorate wealthy individuals or families persist in Athens. Snodgrass has noted the dissonance between the two phenomena the collective action evident in temples and dedications and the clan or individual aggrandizement evident in the Attic iconography: "it is certain that the new undertakings were

---

[47] Snodgrass 2008, 24–25.

the product of collective action ... but no such collective endeavor is detect-able in the Geometric scenes ... they convey the prestige of an individual aristocrat."[48] It might make sense to cast the appearance of regular nudity in public displays involving physical excellence as an attempt by the community to elide the distinctions apparent in the clothing and armor of elites. The collective deposition of wealth in a communal sanctuary, where nudity use-fully expressed the meritocratic sorting of individuals based on strength and physical excellence, while also promoting group solidarity over family loyalty, has been recognized as a strategy designed to redirect wealth that had been previously deposited in burials.[49] In the eighth century, elaborate funerary offerings diminish, while dedications of valuable objects appear in increasing quantities in communal sanctuaries.[50] If there were a collectivist vs. individual-ist or clannist dynamic playing out in eighth century communities, it might have been the case that initiation practices involving nudity at sanctuaries were somehow tied to an ideology in opposition to the assignation of status through individual lineages. Shifting dynamics amongst such ideologies could explain the uneven appearance of naked athletes in art of the seventh century.

Another interesting issue to think about in light of seventh century devel-opments is change in the social role or importance of metalworkers. Even if it is sensible to assign ritual importance to smiths and smithing in the EIA, this role was nowhere apparent by the later Archaic and Classical periods, and most Greek literature expresses disdain rather than reverence for *banausoi*.[51] Presumably, this indicates that the social role of smiths changed at some juncture during the Archaic period. An interesting question, then, revolves around the timing and logic of change in the social role of the smith. In comparative perspective, it has been observed that the link between metal-working and magic is strongest during periods when the technology underpin-ning metalwork is not well understood, and when the procedures for conducting technical work cannot be distributed easily via writing. Malinowski's work suggests that people tend to attribute magic as operational when observed reality extends beyond the boundaries of their comprehension,

[48] Snodgrass 2008, 25.
[49] For the increase of apparent wealth deposition in sanctuaries and concomitant decline in aristocratic grave goods in the eighth century, see Snodgrass 1989–90. We should also recognize (with Morgan 2003, 113) that sanctuaries are "complex entities which both reinforced and transcended other political boundaries and interests."
[50] For weapons and armor disappearing from burials, see Snodgrass 1989–90, 37, 68; Osborne 2009, 163–164. For military paraphernalia from sanctuaries, Carpanos 1878, 101–102; Perdrizet 1908, 93–106; Kunze 1950; 1991; Bol 1989; Philipp 1994; Baitinger 2001; Scott 2010, 149–150.
[51] Although the memory of the powerful and magical smith obviously persisted in Greek myth, in practice such figures do not play a prominent role in Archaic and Classical history (Blakely 1999).

and Gell has expounded at length on the enchanting capabilities of technology that is unfamiliar or that we do not understand.[52] Along these lines, we may posit a process whereby an increasing spread of literacy and technical knowledge enabled easier and more widespread access to information about the banal realities of the metalworking process, so that the supernatural effect of smiths' mastery ceased to function as persuasive ideological grounds for access to ritual power.[53]

Alternatively, we might reconstruct an antagonistic relationship between agricultural, land-owning elites and smith-elites, who may have perceived one another as rivals for political and social power. The disdain for *banausoi* that emerges in the late Archaic period might represent the aftermath of a clash between these two groups, reflecting historical developments whereby agricultural elites ultimately succeeded in establishing a rhetoric that placed artisans at the social margins.[54] If we accept that smiths had ritual power in the EIA, but became marginalized in Archaic Greece, it would be interesting to see some future work addressing how and why ritual spaces in which smiths orchestrated operations could have become coopted by other kinds of elites.

While bronze production in Olympia and other sanctuaries obviously continues beyond the EIA, there is a noticeable change in the nature of votive dedications in the seventh century, perhaps including a decrease in the quantity or proportion of bronze dedications.[55] This development in the archaeological record could signal a change in the way that smiths and smithing were valued, too.[56] The change in depositional practices seems to align with a general cooption of sanctuary space by elites, specifically the use of the space as a venue for competitive status displays. It is interesting, along these lines, to observe that major reorganizations of the sanctuaries of both Olympia and Syme Viannou are evident in the early seventh centuries. These reorganizations coincide with a general decline in the prominence of nude imagery in material culture and the installation of permanent structures in what had previously been open-air sites.[57] In general, the turn of the seventh century seems to have ushered in a period during which elites and communities were manipulating institutions to assert authority over various spheres of society, including economic, judicial, and ritual affairs.[58] Perhaps in the future it might

---

[52] Malinowski 1948, 8–13; Gell 1998.   [53] Blakely 2006, 160.

[54] Along these lines, it is interesting that Metis (skill, cunning, craft), a Titaness who embodied the magical wiles that seemed to still be a source of amazement and wonder among the audiences of the Homeric poems, is set up as a problematic adversary to Zeus in Hesiod's Theogony (Hes. *Th.* 886–900). In the myth, Metis causes Zeus a major headache by hammering at the forge to make Athena's helmet.

[55] Snodgrass 1989; Prent 2005, 420–424.   [56] Prent 2005, 355.

[57] Lebessi and Muhly 1976, 3; Lebessi and Muhly 1990, 318, abb. 3; Kyrieleis 2002.

[58] Murray 1980, 265–266; Kurke 1999, 12–23.

be possible to extend this line of research and to reconstruct two phases in the positioning of power and the role of objects in EIA sanctuaries. In the first, the power of production had ritual value and the finished products were not important. In the second, finished votives themselves had value as visual emblems of the power and wealth of competitive aristocrats. The relationship between these two phases and the processes and conditions under which the role of art for art's sake vs. art for craft's sake inverted might be a productive area of future research.

CONCLUSIONS

This chapter has recapitulated the observations laid out in the preceding chapters and considered how these patterns might cause us to rethink not only nudity and its social meaning in EIA Greece, but also the nonlinear development of religion and ritual between the EIA and the Archaic period. There is a lot to say about nudity and EIA religion based on the material I discuss in this book, but it does not necessarily follow the lines suggested in the usual narratives about Greek history or the trajectory of Greek culture between the LBA and the EIA. While I have suggested some ways that the differences in this story might lead us down new pathways of analysis about Archaic history, I do not really think that an impact on Greek history is the reason that the evidence for EIA nudity and EIA ritual practice presented here is important. Rather it is important because it helps us to see the untidy and complicated society of the EIA as one that was probably largely distinct from and surely mostly indifferent to the Classical world and the world of Bronze Age states, a point upon which I will expand in the subsequent, and final, chapter of this book.

CHAPTER SEVEN

METHOD AND APPROACH IN THE ARCHAEOLOGY OF THE EIA AEGEAN

My purpose in this book has been to reconsider the beginnings of a 'culture of male nudity' in the Aegean through analysis of some of the earliest images of naked males in material culture from the Aegean region. I laid out the evidence for nudity in the archaeological record of the EIA Aegean, especially focusing on the earliest naked figurines from the few sanctuaries on Crete and the mainland where they appear in substantial quantities. I presented a treatment of the earliest naked bronze figurines from EIA that placed their production at the forefront of interpretation and set this in the context of ritual practice and votive deposition. I contended that EIA bronze figurines were not valued for their aesthetic appearance, but accrued value instead through the metal casting processes of production that took place within the sanctuary grounds. This perspective, along with a granular understanding of the casting process, helps to explain their unprepossessing appearance. In contrast to existing views that reconstruct production as a purely economic phenomenon, I posited a meaningful ritual role for bronze working in certain EIA contexts. Specifically, I argued that bronze casting was not practiced at sanctuaries in order to produce votives for the economic benefit of itinerant craftsmen, but that smiths were ritual actors whose casting practices were embedded in and central to some EIA ritual.

In the course of working through the relevant material evidence, I demonstrated that the cultural value and meaning of nakedness was probably regionally diverse during the EIA, with distinct cultures of nudity suggested by evidence from Crete, the Peloponnese, and Central Greece, on the one hand, and from Attica and the eastern Aegean, on the other. This conclusion is useful because it allows us to reconstruct ideologically distinct regional cultures in the EIA, even in the absence of much textual evidence. It also helps make sense of the disconnect between Homeric views on nudity, which fit with a generally eastern iconographic tradition of nudity, and the earliest EIA nude figurines, which come from a few, mainly Cretan and western sanctuaries. It also underpins a caveat that the naked figurines from the EIA can only be used to make limited observations about the way that nudity, figurines, and rituals worked in the context of the regions where they appear rather than general observations about Aegean ritual practice or belief overall.

Although the archaeological remains and images from the EIA present nontrivial interpretational challenges, these challenges are not insuperable, and the material has much to offer as a source for reconstructing Aegean society. I provided some commentary on the way that the evidence I have dealt with in this book might impact the way that we reconstruct the substance of EIA ritual and its relationship to nude bodies in art and practice in Chapter 6.

In this concluding discussion, I return to the methodological points that I briefly highlighted in the preface to the book, and reflect upon whether the efforts and arguments I set out may have broader implications for the study of the Aegean EIA beyond the narrow realm of early rituals involving naked initiates and bronze figurines.

THE EARLY IRON AGE AND GREEK HISTORY

We should remember that the enthusiastically embraced metaphors of each 'new era' can become, like their predecessors, as much the prison house of thought as they first appeared to represent its liberation.[1]

As is the convention for all European prehistory, the periodization of the prehistoric Aegean has been divided into phases derived from the materials used to make tools and weapons through time.[2] Hence the Neolithic, (*ca.* 7000–3000) was a period during which stone tools were used, the Chalcolithic period saw the introduction of copper, and the Bronze Age is characterized by the widespread use of copper alloys. Finally, the start of the EIA coincided with the invention and spread of ironworking. Historical periods in Greece are not called the Middle and Late Iron Ages, but are periodized according to a different logic related to historians' conceptions of

---

[1] Daugman 1990, 33.

[2] This organization of eras goes back to a formulation presented in the Archaic poet Hesiod's *Works and Days*, but was formally introduced as a scheme for prehistory in the twentieth century and has endured to the present day.

the cadence of civilizational rise, apogee, and fall. From humble beginnings in the primitive era of the EIA, the Archaic, Classical, and Hellenistic eras divide Greek history into a tripartite periodization characterized by adolescence and maturation, florescence and achievement, then decadence and decay.

Bronze Age archaeologists in the Aegean have developed their own story of civilization's progress and demise.[3] Most textbooks on the Bronze Age Aegean present a narrative that contains at least some elements of a standard progression starting with simple farming communities in the Neolithic period, the origins of complex states in the Early Bronze Age, the appearance of advanced states that built monumental architecture and developed a distinct ritual and artistic culture on Crete in the Middle Bronze Age, and finally a period of decadent, gaudy, warlike states on the LBA mainland that collapsed under the weight of their own bureaucratic overreach and ideological failures.[4] This collapse is followed by a brief coda or twilight in the postpalatial period (*ca.* 1200–1050) before the story ends with the final onset of darkness, when general poverty and depopulation descend as the first millennium begins in the EIA.

The overarching narratives that frame both Greek history and Aegean prehistory have long been recognized as problematic for archaeologists trying to come to terms with the archaeology of the Aegean between the dissolution of the Mycenaean states and the start of the Archaic period.[5] One of the issues that the narratives create is a tendency for the EIA to fall in between two distinct realms of the discipline, Aegean Prehistory and Classical Archaeology. From the point of view of scholars interested in Aegean prehistory, the seemingly catastrophic events and dramatic cultural changes of the twelfth century represent a logical breaking off point, even though the nature of the evidence does not really change fundamentally after that, meaning prehistorians really are in the best position to interpret the EIA. For a traditionally trained Classicist, the EIA, which lacks texts, is likewise convenient as a stopping point. Since it is largely atextual, the EIA is mostly unknowable and thus of little interest for a scholar trained to analyze and mainly rely upon texts, as many historians are.[6] From that point of view the EIA tends to be seen as something of a void from which literary and historical texts would appear in the context of the eighth-century renaissance.[7]

Despite its marginal position in the discipline, the field of Aegean archaeology has seen the emergence of a strong contingent of scholars focusing their

---

[3] A discussion of this narrative and some of its elements is presented in Tartaron 2008, 93–110.

[4] Among other factors. The cause of the LBA collapse is, of course, a vast and controversial topic; a review is available in Cline 2014.

[5] See Papadopoulos 1993; Morris 1997; Morris 2000, 40–41; Kotsonas 2016; Kotsonas 2020, 78–84.

[6] Whitley 2017, 723.

[7] Papadopoulos and Smithson 2017, 975–976; Papadopoulos 2019, 701.

careers and their scholarship specifically on the EIA.[8] Both in the library and
on the ground in the form of new field and analytical projects, work produced
on the EIA over the last several decades has been successful in bringing this
field into maturity as an area of specialization and publication.[9] Much of the
resulting scholarship is of exemplary quality and has expanded our understanding of the period in manifold ways.[10] The massive *Companion to the Archaeology
of Early Greece and the Mediterranean*, published in 2020, will long stand as an
authoritative monument to how far EIA scholarship progressed between the
publication of the present book and of Snodgrass's *Dark Age of Greece* in 1971.[11]
Judging by the volume of publications that now treat it as a unity, the LBA/
EIA gap seems to have been successfully bridged. The Mycenaean world is
widely recognized as having an important place in accounts of Greek history,
and prehistorians have long since dismantled the idea that LBA Aegean states
were static, oriental institutions unrelated to and structurally distinct from later
Greek historical institutions.[12] Many prehistorians populate faculty positions in
Classics departments, and there is little talk about a Dark Age anymore.[13]

These are positive developments. But having largely succeeded in 'bridging
the divide' between LBA and historical Greek society, it seems to me that we
still struggle with the baggage of the residual master narrative of the Bronze to
Iron Age transition. Our current discourse seems to envision two complex
states (Mycenaean and historical Greek) that are of interest because they
represent notional cultural high points, then places the EIA as a filament of
tissue that binds them together into "one indivisible whole."[14] This new
construction of historical sequences is problematic for the EIA because it

---

[8] See discussion in Kotsonas 2016, 260–264; 2020, 85–89.   [9] Murray 2018, 24.

[10] Notable edited volumes and book length studies of the period spanning the transition from
the LBA to the Archaic period to come out in the last fifteen years include Deger-Jalkotzy
and Lemos 2006; Dickinson 2006; Knapp and van Dommelen 2014; Babbi, Bubenheimer-
Erhart, and Marín Aguilera 2015; Stampolidis, Maner, and Kopanias 2015; Vlachou 2015;
Mazarakis-Ainian, Alexandridou, and Charalambidou 2017; Niesiołowski-Spanò and
Węcowski 2018; Dimitriadou 2019; Lemos and Kotsonas 2020; Middleton 2020. Earlier
highlights include the prolific scholarship of Susan Langdon, e.g., Langdon 1989; 1998; 2001;
2007; 2008; 2015. In the field, John Papadopoulos and his students have revolutionized the
way that we interpret EIA developments through work in the Northern Aegean, among
many other important contributions in the area of ceramic studies, especially for early Athens.
Papadopoulos' contributions to the field are too numerous to distill into a footnote, but
major EIA excavations at Methone (ongoing) and Torone (e.g., Papadopoulos 1989; 2005) as
well as groundbreaking contributions to the archaeology of early Athens are high on the list
(e.g., Papadopoulos and Smithson 2002; 2017; Papadopoulos 2003). See also other important
papers on periodization such as Papadopoulos 1993; 1994; 1996; 1999; 2014; 2019). Also of
great importance is the legacy of Irene Lemos and her students, who have worked hard to
eradicate the formerly common notion of the EIA as a Dark Age (discussed in Kotsonas 2016,
262–263).

[11] Snodgrass 1971; Lemos and Kotsonas 2020.

[12] For example, Parkinson, Nakassis, and Galaty 2011; Nakassis 2013; 2020.

[13] Kotsonas 2016; Murray 2018.   [14] Wace 1973, xxxv.

implicitly subordinates the EIA to earlier and later periods, situating the years between the Mycenaean states' demise and the Archaic period as of essentially relational interest.

As a result, the questions that prehistorians and historians both ask about the EIA tend to be overwhelmingly relational or essentially evolutionary.[15] The questions that prehistorians ask about the EIA tend to revolve around the issue of change and continuity after the events of the twelfth century. How and why are EIA communities different from or the same as LBA ones? What were the processes of transformation that brought society from one phase to the next? The questions Greek historians ask about the EIA tend to revolve around the relationship between later Greek historical institutions and cultural characteristics and EIA ones.[16] When and where can we identify the origins of these institutions and cultural characteristics – the rise of the *polis*, the origins of Greek religion, the underpinnings of a kind of market economy, the appearance of a recognizable tradition of figural art, etc.? In sum, the increasingly large amount of work that attempts to bridge the divide of the EIA, to approach the period from both a Bronze Age and a Greek historical point of view, tends to be framed in terms of durative or evolving institutions: viewed from either end of a dark tunnel, do we see culture and society emerging looking mostly the same over the transitional period or are things more substantially different?

I am not suggesting that these are bad questions or uninteresting framings. The EIA did follow a seemingly dramatic set of events that entailed an end to palatial states and the emergence of some new social, economic, and cultural structures. Historical development does matter – institutions build on prior institutions and tradition and memory can be quite persistent in imbuing objects and social practices with meaning. It is not uninteresting to think about how we may reconstruct these relationships. However, the problem with these approaches is that they have a tendency to *determine* and *limit* the way in which we interpret EIA archaeological evidence.

If we approach EIA material with Bronze Age states in mind, we will tend to focus on certain things that seem to be important in the Bronze Age world – for example, the relationship between long-distance trade networks

---

[15] There are exceptions, however, e.g., Lemos 2002, which simply sets out to treat eleventh and tenth century evidence (mainly pottery), the ARISTEIA project spearheaded by Mazarakis-Ainian (see papers in Mazarakis Ainian, Alexandridou, and Charalambidou 2017), or the majority of Langdon's work cited in n. 10.

[16] Whitley's statement (2017, 723) from the afterword to a recent conference publication is telling: "The principal reason for studying the period . . . is that what emerged from it – the civilization of Archaic and later Greece – was so remarkable, and has left such a major imprint on not only European but also Near Eastern civilisation that what we have come to take its legacy for granted."

and political interaction, the way in which political leaders related to the community, or the economic structure of states. Likewise, if we think about the EIA from the perspective of Greek history, we will structure our thoughts around things that pertain to historical Greece – for example, elite competition and cooperation, the arbitration of political and legal authority, or an aesthetic pursuit of naturalism. Thinking this way is not uninteresting if what we are trying to do is understand the EIA in a relational way – as a period in which culture and society were either different to or the same as what came before and after. However, these approaches are problematic if we want to try to move away from this relational approach to the EIA (seeing it most importantly as a transition from one cultural high point to another) and move toward a reconstruction of what is going on in the EIA from a less relational perspective, that is, an understanding of the EIA that relies on what we can make of the internal logic of its own material remains.

I want to reiterate that the relational approach to the EIA is problematic in part because it tends to *determine* the scope of interpretations. One example of this phenomenon is the proliferation of discussions about state formation, which have often had a profound impact on discourse in EIA archaeology, even though it seems questionable that states by most definitions of the word even existed in many parts of the Aegean during most of the EIA.[17] Another example is the focus on burnt animal sacrifice, which has occupied a prominent place in discussions of the development of ritual practice in early Greece because we know that it had a prominent role in religious activity in historical Greece, not because it had a straightforwardly important one in the LBA.[18] Scholars have been at pains to demonstrate that there is some evidence of burnt animal sacrifice in earlier periods, but it seems unlikely that they would be doing so if not for the desire to connect ritual institutions from the LBA and EIA with later Greek ritual.

Another problem with a relational approach to the EIA is that it tends to *limit* what we can see in the archaeological record. The limiting amounts to a kind of myopia that causes us to preferentially reconstruct and trace the contours of EIA phenomena that are familiar to either a Bronze Age or an historical paradigm. On the other hand, cultural and archaeological features of the EIA that do not fit into those paradigms tend to be written off as failed eccentricities, if they are not elided from analysis entirely. These phenomena become interpretational orphans because of the structure of discourse: they are

---

[17] On the extent to which discussions of state formation have often saturated work on the EIA see Morris' polemics in *Daidalos* and elsewhere (Morris 1992a, 123–124; 1992b, xvii–xviii; 1997, 64–65).

[18] Bergquist 1988; Isaakidou et al. 2002; Hamilakis and Konsolaki 2004; Tartaron 2008, 117–121; Lupack 2020, 162–163.

not located along the strand of development the narrative privileges (Mycenaean states to Archaic Greek ones), so it is hard for us to build them into the narrative at all. One example of this kind of orphaned phenomenon are the stone-built burial tumuli that appear at postpalatial/EIA sites like Chania in the Argolid, several sites in Thessaly, and Anavlochos on Crete that do not have much in common with LBA or Archaic burial customs.[19] Another example is the phenomenon of settlements on tiny offshore islets in the twelfth century, which is difficult to relate to known features of Mycenaean states or Greek *poleis* institutions, and has for this reason been left mostly unexplored.[20] When they are not orphaned, sometimes EIA phenomena are boxed into paradigms into which they fit awkwardly. The most famous example is probably the complete one-off that is the Lefkandi *heröon*. Too spectacular to be ignored, the *heröon* is built into the narrative story of Bronze to Iron Age, but awkwardly so. Its architecture is usually discussed in the context of the origin of monumental temples, even though it had a clearly mortuary function and even though the first real evidence for early temples postdates the Lefkandi structure by at least a century, if not more.[21]

In general, it is often the case that, if some aspect of the EIA does not seem to be in direct dialogue with something in the Mycenaean or Archaic worlds, it is lost from view or pressed into service of more visible categories of cultural history into which it fits awkwardly. This has the net effect of creating an illusion that the structure, institutions, practices, and people of the EIA were essentially similar to the ones in the LBA and the Archaic period. Viewed as the result of our intellectual frameworks, it is easy to see why this similarity is likely to be at least somewhat illusory. I suspect that, in reality, what is happening is that it is easiest for us to pick out and describe entities we recognize from earlier and later periods when we look at the archaeological evidence on account of the relational way that we approach it. However, it is equally easy to conceive of the possibility that a much different set of interpretative results (and a different understanding of EIA society) could be obtained if we only altered the focus.

In this book, I set out to rigorously examine a particular set of EIA objects – naked male bronze figurines – that has often been dismissed as largely of esoteric interest precisely because of the tendency of scholars to see and value the figurines in a relational sense rather than to invest these objects in their own particular historical, social, ritual, and technological context. Doing the

[19] For Chania, see Palaiologou 2013. On Thessaly, Reinders 2003; Malakasioti 2006; Karouzou 2017, 352–356.

[20] Hood 1966; 1970; Kardulias, Gregory, and Sawmiller 1995; Konsolaki-Yannopoulou 2003; 2007; Murray et al. 2020.

[21] See discussion in Wilson Jones 2014, 36–37.

latter suggests a new interpretation that has some relevance for relational histories of the EIA, but ultimately leads to a reconstruction of ritual history in the EIA that is different from anything we would arrive at if we depended on a relational approach. It is unlikely that the interpretation of the EIA figurines that I have presented here would have arisen from a set of assumptions that arose from an understanding of the ritual and material structures of the LBA Aegean world or the Archaic one. Indeed, my reconstruction of EIA worship at rural sanctuaries is one that might seem dissonant with our ideas about Greek culture – it is a shady world of dark places, powerful magicians, and strange cultural inversions in which craftspeople hold ritual power rather than sitting at the margins of society and serving the whims of the elite.

Thinking about the EIA as a period in and of itself, rather than a stretch of connective tissue binding together two periods that are more important, or that at least have traditionally accrued much more sustained and intensive scholarly investigation, reduces the degree to which this dissonance may surprise. Describing the EIA as a transitional period makes it sound like it is not very substantial, and this occasionally has the effect of analytically and intellectually obliterating its quite substantial length. This makes it easier to impose later and earlier realities onto the material, because it causes us to suppose those realities were closer in time to an EIA society than they really were. When we are discussing the tenth century, we should remember that this is fully hundreds of years removed from any recognizable Mycenaean state or the institutions, texts, and culture that characterized Archaic and Classical Greek states. It is not surprising that a lot of characteristics of this culture would have been different from earlier and later conditions: the way that knowledge circulated, the way that people and communities interacted, the demographic realities of population and cultivation of resources, and conceptions of how the world worked almost certainly must have been distinct during the EIA. It is easy to believe, then, that some social and cultural developments during this period might have nothing to do with earlier or later ones. Developments in human society and cultural history involve nonobvious turns, saltations, and eddies that exhaust themselves as often as they manifest linear progressions. Aspects of EIA society that do not involve transparently natural or evolutionary developments linking the thirteenth and the eighth centuries might not help us to link up these two periods, but that does not mean they cannot tell us something important about the EIA.

In the case of the EIA figurines I have dealt with here, the two main distortions that the master narrative has imposed upon them relate to their assessment (a) within society and ritual and (b) as art objects. Both of these issues lead us back to a critique of the role that master narratives have played in organizing our analysis of EIA society. They also give cause to be mindful of the issue of categorization I highlighted in the introduction to the book and touched upon throughout. Because we tend to place EIA figurines within an art historical narrative that is focused on technical skill and aesthetic accomplishment, and to therefore categorize them as art, we may have misunderstood their value. Placing them in an EIA context that is both specifically ritual and closely bound up in the production process pushes us beyond the aesthetic narrative of Greek art and inspires new conclusions. In relation to the way this material is treated as a material constituent of sanctuary assemblages, categorizing the bronze figurines as "votive bronzes" has encouraged us to lump them together with larger, more impressive bronze objects, like tripod cauldrons, and thus to interpret them in light of processes of elite display, which seems like a fundamental misunderstanding of the likely function of these objects. Overall, the focus on elites and elite behavior that has characterized much scholarship on Bronze Age and Archaic Greece has been imposed on EIA nude figurines in a way that does not seem productive for a period in which social hierarchies were likely much less pronounced, and probably much less central to social behavior, than they were in later and earlier periods.

Another issue raised by the research presented here is the way that we categorize different realms of society according to logic that is not inherent to the EIA. We tend not to associate ritual power and craft activity with one another in the past, because these facets of human behavior are not aligned in our view of the world and because extant texts do not suggest that such an association pertained in the Late Bronze or Archaic periods. However, there is thoroughgoing evidence that we should associate these two activities with one another at least in some regions and at some sanctuaries in the EIA. Returning to the problem of categories, analysis has focused on splitting out economic actors – metal workers – from political and ritual actors – elites and priests or priestesses, and to treat metal workers as participants in a market logic which does not sit easily with what we know about the EIA economy. A more plausible scenario for the particular economic and cultural conditions of the EIA confounds these distinctions. We should therefore posit a much more complex interplay of social roles in the EIA that were not rigidly divided among such categories. I suggest that metalworkers in the EIA almost certainly occupied a wide variety of social roles – they were ritual, economic, and political actors all at once.

The evidence for a strong association between metallurgy and ritual in the contexts I review in this book is ample. I anticipate that the most likely opposition to this association would be that ritual and metallurgy are not linked in later or earlier periods. However, the natural implication of such an argument would be that we are only prepared to accept as plausible EIA institutions that are essentially the same as the ones that existed in the Bronze Age and the Archaic period, when we have more evidence to reconstruct such institutions. This kind of approach seems to beg the question of what we think we are doing when we approach the archaeology of the EIA. What is the point of investigating this period in any detail if we are already sure about what we will and will not find there? At the least, it seems like a good way to make the period seem quite boring. While the evidence from the EIA is sufficiently intermittent to resist interpretations that yield certainty, we surely might want to consider the idea that it contains evidence for social and cultural developments that are surprising and distinct, rather than only ones that match what we would expect to find.

Part of the purpose of the book has been to demonstrate what we can achieve if we think more broadly and openly about what might have been happening in the EIA in ways that do not draw on expectations based on material available within the Greco-Roman tradition. Usually, Aegeanists have drawn analogies from the proximate sources of LBA or Homeric society in order to reconstruct EIA institutions. However, casting a wider net when we seek analogical bases for understanding evidence from the EIA, for example by thinking about comparative evidence from the wider Mediterranean or from ethnographic accounts, can help us to escape the rutted intellectual pathways that our disciplinary structure often bogs us down within. While there are many problems with reasoning analogically based on the ethnographic record, and while finding an analogically perfect fit is very difficult, these sources can be helpful because they suggest creative interpretations that lead to original insights. In this case, I think that reaching outside of Classics for sources of analogical insight allows us to find aspects of the EIA that are not necessarily totally unrelated to earlier and later developments within the Aegean but that are not really at all consonant with the ideas that we already have about the Mycenaean world or the Greek historical world. This can be freeing; as a method, perhaps it provides one conduit out of the mental constraints and confining limits of working in a field burdened by a strongly stated and deeply embedded narrative of linear evolutionary development.

Coming to clear and indisputable conclusions about complex ritual and social dynamics in the EIA often presents serious challenges; the evidence is not very copious and the number of well-explored, well-published archaeological sites remains relatively small. While it is no longer accurate to state that EIA archaeologists face an evidence-poor environment, there are certain limitations to analysis of archaeological material that provides little in the way of iconography, visual narratives, or written texts to guide interpretation. We only have small windows through which to glimpse the societies of the EIA, and the regional diversity of the period makes generalizing from these tiny glimpses challenging too. Certainty can be fleeting in analyses of the EIA for these reasons, but certainty is always fleeting in archaeology, and the fact that working on this period is difficult need not prevent us from taking careful stock of the evidence that exists and trying to build a picture of society around it. My conclusions do not represent an undeniable proof of what EIA society and ritual were about, and I anticipate that some will disagree with the conclusions, dismiss them as unimportant because they do not really relate to the rise of the *polis*, or reject them because they cannot be definitively validated. But I contend that they represent a richer and more internally consistent interpretation of EIA nude figurines that takes account of a particular EIA social context than existing ones do.

THE TYRANNY OF THE TEXT

Existing scholarship on the earlier history of nudity in the Aegean directs attention to another issue that often haunts scholars dealing with the EIA, the seemingly intractable problem that John Papadopoulos called the 'tyranny of the text'. Papadopoulos used this term to describe the tendency of historians to afford authority to textual accounts regardless of contradictory information drawn from material culture because of what they perceive as a hierarchical relationship between the validity of interpretations based on the two forms of evidence.[22] For a variety of reasons, many of which are related to the history of the discipline, information in texts often tends to override interpretations that might be drawn from material evidence alone.[23]

As outlined above, the period between 1200 and 700 is widely conceived of as a transitional period. In Aegean periodization, it sits astride the transition between Bronze Age and Iron Ages. It is also considered a transition between prehistory, a period during which textual records are scarce or nonexistent, and history, for which we have access to a relatively robust body of textual evidence.[24] Although there are textual records in Mycenaean Greek from the Aegean LBA, the Linear B texts which mainly record economic transactions, most accounts of ancient Greek history, art, and culture have seen the collapse of the Mycenaean palaces as the end of something distinct from

---

[22] Papadopoulos 1999. See also discussion of the reliance on and valuation of texts in Papadopoulos 2019.

[23] The centrality of texts to the field of Classics not only implicates interpretative practice, but also plays a part in driving research agendas and producing hierarchies of value regarding which periods are considered worthy of study. While I have primarily encountered this in my work on the EIA, and while I believe that the tendency of scholars to impose information from texts (especially Homer) on archaeological evidence is particularly acute in this subfield, it seems to me that the issue has relevance for scholars dealing with any period or region for which textual sources are sparse or marginally related to the geographical or chronological context. Some examples of areas in which textual tyranny might be in play include the early phases of Rome's history, or any provincial or marginal geographic area which are treated in texts by authors who probably did not know very much about them.

[24] Lemos and Kotsonas 2020, xiii.

historical Greece.[25] They begin instead with the period of recovery (often called a renaissance or revolution) in the eighth century when texts written in the Greek alphabet begin to appear.[26] The EIA thus sits somewhat awkwardly as an atextual period between two eras for which there is some textual evidence.[27]

Notwithstanding this consensus – that there are no extant textual records that clearly relate to the EIA – interpretations of and narratives about this period continue to be heavily influenced by texts. While it is often pointed out that relying on Homer as a crutch for interpreting the archaeological evidence from the EIA is problematic, the interpretative tentacles of Homer almost always find their way in to scholarship on the EIA.[28] Despite continued and now quite longstanding warnings about the hazards of using texts to interpret the archaeological record from the twelfth to eighth centuries, Homer is nearly always appealed to in such scholarship, whether the topic relates to the twelfth century, the eighth century, or anything in between, and in areas both central and peripheral to the Attic tradition that ultimately produced the versions of the poems that come down to us. This tendency has the net effect of both greatly flattening the variety and regional nuance of material culture (i.e., assuming that there is a Homeric unity to the EIA world) and imposing interpretations that often sit awkwardly with the material evidence itself.

The point is not to assert that the social and political institutions or realities described in early Greek poetry are any more or less real than inferences we can draw from the archaeological record, but to demonstrate that by taking for granted an analogical relationship between the two distinct sets of evidence, we tend to diminish the nuance of the insights that can be gained from either. In this book, I make a case against the particular way that Homer has been used in the case of understanding the history of the naked male in the Aegean. However, this does not mean that it is possible, or even desirable, to eliminate

---

[25] While this has been the traditional view, it is probably incorrect to say that it is wholly orthodox now, a testament to the quality and impact of scholarly work advocating for a dissolution of the old divide between the Mycenaean and the historical Greek world.

[26] See discussion in Kotsonas 2016, 247. For various formulations of the EIA as the temporal location for the beginnings of the Greek *polis* and a recognizably Hellenic/Hellenizing Greek culture and art or something along those lines see: (a) for history, Ure 1921; Starr 1961; Andrewes 1967, 48–51; Snodgrass 1971; Antonaccio 2011: (b) for art and archaeology, e.g., Starr 1961, 99–103; Carter 1972, 27, 36; Robertson 1975, 14–33; Hägg 1983; Hurwit 1985; Bohen 1991; 1997, 53.

[27] Papadopoulos 2019, 701.

[28] There are too many instances of this sort of haphazard dependence on Homer as a guide to EIA archaeological evidence to cite them systematically here, and it would be inopportune to choose out a few scholars at random to illustrate the tendency. Any reader with experience of EIA scholarship will probably be sufficiently aware of the tendency to obviate the need for extensive references here. For recent criticisms of this sort of reasoning see, e.g. Murray 2017, 67–69; Nakassis 2020, 274–275; Whitley 2020, 172–176.

texts from the study of the EIA. The distinction between 'text and archae-ology' is a misleading one, because archaeologists also work through texts and rely on storytelling, linking narratives about the human experience together.[29] My criticism of the way that Homer has been used in the study of early Greece does not constitute advocacy against the use of texts in archaeology, but a limited criticism of the haphazard way that Homer is often brought into engagement with EIA archaeology.

This limited criticism leads to the equally limited conviction that if we are going to bring Homeric texts to bear on EIA evidence, it is important that the logic and method according to which we do so be explicitly and transparently articulated. Put another way, if we are going to use Homeric poetry as a frame for interpreting material from the EIA, we should be explicit in the fact that when we do this we are effectively reasoning using analogical inference, a method that archaeologists have theorized extensively and that underpins all prehistoric archaeological reasoning.[30] Reasoning by analogy involves explain-ing a poorly known or poorly attested situation by reference to a better known one. While always potentially problematic, it can be a useful tool when it is wielded self-critically and within certain methodological constraints.[31] Crucial to the use of analogy is the issue of fit – whether the source of the inference could be reasonably expected to bear some resemblance to the scenario to which it is being applied. There might be a reasonably good argument that Homeric society provides a good analogy through which to interpret elite contexts in late eighth century Attica, for example, but this case needs to be made explicitly rather than implicitly accepted as useful and appropriate. Using Homeric society as an analogy through which to interpret tenth century evidence from Aetolia, on the other hand, does not seem like it would stand up as well to methodological scrutiny from the point of view of analogical inference and fit.

In another context, my colleagues and I have argued that using analogical inference that looks beyond Homer for inspiration can lead us toward entirely new conclusions that we could never have reached if we depended on the textual record, and which fit better with the EIA material evidence than inferences drawn from Greek literature.[32] My general conviction is that the study of the EIA will benefit if its practitioners further explore the possibility of constructing new texts (narratives) about the archaeological record using inferences and analogies that are critically and carefully constructed to fit the material evidence, rather than working the other way around – constructing

---

[29] See insightful discussion in Lucas 2019.
[30] On analogy in archaeological reasoning see, e.g., Hodder 1982a; 1982b; Wylie 1985.
[31] Wylie 1985, 80; Wendrich 1999, 17–20.   [32] Murray, Chorghay, and MacPherson 2020.

narratives about the evidence from an understanding of society that grows from Greek literary texts that are not relevant to the EIA.

In this book, I have attempted to show how both processes work – first, to show why Homer and Thucydides' ideas about male nudity are probably not a reasonable guide to the nudity that we find in the EIA archaeological record, and second, how viewing the EIA evidence in light of a broader range of alternative models leads us to novel interpretative solutions. Chapters 3 and 5 specifically go even further, flipping the old model of text and archaeology on its head, and arguing that reconstructing EIA institutions from the material record and from ethnographic parallels goes a long way toward explaining some previously perplexing aspects of the Greco-Roman textual tradition, including the persistent attribution of initiatory rituals involving pederasty to a Cretan origin and the presence of ritually powerful metalworkers in myth.

MATERIAL PROCESSES AND PREHISTORIC PEOPLE

One of the additional benefits of approaching EIA archaeological material from an interdisciplinary and ultimately prehistoric perspective is that it allows us to move beyond the paradigm of aesthetic evaluation that tends to dominate interpretations of material culture. It is certainly true that the Greeks of the historical period valued craft objects for their beauty and appreciated the virtuosity of their craftspeople based on the aesthetic achievements that resulted from the technical mastery of their crafts. However, just because this was true of historical Greek communities does not mean that we must interpret EIA material along these lines.

Comparative evidence from a variety of prehistoric and ethnographic contexts demonstrates that there is much more to images and objects than meets the modern eye. When we focus too much on the aesthetic performance of finished objects, "processes of making appear swallowed up in objects made; processes of seeing in images seen."[33] Indeed, craft production processes themselves provided opportunities for communicating values and ideas, often especially "ideas that are cognitively, socially, and emotionally unacceptable to consciousness," which are just the sort of ideas that we might imagine needed transmitting during the ontologically weighty ordeal of a liminal ceremony.[34] The transformations of producing something, such as transforming a piece of wood into a staff or a piece of stone into a statue, are often viewed as fascinating to both mortals and immortals, so that these processes themselves constitute the main realm in which value accrues to objects, irrespective of the

[33] Ingold 2013, 7.   [34] Tuzin 2002, 289.

mundanity of the objects produced.[35] This is in line with Gell's appeal for an abandonment of a strong distinction between technology and magic and his proposal that an appreciation of technical virtuosity often imbues makers with control over supernatural forces that are "intrinsic to the efficacy of works of art in their social context."[36]

These comparative and theoretical perspectives encourage us to move from seeing objects as things that we might admire in a museum to viewing them as the material outcomes of production processes that were themselves a source of wonder by virtue of the fact that they had transformative power. This in turn frees us from a limiting view of objects that situates them within an aesthetic hierarchy, and opens up the possibility of an expansive understanding of material as constitutive of a set of experiences. Thinking about the experience of seeing special objects produced from unusual materials may be a helpful path forward as we seek to animate the static and somewhat sparse artefactual record of the EIA into newly engaging interpretations that give us some insight into its people and society.

The bronze figurines that are among the earliest dedications in Greek sanctuaries in the first millennium and which constitute the first corpus of consistently nude males in early Greek art are quite tiny, highly idiosyncratic, and from unstratified contexts. These figurines are not immediately prepossessing or promising as a medium through which to generate new insights into EIA society. Viewed as aesthetic artworks, they are lumpy, diminutive, and often imperfect. They will never be impressive or captivating in the same way as magisterial, monumental, hollow-cast Greek bronze sculptures of the Archaic and Classical periods. Nonetheless, if we consider the processes and technology behind their production, as well as the personal investment of the artisans to craft and design each, totally *sui generis*, figurine, they become a source of awe and wonderment in a different way. Although unprepossessing aesthetically, viewed as a correlate of certain ritual practices, these figurines serve as valuable guides to many aspects of EIA technology, supernatural belief, and ritual practice.

CONCLUSIONS

In addition to the material revisions to the history of naked ritual activities in the Aegean that I presented in Chapter 6, the book supports a number of methodological points pursuant to the study of the Aegean EIA. First, positioning EIA figurines in a framework of transition ('bridging the divide') has

---

[35] This is especially emphasized in Coupaye's work on, of all things, yams, in Papua New Guinea (Coupaye 2007, 2009, 2012).
[36] Gell 1992, 52.

proven an obstacle for contextual interpretation. Treating naked male EIA figurines as a purely EIA phenomenon, rather than seeing them as a means of connecting Mycenaean and Archaic institutions or conventions, led me to a series of new interpretations and observations. Second, the Homeric texts are clearly a terrible guide to the EIA. We need to set aside the idea that early Greek texts should lead the way in any kind of analysis of EIA material. Third, it may be helpful to think more carefully about processes as opposed to products when we assess EIA material culture in particular, and prehistoric Aegean archaeology in general. It is likely that the characteristics of at least some of the artifacts that we study in this discipline were not as important as the extraordinary and visually awesome processes involved in their production.

Finally, I hope to have convinced readers unaccustomed to thinking about this period that evidence for EIA society can and should sustain interest in its own right. The material I have presented is not really of interest because it contains evidence for some germs of later Archaic and Classical practice, or because it might tell us a little more about a long development of regular nude practice that would culminate in the normative athletic practice that formed a part of historical Greek society. It is also not of interest because it is part of the story of transformation or continuity of institutions after the LBA. To my mind, the interesting thing about the conclusions is that they are especially and most thoroughly about what is going on within a particularly EIA ritual, technological, and social context. These conclusions do not need to be connected to the Mycenaeans or the Athenians and Spartans to engage us. Like any case study of any archaeological context, the material in this book is of interest because it adds to our overall knowledge of the range and varieties of human experience and social organization in the past.

APPENDIX A

Γυμνός AND NUDITY IN HOMER AND HESIOD

THIS APPENDIX DISCUSSES ALL OF THE PASSAGES IN EARLY GREEK EPIC POETRY THAT contain the word *gymnos* (the Greek adjective roughly corresponding to English naked or nude) and related verbs. The material is relevant to the discussion of nudity in Chapter 1 of the book. However, because it is simple to generalize about the nature of this evidence for the purposes of the argument in Chapter 1, it seemed best to avoid interrupting the flow of discussion with a detailed analysis of these passages in the main body of the text and to present the material in an appendix instead. For each passage or group of passages, I provide some commentary and interpretation. The passages are divided into thematic or topically appropriate sections to avoid repetition in the commentary. As in Chapter I, all translations of Homer are from A. T. Murray's Loeb editions (Loeb Classical Libraries No. 104–105 and 170–171).

A THE DEATH OF PATROKLOS (*IL.* 16.815; 17.122; 17.693; 18.21)

Il. 16.813–817

> ὁ μὲν αὖτις ἀνέδραμε, μίκτο δ᾿ ὁμίλῳ,
> ἐκ χροὸς ἁρπάξας δόρυ μείλινον, οὐδ᾿ ὑπέμεινε
> Πάτροκλον **γυμνόν** περ ἐόντ᾿ ἐν δηϊοτῆτι.
> Πάτροκλος δὲ θειοῦ πληγῇ καὶ δουρὶ δαμασθεὶς
> ἂψ ἑτάρων εἰς ἔθνος ἐχάζετο κῆρ᾿ ἀλεείνων.

> . . .he ran back again and mixed with the throng
> after he had drawn out the ashen spear from the flesh, and he did not await
> Patroklos in the fray, unarmed though he was.
> But Patroklos, overcome by the blow of the god and the spear
> drew back into the throng of his comrades, avoiding fate.

Il. 17.120–122

> Αἶαν, δεῦρο, πέπον, περὶ Πατρόκλοιο θανόντος
> σπεύσομεν, αἴ κε νέκυν περ Ἀχιλλῆϊ προφέρωμεν
> **γυμνόν**· ἀτὰρ τά γε τεύχε᾿ ἔχει κορυθαίολος Ἕκτωρ.

> Ajax, come here, good friend, let us hurry in defense of the dead Patroklos
> in the hope that we may bring his corpse at least to Achilleus
> –his naked corpse–but his armor Hektor of the flashing helmet holds.

Il. 17.691–693

ἀλλὰ σύ γ' αἶψ' Ἀχιλῆϊ θέων ἐπὶ νῆας Ἀχαιῶν
εἰπεῖν, αἴ κε τάχιστα νέκυν ἐπὶ νῆα σαώσῃ
γυμνόν· ἀτὰρ τά γε τεύχε' ἔχει κορυθαίολος Ἕκτωρ.

But quickly run to the ships of the Achaians and bring word to Achilleus
in the hope that he may immediately bring the corpse safe to his ship –
the naked corpse; but his armor Hektor of the flashing helmet holds.

Il. 18.20–21

κεῖται Πάτροκλος, νέκυος δὲ δὴ ἀμφιμάχονται
γυμνοῦ· ἀτὰρ τά γε τεύχε' ἔχει κορυθαίολος Ἕκτωρ."

Low lies Patroklos, and around his corpse they are fighting
–his naked corpse–but his armor Hektor of the flashing helmet holds.

Discussion

Patroklos is described as γυμνός once before his death (*Il.* 16.815) and three
times after it (*Il.* 17.122, 17.693, 18.21). The poet's narration of Patroklos'
death has long attracted attention as an interesting and complex moment in the
Iliad. Hektor deals Patroklos the final blow, thus inciting the famously divine
wrath of Achilleus that will carry the poem through to its tragic denouement.
Patroklos is already unarmed (γυμνός) when Hektor strikes him. Prior to the
blow, overzealous Patroklos has had his armor loosened by Apollo.[1] In his
vulnerable state, he is struck first by Euphorbos, who retreats from Patroklos
rapidly notwithstanding his lack of armor (presumably because of the formidable opponent Patroklos represents, armored or not).[2] After these two blows –
one by Apollo that causes his armor to come undone and fall off of his body,
and one by Euphorbos to weaken the hero – Hektor reaches Patroklos' belly
with his sharp spear.

Patroklos' death is exceptional in the poem, and its description therefore had
to be altered from the normal formulaic description of the death of a warrior,
who falls to the ground with his armor clanging around him (ἀράβησε δὲ
τεύχε'ἐπ'αὐτῷ). Presumably the formula would not do in this scenario because
Patroklos' armor had already been removed before he was killed. Instead, his

[1] On the death of Patroklos, the strangely passive role of Hektor in Patroklos' death, and the
role of the gods in his undoing, see Mühlenstein 1987; Janko 1994, 408–9; Nickel 2002; Allan
2005, 6–9; Holmes 2010, 53.
[2] Janko 1994, 415: "The emotive apostrophe marks another stage in Patroklos' demise. Even now
Euphorbos is too wary of his unarmed foe to do more than snatch his spear from the wound and
retreat to the ranks (like Meriones at 13.528–33), before Patroklos withdraws too; this increases our
respect for Patroklos' valor. A bolder man would run up and deliver a fatal blow..."

falling "brings great pain to the host of the Achaians."[3] Notwithstanding the apparent unarmored nature of the corpse when it hits the dust, the poet describes Hektor "stripping the corpse of its armor."[4] The sequence of Patroklos' death sees the poet struggling to fit the normal formulaic sequence of a hero's death into an exceptional case.[5]

The poet uses the adjective γυμνός four times during the narration of Patroklos' death. It is apparent that this concentration is due at least in part to the repetition of the formulaic line "γυμνόν/γυμνοῦ· ἀτὰρ τά γε τεύχε' ἔχει κορυθαίολος Ἕκτωρ." The repetition of this line serves to reinforce the important plot point that although Patroklos' corpse is recoverable, Hektor has already taken possession of Achilleus' armor. This plot point is important because it drives Achilleus' subsequent dilemma, when he decides he would like to return to the battlefield in the aftermath of his friend's death but is no longer in possession of armor. The use of γυμνός to modify Patroklos's corpse has been described as "heavily emphatic,"[6] because in three of its four uses in the scene it is enjambed before a dramatic pause. The first γυμνός describes the state of Patroklos once his armor has been removed, before his body transitions from living being into a corpse; this γυμνόν perhaps serves a premonitory purpose, as the audience will have naturally predicted that any warrior who was γυμνός on the battlefield was shortly to become a corpse.

B ACHILLEUS' PROGRESS FROM GRIEF TO VENGEANCE (IL. 17.711, 21.50)

Il. 17.709–711

> οὐδέ μιν οἴω
> νῦν ἰέναι μάλα περ κεχολωμένον Ἕκτορι δίῳ
> οὐ γάρ πως ἂν **γυμνός** ἐὼν Τρώεσσι μάχοιτο.

But I think that Achilleus will not come out, though he is very angry with noble Hektor,
for in no way would he fight against the Trojans unarmed as he is.

---

[3] Combellack 1965, 47. For death scenes in the *Iliad* in general, see Morrison 1999.

[4] A 'mistake' that is repeated often in lines that describe Hektor's acquisition of Patroklos' armor in the later books of the poem (Combellack 1965, 49–51). Edwards 1991, 74: "Menelaos had to abandon Patroklos' body at 108, so it is now in Hektor's possession. Menelaos' words (122) have reminded us that it is without armor. Then, to show that the pathetic corpse is completely at Hektor's mercy, the poet uses the formulaic ἐπεὶ κλυτὰ τεύχε' ἀπηύρα. Actually, helmet, spear, shield, and corselet were stripped from the living hero by Apollo in superb lines 16.793–804, the description of his fall was altered to fit the fall of an unarmed man and the dying victim protests that the gods struck off his armor. Zeus is similarly misled by the commoner situation of a warrior stripping off his victim's armor."

[5] For the notion that Patroklos' death scene is modeled on a preexisting description of Achilleus' death see Barnes 2011.

[6] Edwards 1991, 74.

Il. 21.49–51

τὸν δ' ὡς οὖν ἐνόησε ποδάρκης δῖος Ἀχιλλεὺς,
γυμνὸν, ἄτερ κόρυθός τε καὶ ἀσπίδος, οὐδ' ἔχεν ἔγχος,
ἀλλὰ τὰ μέν ῥ' ἀπὸ πάντα χαμαὶ βάλε·

When the swift-footed noble Achilleus caught sight of him
all unarmed, without helmet or shield, nor had he a spear,
but he had thrown all these from him to the ground.

Discussion

In book 17, Achilleus is unable to avenge Patroklos on the battlefield while γυμνός. In book 21, he slaughters his unarmed foe Lykaon while Lykaon is γυμνός, having removed his own armor while swimming across the Scamander river. From the moment that Patroklos has been deprived of Achilleus' armor, he is rendered γυμνός. Likewise, Achilleus describes himself in the same terms when he realizes he cannot go out onto the battlefield to avenge his friend, because he does not have his own armor and because it would be ridiculous to attempt to join the fray while γυμνός.[7] Achilleus is the only character described as γυμνός who does not die during the *Iliad*, though this may be a deft foreshadowing of his fated death, something that looms throughout the entirety of the *Iliad*.[8]

Modifying Lykaon at line 21.50, γυμνός is probably likewise meant to prepare the reader for that character's impending doom.[9] The Lykaon episode takes place in the context of Achilleus's *aristeia*, between the death of Patroklos and the final clash between Achilleus and Hektor. Lykaon, a son of Priam, meets Achilleus when he has already shed his armor (he found it too difficult to cross the river while fully armed) and so has no option of attempting to defeat him in battle (*Il.* 21.34–135 presents the full encounter). He therefore presents himself as a suppliant to Achilleus, γυμνός as he is, only to be brutally murdered because, it is implied, Achilleus has ceased to operate according to the normal morals and rules of Homeric society. Several scholars have argued that the

---

[7] For the important role of armor as a marker of identity and the making of a warrior in Homeric poetry, see Davies 2007.

[8] The idea that audiences may have seen Achilleus' death as a reasonable end to the *Iliad* was presented by Wilamowitz (1920), and convincingly demonstrated by Burgess (2009, 43–55, 72–92). A related point is surely that the scene of warriors fighting over Achilleus' corpse (*Od.* 24.36–40) matches almost exactly the scene of fighting over Patroklos' (*Il.* 16.772–76). Barnes argues that the narration of both Hektor's and Patroklos' deaths are modeled on a preexisting source describing the death of Achilleus (Barnes 2011, 5).

[9] Richardson 1993, 58: "Lykaon's helplessness is emphasized by this complex sentence, in anticipation of his desperate plea for salvation. His lack of armor enables Achilleus to recognize him at once. γυμνόν is emphatic at the beginning of the verse."

scene presents Lykaon as a poetic "double" of Hektor.[10] It may therefore be possible that the slaughter of Lykaon while γυμνός is supposed to be a preview of what would happen to Hektor if he does what he is pondering at 22.124, appearing γυμνός in front of Achilleus as a suppliant.[11] As we see in *Il.* 21.122–124, the fate of the man who dies γυμνός and whose corpse is not attended to is not desirable. Achilleus flings Lykaon's corpse into the Scamander, where (he envisions) fish (who "think nothing of him") will "eat the pale fat" of the Trojan prince (*Il.* 21.123). As a further insult, the corpse will never lie properly in state on a bier, nor be mourned properly by family members (*Il.* 21.123–124). The purpose of this passage seems almost certainly to be to provide a salutary reminder about the fate of the warrior who becomes γυμνός on the battlefield both to the audience, and to Hektor, who will shortly ponder approaching Achilleus as a suppliant (as Lykaon has just done).

C THE DEATH OF HEKTOR (*IL.* 22.124, 22.510)

Il. 22.123–125

μή μιν ἐγὼ μὲν ἵκωμαι ἰών, ὁ δέ μ᾽ οὐκ ἐλεήσει
οὐδέ τί μ᾽ αἰδέσεται, κτενέει δέ με **γυμνὸν** ἐόντα
αὔτως ὥς τε γυναῖκα, ἐπεί κ᾽ ἀπὸ τεύχεα δύω.

Let it not be that I approach him as a suppliant, and he not pity me
nor have respect for me, but slay me out of hand unarmed,
as if I were a woman, when I have taken off my armor.

Il. 22.508–511

νῦν δὲ σὲ μὲν παρὰ νηυσὶ κορωνίσι νόσφι τοκήων
αἰόλαι εὐλαὶ ἔδονται, ἐπεί κε κύνες κορέσωνται
    γυμνόν· ἀτάρ τοι εἵματ᾽ ἐνὶ μεγάροισι κέονται
λεπτά τε καὶ χαρίεντα, τετυγμένα χερσὶ γυναικῶν.

But now by the beaked ships far from your parents
will writhing worms devour you, when the dogs have had their fill,
as you lie a naked corpse, yet in your halls lie clothes
finely woven and fair, fashioned by the hands of women.

Discussion

In book 22, Hektor is described as γυμνός twice, once before and once after his death. Like many aspects of his death, this pre- and post-mortuary

---

[10] Lykaon and Hektor are just two possible "doublets" in the poem, along with Meleager and Achilleus, Euphorbos and Paris (on which see Mühlenstein 1987; Nickel 2002; Allan 2005), etc. For a detailed examination of Lykaon and his death, see Ebel 1968; Morrison 1992, 46–47.

[11] For a reading of the two supplication scenes as erotic in undertone, Ready 2005.

characterization parallels the narration of the death of Patroklos.[12] The first passage, describing Hektor before he meets his doom, has attracted the attention of many scholars. Numerous scholars have commented on the fact that Hektor is pondering the loss of face he would experience in relation to his manliness, if he gave up fighting and went as a suppliant to Achilleus without his armor on (γυμνός). We have therefore come to read this passage as an indication that Hektor is pondering whether Achilleus would kill him if he came in front of him naked, when he had stripped off his armor, like a woman. It is the lack of armor and concomitant vulnerability that would render him womanlike if he approached Achilleus to demand mercy.[13] A relatively extreme view along these lines is given by MacCary: "The extraordinary range of meaning in *aideomai*, from shame, to pity, to awe, prepares us for γυμνός: the man without weapons, who is unable to fight, is not a man, but, lacking precisely *aidoia* (male genitalia), it seems, he is a woman."[14] In the second use

---

[12] On the parallels between Patroklos' and Hektor's deaths, see Clarke 1999, 172–173; Morrison 1999, 135; Allan 2005 (both speak after having absorbed the fatal strike). Barnes 2011 discusses further parallels between the heroes' deaths and the possible existence of a death of Achilleus prototype.

[13] Richardson 1993, 119: "*gymnon* must mean unarmed, as at 21.50 etc. αὐτῶς is often used with an implication of helplessness, e.g., 6.400." Janko 1994, 415: "Patroklos is in a tunic, not naked. Thus, Hektor says Achilleus would kill him γυμνός 'like a woman once I take off my armor' (22.124f) – men always carried arms (15.479-82). Warriors wore tunics under their corselets (3.359)"; Bassi 1995, 4–5: "In the epic, it is clearly a sign of his weakness for a warrior to be stripped bare of his armor (i.e. to be γυμνός); It even makes him like a woman (*Il.* 22.122–25). But what is stressed here is the act of stripping the armor, that is, the transition from armed to unarmed." For additional critiques of Hektor's feminine behavior, see Crotty 1994, 85; Loraux 1995, 80–81; Mackie 1996, 44–45; Thornton 1997, 154.

[14] MacCary 1982, 156. MacCary's is not the only possible reading of the phrase, and we might consider it to be an unlikely one, given the use of the term γυμνός throughout the rest of the Homeric corpus. We should wonder how the equivalency of the term γυμνός with a notion of womanly weakness can be squared with the fact that no woman is described as γυμνός at any point in the *Iliad*, in the *Odyssey*, or in Hesiod's works (The earliest appearance of γυμνή comes from Herodotus (1.8.2–3). In addition, the only characters Herodotus describes as nude are very high status individuals, like the Persian king and queen, or the wife of Kypselos (Hdt. 5.92). On dress and nudity in Herodotus, see Burzachini 2001; Soares 2014). Since the term γυμνός only ever applies to males and to inanimate objects in Homer, it seems difficult to find a clear connection between womanliness and γυμνός nudity. Therefore, the equation of the state of being γυμνός with being in a state of womanly weakness does not seem to be an optimal reading of the text. I suggest reading the line as something more like 'going to beg for mercy like a helpless woman might' and to connect this line with the notion that Hektor is going to Achilleus as a suppliant (which is a womanly way to behave), rather than to equate γυμνός with a womanly state of lacking arms. However, the opposite reading is reflected already in most translations, e.g., Murray's (1925: "Let it not be that I approach him as a suppliant, and he not pity me or have respect for me, but slay me out of hand unarmed, as if I were a woman, when I have taken off my armor") and Ready's (2005: "Not will I approach him going to him, and he will not pity nor reverence me, rather he will kill me since I am naked without effort just as a woman, when I strip off my armor.") In any case, based on the abstemious use of γυμνός in the poems, I suspect that the force of γυμνός here does not liken Hektor to a woman, but encourages the audience to think back to book 17 and the fate of

of γυμνός to describe Hektor's fate, we find another parallel to Patroklos's death. In the entirety of the epic tradition only two corpses (and let us recall that the poem describes 240 deaths)[15] are described as γυμνός. Unlike Patroklos' corpse, however, Hektor's is not retrieved from the fray by his comrades, and it is therefore fated to initially suffer the same kinds of indignities that Lykaon's corpse endured: not being mourned properly by the members of his family, not receiving a proper burial, and serving as food for animals.[16]

D γυμνόομαι IN THE *ILIAD*

The only derivation of γυμνός to appear in the *Iliad* is the denominative γυμνόομαι (12.389; 12.399; 12.428; 16.312; 16.400). The use of the denominative is limited to two episodes in books 12 (the *teichomachia*),[17] and 16 (the Greeks fighting under Patroklos' leadership). As opposed to the restricted use of γυμνός to indicate unarmed bodies in danger of becoming corpses, the mediopassive verbal form of the word is used in a variety of circumstances, usually to describe individual parts of the human body that are in danger of immediate damage due to their lack of armor, or to describe inanimate objects, such as the wall of the Achaian camp in book 12.

E ODYSSEUS UNROBED (*OD.* 6.136, 10.301, 10.341, 22.1)

Od. 6.135–136

ὡς Ὀδυσεὺς κούρῃσιν ἐϋπλοκάμοισιν ἔμελλε
μείξεσθαι, **γυμνός** περ ἐών· χρειὼ γὰρ ἵκανε.

Even so Odysseus was about to enter the company of the fair-tressed maidens
naked though he was, for need had come upon him.

Od. 10.299–301

ἀλλὰ κέλεσθαί μιν μακάρων μέγαν ὅρκον ὀμόσσαι,
μή τί τοι αὐτῷ πῆμα κακὸν βουλευσέμεν ἄλλο,
μή σ' **ἀπογυμνωθέντα** κακὸν καὶ ἀνήνορα θήῃ.

But bid her swear a great oath by the blessed gods
that she will not plot against you any fresh mischief to your hurt
for fear that when she has you stripped she may deprive you of your courage and
    your manhood.

Lykaon, who did approach Achilleus as a suppliant described as γυμνός and was killed without pity or respect. The use of the term would also hearken back to Hektor's own slaying of Patroklos, who was already γυμνός when killed.

[15] Garland 1981, 52–53, table 1.

[16] On the theme of the mutilation of the corpse in Homer see Segal 1981.

[17] For the wall as a later interpolation see Page 1959, 332–333; review of scholarship in Porter 2011, 2–12.

Od. 10.339–341

αὐτὸν δ' ἐνθάδ' ἔχουσα δολοφρονέουσα κελεύεις
ἐς θάλαμόν τ'ἰέναι καὶ σῆς ἐπιβήμεναι εὐνῆς
ὄφρα με **γυμνωθέντα** κακὸν καὶ ἀνήνορα θήῃς.

now [you] keep me here, and with guileful purpose bid me
go to your chamber and go up into your bed
that when you have me stripped you may deprive me of my courage and my
    manhood?

Od. 22.1–2

αὐτὰρ ὁ **γυμνώθη** ῥακέων πολύμητις Ὀδυσσεύς,
ἆλτο δ' ἐπὶ μέγαν οὐδὸν ἔχων βιὸν ἠδὲ φαρέτρην

But resourceful Odysseus stripped off his rags
and sprang to the broad threshold with the bow and the quiver

Discussion

In the *Odyssey,* Odysseus is the only character described as γυμνός. He is
γυμνός when Nausicaä finds him after his ship has wrecked upon the
Phaiakian shores (*Od.* 6.136). He fears being made γυμνός (γυμνωθέντα/
ἀπογυμνωθέντα) in front of Circe (*Od.* 10.301 and 10.341) because she may
in those circumstances "render [Odysseus] a weakling and unmanned." He
only agrees to lie with her in such a state of vulnerability if she swears an oath
not to do him any harm. In both cases, there is a sense that complete nudity in
the presence of females is likely to create unpleasant circumstances, either
because it would be inappropriate in front of young, respectable maidens, or
because it created vulnerability in a sexualized, extramarital atmosphere.[18] In
these two instances, the undesirable implications of nudity as shameful or
perilous in inappropriate circumstances are transparent.[19] The adjective also
occurs at *Od.* 11.607 to describe an uncovered weapon (the bow being drawn
from its case, presumably; the Greek reads: γυμνὸν τόξον ἔχων καὶ ἐπὶ

---

[18] Bassi 1995, 4–5: "...to be naked in the presence of a woman is analogous to having
been stripped naked by an enemy."; 14: "In effect, the leafy branch accentuates his
'male parts' in the process of hiding them. But at the same time, the gesture of hiding
himself suggests that he be looked at by other males (cf. 6.221–22). Relevant here is
Odysseus' fear at *Od.* 10.339–41 that being naked before Circe will make him 'weak
and unmanned' (ὄφρα με **γυμνωθέντα** κακὸν καὶ ἀνήνορα θήῃς)...Looking *like* a
woman (as in the example of Achilleus, Ajax, and Hercules), being looked at *as* a
woman (as Hektor imagines in *Iliad* 22) and even being seen *by* a woman (like Circe)
all operate within this economy."

[19] Müller 1906, 73: "Exposure is regarded as a disgrace."

νευρῆφιν ὀϊστόν). Finally, at *Od.* 22.1 Odysseus, dressed as a beggar, reveals himself to the horror of the suitors by shedding his disguise. The meaning and implication of nudity in the *Odyssey* suggests that it is a shameful condition in most circumstances.

F HESIOD'S NAKED EARTH (*OP.* 391–394)

> **γυμνὸν** σπείρειν, **γυμνὸν** δὲ βοωτεῖν,
> **γυμνὸν** δ᾽ ἀμάειν, εἴ χ᾽ ὥρια πάντ᾽ ἐθέλησθα
> ἔργα κομίζεσθαι Δημήτερος, ὥς τοι ἔκαστα
> ὥρι᾽ ἀέξηται.

> . . .sow naked, and plow naked,
> and harvest naked, if you want, in due season, to
> bring in all Demeter's works, so that each crop
> may grow for you in its season. . . (trans. Most)

Discussion

The adjective γυμνός occurs in only one passage of the *Works and Days*. The passage recites a series of orders to the effect that Perses ought to conduct agricultural tasks while naked or lightly clad. The implication is that the farmer is supposed to go naked to the fields for work. Are these reasonable demands? Is it reasonable to reconstruct a situation in which early Greeks thought it appropriate to remove all of their clothing when they went to the fields to plow? While depictions of men plowing in fields from Archaic and Classical Greek art often show nude farmers, this is true of a variety of professions in which nudity must not have been a practical reality (smithing, harvesting olives) and should not implicate Hesiod's meaning in this passage.[20] Likewise, ancient descriptions of working on the farm rarely describe men as nude.[21] In the words of Martin West, then, we might reasonably ask "why is Hesiod so emphatic?"[22]

---

[20] For images of men plowing and working the fields, see Gow 1914.

[21] See West's commentary (1978, 391–2): "artistic representations of men ploughing and sowing. . .sometimes show them naked, sometimes clothed. See also Ar. *Lys.* 1173: ἤδη γεωργεῖν γυμνὸς ἀποδὺς βούλομαι, and the story about Cincinnatus (Liv. 3.26.9; Plin. *HN* 18.20; *De iuris illustribus* 17.1). The plowers in *Sc.* 287, however, wear chitons, the elder Cato farmed naked in the summer but wore an ἐξωμίς in winter, according to Plut. *Cato* 3.2; and Eustathius Macrembolites 4.9.2 portrays a harvester with his chiton modestly wrapped around his loins, and a sunhat."

[22] West 1978, 392.

Some explanations have been put forward for this counterintuitive agrarian advice. According to an ancient scholiast, the message is that it is wise to plow as early as possible in the season, when going outside naked or with few clothes on is reasonable because of the warm weather.[23] However, this rationale is problematic. If the admonition to plow naked relates to the optimal weather conditions, it is strangely reduplicative of the information immediately preceding it; Perses has just learned when during the year certain tasks are to be performed: the plowing when the Pleiades have set (late October or early November), the harvest during early May. These do not seem to be the most obvious times to spend early mornings outside without much covering; and this does not and cannot account for the final phrase in the tricolon, γυμνὸν δ' ἀμάειν.[24] Furthermore, the admonition to plow, plant, and harvest nude or lightly clad cannot produce a logical or coherent conditional or result clause with the following statements, i.e. do these things naked (a) if you want to gather for yourself all Demeter's works in season and (b) so that each crop for you may grow in season. It is difficult to imagine that the attire of the farmer while conducting the business of agriculture could resolve such dire consequences for the crop. We should also take into account that exposing oneself in the presence of the gods is presented elsewhere in the *Works and Days* (lines 730–734) as something to be avoided. When in doubt, of course, it is always plausible to suggest a ritual basis for the rule.

Another option would be to rethink taking the tricolon of γυμνοί as subject accusatives with the infinitive command (a construction that is rare in

[23] Pertusi 1955, 391–393: "γυμνόν σπείρειν: the works of the farmer, to sow, to plow, to harvest, he orders to pursue naked, indicating that these works are made during serene times and not when there is frost or God sends rain; so, in fact the will of good germination quality and the collection of beneficial fruits. Some say you have to turn the fallow after the winter, still move up and down the field when the ground is cool and sow when it is not dry. Plutarch says that it is better that it rains after sowing rather than before; and clear: the corn fields after the time of the Pleiades and before sprout solstice in seven days – in Egypt in three – while those after the solstice struggled in the triple of that time; and so well that the rain comes later rather than sooner. The ancients sowed quite soon, as is evident from the rites of initiation Eleusinian, during which it was said, 'Come, Core, on-embankment, where it is not yet plowed three times.'"; 391a-2: "naked – before the cold, he says in time where you can be naked and follow the oxen. In the sense of: you're an early riser or brisk towards work is not bringing the robe to avoid being embarrassed." The explanation goes back to Virgil (G. 1.299). On farming in Hesiod generally, Marsilio 2000.

[24] West 1978, 391–392: "Sch. vet. Procl. thinks he means that one should plow early while it is still mild enough to go naked; this explanation is already known to Virgil (G. 1.299ff; so also Servius *ad. loc.*) but it takes no account of γυμνὸν δ'ἀμάειν, and we have after all just been given a very much more precise instruction on when to plough. Another interpretation from the scholia is πρόθυμος ἔσῃ πρὸς τὸ ἔργον μὴ φορῶν τὸ ἱμάτιόν σου ἵνα μὴ ἐμποδίζῃ ὑπ' αὐτοῦ. Perhaps originally there was a religious basis to the rule."; 393... "the ὡς clause following naturally, but the connection with γυμνὸν-ἀμάειν is harder to understand, and we lack an exact parallel for the middle κομίζεσθαι."

Hesiod).[25] Instead, it seems plausible to read the passage in parallel with *Op.* 463, taking γυμνόν as a substantive adjective serving as the accusative object of each infinitive (as in, νειὸν δὲ σπείρειν, sow the fallow land)[26] and probably referring back to the χῶρον (s.v. χῶρος) of line 390. In this case, Hesiod would be admonishing his brother to plow the γυμνός land, sow the γυμνός land, reap the γυμνός land, rather than to do these activities while naked or lightly clad. In this translation, the term γυμνός is likely to intend a meaning more along the lines of "uncovered" or "cleared" instead of "nude/naked," as the denominative γυμνόομαι often does in Homeric epic and in *Scutum* (ll. 334, 418, 460 where it describes an unsheathed bow, the unguarded neck of Cycnus, and the unarmored thigh of Ares, respectively).

The precise meaning of this reading remains uncertain as far as it concerns delving into the procedural logic of early Greek farming, but it does a better job of creating a logical sequence of phrases. Instructions about the state of the fields or lands to be plowed, sown, and harvested could be naturally followed by expected results about the seasonal production of crops. According to Halstead's study of pre-modern farming practices in Greece, an aspect of the workload of treating fields that was extremely time-consuming, but to be neglected at great cost, was the process of clearing the fields of weeds, the presence of which would slow plowing, strangle seedlings, and suck up valuable water resources if not removed before sowing, and make the process of harvesting so unmanageable as to render a field of crops effectively lost.[27] If we take the meaning of γυμνόν in *Op.* ll. 391–392 to be something along the lines of *denuded* and apply it to the land (χῶρον) of line 390, assuming that the poet is instructing Perses to ensure that the fields are clear of weeds during the entire planting and growing season, the passage follows far more rationally.

---

[25] Examples can be found in Hesiod *Op.* 423, ὅλμον μὲν τριπόδην τάμνειν; 573, δμῶας ἐγείρειν; 576, καρπὸν ἀγινεῖν; 604, κύνα καρχαρόδοντα κομεῖν; 606, χόρτον δ' ἐσκομίσαι καὶ συρφετόν; 624, γῆν δ' ἐργάζεσθαι.

[26] See also Theognis *Eleg.* 1.106: ἴσον καὶ σπείρειν, "plow in the same measure" the waters of the salty sea. The manuscript tradition is somewhat confused on the case and number of γυμνός, with acc. sg., nom. sg., and acc. pl. all represented. See West 1978 for details.

[27] For example, Halstead 2013, 103: "The area reaped was larger if the crop was sparse and smaller if it was thick, while weeds also slowed progress. In 1939, Mitsos and three friends from Paliambela were hired to reap a large field in another village. 'The field was so tangled with weeds that you could not put down the handful you had just cut. In two days, we reaped only four strémmata [i.e., 0.05 ha/head/day], so we gave up and came home.' At Assiros, Apostolis points out a field once infested so badly with wild vetches (*Vicia spp.*) that cutting a handful of cereal shook the whole stand, scattering grain and slowing progress. A gathering of grandmothers recalls how thistles and brambles hurt their hands while harvesting, making them slow and clumsy."

The compound denominative ἀπογυμνόομαι appears once in Hesiod (*Op.* 730: μηδ᾽ ἀπογυμνωθείς, μακάρων τοι νύκτες ἔασιν; do not completely bare yourself, for the nights belong to the blessed ones), when Hesiod is providing some ideas to Perses about the inadvisability of exposing oneself while urinating in various circumstances. However, given the rarity of γυμνός and its derivatives in the Hesiodic corpus, it is reasonable to conclude that Hesiod had little interest in nudity.

APPENDIX B

CATALOGUE OF BRONZE FIGURINES DISCUSSED IN THE TEXT

THIS APPENDIX PROVIDES A LIST OF THE FIGURINES THAT I STUDIED IN ORDER TO produce the analysis in Chapters 2 and 3. Each entry lists the Museum or Excavation catalogue number of the object and a reference to a publication of a relevant image. Sources are listed in the bibliography provided at the end of the book.

A FIGURINES FROM SITES ON CRETE

Amnisos
Heraklion Museum Inv. No. 2316 (Stürmer 1992, 248, D1.b1)

Archanes
Heraklion Museum Inv. No. 4351 (Sapouna-Sakellarakis 1995, 47, no. 78, fig. 37)

Elounda
Heraklion Giamalakis Collection Inv. No. 574 (Sapouna-Sakellarakis 1995, T19, no. 3)

Aghia Triada
Heraklion Museum Inv. No. Br 744 (Sapouna-Sakellarakis 1995, T19, no. 2)
Heraklion Museum Inv. No. 745 (Naumann 1976, 59, no. 79)
Heraklion Museum Inv. No. 748 (Naumann 1976, 96, P24, pl. 30)
Heraklion Museum Inv. No number (Naumann 1969, 118, 13d)

Kalamafka
London British Museum Inv. No. 1930.6–17.1 (Verlinden 1984, 166–167, 211, pl. 83)

Syme Viannou
Syme Viannou ID No. MH 3137 (Lebessi 2002, pl. 15)
Syme Viannou ID No. MH 3147 (Lebessi 2002, pl. 13)
Syme Viannou ID No. MH 3699 (Lebessi 2002, pl. 20)
Syme Viannou ID No. MH 3700 (Lebessi 2002, pl. 9)
Syme Viannou ID No. MH 4300 (Lebessi 2002, pl. 11)
Syme Viannou ID No. MH 4301 (Lebessi 2002, pl. 14)
Syme Viannou ID No. MH 4301 (Lebessi 2002, pl. 14)
Syme Viannou ID No. MH 4357 (Lebessi 2002, pl. 16)
Syme Viannou ID No. MH 4358 (Lebessi 2002, pl. 18)

Syme Viannou ID No. MH 4359 (Lebessi 2002, pl. 19)

Syme Viannou ID No. MH 4360 (Lebessi 2002, pl. 17)

Syme Viannou ID No. MH 4959 (Lebessi 2002, pl. 10)

Syme Viannou ID No. MH 5055 (Lebessi 2002, 16, pl. 8)

Malibu J. Paul Getty Museum Inv. No. 90.AB.6 (Langdon 2008, 91–92, fig. 2.10)[1]

Kommos

Heraklion Museum Inv. No. 5416 (Koutroumbaki-Shaw 1987, 371–382)

Lasithi Plateau

Oxford Ashmolean Museum Inv. No. AE 16 (Naumann 1969, no. 118, 13k)

Patsos

Heraklion Museum Inv. No. 207 (Naumann 1976, 94, P1, pl. 19)

Heraklion Museum Inv. No. 208 (Naumann 1976, 96, P26, pl. 31)

Heraklion Museum Inv. No. 209 (Verlinden 1984, 220, no. 228, fig. 89)

Oxford Ashmolean Inv. No. G 392 (Naumann 1976, 96, P23, pl. 28)

Phaneromeni

Heraklion Archaeological Museum Inv. No. 2960 (Naumann 1976, 91, S15, pl. 7)

Heraklion Archaeological Museum Inv. No. 2961 (Naumann 1976, 91, S16, pl. 7)

Heraklion Archaeological Museum Inv. No. Br. 2964 (Sapouna-Sakellarakis 1995, T18, no. 2)

Psychro Cave

Heraklion Museum Inv. No. 431 (Naumann 1976, 43, S13, fig. 6)

Oxford Ashmolean Inv. No. AE 620 (Naumann 1976, 91–92, S14)

Oxford Ashmolean Inv. No. AE 20 (Naumann 1976, 91–92, S21)

Unknown Site

Athens National Archaeological Museum Inv. No. 8914 (Sapouna-Sakellarakis 1995, 92, no. 158, fig. 21)

London British Museum Inv. No. 1924.7–15.1 (Verlinden 1984, 223, no. 245, fig. 95)

Heraklion Archaeological Museum Inv. No. 2064 (Padgett 1995, 397)

Heraklion Archaeological Museum Inv. No. 2065 (Naumann 1969, 114–120)

Heraklion Giamalakis Collection Inv. No. 527 (Sapouna-Sakellarakis 1995, 16, no. 12, fig. 20)

Oxford Ashmolean Museum Inv. No. 1946.113 (Naumann 1976, 93, S30, pl. 15)

B FIGURINES FROM SITES ON THE MAINLAND AND ISLANDS

Aetos

No Museum Inv. No. (Langdon 1984, 387, no. C82)

---

[1] Suspected to be from Syme Viannou because of comparable material from the site.

Argive Heraion

No Museum Inv. No. (Waldstein 1905, pl. 71, no. 3)

No Museum Inv. No. (Waldstein 1905, pl. 70, no. 4)

Athens

Athens National Archaeological Museum Inv. No. 6616 (Schweitzer 1969, 132–135)

Delos

Delos Archaeological Museum Inv. No. A454 (Rolley 1973, no. 19)

Delphi

Delphi Archaeological Museum Inv. No. 2654 (Rolley 1969, no. 21)

Delphi Archaeological Museum Inv. No. 2813 (Rolley 1969, no. 45)

Delphi Archaeological Museum Inv. No. 2897 (Rolley 1969, no. 41)

Delphi Archaeological Museum Inv. No. 2903 (Rolley 1969, no. 18)

Delphi Archaeological Museum Inv. No. 2910 (Rolley 1969, no. 22)

Delphi Archaeological Museum Inv. No. 2978 (Rolley 1969, no. 30)

Delphi Archaeological Museum Inv. No. 3240 (Rolley 1969, no. 31)

Delphi Archaeological Museum Inv. No. 3649 (Rolley 1969, no. 28)

Delphi Archaeological Museum Inv. No. 3976 (Rolley 1969, no. 29)

Delphi Archaeological Museum Inv. No. 4019 (Rolley 1969, no. 16)

Delphi Archaeological Museum Inv. No. 5610 (Rolley 1969, no. 44)

Delphi Archaeological Museum Inv. No. 6571 (Rolley 1969, no. 42)

Delphi Archaeological Museum Inv. No. 7230 (Rolley 1969, no. 25)

Delphi Archaeological Museum Inv. No. 7731 (Rolley 1969, no. 20)

Delphi Archaeological Museum Inv. No. 7733 (Rolley 1969, no. 17)

Delphi Archaeological Museum Inv. No. 8922 (Rolley 1977, no. 249)

Delphi Archaeological Museum n.n. (Rolley 1969, no. 23)

Delphi Archaeological Museum n.n. (Rolley 1969, no. 14)

Delphi Archaeological Museum n.n. (Perdrizet 1908, no. 7)

Delphi Archaeological Museum n.n. (Rolley 1969, no. 19)

Mavriki

Tegea Archaeological Museum n.n. (Romaiou 1952, 26, pl. 20d)

Olympia

Athens National Archaeological Museum Inv. No. 6087 (Furtwängler 1890, no. 260)

Athens National Archaeological Museum Inv. No. 6091 (Furtwängler 1890, no. 238)

Athens National Archaeological Museum Inv. No. 6093 (Furtwängler 1890, no. 236)

Athens National Archaeological Museum Inv. No. 6096 (Furtwängler 1890, no. 242)

Athens National Archaeological Museum Inv. No. 6099 (Langdon 1984, no. C19)

Athens National Archaeological Museum Inv. No. 6100 (Langdon 1984, no. C20)

Athens National Archaeological Museum Inv. No. 6105 (Langdon 1984, no. C21)

Athens National Archaeological Museum Inv. No. 6108 (Furtwängler 1890, no. 241)

Athens National Archaeological Museum Inv. No. 6112 (Heilmeyer 1972, 50, no. 110)

Athens National Archaeological Museum Inv. No. 6150 (Furtwängler 1890, no. 256)

Athens National Archaeological Museum Inv. No. 6167 (Furtwängler 1890, no. 240)

Athens National Archaeological Museum Inv. No. 6168 (Kunze 1967, 214, pl. 107)

Athens National Archaeological Museum Inv. No. 6170 (Kunze 1944, taf. 35)

Athens National Archaeological Museum Inv. No. 6182 (Herrmann 1964, 41–42, figs. 22–24)

Athens National Archaeological Museum Inv. No. 6188 (Herrmann 1964, no. 43, figs. 26–27)

Athens National Archaeological Museum Inv. No. 6190 (Heilmeyer 1981, 68–69, pl. 3, nos. 3–4)

Athens National Archaeological Museum Inv. No. 6249 (Schweitzer 1967, pls. 120–121)

Berlin Staatliche Museum Inv. No. 01 3011 (Neugebauer 1931, no. 26)

Berlin Staatliche Museum Inv. No. 01 3680 (Neugebauer 1931, no. 15)

Berlin Staatliche Museum Inv. No. 01 7390 (Neugebauer 1931, no. 27)

Berlin Staatliche Museum Inv. No. 01 8118 (Neugebauer 1931, no. 31)

Berlin Staatliche Museum Inv. No. 01 9000 (Neugebauer 1931, no. 29)

Louvre Museum Inv. No. MND 728 (de Ridder 1913, no. 84)

Olympia Archaeological Museum Inv. No. B 1391 (Kunze 1944, pl. 32, no. 2)

Olympia Archaeological Museum Inv. No. B 1670 (Kunze 1944, no. 110, pl. 35)

Olympia Archaeological Museum Inv. No. B 1671 (Kunze 1944, pl. 34)

Olympia Archaeological Museum Inv. No. B 1754 (Kunze 1944, pl. 32, no. 1)

Olympia Archaeological Museum Inv. No. B 1698 (Kunze 1944, 106, pl. 32, nos. 4–5)

Olympia Archaeological Museum Inv. No. B 4245 (Kunze 1961, 138)

Olympia Archaeological Museum Inv. No. B 5377 (Kunze 1967, pl. 106b)

Olympia Archaeological Museum Inv. No. B 5378 (Kunze 1967, 217–218, pl. 106a)

Olympia Archaeological Museum Inv. No. B 5960 (Kunze 1967, 214, no. 2)

Olympia Archaeological Museum Inv. No. B 5994 (Kunze 1967, pl. 106c)

Olympia Archaeological Museum Inv. No. B 6269 (Kunze 1967, pl. 106)

Olympia Archaeological Museum Inv. No. B 9012 (Langdon 1984, no. C6)

Olympia Archaeological Museum Inv. No. Br 2282 (Langdon 1984, C79)

Petrovouni

Athens National Archaeological Museum Inv. No. 5782 (Langdon 1998, 114–115, fig. 2.25)

Pherai

No Museum Inv. No. (Biesantz 1965, no. L63)

Philia

Ny Carlsberg Glyptothek Inv. No. 3309 (Johansen 1982, 74, fig. 2)

Ny Carlsberg Glyptothek Inv. No. 3310 (Johansen 1982, 73, fig. 1)

Ny Carlsberg Glyptothek Inv. No. 3359 (Johansen 1982, 75, fig. 4)

Ny Carlsberg Glyptothek Inv. No. 3360 (Johansen 1982, 77, fig. 5)

Ny Carlsberg Glyptothek Inv. No. 3607 (Johansen 1982, 74–75, fig. 3)

Volos Archaeological Museum n.n. (Theocharis 1964b, 247, pl. 291b)

Volos Archaeological Museum n.n. (Theocharis 1964b, 247, pl. 291a)

Samos

Samos Archaeological Museum Inv. No. B190 (lost in WWII; Kunze 1930, 146–147)

Sparta

Sparta Archaeological Museum Inv. No. 3244 (Droop 1927, 82, pl. 8)

Sparta Archaeological Museum Inv. No. 2155 (Droop 1927, 99, pl. 11)

Tegea

Tegea Archaeological Museum Inv. No. 323 (Dugas 1921, 354, no. 50, fig. 17)

Tegea Archaeological Museum Inv. No. 356 (Dugas 1921, 355, no. 52)

Tegea Archaeological Museum Inv. No. 359 (Dugas 1921, 355, no. 53, fig. 19)

Tegea Archaeological Museum n.n. (Dugas 1921, 356, no. 54)

Thermon

Athens National Archaeological Museum Inv. No. 14756 (Müller 1929, fig. 293)

Athens National Archaeological Museum Inv. No. 14756 (Romaiou 1915, 275, fig. 41)

Zakynthos

No Museum Inv. No. (Benton 1932, 216)

No Museum Inv. No. (Benton 1932, 216)

APPENDIX C

SAMPLE OF VASE PAINTING IMAGES

THIS APPENDIX PROVIDES A LIST OF THE FIGURED SCENES THAT I STUDIED IN ORDER to produce the analysis in Chapter 3. Each entry lists the Museum or Excavation catalogue number of the vessel and a reference to a publication of the relevant images. In some cases, multiple figured scenes occur on a single vessel; I do not duplicate the entries, but list the multiple image references when relevant alongside the museum or excavation inventory number. Throughout the Appendix, *CVA* is used as an abbreviation for the *Corpus Vasorum Antiquorum* volumes. Other sources are listed in the bibliography provided at the end of the book.

A ATTIC

Amphora in a Private Collection (Tölle 1964, taf. 8)
Amsterdam APM Inv. No. 3491 (Haug 2012, 157, abb. 126a)
Athens Agora Inv. No. P 4990 (Haug 2012, 58 abb. 23)
Athens Agora Inv. No. P 4885 (Coulié 2013, 89, 61)
Athens Benaki Mus. Inv. No. 7675 (Haug 2012, 193, abb. 150)
Athens Goulandris Mus. Inv. No. 136/137 (Haug 2012, 368, abb. 301)
Athens Kerameikos Mus. Inv. No. 268 (Haug 2012, 326, abb. 270)
Athens Kerameikos Mus. Inv. No. 407 (Rombos 1988, pl. 37b)
Athens Kerameikos Mus. Inv. No. 812 (Rombos 1988, pl. 74a)
Athens Kerameikos Mus. Inv. No. 1356 (Haug 2012, 197, abb. 155)
Athens Kerameikos Mus. Inv. No. 1370 (Haug 2015, 103, abb. 41)
Athens Kerameikos Mus. Inv. No. 2159 (Haug 2012, 328, abb. 272)
Athens Kerameikos Mus. Inv. No. 3674 (Haug 2012, 217, abb. 177)
Athens Kerameikos Mus. Inv. No. 5643 (Haug 2012, 83, abb. 49)
Athens Kerameikos Mus. Inv. No. K2 (Haug 2012, 198, abb. 156; 2015, 139, abb. 64)
Athens Kerameikos Mus. No. (Tölle 1964, taf. 16c)
Athens National Archaeological Museum Inv. No. 190 (Haug 2015, 67, abb. 24)
Athens National Archaeological Museum Inv. No. 194 (Haug 2012, 256, abb. 206)
Athens National Archaeological Museum Inv. No. 223 (Haug 2012, 330, abb. 274)
Athens National Archaeological Museum Inv. No. 251 (Haug 2012, 304, abb. 242)
Athens National Archaeological Museum Inv. No. 313 (Coulié 2013, 196, 189)

Athens National Archaeological Museum Inv. No. 784 (Coulié 2013, 93, 66)

Athens National Archaeological Museum Inv. No. 802 (Coulié 2013, 93, fig. 66)

Athens National Archaeological Museum Inv. No. 803 (Coulié 2013, 68, fig. 38)

Athens National Archaeological Museum Inv. No. 804 (Coldstream 1968, pl. 6)

Athens National Archaeological Museum Inv. No. 806 (Coulié 2013, 85, 56)

Athens National Archaeological Museum Inv. No. 810 (Coulié 2013, 91, fig. 63)

Athens National Archaeological Museum Inv. No. 812 (Haug 2012, 68, abb. 35)

Athens National Archaeological Museum Inv. No. 874 (Rombos 1988, pl. 68b)

Athens National Archaeological Museum Inv. No. 894 (Haug 2012, 200, abb. 159)

Athens National Archaeological Museum Inv. No. 990 (Coldstream 1968, pl. 8b)

Athens National Archaeological Museum Inv. No. 7675 (Haug 2015, 94, abb. 36)

Athens National Archaeological Museum Inv. No. 13038 (Haug 2012, 312, abb. 255)

Athens National Archaeological Museum Inv. No. 14423 (Tölle 1964, taf. 6)

Athens National Archaeological Museum Inv. No. 14477 (Haug 2012, 123, abb. 84)

Athens National Archaeological Museum Inv. No. 14960 (Haug 2012, 358, abb. 298)

Athens National Archaeological Museum Inv. No. 16022 (Coldstream 1968, pl. 12d)

Athens National Archaeological Museum Inv. No. 17384 (Athens *CVA* vol. 3, pl. 14)

Athens National Archaeological Museum Inv. No. 17470 (Coldstream 1968, pl. 11d)

Athens National Archaeological Museum Inv. No. 17497 (Athens *CVA* vol. 3, pl. 12)

Athens National Archaeological Museum Inv. No. 17935 (Coldstream 1968, pl. 11c)

Athens National Archaeological Museum Inv. No 18062 (Haug 2015, 72, abb. 29)

Athens National Archaeological Museum Inv. No. 18435 (Haug 2015, 126, abb. 57)

Athens National Archaeological Museum Inv. No. 18542 (Haug 2012, 142, abb. 107)

Athens National Archaeological Museum No Inv. No. (Coldstream 1968, pl. 11f)

Athens Olympeion (Haug 2012, 358, abb. 257)

Athens Passas Priv. Coll. (Tölle 1964, taf. 10)

Athens Stathatos Priv. Coll. (Coldstream 1968, pl. 11g; Haug 2012, 97, abb. 37)

Athens Vlastos Priv. Coll. (Tölle 1964, taf. 16d)

Baltimore Museum Inv. No. 48.2231 (Haug 2015, 93, abb. 35)

Basel Museum Inv. No. 61.232 (Haug 2015, 120, abb. 53)

Basel Museum Inv. No. GS 61 (Haug 2015, 70, abb. 70)

Basel Museum Inv. No. BS 406 (Basel *CVA* vol. 1, pl. 3)

Berlin Museum Inv. No. 3203 (Haug 2015, 103, abb. 40)

Berlin Museum Inv. No. 4506 (Rombos 1988, pl. 71b)

Berlin Museum Inv. No. 31106 (Haug 2012, 314, abb. 256)

Berlin Staatliche Museum Inv. No. V.I. 3374 (Haug 2015, 109, abb. 44)

Berlin Staatliche Museum Inv. No. V.I. 4506 (Haug 2012, 133, abb. 94)

Berlin Staatliche Museum Inv. No. 31045 (Tölle 1964, taf. 7)

Bern Historical Museum Inv. No. 23270 (Tölle 1964, taf. 15)

Bochum Museum Inv. No. 1066 (Haug 2012, 140, abb. 102)

Boston Museum of Fine Arts Inv. No. 25.42 (Haug 2015, abb. 42)

Brauron Museum Inv. No. 8a (Haug 2015, 134, abb. 62)

Brauron Museum Inv. No. 155 (Haug 2012, 338, abb. 281)

Brauron Museum Inv. No. 315 (Rombos 1988, pl. 66a)

Brauron Museum Inv. No. 1890.2 (Haug 2012, 93, abb. 62)

Brussels Museum Inv. No. 1506 (Brussels *CVA* vol. 3, pl. 1)

Brussels Museum Inv. No. A 1376 (Haug 2012, 261, abb. 214)

Brussels Museum Inv. No. A 1941 (Brussels *CVA* vol. 3, pl. 1)

Buffalo Museum Inv. No. C12847 (Haug 2012, 199, abb. 158)

Cambridge Museum Inv. No. 345 (Tölle 1964, taf. 18)

Cambridge Museum Inv. No. GR 1-1935 (Coldstream 1968, pl. 13e–f)

Cleveland Museum Inv. No. 27.6 (Cleveland *CVA* vol. 1, pls. 2–3)

Copenhagen Museum Inv. No. 1628 (Copenhagen NM *CVA* vol. 3, pl. 73; Haug
    2012, 262, Abb. 216a–b)

Copenhagen Museum Inv. No. 2680 (Haug 2012, 60, abb. 25)

Copenhagen Museum Inv. No. 7029 (Copenhagen NM *CVA* vol. 3, pl. 73)

Copenhagen Museum Inv. No. 726 (Coulié 2013, 82, fig. 54)

Copenhagen Museum Inv. No. 727 (Copenhagen NM *CVA* vol. 3, pl. 73; Coulié
    2013, 92, fig. 65)

Dresden Museum Inv. No. ZV 1635 (Haug 2012, 66, abb. 32)

Dusseldorf Museum Inv. No. 1970.19 (Haug 2015, 107, abb. 43)

Eleusis Museum Inv. No. 741 (Coulié 2013, 65, fig. 34)

Eleusis Museum Inv. No. 741 (Coulié 2013, 65, fig. 34)

Eleusis Museum Inv. No. 1045 (Coulié 2013, 88, fig. 59)

Erlangen Museum Inv. No. I 458 (Erlangen *CVA* vol. 1, pls. 10–11)

Essen Museum Inv. No. K969 (Tölle 1964, taf. 13)

German Priv. Coll. (Haug 2012, 121, abb. 81–82)

Hamburg Museum Inv. No. 1936.2 (Hamburg *CVA* vol. 1, pl. 1)

Hamburg Museum Inv. No. 1966.89 (Hamburg *CVA* vol. 1, pls. 10–11)

Hannover Museum Inv. No. 1953,148 (Hannover *CVA* vol. 1, pl. 1)

Heidelberg Museum Inv. No. G 140 (Heidelberg *CVA* vol. 3, pl. 116)

Hobart Priv. Coll. No. 31 (Coldstream 1968, pl. 12f)

Karlsruhe Museum Inv. No. 60/12 (Karlsruhe *CVA* vol. 3, pl. 1)

Karlsruhe Museum Inv. No. B 2674 (Karlsruhe *CVA* vol. 3, pl. 13)

Karlsruhe Museum Inv. No. B 2675a (Karlsruhe *CVA* vol. 3, pl. 3)

Karlsruhe Museum Inv. No. B 2676 (Karlsruhe *CVA* vol. 3, pl. 3)

Laon Museum Inv. No. 37769 (Haug 2012, 340–341, abb. 283b)

Leiden Museum Inv. No. I.1909/1.1 (Coldstream 1968, pl. 11a)

Liverpool Priv. Coll. (Haug 2012, 163, abb. 131)

London British Museum Inv. No. 1899 (Coulié 2013, 89, fig. 60)

London British Museum Inv. No. 1916.1–8.2 (Coldstream 1968, pl. 12b)

Mainz Museum Inv. No. 46 (Mainz *CVA* vol. 1, pl. 2)

Mainz Museum Inv. No. 53 (Mainz *CVA* vol. 1, pl. 7)

Mannheim Museum Inv. No. 66 (Mannheim *CVA* vol. 1, pl. 2)

Mannheim Museum Inv. No. 68 (Mannheim *CVA* vol. 1, pl. 3)

Mannheim Museum Inv. No. 69 (Mannheim *CVA* vol. 1, pl. 3)

Marathon Museum Inv. No. K 2207 (Coulié 2013, 86, fig. 57)

Marseille Museum Inv. No. 7471 (Haug 2012, 354, abb. 290)

Merenda Museum Inv. No. 100 53.1578 (Xagorari-Gleißner 2005, pl. 127a)

Merenda Museum Inv. No. 236 1890,2 (Xagorari-Gleißner 2005, pl. 36b)

Mt. Holyoke Museum n.n. (Haug 2012, 143, abb. 109)

Munich Museum Inv. No. 6029 (Munich *CVA* vol. 3, pl. 124)

Munich Museum Inv. No. 6183 (Munich *CVA* vol. 3, pl. 108)

Munich Museum Inv. No. 6228 (Munich *CVA* vol. 3, pl. 109)

Munich Museum Inv. No. 8696 (Coulié 2013, 93, fig. 68)

Munich Museum Inv. No. 8748 (Coldstream 1968, pl. 8d)

Munich Museum Inv. No. 8936 (Haug 2012, 267, abb. 221)

New York Metropolitan Museum Inv. No. 10.210.7 (Metropolitan Mus. *CVA* vol. 5, pl. 28)

New York Metropolitan Museum Inv. No. 10.210.8 (Haug 2015, 101, abb. 39)

New York Metropolitan Museum Inv. No. 14.130.14 (Metropolitan Mus. *CVA* vol. 5, pls. 8–9)

New York Metropolitan Museum Inv. No. 14.130.15 (Coulié 2013, 87, fig. 58)

New York Metropolitan Museum Inv. No. 14.11.2 (Metropolitan Mus. *CVA* vol. 5, pl. 1)

New York Metropolitan Museum Inv. No. 34.11.12 (Coulié 2013, 46, pl. 12)

New York Metropolitan Museum Inv. No. 35.11.12 (Metropolitan Mus. *CVA* vol. 5, pl. 21)

New York Priv. Coll. (Haug 2012, 357, abb. 296)

Nordrhein Museum No. 1970-19 (Nordrhein *CVA* vol. 1, pl. 2)

Oxford Ashmolean Museum Inv. No. 1916.55 (Haug 2012, 62, abb. 26a–b)

Oxford Ashmolean Museum Inv. No. 1925.22a (Tölle 1964, taf. 16a)

Oxford Ashmolean Museum Inv. No. 1929.24 (Haug 2012, 340, abb. 284)

Oxford Ashmolean Museum Inv. No. 1936.599 (28) (Tölle 1964, taf. 9)

Paris Louvre Museum Inv. No. A 517 (Coldstream 1968, pl. 7a; Louvre *CVA* vol. 3, pl. 1.1–4, 7)

Paris Louvre Museum Inv. No. A 519 (Coulié 2013, 77, fig. 47)

Paris Louvre Museum Inv. No. A 522 (Coulié 2013, 74, fig. 44)

Paris Louvre Museum Inv. No. A 523 (Louvre *CVA* vol. 3, pl. 5)

Paris Louvre Museum Inv. No. A 526 (Haug 2015, 73, abb. 30)

Paris Louvre Museum Inv. No. A 527 (Louvre *CVA* vol. 3, pls. 2–3)

Paris Louvre Museum Inv. No. A 528 (Louvre *CVA* vol. 3, pl. 7)

Paris Louvre Museum Inv. No. A 530 (Haug 2012, 305, abb. 247; Louvre *CVA* vol. 3, pl. 6)

Paris Louvre Museum Inv. No. A 532 (Louvre *CVA* vol. 3, pl. 7)

Paris Louvre Museum Inv. No. A 534 (Haug 2012, 260, abb. 213)

Paris Louvre Museum Inv. No. A 538 (Haug 2012, 305, abb. 246)

Paris Louvre Museum Inv. No. A 541 (Louvre *CVA* vol. 3, pl. 13)

Paris Louvre Museum Inv. No. A 542 (Louvre *CVA* vol. 18, pl. 17)

Paris Louvre Museum Inv. No. A 545 (Louvre *CVA* vol. 3, pl. 9)

Paris Louvre Museum Inv. No. A 547 (Coulié 2013, 69, fig. 69)

Paris Louvre Museum Inv. No. A 551 (Louvre *CVA* vol. 3, pl. 8)

Paris Louvre Museum Inv. No. A 552 (Coldstream 1968, pl. 8a; Coulié 2013, 78, fig. 48)

Paris Louvre Museum Inv. No. A 555 (Louvre *CVA* vol. 3, pl. 8)

Paris Louvre Museum Inv. No. A 560 (Louvre *CVA* vol. 3, pl. 8)

Paris Louvre Museum Inv. No. CA 1179 (Louvre *CVA* vol. 16, pl. 55)

Paris Louvre Museum Inv. No. CA 1333 (Tölle 1964, taf. 5)

Paris Louvre Museum Inv. No. CA 1779 (Rombos 1988, pl. 68a; Louvre *CVA* vol. 16, pl. 39)

Paris Louvre Museum Inv. No. CA 1780 (Louvre *CVA* vol. 16, pl. 39)

Paris Louvre Museum Inv. No. CA 1823 (Louvre *CVA* vol. 16, pl. 52)

Paris Louvre Museum Inv. No. CA 1940 (Louvre *CVA* vol. 16, pl. 25)

Paris Louvre Museum Inv. No. CA 2503 (Louvre *CVA* vol. 3, pl. 34)

Paris Louvre Museum Inv. No. CA 2509 (Louvre *CVA* vol. 17, pl. 16–17)

Paris Louvre Museum Inv. No. CA 3256 (Coulié 2013, 90, fig. 62)

Paris Louvre Museum Inv. No. CA 3272 (Louvre *CVA* vol. 18, pl. 9)

Paris Louvre Museum Inv. No. CA 3282 (Coldstream 1968, pl. 14d)

Paris Louvre Museum Inv. No. CA 3283 (Louvre *CVA* vol. 3, pl. 28–29)

Paris Louvre Museum Inv. No. CA 3362 (Louvre *CVA* vol. 3, pl. 7)

Paris Louvre Museum Inv. No. CA 3376 (Louvre *CVA* vol. 3, pl. 8)

Paris Louvre Museum Inv. No. CA 3382 (Louvre *CVA* vol. 3, pl. 9)

Paris Louvre Museum Inv. No. CA 3385 (Louvre *CVA* vol. 3, pl. 9)

Paris Louvre Museum Inv. No. CA 3419 (Louvre *CVA* vol. 18, pl. 23)

Paris Louvre Museum Inv. No. CA 3421 (Louvre *CVA* vol. 3, pl. 10)

Paris Louvre Museum Inv. No. CA 3422 (Louvre *CVA* vol. 3, pl. 10)

Paris Louvre Museum Inv. No. CA 3448 (Louvre *CVA* vol. 18, pl. 23)

Paris Louvre Museum Inv. No. CA 3468 (Louvre *CVA* vol. 16, pl. 40)

Paris Louvre Museum Inv. No. CA 4615 (Louvre *CVA* vol. 18, pl. 18)

Paris Louvre Museum Inv. No. CA 4626 (Louvre *CVA* vol. 18, pl. 18)

Paris Louvre Museum Inv. No. CA 4637 (Louvre *CVA* vol. 18, pl. 18)

Paris Louvre Museum Inv. No. CA 4667 (Louvre *CVA* vol. 18, pl. 7)

Paris Louvre Museum Inv. No. CA 6509 (Haug 2012, 278, abb. 231)

Paris Louvre Museum Inv. No. MNE 1020 (Haug 2012, 263, abb. 217)

Philadelphia Museum Inv. No. MS 5464 (Haug 2012, 84, abb. 52)

Prague Inv. No. 6016 (Prague *CVA* vol. 1, pl. 11)

Piraeus Museum n.n. (Haug 2012, 369, abb. 302)

Rodin Museum n.n. (Rodin *CVA* vol. 16, pl. 8.7)

Rodin Museum n.n. (Rodin *CVA* vol. 16, pl. 9.1)

Röhss Museum Inv. No. 55–59 (Göteborg *CVA* pl. 17)

Stockholm National Museum Inv. No. 1976.11 (Stockholm *CVA* vol. 2, pl. 6)

Stockholm National Museum Inv. No. Ant 1714 (Stockholm *CVA* vol. 2, pl. 7)

Stuttgart Museum Inv. No. KAS 10 (Stuttgart *CVA*, pl. 6)

Sydney Museum Inv. No. 46.41 (Haug 2012, 66, abb. 30)

The Hague Museum Inv. No. 2010 (Pays Bas *CVA* vol. 3, pl. 3)

The Hague Museum Inv. No. 2015 (Pays Bas *CVA* vol. 3, pl. 3)

Thorikos Royal Ontario Museum Inv. No. T C 65.666 (Rombos 1988, pl. 11a)

Toronto Museum Inv. No. C 951 (Haug 2015, 114, abb. 47)

Tübingen Museum Inv. No. 10.1086 (Tübingen *CVA* vol. 2, pl. 22)

Tübingen Museum Inv. No. 10.1465 (Tübingen *CVA* vol. 2, pl. 26)

Tübingen Museum Inv. No. 10.1466 (Tübingen *CVA* vol. 2, pl. 26)

Tübingen Museum Inv. No. 28.5450 (Tübingen *CVA* vol. 2, pl. 16)

Tübingen Museum Inv. No. 2657 (Tübingen *CVA* vol. 2, pl. 14–15)

Tübingen Museum Inv. No. 5629 (Tübingen *CVA* vol. 2, pl. 26)

Warsaw Museum Inv. No. 142172 (Haug 2012, 261, abb. 215)

B ARGIVE

Argive Heraion Amphora (Courbin 1966, pl. 8)

Argive Heraion Frag. (Courbin 1966, pl. 145)

Argive Heraion Frag. (Courbin 1966, pl. 147)

Argive Heraion Frag. (Courbin 1966, pl. 147)

Argive Heraion Frag. (Courbin 1966, pl. 147)

Argive Heraion Frag. (Waldstein 1905, pl. 57.1)

Argive Heraion Frag. (Waldstein 1905, pl. 57.3)

Argive Heraion Frag. (Waldstein 1905, pl. 57.4)

Argive Heraion Frag. (Waldstein 1905, pl. 57.6)

Argive Heraion Frag. (Waldstein 1905, pl. 57.7)

Argive Heraion Frag. (Waldstein 1905, pl. 57.10)

Argive Heraion Frag. (Waldstein 1905, pl. 57.11)

Argive Heraion Frag. (Waldstein 1905, pl. 57.12)

Argive Heraion Frag. (Waldstein 1905, pl. 57.19)

Argos Museum Inv. No. C 1 (Coldstream 1968, pl. 29e)

Argos Museum Inv. No. C 4 (Courbin 1966, pl. 61)

Argos Museum Inv. No. C 201 (Courbin 1966, pls. 43–45)

Argos Museum Inv. No. C 208 (Courbin 1966, pl. 46)

Argos Museum Inv. No. C 209 (Courbin 1966, pl. 102)

Argos Museum Inv. No. C 210 (Courbin 1966, pl. 41)

Argos Museum Inv. No. C 229 (Courbin 1966, pl. 40)

Argos Museum Inv. No. C 240 (Courbin 1966, pl. 40)

Argos Museum Inv. No. C 871 (Courbin 1966, pl. 57)

Argos Museum Inv. No. C 890 (Courbin 1966, pl. 64)

Argos Museum Inv. No. C 1146 (Courbin 1966, pl. 65)

Argos Museum Inv. No. C 1263 (Courbin 1966, pl. 141)

Argos Museum Inv. No. C 2441 (Courbin 1966, pl. 63)

Argos Museum Inv. No. C 3462 (Courbin 1966, pl. 141)

Athens DAI n.n. (Courbin 1966, pl. 62)

Athens DAI n.n. (Courbin 1966, pl. 81)

Athens Kerameikos Museum Inv. No. 1306 (Courbin 1966, pl. 149)

Athens National Archaeological Museum Inv. No. 877 (Coldstream 1968, pl. 29d)

Corinth Museum Inv. No. T 2545 (Coldstream 1968, pl. 30a–b)

Nafplion Museum Inv. No. 1915 (Coldstream 1968, pl. 29f)

Nafplion Museum Inv. No. 1973 (Coldstream 1968, pl. 30d)

Nafplion Museum n.n. (Coldstream 1968, pl. 30c)

Würzburg n.n. (Courbin 1966, pl. 78)

C BOEOTIAN

Athens National Archaeological Museum Inv. No. 5893 (Coldstream 1968, pl. 45d)

Athens National Archaeological Museum Inv. No. 12896 (Coldstream 1968, pl. 44j)

Röhss Mus. Inv. No. GA 1641 (Göteborg *CVA* pl. 18)

Hamburg Museum Inv. No. 1936.2 (Hamburg *CVA* vol. 1, pl. 1)

Heidelberg Museum Inv. No. G 60 (Heidelberg *CVA* vol. 3, pl. 119)

London British Museum Inv. No. 1910.10–13.1 (Coldstream 1968, pl. 44b)

Paris Louvre Inv. No. A 568 (Coulié 2013, 103, fig. 80)

Sarajevo Museum Inv. No. 36 (Rombos 1988, pl. 57b)

Thebes Archaeological Museum Inv. No. 43488

D LAKONIAN

Athens National Archaeological Museum Inv. No. 234 (Coldstream 1968, pl. 46n)

Sparta Acropolis Frag. (Margreiter 1988, taf. 41, 481)

Sparta Acropolis Excavation Inv. No. 2943 (Margreiter 1988, taf. 26, 304)

Sparta Amyklaion Frag. (Margreiter 1988, taf. 40, 472)

Sparta Amyklaion Excavation Inv. No. 389, 75/770 (Margreiter 1988, taf. 25, 290)

Sparta Artemis Orthia Frag. (Margreiter 1988, taf. 25, 294; abb. 12–47)

Sparta Mus. n.n. (Coldstream 1968, pl. 46j)

Sparta Mus. n.n. (Coldstream 1968, pl. 46p)

Unknown Sherd (Woodward, Droop, and Lamb 1926/1927, fig. 1d)

Object illustrated in Vlachou 2012, 120, fig. 5

Object illustrated in Vlachou 2018, 112, fig. 4.10

BIBLIOGRAPHY

Adrimi-Sismani, V. 2006. "The Palace of Iolkos and Its End," in S. Deger-Jalkotzy and I. Lemos, eds., *Ancient Greece: From the Mycenaean Palaces to the Age of Homer,* Edinburgh, 151–179.

Ahlberg, G. 1967. "A Late Geometric Grave-Scene Influenced by North Syrian Art," *Opuscula Atheniensia* 7: 177–186.

Ahlberg, G. 1971a. *Fighting on Land and Sea in Greek Geometric Art,* Stockholm.

Ahlberg, G. 1971b. *Prothesis and Ekphora in Greek Geometric Art: Studies in Mediterranean Archaeology* 32, Göteborg.

Ahlberg-Cornell, G. 1987. "Games, Play, and Performance in Early Greek Art," *Acta Archaeologica* 58: 55–86.

Ahlberg-Cornell, G. 1992. *Myth and Epos in Early Greek Art: Representation and Interpretation, Studies in Mediterranean Archaeology* 100, Jonsered.

Albenda, P. 1987. "Women, Child, and Family: Their Imagery in Assyrian Art," in J.-M. Durand, ed., *La femme dans le Proche-Orient antique,* Paris, 17–21.

Albers, G. 1994. *Spätmykenische Stadtheiligtümer: Systematische Analyse und vergleichende Auswertung der archäologischen Befunde,* Oxford.

Alberti, B. 2002. "Gender and the Figurative Art of Late Bronze Age Knossos," in Y. Hamilakis, ed., *Labyrinth Revisited: Rethinking Minoan Archaeology,* Oxford, 98–117.

Alberti, B. 2014. "Fare storia nella protostoria: la questione della presenza micenea a Cnosso alla luce dei dati archeologici e dei nuovi approcci antropologici," *Historika* 4, 11–51.

Aldenderfer, M. 1993. "Ritual, Hierarchy, and Change in Foraging Societies," *Journal of Anthropological Archaeology* 12: 1–40.

Alexiou, S. 1956. "Ἱερὸν παρὰ τὸ Καβοῦσι Ἱεραπέτρας," *Cretica Chronica* 10: 7–19.

Alexiou, S. 1958. "Ἡ μινωϊκὴ θεὰ μεθ' ὑψωμένων χειρῶν," *Cretica Chronica* 12: 179–299.

Alexiou, S. 1963a. "Τσούτσουρος," in *Archaeologikon Deltion* 18 *Chronika* B'2: 310–311.

Alexiou, S. 1963b. "Χρονικά," *Cretica Chronica* 25: 457–478.

Ålin, P. 1962. *Das Ende der mykenischen Fundstätten auf dem griechischen Festland, Studies in Mediterranean Archaeology* 1, Lund.

Allan, W. 2005. "Arms and the Man: Euphorbus, Hector, and the Death of Patroclus," *Classical Quarterly n.s.* 55.1: 1–16.

Allen, T. 1921. *The Homeric Catalogue of Ships,* Oxford.

Altheim, F. 1952. *Attila,* Paris.

Amiet, P. 1976. *L'art d'Agadé au Musée du Louvre,* Paris.

Amiet, P. 1980. *La glyptique mésopotamienne archaïque,* Paris.

Anderson, L. 1975. "Relief Pithoi from the Archaic Period of Greek Art," Unpublished PhD Dissertation, University of Colorado.

Andrewes, A. 1961. "Phratries in Homer," *Hermes* 89: 129–140.

Andrewes, A. 1967. *Greek Society,* London.

Antonaccio, C. 2011. "8th-Century Renaissance," in M. Finkelberg, ed., *The Homer Encyclopedia,* Chichester, 241–242.

Antoniadis, V. 2017. *Knossos and the Near East: A Contextual Approach to Imports and Imitations in Early Iron Age Tombs,* Oxford.

Appadurai, A., ed. 1986. *The Social Life of Things,* Cambridge.

Aravantinos, V. 1989–1990. "Santuari e palazzo: Appunti sui rapporti economicoamministrativi tra la sfera del culto e il potere politico in età micenea," *Scienze dell'Antichita: Storia, archeologia, antropologia* 3–4: 243–261.

Aravantinos, V. 2014. "The Inscriptions from the Sanctuary of Herakles at Thebes: An Overview," in N. Papazarkades, ed., *The Epigraphy and History of Boeotia: New Finds, New Prospects*, Leiden, 149–210.

Aravantinos, V. 2015. "Το Τέμενος του Ηρακλέους στη Θήβα," in S. Oikonomou, ed., *Αρχαιολοφικές Σύμβολες 3: Βοιοτία και Εύβοια*, Athens, 85–106.

Aravantinos, V. 2017. "The Sanctuaries of Herakles and Apollo Ismenios at Thebes: New Evidence," in X. Charalambidou and C. Morgan, eds., *Interpreting the Seventh Century BC: Tradition and Innovation*, Oxford, 221–230.

Arieti, J. W. 1975. "Nudity in Greek Athletics," *Classical World* 68: 431–436.

Arrington, N. 2016. "Talismanic Practice at Lefkandi: Trinkets, Burials, and Belief in the Early Iron Age," *Cambridge Classical Journal* 62: 1–30.

Aruz, J., ed. 2003. *Art of the First Cities: The Third Millenium B.C. from the Mediterranean to the Indus*, New York.

Asher-Greve, J. 1997. "The Essential Body. Mesopotamian Conceptions of the Gendered Body," *Gender and History* 9: 432–461.

Asher-Greve, J. and D. Sweeney. 2006. "On Nakedness, Nudity, and Gender," in S. Schoer, ed., *Images and Gender: Contributions to the Hermeneutics of Reading Ancient Art*, Göttingen, 125–176.

Åstrom, P. 1987. "Votive Deposits in the Late Cypriote Bronze Age," in *Gifts to the Gods. Proceedings of the Uppsala Symposium 1985*, Boreas 15, Uppsala, 177–179.

Auffarth, C. 2006. "Das Heraion von Argos oder das Heraion der Argolis? Religion im Prozeß der Polisbildung," in K. Freitag, P. Funke, and M. Haake, eds., *Kult–Politik–Ethnos: Überregionale Heiligtümer im Spannungsfeld von Kult und Politik*, Stuttgart, 73–88.

Aupert, P. 1976. "Chronique des fouilles et découvertes archéologiques en Grèce en 1975," *Bulletin de Correspondance Hellénique* 100: 591–745.

Aurigny, H. 2019. *Bronzes du haut-archaïsme à Delphes: Trépieds, chaudrons, et vaisselle de bronze (fin VIIIe–VIIe siècle). Fouilles de Delphes V.5*, Athens.

Austin, R. P. 1937. "Geometric Man," *Greece and Rome* 7.1: 18–24.

Averett, E. 2007. "Dedications in Clay: Terracotta Figurines in Early Iron Age Greece (c. 1100–700 BCE)," Unpublished PhD Dissertation, University of Missouri–Columbia.

Azhar Ali Khan, M., A. Khalil Sheikh, and B. Suleiman Al-Shaer. 2017. *Evolution of Metal Casting Technologies: A Historical Perspective*, Cham.

Babbi, A., 2008. *La piccola plastica fittile antropomorfa dell'Italia antica: dal Bronzo Fnale all'Orientalizzante*, Pisa.

Babbi, A., F. Bubenheimer-Erhart, and B. Marín Aguilera, eds., 2015. *The Mediterranean Mirror: Cultural Contacts in the Mediterranean Sea between 1200 and 750 B.C.*, Mainz.

Bachvarova, M. 2016. *From Hittite to Homer: The Anatolian Background of Ancient Greek Epic*, Cambridge.

Badre, L. 1980. *Les figurines anthropomorphes en terre cuite à l'âge du Bronze en Syrie*, Paris.

Badre, L. 2006. "Tell Kazel-Simyra: A Contribution to a Relative Chronological History in the Eastern Mediterranean during the Late Bronze Age," *Bulletin of the American Schools for Oriental Research* 343: 65–95.

Badre, L. 2011. "Cultural Interconnections in the Eastern Mediterranean: Evidence from Tell Kazel in the Late Bronze Age," in K. Duistermaat and I. Regulski, eds., *Intercultural Contacts in the Ancient Mediterranean*, Leuven, 205–223.

Badre, L., M. C. Boileau, R. Jung, H. Mommsen, and M. Kerschner. 2005. "The Provenance of Aegean- and Sryian-type pottery found at Tell Kazel (Syria)," *Ägypten und Levante* 15: 15–47.

Badre, L. and E. Capet. 2014. "The Late Bronze Age Pottery from Tell Kazel. Links with the Aegean, Cyprus, and the Levant," in M. Luciani and A. Hausleiter, eds., *Recent Trends in the Study of Late Bronze Age Ceramics in Syro-*

Mesopotamia and Neighbouring Regions, Rahden, 157–180.

Badre, L. and E. Gubel. 1999/2000. "Tell Kazel, Syria: Excavations of the AUB Museum 1993–1998, Third Preliminary Report," *Berytus* 44: 123–203.

Badre, L., E. Gubel, E. Capet, and N. Panayot. 1994. "Tell Kazel (Syrie): Rapport préliminaire sur les 4ᵉ–8ᵉ campagnes de fouilles (1988–1992)," *Syria* 71: 259–359.

Bailey, D. 2005. *Prehistoric Figurines: Representation and Corporeality in the Neolithic*, London and New York.

Bailey, D. 2013. "Figurines, Corporeality and the Origins of the Gendered Body," in D. Bolger, ed., *A Companion to Gender History*, Oxford, 244–264.

Baitinger, H. 2001. *Olympische Forschungen vol. 29: Die Angriffswaffen aus Olympia*, Berlin.

Bakker, E. 2018. *Poetry in Speech: Orality and Homeric Discourse*, Ithaca and London.

Banti, L. 1943. "I culti minoici e greci di Haghia Triada," *Annuario della Scuola Archeologica di Atene* 3–4: 10–74.

Barber, E. 1991. *Prehistoric Textiles: The Development of Cloth in the Neolithic and Bronze Ages*, Princeton.

Barndon, R. 1999. "Iron Working and Social Control: The Use of Anthropomorphic Symbols in Recent and Past East African Contexts," *Kvinner I Arkelogi I Norge* 22/23: 59–76.

Barnes, T. 2011. "Homeric ἀνδροτῆτα καὶ ἥβην," *Journal of Hellenic Studies* 131: 1–13.

Barnes, S. and P. Ben-Amos. 1983. "Benin, Oyo, and Dahmey: Warfare, State Building, and the Sacralization of Iron in West African History," *Expedition* 25.2: 5–14.

Barnett, R., E. Bleibtrau, and G. Turner. 1998. *Sculptures from the Southwest Palace of Sennacherib at Ninevah*, London.

Barsalou, L. 1983. "Ad-hoc categories," *Memory and Cognition* 11: 211–217.

Barsalou, L. 1985. "Ideals, Central Tendency, and Frequency of Instantiation as Determinants of Graded Structure in Categories," *Journal of Experimental Psychology: Learning, Memory, and Cognition* 11.4: 629–654.

Barthes, R. 1977. "Diderot, Brecht, Eisenstein," in *Image-Music-Text*, trans. S. Heath, New York, 69–78.

Bass, G. 1967. *Cape Gelidonya: A Bronze Age Shipwreck*, Philadelphia.

Bassi, K. 1995. "Male Nudity and Disguise in the Discourse of Greek Historionics," *Helios* 22.1: 3–22.

Baumann, E. 1950. *De mythe van den Manken God*, Leiden.

Beal, C. 1994. *Boys and Girls: The Development of Gender Roles*, New York.

Beck, F. 1988. Review of M. Poliakoff, *Combat Sports in the Ancient World: Competition, Violence, and Culture. Echos du Monde Classique* 23: 420–423.

Beeley, P. and R. Smart, eds. 1995. *Investment Casting*, London.

Beidelmann, T. 1989. "Agonistic Exchange: Homeric Reciprocity and the Heritage of Simmel and Mauss," *Cultural Anthropology* 4: 227–259.

Bell, C. 1997. *Ritual: Perspectives and Dimensions*, Oxford.

Bell, C. 2009 [1992]. *Ritual Theory, Ritual Practice*, Oxford.

Bendall, L. 2007. *Economics of Religion in the Mycenaean World: Resources Dedicated to Religion in the Mycenaean Palace Economy*, Oxford.

Bendall, L. and M. West. 2020. "Evidence from Written Sources," in I. Lemos and A. Kotsonas, eds., *A Companion to the Archaeology of Early Greece and the Mediterranean*, Hoboken, 55–74.

Bennet, J. 1997. "Homer and the Bronze Age," in I. Morris and B. Powell, eds., *A New Companion to Homer*, Leiden, 511–534.

Bennet, J. 2014. "Linear B and Homer," in Y. Duhoux and A. Morpurgo Davies, eds., *A Companion to Linear B: Mycenaean Greek Texts and Their World*, vol. 3, Louvain-la-Neuve, 187–233.

Bennett, M. 1997. *Belted Heroes and Bound Women: The Myth of the Homeric Warrior King*, Lanham, MD.

Benson, J. 1970. *Horse, Bird, and Man: The Origins of Greek Painting,* Amherst.

Benson, J. 1982. "Picture, Ornament, and Periodicity in Attic Geometric Vase-Painting," *The Art Bulletin* 64.4: 535–549.

Benton, S. 1932. "The Ionian Islands," *Annual of the British School at Athens* 33: 213–246.

Benton, S. 1935. "Excavations in Ithaca III," *Annual of the British School at Athens* 35: 45–73.

Benton, S. 1953. "Further Excavations at Aetos," *Annual of the British School at Athens* 48: 255–358.

Benzi, M. 1999. "Riti di passagio sulla larnax dalla Tomba 22 di Tanagra," in V. La Rosa, D. Palermo, and L. Vagnetti, eds., *Epi ponton plazomenoi: Simposio italiano di studi egei dedicato a Luigi Barnabò Brea e Giovanni Pugliese Carratelli,* Rome, 215–233.

Berger, J. 1972. *Ways of Seeing,* London.

Bergquist, B. 1988. "Archaeology of Sacrifice: Minoan-Mycenaean versus Greek. A Brief Query into Two Sites with Contrary Evidence," in R. Hägg, N. Marinatos, and G. Nordquist, eds., *Early Greek Cult Practice,* Stockholm, 21–34.

Bernard, F. 1969. *J.G. Herder on Social and Political Culture,* Cambridge.

Bernus, E. 1983. "Place et rôle du forgeron dans la société touarègue," in N. Echard, ed., *Métallurgies Africaines,* Paris, 237–251.

Bessios, M., J. G. Tzifopoulos, and A. Kotsonas. 2012. Μεθώνη Πιερίας I: Επιγραφές χαράγματα και εμπορικά σύμβολα στη γεωμετρική και αρχαϊκή κεραμική από το 'Υπόγειο' της Μεθώνης Πιερίας στη Μακεδονία, Thessaloniki.

Bethe, E. 1907. *Die dorische Knabenliebe. Rheinisches Museum für Philologie,* Frankfurt.

Bianchi, R. S. 1990. "Egyptian Metal Statuary of the Third Intermediate Period (circa 1070–656 BC), from Its Egyptian Antecedents to Its Samian Examples," in M. True and J. Podany, eds., *Small Bronze Sculpture from the Ancient World,* Los Angeles, 61–84.

Biesantz, H. 1954. *Kretisch-mykenische Siegelbilder,* Marburg.

Biesantz, H. 1965. *Die thessalischen Grabreliefs: Studien zur nordgriechischen Kunst,* Mainz am Rhein.

Birringer, J. 2015. "Les ateliers de production dans les sanctuaires de Kommos et de Kato Symi," in D. Lefèvre-Novaro, L. Martzolff, and M. Ghilardi, eds., *Géosciences, archéologie et histoire en Crète de L'âge du bronze récent à l'époque archaïque,* Padua, 293–302.

Blackwell, N. 2014. "Making the Lion Gate Relief at Mycenae: Tool Marks and Foreign Influence," *American Journal of Archaeology* 118.3: 451–488.

Blackwell, N. 2018. "Contextualizing Mycenaean Hoards: Metal Control on the Greek Mainland at the End of the Bronze Age," *American Journal of Archaeology* 122.4: 509–539.

Blackwell, N. 2020. "Tools," in I. Lemos and A. Kotsonas, eds., *A Companion to the Archaeology of Early Greece and the Mediterranean,* Hoboken, 523–538.

Blakely, S. 1999. "Smelting and Sacrifice: Comparative Analysis of Greek and Near Eastern Cult Sites from the Late Bronze through Classical Periods," in S. Young, ed., *Metals in Antiquity,* Oxford, 86–90.

Blakely, S. 2006. *Myth, Ritual, and Metallurgy in Ancient Greece and Recent Africa,* Cambridge.

Blegen, C., M. Rawson, W. Taylour, and W. Donovan. 1973. *The Palace of Nestor at Pylos in Western Messenia III: Acropolis and Lower Town, Tholoi, Grave Circle, and Chamber Tombs. Discoveries outside the Citadel,* Princeton.

Blinkenberg, C. 1931. *Lindos. Fouilles de l'Acropole 1902–1914. I. Les petits objets,* Berlin.

Blocher, F. 1992. "Gaukler im alten Orient," in V. Haas, ed., *Aussenseiter und Randgruppen. Beiträge zu einer Sozialgeschichte des Alten Orients,* Konstanz, 79–111.

Block, E. 1985. "Clothing Makes the Man: A Pattern in the Odyssey," *Transactions of the American Philological Association* 115: 1–11.

Bloedow, E. 1997. "Itinerant Craftsmen and Trade in the Aegean Bronze Age," in R. Laffineur and P. Betancourt, eds., *TEXNH: Craftsmen, Craftswomen, and Craftsmanship in the Aegean Bronze Age, Aegaeum* 16, vol. 2, Liège and Austin, 439–447.

Blok, J. 2014. "A 'Covenant' between Gods and Men: *Hiera kai hosia* and the Greek *polis*," in C. Rapp and H. Drake, eds., *The City in the Classical and Post-Classical World: Changing Contexts of Power and Identity*, Cambridge, 14–37.

Blome, P. 1982. *Die figürliche Bildwelt Kretas in der geometrischen und früharchaischen Periode*, Mainz am Rhein.

Boardman, J. 1961. *The Cretan Collection in Oxford. The Dictaean Cave and Iron Age Crete*, Oxford.

Boardman, J. 1967. *Excavations in Chios 1952–1955: Greek Emporio, British School at Athens Supplement 6*, London.

Boardman, J. 1978. *Greek Sculpture. The Archaic Period*, London.

Boardman, J. 1980. *The Greeks Overseas*, New York.

Boardman, J. 2004. "Nudity in Art," in D. Kurtz, ed., *Reception of Classical Art*, Oxford, 47–54.

Bocher, S. 2006–2007. "Reconstructing Votive Cult Practices in Early Greek Sanctuaries – The Example of the Geometric Votive Bronzes from Olympia," *Anodos: Studies of the Ancient World* 6–7: 85–90.

Boehmer, R. 1965. *Die Entwicklung der Glyptik während der Akkad-Zeit*, Berlin.

Boehmer, R. 1999. *Uruk. früheste Siegelabrollungen. Ausgrabungen in Uruk-Warka, Endberichte 24*, Mainz.

Bohen, B. 1991. "The Dipylon Amphora: Its Role in the Development of Greek Art," *Journal of Aesthetic Education* 25.2: 59–65.

Bohen, B. 1997. "Aspects of Athenian Grave Cult in the Age of Homer," in S. Langdon, ed., *New Light on a Dark Age*, Colombia, MO, 44–55.

Böhm, S. 1990. *Die 'nackte Göttin': zur Ikonographie und Deutung unbekleideter weiblicher Figuren in der frühgriechischen Kunst*, Mainz.

Bol, P. 1985. *Antik Bronzetechnik: Kunst und Handwerk antiker Erzbildner*, Beck.

Bol, P. 1989. *Olympische Forschungen vol. 17: Argivische Schilde*, Berlin.

Bol, C. 2004. *Frühgriechische Bilder und die Entstehung der Klassik: Perspektive, Kognition und Wirklichkeit*, Munich.

Bolger, D. 1996. "Figurines, Fertility, and the Emergence of Complex Society in Prehistoric Cyprus," *Current Anthropology* 37: 365–373.

Bonfante, L. 1989. "Nudity as a Costume in Classical Greece," *American Journal of Archaeology* 93.4: 543–570.

Bonfante, L. 1990. "The Naked Greek," *Archaeology* 43: 28–35.

Bonfante, L. 1993. "Etruscan Nudity," *Source: Notes in the History of Art* 12: 47–55.

Bonfante, L. 2000. "Classical Nudity in Italy and Greece," in D. Ridgway, ed., *Ancient Italy in its Mediterranean Setting*, London, 271–293.

Borda, M. 1946. *Arte cretese-micenea nel Museo Pigorini di Roma*, Rome.

Borgna, E. 1995. "I ripostigli delle acropoli micenee e la circolazione del bronzo all fine dell'età palaziale," *Studi Micenei ed Egeo-Anatolici* 35: 7–56.

Born, H. and A. Moustaka. 1982. "Eine geometrische Bronzestatuette im originalen Gussmantel aus Olympia," *Mitteilungen des Deutschen Archäologischen Instituts, Athenische Abteilung* 97: 17–23.

Borrell, B. and D. Rittig. 1998. *Orientalische und griechische Bronzereliefs aus Olympia, Olympische Forschungen 26*, Berlin.

Bossert, H. 1923. *Altkreta*, Berlin.

Bouzek, J. 1983. "The Legacy of Late Geometric Art," in R. Hägg, ed., *The Greek Renaissance of the 8th Century B.C.: Tradition and Innovation*, Stockholm, 69–73.

Bradley, R. 2000. *An Archaeology of Natural Places*, London.

Bradley, R. 2005. *Ritual and Domestic Life in Prehistoric Europe*, London.

Brelich, A. 1962. *Le iniziazioni: Parte seconda. Sviluppi storici nelle civiltà superiori, in particolare nella Grecia antica*, Rome.

Brelich, A. 1969. *Paides e Parthenoi*, Rome.

Bremer, J.-M. 1998. "The Reciprocity of Giving and Thanksgiving in Greek Worship," in C. Gill, N. Postlethwaite, and R. Seaford, eds.,

Reciprocity in the Ancient World, Oxford, 127–137.

Bremmer, J. 1980. "An Enigmatic Indo-European Rite: Paederasty," *Arethusa* 13.2: 279–298.

Brock, J. 1957. *Fortetsa: Early Greek Tombs Near Knossos*, London.

Brod, H. and M. Kaufman, eds. 1994. *Theorizing Masculinities*, Thousand Oaks and London.

Broodbank, C. 2004. "Minoanization," *Proceedings of the Cambridge Philological Society* 50: 46–91.

Broodbank, C. 2013. *The Making of the Middle Sea*, London and New York.

Brown, A. and A. Peatfield. 1987. "Stous Anthropolitous: A Minoan Site Near Epano Zakro, Sitias," *Annual of the British School at Athens* 82: 23–34.

Bruer, S.-G. 2010. "Suche nach den Anfängen der Kunst: Idole in der klassischen Archäologie im 18. und frühen 19. Jahrhundert," in M. Kunze, C. Prinz, and G. Walinda, eds., *Götzen, Götter, und Idole: frühe Menschenbilder aus 10 Jahrtausenden*, Mainz, 79–88.

Brunner-Traut, E. 1955. "Die Wochenlaube," *Mitteilungen des Instituts für Orientforschung* 3: 11–30.

Brysbaert, A. and M. Vetters. 2013. "A Moving Story about Exotica: Objects' Long-Distance Production Chains and Associated Identities at Tiryns, Greece," *Opuscula: Annual of the Swedish Institutes at Athens and Rome* 6: 175–210.

Budd, P. and T. Taylor. 1995. "The Faerie Smith Meets the Bronze Industry: Magic Versus Science in the Interpretation of Prehistoric Metal-Making," *World Archaeology* 27.1: 133–143.

Buffière, F. 1956. *Les mythes d'Homère et la pensée grecque*, Paris.

Buikstra, J. and C. Douglas. 1999. "Centering the Ancestors: Cemeteries, Mounds, and Sacred Landscapes of the Ancient North American Mid-Continent," in W. Ashmore and A. B. Knapp, eds., *Archaeologies of Landscape: Contemporary Perspectives*, Malden, 201–228.

Burgess, J. 2009. *The Death and Afterlife of Achilles*, Baltimore.

Burkert, W. 1975. "Rešep-Figuren, Apollon von Amyklai und die 'Erfindung' des Opfers auf Cypern. Zur Religionsgeschichte der 'Dunklen Jahrhunderte'," *Grazer Beiträge* 4: 51–79.

Burkert, W. 1983. *Homo Necans, the Anthropology of Ancient Greek Sacrificial Ritual and Myth*, trans. P. Bing, Berkeley.

Burkert, W. 1992. *The Orientalizing Revolution: Near Eastern Influence on Greek Culture in the Early Archaic Age*, trans. M. Pinder and W. Burkert, Cambridge and London.

Burkert, W. 1996. "Greek Temple-Builders: Who, Where, and Why?" in R. Hägg, ed., *The Role of Religion in the Early Greek Polis*, Stockholm, 21–29.

Burzachini, G. 2001. "Nudità e vergogna presso Lidi e barbari (Hdt. I 10, 3)," *Eikasmos* 12: 85–88.

Buschor, E. 1934. "Kentauren," *American Journal of Archaeology* 38: 128–132.

Buschor, E. 1943. *Satyrtänze und frühes Drama*, Munich.

Buschor, E. 1951. "Spendekanne aus Samos," *Annual of the British School at Athens* 46: 32–41.

Buschor, E. and W. von Marrow. 1927. "Vom Amyklaion," *Mitteilungen des Deutschen Archäologischen Instituts, Athenische Abteilung* 52: 1–204.

Butler, J. 1993. *Bodies that Matter: On the Discursive Limits of Sex*, New York.

Byrne, M. 1991. *The Greek Geometric Warrior Figurines: Interpretation and Origin. Archaeologica Transatlantica X*, Louvain.

Cambitoglou, A., ed., 1971. *Zagora I. Excavation of a Geometric Town on the Island of Andros*, Sydney.

Carpanos, C. 1878. *Dodone et ses ruines*, Paris.

Carter, J. 1972. "The Beginning of Narrative Art in the Greek Geometric Period," *Annual of the British School at Athens* 67: 25–58.

Cartledge, P. 1981. "The Politics of Spartan Pederasty," *Cambridge Classical Journal* 27: 17–36.

Caskey, J. 1964. "Excavations in Keos, 1963," *Hesperia* 33: 314–335.

Caskey, M. 1976. "Notes on Relief Pithoi of the Tenian-Boiotian Group," *American Journal of Archaeology* 80.1: 19–41.

Casson, S. 1921. *Catalogue of the Acropolis Museum II*, Cambridge.

Catling, H. 1969. "The Cypriot Copper Industry," *Archaeologia Viva* 2.3: 81–88.

Catling, H. 1971. "A Cypriot Bronze Statuette in the Bomford Collection," in C. Schaeffer, ed., *Alasia I*, Paris, 15–32.

Catling, R. 1980–1981. "Archaeology in Greece, 1980–1981," *Archaeological Reports* 27: 3–48.

Cavanagh, P. 1990. "Practical Considerations and Problems of Bronze Casting," in M. True and J. Podany, eds., *Small Bronze Sculpture from the Ancient World*, Los Angeles, 145–160.

Cavanagh, W. and C. Mee. 1999. "Building the Treasury of Atreus," in P. Betancourt, V. Karageorghis, R. Laffineur, and W.-D. Niemeier, eds., *Meletemata: Studies in Aegean Archaeology Presented to Malcolm H. Weiner as he Enters his 65th Year*, Liège, 93–102.

Chadwick, J. 1988a. "The Women of Pylos," in J.-P. Olivier and T. Palaima, eds., *Texts, Tablets and Scribes: Studies in Mycenaean Epigraphy Offered to Emmett L. Bennett Jr.*, Salamanca, 43–95.

Chadwick, J. 1988b. "What Do We Know about Mycenaean Religion," in A. Morpurgo-Davies and Y. Duhoux, eds., *Linear B: A 1984 Survey*, Leuven, 191–202.

Chaniotis, A. 1996. *Die Verträge zwischen kretischen Städten in der hellenistischen Zeit*, Stuttgart.

Chaniotis, A. 2006. "Heiligtümer überregionaler Bedeutung auf Kreta," in K. Freitag, P. Funke, and M. Haake, eds., *Kult–Politik–Ethnos: Überregionale Heiligtümer im Spannungsfeld von Kult und Politik*, Stuttgart, 197–210.

Chantraine, P. 1968. *Dictionnaire Étymologique de la Langue Grecque: Histoire des mots*, Paris.

Chapin, A. 2002. "Maidenhood and Marriage: The Reproductive Lives of the Girls and Women from Xeste 3, Thera," *Aegean Archaeology* 4: 7–25.

Chapin, A. 2007a. "Boys Will Be Boys: Youth and Gender Identity in the Theran Frescoes," in A. Cohen and J. Rutter, eds., *Constructions of Childhood in Ancient Greece and Italy*, Princeton, 229–255.

Chapin, A. 2007b. "A Man's World? Gender and Male Coalitions in the West House Miniature Frescoes," in P. Betancourt, M. Nelson, and H. Williams, eds., *Krinoi kai Limenai: Studies in Honor of Joseph and Maria Shaw*, Philadelphia, 139–144.

Chapin, A. 2009. "Constructions of Youth and Gender in Aegean Art: The Evidence from Crete and Thera," in K. Kopaka, ed., *FYLO: Engendering Prehistoric 'Stratigraphies' in the Aegean and the Mediterranean*, Liège, 175–182.

Chapin, A. 2012. "Do Clothes Make the Man (or Woman)? Sex, Costume, and the Color Convention in Aegean Art," in M.-L. Nosch and R. Laffineur, eds., *KOSMOS: Jewellry, Adornment, and Textiles in the Aegean Bronze Age*, Liège, 297–304.

Chapin, A. 2014. "Aegean Painting in the Bronze Age," in J. Pollitt, ed., *The Cambridge History of Painting in the Classical World*, New York, 1–65.

Charalambidou, X. and C. Morgan, eds. 2017. *Interpreting the Seventh Century BC: Tradition and Innovation*, Oxford.

Childe, G. 1944. "Archaeological Ages as Technological Stages," *Journal of the Royal Anthropological Institute* 74: 7–24.

Childs, S. and D. Killick. 1993. "Indigenous African Metallurgy. Nature and Culture," *Annual Review of Anthropology* 22: 317–337.

Christesen, P. 2002. "On the Meaning of γυμνάζω," *Nikephoros (Zeitschrift für Sport und Kultur im Altertum)* 15: 7–37.

Christesen, P. 2007. *Olympic Victor Lists and Ancient Greek History*, Cambridge.

Christesen, P. 2012a. *Sport and Democracy in the Ancient and Modern Worlds*, Cambridge.

Christesen, P. 2012b. "Athletics and Social Order in Sparta in the Classical Period," *Classical Antiquity* 31: 193–255.

Christesen, P. 2013. "Sport and Democratization in Ancient Greece (with an Excursus on Athletic Nudity)," in P. Christesen and D.

Kyle, eds., *A Companion to Sport and Spectacle in Greek and Roman Antiquity*, Malden, 211–235.

Christesen, P. 2018. "Sparta and Athletics," in A. Powell, ed., *A Companion to Sparta*, Malden, 543–564.

Christiansen, J. 1992. *Greece in the Geometric Period*, Copenhagen.

Christou, S. 2012. *Sexually Ambiguous Imagery in Cyprus from the Neolithic to the Cypro-Archaic Period*, Oxford.

Chrysoulaki, S. and L. Platon. 1987. "Relations between the Town and Palace of Zakro," in R. Hägg and N. Marinatos, eds., *The Function of Minoan Palaces*, Stockholm, 77–84.

Clairmont, C. 1993. *Classical Attic Tombstones: Introduction*, Berlin.

Clark, K. 1960. *The Nude. A Study of Ideal Art*, 2nd ed., Harmondsworth.

Clarke, M. 1999. *Flesh and Spirit in the Songs of Homer: A Study of Words and Myths*, Oxford.

Cline, E. 2014. *1177 B.C.: The Year Civilization Collapsed*, Princeton.

Cohen, C., J. Maran, and M. Vetters. 2010. "An Ivory Rod with a Cuneiform Inscription, Most Probably Ugaritic, from a Final Palatial Workshop in the Lower Citadel of Tiryns," *Archäologischer Anzeiger* 2010.2: 1–22.

Coldstream, J. 1968. *Greek Geometric Pottery*, London.

Coldstream, J. 1977. *Geometric Greece*, London.

Coldstream, J. 1981. "Knossian Figured Scenes," in Πεπραγμένα τοῦ Δ' Διεθνοῦς Κρητολογικοῦ Συνεδρίου, vol. A1, Athens, 67–73.

Coldstream, J. 1984. *The Formation of the Greek Polis. Aristotle and Greek Archaeology*, Opladen.

Coldstream, J. 2000. "Knossos and Egypt in the Early Iron Age," in A. Karetsou, ed., Κρήτη - Αίγυπτος: Πολιτισμικοί δεσμοί τριών χιλιετιών. Μελέτες, Athens, 172–173.

Coldstream, J. 2003 [1977]. *Geometric Greece*, London.

Coldstream, J. 2006a. "Knossos in Early Greek Times," in S. Deger-Jalkotzy and I. Lemos, eds., *From Mycenae to Homer*, Edinburgh, 581–596.

Coldstream, J. 2006b. "The Long, Pictureless Hiatus. Some Thoughts on Greek Figured Art between Mycenaean Pictorial and Attic Geometric," in E. Rystedt and B. Wells, eds., *Pictorial Pursuits: Figurative Painting on Mycenaean and Geometric Pottery*, Stockholm, 159–163.

Coldstream, J. 2008. *Greek Geometric Pottery*, Bristol.

Coldstream, J. N., and H. W. Catling, 1996. *Knossos North Cemetery: Early Greek Tombs*, London.

Coldstream, J., L. Eiring, and G. Foster. 2001. *Knossos Pottery Handbook: Greek and Roman*, Athens.

Cole, S. 1984. "The Social Function of Rituals of Maturation: the Koureion and the Arkteia," *Zeitschrift für Papyrologie und Epigraphik* 55: 233–244.

Combellack, F. 1965. "Some Formulary Illogicalities in Homer," *Transactions of the American Philological Association* 96: 41–56.

Connell, R. 1995. *Masculinities*, Oxford.

Cook, A. 1925. *Zeus, vol. II.1*, Cambridge.

Cook, E. 2004. "Near Eastern Sources for the Palace of Alkinoos," *American Journal of Archaeology* 108.1: 43–77.

Cook, J. 1975. Review of W.-D. Heilmeyer, *Frühe olympische Tonfiguren. Classical Review* 25.1: 158.

Cook, R. M. 1997. *Greek Painted Pottery*, 3rd ed., London and New York.

Cooper, F. 1977. Review of W.-D. Heilmeyer, *Frühe olympische Tonfiguren. Classical World* 70: 343–345.

Cornwall, A. and N. Lindisfarne. 1994. *Dislocating Masculinities: Comparative Ethnographies*, London.

Coulié, A. 2013. *La céramique grecque aux époques géométrique et orientalisante (XIe-VIe siècle av. J.-C.)*, Paris.

Coupaye, L. 2007. "Beyond Mediation: The Long Yams of Papua New Guinea," in C. Jeffrey and G. Minissale, eds., *Art Histories: Global and Local Mediations*, Cambridge, 205–20.

Coupaye, L. 2009. "Ways of Enchanting: Chaînes Opératoires and Yam Cultivation in Nyamikum Village, Maprik, Papua New

Guinea," *Journal of Material Culture* 14.4: 433–458.

Coupaye, L. 2012. *Growing Artefacts, Displaying Relationships: Yams, Art and Technology amongst the Abelam of Papua New Guinea*, Oxford and New York.

Courbin, P. 1954. "Chronique des fouilles et découvertes archéologiques en Grèce en 1953," *Bulletin de Correspondance Hellénique* 78: 95–224.

Courbin, P. 1957. "Argos: Quartier Sud," *Bulletin de Correspondance Hellénique* 81: 665–681.

Courbin, P. 1966. *La céramique géométrique de l'Argolide*, 2 vols., Paris.

Courbin, P. 1992. "La signification du géométrique argien," in M. Piérart, ed., *Polydipsion Argos: Argos de la fin des palais mycéniens à la constitution de l'État classique*, Athens, 55–68.

Courby, F. 1922. *Les vases grecs à reliefs*, Paris.

Crielaard, J.-P. 1995. "Homer, History, and Archaeology: Some Remarks on the Date of the Homeric World," in J.-P. Crielaard, ed., *Homeric Questions*, Leiden, 201–288.

Crielaard, J.-P. 1999. "Production, Circulation, and Consumption of Early Iron Age Greek Pottery (Eleventh to Seventh Centuries BC)," in J.-P. Crielaard, V. Stissi, and G. van Wijngaarden, eds., *The Complex Past of Pottery: Production, Circulation, and Consumption of Mycenaean and Greek Pottery*, Leiden, 49–81.

Crielaard, J.-P. 2011. "The *Wanax* to *Basileus* Model Reconsidered," in A. Mazarakis Ainian, ed., *The Dark Ages Revisited*, Volos, 83–111.

Crielaard, J.-P. 2015. "Powerful Things in Motion: A Biographical Approach to Eastern Elite Goods in Greek Sanctuaries," in E. Kistler, B. Öhlinger, M. Mohr, and M. Hoernes, eds., *Sanctuaries and the Power of Consumption*, Wiesbaden, 351–372.

Croissant, F. 1992. "Les débuts de la plastique argienne," in M. Piérart, ed., *Polydipsion Argos: Argos de la fin des palais mycéniens à la constitution de l'État classique*, Athens, 69–97.

Croissant, F. 2008. "Batailles géométriques pariennes," in E. Greco and E. Carando, eds.,

Alba della città, alba delle immagini?, Athens, 31–62.

Crotty, K. 1994. *The Poetics of Supplication*, Ithaca.

Crowley, J. 2008. "Mycenaean Art and Architecture," in C. Shelmerdine, ed., *The Cambridge Companion to the Aegean Bronze Age*, Cambridge, 258–288.

Crowther, N. 1982. "Athletic Dress and Nudity in Greek Athletics," *Eranos* 80: 163–168.

Crowther, N. 1988. "The Age-Category of Boys at Olympia," *Phoenix* 42: 304–308.

Currie, B. 2016. *Homer's Allusive Art*, Oxford.

D'Agata, A. 1997. "Shrines on the Piazzale dei Sacelli at Ayia Triadha. The LM IIIC and SM material: A Summary," in J. Driessen and A. Farnoux, eds., *La Crète mycénienne*, Paris, 85–100.

D'Agata, A. 1998. "Changing Patterns in a Minoan and Post-Minoan Sanctuary: The Case of Ayia Triada," in W. Cavanagh and M. Curtis, eds., *Post-Minoan Crete. BSA Studies 2*, London, 19–26.

D'Agata, A. 1999. *Statuine minoiche e post-minoiche dai vecchi scavi de Haghia Triada (Creta). Haghia Triada 2*, Padua.

D'Agata, A. 2006. "Cult Activity on Crete in the Early Dark Age: Changes, Continuities, and the Development of a 'Greek' Cult System," in S. Deger-Jalkotzy and I. Lemos, eds., *From Mycenae to Homer*, Edinburgh, 397–414.

D'Agata, A. 2012. "The Power of Images: A Figured Krater from Thronos Kephala (Ancient Sybrita) and the Process of Polis Formation in Early Iron Age Crete," *Studi micenei ed egeo-anatolici* 54: 207–247.

D'Agata, A. 2014. "Warrior Dance, Social Ordering, and the Process of Polis Formation in Early Iron Age Crete," in K. Soar and C. Aamodt, eds., *Archaeological Approaches to Dance Performance*, Oxford, 75–83.

D'Agostino, B., M. Palmieri, F. Poole, and A. Cassio. 2017. "Potters, *hippeis*, and Gods at Penteskouphia (Corinth), Seventh to Sixth Centuries BC," in J. Bintliff and N. Rutter, eds., *The Archaeology of Greece and Rome: Studies in Honour of Anthony Snodgrass*, Edinburgh, 155–182.

Dalby, A. 1995. "The *Iliad*, the *Odyssey*, and their Audiences," *Classical Quarterly* 45.2: 269–279.

Damiani-Indelicato, S. 1988. "Were Cretan Girls Playing at Bull Leaping?" *Cretan Studies* 1: 39–47.

Dardaillon, E. 2012. "The Evidence for Metallurgical Workshops of the Second Millennium in Ugarit," in V. Kassianidou and G. Papasavvas, eds., *Eastern Mediterranean Metallurgy and Metalwork,* Oxford, 169–179.

Daugman, J. 1990. "Brain Metaphor and Brain Theory," in E. Schwartz, ed., *Computational Neuroscience,* Cambridge, 9–18.

Daux, G. 1959. "Chronique des Fouilles," *Bulletin de Correspondance Hellénique* 83: 567–793.

David, E. 2010. "Sparta and the Politics of Nudity," in A. Powell and S. Hodkinson, eds., *Sparta: The Body Politic,* Swansea, 137–163.

Davies, M. 2007. "The Hero and His Arms," *Greece and Rome* 54.2: 145–155.

Davies, P. 2017. "Articulating Status in Ancient Greece: Status (In)consistency as a New Approach," *Cambridge Classical Journal* 63: 29–52.

Davies, V. and R. Friedman. 2002. "The Narmer Palette. An Overlooked Detail," in M. Edamaty and M. Trad, eds., *Egyptian Museum Collections around the World,* Cairo, 243–246.

Davis, E. 1986. "Youth and Age in the Thera Frescoes," *American Journal of Archaeology* 90: 399–406.

Davison, J. 1961. *Attic Geometric Workshops,* New Haven.

Dawkins, R., C. H. Hawes, and R. Bosanquet. "Excavations at Palaikastro, IV," *Annual of the British School at Athens* 11: 258–308.

De Garis Davies, N. 1925. *The Tomb of Two Sculptors at Thebes,* New York.

De la Croix, H. and R. Tansey. 1986. *Gardner's Art Through the Ages,* 8th ed., San Diego.

De Polignac, F. 1984. *La naissance de la cité grecque,* Paris.

De Polignac, F. 1994. "Mediation, Competition, and Sovereignty: The Evolution of Rural Sanctuaries in Geometric Greece," in S. Alcock and R. Osborne, eds., *Placing the Gods. Sanctuaries and Sacred Space in Ancient Greece,* Oxford, 3–18.

De Polignac, F. 1995. *Cults, Territory, and the Origins of the Greek City State,* Chicago.

De Ridder, S. 1896. *Catalogue des bronzes trouvés sur l'acropole d'Athènes,* Paris.

De Ridder, S. 1898. "Amphores béotiennes à reliefs," *Bulletin de Correspondance Hellénique* 22: 439–471.

De Ridder, S. 1913. *Bronzes antiques du Louvre,* Paris.

de Ste. Croix, G. E. M. 1981. *The Class Struggle in the Ancient Greek World,* Oxford.

Decker, W. 1978. *Annotierte Bibliographie zum Sport im alten Ägypten,* Hildesheim.

Deger-Jalkotzy, S. 2008. "Decline, Destruction, Aftermath," in C. Shelmerdine, ed., *The Cambridge Companion to the Aegean Bronze Age,* Cambridge, 387–415.

Deger-Jalkotzy, S. 2014. "A Very Underestimated Period: The Submycenaean Phase of Early Greek Culture," in D. Nakassis, J. Gulizio, and S. James, eds., *KE-RA-ME-JA: Studies Presented to Cynthia W. Shelmerdine,* Philadelphia, 41–52.

Deger-Jalkotzy, S. and I. Lemos, eds. 2006. *Ancient Greece: From the Mycenaean Palaces to the Age of Homer,* Edinburgh.

Dekoulakou, I. 1972. "Ἀλίκυρνα," *Archaiologikon Deltion* 27 *Chronika B'2:* 438–439.

Delcourt, M. 1957. *Héphaistos ou la légende du magicien,* Paris.

Del Freo, M. 2005. "L'expression *ka-ko na-wi-jo* de la tablette Jn 829 de Pylos," in R. Laffineur and E. Greco, eds., *Emporia: Aegeans in the Central and Eastern Mediterranean. Aegaeum 25,* Liège and Austin, 793–803.

Demakopoulou, K. 1970. "Μυκηναϊκή πηλίνη κεφαλή," *Archaiologikon Deltion* 25: 174–183.

Demakopoulou, K. 1982. "Το μυκηναϊκό ιερό στο Αμυκλαίο και η ΥΕ ΙΙΙΓ περίοδος στη Λακωνία," Unpublished PhD Dissertation, University of Athens.

Demakopoulou, K. 1989. "Contest in the Bronze Aegean: Crete, Thera, and

Mycenaean Greece," in O. Tzachou-Alexandri, ed., *Mind and Body: Athletic Contests in Ancient Greece*, Athens, 25–30, 111–125.

Demargne, P. 1929. "Terres cuites archaïques de Lato," *Bulletin de Correspondance Hellénique* 53: 382–429.

Demargne, P. 1931. "Recherches sur le site de l'Anavlochos," *Bulletin de Correspondance Hellénique* 55: 365–407.

Demargne, P. 1947. *La Crète dédalique*, Paris.

Déonna, W. 1938. "Notes d'archéologie délienne," *Bulletin de Correspondance Hellénique* 62: 209–235.

Desborough, V. 1952. *Protogeometric Pottery*, Oxford.

Desborough, V., R. Nicholls, and M. Popham. 1970. "A Euboean Centaur," *Annual of the British School at Athens* 65: 21–30.

Dessenne, A. 1949. "Têtes minoennes," *Bulletin de Correspondance Hellénique* 73: 307–315.

Dickinson, O. 1986. "Homer, the Poet of the Dark Age," *Greece and Rome* 33: 20–37.

Dickinson, O. 2006. *The Aegean from Bronze Age to Iron Age: Continuity and Change between the Twelfth and Eighth Centuries BC*, London and New York.

Dickinson, O. 2020. "The Irrelevance of the Greek 'Tradition'," in G. Middleton, ed., *Collapse and Transformation: The Late Bronze Age to Early Iron Age in the Aegean*, Oxford and Philadelphia, 153–160.

Dietrich, B. 1983. "Tradition in Greek Religion," in R. Hägg, ed., *The Greek Renaissance of the Eighth Century B.C. Tradition and Innovation*, Stockholm, 85–89.

Dimitriadou, E. 2019. *Early Athens: Settlements and Cemeteries in the Submycenaean, Geometric, and Archaic Periods*, Los Angeles.

Dimopoulou, N. 1997. "Workshops and Craftsmen in the Harbour-Town of Knossos at Poros-Katsambas," in R. Laffineur and P. Betancourt, eds., *TEXNH. Craftsmen, Craftswomen and Craftsmanship in the Aegean Bronze Age*, vol. 2, Liège, 433–438.

Dimopoulou, N. 2004. "Το επίνειο της Κνωσού στον Πόρο-Κατσαμπά," in G. Cadogan, E. Hatzaki, and A. Vasilakis, eds., *Knossos:*

Palace, City, State, BSA Studies 12, London, 363–380.

Dimopoulou, N. 2012. "Metallurgy and Metalworking in the Harbor Town of Knossos at Poros-Katsambas," in V. Kassianidou and G. Papasavvas, eds., *Eastern Mediterranean Metallurgy and Metalwork in the Second Millenium BC*, Oxford, 135–141.

Dinsmoor, W. 1921. "Attic Building Accounts IV: The Statue of Athena Promachos," *American Journal of Archaeology* 25: 118–129.

Dobres, M.-A. 2000. *Technology and Social Agency*, Malden.

Dobres, M.-A. 2010. "Archaeologies of Technology," *Cambridge Journal of Economics* 34.1: 103–114.

Doonan, R. and A. Mazarakis Ainian. 2007. "Forging Identity in Early Iron Age Greece: Implications of the Metalworking Evidence from Oropos," in A. Mazarakis Ainian, ed., *Oropos and Euboea in the Early Iron Age*, Volos, 361–378.

Dolan, B. 2016. "Making Iron in the Irish Midlands: The Social and Symbolic Role of Iron Age Ironworkers," *The Journal of Irish Archaeology* 25: 31 48.

Donlan, W. 1997. "The Homeric Economy," in I. Morris and B. Powell, eds., *A New Companion to Homer*, Leiden, 649–667.

Dörpfeld, W. 1935. *Alt-Olympia: Untersuchungen und Ausgrabungen zur Geschichte des ältesten Heiligtums von Olympia und der älteren griechischen Kunst*, Berlin.

Dothan, M. 1956. "The Excavations at Nahariya," *Israel Exploration Journal* 6: 14–25.

Douglas, M. 1966. *Purity and Danger: An Analysis of Concepts of Pollution and Taboo*, London.

Douglas, M. 1970. *Natural Symbols, Explorations in Cosmology*, London.

Doumas, C. 1987. "Η Ξεστή 3 καί οἱ κυανοκέφαλοι στήν τέχνη τῆς Θήρας," in L. Kastrinaki, G. Orphanou, and N. Giannadakis, eds., *ΕΙΛΑΠΙΝΗ. Τόμος Τιμητικός γιά τόν Καθηγητή Νικόλαο Πλάτωνα*, Heraklion, 151–159.

Doumas, C. 1992. *The Wall-Paintings of Thera*, Athens.

Dougherty, C. and L. Kurke, eds. 1993. *Cultural Poetics in Archaic Greece: Cult, Performance, Politics*, Cambridge.

Dover, K. 1978. *Greek Homosexuality*, London.

Dover, K. 1992. "Greek Homosexuality and Initiation," in W. Dynes and S. Donaldson, eds., *Homosexuality in the Ancient World*, New York and London, 127–148.

Droop, J. 1927. "Excavations at Sparta," *Annual of the British School at Athens* 28: 49–81.

Ducat, J. 2006. *Spartan Education*, trans. E. Stafford, P.-J. Shaw, and A. Powell, Swansea.

Duerr, H. 1988–99. *Der Mythos vom Zivilisationsprozess*, 5 vols., Frankfurt am Mainz.

Dugas, C. 1921. "Le sanctuaire d'Aléa Athéna à Tegée avant le IVᵉ siècle," *Bulletin de Correspondance Hellénique* 45: 335–435.

Dunand, M. 1958. *Fouilles de Byblos II, 1933–1938*, Paris.

Duplouy, A. and R. Brock, eds., *Defining Citizenship in Archaic Greece*, Oxford.

Durkheim, E. 1965 [1915]. *The Elementary Forms of Religious Life*, trans. J. Swain, New York.

Ebel, H. 1968. "The Killing of Lykaon: Homer and Literary 'Structure'," *College English* 29.7: 503–529.

Eco, U. 2004. *History of Beauty*, New York.

Edelman, M. 1971. *Politics as Symbolic Action*, Chicago.

Eder, B. 2001a. "Continuity of Bronze Age Cult at Olympia? The Evidence of the Late Bronze Age and Early Iron Age pottery," in R. Laffineur and R. Hägg, eds., *Potnia: deities and religion in the Aegean Bronze Age,* Liège, 201–209.

Eder, B. 2001b. "Die Anfänge von Elis und Olympia: zur Siedlungsgeschichte der Landschaft Elis am Übergang von der Spätbronze-zur Früheisenzeit," in V. Mitsopoulos-Leon, ed., *Forschungen in der Peloponnes*, Athens, 233–243.

Eder B. 2006a. "The World of Telemachus: Western Greece 1200–700 BC," in S. Deger-Jalkotzy and I. Lemos, eds., *Ancient Greece: From the Mycenaean Palaces to the Age of Homer,* Edinburgh, 549–580.

Eder, B. 2006b. "Die spätbronze und früheisenzeitliche Keramik," in H. Kyrieleis,

ed., *Anfänge und Frühzeit des Heiligtums von Olympia: die Ausgrabungen am Pelopion 1987–1996*, Berlin, 141–246.

Eder, B. 2016. "Ideology in Space: Mycenaean Symbols in Action," in E. Alram-Stern, F. Blakolmer, S. Deger-Jalkotzy, R. Laffineur, and J. Weilharnter, eds., *Metaphysis: Ritual, Myth, and Symbolism in the Aegean Bronze Age*, Leuven, 175–185.

Eder, B. 2019. "The Role of Sanctuaries and the Formation of Greek Identity in the Late Bronze Age/Early Iron Age Transition," in A. Tsingarada and I. Lemos, eds., *Beyond the Polis: Rituals, Rites, and Cults in Early and Archaic Greece*, Brussels, 25–52.

Eder, B. and I. Lemos. 2020. "The Emergence of Early Iron Age Communities," in I. Lemos and A. Kotsonas, eds., *A Companion to the Archaeology of Early Greece and the Mediterranean*, Hoboken, 133–160.

Edsman, C.-M. 1949. *Ignus Divinus*, Lund.

Edwards, M. 1991. *The Iliad: A Commentary. Volume V: Books 17–20*, Cambridge.

Eiteljorg, H. 1980. "The Fast Wheel, the Multiple-Brush Compass, and Athens as Home of the Protogeometric Style," *American Journal of Archaeology* 84.4: 445–452.

Eliade, M. 1955. "Smiths, Shamans, and Mystagogues," *East and West* 6.3: 206–215.

Eliade, M. 1958. *Rites and Symbols of Initiation: The Mysteries of Birth and Rebirth*, trans. W. Trask, New York.

Eliade, M. 1962. *The Forge and the Crucible*, New York.

Erb-Satullo, N., B. Gilmour, and N. Khakhutaishvili. 2014. "Late Bronze and Early Iron Age Copper Smelting Technologies in the South Caucasus: The View from Ancient Colchis c. 1500–600 BC," *Journal of Archaeological Science* 49: 147–159.

Erbse, H., ed. 1969. *Scholia Graeca in Homeri Iliadem*, vol. 1, Berlin.

Erickson, B. 2002. "Aphrati and Syme Viannou: Pottery, Continuity, and Cult in Late Archaic and Classical Crete," *Hesperia* 71: 41–90.

Ervin, M. 1963. "A Relief Pithos from Mykonos," *Archaiologikon Deltion* 18 A' *Meletemata*: 37–75.

Evans, A. J. 1928. *The Palace of Minos at Knossos III*, London.

Evans, I. 1953. *The Religion of Temasuk Dusuns of North Borneo*, Cambridge.

Evely, D. 1993. *Minoan Crafts: Tools and Techniques. An Introduction*, Göteborg.

Faro, E. Z. 2008. "Minoan Extra Urban Ritual," Unpublished PhD Dissertation, University of Michigan.

Faure, P. 1967. "Nouvelles recherches sur trois sortes de sanctuaires Crétois," *Bulletin de Correspondance Hellénique* 91: 114–150.

Faure, P. 1969. "Sure trois sortes de sanctuaires crétois," *Bulletin de Correspondance Hellénique* 93: 174–213.

Faure, P. 1972. "Cultes populaires dans la Crète antique," *Bulletin de Correspondance Hellénique* 96: 389–426.

Fausto-Sterling, A. 1993. "The Five Sexes: Why Male and Female Are Not Enough," *The Sciences* 33.2: 20–25.

Feinberg, W. 1983. *Lost-Wax Casting: A Practitioner's Manual*, London.

Felsch, R. 1980. "Apollon und Artemis oder Artemis und Apollon? Bericht von den Grabungen im neu entdecken Heiligtum bei Kalapodi 1973–1977," *Archäologischer Anzeiger* 38: 38–123.

Felsch, R. 1983. "Zur Chronologie und zum Stil geometrischer Bronzen aus Kalapodi," in R. Hägg, ed., *The Greek Renaissance of the Eighth Century BC: Tradition and Innovation*, Stockholm, 123–129.

Felsch, R. 1987. "Kalapodi. Bericht über die Grabungen im Heiligtum der Artemis Elaphebolos und des Apollo von Hyampolis 1978–1982," *Archäologischer Anzeiger* 1987: 1–26.

Felsch, R. 1996. *Kalapodi: Ergebnisse der Ausgrabungen im Heiligtum der Artemis und des Apollon von Hyampolis in der antiken Phokis*, Mainz am Rhein.

Felsch, R. 2001. "Opferhandlungen des Alltagslebens im Heiligtum der Artemis Elaphebolos bei Kalapodi," in R. Laffineur and R. Hägg, eds., *Potnia. Deities and Religion in the Aegean Bronze Age. Aegaeum 22*, Liège and Austin, 193–199.

Felsch, R. 2007. *Kalapodi II: Zur Stratigraphie des Heiligtums; die Bronzefunde; die Angriffswaffen*, Mainz am Rhein.

Ferrari, G. 2002. *Figures of Speech. Men and Maidens in Ancient Greece*, Chicago.

Feyel, C. 2006. *Les artisans dans les sanctuaires grecs aux époques classiques et hellénistique à travers la documentation financière en Grèce*, Athens.

Finley, M. 1954. *The World of Odysseus*, New York.

Finley, M. 1981. *Economy and Society in Ancient Greece*, London.

Finné, M., K. Holmgren, C.-C. Shen, H.-M. Hu, M. Boyd, and S. Stocker. 2017. "Late Bronze Age Climate Change and the Destruction of the Mycenaean Palace of Nestor at Pylos," *PLOS One* 12.12: e0189447.

Fittschen, K. 1969. *Untersuchungen zum Beginn der Sagendarstellungen bei den Griechen*, Berlin.

Fogelin, L. 2003. "Ritual and Presentation in Early Buddhist Religious Architecture," *Asian Perspectives* 42: 129–154.

Fogelin, L. 2004. "Sacred Architecture, Sacred Landscape: Early Buddhism in Coastal Andhra Pradesh," in H. P. Ray and C. M. Sinopoli, eds., *Archaeology as History in South Asia*, New Delhi, 376–391.

Fogelin, L. 2006. *Archaeology of Early Buddhism*, Walnut Creek.

Fogelin, L. 2007. "The Archaeology of Religious Ritual," *Annual Review of Anthropology* 44: 329–345.

Forbes, R. 1964. *Studies in Ancient Technology*, vol. 8, Leiden.

Forster, E. 1901–1902. "Praisos. The Terracottas," *Annual of the British School at Athens* 8: 271–281.

Foucault, M. 1985. *The History of Sexuality: Volume 2, The Use of Pleasure*, London.

French, E. 1971. "The Development of Mycenaean Terracotta Figurines," *Annual of the British School at Athens* 66: 101–187.

French, E. 1981a. "Mycenaean Figures and Figurines, their Typology and Function," in R. Hägg and N. Marinatos, eds., *Sanctuaries and Cults in the Aegean Bronze Age*, Stockholm, 173–178.

French, E. 1981b. "Cult places at Mycenae," in R. Hägg and N. Marinatos, eds., *Sanctuaries and Cults in the Aegean Bronze Age,* Stockholm, 41–48.

French, E. 1985. "The Figures and Figurines," in C. Renfrew, ed., *The Archaeology of Cult: The Sanctuary at Phylakopi,* London, 209–280.

French, E. 2006. "The Terracotta Figurines," in D. Evely, ed., *Lefkandi IV: The Bronze Age. The Late Helladic IIIC Settlement at Xeropolis,* London, 257–263.

Frisk, H. 1960. *Griechisches Etymologisches Wörterburch,* Band I: A–Ko, Heidelberg.

Fuchs, W. and J. Floren. 1987. *Die geometrische und archaische Plastik. Die griechische Plastik I,* Munich.

Furtwängler, A. 1880. *Die Bronzefunde aus Olympia und deren Kunstgeschichtliche Bedeutung,* Berlin.

Furtwängler, A. 1890. *Die Bronzen und die Übrigen Kleineren Funde von Olympia. Tafelband,* Berlin.

Furtwängler, A. 1890–1897. *Olympia: die Ergebnisse der von dem Deutschen Reich veranstalteten Ausgrabung IV, die Bronzen,* Berlin.

Gadolou, A. 2017. "The Formation of Religious Landscapes in Achaia during the Early Historical Era," in A. Mazarakis Ainian, A. Alexandridou, and X. Charalambidou, eds., *Regional Stories: Towards a New Perception of the Early Greek World,* Volos, 279–291.

Galaty, M. and W. A. Parkinson. 2007. "Introduction: Mycenaean Palaces Rethought," in M. Galaty and W. Parkinson, eds., *Rethinking Mycenaean Palaces II,* 2nd ed., Los Angeles, 1–17.

Gallett de Santerre, H. 1987. "Les statuettes de bronze mycéniennes au type dit du 'dieu Reshef' dans leur contexte égéen," *Bulletin de Correspondance Hellénique* 111: 7–29.

Gardiner, E. 1930. *Athletics of the Ancient World,* Oxford.

Garland, R. 1981. "The Causation of Death in the *Iliad,*" *Bulletin of the Institute of Classical Studies* 28: 43–60.

Garrison, D. 2010. "Introduction," in D. Garrison, ed., *A Cultural History of the Human Body in Antiquity,* Oxford, 1–24.

Gauer, W. 2003. Review of *Olympia XI. Bericht über die Ausgrabungen in Olympia. Gnomon* 75.3: 243–248.

Gauß, W. and F. Ruppenstein. 2020. "Pottery," in I. Lemos and A. Kotsonas, eds., *A Companion to the Archaeology of Early Greece and the Mediterranean,* Hoboken, 433–470.

Geertz, C. 1973. "Religion as a Cultural System," in *The Interpretation of Cultures,* New York, 87–125.

Geertz, C. 1980. *Negara: The Theatre State in Nineteenth Century Bali,* Princeton.

Gehrig, U. 1964. "Die geometrischen Bronzen von dem Heraion von Samos," Unpublished PhD Dissertation, University of Hamburg.

Gehrig, U. 1979. "Frühe Griechische Bronzegüsstechniken," *Archäologischer Anzeiger* 1979: 547–558.

Gell, A. 1992. "The Technology of Enchantment," in J. Coote and A. Shelton, eds., *Anthropology, Art, and Aesthetics,* 40–63, Oxford.

Gell, A. 1998. *Art and Agency: An Anthropological Theory,* Oxford.

Georganas, I. 2008. "Between Admetus and Jason: Pherai in the Early Iron Age," in C. Gallou, M. Georgiadis, and G. Muskett, eds., *Dioskouroi: Studies Presented to W.G. Cavanagh and C.B. Mee on the Anniversary of Their 30-Year Joint Contribution to Aegean Archaeology,* Oxford, 274–280.

Gesell, G. 1972. "The Archaeological Evidence for the Minoan House Cult and Its Survival in Iron Age Crete," Unpublished PhD Dissertation, University of North Carolina.

Gesell, G. 1976. "The Minoan Snake Tube: A Survey and Catalogue," *American Journal of Archaeology* 80: 247–259.

Gesell, G. 1985. *Town, Palace, and House Cult in Minoan Crete, Studies in Mediterranean Archaeology* 67, Göteborg.

Gillis, C. 1997. "The Smith in the Late Bronze Age – State Employee, Independent Artisan, or Both?" in R. Laffineur and P. Betancourt, eds., *TEXNH: Craftsmen, Craftswomen, and Craftsmanship in the Aegean Bronze Age,* Liège and Austin, 505–513.

Gilmour, G. 1993. "Aegean Sanctuaries and the Levant in the Late Bronze Age," *Annual of the British School at Athens* 88: 125–134.

Gimatzidis, S. 2010. *Die Stadt Sindos: Eine Siedlung von der späten Bronze- bis zur klassischen Zeit am Thermäischen Golf in Makedonien*, Rahden.

Gimbutas, M. 1991. *The Civilization of the Goddess: The World of Old Europe*, San Francisco.

Gjerstad, E., J. Lindros, E. Sjöqvist, and A. Westholm. 1935. *The Swedish Cyprus Expedition: Finds and Results of the Excavations in Cyprus, 1927–1931*, Vol. 2, Stockholm.

Goelet, O. 1993. "Nudity in Ancient Egypt," *Source: Notes in the History of Art* 12.2: 20–31.

Goffman, E. 1956. *The Presentation of Self in Everyday Life*, Edinburgh.

Gombrich, E. 1960. *Art and Illusion*, Princeton.

Gomme, H. 1945–1951. *A Historical Commentary on Thucydides*, Oxford.

Gordon, C. 1950–1951. "Belt-Wrestling in the Bible World," *Hebrew Union College Annual* 23: 131–136.

Goris, R. 1960. "The Position of the Blacksmiths," in J. Swellengebel, ed., *Bali: Studies in Life, Thought, and Ritual*, The Hague, 291–297.

Gosselain, O. 1998. "Social and Technical Identity in a Clay Crystal Ball," in M. Stark, ed., *The Archaeology of Social Boundaries*, Washington DC, 78–106.

Gottschall, J. 2008. *The Rape of Troy: Evolution, Violence, and the World of Homer*, Cambridge.

Gow, A. 1914. "The Ancient Plough," *Journal of Hellenic Studies* 34: 249–275.

Graça da Silva, S. and J. Tehrani. 2016. "Comparative Phylogenetic Analyses Uncover the Ancient Roots of Indo-European Folktales," *Royal Society Open Science* 3: 150645.

Graindor, P. 1905. "Vases archaïques à reliefs de Tinos," *Revue archéologique* 6: 286–291.

Greiveldinger, A. 2003. "Sur l'identité des dédicants des *pinakes* de Penteskouphia (Corinthe)," in B. Schlamtz and M. Söldner,

eds., *Griechische Keramik im kulturellen Kontext*, Münster, 80–82.

Grethlein, J. 2009. "The *Iliad* and the Trojan War," in D. Konstan and K. Raaflaub, eds., *Epic and History*, Oxford and Malden, 122–144.

Grosz, E. 1995. *Space, Time, and Perversion*, London.

Grote, G. 1846–1856. *A History of Greece*, 12 vols., New York.

Grottanelli, C. 1988. "Of Gods and Metals. On the Economy of Phoenician Sanctuaries," *Scienze dell'Antichita: Storia, archeologia, antropologia* 2: 243–255.

Grottanelli, C. 1989–1990. "Do ut des?" in G. Bartolini, G. Colonna, and C. Grottanelli, eds., *Anathema. Regime dell Offerte e Vita dei Santuari nel Mediteranneo Antico*, Rome, 45–54.

Guggisberg, M. 1996. *Frühgriechische Tierkeramik: Zur Entwicklung und Bedeutung der Tiergefäße und der hohlen Tierfiguren in der späten Bronze- und frühen Eisenzeit (ca. 1600–700 v. Chr.)*, Mainz.

Hachmann, R. 1980. *Bericht über die Ergebnisse der Ausgrabungen in Kamid el-Loz in den Jahren 1968 bis 1970*, Bonn.

Hägg, R. ed., 1983. *The Greek Renaissance of the Eighth Century BC: Tradition and Innovation*, Stockholm.

Hägg, R. 1992. "Sanctuaries and Workshops in the Bronze Age Aegean," in T. Linders and B. Alroth, eds., *Economics of Cult in the Ancient Greek World*, Uppsala, 29–32.

Halbherr, F. 1903. "Resti dell'età Micenea scoperti ad Haghia Triada presso Phaestos," *Monumenti Antichi* 13: 5–76.

Hall, E. 1914. *Excavations in Eastern Crete; Vrokastro*, Philadelphia.

Hall, J. 2002. *Hellenicity: Between Ethnicity and Culture*, Chicago and London.

Hall, J. 2013. *A History of the Archaic Greek World, ca. 1200–479 BCE*, Chichester.

Halpern, D. 2000. *Sex Differences in Cognitive Abilities*, 3rd ed., Mahwah.

Halstead, P. 2013. *Two Oxen Ahead*, Hoboken.

Hamilakis, Y. and E. Konsolaki. 2004. "Pigs for the Gods: Burnt Animal Sacrifices as

Embodied Rituals at a Mycenaean Sanctuary," *Oxford Journal of Archaeology* 23: 35–151.

Hamilton, N. 2000. "Ungendering Archaeology: Concepts of Sex and Gender in Figurine Studies in Prehistory," in M. Donald and L. Hurcombe, eds., *Representations of Gender from Prehistory to the Present*, London, 17–30.

Hampe, R. and Jantzen, U. 1937. "Bericht über die Ausgrabungen in Olympia. Die Grabung im Frühjahr 1937," *Jahrbuch des Deutschen Archäologischen Instituts* 52: 28–41.

Hannah, P. 1998. "The Reality of Greek Male Nudity: Looking to African Parallels," *Scholia* 7: 17–40.

Hardie, P. 1985. "Imago Mundi: Cosmological and Ideological Aspects of the Shield of Achilles," *Journal of Hellenic Studies* 105: 11–31.

Harloe, K. 2013. *Winckelmann and the Invention of Antiquity*, Oxford.

Harper, M. 1987. "Possible Toxic Metal Exposure of Prehistoric Bronze Workers," *British Journal of Industrial Medicine* 44: 652–656.

Harpur, Y. 1987. *Decoration in Egyptian Tombs of the Old Kingdom, Studies in Orientation and Scene Content*, London.

Harris, H. 1964. *Greek Athletes and Athletics*, New Haven.

Hartt, F. 1989. *Art: A History of Painting, Sculpture, Architecture*, 3rd ed., New York.

Hasaki, E. 2002. "Ceramic Kilns in Ancient Greece: Technology and Organization of Ceramic Workshops," Unpublished PhD Dissertation, University of Cincinnati.

Hatzaki, E. and A. Kotsonas. 2020. "Knossos and North Central Crete," in I. Lemos and A. Kotsonas, eds., *A Companion to the Archaeology of Early Greece and the Mediterranean*, Hoboken, 1029–1053.

Haug, A. 2012. *Die Entdeckung des Körpers: Körper- und Rollenbilder im Athen des 8. und 7. Jahrhunderts v. Chr.*, Berlin.

Haug, A. 2015. *Bild und Ornament im frühen Athen*, Regensburg.

Hayden, B. 1991. "Terracotta Figures, Figurines, and Vase Attachments from Vrokastro, Crete," *Hesperia* 60: 103–144.

Hayes, K. 1993. "When Is a Symbol Archaeologically Meaningful? Meaning, Function, and Prehistoric Visual Arts," in N. Yoffee and A. Sherratt, eds., *Archaeological Theory: Who Sets the Agenda,* Cambridge, 81–92.

Haynes, D. 1992. *The Technique of Greek Bronze Statuary*, Mainz am Rhein.

Haysom, M. 2011. "The Strangeness of Crete: Problems for the Protohistory of Greek Religion," in M. Haysom and J. Wallensten, eds., *Current Approaches to Religion in Ancient Greece,* Stockholm, 95–110.

Heilmeyer, W.-D. 1969. "Geissereibetriebe in Olympia," *Jahrbuch des Deutschen Archäologischen Instituts* 84: 1–69.

Heilmeyer, W.-D. 1972. *Olympia Forschungen VII: Frühe Olympische Tonfiguren*, Berlin.

Heilmeyer, W.-D. 1979. *Olympia Forschungen XII: Frühe Olympische Bronzefiguren: Die Tiervotive*, Berlin.

Heilmeyer, W.-D., G. Zimmer, and G. Schneider. 1987. "Die Bronzegiesserei unter der Werkstatt des Phidias in Olympia," *Archäologischer Anzeiger* 1987: 239–299.

Helgeson, V. 2002. *The Psychology of Gender*, Upper Saddle River.

Helms, M. 1993. *Craft and the Kingly Ideal. Art, Trade, and Power*, Austin.

Helms, M. 2006. "Joseph the Smith and the Salvational Transformation of Matter in Early Medieval Europe," *Anthropos* 101.2: 451–471.

Hemingway, S. 2000. "Bronze Sculpture," in R. Ling, ed., *Making Classical Art: Process and Practice,* Charleston, 37–46.

Herder, J. 1877. *Sämtliche Werke*, B. Suphan, ed., 33 vols., Berlin.

Herrmann, H.-V. 1962. "Zur ältesten Geschichte von Olympia," *Mitteilungen des Deutschen Archäologischen Instituts, Athenische Abteilung* 77: 3–34.

Herrmann, H.-V. 1964. "Werkstätten geometrischer Bronzeplastik," *Jahrbuch des Deutschen Archäologischen Instituts* 79: 17–71.

Herzfeld, M. 1985. *The Poetics of Manhood: Contest and Identity in a Cretan Mountain Village*, Princeton.

Heymans, E. and G. van Wijngaarden. 2011. "Low-Value Manufactured Exotics in the Eastern Mediterranean in the Late Bronze and Early Iron Ages," in A. Vianello, ed., *Exotica in the Prehistoric Mediterranean*, Oxford, 124–136.

Higgins, R. 1967. *Greek Terracottas*, London.

Higgins, R. 1984. "Terracotta Figurines," in M. Popham, ed., *The Minoan Unexplored Mansion at Knossos, BSA Supplement 17*, Oxford, 199–202.

Hill, E. 2003. "Sacrificing Moche Bodies," *Journal of Material Culture* 8: 285–299.

Hiller, F. 1977. "Nochmals zu den Lanzenschwingern Olympia B 1701 und B 1999," *Archäologischer Anzeiger* 1977: 149–159.

Hiller, S. 1972. "Allgemeine Bemerkungen zur JN-Serie," *Studi Micenei ed Egeo-Anatolici* 55: 51–72.

Hiller, S. 1979. "*Ka-ko na-wi-jo.* Notes on Interdependence of Temple and Bronze in the Aegean Bronze Age," in E. Risch and H. Mühlenstein, eds., *Colloquium Mycenaeum*, Neuchâtel and Genève, 189–195.

Hiller, S. 1981. "Mykenische Heiligtümer: Das Zeugnis der Linear B-Texte," in R. Hägg and N. Marinatos, eds., *Sanctuaries and Cults in the Aegean Bronze Age*, Stockholm, 95–126.

Hiller, S. 1988. "Dependent Personnel in Mycenaean Texts," *Orientalia Lovaniensia Analecta* 23: 53–68.

Himmelmann, N. 1980. *Über Hirten-Genre in der antiken Kunst*, Opladen.

Himmelmann, N. 1985. *Ideale Nacktheit*, Opladen.

Himmelmann, N. 1990. *Ideale Nacktheit in der griechischen Kunst*, Berlin.

Himmelmann, N. 2002. "Frühe Weihgeschenke," in H. Kyrieleis, ed., *Olympia 1875–2000*, Mainz, 91–108.

Himmelmann–Wildschutz, N. 1974. "Die Lanzenschwinger-Bronzen Olympia B 1701 und 1999," *Archäologischer Anzeiger* 1974: 538–544.

Hirschfeld, N. 2000. "Marked Late Bronze Age Pottery from the Kingdom of Ugarit," in M. Yon, V. Karageorghis, and N. Hirschfeld, *Céramiques mycéniennes. Ras Shamra Ugarit, XIII*, Paris, 163–200.

Hitchcock, L. 1997. "Engendered Domination: A Structural Analysis of Minoan Neopalatial Bronze Figurines," in J. Moore and E. Scott, eds., *Invisible People and Processes: Writing Gender and Childhood in European Archaeology*, London and New York, 113–130.

Hitchcock, L. 2000. "Engendering Ambiguity in Minoan Crete: It's a Drag to Be a King," in M. Donald and L. Hurcombe, eds., *Representations of Gender from Prehistory to the Present*, London, 69–86.

Hodder, I. 1982a. *Symbols in Action: Ethnoarchaeological Studies of Material Culture*, Cambridge.

Hodder, I. 1982b. "Theoretical Archaeology: A Reactionary View," in I. Hodder, ed., *Symbolic and Structural Archaeology*, Cambridge, 1–16.

Hodder, I. 1982c. *The Present Past*, London.

Hodkinson, S. 1983. "Social Order and the Conflict of Values in Classical Sparta," *Chiron* 13: 239–281.

Hodkinson, S. 1997. "The Development of Spartan Society and Institutions in the Archaic Period," in L. Mitchell and P. Rhodes, eds., *The Development of the Polis in Archaic Greece*, London, 83–102.

Hodkinson, S. 1999. "An Agonistic Culture? Athletic Competition in Archaic and Classical Spartan Society," in S. Hodkinson and A. Powell, eds., *Sparta: New Perspectives*, Swansea and London, 147–187.

Hoffman, G. 1997. *Imports and Immigrants: Near Eastern Contacts with Iron Age Crete*, Ann Arbor.

Hogarth, D. 1899–1900. "The Dictaean Cave," *Annual of the British School at Athens* 6: 94–116.

Hogarth, D. 1903. "The Cretan Exhibition," *Cornhill Magazine (March)*: 319–332.

Holmes, B. 2010. *The Symptom and the Subject: The Emergence of the Physical Body in Ancient Greece*, Princeton.

Homès-Fredericq, D. and J. Hennessey, eds. 1989. *Archaeology of Jordan II: Field Reports, Surveys, and Sites*, Leuven.

Hood, S. 1953. "Part V, A Mycenaean Cavalryman," *Annual of the British School at Athens* 48: 84–93.

Hood, S. 1966. "An Aspect of the Slav Invasions of Greece in the Early Byzantine Period," *Sborník Národhního Musea v Praze (Acta Musei Nationalis Pragae) A: Historia* 20: 165–171.

Hood, S. 1970. "Isles of Refuge in the Early Byzantine Period," *Annual of the British School at Athens* 65: 37–45.

Hood, S. 1978. *The Arts in Prehistoric Greece*, Harmondsworth.

Hornung, E. 1968. *Altägyptische Höllenvorstellungen*, Berlin.

Houby-Nielsen, S. 2000. "Child burials in Ancient Athens," in J. Sofaer Derevenski, ed., *Children and Material Culture*, London, 151–166.

Howey, M. and J. O'Shea. 2009. "On Archaeology and the Study of Ritual: Considering Inadequacies in the Culture-History Approach and Quests for Internal Meaning," *American Antiquity* 74.1: 193–201.

Huber, S. 1991. "Un atelier de bronzier dans le sanctuaire d'Apollon à Érétrie," *Antike Kunst* 34: 137–154.

Huber, S. 1997. "Activité métallurgique dans le sanctuaire d'Apollon à Érétrie," in C. Gillis, C. Risberg, and B. Sjöberg, eds., *Trade and Production in Premonetary Greece. Production and the Craftsman*, Jonsered, 173–181.

Huber, S. 2003. *L'aire sacrificielle au nord du Sanctuaire d'Apollon Daphnéphoros. Un rituel des époques géométrique et archaïque Eretria XIV*, Gollion.

Humphrey, C. and J. Laidlaw. 1994. *Archetypal Actions of Ritual: A Theory of Ritual Illustrated by the Jain Rite of Worship*, Oxford.

Hurwit, J. 1985. *The Art and Culture of Early Greece, 1100–480 B.C.*, Ithaca.

Hurwit, J. 2007. "The Problem with Dexileos: Heroic and Other Nudities in Greek Art," *American Journal of Archaeology* 111.1: 35–60.

Hurwit, J. 2011. "The Shipwreck of Odysseus: Strong and Weak Imagery in Late Geometric Art," *American Journal of Archaeology* 115.1: 1–18.

Iacovou, M. 2012. "External and Internal Migrations during the 12th Century BC: Setting the Stage for an Economically Successful Early Iron Age on Cyprus," in M. Iacovou, ed., *Cyprus and the Aegean in the Early Iron Age: The Legacy of Nicolas Coldstream*, Nicosia, 207–227.

Immerwahr, S. 1990. *Aegean Painting in the Bronze Age*, University Park.

Ingold, T. 1993. "The Reindeerman's Lasso," in P. Lemonnier, ed., *Technological Choices: Transformation in Material Cultures since the Neolithic*, London, 108–125.

Ingold, T. 2013. *Making: Anthropology, Archaeology, Art, and Architecture*, Abingdon and New York.

Inomata, T. 2006. "Plazas, Performers, and Spectators," *Current Anthropology* 47: 805–842.

Inomata, T. and L. Coben, eds. 2006. *Archaeology of Performance: Theaters of Power, Community, and Politics*, Walnut Creek.

Insoll, T. 2004. *Archaeology, Ritual, Religion*, London.

Insoll, T. 2011, ed., *The Oxford Handbook of the Archaeology of Ritual and Religion*, Oxford.

Insoll, T., ed. 2017. *The Oxford Handbook of Prehistoric Figurines*, Oxford.

Isaakidou, V., P. Halstead, J. Davis, and S. Stocker. 2002. "Burnt Animal Sacrifice in Late Bronze Age Greece: New Evidence from the Mycenaean 'Palace of Nestor', Pylos," *Antiquity* 76: 86–92.

Jacopi, G. 1932–1933. *Clara Rhodos VI-VII*, Rhodes.

Jameson, M. 1990. "Perseus, the Hero of Mykenai," in R. Hägg and G. Nordquist, eds., *Celebrations of Death and Divinity in the Bronze Age Argolid*, Stockholm, 213–222.

Janko, R. 1994. *The Iliad: A Commentary. Volume IV: books 13–16*, Cambridge.

Janson, H. and A. Janson. 1991. *History of Art*, 4th ed., Englewood Cliffs.

Janssen, R. and J. Janssen. 1990. *Growing Up in Ancient Egypt*, London.

Jantzen, U. 1955. *Griechische Greifenkessel*, Berlin.

Jantzen, U. 1972. *Ägyptische und Orientalische Bronzen aus dem Heraion von Samos, Samos VIII*, Bonn.

Jarosch, V. 1994. *Samische Tonfiguren, des 10. bis 7. Jahrhunderts v. Chr. aus dem Heraion von Samos, Samos XVIII*, Bonn.

Jeanmaire, H. 1939. *Couroi et Courètes: Essai sur l'éducation spartiate et sur les rites d'adolescence dans l'antiquité hellénique*, Lille.

Jenkins, I. and V. Turner. 2010. *The Greek Body*, London.

Jochelson, W. 1931. "The Yakut," *Anthropological Papers of the Museum of Natural History* 33: 37–225.

Johansen, P. 1982. "Graeske Geometriske Bronzer," *Meddelelser fra Ny Carlsberg Glyptotek* 38: 73–98.

Jordan, P. 2003. *Material Culture and the Sacred Landscape: The Anthropology of the Siberian Khanty*, Walnut Creek.

Joyce, R. 1993. "Women's Work: Images of Production and Reproduction in Pre-Hispanic Southern Central America," *Current Anthropology* 34: 255–274.

Jullien, F. 2000. "Le nu impossible," in F. Jullien, ed., *De l'essence ou du nu*, Paris, 54–152.

Jung, R. 2007. "Tell Kazel and the Mycenaean contacts with Amurru (Syria)," in M. Bietak, ed., *The Synchronization of Civilizations in the Eastern Mediterranean in the Second Millennium B.C., 3. Proceedings of the SCIEM 2000, 2nd EuroConference Vienna, 28th of May – 1st of June 2003*, Vienna, 551–570.

Kaiser, I. 2013. *Kretisch geometrische Keramik – Form und Dekor: Entwicklung aus Tradition und Rezeption*, Möhnsee.

Kalligas, P. 1968. "Αρχαιότητες και Μνημεία Ιονίων Νησών," *Archaiologikon Deltion* 23 B' 2 Chronika: 302–322.

Kalligas, P. 1969. "Τὸ ἐν Κερκύρᾳ ἱερὸν τῆς Ἀκραίας Ἥρας," *Archaiologikon Deltion* 24 A' Meletemata: 51–58.

Kaniewski, D., E. Paulissen, E. Van Campo, H. Weiss, T. Otto, J. Bretschneider, and K. Van Lerberghe. 2010. "Late Second–Early First Millennium BC Abrupt Climate Changes in Coastal Syria and Their Possible Significance for the History of the Eastern Mediterranean," *Quaternary Research* 74: 207–215.

Kanta, A. 1991. "Cult, Continuity, and the Evidence of Pottery at the Sanctuary of Syme Viannou, Crete," in D. Musti, A. Sacconi, L. Rocchi, L. Rocchetti, R. Scafa, L. Sportiello, and M. Giannotta, eds., *La transizione dal miceneo all'alto arcaismo. Dal palazzo alla città*, Rome, 479–505.

Karageorghis, V. 1958. "Myth and Epic in Mycenaean Vase Painting," *American Journal of Archaeology* 62.4: 383–387.

Karageorghis, V. 1966. "Notes on some Centaurs from Cyprus," in Χαριστήριον εις Αναστάσιον Κ. Ορλάνδον, Athens, 160–173.

Karageorghis, V. 1973. *Excavations in the Necropolis of Salamis III*, Haarlem.

Karageorghis, V. 1976. *Kition. Mycenaean and Phoenician discoveries in Cyprus*, London.

Karageorghis, V. 1985. *Excavations at Kition, V. The Pre-Phoenician Levels*, Nicosia.

Karageorghis, V. 1993. *The Coroplastic Art of Ancient Cyprus II: Late Cypriote II – Cypro-Geometric III*, Nicosia.

Karageorghis, V., A. Kanta, N. Stampolidis, and Y. Sakellarakis, eds. 2014. *Kypriaka in Crete: From the Bronze Age to the End of the Archaic Period*, Nicosia.

Karageorghis, V. and E. Masson. 1975. "A propos de la découverte d'écailles d'armure en bronze à Gastria-Alaas (Chypre)," *Archäologischer Anzeiger* 1975: 209–222.

Karageorghis, V. and N. Stampolidis, eds. 1998. *Eastern Mediterranean: Cyprus-Dodecanese-Crete 16th–6th centuries BC*, Athens.

Kardamaki, E. 2015. "A New Group of Figures and Rare Figurines from a Mycenaean Workshop Installation at Kontopigado, Alimos (Athens)," *Mitteilungen des Deutschen Archäologischen Instituts, Athenische Abteilung* 127/128: 47–90.

Kardara, C. 1968. "The Itinerant Art," in *Atti e memorie del 1° congress internazionale di Micenologia*, Rome, 222–227.

Kardulias, N., T. Gregory, and J. Sawmiller. 1995. "Bronze Age and Late Antique Exploitation of an Islet in the Saronic Gulf, Greece," *Journal of Field Archaeology* 22.1: 3–21.

Karetsou, A. and G. Rethemiotakis. 1990. "Κόφινας. Ιερό κορυφής," *Archaiologikon Deltion* 45 B'2 Chronika: 429–430.

Karo, G. 1930. *Die Schachtgräber von Mykenai*, Munich.

Karouzou, E. 2017. "Thessaly from the Protogeometric to the Early Archaic Period (1100–600 BC)," in A. Mazarakis-Ainian, A. Alexandridou, and X. Charalambidou, eds., *Regional Stories: Towards a New Perception of the Early Greek World*, Volos, 343–380.

Karouzou, S. 1960. "Χάλκινος Ἀρχαϊκὸς Ζωστήρ," *Archaiologikon Deltion* 16: 60–71.

Kassianidou, V. 2012. "Metallurgy and Metalwork in Enkomi: The Earliest Phases," in V. Kassianidou and G. Papasavvas, eds., *Eastern Mediterranean Metallurgy and Metalwork in the Second Millennium BC*, Oxford, 94–106.

Kertzer, D. 1988. *Ritual, Politics, and Power*, New Haven.

Kiderlen, M. 2010. "Zur Chronologie griechischer Bronzedreifüße des geometrischen Typs und den Möglichkeiten einer politisch-historischen Interpretation der Fundverteilung," *Archäologischer Anzeiger* 2010: 91–104.

Kiderlen, M., M. Bode, A. Hauptmann, and Y. Bassiakos. 2016. "Tripod Cauldrons Produced at Olympia Give Evidence for Trade with Copper from Faynan (Jordan) to South West Greece, c. 950–750 BCE," *Journal of Archaeological Science: Reports* 8: 303–313.

Kiderlen, M., A. Hein, H. Mommsen, and N. Müller. 2017. "Production Sites of Early Iron Age Greek Bronze Tripod Cauldrons: First Evidence from Neutron Activation Analysis of Casting Ceramics," *Geoarchaeology* 32: 321–342.

Kilian, K. 1975. *Fibeln in Thessalien*, Munich.

Kilian, K. 1980. "Ἀρκαδικὲς καὶ Λακωνικὲς ἰδιομορφίες στὰ χαλκᾶ κοσμήματα τῆς ὑστέρας Γεωμετρικῆς ἐποχῆς," *Lakonikai Spoudai* 3: 33–38.

Kilian, K. 1983. "Ausgrabungen in Tiryns 1982/1983," *Archäologischer Anzeiger*: 105–151.

Kilian-Dirlmeier, I. 1985. "Fremde Weihungen in griechischen Heiligtümern vom 8. bis zum Beginn des 7. Jahrhunderts v. Chr.," *Jahrbuch des Römisch-Germanischen Zentralmuseums, Mainz* 32: 215–254.

Kilian-Dirlmeier, I. 2002. *Kleinfunde aus dem Athena Tonia-Heiligtum bei Philia (Thessalien)*, Mainz.

Klebinder-Gauß, G. 2015. "Interpreting Votive Offerings from Early Archaic Deposits at the Artemision of Ephesos," in P. Pakkanen and S. Bocher, eds., *Cult Material: From Archaeological Deposits to Interpretation of Early Greek Religion*, Helsinki, 107–121.

Knapp, A. B. 1986. *Copper Production and Divine Protection: Archaeology, Ideology, and Social Complexity on Bronze Age Cyprus*, Göteborg.

Knapp, A. B. 1997. "Boys will be Boys: Masculinist Approaches to a Gendered Archaeology," in J. Hope, M. Casey, D. Donlon, and S. Wellfare, eds., *The Third Australian Women in Archaeology Conference*, Canberra, 32–36.

Knapp, A. B. 1998. "Who's Come a Long Way, Baby? Gendering Society, Gendering Archaeology," *Archaeological Dialogues* 5: 91–106, 115–125.

Knapp, A. B. and J. F. Cherry. 1994. *Provenience Studies and Bronze Age Cyprus: Production, Exchange, and Politico-Economic Change*, Madison.

Knapp, A. B. and S. Manning. 2016. "Crisis in Context: The End of the Late Bronze Age in the Eastern Mediterranean," *American Journal of Archaeology* 120.1: 99–149.

Knapp, A. B. and L. Meskell. 1997. "Bodies of Evidence on Prehistoric Cyprus," *Cambridge Archaeological Journal* 7: 183–204.

Knapp, A. B. and P. van Dommelen. 2014. *The Cambridge Prehistory of the Bronze and Iron Age Mediterranean*, Cambridge.

Knauss, J., B. Heinrich, and H. Kalyk. 1984. *Die Wasserbauten der Minyer in der Kopais – die älteste Flußregulierung Europas*, Munich and Obernach.

Knobloch, J. 1993. "Gr. γυμνός – ein Relikt der mediterranen Frauensprache," *Historische Sprachforschung/Historical Linguistics* 106.2: 303–304.

Knodell, A. 2021. *Societies in Transition in Early Greece: An Archaeological History*, Berkeley.

Knox, B. 1991. "The Human Figure in Homer," in D. Buitron-Oliver, ed., *New Perspectives in Early Greek Art*, Washington: 93–96.

Koehl, R. 1986. "The Chieftain Cup and a Minoan Rite of Passage," *Journal of Hellenic Studies* 106: 99–110.

Koehl, R. 2000. "The Ritual Context," in S. MacGillivray, J. Driessen, and H. Sackett, eds., *The Palaikastro Kouros: A Minoan Chryselephantine Statuette and Its Aegean Bronze Age Context, BSA Studies 6*, London.

Koehl, R. 2016. "Beyond the 'Chieftain Cup': More Images Relating to Minoan Male Rites of Passage," in R. Koehl, ed., *Studies in Aegean Art and Culture: A New York Aegean Bronze Age Colloquium in Memory of Ellen N. Davis*, Philadelphia, 113–132.

Kolia, E. 2011. "A Sanctuary of the Geometric Period in Ancient Helike, Achaea," *Annual of the British School at Athens* 106: 201–246.

Kolonas, L., K. Sarri, C. Margariti, I. Vanden Berghe, I. Skals, and M.-L. Nosch. 2017. "Heirs of the Loom? Funerary Textiles from Stamna (Aitolia, Greece): A Preliminary Analysis," in M. Fotiadis, R. Laffineur, Y. Lolos, and A. Vlachopoulos, eds., *Hesperos. The Aegean Seen from the West*, Leuven, 533–544.

Kopcke, G. 1968. "Heraion von Samos: Die Kampagnen 1961/1965 im Südtemenos (8.-6. Jahrhundert)," *Mitteilungen des Deutschen Archäologischen Instituts, Athenische Abteilung* 83: 250–234.

König, O. 1990. *Nacktheit: Soziale Normierung und Moral*, Opladen.

Konsolaki-Yannopoulou, E. 2003. "Η Μυκηναϊκή Εγκατάσταση στο νησάκι Μόδι της Τροιζινίας," in N. Kyparissi-Apostolika and M. Papakonstantinou, eds., *The Periphery of the Mycenaean World*, Athens, 417–432.

Konsolaki-Yannopoulou, E. 2004. "Mycenaean Religious Architecture. The Archaeological Evidence from Ayios Konstantinos, Methana," in M. Wedde, ed., *Celebrations: Sanctuaries and the Vestiges of Cult Practice*, Bergen, 61–94.

Konsolaki-Yannopoulou, E. 2007. "Η Υστερομυκηναϊκή εγκατάσταση στην ερημονησίδα Μόδι του Σαρωνικού," in E. Konsolaki-Yannopoulou, ed., *ΕΠΑΘΛΟΝ: Αρχαιολογικό Συνέδριο προς τιμήν του Αδώνιδος Κ. Κύρου*, Athens, 171–198.

Kontoleon, N. 1950. "Τῆνος, Ξώμπουργο," *Praktika tes en Athenais Archaiologikes Hetaireias* 1950: 264–268.

Kontoleon, N. 1952. "Τῆνος, Ξώμπουργο," *Praktika tes en Athenais Archaiologikes Hetaireias* 1952: 531–546.

Kontoleon, N. 1953. "Τῆνος, Ξώμπουργο," *Praktika tes en Athenais Archaiologikes Hetaireias* 1953: 258–267.

Kontoleon, N. 1955. "Τῆνος, Ξώμπουργο," *Praktika tes en Athenais Archaiologikes Hetaireias* 1955: 258–263.

Kontoleon, N. 1958. "Τῆνος, Ξώμπουργο," *Praktika tes en Athenais Archaiologikes Hetaireias* 1958: 220–227.

Kontoleon, N. 1961. "Das heutige Bild der archaischen Kunst der Kykladen," *Atti del Settimo Congresso Internazionale di Archeologia Classica*, vol. 1, Rome, 267–272.

Korfmann, M. 1995. "Troia: A Residential and Trading City at the Dardanelles," in R. Laffineur and W.-D. Niemeier, eds., *Politeia. Society and State in the Aegean Bronze Age*, Liège, 173–183.

Kotsonas, A. 2009. "Central Greece and Crete in the Early Iron Age," in A. Mazarakis Ainian, ed., *Αρχαιολογικό Έργο Θεσσαλίας και Στερεάς Ελλάδας 2003–2005*, Volos, 1051 1065.

Kotsonas, A. 2012a. "Η ενεπίγραφη κεραμική του 'Υπογείου'," in M. Bessios, Y. Tzifopoulos, and A. Kotsonas, eds., *Μεθώνη Πιερίας I: Επιγραφές, χαράγματα και εμπορικά σύμβολα στη γεωμετρική και αρχαϊκή κεραμική από το 'Υπόγειο' της Μεθώνης Πιερίας στη Μακεδονία*, Thessaloniki, 113–303.

Kotsonas, A. 2012b. "'Creto-Cypriot' and 'Cypro-Phoenician' Complexities in the Archaeology of Interaction between Crete and Cyprus," in M. Iacovou, ed., *Cyprus and the Aegean in the Early Iron Age*, Nicosia, 155–181.

Kotsonas, A. 2016. "Politics of Periodization and the Archaeology of Early Greece," *American Journal of Archaeology* 120.2: 239–270.

Kotsonas, A. 2020. "History of Research," in I. Lemos and A. Kotsonas, eds., *A Companion to the Archaeology of Early Greece and the Mediterranean*, Hoboken, 75–96.

Kourou, N. 1996. "Ἀνασκαφὲς στὸ Ξώμπουργο Τήνου 1995–1996," *Praktika tes en Athenais Archaiologikes Hetaireias* 1996: 261–270.

Kourou, N. 2002a. "Aegean and Cypriot Wheelmade Terracotta Figures of the Early Iron Age. Continuity and Disjunction," in E. Braun-Holzinger and H. Matthäus, eds., *Die nahöstlichen Kulturen und Griechenland an der Wende vom 2. zum 1. Jahrtausend v. Chr. Kontinuität und Wandel von Strukturen und Mechanismen kultureller Interaktion*, Möhnsee, 11–38.

Kourou, N. 2002b. *Attic and Atticizing amphoras of the Protogeometric and Geometric periods, CVA Greece fasc. 8, Athens National Museum*, Athens.

Kourou, N. 2008. "The Dawn of Images and Cultural Identity: The Case of Tenos," in E. Greco and E. Carando, eds., *Alba della città, alba delle immagini?*, Athens, 63–90.

Kourou, N. and A. Karetsou. 1994. "Το ιερό του Ερμού Κραναίου στην Πατσό Αμαρίου," in L. Rocchetti, ed., *Sybrita, La Valle di Amari fra Bronzo e Ferro I*, Rome, 81–164.

Koutroumbaki-Shaw, M. 1987. "A Bronze Figurine of a Man from the Sanctuary at Kommos, Crete," in *Εἰλαπίνη. Τόμος τιμητικός γιὰ τὸν Καθηγητὴ Νικόλαο Πλάτωνα*, Heraklion, 371–382.

Kramer-Hajos, M. 2015. "Mourning on the Larnakes at Tanagra: Gender and Agency in Late Bronze Age Greece," *Hesperia* 84.4: 627–667.

Kramer-Hajos, M. 2016. *Mycenaean Greece and the Aegean World: Palace and Province in the Late Bronze Age*, Cambridge.

Krause, C. 1981. "Eretria: Ausgrabungen 1979–1980," *Antike Kunst* 24: 83–84.

Kroll, J. 2008. "The Monetary Use of Weighed Bullion in Archaic Greece," in W. Harris, ed., *The Monetary Systems of the Greeks and Romans*, Oxford, 12–37.

Kühne, H. 1978. "Das Motiv der nährenden Frau oder Göttin in Vorderasien," in E. Schwertheim, S. Sahin, and J. Wagner, eds., *Studien zur Religion und Kultur Kleinasiens*, vol. 2, Leiden, 504–515.

Kunze, E. 1930. "Anfänge der griechischen Plastik," *Mitteilungen des Deutschen Archäologischen Instituts, Athenische Abteilung* 55: 141–162.

Kunze, E. 1931. *Kretische Bronzereleifs*, Stuttgart.

Kunze, E. 1944. "Bronzestatuetten," *Bericht über die Ausgrabungen in Olympia* 4: 105–142.

Kunze, E. 1946. "Zeusbilder in Olympia," *Antike und Abendland* 2: 95–113.

Kunze, E. 1948. *Neue Meisterwerke griechischer Kunst aus Olympia*, Munich.

Kunze, E. 1950. *Olympia II: Archaische Schildbänder*, Berlin.

Kunze, E. 1961. "Kleinplastik aus Bronze," *Bericht über die Ausgrabungen in Olympia* 7: 138–180.

Kunze, E. 1967. "Kleinplastik aus Bronze," *Bericht über die Ausgrabungen in Olympia* 8: 213–250.

Kunze, K. 1991. *Olympische Forschungen vol. 21: Beinscheinen*, Berlin.

Kurke, L. 1999. *Coins, Bodies, Games, and Gold*, Princeton.

Kyrieleis, H. 1990. "Samos and Some Aspects of Archaic Greek Bronze Casting," in M. True and J. Podany, eds., *Small Bronze Sculpture from the Ancient World*, Los Angeles, 15–30.

Kyrieleis, H. 2002. "Zu den Anfängen des Heiligtums von Olympia," in H. Kyrieleis, ed., *Olympia 1875–2000: 125 Jahre deutsche Ausgrabungen*, Mainz am Rhein, 213–220.

Kyrieleis, H., 2006. *Anfänge und Frühzeit des Heiligtums von Olympia: Die Ausgrabungen am Pelopion 1987– 1996, Olympia Forschungen 31*, Berlin.

Lagogianni-Georgakarakos, M. 2000. "Έξι χάλκινα γυναικεία ειδώλια από το Ιδαίον Άντρον," in A. Karetsou, ed., *Πεπραγμένα του Η' Διεθνούς Κρητολογικού Συνεδρίου, vol. Α2, Ηράκλειο, 9-14 Σεπτεμβρίου 1996*, Heraklion, 117–135.

Laistner, M. 1912/1913. "Geometric Pottery at Delphi," *Annual of the British School at Athens* 19: 61–69.

Lakoff, G. 1987. *Women, Fire, and Dangerous Things: What Categories Reveal about the Mind*, Chicago.

Lamb, W. 1929. *Greek and Roman Bronzes*, London.

Lambrinoudakis, V. 1981. "Remains of the Mycenaean Period in the Sanctuary of Apollo Maleatas," in R. Hägg and N. Marinatos, eds., *Sanctuaries and Cults in the Aegean Bronze Age,* Stockholm, 59–65.

Lambrinoudakis, V. 1992. ""Εξι χρόνια αρχαιολογικῆς ἔρευνας στὰ "Υρια τῆς Νάξου," *Archaiologike Ephemeris* 1992: 201–216.

Langdon, S. 1984. "Art, Religion, and Society in the Greek Geometric Period," Unpublished PhD Dissertation, Indiana University.

Langdon, S. 1987. "Gift Exchange in the Geometric Sanctuaries," in T. Linders and G. Nordquist, eds., *Gifts to the Gods,* Uppsala, 107–113.

Langdon, S. 1989. "The Return of the Horse-Leader," *American Journal of Archaeology* 93.2: 185–201.

Langdon, S. 1991. "A Votive Figurine from Early Crete," *Muse* 25: 21–29.

Langdon, S. 1998. "Significant Others: The Male-Female Pair in Greek Geometric Art," *American Journal of Archaeology* 102.2: 251–270.

Langdon, S. 2001. "Beyond the Grave: Biographies from Early Greece," *American Journal of Archaeology* 105: 579–606.

Langdon, S. 2007. "The Awkward Age: Art and Maturation in Early Greece," in A. Cohen and J. Rutter, eds., *Constructions of Childhood in Ancient Greece. Hesperia Supplement 41,* Princeton, 173–191.

Langdon, S. 2008. *Art and Identity in Dark Age Greece,* Cambridge.

Langdon, S. 2015. "Geometric Pottery for Beginners: Children and Production in Early Greece," in V. Vlachou and A. Tsingarida, eds., *Pots, Workshops, and Early Iron Age Society: Function and Role of Ceramics in Early Greece,* Brussels, 21–36.

Lapatin, K. 2014. "The Materials and Techniques of Greek and Roman Art," in C. Marconi, ed., *The Oxford Handbook of Greek and Roman Art and Architecture,* Oxford, 203–240.

Latacz, J. 2004. *Troy and Homer: Towards the Solution of an Old Mystery,* Oxford.

Latacz, J. 2005. *Troia und Homer. Der Weg zur Lösung eines alten Rätsels,* 5th ed., Munich.

Laurent, M. 1901. "Sur un vase de style géométrique," *Bulletin de Correspondance Hellénique* 25: 143–155.

Leaf, W. 1900–1902. *The Iliad,* 2 vols., London and New York.

Lear, A. 2013. "Eros and Greek Sport," in P. Christesen and D. Kyle, eds., *A Companion to Sport and Spectacle in Greek and Roman Antiquity,* London and Malden, 246–257.

Lebessi, A. 1975. "Ιερόν Ερμού και Αφροδίτης εις Σήμη Βιάννου," *Praktika tes en Athenais Archaiologikes Hetaireias* 1975: 322–339.

Lebessi, A. 1985. *Το ιερό του Ερμή και της Αφροδίτης στη Σύμη Βιάννου Ι. Χάλκινα κρητικά τορεύματα,* Athens.

Lebessi, A. 1991a. "Το ιερό του Ερμή και της Αφροδίτης στη Σύμη βιάννου," *Praktika tes en Athenais Archaiologikes Hetaireias* 1991: 306–330.

Lebessi, A. 1991b. "Flagellation and authoflagellation: Données iconographiques pour une tentative d'interprétation," *Bulletin de Correspondance Hellénique* 115: 99–123.

Lebessi, A. 1996. "The Relations of Crete and Euboea in the Tenth and Ninth Centuries B.C. The Lefkandi Centaur and his Predecessors," in D. Evely, I. Lemos, and S. Sherratt, eds., *Minotaur and Centaur: Studies in the Archaeology of Crete and Euboea presented to Mervyn Popham,* Oxford, 146–154.

Lebessi, A. 2002. *Το Ιερό του Ερμή και της Αφροδίτης στη Σύμη Βιάννου ΙΙΙ: Τα χάλκινα ανθρωπόμορφα ειδώλια,* Athens.

Lebessi, A. 2009. "The Erotic Goddess of the Syme Sanctuary, Crete," *American Journal of Archaeology* 113.4: 521–545.

Lebessi, A. and P. Muhly. 1976. "The Sanctuary of Hermes and Aphrodite in Crete," *Expedition* 18.3: 2–13.

Lebessi, A. and P. Muhly. 1987. "The Sanctuary of Hermes and Aphrodite at Syme, Crete," *National Geographic Research* 3: 102–113.

Lebessi, A. and P. Muhly. 1990. "Aspects of Minoan Cult. Sacred Enclosures: The Evidence from the Syme Sanctuary (Crete)," *Archäologischer Anzeiger* 1990: 315–336.

Lebessi, A. and P. Muhly. 2003. "Ideology and Cultural Interaction: Evidence from the Syme Sanctuary, Crete," in Y. Duhoux, ed., *Briciaka: A Tribute to W. C. Brice*, Amsterdam, 95–103.

Lebessi, A., P. Muhly, and G. Papasavvas. 2004. "The Runner's Ring: A Minoan Athlete's Dedication at the Syme Sanctuary, Crete," *Mitteilungen des Deutschen Archäologischen Instituts, Athenische Abteilung* 119: 1–31.

Lee, M. 2015. *Body, Dress, and Identity in Ancient Greece*, Cambridge.

Legakis, B. 1977. "Athletic Contests in Archaic Greek Art," Unpublished PhD Dissertation, University of Chicago.

Le Goff, J. 1988. *Medieval Civilization 400–1500*, New York.

Leitao, D. 1995. "The Perils of Leukippos," *Classical Antiquity* 14: 130–163.

Leitao, D. 2012. *The Pregnant Male as Myth and Metaphor in Classical Greek Literature*, Cambridge.

Lemonnier, P. 1992. *Elements for an Anthropology of Technology*, Ann Arbor.

Lemonnier, P. 2012. *Mundane Objects: Materiality and Non-verbal Communication*, Walnut Creek.

Lemos, I. 2002. *The Protogeometric Aegean*, Cambridge.

Lemos, I. 2006. "A New Figurine from Xeropolis on Lefkandi," in E. Herring, I. Lemos, F. Lo Schiavo, L. Vagnetti, R. Whitehouse, and J. Wilkins, eds., *Across Frontiers: Etruscans, Greeks, Phoenicians, and Cypriots*, London, 89–94.

Lemos, I. 2010. "The Excavations at Lefkandi – Xeropolis," *Bulletin of the Institute of Classical Studies* 53: 134–135.

Lemos, I. 2011–2012. "Euboea and Central Greece in the Post-Palatial and Early Greek Periods," *Archaeological Reports* 19–27.

Lemos, I. 2012. "A Northern Aegean Amphora from Xeropolis, Lefkandi," in P. Adam-Veleni and K. Tzanavari, eds., *Δινήεσσα: Τιμητικός τόμος για την Κατερίνα Ρωμιοπούλου*, Thessaloniki, 177–182.

Lemos, I. and A. Kotsonas, eds. 2020. *A Companion to the Archaeology of Early Greece and the Mediterranean*, 2 vols., Hoboken.

Lerat, L. 1961. "Fouilles à Delphes à l'Est du Grand Sanctuaire," *Bulletin de Correspondance Hellénique* 85: 316–366.

Lesure, R. 2001. *Ancient Figurines: Context, Comparison, and Prehistoric Art*, Cambridge.

Letterman, H. and F. Hiller von Gaertringen. 1911. "Arkadische Forschungen," *Akademie der Wissenschaften* 4: 41–42.

Leukart, A. 1979. "Autour de *ka-ko na-wi-jo*: quelques critères," in E. Risch and H. Mühlenstein, eds., *Colloquium Mycenaeum*, Neuchâtel and Geneva, 183–187.

Levi, D. 1945. *Early Hellenic Pottery of Crete*, Princeton.

Levi, D. 1959. "La villa rurale minoica de Gortina," *Bollettino d'Arte* 44: 237–265.

Levy, T. 2009. "Pastoral Nomads and Iron Age Metal Production in Ancient Edom," in J. Szuchman, ed., *Nomads, Tribes, and the State in the Ancient Near East*, Chicago, 147–176.

Levy, T., R. Adams, and A. Muniz. 2004. "Archaeology and the Shasu Nomads – Recent Excavations in the Jabal Hamrat Fidan, Jordan," in W. Propp and R. Friedman, eds., *Le-David Maskil: A Birthday Tribute for David Noel Freedman*, Winona Lake, 63–89.

Levy, T., R. Adams, M. Najjar, A. Hauptmann, J. Anderson, B. Brandl, M. Robinson, and T. Higham. 2004. "Reassessing the Chronology of Biblical Edom: New Excavations and 14C Dates from Khirbat en-Nahas (Jordan)," *Antiquity* 78: 863–876.

Liagkouras, A. 1963. "Καινούργιον Φθιώτιδος," *Archaiologikon Deltion* 18 B'1 Chronika: 144.

Linke, B. 2006. "Zeus als Gott der Ordnung. Religiöse Autorität im Spannungsfeld von überregionalen Überzeugungen und lokalen Kulten am Beispiel der Zeuskulte im archaischen Griechenland," in K. Freitag, P. Funke, and M. Haake, eds., *Kult–Politik–Ethnos: Überregionale Heiligtümer im Spannungsfeld von Kult und Politik*, Stuttgart, 89–120.

Loraux, N. 1995. *The Experiences of Tiresias: The Feminine and the Greek Man*, trans. P. Wissing, Princeton.

Lorimer, H. 1950. *Homer and the Monuments*, London.

Lucas, A. and J. Harris. 1962. *Ancient Egyptian Materials and Industries*, 4th ed., London.

Lucas, G. 2019. *Writing the Past: Knowledge and Literary Production in Archaeology*, London and New York.

Luckenbill, D., trans. 1924. *The Annals of Sennacherib*, 2 vols., Chicago.

Luce, J. 1975. *Homer and the Heroic Age*, London.

Ludwig, P. 2002. *Eros and Polis: Desire and Community in Greek Political Theory*, Cambridge.

Lupack, S. 2010. "Mycenaean Religion," in E. Cline, ed., *The Oxford Handbook of the Bronze Age Aegean*, Oxford, 263–276.

Lupack, S. 2020. "Continuity and Change in Religious Practice from the Late Bronze Age to the Iron Age," in G. Middleton, ed., *Collapse and Transformation: The Late Bronze Age to Early Iron Age in the Aegean*, Oxford and Philadelphia, 161–167

Lyttkens, C. 2013. *Economic Analysis of Institutional Change in Ancient Greece: Politics, Taxation, and Rational Behavior*, London and New York.

Maass, M. 1977. "Kretische Votivdreifüsse," *Mitteilungen des Deutschen Archäologischen Instituts, Athenische Abteilung* 92: 33–59.

Maass, M. 1978. *Olympische Forschungen X. Die Geometrischen Dreifüsse von Olympia*, Berlin.

Maass, M. 1981. "Die Geometrischen Dreifüsse von Olympia," *Antike Kunst* 24: 6–20.

MacCary, W. 1982. *Childlike Achilles: Ontogeny and Phylogeny in the Iliad*, New York.

Macdonald, C., E. Hallager, and W.-D. Niemeier. 2009. *The Minoans in the Central, Eastern, and Northern Aegean: New Evidence*, Athens.

MacDonald, W., D. Coulson, and J. Rosser, eds. 1983. *Excavations at Nichoria in Southwest Greece Volume III: Dark Age and Byzantine Occupation*, Minneapolis.

Mackie, H. 1996. *Talking Trojan: Speech and Community in the Iliad*, Lanham.

MacVeigh Thorne, S. and M. Prent 2000. "The Sanctuary of Diktaean Zeus at Palaikastro: A Re-Examination of the Excavations by the British School in 1902–1906," in *Πεπραγμένα του Η´ Διεθνούς Κρητολογικού Συνεδρίου*, Heraklion, 169–178.

Maddin, R. 2011. "The Metallurgy of Iron During the Early Years of the Iron Age," in P. Betancourt and S. Ferrence, eds., *Metallurgy: Understanding How, Learning Why. Studies in Honor of James D. Muhly*, Philadelphia, 203–210.

Malakasioti, Z. 2006. "Νέα στοιχεία για την Πρώιμη Εποχή του Σιδήρου στην περιοχή του Αλμυρού 1100-700 π.Χ.: η παρουσία της Άλου," in A. Mazarakis Ainian, ed., *Archaeological Work on Thessaly and Central Greece: From Prehistory to the Contemporary Period*, Volos, 111–121.

Malinowksi, B. 1948. *Magic, Science, Religion, and Other Essays*, Boston.

Mallwitz, A. 1966. "Das Heraion von Olympia und seine Vorgänger," *Jahrbuch des Deutschen Archäologischen Instituts* 81: 310–376.

Mallwitz, A. 1988. "Cult and Competition Locations at Olympia," in W. Raschke, ed., *The Archaeology of the Olympics: The Olympics and Other Festivals in Antiquity*, Madison, 79–109.

Mallwitz, A. 1999. *Olympia XI. Bericht über die Ausgrabungen in Olympia*, Berlin.

Mallwitz, A. and W. Schiering. 1964. *Die Werkstatt des Pheidias in Olympia, Olympische Forschungen V*, Berlin.

Maner, Ç. 2012. "A Comparative Study of Hittite and Mycenaean Fortification Architecture," in C. Stampolidis, A. Kanta, and A. Giannikouri, eds., *Athanasia: The Earthly, Celestial, and the Underworld in the Mediterranean from the Late Bronze Age and the Early Iron Age*, Heraklion, 56–66.

Mann, J. 1947. "*Gymnazo* in Thucydides, 1.6.5–6," *Classical Review* 24: 17–78.

Manning, S. 2008. "Formation of the Palaces," in C. Shelmerdine, ed., *The Cambridge Companion to the Aegean Bronze Age*, Cambridge, 105–120.

Mantzourani, E. "Sexuality or Fertility Symbol? The Bronze Figurine from Makrigialos," in E. Mantzourani and P. Betancourt, eds., *PHILISTOR: Studies in Honor of Costas Davaras*, Philadelphia, 105–112.

Maraghiannis, G. n.d. *Antiquités Crétoises I,* Vienna.

Maran, J. 2004. "The Spreading of Objects and Ideas in the Late Bronze Age Eastern Mediterranean: Two Case Examples from the Argolid of the 13th and 12th Centuries B.C.," *Bulletin of the American Schools of Oriental Research* 336: 11–30.

Maran, J. and J. Wright. 2020. "The Rise of Mycenaean Culture, Palatial Administration, and Its Collapse," in I. Lemos and A. Kotsonas, eds., *A Companion to the Archaeology of Early Greece and the Mediterranean,* Hoboken, 99–132.

Margreiter, I. 1988. *Frühe lakonische Keramik der geometrischen bis archaischen Zeit (10. bis 6. Jahrhundert v. Chr.),* Waldsassen-Bayern.

Markoe, G. 1989. "The 'Lion Attack' in Archaic Greek Art: Heroic Triumph," *Classical Antiquity* 8: 86–115.

Marinatos, N. 1984. *Art and Religion in Thera: Reconstructing a Bronze Age Society,* Athens.

Marinatos, N. 1993. *Minoan Religion: Ritual, Image, and Symbol,* Columbia.

Marinatos, N. 1996. "Cults by the Seashore: What Happened at Amnisos?" in R. Hägg, ed., *The Role of Religion in the Early Greek Polis,* Stockholm, 135–139.

Marinatos, S. 1929. "Ἀνασκαφαί ἐν Κρήτῃ," *Praktika tes en Athenais Archaiologikes Hetaireias* 1929: 91–99.

Marinatos, S. 1962. "Zur Frage der Grotte von Arkalochori," *Kadmos* 1: 87–94.

Marinatos, S. 1971. *Excavations at Thera 4: 1970 Season,* Athens.

Marinatos, S. 1976. *Excavations at Thera 8: 1973 Season,* Athens.

Marsilio, M. S. 2000. *Farming and Poetry in Hesiod's "Works and Days,"* Lanham.

Mastrapas, A. 1996. "Ὑδρία με ηθμωτό κυάθιο από το ΥΚ/ΥΕ ΙΙΙ Γ νεκροταφείο Καμινιού Νάξου," in E. DeMiro, L. Godart, and A. Sacconi, eds., *Atti e Memorie del Secondo Congresso Internazionale di Micenologia,* Rome, 797–803.

Matthäus, H. 2000. "Crete and the Near East during the Early 1st Millennium B.C. – New Investigations on Bronze Finds from the Idaean Cave of Zeus," in A. Karetsou, ed., *Πεπραγμένα του Η' Διεθνούς Κρητολογικού Συνεδρίου,* vol. Α2, Ηράκλειο, 9-14 Σεπτεμβρίου 1996, Heraklion, 267–280.

Matthaus, H. 2005. "Toreutik und Vasenmalerei im früheisenzeitlichen Kreta: Minoisches Erbe, lokale Traditionen und Fremdeinflüsse," in C. Suter and C. Uelinger, eds., *Crafts and Images in Contact: Studies in Eastern Mediterranean Art of the First Millennium BCE,* Fribourg, 291–350.

Mattusch, C. 1975. "Casting Techniques of Greek Bronze Sculpture: Foundries and Foundry Remains from the Athenian Agora with Reference to Other Ancient Sources," Unpublished PhD Dissertation, University of North Carolina.

Mattusch, C. 1988. *Greek Bronze Statuary from the Beginnings through the Fifth Century B.C.,* Ithaca and London.

Mattusch, C. 1990. "The Casting of Greek Bronzes: Variation and Repetition," in M. True and J. Podany, eds., *Small Bronze Sculpture from the Ancient World,* Los Angeles, 125–144.

Mattusch, C. 1991. "Corinthian Metalworking: The Gymnasium Bronze Foundry," *Hesperia* 60.3: 383–395.

Mattusch, C. 2008. "Bronzeworking and Tools," in J. Oleson, ed., *The Oxford Handbook of Engineering and Technology in the Classical World,* Oxford, 418–438.

Matz, F. 1950. *Geschichte der Griechischen Kunst,* Frankfurt am Main.

Mazarakis Ainian, A. 1997. *From Rulers' Dwellings to Temples: Architecture, Religion, and Society in Early Iron Age Greece (1100–700 BC),* Jonsered.

Mazarakis Ainian, A., A. Alexandridou, and X. Charalambidou, eds. 2017. *Regional Stories: Towards a New Perception of the Early Greek World,* Volos.

McDonald, W. and G. Rapp. 1972. *The Minnesota Messenia Expedition: Reconstructing a Bronze Age Regional Environment,* Minneapolis.

McDonnell, M. 1991. "The Introduction of Athletic Nudity," *Journal of Hellenic Studies* 111: 182–193.

Mealey, L. 2000. *Sex Differences: Development and Evolutionary Strategies,* San Diego.

Mervis, C. 1986. "Child-basic Object Categories and Early Lexical Development," in U. Neisser, ed., *Concepts Reconsidered: The Ecological and Intellectual Bases of Categorization,* New York, 201–233.

Mervis, C. and E. Rosch. 1981. "Categorization of Natural Objects," *Annual Review of Psychology* 32: 89–115.

Meskell, L. 1998. "Twin Peaks. The Archaeologies of Çatalhöyük," in L. Goodison and C. Morris, eds., *Ancient Goddesses: Myths and the Evidence,* Madison, 46–62.

Michailidou, A. 2001. "Recording Quantities of Metal in Bronze Age Societies in the Aegean and the Near East," in A. Michailidou, ed., *Manufacture and Measurement: Counting, Measuring and Recording. Craft Items in Early Aegean Societies,* Athens, 84–119.

Middleton, G., ed. 2020. *Collapse and Transformation: The Late Bronze to Early Iron Age in the Aegean,* Oxford.

Mikrakis, M. 2015. "Pots, Early Iron Age Athenian Society and the Near East: The Evidence of the Rattle Group," in V. Vlachou, ed., *Pots, Workshops, and Early Iron Age Society: Function and Role of Ceramics in Early Greece,* Brussels, 277–289.

Mikrakis, M. 2016. "'It's War, Not a Dance': Polarising Embodied Identities in the Eastern Mediterranean from the End of the Bronze Age to the Early Iron Age," in M. Mina, Y. Papadatos, and S. Triantaphyllou, eds., *An Archaeology of Prehistoric Bodies and Embodied Identities in the Eastern Mediterranean,* Oxford, 89–95.

Mikrakis, M. 2017. "Musical Performance and Society in Protohistoric Cyprus: Coroplastic and other Visual Evidence," in A. Bellia and C. Marconi, eds., *Musicians in Ancient Coroplastic Art: Iconography, Ritual Contexts, and Functions,* Rome, 57–72.

Militello, P. 2003. "Il rhyton dei Lottatori e le scene di combattimento: battaglie, duelli, agoni e competizioni nella Creta neopalaziale," *Creta Antica* 4: 359–401.

Miller, S. 2002. "The Shrine of Opheltes and the Earliest Stadium at Nemea," in H. Kyrieleis, ed., *Olympia 1875–2000,* Mainz, 239–250.

Miniaci, G. 2018. "Deposit F (Nos. 15121–15567) in the Obelisk Temple at Byblos: Artefact Mobility in the Middle Bronze Age I–II (1850–1650 BC) between Egypt and the Levant," *Ägypten und Levante* 28: 379–408.

Miron, R. 1990. *Kamid el-Loz 10: Das 'Schatzhaus' im Palastbereich: Die Funde,* Bonn.

Mommsen, H., T. Beier, and A. Hein. 2002. "A Complete Chemical Grouping of the Berkeley Neutron Activation Analysis Data on Mycenaean Pottery," *Journal of Archaeological Science* 29: 613–637.

Monroe, C. 2009. *Scales of Fate: Trade, Tradition, and Transformation in the Eastern Mediterranean ca. 1350–1175 BCE,* Münster.

Moore, G., ed. 2006. *Selected Writings on Aesthetics by Johann Gottfried Herder,* Princeton.

Moore, H. 1994. *A Passion for Difference,* Cambridge.

Moorey, P. and S. Fleming. 1984. "Problems in the Study of the Anthropomorphic Metal Statuary from Syro-Palestine before 330 B.C.," *Levant* 16: 67–90.

Moretti, L. 1957. *Olympionikai: i vincitori negli antichi Agoni Olimpici,* Rome.

Morgan, C. 1990. *Athletes and Oracles: The Transformation of Olympia and Delphi in the Eighth Century B.C.,* Cambridge.

Morgan, C. 1993. "The Origins of Pan-Hellenism," in N. Marinatos and R. Hägg, eds., *Greek Sanctuaries: New Approaches,* London, 18–44.

Morgan, C. 1994. "The Evolution of a Sacred Landscape: Isthmia, Perachora, and the Early Corinthian State," in S. Alcock and R. Osborne, eds., *Placing the Gods: Sanctuaries and Space in Ancient Greece,* Oxford, 105–142.

Morgan, C. 1996. "From Palace to Polis? Religious Developments on the Greek Mainland during the Bronze Age/Iron Age Transition," in P. Hellström and B. Alroth, eds., *Religion and Power in the Ancient Greek World,* Uppsala, 41–58.

Morgan, C. 1997. "The Archaeology of Sanctuaries in Early Iron Age and Archaic *Ethne*: A Preliminary View," in L. Mitchell and P. Rhodes, eds., *The Development of the Polis in Archaic Greece*, London and New York, 168–198.

Morgan, C. 1999. *Isthmia. The Late Bronze Age Settlement and Early Iron Age Sanctuary*. 8, Princeton.

Morgan, C. 2003. *Early Greek States beyond the Polis*, London.

Morgan, C. 2010. "Early Ithacesian Vase Painting and the Problem of Homeric Depictions," in E. Walter-Karydi, ed., *Μύθοι, Κείμενα, Εικόνες. Ομηρικά Έπη και αρχαία Ελληνική Τέχνη*, Ithaca, 65–94.

Morgan, C. and T. Whitelaw. 1991. "Pots and Politics: Ceramic Evidence for the Rise of the Argive State," *American Journal of Archaeology* 95.1: 79–108.

Morgan, L. 2000. "Form and Meaning in Figurative Painting," in S. Sherratt, ed., *The Wall Paintings of Thera: Proceedings of the First International Symposium,* Athens, 925–944.

Morris, C. 1993. "Hands Up for the Individual! The Role of Attribution Studies in Aegean Prehistory," *Cambridge Archaeological Journal* 3.1: 41–66.

Morris, C. 2001. "The Language of Gesture in Minoan Religion," in R. Laffineur and R. Hägg, eds., *POTNIA: Deities and Religion in the Aegean Bronze Age*, Liège, 245–251.

Morris, C. 2009. "Configuring the Individual: Bodies of Figurines in Minoan Crete," in A. D'Agata, A. van de Moortel, and M. Richardson, eds., *Archaeologies of Cult: Essays on Ritual and Cult in Crete*, Princeton, 179–187.

Morris, C. 2017. "Minoan and Mycenaean Figurines," in T. Insoll, ed., *The Oxford Handbook of Prehistoric Figurines*, Oxford, 659–680.

Morris, C. and A. Peatfield. 2002. "Feeling through the Body: Gesture in Cretan Bronze Age Religion," in Y. Hamilakis, M. Pluciennik, and S. Tarlow, eds., *Thinking through the Body: Archaeologies of Corporeality*, New York, 105–120.

Morris, I. 1986. "The Use and Abuse of Homer," *Classical Antiquity* 5: 81–129.

Morris, I. 1991. "The Early Polis as City and State," in J. Rich and A. Wallace-Hadrill, eds., *City and Country in the Ancient World*, London and New York, 25–57.

Morris, I. 1996. "The Strong Principle of Equality and the Origins of Greek Democracy," in J. Ober and C. Hedrick, eds., *Demokratia*, Princeton, 19–48.

Morris, I. 1997. "The Art of Citizenship," in S. Langdon, ed., *New Light on a Dark Age,* Columbia, 9–43.

Morris, I. 1999. "Archaeology and Gender Ideologies in Early Archaic Greece," *Transactions of the American Philological Association* 129: 305–317.

Morris, I. 2000. *Archaeology as Cultural History: Words and Things in Iron Age Greece*, Oxford and Malden.

Morris, I. 2007. "Early Iron Age Greece," in I. Morris, W. Scheidel, and R. Saller, eds., *The Cambridge Economic History of the Ancient World*, Cambridge, 211–241.

Morris, I. 2014. *War! What Is It Good For? Conflict and the Progress of Civilization from Primates to Robots*, Princeton.

Morris, S. 1992a. *Daidalos and the Origins of Greek Art*, Princeton.

Morris, S. 1992b. "Introduction. Greece beyond East and West: Perspectives and Prospects," in G. Kopcke and I. Tokumaru, eds., *Greece between East and West: 10th–8th Centuries BC,* Mainz, xiii–xviii.

Morris, S. 1997. "Greek and Near Eastern Art in the Age of Homer," in S. Langdon, ed., *New Light on a Dark Age: Exploring the Culture of Geometric Greece*, Columbia and London, 56–71.

Morris, S. 2007. "Troy between Bronze and Iron Ages: Myth, Cult, and Memory in a Sacred Landscape," in S. Morris and R. Laffineur, eds., *Epos: Reconsidering Greek Epic and Aegean Bronze Age Archaeology. Aegaeum 28*, Liège and Austin, 59–68.

Morrison, I. 1992. *Homeric Misdirection: False Predictions in the Iliad*, Ann Arbor.

Morrison, I. 1999. "Homeric Darkness: Patterns and Manipulation of Death Scenes in the *Iliad*," *Hermes* 127.2: 129–144.

Mountjoy, P. 1986. *Mycenaean Decorated Pottery: A Guide to Identification, Studies in Mediterranean Archaeology* 73, Göteborg.

Mountjoy, P. 1999. *Regional Mycenaean Decorated Pottery*, Rahden.

Mouratidis, J. 1985. "The Origin of Nudity in Greek Athletics," *Journal of Sport History* 12.3: 213–232.

Mühlenstein H. 1987. "Euphorbus und der Tod des Patroklos," *Homerische Namenstudien*, Frankfurt, 78–89.

Muhly, P. 2008. *The Sanctuary of Hermes and Aphrodite at Syme Viannou IV: Animal Images of Clay, Handmade Figurines; Attachments; Mouldmade Plaques*, Athens.

Müller, K. 1852. *Ancient Art and Its Remains, or, A Manual of the Archaeology of Art*, London.

Müller, V. 1929. *Frühe Plastik in Griechenland und Vorderasien. Ihre Typenbildung von der neolithischen bis in die griechisch-archaische Zeit (rund 3000 bis 600 v.Chr.)*, Augsburg.

Müller, W. 1906. *Nacktheit und Entblößung in der altorientalischen und älteren griechischen Kunst*, Leipzig.

Müller, W. and F. Oelmann. 1912. "Die Nekropole der Geometrischen Periode," in G. Karo, ed., *Tiryns I: Die Ergebnisse der Ausgrabungen des Instituts*, Athens, 127–164.

Murphy, C. 2020. "Ceramicists, Apprentices, or Part-Timers? On the Modelling and Assembling of Peak Sanctuary Figurines," *EXARC* 2020.3: https://exarc.net/ark:/88735/10518.

Murray, O. 1980. *Early Greece*, Brighton.

Murray, O. 1991. "The Social Function of Art in Early Greece," in D. Buitron-Oliver, ed., *New Perspectives in Early Greek Art*, Washington, 23–32.

Murray, O. 1993. *Early Greece*. 2nd ed. Cambridge, MA.

Murray, S. 2013. "The Role of Religion in Greek Sport and Spectacle," in D. Kyle and P. Christesen, eds., *A Companion to Sport and Spectacle in Greek and Roman Antiquity*, Malden, 309–319.

Murray, S. 2015. "Athletics and Education in Ancient Greece and Rome," in M. Bloomer, ed., *A Companion to Ancient Education*, Malden, 430–443.

Murray, S. 2017. *The Collapse of the Mycenaean Economy: Trade, Imports, and Institutions, 1300–700 BCE*, Cambridge.

Murray, S. 2018. "Lights and Darks: Data, Labeling, and Language in the History of Scholarship on Early Greece," *Hesperia* 87: 17–54.

Murray, S. 2020. "The Changing Economy," in G. Middleton, ed., *Collapse and Transformation: The Late Bronze to Early Iron Age in the Aegean*, Oxford and Philadelphia, 199–205.

Murray, S. 2021. "Rules and Order," in P. Christesen and C. Stocking, eds., *A Cultural History of Sport in Antiquity*, London, 95–120.

Murray, S., I. Chorghay, and J. MacPherson. 2020. "The Dipylon Mistress: Social and Economic Complexity, the Gendering of Craft Production, and Early Greek Ceramic Material Culture," *American Journal of Archaeology* 124.2: 215–244.

Murray, S., C. Pratt, R. Stephan, M. McHugh, G. Erny, B. Lis, A. Psoma, and P. Sapirstein. 2020. "The 2019 Bays of East Attica Regional Survey (BEARS) Project," *Mouseion* 17.2: 323–393.

Mylonas, G. 1966. *Mycenae and the Mycenaean Age*, Princeton.

Myres, J. 1897. "Excavations in Cyprus in 1894," *Journal of Hellenic Studies* 17: 134–173.

Myres, J. 1903. "Excavations at Palaikastro II. The Sanctuary Site at Petsofa," *Annual of the British School at Athens* 9: 356–387.

Nafplioti, A. 2008. "Mycenaean Political Domination of Knossos Following the LM IB Destructions on Crete: Negative Evidence from Strontium Isotope Ratio Analysis ($^{87}St/^{86}Sr$)," *Journal of Archaeological Science* 35: 2307–2317.

Nagy, G. 1986. "Pindar's *Olympian* 1 and the Aetiology of the Olympic Games," *Transactions of the American Philological Association* 116: 71–88.

Nagy, G. 2003. *Homeric Responses*, Austin.

Nakassis, D. 2013. *Individuals and Society in Mycenaean Pylos*, Leiden.

Nakassis, D. 2020. "The Economy," in I. Lemos and A. Kotsonas, eds., *A Companion to the Archaeology of Early Greece and the Mediterranean*, Hoboken, 271–292.

Nakassis, D., W. Parkinson, and M. Galaty, eds. 2011. "Forum: Redistribution in Aegean Palatial Societies," *American Journal of Archaeology* 115.2: 175–244.

Naumann, U. 1969. "Eine geometrische Bronzestatuette von Kreta," in P. Zazoff, ed., *Opus Nobile. Festschrift zum 60. Geburtstag von Ulf Jantzen*, Weisbaden, 114–20.

Naumann, U. 1976. *Subminoische und protogeometrische Bronzeplastik auf Kreta*, Berlin.

Neal, L. 1992. *The Female Body: Art, Obscenity, and Sexuality*, London.

Neer, R. 2012. *Art and Archaeology of the Greek World: A New History, c. 2500–150 BCE*, New York.

Negbi, O. 1976. *Canaanite Gods in Metal. An Archaeological Study of Ancient Syro-Palestinian Figurines*, Tel Aviv.

Negbi, O. 1988. "Levantine Elements in the Sacred Architecture of the Aegean at the Close of the Bronze Age," *Annual of the British School at Athens* 83: 339–357.

Neugebauer, K. 1931. *Staatliche Museen zu Berlin: Katalog der statuarischen Bronzen im Antiquarium I. Die minoischen und archaischen griechischen Bronzen*, Berlin.

Nicholls, R. 1970. "Greek Votive Statuettes and Religious Continuity, c. 1200–700 B.C.," in B. Harris, ed., *Auckland Classical Essays Presented to E. M. Blaiklock*, Auckland, 1–37.

Nicholls, R. 1975. Review of W.-D. Heilmeyer, *Frühe Olympische Tonfiguren. Journal of Hellenic Studies* 95: 289–290.

Nickel, R. 2002. "Euphorbus and the Death of Achilles," *Phoenix* 56.3/4: 215–233.

Niemeier, W.-D. 1999. "Mycenaeans and Hittites in Western Asia Minor," in R. Laffineur, ed., *Polemos. Le contexte guerrier en Egée à l'âge du Bronze*, Liège and Austin, 141–155.

Niemeier, W.-D. 2016. "Ritual in the Mycenaean Sanctuary at Abai (Kalapodi)," in E. Alram-Stern, F. Blakolmer, S. Deger-Jalkotzy, R. Laffineur, and J. Weilhartner, eds., *Metaphysis: Ritual, Myth, and Symbolism in the Aegean Bronze Age*, Leuven and Liège, 303–310.

Niesiołowski-Spanò, L. and M. Węcowski, eds. 2018. *Change, Continuity, and Connectivity: North Eastern Mediterranean at the Turn of the Bronze Age and in the Early Iron Age*, Wiesbaden.

Noble, J. V. 1975. "The Wax of the Lost Wax Process," *American Journal of Archaeology* 79: 368–369.

North, D., J. Wallis, and B. Weingast. 2009. *Violence and Social Orders: A Conceptual Framework for Interpreting Recorded Human History*, Cambridge.

Nottbohm, G. 1943. "Der Meister der grossen Dipylon-Amphora in Athen," *Jahrbuch des Deutschen Archäologischen Instituts* 58: 1–31.

Nowicki, K. 2000. *Defensible Sites in Crete, c. 1200–800 BC. Aegaeum 21*, Liège and Austin.

Nriagu, J. 1983. *Lead and Lead Poisoning in Antiquity*, New York.

O'Connor, S. 1975. "Iron Working as Spiritual Inquiry in the Indonesian Archipelago," *History of Religions* 14.3: 173–190.

O'Connor, S. 1985. "Metallurgy and Immortality at Candi Sukuh, Central Java," *Indonesia* 39: 52–70.

Olivier, J.-P. 1997. "La collecte et la circulation de l'information économique dans la Crète mycénienne," in J. Driessen and A. Farnoux, eds., *La Crète Mycénienne*, Paris, 313–317.

Olsen, B. 2014. *Women in Mycenaean Greece: The Linear B tablets from Pylos and Knossos*, London.

Orfanou, S. 2020. "Early Iron Age Greek Copper-Based Technology: Votive Offerings from Thessaly," Unpublished PhD Dissertation, University College London.

Orthmann, W. 1975. *Der Alte Orient, Propyläen Kunstgeschichte 18*, Berlin.

Osborne, R. 1997. "Men Without Clothes: Heroic Nakedness and Greek Art," *Gender and History* 9: 504–528.

Osborne, R. 1998. "Sculpted Men of Athens: Masculinity and Power in the Field of Representation in the Classical Tradition," in L. Foxhall and J. Salmon, eds., *Thinking Men: Masculinity and Self-Representation in the Classical Tradition*, London, 23–42.

Osborne, R. 2004. "Hoards, Votives, Offerings: The Archaeology of the Dedicated Object," *World Archaeology* 36: 1–10.

Osborne, R., ed. 2004. *Objects of Dedication: World Archaeology* 36 (special issue).

Osborne, R. 2009 [1996]. *Greece in the Making 1200-478 BC*, 2nd ed., London and New York.

Osborne, R. 2014. Review of A. Haug (2012) *Die Entdeckung des Körpers, Sehepunte* 14.4.

Østby, E. 1997. "Early Iron Age in the sanctuary of Athena Alea at Tegea. Recent Excavations," *Acta ad archaeologiam et atrium historium pertinentia* 9: 79–107.

Østby, E., J.-M. Luce, G. Nordquist, C. Tarditi, and M. Voyatzis. 1994. "The Sanctuary of Athena Alea at Tegea: First Preliminary Report (1990–1992)," *Opuscula Atheniensia* 20: 89–141.

Padgett, J. 1995. "A Geometric Bard," in J. Carter and S. Morris, eds., *The Ages of Homer: A Tribute to Emily Townsend Vermeule*, Austin.

Padgett, J., W. Childs, and D. Tsiafakis, eds. 2003. *The Centaur's Smile: The Human Animal in Early Greek Art*, Princeton.

Page, D. 1959. *History and the Homeric Iliad*, Berkeley.

Palaima, T. 1987. "Mycenaean Seals and Sealings in Their Economic and Administrative Contexts," in P. Ilievski and L. L. Crepajac, eds., *Tractata Mycenaea*, Skopje, 249–266.

Palaima, T. 1991. "Maritime Matters in the Linear B Tablets," in R. Laffineur and L. Basch, eds., *Thalassa: L'Egée préhistorique et la mer, Aegaeum* 7, Liège, 273–310.

Palaima, T. 2003. "'Archives' and 'Scribes' and Information Hierarchy in Mycenaean Linear B Records," in M. Brosius, ed., *Ancient Archives and Archival Traditions: Concepts of Record-Keeping in the Ancient World*, Oxford, 153–194.

Palaima, T. 2004. "Sacrificial Feasting in the Linear B Documents," in J. Wright, ed., *The Mycenaean Feast*, Princeton, 97–126.

Palaima, T. 2015. "The Mycenaean Mobilization of Labor in Agricultural and Building Projects: Institutions, Individuals, Compensation, and Status in the Linear B Tablets," in P. Steinkeller and M. Hudson, eds., *Labor in the Ancient World: A Colloquium Held at Hirschbach*, Dresden, 617–648.

Palaiologou, H. 2013. "Late Helladic IIIC Cremation Burials at Chania of Mycenae," in M. Lochner and F. Ruppenstein, eds., *Brandbestattungen von der mittleren Donau bis zur Ägäis zwischen 1300 und 750 v. Chr.*, Vienna, 249–280.

Palmieri, M. 2009. "Navi mitiche, artigiani e commerci sui *pinakes* corinzi da Penteskouphia: alcune riflessioni," in F. Camia and S. Privitera, eds., *Obeloi: Contatti, scambi, e valori nel Mediterraneo antico*, Paestum and Athens, 85–104.

Pálsson, G. 1994. "Enskilment at Sea," *Man* 29: 901–927.

Papadimitriou, A. 2006. "The Early Iron Age in the Argolid. Some New Aspects," in S. Deger-Jalkotzy and I. Lemos, eds., *From Mycenae to Homer*, Edinburgh, 531–547.

Papadopoulos, J. 1989. "An Early Iron Age Potter's Kiln at Torone," *Mediterranean Archaeology* 2: 9–44.

Papadopoulos, J. 1993. "To Kill a Cemetery: The Athenian Kerameikos and the Early Iron Age in the Aegean," *Journal of Mediterranean Archaeology* 6: 175–206.

Papadopoulos, J. 1994. "Early Iron Age Potters' Marks in the Aegean," *Hesperia* 63.4: 437–507.

Papadopoulos, J. 1996. "Dark Age Greece," in B. Fagan, ed., *The Oxford Companion to Archaeology*, Oxford, 253–255.

Papadopoulous, J. 1997. "Innovations, Imitations, and Ceramic Style: Modes of Production and Modes of Dissemination," in R. Laffineur and P. Betancourt, eds., *TEXNH: Craftsmen, Craftswomen, and Craftsmanship in the Aegean Bronze Age*, Liège, 449–462.

Papadopoulos, J. 1999. "Archaeology, Myth-History, and the Tyranny of the Text:

Chalkidike, Torone, and Thucydides," *Oxford Journal of Archaeology* 18.4: 377–394.

Papadopoulos, J. 2003. *Ceramicus Redivivus: The Early Iron Age Potters' Field in the Area of the Classical Athenian Agora*, Princeton.

Papadopoulos, J., ed., 2005. *The Early Iron Age Cemetery at Torone: Excavations conducted by the Australian Archaeological Institute at Athens in collaboration with the Athens Archaeological Society*, Los Angeles.

Papadopoulos, J. 2014. "Greece in the Early Iron Age: Mobility, Commodities, Polities, and Literacy," in A. Knapp and P. van Dommelen, eds., *The Cambridge Prehistory of the Bronze and Iron Age Mediterranean*, Cambridge, 178–195.

Papadopoulos, J. 2019. "Greek Protohistories," *World Archaeology* 50.5: 690–705.

Papadopoulos, J., B. Damiata, and J. Marston. 2011. "Once More with Feeling: Jeremy Rutter's Plea for the Abandonment of the Term Submycenaean Revisited," in W. Gauss, M. Lindblom, R. Smith, and J. Wright, eds., *Our Cups Are Full: Pottery and Society in the Aegean Bronze Age*, Oxford, 187–202.

Papadopoulos, J. and E. Smithson. 2002. "The Cultural Biography of a Cycladic Geometric Amphora: Islanders in Athens and the Prehistory of Metics," *Hesperia* 71: 149–199.

Papadopoulos, J. and E. Smithson. 2017. *The Early Iron Age: The Cemeteries. The Athenian Agora 36*, Princeton.

Papadopoulos, J., J. Vedder, and T. Schreiber. 1998. "Drawing Circles: Experimental Archaeology and the Pivoted Multiple Brush," *American Journal of Archaeology* 102.3: 507–529.

Papakonstantinou, E. 1992. "Ολυμπία: Στάδια εξέλιξης και οργάνωσης του χώρου," in W. Coulsen and H. Kyrieleis, eds., *Proceedings of an International Symposium on the Olympic Games,* Athens, 51–57.

Papasavvas, G. 2001. *Χάλκινοι υποστάτες από την Κύπρο και την Κρήτη*, Nicosia.

Papasavvas, G. 2003. "Cypriot Casting Technology 1: The Stands," *Annual Report of the Director of the Department of Antiquities, Republic of Cyprus* 2003: 23–52.

Papasavvas, G. 2014. "Bronze Stands of Cypriot types from Crete: Rod Tripods and Four-Sided Stands," in V. Karageorghis, A. Kanta, N. Stampolidis, and Y. Sakellarakis, eds., *Kypriaka in Crete*, Nicosia 312–324.

Papaspyridi–Karouzou, S. 1952. "Αρχαϊκὰ Μνημεῖα τοῦ Ἐθνικοῦ Μουσείου," *Archaiologike Ephemeris* 1952: 137–166.

Pappalardo, E. 2002. "Il 'Tripillar shrine' di Kommos: alcune considerazioni," *Cretica Antica* 3: 263–274.

Paribeni, R. 1903. "Lavori eseguiti dalla Missione Archeologica Italiana nel palazzo e nella necropoli di Haghia Triadha," *Rendiconti della R. Academia dei Lincei* 12: 317–362.

Parker, R. 1998. "Pleasing Thighs: Reciprocity in Greek Religion," in C. Gill, N. Postlethwaite, and R. Seaford, eds., *Reciprocity in Ancient Greece*, Oxford, 105–125.

Pautasso, A. 2018. "'The Result can be Bold and Startling'. Crateri Figurati d'Età Geometrica dalla Necropoli di Siderospilia (Priniàs)," *Annuario della Scuola archeologica di Atene e delle Missioni italiane in Oriente* 96: 497–518.

Pautasso, A. 2019. "La ceramica figurate d'età geometrica dalla necropoli di Siderospilia (Priniàs): alcune riflessioni sul tema della mobilità," in *Proceedings of the 12th International Congress of Cretan Studies,* https://12iccs.proceedings.gr/en/proceedings/category/39/35/523.

Percy, W. 1996. *Pederasty and Pedagogy in Archaic Greece*, Urbana and Chicago.

Perdrizet, P. 1908. *Les Fouilles de Delphes vol. 5: Monuments figurés, Petits bronzes, terres-cuites, antiquités diverses*, Paris.

Pertusi, A. 1955. *Scholia Vetera in Hesiodi Opera et Dies,* Milan.

Petersen, G. 2010. *Mining and Metallurgy in Ancient Peru*, trans. W. Brooks, Boulder, CO.

Petropoulos, M. 2002. "The Geometric Temple at Ano Mazaraki (Rakita) in Achaia," in E. Greco, ed., *Gli Achei e l'Identita etnica degli Achei d'Occidente*, Paestum and Athens, 143–164.

Philipp, H. 1994. "Olympia, die Peloponnes und die Westgriechen," *Jahrbuch des Deutschen Archäologischen Instituts* 109: 77–92.

Pilafidis-Williams, K. 1998. *The Sanctuary of Aphaia on Aigina in the Bronze Age,* Munich.

Pilz, O. 2011. *Frühe matrizengeformte Terrakotten auf Kreta, Votivpraxis und Gesellschaftsstruktur in spätgeometrischer und frin üharchaischer Zeit,* Möhnsee.

Pilz, O. 2014. "Narrative Art in Archaic Crete," in O. Pilz and G. Seelentag, eds., *Cultural Practices and Material Culture in Archaic and Classical Crete,* Berlin and Boston, 243–261.

Pinch, G. 1993. *Votive Offerings to Hathor,* Oxford.

Platon, N. 1951. "Τὸ Ἱερὸν Μαζᾶ (Καλοῦ Χωριοῦ Πεδιάδος) καὶ τὰ Μινωικὰ Ἱερὰ Κορυφῆς Μινωικοὶ θρόνοι," *Cretica Chronica* 5: 96–160.

Platon, N. and K. Davaras. 1961–1962. "Ἀρχαιότητες καὶ μνημεῖα Κρήτης. Κεντρικὴ καὶ Ἀνατολικὴ Κρήτη," *Archaiologikon Deltion* 17: 281–291.

Podro, M. 1982. *The Critical Historians of Art,* Yale.

Poliakoff, M. 1987. *Combat Sports in the Ancient World,* New Haven.

Popham, M., L. Sackett, and P. Thelemis, eds. 1980. *Lefkandi I. The Iron Age. Text. The Settlement. The Cemeteries,* London.

Popham, M., E. Touloupa, and L. Sackett. 1982. "The Hero of Lefkandi," *Antiquity* 56: 169–174.

Porada, E. 1980. "The Iconography of Death in Mesopotamia in the Early Second Millennium B.C.," in B. Alster, ed., *Death in Mesopotamia,* Copenhagen, 259–270.

Porter, J. 2011. "The Achaean Wall and the Limits of Fictionality in Homeric Criticism," *Transactions of the American Philological Association* 2011: 1–36.

Poursat, J.-C. 1983. "Ateliers et sanctuaires à Malia: Nouvelles données sur l'organistion sociale à l'époque des premiers palais," in O. Krzyskowska and L. Nixon, eds., *Minoan Society,* Bristol, 277–281.

Powell, A. 1998. "Sixth-century Lakonian Vase-Painting: Continuities and Discontinuities with the Lykourgan Ethos," in H. van Wees and N. Fisher, eds., *Archaic Greece: New Approaches and New Evidence,* London, 119–146.

Pratt, C. 2015. "The SOS Amphora: An Update," *Annual of the British School at Athens* 110: 213–245.

Prent, M. 2005. *Cretan Sanctuaries and Cults: Continuity and Change from Late Minoan IIIC to the Archaic Period: Religions in the Graeco-Roman World* 154, Leiden.

Preziosi, P. 1975. "An Early Cycladic Sculptor," *Antike Kunst* 18: 47–50.

Prost, L. 2018. "Laconian Art," in A. Powell, ed., *A Companion to Sparta,* vol. 1, Hoboken and Chichester, 154–176.

Raaflaub, K. and H. van Wees. 2009. *A Companion to Archaic Greece,* Chichester and Malden.

Rasmussen, K. 1938. *Knud Rasmussen's Posthumous Notes on the Life and Doings of the East Greenlanders in Olden Times, Meddelelser om Grønland* 109.1, New York.

Raubitschek, I. 1988. *The Metal Objects (1952–1989), Isthmia VII,* Princeton.

Raven-Hart, R. 1958. "The Casting-Technique of Certain Greek Bronzes," *Journal of Hellenic Studies* 78: 87–91.

Ready, J. 2005. "*Iliad* 22.123–128 and the Erotics of Supplication," *Classical Bulletin* 81.2: 145–164.

Ready, J. 2019. *Orality, Textuality, and the Homeric Epics: An Interdisciplinary Study of Oral Texts, Dictated Texts, and Wild Texts,* Oxford.

Rehak, P. 1996. "Aegean Breechcloths, Kilts, and the Keftiu Paintings," *American Journal of Archaeology* 100: 35–51.

Rehak, P. 1999a. "The Aegean Landscape and the Body: A New Interpretation of the Thera Frescoes," in N. Wicker and B. Arnold, eds., *From the Ground Up: Beyond Gender Theory in Archaeology: Proceedings of the Fifth Gender and Archaeology Conference,* Oxford, 11–22.

Rehak, P. 1999b. "The Construction of Gender in Late Bronze Age Aegean Art: A Prolegomenon," in M. Casey, D. Donlon, J. Hope, and S. Wellfare, eds., *Redefining Archaeology: Feminist Perspectives,* Canberra, 191–198.

Rehak, P. 2007. "Children's Work: Girls as Acolytes in Aegean Ritual and Cult," in A.

Cohen and J. Rutter, eds., *Constructions of Childhood in Ancient Greece and Italy*, Princeton, 205–225.

Rehder, J. 2000. *The Mastery and Uses of Fire in Antiquity*, Montreal.

Reinders, R. 2003. "Beginning and End of the Occupation at New Halos," in R. Reinders and W. Prummel, eds., *Housing in New Halos: A Hellenistic Town in Thessaly, Greece*, Lisse, 231–247.

Renfrew, C. 1981. "Questions of Minoan and Mycenaean Cult," in R. Hägg and N. Marinatos, eds., *Sanctuaries and Cults in the Aegean Bronze Age*, Stockholm, 27–33.

Renfrew, C., ed., 1985. *The Archaeology of Cult: The Sanctuary at Phylakopi,* London.

Renfrew, C. 1994. "The Archaeology of Religion," in C. Renfrew and E. Zubrow, eds., *The Ancient Mind*, Cambridge, 47–54.

Renfrew, C. and J. Cherry. 1985. "The Other Finds," in C. Renfrew, ed., *The Archaeology of Cult: The Sanctuary at Phylakopi*, London, 299–360.

Rethemiotakis, G. 1997. "Minoan Clay Figures and Figurines: Manufacturing Techniques," in R. Laffineur and P. Betancourt, eds., *TEXNH: Craftsmen, Craftswomen, and Craftsmanship in the Aegean Bronze Age*, Liège, 117–121.

Rethemiotakis, G. 1998. *Ανθρωπομορφική πηλοπλαστική στην Κρήτη από τη Νεοανακτορική έως την Υπομινωϊκή περίοδο*, Athens.

Rethemiotakis, G. 2001. *Minoan Clay Figures and Figurines from the Neopalatial to the Subminoan period*, trans. A. Doumas, Athens.

Richardson, N. 1993. *The Iliad: A Commentary*, Cambridge.

Richter, G. 1944. "Five Bronzes Recently Acquired by the Metropolitan Museum," *American Journal of Archaeology* 48.1: 1–9.

Riemann, H. 1946/1947. "Die Bauphasen des Heraions von Olympia," *Jahrbuch des Deutschen Archäologischen Instituts* 61/62: 30–54.

Riggsby, B. 1992. "Sex and Gender, Biology and Culture," in G. Lupton, P. Short, and R. Whip, eds., *Society and Gender – An Introduction to Sociology*, Melbourne, 26–37.

Rink, H. 1885. *Tales and Traditions of the Eskimo*, London.

Risberg, C. 1998. "Production in a Sacred Space," *TOPOI* 8: 671–679.

Risberg, C. 1992. "Metalworking in Greek Sanctuaries," in T. Linders and B. Alroth, eds., *Economics of Cult in the Greek World*, Uppsala, 33–40.

Rivière, K. 2016. "Le *témenos* grec archaïque: une affaire politique," in P.A. Caltot, A. Boiché, H. Berthelot, M. Diarra, Fl. Réveillhac, and E. Romieux-Brun, eds., *Vivre et penser les frontiers dans le monde méditerranéen antique*, Bordeaux, 81–90.

Rivière, K. 2018. "Performances rituelles et expression des hiérarchies sociales dans la Grèce de l'âge du Fer," *PALLAS* 107, 57–74.

Rizza, G. 1967–1968. "Le terracotta di Axòs," *Annuario della Scuola archeologica di Atene e delle Missioni italiane in Oriente* 65–66 (n.s. 29–30): 211–302.

Rizza, G. 1974. "Ceramiche figurate di Prinias," in *Πεπραγμένα του Γ' Διεθνούς Κρητολογικού Συνεδρίου*, Athens, 286–289.

Rizza, G. 1978. "Gli Scavi di Priniàs e il Problema delle origini dell'arte greca," in *Un decennio di ricerche archeologiche 1. Quaderni de la Ricerca Scientifica*, Rome, 85–137.

Rizza, G. 1991. "Priniàs. La città arcaica sulla Patela," in D. Musti, A. Sacconi, L. Rocchi, L. Rocchetti, R. Scafa, L. Sportiello, and M. Giannotta, eds. *La Transizione dal Miceneo all' alto Arcaismo. Dal palazzo alla città*, Rome, 331–347.

Robertson, C. 1975. *A History of Greek Art*, Cambridge.

Robins, F. 1953. *The Smith:. The Traditions and Lore of an Ancient Craft*, New York.

Robins, G. 1993. *Women in Ancient Egypt*, London.

Rolley, C. 1967. *Monumenta Graeca et Romana V.1 Greek Minor Arts, the Bronzes*, Leiden.

Rolley, C. 1969. *Fouilles de Delphes V. Monuments figurés. Les statuettes de bronze*, Paris.

Rolley, C. 1973. "Bronze géometriques et orientaux à Délos," in École française d'Athènes, ed., *Études déliennes, publiées à l'occasion du centième anniversaire du début des Fouilles de l'École française d'Athènes à Délos*, Paris, 491–524.

Rolley, C. 1977. *Fouilles de Delphes V. 3: Monuments figurés, les trépieds à cuve clouée*, Paris.

Rolley, C. 1984. *Die Griechischen Bronzen*, Munich.

Rolley, C. 1986. *Greek Bronzes*, trans. R. Howell, London.

Rolley, C. 1993. "Les bronzes grecs et romains. Recherches récentes," *Revue archéologique*: 387–400.

Rolley, C. 1994. *La sculpture grecque*, Paris.

Rolley, C. 1998. "Les bronzes grecs et romains. Recherches récentes," *Revue archéologique*: 291–310.

Romaiou, K. 1915. "Ἐκ τοῦ προϊστορικοῦ Θέρμου," *Archaiologikon Deltion* 1: 225–279.

Romaiou, K. 1952. "Τεγεατικὸν ἱερὸν Ἀρτέμιδος Κνακεάτιδος," *Archaiologike Ephemeris* 1952: 1–31.

Romalis, S. 1983. "The East Greenland Tupilaq Image: Old and New Versions," *Études/Inuit/Studies* 7.1: 152–159.

Romano, D. 2005. "A New Topographical and Architectural Survey of the Sanctuary of Zeus at Mt. Lykaion," in E. Østby, ed., *Ancient Arcadia*, Athens, 381–396.

Romano, D. 2013. "Athletic Festivals in the Northern Peloponnese and Central Greece," in P. Christesen and D. Kyle, eds., *A Companion to Sport and Spectacle in Greek and Roman Antiquity*, Malden, 176–191.

Romano, D. and M. Voyatzis. 2010. "Excavating at the Birthplace of Zeus," *Expedition* 52: 9–21.

Rombos, Th. 1988. *The Iconography of Attic Late Geometric II Pottery*, Jonsered.

Rosner, E. 1955. "Die Lahmheit des Hephaistos," *Forschungen und Fortschritte* 29: 362–363.

Rostocker, W. and E. Gebhard. 1980. "The Sanctuary of Poseidon at Isthmia: Techniques of Metal Manufacture," *Hesperia* 49.4: 347–363.

Rowlands, M. 1971. "The Archaeological Interpretation of Prehistoric Metalworking," *World Archaeology* 3: 210–224.

Rückl, S. 2008. "The Spatial Layout of the Protogeometric Settlement at Mitrou, East Lokris (Central Greece): Social Reality of a Greek village in the 10th century BC," Unpublished MA Thesis, University of Sheffield.

Ruijgh, C. 1995. "D'Homère aux origines proto-mycéniennes de la tradition épique. Analyse dialectologique du lange homérique, avec un excursus sur la création de l'alphabet grec," in J. P. Crielaard, ed., *Homeric Questions*, Amsterdam, 1–96.

Russell, J. 1987. "Bulls for the Palace and Order in the Empire," *Art Bulletin* 69.4: 520–539.

Rutherford, R. 2013. *Homer*, 2nd ed., Cambridge.

Rutherford, R. 2019. *Iliad. Book XVIII*, Cambridge.

Rutkowski, B. 1986. *The Cult Places of the Aegean*, New Haven.

Rutkowski, B. 1988. "Cretan Open-air Shrines," *Archeologia: Rocznik Instytutu historii kultury materialnej Polskiej akademii nauk* 39: 9–26.

Rutkowski, B. 1989. "Clay Votive Sculpture from Pyrgos: Part 1," *Archeologia: Rocznik Instytutu historii kultury materialnej Polskiej akademii nauk* 40: 55–84.

Rutkowski, B. 1991. *Petsofas: A Cretan Peak Sanctuary. Studies and Monographs in Mediterranean Archaeology and Civilization 1*, Warsaw.

Rutkowski, B. and K. Nowicki. 1986. "Report on Investigations in Greece IV," *Archeologia: Rocznik Instytutu historii kultury materialnej Polskiej akademii nauk* 37: 159–170.

Rutkowski, B. and K. Nowicki. 1996. *The Psychro Cave and other Sacred Grottoes in Crete*, Warsaw.

Rutter, J. 1999. "Cretan External Relations duing LM IIIA2–B (ca. 1370–1200 B.C.): A View from the Mesara," in W. Phelps, Y. Lolos, and Y. Vichos, eds., *The Point Iria Wreck: Interconnections in the Mediterranean ca. 1200 B.C. Proceedings of the International*

Conference, Island of Spetses, 19 September 1998, Athens, 139–186.

Rutter, J. 2006. "Ceramic Imports of the Neopalatial and Later Bronze Age Eras," in J. Shaw and M. Shaw, eds., *Kommos V,* 646–688, 712–715.

Rutter, J. 2013. "Sport in the Aegean Bronze Age," in P. Christesen and D. Kyle, eds., *A Companion to Sport and Spectacle in Greek and Roman Antiquity,* Malden, 36–52.

Rystedt, E. 1986. "The Foot-Race and Other Athletic Contests in the Mycenaean World," *Opuscula Atheniensia* 16: 103–116.

Rystedt, E. 1988. "Mycenaean Runners – including Apobatai," in E. French and K. Wardle, eds., *Problems in Greek Prehistory,* Bristol, 437–442.

Rystedt, E. 1999. "No Words, Only Pictures: Iconography in the Transition between the Bronze Age and the Iron Age in Greece," *Opuscula Atheniensia* 24: 89–98.

Sackett, H. 1976. "A New Figured Krater from Knossos," *Annual of the British School at Athens* 71: 117–129.

Sakellarakis, Y. 1983. "Ἀνασκαφή Ἰδαίου Ἄντου," *Praktika tes en Athenais Archaiologikes Hetaireias* 1983: 415–500.

Sakellarakis, Y. 1988. "Some Geometric and Archaic Votives from the Idaean Cave," in R. Hägg, N. Marinatos, and G. Nordquist, eds., *Early Greek Cult Practice,* Stockholm, 173–193.

Sakellarakis, Y. 1992. "The Idaean Cave Ivories," in J. Fitton, ed., *Ivory in Greece and the Eastern Mediterranean from the Bronze Age to the Hellenistic Period,* London, 113–140.

Sakellarakis, Y. 2013. *Το Ιδαίο Άντρο: Ιερό και μαντείο,* 3 vols., Athens.

Salavoura, E. 2015. *Μυκηναϊκή Αρκαδία: Αρχαιολογική και τοπογραφική θεώρηση,* Athens.

Sallares, R. 1991. *The Ecology of the Ancient Greek World,* Ithaca.

Sansone, D. 1988. *Greek Athletics and the Genesis of Sport,* Berkeley.

Sapirstein, P. 2018. "Work, Skill, and Technology," in E. Lytle, A. Montenach, and D. Simpson eds., *A Cultural History of Work in Antiquity,* London, 95–111.

Sapirstein, P. 2021. "The First Doric Temple in Sicily, its Builder, and IG XIV 1," *Hesperia* 90.3: 411–477.

Sapouna-Sakellarakis, E. 1995. *Die bronzenen Menschenfiguren auf Kreta und in der Ägäis,* PBF I.5, Stuttgart.

Saxe, L. 2002. "How Common Is Intersex? A Response to Anne Fausto-Sterling," *Journal of Sex Research* 39.3: 174–178.

Scanlon, T. 2002. *Eros and Greek Athletics,* Oxford.

Scanlon, T. 2005. "The Dispersion of Pederasty and the Athletic Revolution in Sixth-Century BC Greece," *Journal of Homosexuality* 49.3–4: 63–85.

Schachermeyr, F. 1962. "Forschungsbericht zur ägäischen Frühzeit," *Archäologischer Anzeiger* 1962: 105–382.

Schäfer, J. 1957. *Studien zu den griechischen Reliefpithoi des 8-6 Jahrhunderts v. Chr. aus Kreta, Rhodos, Tenos, und Boiotia,* Kallmünz.

Schäfer, J. 1991. "Das problem der Kultkontinuität im Falle des Heiligtums des Zeus Thenatas," in D. Musti, A. Sacconi, L. Rocchi, L. Rocchetti, R. Scafa, L. Sportiello, and M. Giannotta, eds., *La transizione dal miceneo all'alto arcaismo. Dal palazzo alla cittá,* Rome, 349–359.

Schäfer, W. ed., 1992. *Amnisos: nach den archäologischen, historischen und epigraphischen Zeugnisse des Altertums und Neuzeit,* 2 vols., Berlin.

Schefold, K. 1964. *Frühgriechische Sagenbilder,* Munich.

Schefold, K. 1966. *Myth and Legend in Early Greek Art,* New York.

Schefold, K. 1993. *Götter- und Heldensagen der Griechen in der Spätarchaischen Kunst,* Munich.

Schliemann, H. 1880. *Ilios: The City and Country of the Trojans. The Results of Researches and Discoveries on the Site of Troy and throughout the Troad in the Years 1871, 72, 73, 78, 79,* London.

Schmaltz, B. 1980. *Metallfiguren aus dem Kabirenheiligtum bei Theben. Die Statuetten aus Bronze und Blei,* Berlin.

Schmidt, P. and B. Mapunda. 1997. "Ideology and the Archaeological Record in Africa: Interpreting Symbolism in Iron Smelting Technology," *Journal of Anthropological Archaeology* 16: 73–102.

Schmitt-Pantel, P. 1990. "Sacrificial Meal and *Symposion*: Two Models of Civic Institutions in the Archaic City?" in O. Murray, ed., *Sympotica: A Symposium on the Symposium*, Oxford, 14–33.

Schneider, G. and G. Zimmer. 1984. "Technische Keramik aus antiken Bronzegußwerkstätten in Olympia und Athen," *Berliner Beiträge zur Archäometrie* 9: 17–60.

Schoinas, C. 1999. "Εικονιστική παράσταση σε όστρακα κρατήρα από την Αγία Τριάδα Ηλείας," in E. Froussou, ed., *Η Περιφέρεια του Μυκηναϊκού Κόσμου, Α'*, Athens, 257–262.

Schröder, B. 1927. *Der Sport in Altertum*, Berlin.

Schrott, R. 2008. *Homers Heimat. Der Kampf um Troia und seine realen Hintergründe,* Munich.

Schürmann, W. 1996. *Das Heiligtum des Hermes und der Aphrodite in Syme Viannou II: Die Tierstatuetten aus Metall,* Athens.

Schweitzer, B. 1967. *Die geometrische Kunst Griechenlands: frühe Formenwelt im Zeitalter Homers,* Cologne.

Schweizter, B. 1969. *Greek Geometric Art*, trans. P. and C. Usborne, London.

Scott, M. 2010. *Delphi and Olympia: The Spatial Politics of Panhellenism in the Archaic and Classical Periods*, Cambridge.

Scott, M. 2014. *Delphi: A History of the Center of the Ancient World*, Princeton.

Seeden, H. 1980. *The Standing Armed Figurines in the Levant*, Munich.

Segal, C. 1981. *The Theme of the Mutilation of the Corpse in the Iliad*, Leiden.

Segal, C. 2018. *Singers, Heroes, and Gods in the Odyssey*, Ithaca and London.

Shapiro, H. 2000. "Modest Athletes and Liberated Women: Etruscans on Attic Black-Figure Vases," in B. Cohen, ed., *Not the Classical Ideal: Athens and the Construction of the Other in Greek Art*, Leiden, 313–337.

Shaw, J. 1989. "Phoenicians in Southern Crete," *American Journal of Archaeology* 93: 165–183.

Shaw, J. 2006. "Kommos in the Mesara Landscape," in J. Shaw and M. Shaw, eds., *Kommos V*, Princeton, 863–875.

Shaw, J. and M. Shaw. 2000. *Kommos IV: The Greek Sanctuary*, Princeton.

Shaw, M. 2000. "The Sculpture from the Sanctuary," in J. Shaw and M. Shaw, eds., *Kommos IV: The Greek Sanctuary,* Princeton, 135–209.

Shelmerdine, C. "Mycenaean Society," in Y. Duhoux and A. Morpurgo Davies, eds., *A Companion to Linear B: Mycenaean Greek Texts and their World,* Louvain-la-Neuve and Dudley, MA, 115–158.

Shelmerdine, C. and J. Bennet. 2008. "Economy and Administration," in C. Shelmerdine, ed., *The Cambridge Companion to the Aegean Bronze Age*, Cambridge, 289–309.

Sherratt, S. 1990. "Reading the Texts: Archaeology and the Homeric Question," *Antiquity* 64: 807–824.

Sherratt, S. 1994. "Commerce, Iron, and Ideology: Metallurgical Innovation in the 12th–11th Century Cyprus," in V. Karageorghis, ed., *Cyprus in the 11th Century BC*, Nicosia, 59–106.

Sherratt, S. 1996. "With Us but Not Of Us: The Rôle of Crete in Homeric Epic," in D. Evely, I. Lemos, and S. Sherratt, eds., *Minotaur and Centaur: Studies in the Archaeology of Crete and Euboea presented to Mervyn Popham*, Oxford, 87–99.

Sherratt, S. 2004. "Feasting in Homeric Epic," *Hesperia* 73.2: 301–337.

Sherratt, S. 2020. "From the Near East to the Far West," in I. Lemos and A. Kotsonas, eds., *A Companion to the Archaeology of Early Greece and the Mediterranean*, Hoboken, 187–216.

Simantoni-Bournia, E. 2004. *La Céramique Grecque à Reliefs: Ateliers insulaires du VIIIᵉ au VIᵉ Siècle avant J.–C.,* Geneva.

Simantoni-Bournia, E. 2017. "On Women and on Lions," in X. Charalambidou and C. Morgan, eds., *Interpreting the Seventh Century BC: Tradition and Innovation*, Oxford, 31–37.

Simon, C. 1997. "The Archaeology of Cult in Geometric Greece: Ionian Temples, Altars, and Dedications." in S. Langdon, ed., *New Light on a Dark Age: Exploring the Culture of Geometric Greece,* Columbia, 125–43.

Sinn, U. 1981. "Das Heiligtum der Artemis Limnatis bei Kombothekra," *Mitteilungen des Deutschen Archäologischen Instituts, Athenische Abteilung* 96: 25–91.

Sinn, U. 1988. "Der Kult der Aphaia auf Aegina," in R. Hägg, N. Marinatos, and G. Nordquist, eds., *Early Greek Cult Practice,* Stockholm, 149–159.

Smith, C. 1981. "The Early History of Casting, Molds, and the Science of Solidification," in *A Search for Structure,* Cambridge and London, 127–173.

Smith, J. 1987. "The Domestication of Sacrifice," in R. Hamerton-Kelly, ed., *Violent Origins,* Stanford, 191–205.

Smith, R. 1962. "Near Eastern Forerunners of the Striding Zeus," *Archaeology* 5: 176–183.

Snodgrass, A. 1971. *The Dark Age of Greece,* Edinburgh.

Snodgrass, A. 1977. *Archaeology and the Rise of the Greek State: An Inaugural Lecture,* Cambridge.

Snodgrass, A. 1980. *Archaic Greece: The Age of Experiment,* Berkeley.

Snodgrass, A. 1989. "The Coming of the Age of Iron in Greece: Europe's Earliest Bronze/Iron Transition," in M. Stig Sørensen and R. Thomas, eds., *The Bronze Age-Iron Age Transition in Europe: Aspects of Continuity and Change in European Societies, c. 1200 to 500 BC,* Oxford, 22–35.

Snodgrass, A. 1989–90. "The Economics of Dedication at Greek Sanctuaries," *Scienze dell'Antichita: Storia, archeologia, antropologia* 3-4: 287–294.

Snodgrass, A. 1993. "The Rise of the Greek Polis. The Archaeological Evidence," in M. Hansen, ed., *The Ancient Greek City-State,* Copenhagen, 30–40.

Snodgrass, A. 1998. *Homer and the Artists: Text and Picture in Early Greek Art,* Cambridge.

Snodgrass, A. 2008. "Descriptive and Narrative Art at the Dawn of the Polis," in E. Greco and E. Carando, eds., *Alba della città, alba delle immagini?,* Athens, 21–30.

Soares, C. 2014. "Dress and Undress in Herodotus' *Histories,*" *Phoenix* 68/3–4: 222–234.

Sourvinou-Inwood, C. 1988. "Further Aspects of *polis* Religion," *AION* 10: 259–274.

Sourvinou-Inwood, C. 1990. "What Is *polis* Religion?" in O. Murray and S. Price, eds., *The Greek City: From Homer to Alexander,* Oxford, 295–322.

Spantidaki, Y. and Moulhérat, C. 2011. "Greece," in M. Gleba and U. Mannering, eds., *Textiles and Textile Production in Europe from Prehistory to AD 400,* Oxford, 185–200.

Spencer, A. 1993. *Early Egypt. The Rise of Civilization in the Nile Valley,* London.

Spivey, N. 2004. *The Ancient Olympics,* Oxford.

Sporn, K. 2002. *Heiligtümer und Kulte Kretas in klassischer und hellenistischer Zeit,* Heidelberg.

Spyropoulos, Th. 1971. "Καμηλόβρυση Παραλίμνης," *Archaiologikon Deltion* 26 B'1 *Chronika:* 215–217.

Stähli, A. 2006. "Nacktheit und Körperinszenierung in Bildern der griechischen Antike," in S. Schroer, ed., *Images and Gender: Contributions to the Hermeneutics of Reading Ancient Art,* Göttingen, 209–227.

Stampolidis, N. 1992. "Four Ivory Heads from the Geometric/Archaic Cemetery at Eleutherna," in J. L. Fitton, ed., *Ivory in Greece and the Eastern Mediterranean from the Bronze Age to the Hellenistic Period,* London, 141–161.

Stampolidis, N. and A. Kotsonas. 2006. "Phoenicians in Crete," in S. Deger-Jalkotzy and I. Lemos, eds., *Ancient Greece: From the Mycenaean Palaces to the Age of Homer,* Edinburgh, 337–360.

Stampolidis, N., Ç. Maner, and K. Kopanias, eds. 2015. *NOSTOI: Indigenous Culture, Migration + Integration in the Aegean Islands + Western Anatolia during the Late Bronze and Early Iron Ages,* Istanbul.

Stampolidis, N., E. Papadopoulou, I. Lourentzatou, and I. Fappas, eds. 2019. *Crete: Emerging Cities: Aptera, Eleutherna, Knossos,* Athens.

Stansbury-O'Donnell, M. 2015. *A History of Greek Art,* Hoboken.

Starr, C. 1961. *The Origins of Greek Civilization, 1100–650 BCE*, New York.

Starr, C. 1986. *Individual and Community*, New York.

Stewart, A. 1990. *Greek Sculpture: An Exploration*, New Haven.

Stewart, A. 1997. *Art, Desire, and the Body in Ancient Greece*, Cambridge.

Stürmer, V. 1992. "Area A: Die Villa der Lilien," in J. Schäfer, ed., *Amnisos*, Berlin, 219–223.

Sturtevant, E. 1912. "Γυμνός and Nudus," *American Journal of Philology* 33.3: 324–329.

Sweet, W. 1985. "Protection of the Genitals in Greek Athletics," *Ancient World* 11: 43–52.

Swenson, E. 2015. "The Archaeology of Ritual," *Annual Review of Anthropology* 44: 329–345.

Swenson, E. and J. Warner. 2012. "Crucibles of Power: Forging Copper and Forging Subjects at the Moche Ceremonial Center of Huaca Colorada, Peru," *Journal of Anthropological Archaeology* 31: 314–333.

Talalay, L. 1987. "Rethinking the Function of Clay Figurine Legs from Neolithic Greece: An Argument by Analogy," *American Journal of Archaeology* 91: 161–169.

Talalay, L. 1993. *Deities, Dolls, and Devices: Neolithic Figurines from Franchthi Cave, Greece. Franchthi 9*, Bloomington.

Talalay, L. 2000. "Archaeological Ms.conceptions: Contemplating Gender and Power in the Greek Neolithic," in M. Donald and L. Hurcombe, eds., *Representations of Gender from Prehistory to the Present*, London, 3–16.

Tanner, J. 2001. "Nature, Culture, and the Body in Classical Greek Religious Art," *World Archaeology* 33.2: 257–276.

Taplin, O. 1980. "The Shield of Achilles within the *Iliad*," *Greece and Rome* 27: 1–21.

Tartaron, T. 2008. "Aegean Prehistory as World Archaeology: Recent Trends in the Archaeology of Bronze Age Greece," *Journal of Archaeological Research* 16: 83–161.

Tatton-Brown, V., ed., 1979. *Cyprus B.C.: 7,000 Years of History*, London.

Themelis, P. 1965. "Καλαμάτα – Πέρα Καλαμίτσα," *Archaiologikon Deltion* 20 *B'2 Chronika*: 207.

Theocharis, D. 1963, "Φίλια," *Archaiologikon Deltion* 18 *B'1 Chronika*: 135–139.

Theocharis, D. 1964a. "Ἀρχαιολογικὴ Συλλογὴ Λαμίας," *Archaiologikon Deltion* 19 *B'2 Chronika*: 241–243.

Theocharis, D. 1964b. "Ἱερὸν Ἀθηνᾶς Φίλια Καρδίτσης," *Archaiologikon Deltion* 19 *B'2 Chronika*: 244–249.

Thomas, C. and C. Conant. 1999. *Citadel to City-State: The Transformation of Greece, 1200–700 B.C.E.*, Bloomington.

Thomas, G. 1995. *Bronze Casting: A Manual of Techniques*, Marlborough.

Thomas, R. 1992. *Griechische Bronzestatuetten*, Darmstadt.

Thomason, A. 2004. "From Sennacherib's Bronzes to Taharqa's Feet: Conceptions of the Material World at Ninevah," *Iraq* 66: 151–162.

Thommen, L. 1996. "Nacktheit und Zivilisationsprozeß," *Historische Anthropologie* 4: 438–450.

Thommen, L. 2007. *Antike Körpergeschichte*, Zurich.

Thornton, B. 1997. *Eros: The Myth of Ancient Greek Sexuality*, Boulder, CO.

Thuillier, J.-P. 1988. "La nudité athlétique (Grèce, Étrurie, Rome)," *Nikephoros* 1: 29–48.

Thurston, C. 2015. "The Co-Occurrence of Terracotta Wheelmade Figures and Handmade Figurines in Mainland Greece, Euboea, the Dodecanese, the Cyclades, and the Northern Aegean Islands, 1200–700 BC," Unpublished PhD Dissertation, Cambridge University.

Tilly, C. 1990. *Coercion, Capital, and European States, AD 990–1992*, Malden.

Tölle, R. 1964. *Frühgriechische Reigentänze*, Waldsassen and Bayern.

Tomlinson, J., J. Rutter, and S. Hoffmann. 2010. "Mycenaean and Cypriot Late Bronze Age Ceramic Imports to Kommos: An Investigation by Neutron Activation Analysis," *Hesperia* 79.2: 191–231.

Touchais, G. 1980. "Chronique des fouilles en 1979," *Bulletin de Correspondance Hellénique* 104: 581–688.

Treister, M. 1996. *The Role of Metals in Ancient Greek History*, Leiden.

Tsipopoulou, M. 2005. *Η Ανατολική Κρήτη στην Πρώιμη Εποχή του Σιδήρου*, Heraklion.

Turner, T. 1977. "Transformation, Hierarchy, and Transcendence: A Reformulation of van Gennep's Model of the Structure of Rites de Passage," in S. Moore and B. Myerhoff, eds., *Secular Ritual*, Assen, 53–70.

Turner, V. 1967. *The Forest of Symbols: Aspects of Ndembu Ritual*, Ithaca.

Tuzin, D. 2002. "Art, Ritual, and the Crafting of Illusion," *The Asia Pacific Journal of Anthropology* 3.1: 1–23.

Tylecote, R. 1976. *A History of Metallurgy*, London.

Tzachili, I. 2012. "Some Particular Figurines from the Peak Sanctuary of Vrysinas, near Rethymnon, Crete," in E. Mantzourani and P. Betancourt, eds., *PHILISTOR: Studies in Honor of Costis Davaras*, Philadelphia, 233–238.

Ucko, P. 1962. "The Interpretation of Prehistoric Anthropomorphic Figurines," *Journal of the Royal Anthropological Institute* 92: 38–54.

Ucko, P. 1968. *Anthropomorphic Figurines of Predynastic Egypt and Neolithic Crete with Comparative Material from the Prehistoric Near East and Mainland Greece*, London.

Ulf, C. 2003. *Der neue Streit um Troja. Eine Bilanz*, Munich.

Ulf, C. 2009. "Rethinking Cultural Contacts," *Ancient West and East* 8: 81–132.

Ure, P. 1921. *The Greek Renaissance*, London.

Van Baal, J. 1966. *Dema*, The Hague.

Van den Eijnde, F. 2010. "Cult and Society in Early Athens 1000–600 B.C.," Unpublished PhD Dissertation, University of Utrecht.

Van Dyke, R. 2004. "Memory, Meaning, and Masonry: The Late Bonito Chacoan Landscape," *American Antiquity* 60: 413–431.

Van Gennep, A. 1909. *Les rites de passage*, Paris.

Van Leuven, J.-C. 1978. "The Mainland Tradition of Sanctuaries in Prehistoric Greece," *World Archaeology* 10.2: 139–148.

Van Straten, F. 1981. "Gifts for the Gods," in H. Vernsel, ed., *Faith, Hope, and Worship: Aspects of Religious Mentality in the Ancient World.*

Studies in Greek and Roman Religion 2, Leiden, 65–151.

Van Wees, H. 1992. *Status Warriors: War, Violence, and Society in Homer and History*, Amsterdam.

Van Wees, H. 1994. "The Homeric Way of War: the *Iliad* and the Hoplite Phalanx (II)," *Greece and Rome* 41: 131–155.

Van Wees, H. 1995. "Clothes, Class, and Gender in Homer," in D. Cairns, ed., *Body Language in the Greek and Roman Worlds*, Swansea, 1–36.

Van Wees, H. 2010. "Trailing Tunics and Sheepskin Coats: Dress and Status in Early Greece," in L. Cleland, M. Harlow, and L. Llewellyn-Jones, eds., *The Clothed Body in the Ancient World*, Oxford, 44–51.

Vandier d'Abbadie, J. 1937. *Catalogue des ostraca figurés de Deir el Médineh (nos. 2256 à 2722), Documents de fouilles publiés par les members de l'institut français II.2*, Cairo.

Vandier d'Abbadie, J. 1959. *Catalogue des ostraca figurés de Deir el Médineh (nos. 2734 à 3035), Documents de fouilles publiés par les members de l'institut français II.4*, Cairo.

Venclová, N. 1998. *Mšecké Zehrovice in Bohemia: Archaeological Background to a Celtic Hero*, Sceaux.

Verbruggen, H. 1981. *Le Zeus Crétois*, Paris.

Verdan, S. 2013. *Le sanctuaire d'Apollon Daphnéphoros à l'époque géometrique. Eretria XXII*, Bern.

Verdan, S. 2015. "Geometric Eretria: Some Thoughts on Old Data," in J.-P. Descœudres and S. Paspalas, eds., *Zagora in Context: Settlements and Intercommunal Links in the Geometric Period (900–700 BC)*, Sydney, 181–190.

Verdelis, N. 1959. "Ανασκαφή μυκηναϊκής επιχώσεως εν Τίρυνθι," *Archaiologike Ephemeris* 1956: 5–8.

Verdelis, N. 1963. "Neue geometrische Gräber in Tiryns," *Mitteilungen des Deutschen Archäologischen Instituts, Athenische Abteilung* 78: 1–62.

Verdelis, N., D. French, and E. French. 1965. "Τίρυνς: Μυκηναϊκή επίχωσις έξωθεν του δυτικού τείχους της ακροπόλεως,"

Archaiologikon Deltion 60 A' Meletemata: 137–152.

Verlinden, C. 1984. *Les statuettes anthropomorphes crétoises en bronze et en plomb, du IIIe millénaire au VIIe siècle av. J.–C. Archaeologia Transatlantica IV*, Louvain la Neuve.

Verlinden, C. 1986. "La métallurgie minoenne et la fonte à la cire perdue. Expérimentations sur un proceed antique," *Bulletin de Correspondance Hellénique* 110: 41–52.

Vetters, M. 2009. "Die Spätbronzezeitlichen Terrakotta-Figurinen aus Tiryns. Überlegungen zu religiös motiviertem Ritualverhalten in mykenischer Zeit anhand von Kontextanalysen ausgewählter Siedlungsbefunde," Unpublished PhD Dissertation, University of Heidelberg.

Vetters, M. 2011. "A Clay Ball with a Cypro-Minoan Inscription from Tiryns," *Archäologischer Anzeiger* 2011.2: 1–49.

Vetters, M. 2020. "Figurines and Sculpture," in I. Lemos and A. Kotsonas, eds., *A Companion to the Archaeology of Early Greece and the Mediterranean*, Hoboken, 539–570.

Vetters, M. and J. Weilhartner. 2017. "A Nude Man Is Hard to Find: Tracing the Development of Mycenaean Late Palatial Iconography for a Male Deity," *Mitteilungen des Deutschen Archäologischen Instituts, Athenische Abteilung* 131/132: 31–78.

Vickers, M. and D. Gill. 1994. *Artful Crafts: Ancient Greek Silverware and Pottery*, Oxford.

Vidal-Naquet, P. 1986. *The Black Hunter: Forms of Thought and Forms of Society in the Ancient World*, trans. A. Szegedy-Maszak, Baltimore and London.

Vikatou, O. 2001. "Σκηνή πρόθεσης από το μυκηναϊκό νεκροταφείο της Αγίας Τριάδας," in V. Mitsopoulos-Leon, ed., *Forschungen in der Peloponnes*, Athens, 273–284.

Vlachou, V. 2012. "The Spartan Amyklaion: The Early Iron Age Pottery from the Sanctuary," *Journal of the Benaki Museum* 11–12: 113–124.

Vlachou, V., ed. 2015. *Pots, Workshops, and Early Iron Age Society: Function and Role of Ceramics in Early Greece*, Brussels.

Vlachou, V. 2018. "Feasting at the Sanctuary of Apollo Hyakinthos at Amykles: The Evidence of the Early Iron Age," in F. van den Eijnde, J. Blok, and R. Strootman, eds., *Feasting and Polis Institutions*, Leiden and Boston, 93–124.

Voigtländer, W. 1973. "Zur Chronologie der spätmykenischen Burgen in Tiryns," in U. Jantzen, ed., *Tiryns VI*, Mainz, 241–266.

Voigtländer, W. 2003. *Die Palaststilkeramik. Tiryns X*, Mainz.

Vokotopoulou, I. 1968. "Βίτσα Ζαγορίου," *Archaiologikon Deltion* 23 B'2 *Chronika*: 287–291.

Voyatzis, M. 1990. *The Early Sanctuary of Athena Alea at Tegea*, Göteborg.

Voyatzis, M. 1995. "Geometric Arcadia," in C. Morris, ed., *Klados. Essays in Honour of J. N. Coldstream*, London, 271–283.

Wace, A. 1973. "Foreward," in M. Ventris and J. Chadwick, eds., *Documents in Mycenaean Greek*, Cambridge, xxi–xxxv.

Wace, A. and F. Stubbings, eds. 1962. *A Companion to Homer*, London.

Waldbaum, J. 1978. *From Bronze to Iron: The Transition from the Bronze Age to the Iron Age*, Göteborg.

Waldstein, C. 1905. *The Argive Heraeum*, vol. 2, Boston.

Wallace, S. 2010. *Ancient Crete: From Successful Collapse to Democracy's Alternatives*, Cambridge.

Walker, W. 1998. "Where Are the Witches of Prehistory?," *Journal of Archaeological Method and Theory* 5: 245–308.

Walter, H. 2019. *Ursprung und Frühzeit des Heraion von Samos*, Wiesbaden.

Watrous, V. 1985. "Late Bronze Age Kommos: Imported Pottery as Evidence for Foreign Contact," in J. Shaw and M. Shaw, eds., *A Great Minoan Triangle in South-Central Crete: Kommos, Hagia Triadha, Phaistos*, Toronto, 7–11.

Watrous, V. 1992. *Kommos III: The Late Bronze Age Pottery*, Princeton.

Watrous, V. 1995. "Some Observations on Minoan Peak Sanctuaries," in R. Laffineur and W.-D. Niemeier, eds., *Society and State in the Aegean Bronze Age*, Liège, 393–403.

Watrous, V. 1996. *The Cave Sanctuary of Zeus at Psychro: A Study of Extra-Urban Sanctuaries in Minoan and Early Iron Age Crete*, Liège.

Webb, J. 1999. *Ritual Architecture, Iconography, and Practice in the Late Cypriot Bronze Age*, Jonsered.

Webster, T. B. L. 1955. "Homer and Geometric Vases," *Annual of the British School at Athens* 50: 38–50.

Weege, F. 1911. "Einzelfunde von Olympia 1907–1909," *Mitteilungen des Deutschen Archäologischen Instituts, Athenische Abteilung* 36: 163–192.

Wells, B. 1983. *Asine II, Fasc. 4. The Protogeometric Period, Part 2: The Analysis of the Settlement*, Stockholm.

Wendrich, W. 1999. *The World According to Basketry: An Ethno-Archaeological Interpretation of Basketry Production in Egypt*, Leiden.

Werbrouck, M. 1938. *Les pleureuses dans l'Égypte ancienne*, Brussels.

Wertime, T. 1983: "The Furnace versus the Goat: the Pyrotechnologic Industries and Mediterranean Deforestation in Antiquity," *Journal of Field Archaeology* 10.4: 445–452.

West, M. 1978. *Hesiod's Works and Days, edited with prolegomena and commentary*, Oxford.

West, M. 2011. *Hellenica: Selected Papers on Greek Literature and Thought, Volume I: Epic*, Oxford.

West, M. 2014. *The Making of the Odyssey*, Oxford.

Whitley, J. 1991a. *Style and Society in Dark Age Greece: The Changing Face of a Pre-Literate Society, 1100–700 BC*, Cambridge.

Whitley, J. 1991b. "Social Diversity in Dark Age Greece," *Annual of the British School at Athens* 86: 341–346.

Whitley, J. 2002. "Objects with Attitude: Biographical Facts and Fallacies in the Study of Bronze Age and Early Iron Age Warrior Graves," *Cambridge Archaeological Journal* 12.2: 217–232.

Whitley, J. 2017. "Afterword: Regional Stories: Towards a new Perception of the Early Greek World," in A. Mazarakis Ainian, A. Alexandridou, and X. Charalambidou, eds., *Regional Stories: Towards a New Perception of the Early Greek World*, Volos, 723–729.

Whitley, J. 2020. "The Re-Emergence of Political Complexity," in I. Lemos and A. Kotsonas, eds., *A Companion to the Archaeology of Early Greece and the Mediterranean*, Hoboken, 161–186.

Wilamowitz, U. 1920. *Die Ilias und Homer*, Berlin.

Wilde, O. 1966. *The Complete Works of Oscar Wilde*, edited by J. B. Foreman, London.

Willemsen, F. 1954–1955. "Das Datum der sogennanten Steinerschen Bronzen," *Mitteilungen des Deutschen Archäologischen Instituts, Athenische Abteilung* 69/70: 12–32.

Willemsen, F. 1957. *Dreifusskessel von Olympia*, Ol. Forsch. III, Berlin.

Willer, F. 2007. "Experimental Reconstruction of the Bronze Casting Process of the Smiting God on a Bull," *Berytus* 50: 49–57.

Willetts, R. 1955. *Aristocratic Society in Ancient Crete*, London.

Willetts, R. 1962. *Cretan Cults and Festivals*, London.

Willetts, R. 1965. *Ancient Crete. A Social History from the Early Times until the Roman Occupation*, London.

Wilson Jones, M. 2014. *Origins of Classical Architecture: Temples, Orders, and Gifts to the Gods in Ancient Greece*, New Haven.

Winckelmann, J. 1763. *Geschichte der Kunst des Alterthums*, Vienna.

Winkler, J. 1990. "Laying Down the Law: The Oversight of Men's Sexual Behavior in Classical Athens," in D. Halperin, J. Winkler, and F. Zeitlin, eds., *Before Sexuality: The Construction of Erotic Experience in the Ancient Greek World*, Princeton, 171–210.

Winter, I. 2003. "Mastery of Materials and the Value of Skilled Production in Ancient Sumer," in T. Potts, M. Roaf, and D. Stein, eds., *Culture through Objects: Ancient Near Eastern Studies Presented to P.R.S. Moorey*, Oxford, 403–421.

Winter, U. 1983. *Frau und Göttin*, Freiburg.

Winter, U. 1985. "After the Battle Is Over. The Stele of Vultures and the Beginning of Historical Narrative in the Art of the Ancient Near East," in H. Kesster and M. Simpson, eds., *Pictorial Narrative in Antiquity and the Middle Ages, Studies in the History of Art 16*, Washington, 11–31.

Wolters, P. 1925. "Forschungen auf Ägina," *Archäologischer Anzeiger*: 1–12.

Woodward, A., J. Droop, and W. Lamb. 1926/ 1927. "Excavations at Sparta, 1927," *Annual of the British School at Athens* 28: 1–106.

Wright, J. 1994. "The Spatial Configuration of Belief: The Archaeology of Mycenaean Religion," in S. Alcock and R. Osborne, eds., *Placing the Gods: Sanctuaries and Space in Ancient Greece*, Oxford, 37–78.

Wright, J. 1995. "The Archaeological Correlates of Religion: Case Studies in the Aegean," in R. Laffineur and W.-D. Niemeier, eds., *Politeia: Society and State in the Aegean Bronze Age, 2 vols.*, Liège, 341–348.

Wright, J. 2008. "Early Mycenaean Greece," in C. Shelmerdine, ed., *The Cambridge Companion to the Aegean Bronze Age*, Cambridge, 230–257.

Wylie, A. 1985. "The Reaction against Analogy," in M. Schiffer, ed., *Advances in Archaeological Method and Theory*, vol. 8, London, 63–111.

Xagoragi-Gleißner, M. 2005. *Die Geometrische Nekropole von Merenda: Die Funde aus der Grabung von Papadimitriou 1960–1961*, Dettelbach.

Yalouris, N. 1959. "Δοκιμαστικὴ ἀνασκαφὴ εἰς τὸν Ναὸν τοῦ Ἐπικουρίου Ἀπόλλωνος Βασσῶν," *Praktika tes en Athenais Archaiologikes Hetaireias* 1959: 155–159.

Yalouris, N. 1974. "Three Geometric Figurines," *Antike Kunst* 17: 21–23.

Yalouris, N. 1978. "Problems Relating to the Temple of Apollo Epikouros at Bassae," in J. Coldstream and M. Colledge, eds., *Greece and Italy in the Classical World*, London, 89–104.

Yamagata, N. 2005. "Clothing and Identity in Homer: The Case of Penelope's Web," *Mnemosyne* 58.4: 539–546.

Yasur-Landau, A. 2010. *The Philistines and Aegean Migration at the End of the Late Bronze Age*, Cambridge.

Yates, T. 1993. "Frameworks for an Archaeology of the Body," in C. Tilley, ed., *Interpretative Archaeology*, Oxford, 31–72.

Yoffee, N. 1985. "Perspectives on 'Trends towards Social Complexity' in Prehistoric Australia and Papua New Guinea," *Archaeology in Oceania* 20.2: 41–48.

Younger, J. 1976. "Bronze Age Representations of Aegean Bull-Leaping," *American Journal of Archaeology* 80: 125–137.

Younger, J. 1995. "Bronze Age Representations of Aegean Bull-Games, III," in R. Laffineur and W.-D. Niemeier, eds., *Politeia: Society and State in the Aegean Bronze Age*, 2 vols., Liège, 507–545.

Zaccagnini, P. 1983. "Patterns of Mobility among Ancient Near Eastern Craftsmen," *Journal of Near Eastern Studies* 24: 245–264.

Zafeiropoulou, F. and A. Agelarakis. 2005. "Warriors of Paros," *Archaeology* 58.1: 30–35.

Zafeiropoulou, F. 2000. "Το αρχαίο νεκροταφείο της Πάρου στη Γεωμετρική και Αρχαϊκή Εποχή," *Archaiologike Ephemeris* 2000: 283–293.

Zafeiropoulou, P. 2006. "Geometric Battle Scenes on Vases from Paros," in E. Rystedt and B. Wells, eds., *Pictorial Pursuits: Figurative Painting on Mycenaean and Geometric Pottery*, Stockholm, 271–277.

Zamora Lopez, J. 2015. "Bronze and Metallurgy in Phoenician Sources," in J. Jimenez Avila, ed., *Phoenician Bronzes in Mediterranean*, Madrid, 29–45.

Zarifis, N. 2007. "Η αρχιτεκτονική του ιερού του Ερμή και της Αφροδίτης στην Κάτω Σύμη Βιάννου," Unpublished PhD Dissertation, University of Thessaloniki.

Zeimbekis, M. 1998. "The Typology, Forms, and Functions of Animal Figures from Minoan Peak Sanctuaries with Special Reference to Juktas and Kophinas," Unpublished PhD Dissertation, University of Bristol.

Zerner, C. 1981. "Signs of the Spirit, Signature of the Smith: Iron Forging in Tana Toraja," *Indonesia* 31: 88–112.

Zervos, C. 1956. *L'art de la Crete, Néolithique et Minoenne*, Paris.

Zimmer, G. 1990. *Griechische Bronzegußwerkstätten. Zur Technologieentwicklung eines antiken Kunsthandwerkes*, Mainz.

Zimmermann, J.-L. 1989. *Les chevaux de bronze dans l'art géométrique grec*, Mayence.

Zurbach, J. 2016. "Aegean Economies from Bronze Age to Iron Age," in J. Moreno García, ed., *Dynamics of Production in the Ancient Near East*, Oxford and Philadelphia, 358–368.

INDEX